Freud and the Limits of Bourgeois Individualism

Historical Materialism
Book Series

Editorial Board

Loren Balhorn (*Berlin*)
David Broder (*Rome*)
Sebastian Budgen (*Paris*)
Steve Edwards (*London*)
Juan Grigera (*London*)
Marcel van der Linden (*Amsterdam*)
Peter Thomas (*London*)

VOLUME 240

The titles published in this series are listed at *brill.com/hm*

Freud and the Limits of Bourgeois Individualism

By

Léon Rozitchner

Translated and introduced by

Bruno Bosteels

BRILL

LEIDEN | BOSTON

Originally published in Spanish as *Freud y los límites del individualismo burgués* by Siglo XXI Editores, 1972. The translation has been generously supported by the Sur Program of the Ministry of Foreign Affairs, International Trade and Worship of the Argentine Republic.

The Library of Congress Cataloging-in-Publication Data is available online at https://catalog.loc.gov
LC record available at https://lccn.loc.gov/2021050150

Typeface for the Latin, Greek, and Cyrillic scripts: "Brill". See and download: brill.com/brill-typeface.

ISSN 1570-1522
ISBN 978-90-04-47157-3 (hardback)
ISBN 978-90-04-47158-0 (e-book)

Copyright 2022 by Koninklijke Brill NV, Leiden, The Netherlands.
Koninklijke Brill NV incorporates the imprints Brill, Brill Nijhoff, Brill Hotei, Brill Schöningh, Brill Fink, Brill mentis, Vandenhoeck & Ruprecht, Böhlau Verlag and V&R Unipress.
All rights reserved. No part of this publication may be reproduced, translated, stored in a retrieval system, or transmitted in any form or by any means, electronic, mechanical, photocopying, recording or otherwise, without prior written permission from the publisher. Requests for re-use and/or translations must be addressed to Koninklijke Brill NV via brill.com or copyright.com.

This book is printed on acid-free paper and produced in a sustainable manner.

I have told you that psycho-analysis began as a method of treatment; but I did not want to commend it to your interest as a method of treatment but on account of the truths it contains, on account of the information it gives us about what concerns human beings most of all – their own nature – and on account of the connections it discloses between the most different of their activities.

SIGMUND FREUD

Contents

Translator's Introduction   1

Introduction   19

PART 1
The Internal Distance

1   The Articulation and the Breach   27

PART 2
The External Distance

2   Civilisation and Its Discontents   107
     I   The Historical Categories, Foundation of the Psychic Apparatus   107
     II   Techniques to Elude the Reality of the External World   120
     III   Analysis of the Real Obstacle   136
     IV   The Historical Foundation of the Lack of Discernment   153
     V   The Negation of Aggressiveness   171
     VI   Out of Hunger Not Being Capable of Love   190
     VII   The Halting of Aggressiveness Due to Guilt   209
     VIII   Ideology, the Concealment of Guilt's True Content   253
     IX   Transformation of the Fundamental Bourgeois Categories   263

3   Group Psychology and the Analysis of the Ego   290
     I   Introduction   290
     II   Critique of the Bourgeois Conceptions of the Group (Continuation)   327
     III   The Amplification of the Body beyond Dependency   335
     IV   The Official Institutions Are Groups Congruent with the System   351
     V   The Discernment Repressed   368
     VI   The Human Form as Index of the Coherence of the Social System   388
     VII   Being in Love and Hypnosis: From Individual Dependency to Social Dependency   408

VIII	The Return to the Historical Origin	435
IX	Dialectic of Collective Forms: From the Primal Horde to the Fraternal Alliance	449
X	The Mass, Stage or Battlefield	477

Bibliography 511
Index 512

Translator's Introduction

The work of the Argentine philosopher Moishe Leib (León) Rozitchner (1924–2011) has had a strange fate. On the one hand, we benefit enormously from the decision of the National Library of Argentina, when it was under the directorship of his longtime friend Horacio González, to publish Rozitchner's complete works, including a significant number of previously unpublished or hard-to-find materials. This decision without a doubt has contributed to the momentum of Rozitchner's posthumous recognition. In fact, even though he would not have liked the expression, linked as it is to the latest intellectual fashions of French thought, we could say that this editorial project marks a true 'event' in the panorama of contemporary theory and philosophy. At least in Spanish, the reader is now able to appreciate the secret force and originality of this philosopher's thought as a unified whole that spans more than half a century, beginning in 1962 (the year in which he published *Persona y comunidad*, based on his doctoral thesis on Max Scheler's theory of affectivity that he had defended in 1960 under the guidance of Maurice Merleau-Ponty at the Sorbonne) until the posthumous publication of *Materialismo ensoñado* (with four short texts on 'oneiric materialism' that he was able to oversee at the end of his life). On the other hand, we should give pause to reflect on the fact that even in his home country of Argentina Rozitchner was only rarely appreciated in public as one of the most important philosophers of his time, a writer and intellectual whose thought exceeds from all sides the scope of professional academic philosophy. Rozitchner often complained about the scant reaction – whether positive or negative – that his works provoked. He regretted this all the more in that his works were always meant to be precisely that: provocations. Instead of setting up fake Socratic dialogues or participating in insipid democratic roundtables, here is a thinker who admittedly was always looking for polemics and controversies, sometimes going straight for the ad hominem attack. At least now, with the recent editorial project of the Argentinian National Library, there are no more excuses for continuing to ignore the theoretical force of these provocations. More importantly, we can begin to appreciate the systematic impulse that runs through each of these works as their originating hypothesis. For English-language readers, finally, the situation is still dire, insofar as few of Rozitchner's essays – and none of his full-length books – have been translated until now.[1] The present translation of *Freud and*

---

1 Previous translations into English include Rozitchner 2008a, pp. 33–53; Rozitchner 2008b,

the Limits of Bourgeois Individualism seeks to remedy this imbalance by supplementing the few existing translations of individual essays with a rendering of Rozitchner's most extensive and systematic take on the so-called 'social' or 'collective' works of the founder of psychoanalysis. Thus, after a brief commentary on Freud's *New Introductory Lectures on Psychoanalysis*, the book provides the reader with a chapter-by-chapter analysis of *Civilisation and Its Discontents* and *Group Psychology and the Analysis of the Ego*.[2]

More than just treatises in academic philosophy, Rozitchner's books are like bricks thrown into the window of an unsuspecting neighbour, or Molotov cocktails whose long wick has yet to be ignited. The image of the brick is apt to evoke the mischievous child that León in a certain way continued to be until the end, with his loud sardonic laughter and his seemingly inexhaustible vital energy. Someone not unlike the young Augustine who, when he was still a pagan and long before he was to become canonised as a Christian saint, with a group of friends stole a few pears from a neighbour's garden. In Rozitchner's analysis of this famous episode, narrated at the beginning of the *Confessions* by the adult and converted Augustine, it is indeed a small act of rebellion, a collective petty crime whose fond recollection of companionship and law-breaking – in this case the infraction of the law of private property – is quickly erased under the repressive effects of guilt and shame, but not without leaving unconscious traces in the memory of its author, as if they were the rumours of an ancient drama that would never be completely forgotten. Saint Augustine thus writes, opening his joyful heart before the Lord: 'Let my heart now tell you what caused me to do wrong for no purpose, and why it was only my own love of mischief that made me do it. The evil in me was foul, but I loved it. I loved my own perdition and my own faults, not the things for which I committed wrong, but the wrong itself. My soul was vicious and broke away from your safe keeping to seek its own destruction, looking for no profit in disgrace but only for disgrace itself'.[3] This cause (*causa*), or this thing (*cosa*), which forms the real object-cause of desire behind the phantasmatic scene of the theft of pears in Augustine's *Confessions*, for Rozitchner recalls nothing so much as the maternal 'thing', the sensual and affective primordial matrix for that which Freud calls *das Ding*.

---

pp. 41–50; Rozitchner 2012a, pp. 147–57; and Rozitchner 2017, pp. 738–45. Parts of this Translator's Preface also appear in the presentation of this last translation, in Bosteels 2017, pp. 726–37.

2 Rozitchner 1979 [1972]. For further discussions of this work in English, see Plotkin 2001, pp. 166–90; Chapters 4 and 5 in Bosteels 2012, pp. 97–157; and Benezra 2016, pp. 515–32.

3 Augustine 1961, pp. 47–8 (translation modified to retain the reference to *causa*).

In the process of conversion to Christianity that constitutes the key moment of the *Confessions*, however, this maternal 'thing' will be painfully supplanted by the new law of the Father-God, representative of an abstract and purely quantitative infinity without which – according to Rozitchner's provocative thesis – capitalism would not have been able to take root in subjectivity much later in history: 'Triumphant capitalism, the quantitative and infinite accumulation of wealth in the abstract monetary form, would not have been possible without the human model of religious infinity promoted by Christianity, without the imaginary and symbolical reorganization operated in subjectivity by the new religion of the Roman Empire'.[4] It is for this reason that a reading of Augustine's *Confessions* can help us understand the new catastrophe that we are living again in the present, analogous to the times of decadence of the Roman Empire:

> Augustine becomes a model of the vicissitudes faced by the terrified men and women of his time. In that sense his *Confessions* offer the possibility of discerning and exposing the psychic mechanisms that the Christian Church has created over time to deepen and create a new availability to political power. This is achieved by opening, as a refuge from Roman despotic terror, an imaginary subjective refuge restricted to one's own devalued body, separated from the others who are also subjected, in order to produce human beings overcome in life by death.[5]

In fact, the episode of the theft of pears exemplifies a kind of original or primordial scene characteristic of Rozitchner's form of reading and writing in all of his works, not just in the analysis of the *Confessions* in the book *The Thing and the Cross: Christianity and Capitalism*, but also in an even more systematic way at the level of collective, group, or mass psychology, for example, in *Freud and the Limits of Bourgeois Individualism*. What is involved in this reading strategy always comes down to rescuing the original moment of collective rebellion over and against the existing legal, moral, and politico-theological order. When Freud, in his 'social' works such as *Totem and Taboo*, *Civilisation and Its Discontents*, or *Moses and Monotheism*, situates the origin of moral conscience in the crime of parricide on the part of a fraternal alliance, according to Rozitchner he is indicating precisely to what extent the transition from infancy to adulthood, both for the individual and by analogy for the human species, always

---

4 Rozitchner 1997, p. 9.
5 Rozitchner 1997, pp. 95–6.

presupposes and builds on a prior act of rebellion. Power does not impose its dominion on the child without first hiding the truth of the rebellion that supports it. Thus, we can understand what Rozitchner says in *Freud and the Limits of Bourgeois Individualism*, a book whose first publication coincides with the moment of Gilles Deleuze and Félix Guattari's *Anti-Oedipus* in post-68 France:

> Civilisation does not triumph over the child because, subjected from birth, the latter would prolong and extend this submission into adulthood. The child is a rebel and an aggressor and a victor; only the remorse over its triumph leads to the guilt that subsequently bends and subjects the child. It is because the child is deeply moral and pays with its guilt for the imaginary murder that the adult's morality, which is the true assassin, takes power over this noble sense and ratifies with its judgment an imaginary situation as if it were real.[6]

To go back to the example of the theft of pears in Augustine's *Confessions*, in this case too what is at stake for Rozitchner is to recover the moment of collective rebelliousness on the part of a group of companions ('the beardless plebes' says Rozitchner), subsequently betrayed in Augustine's implacable retrospective glance, when he accuses his friends as the true culprits of the crime. 'By myself I would not have committed that robbery. It was not the takings that attracted me but the raid itself, and yet to do it by myself would have been no fun and I should not have done it', Augustine remarks in the conclusion to his recounting of the episode in question. 'This was friendship of a most unfriendly sort, bewitching my mind in an inexplicable way. For the sake of a laugh, a little sport, I was glad to do harm and anxious to damage another; and that without thought of profit for myself or retaliation for injuries received! And all because we are ashamed to hold back when others say "Come on! Let's do it!"'[7] Rozitchner, unlike St. Augustine, does not shrink in his conviction that it is possible to traverse this labyrinthian path in the opposite direction, in order to recover the bewitching enthusiasm of collective rebellion as the sole source of all the existing power in the world.

In the beginning there was rebellion. This is how we could summarise the fundamental orientation behind all of Rozitchner's thinking. Such is the origin and principle of the world of historical action in general, where action always means transaction, so that the origin is marked by constant conflict and no

---

6 Rozitchner 1979 [1972], p. 221; see below, p. 227.
7 Augustine 1961, p. 52.

stable principle offers any protective safety for a good moral conscience. 'Transaction: objective-subjective elaboration of an agreement, the result of a prior struggle, of a combat in which the one who will become subject, that is, the I or the ego, is not that sweet angelical being called child, such as the adult imagines it, which would come to be molded with impunity by the system without resistance', Rozitchner insists. Rather, it is the other way around: 'If there is transaction, if the I is its locus, there was a struggle at the origin of individuality: there were winners and losers, and the formation of the subject is the description of this process'.[8] For Rozitchner, the real task of thought, regardless of whether it is called philosophy, theory, or still something else, is to reanimate the possible return to that forgotten origin of our subjectivity. Instead of being trapped in a closed structure of compulsive repetition, the aim would be to restore the force of historical possibility condensed in our subjective structures. The act of thinking thus participates in a common effort at defatalisation that exposes the contingency of the event nested in each structure, the rebellion prior to each submission, and the forgotten resistance behind each defeat.

The powerful originality of Rozitchner's work lies in the proposal of a combined history and theory of the subject, marked by at least two major thresholds: the institution of Christianity as the dominant monotheistic religion under the Roman Empire and the bloody origins of capitalism in the process of so-called primitive or originary accumulation and colonialist expansion of the West. Methodologically if not thematically speaking, Rozitchner's work in this regard is closer to Michel Foucault's *History of Sexuality* and its subsequent elaborations leading up to his lecture course on *The Hermeneutics of the Subject* than to Alain Badiou's *Theory of the Subject*. He seeks not only to map out an event-based theory of the subject, one that would be valid for all times, but also to elaborate on some of the major historic events that mark the thresholds and change the structures of subjectivity itself.

History and theory in this interpretation of the subject are as inextricably linked as the twin dimensions of structure and event. They are not opposed to one another but must be understood as being closely intertwined. Referring to the murder of the 'primordial father' as described by Freud, for example, Rozitchner points out:

> Thus, in the originary drama there lies hidden the structural meaning of the ground of every human being: there where event (the murder) and structure (the transition from natural individuality to cultural individu-

---

8 Rozitchner 2003a, pp. 20–1.

ation through the fraternal alliance) constitute the originary point from which all human rationality was produced. In the relation of individual to individual (between father and son), the mediating third was a collective being: the fraternal alliance. This initial moment is crucial because it is from this first opposition that, in the ambiguity of love and hatred toward the father, the point of insertion of the cultural dialectic takes shape – that is, of reason that supports itself in the flesh of the other but at the same time in the common body sketched out by the brothers, as a necessary process for one's own coming-into-being.[9]

By articulating the twin aspects of event and structure in the constitution of subjectivity, the latter also becomes open to its own transformation. Far from being wholly and strictly determining, the structure can be made to reveal the point of contingency from where it becomes subject to change.

This is, then, the lesson that we can draw from the image of the mischievous child stealing pears from a neighbor's garden or throwing stones into his window: there is an eventful act of rebellion at the origin of every structure of subjection. The image of the Molotov cocktail, on the other hand, can serve to evoke a particular historical figure of the collective militant subject who, especially in the last two decades, has become common throughout the world: from the crisis of 19–20 December 2001 in Argentina to the activists who in 2011 began to take to the squares in Egypt, Spain, Turkey, or the United States. There are many ties, some explicit and others still muted and subterranean, that link Rozitchner's work to this recent wave of militant politics which, more than revolutionary in the classical sense, would have to be called autonomist or insurrectionist – yet more proof, if any were needed, of the enormous value of the work of this philosopher for the twenty-first century. Following this image of the rioter, we could consider Rozitchner a street fighting philosopher in the best tradition of revolutionary anarchism, or what in the nineteenth century would have been called libertarian socialism. But, insofar as the subject of politics for Rozitchner is never an individual but a collective body, based on the generic force of a common power in feeling, acting, and thinking, it would be more appropriate to speak of him as a sensuous – he himself would have said *ensoñado*, 'sensuous-oneiric' or 'dreamed up' – anarcho-communist thinker of collective praxis. Philosophy, or theory, in relation to the event-like origin to be recovered from the existing power structures, in this sense is always a reflection on what we do in fact know, even if only unconsciously, about what a

---

9   Rozitchner 1979 [1972], p. 236; see below, p. 242.

body can do. And this knowledge, in turn, is not only a matter of reflection or contemplation: it also entails the verification and experimentation of what we unconsciously already know and feel, that is, the infinite power of the collective body, prolonged or inhibited as the case may be in the capacities of our very own flesh.

León Rozitchner's work includes four major books, devoted to polemical controversies with four major figures of philosophy and world politics: Max Scheler (*Person and Community*), Sigmund Freud (*Freud and the Limits of Bourgeois Individualism*), Juan Domingo Perón (*Perón: Between Blood and Time*) and Saint Augustine (*The Thing and the Cross*).[10] To these books, published during his lifetime, we can add several posthumous editions that are available thanks to the extraordinary work of Diego Sztulwark and Cristián Sucksdorf, the editors who also prepared an excellent series of individual introductions to each of the works of Rozitchner published by the National Library in Argentina: on the Venezuelan educator Simón Rodríguez (*Philosophy and Emancipation*), on Emmanuel Levinas (*Levinas or the Philosophy of Consolation*), on Karl Marx (*Marx and Infancy*), and on Hegel (*Psychic Hegel*), as well as a series of more circumstantial texts that sometimes had been difficult to find (the early *Bourgeois Morality and Revolution* about the hearings of the *contras* of the Bay of Pigs invasion in Cuba; his reflections on the 1967 Arab-Israeli conflict in *Being Jewish*; the posthumous compilation *Christian Questions*; or the even heftier collection of *Political Writings*) and more personal collections that León himself was able to oversee at the end of his life (the already mentioned slender volume *Oneiric Materialism*; the booklet *About the Defeat and the Vanquished*, which includes his polemic over the question of revolutionary violence with the Argentinian philosopher Óscar del Barco; and the mini-book *Live Tongues*, printed and packaged in the size of a cigarette box as part of another initiative of the National Library, dedicated to his young twin daughters Lara and Nathy).[11]

The central figures behind Rozitchner's philosophical legacy are undoubtedly Marx and Freud. As he explains from exile, in a series of six lectures delivered in Mexico and published under the slightly misleading title *Freud and the Problem of Power* (the volume more aptly could be called *Marx, Freud, and the Problem of Power*), these two figures should always be read together, not because one would add a part of the problem that the other, in a perfect chiasm of complementary blindness, would have failed to address, but because

---

10   See Rozitchner 1962; 1972 [1979]; 1985; 1997.
11   See Rozitchner 2012b; 2013a; 2015a; 2015b; 2012c [1962]; 2016 [1967]; 2013b; 2015c; 2011a; 2011b; 2009.

both think fundamentally the same problem from different angles, with more emphasis on the so-called 'objective' factors in Marx's case and on the 'subjective' factors in Freud's case. 'To try to understand this place, which is also individual, where that collective power continues somehow to generate itself and at the same time – as is all too clear – to inhibit itself in its development', such would be the goal. 'In short: What is the significance of the so-called "subjective" conditions in the development of collective processes that tend toward a radical transformation of social reality? Is the condition of radicality not determined precisely by deepening this repercussion of the so-called "objective" conditions in subjectivity, without which politics is bound to remain ineffective?'[12] These are some of the questions that Rozitchner asks about the unity of the objective and subjective aspects of political struggle at the beginning of *Freud and the Problem of Power*. But they reiterate a hypothesis that he had already formulated in an even more controversial way in his programmatic text 'The Left Without Subject', first published in 1966 in the Argentine leftwing journal *La Rosa Blindada* and reprinted in 1968 in the influential Cuban journal *Pensamiento crítico*.[13] According to Rozitchner, unless the Left is able to tackle the question of the subjective inscription of power, it also will not be able to organise the popular forces of rebellion. This is why he is so fond of quoting the phrase from the *Grundrisse* where Marx mentions 'both the objective and the subjective conditions, which are only the two distinct forms of the same conditions', just as he likes to repeat one of the initial phrases from *Group Psychology and the Analysis of the Ego*, where Freud affirms that 'from the very first individual psychology, in this extended but entirely justifiable sense of the words, is at the same time social psychology as well'.[14] Between the interpretations of both thinkers there exists a profound dialectic that still today should explain the interest of what not long ago used to be called Freudo-Marxism – a tradition parallel, as far as Rozitchner is concerned, to what at the same time begins to be developed in France in terms of Lacano-Althusserianism in a dialogue between the Marxism of Louis Althusser and the psychoanalysis of Jacques Lacan that would inspire such important contemporary philosophers as Badiou but also Slavoj Žižek and, in an expanded dialogue with Foucault, Judith Butler.

In fact, the title of one of the works of this last philosopher, *The Psychic Life of Power: Theories in Subjection*, could also serve to describe the entire traject-

---

12 Rozitchner 2003a, p. 11.
13 Rozitchner 1966, reprinted in the Cuban journal *Pensamiento crítico* 12 (1968), pp. 151–83; and again in the excellent anthology Rozitchner 1996, pp. 45–75.
14 Marx 1973, p. 832; and Freud 1959, p. 3.

ory of Rozitchner's thought, especially if we remember that for him the psychic element, far from being reducible to the Christian interpretation of the Greek *psychè* as soul, is inseparable from its inscription in the sensual, affective, and material density of the body. The Christian soul is rather the prison of the flesh, as Foucault also suggested in an ingenious inversion of the old saying according to which the body is the prison of the soul. How is it that we submit so commonly with body and soul to a regime of voluntary servitude? What role do imaginary dispositions such as Christianity or Judaism play in this subjection? And what do such dispositions have to do both with the generalised imposition of the capitalist regime of the commodity-form and with the possibility of revolt against its worldwide wall-to-wall domination today?

In articulating these questions throughout his work, Rozitchner in a certain sense does nothing more than cover the ground of the young Marx's intellectual path again and again: the trajectory in which, between 1841–3, he moved quickly from the critique of religion, via the critique of the Hegelian theory of the state, to the critique of political economy. These three critiques according to Rozitchner are historically and conceptually linked, so that none of them can be completely abandoned without betraying the overall revolutionary impulse behind all of Marx's thought. As we can read in the posthumously published manuscript that gives its title to the volume *Marx and Infancy*: 'As long as Marx is understood only in the field of economics, he will continue to hide the implicit refutation of all metaphysics and all theology'.[15] This explains the keen interest that Rozitchner has always shown for a polemical text such as 'On the Jewish Question', in which Marx takes up the question of religion – even though in 1843, according to the German thinker, the critique of religion already could be considered a closed matter, having been settled by young Hegelians like Ludwig Feuerbach – to show that the development of modern capitalism is inseparable from Christianity, as can be seen most emblematically according to Marx in the case of the United States. The supposed separation of Church and state does not contradict but rather confirms the fact that this youthful democracy represents the culmination of the Christian essence of the modern state. In fact, as is already indicated in the strange split between 'man' and 'citizen' in the 'Universal Declaration of the Rights of Man and of the Citizen', the religious separation between the earthly and the heavenly realms serves as an ideological matrix to maintain a homologous separation in the field of politics between the private individual (selfish holder of inalienable rights that make one formally free) and the public person (subject of the civic order of

---

15   Rozitchner 2015a, p. 74.

the republic which is supposed to be secular but in reality continues to be profoundly religious).

Again, what we can witness here is the deep unity of Rozitchner's entire thought, despite the presence of different stages as enumerated by the editors in their general presentation of his complete works. The illusory division between the individual and the collective, in effect, was already the subject of the author's first texts: not only in *Person and Community* but also in *Bourgeois Morality and Revolution*. *Freud and the Limits of Bourgeois Individualism* serves to give this topic its most systematic theoretical framework, which would subsequently enable Rozitchner to understand the failure of the Peronist movement to sustain a truly revolutionary popular power, as analysed in *Perón: Between Blood and Time*. Finally, as far as the thesis on the historical link between capitalism and Christianity is concerned, after *The Thing and the Cross* this is the problematic that would occupy Rozitchner's final philosophical reflections until his death, most notably in the interviews and journalistic texts compiled after the attacks of 9/11 on the Twin Towers and the wars in Iraq and Afghanistan, in the volume *Terror and Grace*.[16]

Thus, we see how the task proposed by León Rozitchner at the end of his life has its remote source in the combination of interests of the young Marx and the late Freud: to study not only the origin and limits of the capitalist economic system but also its political implications and its links with the imaginary and affective apparatuses of Christianity for the production of submissive and docile subjectivities. Following this track, Rozitchner seeks to retrace the steps leading to the fulfillment of the Christian spirit in the modern secular state. In a time still dominated by the war on terror and fundamentalism, justified in the name of the supposedly democratic but actually deeply racist values of Western Christian civilisation, the actuality of this proposal could not be more obvious.

In addition to developing a Freudo-Marxist theory of the subject, Rozitchner's reading of texts like Marx's 'On the Jewish Question' requires a reconstruction of the history not only of capitalist but also of pre-capitalist forms of subjectivity, in the style of what Rozitchner offers in *The Thing and the Cross*. 'We therefore must reach back from political to religious alienation in order to understand the persistence of the religious within the political', Rozitchner proposes in his careful commentary on Marx's youthful text. 'We must show that the Christian essence, which "critical criticism" claims to have overcome, remains and is objectified in the material social relations of the democratic sec-

---

16   Rozitchner 2003b.

ular state whose terminal form, as Marx demonstrates, is the United States of America; and show, moreover, how it persists to this very day'.[17] Even for the future author of *Capital*, who will delight in indicating the 'metaphysical subtleties' and 'theological niceties' of that demoniacal object that is the commodity, it is not enough to argue for the total emancipation of and from religion. In fact, the political abolition of religion runs the risk of leaving intact the religious and more properly Christian core of the dominant modern form of politics, that is to say, the religious matrix of the modern state as defended by Bruno Bauer and other young Hegelians, with whom Marx in 1843 is about to break. It is not simply a question of secularising religion in the name of an atheist materialism, but of travelling down the genealogical path back to that religious alienation in which political and economic alienation is still rooted today.

If Judaism and Christianity in different ways have shaped the organisation of subjectivity in the West, Rozitchner admittedly never considered addressing the function of Islam along the same lines as the third religion of the Book. Instead, he restricted himself to investigating the role of the first two religions in shaping our imaginary and symbolic structures of domination and servitude. In the final stage of his philosophical trajectory, a fundamental task in this regard amounted to gaining an understanding of the substance or matter on which such dispositions work. If religion constitutes a formal matrix for the constitution of historically changing modes of subjectivity, how can we describe the subject-matter on which these forms exert their power? Following the young Marx, Rozitchner sometimes chooses to call this substance the 'generic being' of the human species. Other times, he picks up on the implicit question left unanswered in the opening sentence of *Capital*. Indeed, although almost all readers of Marx assume that this book begins directly with the analysis of the commodity, the first noun of *Das Kapital* actually refers to the 'wealth' (*Reichtum*) of the human being as it could be imagined prior to, outside of, or beyond its incorporation into the logic of capitalist societies: 'The wealth of those societies in which the capitalist mode of production prevails, presents itself as "an immense accumulation of commodities", its unit being a single commodity'.[18] This suggests that there is another kind or at least another understanding of wealth, which does not present itself in the capitalist form of an accumulation of commodities. What, then, is this other kind of wealth and how can we think of it outside and beyond the societies where the capitalist mode of production dominates?

---

17   Rozitchner, 'La cuestión judía', in Vernik (ed.) 2011, p. 199.
18   Marx 1976, p. 125. For a fascinating interpretation of the opening line of *Capital*, an analysis openly declared to be in tune with Rozitchner's work, see Holloway 2015, pp. 3–26.

Rozitchner ultimately decided to answer this question by choosing to interpret the wealth of our generic being in terms of the maternal thing: the *mater* of *mater*ialism as the archaic or originary foundation, without which neither Marx nor Freud could have carried out their respective critiques – even if the maternal element in their mature works is as absent as the Christian essence remains invisible in the secular modern state, all while being omnipresent. Undoubtedly, this decision in favour of a sensuous and dreamlike materialism raises a number of questions that Rozitchner was not able fully to address at the end of his life. Not only does this *mater*ialism or *mother*ialism seem to imprint a limited heteronormativity on all sexual relationships, but in its emphasis on the plenitude of the child's bond with the mother it also may suggest a phantasmatic state that could easily be termed imaginary, in the pejorative sense that this adjective often has for someone like Lacan. Much of Rozitchner's interpretation in *Freud and the Limits of Bourgeois Materialism*, in fact, is already devoted to debunking the narcissistic imaginary of the child's blissful fusion with the mother, of which the oceanic feeling of religion for Freud represents a belated collective version or mass delusion. More so than the mere image of a lost paradise, however, the maternal thing for Rozitchner offers a necessary lever for the criticism of our present. Like the supposition of human wealth outside the eternal present dominated by the capitalist social relation, it is a dream-like fiction necessary to think of a pre-capitalist past without which we would not be able to imagine a post-capitalist future. Past and future at the same time, the maternal is the future past of a potentiality – to think, enact, and enliven the wealth of human intercorporeality outside of capitalism – to which Rozitchner's thought never will have ceased to be loyal.

Rozitchner's extended reading of two of Freud's best-known social works, in this sense, allows us to revisit a series of open questions: What is the logic of the social bond and how might psychoanalysis contribute to an elucidation of such a logic? Does taking psychoanalysis as a point of departure necessarily mean that the social bond is constituted primarily at the level of the psychic life of an individual? Or is it rather the other way around, so that our psychic life is ultimately determined by the historically changing nature of the social bond? And, if the understanding of this determination requires an articulation between the study of the psyche and the study of society, can such an articulation be achieved with that unique amalgamation once known as Freudo-Marxism? Is this tradition today bound to appear hopelessly outdated, if it was not stillborn? Or can we still draw useful parallels between what Freud did for the subject's conscious and unconscious psychic life and what Marx did for the production and reproduction of our social, economic, political, and ideological life? Does a mere parallelism between two supposedly autonomous traditions of self-described 'scientific' thought – even considering their respective critiques of the sciences of psychology and political economy – suffice to constitute a materialist and historical theory of the subject capable of understanding and, ideally, transforming the current state of affairs as well? Or must the alleged autonomy and internal consistency of each of these traditions – psychoanalysis and historical materialism – be put to the test of the radical insights of the other?

These are some of the fundamental questions directly or indirectly tackled in *Freud and the Limits of Bourgeois Individualism*, to which the reader hereby gains access in English, almost fifty years after the book's first edition in Spanish. I will not pretend to summarise Rozitchner's original answers to those questions. On the contrary, readers should be able to conclude for themselves if and to what extent the interpretation painstakingly elaborated in the more than five hundred pages that follow, always in close proximity to the letter and spirit of Freud's texts, is as productive today as it was for Latin American audiences in the 1970s, when the book quickly went through three editions. The sheer fact of the book's belated translation into English as well as some of the unique obstacles that I faced as its translator, though, deserve to be addressed in a few final comments to conclude this Introduction.

On the one hand, to translate a book of theory or philosophy is never just a matter of finding equivalences between two linguistic traditions. It also involves creating bridges or, alternatively, leaving productive gaps of incomprehension between different historical moments, theoretical trends, and discursive paradigms. There is, of course, a reason for why I think Rozitchner's Freud deserves to be put into a creative dialogue with contemporary thinkers such as Butler or Badiou. This is because, even though the period in which he wrote *Freud and the Limits of Bourgeois Individualism* coincided with the post-1968 atmosphere best captured in Deleuze and Guattari's *Anti-Oedipus*, Rozitchner reserves the greatest venom of his scorn for the school of Althusserians who at the time were rapidly gaining ascendancy in Latin America as much as, if not more so than, in France. For Louis Althusser and his followers, however, there was no point in developing a theory of the subject, except as an effect of pure ideology. At best, the subject was the 'bearer' of structural relationships or the 'placeholder' called upon to fill an empty slot within a structure that was to be mapped out with the rigour of Marxism as a new science, the science of history or historical materialism, for which a new philosophy would provide the conceptual scaffolding in the guise of dialectical materialism, or the materialist dialectic, already at work in a practical state in Marx's oeuvre. With thinly disguised attacks against the fashions of 'science' and 'theoretical practice', this is the classical Althusserian standpoint that Rozitchner repeatedly takes to task in the following pages. And yet, because of the way in which he mobilises Freud's 'social' or 'collective' works for the sake of a theory of the subject as the nucleus of historical verification, Rozitchner's book also anticipates a turn or return toward the subject that paradoxically would come to unite a great many ex-Althusserians in their attempts beginning in the early 1970s both to break with their former teacher and to develop a theory of political agency capable of accounting for the subject-effects of both subjection and subjectivization. As Badiou would claim in his *Theory of the Subject*, explaining why a disciple of Althusser would even bother with such a topic in the first place, it became clear that Marxists had to produce precisely a materialist theory of that very category of the subject which previously was considered to be the embodiment of humanist idealism: 'We demand of *materialism* that it include what we need and which Marxism, even without knowing it, has always made into its guiding thread: a theory of the subject'.[19] And this demand or this requirement, finally, is very much a conviction shared not only by other ex-Althusserians such as Jacques Rancière or Étienne Balibar but also, as the latter in particular would repeatedly come to insist, by thinkers such as Judith Butler in *The Psychic Life of Power*. Indeed, with chapters devoted to Hegel, Nietzsche, Freud, Foucault and Althusser (but none to Marx), Butler's book openly inscribes itself in the French linguistic and theoretical tradition structured around the double meaning of subject as both subjection and subjectivation: 'The term "subjectivation" carries the paradox in itself: *assujetissement* denotes both the becoming of the subject and the process of subjection – one inhabits the figure of autonomy only by becoming subjected to power, a subjection which implies a radical dependency'.[20]

Thus, too, in spite of Rozitchner's open antagonism against Althusser, or in part thanks to this opposition, there is something in his peculiar version of Freudo-Marxism that anticipates a productive dialogue with the Lacano-Althusserianism of several of Althusser's former students. Similarly, even though he only rarely invokes the name or work of the author of *History of Sexuality*, Rozitchner's reading of the genealogy of the subject in the wake of Christianity, the long and potentially still ongoing period of primitive capitalist accumulation, or the role of what he calls the three Oedipuses (Greek, Jewish, and Christian), can be understood productively in conjunction with Foucault's final seminars at the Collège de France.

---

19 Badiou 2013, p. 182.
20 Butler 1997, p. 83. See also Étienne Balibar, Barbara Cassin, and Alain de Libera, 'Subject', in Cassin (ed.) 2014, pp. 1069–91; and Rancière 1995, pp. 63–72.

All this, however, is not meant as a way to retrieve or salvage a Latin American author only in the name of his possible anticipations of better-known voices and theories from Europe and the United States. Nor should the suggestion of these comparisons be seen as an attempt to erase the discomfort that certain elements in Rozitchner's views on gender, race, or sexuality might cause in the contemporary reader. At the same time, I also do not believe that we should strive to read and translate only those texts that already coincide fully with our own ideas, presuppositions, biases, or preferences. My wager as a reader and a translator has always been that it is worth more to work through the logic of a given text, complete with its problems and promises, than to strive for an ideal norm that even in the best scenario would give us only the good conscience of a shortsighted and ahistorical moral superiority. Especially in the case of a book like Rozitchner's *Freud and the Limits of Bourgeois Individualism*, which on page after page argues for an understanding of the subject as the place of verification of history, such a wager has strengthened my conviction that it would have been counterproductive to clean up the translation for readers who come to this interpretation in the twenty-first century with a lot of new baggage as well as problems and promises of their own.

On the other hand, the present translation faced a number of other challenges that could be helpful for the reader to understand. Many of these challenges are typical of translations of Freud's works in general, for which Rozitchner's text requires us to switch back and forth between German, Spanish, and English:

Cultura, in Spanish, serves to translate Freud's term *Kultur* typically translated as 'civilisation' in English, as in *Civilisation and Its Discontents*. For the sake of consistency with Rozitchner's own paraphrases, I have sometimes used both English terms, 'culture or civilisation', and 'the world of culture or civilisation' for *el mundo cultural*.

Masas, 'masses' or 'multitudes', is the official Spanish translation of Freud's *Massen*, as in *Massenpsychologie und Ich-analyse*, rather unfortunately rendered into English as *Group Psychology and the Analysis of the Ego*.

El yo, el superyó, el ello are the Spanish renderings of Freud's *das Ich, das Über-ich* and *das Es*, again rather unfortunately but officially translated into English with the Latinate expressions 'the ego', 'the super-ego' and 'the id'. Like Freud's German, the Spanish language gives Rozitchner much greater freedom to play on the grammatical flexibility of these personal pronouns and neologisms, leading me on occasion to use analogous English expressions such as 'the *it*'.

Instintos for the most part has been left as 'instincts' as in the standard English translations of Freud's work, even though 'drives' would have been better from a contemporary theoretical perspective.

Conciencia in Spanish can mean both 'consciousness' and 'conscience'. Sometimes, when Rozitchner and Freud's Spanish translator mean exclusively the latter, they will use *conciencia moral*. When the meaning is unstable, I often alternate between the two English words, or use both at the same time.

Enfermo is the official Spanish translation that corresponds to 'patient' in the English version of Freud's writings (*Kranke* in German). I frequently translate this as 'sick person' or 'the sick' in keeping with the context of Rozitchner's explanations.

Líder, *jefe*, and *caudillo* in the Spanish text are used almost indistinctly to refer to the 'leader' or 'chief' in Freud's account of the primordial or primal father, whom Rozitchner compares and contrasts with the figure of the Latin American *caudillo*, the 'leader' or 'strongman'.

Proto-, *primigenio* and *primordial* are rendered as 'primeval', 'primordial', or 'primal', but sometimes are left in German with *Ur-* as prefix.

Semejante and *semejanzas* refer to the 'similitudes', 'similarities' or 'likenesses' that are the result of the psychic mechanism of identification.

Prójimo refers to one's 'neighbour', as in the Judeo-Christian tradition frequently referenced by Freud.

Other translation issues, finally, have to do with idiosyncrasies of Rozitchner's style and vocabulary:

Desentrañar, typically translated as 'to disentangle', is Rozitchner's preferred expression for talking about the task of analysis. It also includes a wordplay on *entrañas*, 'guts' or 'entrails', and *entrañable*, meaning 'endearing' or, more literally, 'having to do with a deep feeling'. Something *entrañablemente moral* therefore becomes 'a deeply moral gut feeling'.

Discriminación and *indiscriminación*, like *discernimiento* and *indiscernimiento*, should be understood in the sense of the capacity for establishing or discerning differences, and not in the legal or political sense of racial or sexual discrimination. For this reason, I have opted as often as possible for 'discernment' and 'lack of discernment', 'indiscriminateness', or 'indistinction'.

Cortar por lo sano means 'to make a clean break', but insofar as the expression also includes a reference to 'healthy', *sano*, it becomes a pun that conveys something like 'opting for the normalcy of health'.

Detener is alternatively translated as 'halt', 'hold back', 'hold at bay', 'thwart', 'detain' or '(keep in) check'.

Salida and *salida en falso* refer to the 'escape', 'exit (scenario)' or 'way out', including the 'false way out' of pathological formations.

El cuerpo a cuerpo is a common expression with which Rozitchner refers to the 'one-on-one conflict', the 'bodily encounter', or the 'clash' among bodies that makes up what he elsewhere calls human intercorporeality.

Hecho histórico is not so much a 'historic fact' in the positivistic sense but rather a 'historic deed', something that is the result of a 'doing' or *hacer*. It can be understood in accordance with to Giambattista Vico's principle of *verum factum*, which holds that the truth is humanly made and therefore, for Rozitchner, can be unmade and remade.

Bibliography

Saint Augustine, *Confessions*, translated by R.S. Pine-Coffin, London: Penguin, 1961.

Badiou, Alain 2013, *Theory of the Subject*, translated by Bruno Bosteels, London: Bloomsbury.

Benezra, Karen 2016, 'León Rozitchner's Mass Psychology', *Journal of Latin American Cultural Studies*, 25.4.

Bosteels, Bruno 2012, *Marx and Freud in Latin America: Politics, Psychoanalysis, and Religion in Times of Terror*, London: Verso.

Bosteels, Bruno 2017, 'The Psychic Life of the Power of Rebellion: Introducing León Rozitchner's "Philosophy and Terror"', *Theory & Event*, 20.2.

Butler, Judith 1997, *The Psychic Life of Power: Theories in Subjection*, Stanford: Stanford University Press.

Cassin, Barbara (ed.) 2014, *Dictionary of Untranslatables: A Philosophical Lexicon*, translated by Emily Apter, Jacques Lezra, and Michael Wood, Princeton: Princeton University Press.

Freud, Sigmund 1959, *Group Psychology and the Analysis of the Ego*, trans. James Strachey, New York: W.W. Norton.

Holloway, John 2015, 'Read Capital: The First Sentence, or, Capital Starts with Wealth, not with the Commodity', *Historical Materialism*, 23.3: 3–26.

Marx, Karl 1972, *Grundrisse: Foundations of the Critique of Political Economy (Rough Draft)*, translated by Martin Nicolaus, London–New York: Penguin.

Marx, Karl 1976, *Capital: A Critique of Political Economy*, Volume I, translated by Ben Fowkes, London: Penguin.

Plotkin, Mariano 2001, 'When Marx Meets Freud', in *Freud in the Pampas: The Emergence and Development of a Psychoanalytic Culture in Argentina*, Stanford: Stanford University Press.

Rancière, Jacques 1995, 'Politics, Identification, and Subjectivization', *The Identity in Question*, edited by John Rajchman, New York-London: Routledge.

Rozitchner, León 1962, *Persona y comunidad: Ensayo sobre la significación ética de la afectividad en Max Scheler*, Buenos Aires: Eudeba.

Rozitchner, León 1966, 'La izquierda sin sujeto', *La rosa blindada* 9.

Rozitchner, León 1979 [1972], *Freud y los límites del individualismo burgués*, Mexico City: Siglo Veintiuno.

Rozitchner, León 1985, *Perón: Entre la sangre y el tiempo: Lo inconsciente y la política*, Buenos Aires: Centro Editor de América Latina.

Rozitchner, León 1996, *Las desventuras del sujeto político: Ensayos y errores*, Buenos Aires: El Cielo por Asalto.

Rozitchner, León 1997, *La Cosa y la Cruz: Cristianismo y Capitalismo (en torno a las Confesiones de san Agustín)*, Buenos Aires: Losada.

Rozitchner, León 2003a, *Freud y el problema del poder*, Buenos Aires: Losada.

Rozitchner, León 2003b, *El terror y la gracia*, edited by Rubén H. Ríos, Buenos Aires: Norma.

Rozitchner, León 2008a, 'The Thing and the Cross: Christianity and Capitalism (About Saint Augustine's *Confessions*)', translated by Karen Benezra and Rachel Price, *Polygraph*, 19–20.

Rozitchner, León 2008b, 'Exile, War and Democracy: An Exemplary Sequence', translated by Philip Derbyshire, *Radical Philosophy*, 152.

Rozitchner, León 2009, *Lenguas vivas*, Buenos Aires: Biblioteca Nacional.

Rozitchner, León 2011a, *El materialismo ensoñado: Ensayos*, Buenos Aires: Tinta Limón.

Rozitchner, León 2011b, *Acerca de la derrota y de los vencidos*, Buenos Aires: Quadrata/Biblioteca Nacional.

Rozitchner, León 2012a, 'Terror and Grace', translated by Philip Derbyshire, *Journal of Latin American Cultural Studies*, 21.1.

Rozitchner, León 2012b, *Filosofía y emancipación: Simón Rodríguez: el triunfo de un fracaso ejemplar*, Buenos Aires: Biblioteca Nacional.

Rozitchner, León 2012c [1962], *Moral burguesa y revolución*, Buenos Aires: Biblioteca Nacional; original edition Procyon.

Rozitchner, León 2013a, *Levinas o la filosofía de la consolación*, Buenos Aires: Biblioteca Nacional.

Rozitchner, León 2013b, *Cuestiones cristianas*, Buenos Aires: Biblioteca Nacional.

Rozitchner, León 2015a, *Marx y la infancia*, Buenos Aires: Biblioteca Nacional.

Rozitchner, León 2015b, *Hegel psíquico 1*, Buenos Aires: Biblioteca Nacional.

Rozitchner, León 2015c, *Escritos políticos*, Buenos Aires: Biblioteca Nacional.

Rozitchner, León 2016 [1967], *Ser judío y otros ensayos afines*, Buenos Aires: Biblioteca Nacional; original Ediciones de la Flor, 1967; reedition Losada 2011.

Rozitchner, León 2017, 'Philosophy and Terror', translated by Don T. Deere and Ricardo Ortiz Vázquez, *Theory & Event*, 20.3.

Vernik, Esteban (ed.) 2011, *Volver a 'La cuestión judía'*, Barcelona: Gedisa.

Introduction

How to justify, between us, one more book? This is not a rhetorical question: Is it possible to write without shame anything else that is not about torture, assassinations, humiliation, and dispossession, when the order of reality in which we live is built on their foundation? And yet, this is what I write about; and it is against this backdrop that we propose to think here. This also does not mean to relegate violence to the field of mere signs. A violent book must sound like a mockery for those who really confront torture and death. There exists, in any literary expression, a step not yet taken, a distance that no word can overcome, because this step exists in some beyond in the direction of which language is gesturing: the space where, if we dared to take the step, what would appear is the presence of death.

Perhaps this book, in the ideality of its paper and ink, is only the intent to understand a distance that the bourgeoisie opened up in each one of us: to know what it is that resists within us in order to go beyond our own limits. This work therefore is dedicated, with a preference, to the Left: the book is inscribed in the very problems that are discussed in it. That is to say, it is inscribed in a new stage of the class struggle in Argentina, where popular commotion and resistance have produced the unprecedented reality of our situation: the uprisings of entire cities against the occupying army that one class gave itself, so it thinks, in order to stop the dialectic of history. In these years that reach all the way to the present, much pain, frustration, and suffering continue to delimit the boundaries of the distance covered – in the torture, rape, and killing that power prolongs. This is why the present book asks, indirectly, about the conditions of personal and collective effectiveness in the sphere of political action. It should not be read, nor should its title be understood, as a 'scientific' work, written in the third person: it was written in the first person. It is, if you want, a book 'with a subject'. And when I say 'Freud and the limits of bourgeois individualism', I am not talking only about the limits of some other, but through analysis about my own. In writing this book I wanted above all to erase the distance and the restraint to which we are introduced by the 'scientific' formulations that are so fashionable today in their pretense of truth, in which the wisdom of well-read meanings – in this case psychoanalysis – is always inscribed in the framework of the sick person: always the other, but never one's own subjectivity. Everyone can read Freud, we can all realise this miracle that reading makes possible: to pass on to others this 'dedicated' meaning that language brings up within ourselves, this meaning that, coming from the outside, we had to animate with our personal reading in order for it really to emerge. The clandestine nature of reading, in its solitude, though seemingly the most personal act, in reality makes possible the greatest distance and the maximum of depersonalisation. This is the miracle: always to situate the 'object' outside of oneself, distancing it from the irreducibly individual place where nonetheless meaning comes to be thought in the process of reading, in order to transfer it to a beyond which leaves us untouchable, as if language – now called 'discourse', with a further increment in the distancing – always described the foreign. *De te fabula narratur*, Marx reminds us; we speak about *our very own ego*, Freud signals. This return to the subject is now more necessary than ever; thanks to structuralism, we end up not speaking but being spoken. We dissolve ourselves in the impersonal, which is conceptualised within us as the anonymous space of signification and, thus, devoid of responsibility.

Science 'has no subject', we are told. But we know that politics does have a subject. Beyond the negated subject, who suffers? Who suffers the torture? Politics has torture and death at its disposal, given that pain and the end of life are never anonymous, despite the fact that the aim of the repressor, too, consists in annihilating the subject. In its limit-case politics shows the two extremes in dissociation, which is something the 'scientist' – as well as the police officer – eludes in his spiritual and anonymous practice: the union of the most individual and the most collective. If science were to talk about the subject doing science, it would not be able to avoid including within its discourse the total dimension in which the being or non-being of that humanity referred to in science is at stake. It would not be able to do without including the subject's own self in its quest for truth. *Politics* also means to give rise to this distance hidden within oneself by the bourgeois mode of reading, in order to open up in one's own terrorised flesh the place of personal contradiction; it means to unravel the limits that link us to the others in a closeness that erases the distances and false differences with their meagre oppositions. But if this kind of thinking is already political, it is because it vanquishes a distance and opens up a real path through the work of one's own transformation. Because it manages to include in one's self, and to extend in its compass, the collective power from which we were separated. This is why in the present work I was interested in reaching that dimension where the ideology that is present even in the politics of the Left, in the form of a distancing of the subject – as well as the obfuscations that this generates – continues to be through and through ideological, albeit leftist, *because of the way in which it is used*. The 'scientific' truth serves all purposes, including – why not? – to hide, by showing itself, the truth of one's own subjectivity. The same holds for 'theory': it serves to reach the truth of 'knowledge', but only in its structural generality, which is used as a new shield and a new trap, in order to install oneself in conventional reality. Also revolutionary theory and Marxism and psychoanalysis, even Freud and Marx themselves, offer a warm place of refuge from the storm of violence and persecution. The 'functionary of humanity', as Husserl defined the philosopher, has been converted without further ado into the bureaucrat of the ideas of others: knowledge became institutionalised, and 'theoretical practice' separated. But separated not only from politics: also from itself. If there is an exterior distance that the structure articulates – and people take pleasure these days in showing this ironclad determination – this exterior distance must also exist for the subject who is, they say, the 'bearer' of this articulation. But in that case the subject is also the place of the historical debate and it is there that the truth of the system that traverses it becomes verified.

So we ask ourselves in this book what limits the knowledge and transformation that the Left proposes for itself must cross in order to provide the adequate theory that would prolong itself in political activity. We think that in this context Freud's word has something to offer: in order to understand what is popular culture, what is collective action, what it means to form a militant. Or, if you want: how far must the revolution reach, even in its urgency, in order to be effective? What unknown determinisms must it combat and, among them, which ones are those that continue to sustain in spite of everything the project of radical transformation *without radicalness*? For one, the impoverishment of theory, which in bringing out the objective moment of the structure of production as its sole enemy leaves by the wayside the problem of the subjects determined by this structure. It only considers them as instruments of the transformation and passive ones to boot, even in their militant activity. It leaves out, as if this were not part of the productive force of reality itself, the personified place in which the power of opposition also is generated to the point of including itself in the decision collectively to transform the system.

And do not tell me that to negate the subject means to negate, in science as much as in politics, one's own bourgeois subjectivity. In one case as in the other, this negation cannot be obtained by way of a leap but only at the end of a process. By negating it in one leap, the bourgeois subject who makes the transition to the revolution also throws overboard, together with the effective negativity that constitutes it, an effective power that it abandons perhaps too lightly. What is it that one thus abandons?

What one abandons is precisely this nucleus which in the subject, because of its class determination, would have had to keep it closely tied to its old privileges: one abandons in oneself the nucleus of a valid affirmation. Because it was also one's – class? – privilege to be able to discern the truth of one's insertion *in spite of determinism*. This power, which it was allowed to discern, is not meant to be delegated. The invitation that we transform reality will always be 'exterior' if it is not also included in the 'place' where the elaboration of the revolutionary transition appears as organising the subjective structure of the political subject. Is it not the case that by negating the 'subject' as private property and class privilege, a fundamental and bourgeois pessimism subsists with regard to the contents of one's thought? Will we not have generalised too lightly this 'viper's nest' of one's own subjectivity as being irreducible to all transformation? Perhaps it is also from this pessimism that the 'activist' decision is borne that requires 'man' to be a mere function carried out in a given context. They need its punctual efficacy, which they say is political, but not its personal transformation. Or perhaps, in prolonging their own negation, they need to subdue, always in function of efficacy and urgency, that aspect of the other which appears in terms of the 'subject'. Here words abound to justify in theory, with a certain taste of Stalinism, the self-deprecation of the human being: ideological 'support', bearer, always messenger, harbinger of someone else's truth, and, in the final instance, slave. This disdain occurs in the guise of an instrumental justification, always in the service of the best cause. Althusser writes with great realism, and our realist friends repeat, without blushing:

> In a classless society, just as in a class society, ideology has the function to guarantee the *linkage* of men and women among themselves within the ensemble of the forms of their existence, the *relation* of individuals to the tasks that the social structure fixates for them.[1]

This much is clear: the anonymous power of the structure fixates the anonymous place of the supports. By eliminating the subject one eliminates at the same time the problem of subjective submission: qua ideological subject, its necessity is to be subjected, in the way the tasks of the social structure prescribe. Already the 'knowledge' expert anticipates, from within the bourgeoisie, where he will end up: he will end up falling in line, on the side of power, bringing with him his transparent scientific purity against the opacity of the 'bearers'.

If the subject is an illusion, and it is our own bourgeois subjectivity that makes the transition impossible, let us abandon this illusion – they tell us – together with the debris of the society that we must overcome. And there, amidst the old junk of the bourgeoisie, what remains is also the field of an essential contradiction that was not assumed or taken to its extreme limit. As if the contradiction of the system were not also elaborated in the contents and relations of these subjects who overextended themselves beyond their class

---

1 Althusser 1974, pp. 54–5.

destiny and decided not to bother anymore with their 'petty bourgeois' ideas. Trunks of the Left, stripped of what is most proper to them by the Althusserian defoliation, remain without sap and without leaves, just mere skeletons of a previous or possible density. Colonised in the end by the fashion of the European centres, of which they also scream the latest slogan, what better proof of the colonising submission than this demand before which those humiliated by knowledge give up what is most proper, their own difference, that most particularised place from which this difference could emerge: their own submitted subjectivity? Because it is another reality that is screaming here, and not our own. But this does not mean that the petty bourgeois in each one of us who started to make the transition ended up accepting the 'science' of Marxism: that which is negated in the abstract subsists and, as Freud teaches us, it continues to determine us, except now by dedicating our energies to making sure that it does not appear. These are the meanderings of the repressive logic that no political privilege would be able to annul.

Why just *now* does this problem appear? Each author accentuates that which, coming from the bourgeois determination, was previously the place of a blind spot that the others were also not able to illuminate, for which there was not yet an adequate answer, but which must be included in the discernment of the real. I think that it is Freud who illuminates this personal and social blind spot for Marxism, which previously had already determined its location. The insistence of the problem of the subject, blind spot in political Marxism, only gains validity precisely insofar as it is denied. For it constitutes one of the extremes of the historical dialectic, without which the meaning of the revolution is lost.

Because this too is inscribed in the class struggle, which by force means ideological struggle. An ideological struggle, which means not only to struggle against the bourgeoisie that confronts us, but also, in addition, to undo the traps that the bourgeoisie has included in ourselves as its most profound effectiveness, which thereby produces our ineffectiveness, despite our declared intent to destroy it. How can we effectively think the transition toward the revolution if we have been made with the categories of the bourgeoisie, if we still live within the boundaries marked out by its reality? Science, the knowledge of the structure that determines us, must reach all the levels of our reference to the real in order to revitalise them and convert them into adequate receptacles to decipher its signs, its symbols and its institutions, as well as the gestures, words, and images with which they inundate us. Subjectivity is also an institution. If the most general system of rational deciphering, which Marxist theory announced and which is present in the work of Freud, is not prolonged and enervated in the corporeity of a subject exercising it as an instrument that situates reason in the density of its own life, how can we *see* reality, how can we *act* as mediator between theory and the specific practice of the here and now in which it should be applied if it has to have human meaning? How, if not, could we elaborate our insertion and motivate that of others in the same process? Dispersion and abandonment are present, as the future that awaits us, in any political determination that would appear to animate the actors only from the outside, without therefore including the subject within it.

This is why Freud's teachings are so important for Marxism and politics: because in the analysis of the subject extended to the point of showing the determinations of the system in its most profound subjectivity they converge with and ratify the truths that Marx analysed in the 'objective' structures of the system of production. A message and a truth that the majority of psychoanalysts ignore, but that the revolutionary militants should incorporate as a form of knowledge that belongs to them as well. As long as psychoanalytic theory does not re-encounter the foundation of individual liberation in the recuperation of a collective power, which only the organisation for the struggle renders effective; as long as it does not re-encounter as the foundation of every 'cure' the – non-aleatory – necessity of aiming that violence, which the normal and the sick persons exert upon themselves, *now against the repressive system*; and until this necessity appears as a necessity inscribed in the essence and foundation of the 'psychic apparatus', this apparatus will be, in each one of us, an infernal machine mounted by the enemy in what is most proper to us. And as long as it fails to do this, psychoanalytical theory will only be an ideology, which stands still, fearful, on the threshold of its most fruitful discovery: the discovery of the class struggle included within human subjectivity as the nucleus of its most individual existence, which because of the form imposed on it by bourgeois individualism, is ignorant about itself.

Our thesis consists in affirming that every subject is also the nucleus of *historical truth* and it is with the aim of demonstrating this thesis that the present work sets out. To that end we will look for support, especially, in two 'social' works by Freud: *Civilisation and Its Discontents* and *Group Psychology and the Analysis of the Ego*.

PART 1

The Internal Distance

CHAPTER 1

The Articulation and the Breach

All the quotations and page numbers in this Chapter, unless otherwise indicated, correspond to the *New Introductory Lectures on Psycho-Analysis*, *The Standard Edition of the Complete Psychological Works of Sigmund Freud*, vol. XXII (1932–1936). Other references to Freud will also be provided in the text.

To pass over into reality: such is the distance to be overcome. But how can we comprehend the distance that opens up in reality in order to be crossed, if by definition we are installed in it? The first problem of a theory of action supposes, therefore, that we previously make visible that which cannot be seen, because it forms a system with what we are. This is the paradoxical aspect of the radical beginning: to discover a distance that exists in being already covered over by proximity as if, as a result, it were inexistent.

It is in dreams that Freud proposes to surprise this invisibility of the distance by putting into relief that which all proximity promises to us, there where the distance appears already filled with the unitary coincidence of the two extremes that define it: desire and the object of its satisfaction. In this distance is where the psychic apparatus opens up, the place in which the drama of unsatisfied desire unfolds.

The adult's dream continues to fulfil the desire just as the first object relation fulfilled it in the child. At the origin need became desire, Freud tells us, because the inaugural distance was shortened by the other: the mother recognised the child's cries of despair, and came closer so as to satisfy it. This suturing without hiatus and without distance, this covering of space that the other accomplished by coming closer when the need was only convulsively proffered by the child in the form of a scream, remains forever as a privileged form of satisfaction:

> A hungry baby screams or kicks helplessly. But the situation remains unaltered, for the excitation arising from an internal need is not due to a force producing a momentary impact but to one which is in continuous operation. A change can only come about if in some way or other (in the case of the baby, through outside help) an 'experience of satisfaction' can be achieved which puts an end to the internal stimulus [...] As a result of the link that has thus been established, next time this need arises a psychical impulse will at once emerge which will seek to re-cathect the mnemic image of the perception and to re-evoke the perception itself, that is to say,

> to re-establish the situation of the original satisfaction. An impulse of this kind is what we call a wish; the reappearance of the perception is the fulfilment of the wish; and the shortest path to the fulfilment of the wish is a path leading direct from the excitation produced by the need to a complete cathexis of the perception. (Freud, *The Interpretation of Dreams*, SE 5: 565–6)

We already see: the distance with regard to the external world, which is maximal and unknown, is covered by the child by following the *shortest path* from within its own nascent subjectivity: it traverses this distance within itself.

> Nothing prevents us from assuming that there was a primitive state of the psychical apparatus in which this path was actually traversed, that is, in which wishing ended in hallucinating. Thus the aim of this first psychical activity was to produce a 'perceptual identity' – a repetition of the perception which was linked with the satisfaction of the need. (*The Interpretation of Dreams*, SE 5: 566)

The magic repeats itself, but little by little it becomes distended in its invocation, defrauded by repetition. Only hallucination brings the object back in its indelible and shining first presence, in being the object that is truly full, though *now* ineffective. But what the adult's time solidified, the dream returns and opens up day after day. For this reason, when the need arises again, converted forever into the desire of a wish by the form of the other, it lacks the distance from its object: it chooses the shortest path. But what separates the need from the object, this path, which is necessarily unknown and which extends itself, indomitable and surprising, is reality itself. Reality is the announcement of possible presence, but against the background of the very absence of this first object, which, in its case for real, would fully satisfy the wish. The distance from the real and effective object is redoubled on the basis of the absence of the first recovery. And from there, from its separation, what will gradually emerge and produce itself is the density of its reality: perspectives that become integrated, that qualify it and discover it, all the while covering it up, that give it a profile and define it as 'real', but simultaneously adding the time and space of a finitude and an independence that from now on will be our misfortune. Because compared to this actual and laborious density of the adult, the other, infantile satisfaction, in its punctual and instantaneous coincidence, which is infinite in its own way, continues to be for unconscious desire the most real, for being the first one. To hallucinate it means to coincide: the supremely satisfying coincidence took place without distance. But there really was a distance, even though the newborn could not know it. From this first distance, from the distance brought near without a path to cross because it is from there that the path opened up in the first place, there will later open up the terror of remoteness, *and reality*. All real distance, all non-coincidence, will become remote and infinite distance for desire.

This permanence of unsatisfied desire in the midst of reality is what Freud attempts to capture. His mode of access, denied by the wakefulness of normality, only opens up clearly – darkly – in dreams and in madness. But this is not to say that everyday life has disappeared. The magic of desire subsists within us, but it disguises itself in the real and appears as though surrounding the real with the halo of the supplementary infinity of a time halted in its secured repetition: thus the most prosaic element is sustained in wakefulness by the same mechanism as in hallucination. The hallucination, the one that revives in the act of dreaming, does not disappear: it prolongs itself, once we are already awake, like an invisible shadow in the thickness of the real, and its absence is terrifying and moving in every visible presence. Whence the attempt at consolation: as if only to redouble the ever more categorical presence of what is given could scare away its past halo. As if the supreme empirical and material coincidence with the object could once again, at last, produce the 'identity of perception' within the 'identity of reality': in the repetition of a world and an order always identical with itself. The 'normal' person is a person sick with reality. Except that now, as opposed to the one asleep, the normal person projects this reality as permanence and thereby obtains the constant identity of the real itself. The conventional reality that tranquillises and no longer terrifies, as in the consoling hallucination, is that which remains identical. If reality did not console the desire at the same time as it defrauds it, the unsatisfied wish would push it to transform that reality which denies it: perhaps we would dream less, perhaps we would act more.

This is the task: to formulate the problem of the origin of the social and historical distance – the objective path – by going back to the distance that opens up in the seminally unsatisfied desire – the subjective path; to include the historical space within the psychic space. There exists, in other words, a complementary and correlative mode of access to the comprehension of the historical distance that politics confronts – the distance that opens up in the class struggle – from that original distance which links the interior with the exterior, the subjective with the real space in which the unsatisfied desire prolongs itself, not without residue, looking for its satisfaction.

1   The 'Harmless Dream-Psychosis'

What function does sleeping perform, given that it is part of the unity of life, but keeping in mind that its meaning appears given in wakefulness? To what form of real organisation does the dream take us back by extricating us, every day, necessarily, from the world in order to prepare us, after sleeping, to submerge ourselves once more in it? What distance opens up between being awake and being asleep? Because sleeping is the withdrawing of human beings from the world *within* the world, once their active relation with reality is suspended.

> The state of sleep involves a turning-away from the real external world ... (16)

This 'normal' withdrawal from reality will serve to put into relief the extreme limit of the habitual – but invisible – distancing that the subject opens up within itself with regard to the world. In his attempt to understand and explain the psychic activity in the dream, Freud will show us these elaborations in a moment of the organism's rest, repose, or passivity. In other words, he will show us what happens in the psychic space when the relation of the subject with reality momentarily finds itself suspended. In its everyday aspect, this is an extreme case that every human being normally lives through. What processes – Freud asks himself – are produced in this case? In the most habitual of everyday acts, in this rhythm that biology prolongs without surprises in every human being, in the repose of sleep, the conflicted activity of dreaming nevertheless introduces itself. In the most irreducible of 'biological' activities the presence of the historical determination that continues to elaborate itself intrudes precisely there. There is a distance that needs to be understood between biological sleeping and cultural dreaming.

> ... the dream is a pathological product, the first member of the class which includes hysterical symptoms, obsessions and delusions, but ... it is distinguished from the others by its transitoriness and by its occurrence under conditions which are part of normal life. (15–16)

The dream is not read here from the point of view of the official cultural link, congruent with 'reality': this is why it appears as pathological. Freud took the dream seriously. From the point of view of the unsatisfied wish that must find satisfaction in reality, and also from the point of view of a theory of the true action which opens the framework of satisfaction within reality, *the dream – not sleep – is a sickness*. Because in the dream there is no true satisfaction.

Which would mean: for human beings to be able to satisfy their desire in reality, to sleep would not be to dream. The dream only tries to compensate the defective relation to reality: because of this, and because it does not manage to do this, it is pathological. So this much is clear: if Freud talks about the dream, it is because he wants to analyse the *normal* modalities of withdrawal and concealment of reality, those of a false act which does not reveal – therein lies its specific structure – the meaning of the lack of reality for which it comes in as a compensation.

The dream is, moreover, an extreme case in which our own delirium does not bother us: it only bothers us in the delirious person, in the sick person who does this for real, but not in us. The dream is this peculiar object that managed to conceal, in all its marvel, the astonishment that it should arouse in us: this power of oblivion that is present precisely in what is most significant. Its power of oblivion resides precisely in that there is no distance between the lived and the signified. Its only distance, wherein lies the actual power of illusion of the dream, is not with itself – there is no difference – but with its opposite; and its opposite is wakefulness. But wakefulness has the same characteristics as the dream: it also does not open up any distance, usually, within itself. Both in the dream and in wakefulness we coincide with the object: we *are* the dream, we *are* the wakefulness. And the distance that knowledge habitually introduces does not affect the unshakable certainty of being, in which *in spite of everything we remain*.

What is left, then, is the fact that, coming from the state of wakefulness, sleep separates us from reality.

> The state of sleep involves a turning-away from the real external world, and there we have the necessary condition for the development of a psychosis. (16)

The dream's psychosis only prolongs itself in the pathology of the wakeful state: there we have the transition from the dream to wakefulness. Even though the 'normal' person does not know it, because for him 'the dreams are but dreams' (*los sueños, sueños son*). But what interests Freud, as production of a normal psychosis, are the processes which are being elaborated here, and which facilitate access to the phenomena of the unconscious: the distance between us and ourselves.

> The process of the dream-work, then, is something entirely new and strange, nothing resembling which was known before. It has given us our first glimpse of the processes which take place in the unconscious system

and has shown us that they are *quite other* than what we know from our conscious thinking and are bound to appear to the latter preposterous and incorrect. (17, emphasis added)

Thus, the dream has allowed us to gain access to the unconscious of the conscious, just when the vigilant consciousness of the wakeful ego disappears into the dream: when the judgment disappears which signals it as 'preposterous and incorrect'. The same mechanisms organise both the sickness and the dream: the 'abnormal' person who is awake operates as in the dream.

> ... in the construction of neurotic symptoms the same mechanisms (we do not venture to say 'processes of thought') are operative as those which have transformed the latent dream-thoughts into the manifest dream. (18)

But this also gives us an indication in the guise of a link: the normal aspect of the dream fuses with the pathological aspect of sickness. And both can do so, insofar as they are not integrated by conscious reason. In this way, in the dream we lay out and walk down the historical road of the constitution of cultural-personal significations and we come back from the representation to the image. But we also return to the imaginary as if it were real. The dream works beyond 'real' time and space. But it works to a certain end: the dream opens a 'scene' in which what is at play is once again the drama of the peremptory satisfaction of one's wish, unsatisfied in reality.

> The shutting-off of mental life from reality at night and the regression to primitive mechanisms which this makes possible enable this wished-for instinctual satisfaction to be experienced in a hallucinatory manner as occurring in the present. As a result of this same regression, ideas are transformed in the dream into visual pictures: the latent dream-thoughts, that is to say, are dramatised and illustrated. (19)

To live, while being absent, is the *as if* of presence. The hallucinatory satisfaction conforms itself with this 'as if' of the presence that it hallucinates. Presence, by contrast, is the real, with which we believe we coincide in the wakeful state. There would be no distance in reality for the normal person: here the thing really would be present. But Freud shows us that if there is satisfaction in the reality of the presence, it is because there also was, in the act of dreaming, an ideal satisfaction: with the presence of an absence. *As if* the absent were present in the dream. But also: *as if* there were no absence in the presence of the wakeful state.

What matters for the question that guides us is this other feature that appears in sleep: the *'intentional* turning away from the external world' (19, emphasis added). The intention that leads us to go to sleep is rest: for this we must turn away from reality. We must take a rest from the exterior world. And thus arises the question: what happens when the instinctive impulses find their road to motility blocked off for them, that is to say, the possibility of connecting with the objective presence of the exterior world? They must be content with a hallucinatory satisfaction. I sleep, but my impulses do not. Yet these hallucinatory mechanisms of satisfaction – and this is what matters – also appear in those connections with the wakeful reality in which the repressed action takes reality itself as its field of dramatisation, as happens in the case of the sick person. I mean: reality and presence also appear, just as in the dream, as the *scene* of a *real* activity that we cannot develop. To what extent do these mechanisms of the dream determine and regulate, by way of compensation, the lack of satisfaction of the wish *within* reality itself? To what extent can we say that reality itself, full of its objective presence, is sometimes nothing more than a 'scene' for representing the drama of unsatisfied desire? By asking about the interior distance, Freud in reality points at the invisible exterior desire.

This example of the dream will serve as the 'natural' model for the withdrawal in the attempt to understand the radical and effective separation from reality, as well as the mechanisms of apparent satisfaction:

> Like every instinctual impulse, it [the dream] too presses for satisfaction by action; but its path to motility is blocked by the physiological regulations implied in the state of sleep; it is compelled to take the backwards course in the direction of perception and to be content with a hallucinated satisfaction. (19–20)

What this means is that the action aimed at reality is the adequate and normal form adopted by individuals in their search for satisfaction. But we should not think, therefore, that the material, 'biological' mode of coincidence is that which determines this as the true action. The reality principle is the principle of symbolic reality, of material reality signified and culturally articulated and valorised. When Freud says 'action' and 'motility' of the physiological dispositions, he is saying at the same time: materiality and signification, body and meaning. Hence, what mobilises the body that sleeps are the 'latent thoughts', that is to say, significant relationships that organise the whole unsatisfied wish. But the 'ideality' of what is latent is not a privilege of the dream; rather, it also corresponds to the 'ideality' of culture, even if the latter, in the wakeful state, imposes itself on us only as material. But we don't know it: we are in the real. Because the unsatisfied wishes that are mobilised in the dream do not come only from the abyss of subjectivity. They are what is left hanging in wait of satisfaction in a context that is also ideal: in the framework of that invisible rationality with which the historical system of production orders and organises the materiality of the real world. Here the latent 'idea' that beats[1] within the one who dreams does not represent a purely abstract formulation: it finds itself depicted in the trail that the super-ego left engraved in the flesh as the determining form of all desire. These 'latent ideas' that remain as 'the day's residues', residues of the lack of satisfaction lived in the wakeful state, this is what in the reality of culture – also official culture – could not be satisfied. The fact that the day's residues, which come from the reality lived as merely empirical, remain in one as 'latent ideas' means that their latency, invisibly, continues to be supported without knowing it by the very personal foundation that integrated us in the repressive ideality of culture: in the form of the Other that regulates us from within. The ideas that now are latent were in reality – the reality with whose meaning they animated and interrogated it – unconscious significations that were lived among the facts: in the wakeful state they were not distinguished as 'ideas' because they were incarnated without distance in the relations to the world and in the motility of the body in search of their satisfaction. But the 'latent ideas' that are awakened in the dream are the return to the personal foundation of the idea, to the body of signification that disappears as a mere thought-idea in order to beat in the carnal sense. But the latter already is only the lived experience of the meaning, affectivity, and images that transmit them, just as in their origin the first significations were transmitted. The latent idea that stands out in the dream is the repressed idea, *this one* thought, Freud says, which is, like the impulse that sustains it, 'a child of night', the idea which is strange to the ego and perhaps even repellent (18). Everything is organised around this repudiated thought. But this means, in addition, that this central 'latent idea' that the dream awakens was not a thought that was thinkable and conscious in the wakeful state: it was necessary for me to be asleep for it to be able to appear and stand out, embodied in the sensibility of the image and its presence.

What is of interest, then, is the dream as *model of any transaction* that takes place when 'we turn away from the real world' (16). And it is Freud who interrogates himself, immersed in the dream. Freud is going to interrogate the dream about the transaction that compensates by way of hallucination for the lack of

---

1 *Translator's note*: The author plays on the verbal meaning of 'latent' or *latente*, from *latir* in Spanish: *la 'idea' que late*, thus, refers to a 'latent idea' but also to an idea that 'beats', like a heart, making it at once a bodily and not just a mental or ideal phenomenon. I have tried to keep this wordplay by using both images at the same time in English.

satisfaction. For if the normal here is pathological: 'the dream is a pathological product', he told us, 'the first member of the *class* which includes hysterical symptoms, obsessions and delusions' (15–16), it is also *this pathology inherent in normality* which Freud studies in the objective field where social relations are knotted together, and also where the drama of the repressed and of repression is resolved in a transaction. The individual dream is as 'normal', qua transaction, as is the field of the artificial mass – army or Church – in the collective domain. This is why this 'harmless dream-psychosis' (16) puts us on the track of other, less innocent ones: the wakeful 'psychosis' of the normal social human being.

The 'harmless dream-psychosis' differs from psychosis in its alternating, voluntary, and intentional character:

> The harmless dream-psychosis is the result of a withdrawal from the external world which is consciously willed and only temporary, and it *disappears* when relations to the external world are resumed. (16, emphasis added)

The psychosis disappears, Freud tells us, when we wake up: it disappears because the reality of the external world goes back to being the only dominant support, which is something that does not occur in the case of the psychotic. This is why it is here only a 'harmless dream-psychosis'.

What appears in the dream? The 'preposterous' and the 'incorrect'. The maximal opposition occurs in the midst of a subject who, for this very reason, repudiates it as such. But Freud is telling us: we live in the preposterous and we rid ourselves of it as if nothing happened. We live in the marvellous and distance ourselves from the incorrect. Day after day, night after night, we pass from sleep to wakefulness and we walk around in real life as if this marvel that happens to us at night, as if those dark children of the night disappeared and their faces were erased as soon as the pale children of the morning appear. In the bosom of any human being this marvellous power is at work that we chase away in one breath when the light of day surprises us and takes us out of bed and, so we believe, into reality. But there are those of us who hang on, nevertheless, to the dream: psychosis is the attempt to sleep by day, to prolong the dream as if reality necessarily scared away desire and there were no transition from the imaginary to the real; as if the sick refused to admit that the marvellous is possible only at night and in dreams.

The opposition that conscious wakefulness puts up against the truth of the dream is tenacious: it becomes understandable in interpretation, when we approach the dream in order to extract from it its significance relative to the wakeful state, relative to the reality that consciousness, immersed in reality itself, rejects. We accept all ideas *except one* – Freud tells us – which is contradictory to all the others. This is the black child among the white. But this 'idea' is a thought so grave that even the ideality of consciousness, in its coherence and its logic, rejects it. What happens is that it is not just a 'mere' idea that can be thought without consequences, like almost everything we think: this idea is thick, dense, heavy: *it has body*. It is the child of the night, we have engendered it in our sleep, like a natural child, clandestine and illegitimate: it lacks identity, we cannot recognise it. The other ideas, yes, they are our children, their white brothers, the latent ideas that consciousness recognises as compatible: they are the fruit of legal and official relationships. But this one, on the other hand, is our only true child, the black child: the one who was created in a night of love, when we went to lay down with ourselves, we believe, and one went to sleep, when the ego went to bed with its body and could not avoid giving birth, could not elude that the impulses of the id gave it this plebeian child of unsatisfied desire. And where do we discover that which consciousness denies? In the fact that even now, in spite of everything, consciousness is the consciousness of a body that does not forget and because of this, feels. In the passion with which the ego, already awake, looks at its face in the light of day and rejects it, but negating it in a peculiar way, that is where we recognise the clandestine fruit: 'he may possibly reject it [this idea] *with passionate feeling*', says Freud (18, emphasis added). *The ego is still pregnant with emotion; it still conserves the flavour of the forbidden fruit that it has tasted*. But this child must give proof of blood and lineage: 'this expression is a weakened, distorted and disguised one' (18). This 'idea' or this 'thought' is like the illegitimate son thrown into the waters and saved by Freud, rejected, expulsed, disguised like a townsman in order to survive. Its spurious origin does not carry on its forehead, as Marx says of value, what it is: it must be deciphered. It is Moses, it is Oedipus. It suffices that the analyst denounces it and shows its lineage in order for it to be rejected, in the same act as the irrefutable proof, with horror: this is not *my* child, this is not the one that *I* had: this is the son of … an Other. The child of the night is the child of psychotic adultery, but we believed it was 'innocent', 'temporary', without consequences: Did we not settle that the dream was harmless? This child of scorn is not of my own making.

2 The Originary Distancing

The dream is, as we saw, the most proximate within the most foreign: *next to* normality, psychosis. The dream is a transaction in order to be able to sleep.

And the same occurs, in sickness, with the symptom: it is right next to the patient, it rises or surges forth within the latter as something strange, incomprehensible, a foreign body within my own, with which we end up becoming familiar: 'what is, of all the contents of the mind, most foreign to the ego' (57). Just as foreign is the symptom in the sick person as the dream in the person who is awake. The dream in its alternation with wakefulness would open up the widest field, within the subject, of a distance: the distance that shows us the internal difference, which has not been assimilated and is assumed only as foreign. It would give us the measure of how difference – day and night – maintains and sustains itself at the heart of the same – of the imperturbable resemblance of the ego – apparently without determining it. It shows us the degree to which we are capable of living normally in the proximity of the irrational at the heart of rationality and order, without seeing it. What thus opens up would be an internal distance at the heart of the subject, between self and itself, without any common measure in the person who is awake with the external distance that wakefulness all of a sudden opens for us when we wake up. And this is because it rests on an alternation that chases it away: that of the dream, which follows upon the wakefulness. If in our sleep, disturbing everything, dreaming did not make its appearance ...

This internal distance that sleeping reveals is not a natural but a cultural distance. Within this sphere that the dream opens up within ourselves what emerges in all its nakedness is the drama of culture or civilisation. To dream is not a physiological act: it is a cultural combat against our demons, a drama renewed once more between nature and culture within the subject itself, within *each* subject. Here, in the pure passivity of the sleeping person, we can observe how culture is fought out even in the flesh that sleeps off its fatigue and is far removed from reality, as far away from reality as possible as all the living can be while continuing to live.

The symptom is the most alien to the ego, Freud tells us: the maximum distance at the heart of the subject. The most foreign means: the not-I. The ego or I does not perceive it as its own, they do not speak the same language, so it has nothing to do with the other: it rejects it as strange. The symptom is a *representative*, it is not the repressed itself: the repressed announces itself through the symptom. The repressed is not present in person, for the ego, in our own body. It is thus through a representative, a mediator, that the repressed appears, as if it came from afar, from foreign lands and speaking another language, when in reality it surges up from deep inside the subject itself. It so happens that the subject is mediated between it and itself by a distance that the representation, the sign, opens up in its own interior: culture distanced it at its very heart from its own being in order for it to exist. But we already know that the internal distance is the result of a cultural distance, the sedimentation worked by history, the distance which was not reanimated but moves contradictorily from the inside. This internal distance is in reality its good fortune, thanks to which it may set off on a path and open up an external distance still to be traversed. If there is a path outwards, toward the world of culture or civilisation, it is because previously a distance toward the inside was opened up. And in this adequate transformation between the internal distance that is recuperated, for psychoanalysis, in the external distance – in the world – there also resides the power for the subject to disentangle the origin and meaning of the life of culture or civilisation.

In the dream, as normal psychosis, the internal opposition was positioned between two fields, the daily and the nocturnal, of which Freud offered us the dialectic. What did this tell us? That in the dream the task of wakefulness is elaborated and continues, except with other means. The objective, both of the dream and of wakefulness, is thus the same: the satisfaction of the unsatisfied desire. But so is its elaboration. To discover that the dream too seeks to satisfy the desire that was unsatisfied in wakefulness meant to prolong the debate of wakeful life in sleeping, to find the unity in the habitual and alternating separation, anchoring both and making them go in one and the same direction. It means to find the complementary unity of the universal law of the human being, the one which rules everything and provides us with the master key to its meaning for all: the foundation of the human subject is to be unsatisfied desire in the uninterrupted search for satisfaction.

Supposing that in reality we satisfy our desires, if this is to be our conviction, what happens in the dream? Moreover, what happens then with those, like the psychotic, who *dream awake?* Those who dream while being awake dared to unite the separate: they brought the dream out of the shadows of sleep into the light and *they do in wakefulness what we all do in our dreams*. Except that the alternation of the day that follows the night is converted for them in the simultaneity of wakefulness and the interior attempt at a resolution of the conflict: no longer first one (the day) and then the other (the night), but one next to and together with the other, given that both are contradictory and yet – this is their wisdom and their madness – *they must be affirmed at the same time*. But in order to accomplish this, they too in their extreme coherence had to make compromises: the transaction, the symptom, articulates the two. But this does not mean that the difference separating them disappeared: they continue one *next to* the other.

Let us recall how satisfaction appeared in dreams:

> Like every instinctual impulse, it too presses for satisfaction by action; but its path to motility is blocked by the physiological regulations implied in the state of sleep; it is compelled to take the backwards course in the direction of perception and to be content with a hallucinated satisfaction. (19–20)

Here the body remains locked into itself, reduced only to whatever culture internalised as the domain for displaying this combat toward the pursuit of satisfaction. This is a key 'normal' experience in order to observe the functioning of the psychic apparatus in a vacuum. What is the real here? The world – the world of the one who dreams – is internalised in the repressive structure of the subject, of the ego or I who dreams. Repression counts on one, not on all: only one who is dreaming. And the repressed is animated in the dream, it animates one, the ego: it grows gigantic in the body and *the repressed wakes up in the dream*. It does not have to confront, as in wakefulness, the real power of the system's force, or of the vigilant ego, when it pretends to move into action.

But its force is at the same time its weakness: the ego closes the doors to action, to motility. Even though, as we will see, the id that seeks to satisfy itself knows nothing about reality: hallucination is enough, with the illusion of presence, in order to calm itself. It has enough with the simulacrum of satisfaction with which the ego satisfies it. I want to sleep and for them to stop harassing me: I thus close the body to the outside. But I cannot avoid that it opens itself ever more to the inside.

What continues to beat in the body of the one who dreams? Freud said: the latent thoughts, day rests that our wakeful relation with the world left unsatisfied in ourselves. Thus the elaboration of the dream continues, with our own means, the labour of a now subjectivised relation, which unfolds only in the psychic apparatus of the sleeping person:

> The latent dream-thoughts are thus transformed into a collection of sensory images and visual scenes. (20)

The representation follows along, in the dream, down the path of culture or civilisation and becomes sensible presence. One senses without sensing the exterior relation, one sees without seeing the exterior object. Precisely when I cut off my relation to the world, the subjective significations become gigantic and take on corporeal form:

> It is as they travel on this course that what seems to us so novel and so strange occurs to them. All the linguistic instruments by which we express

> the subtler relations of thought – the conjunctions and prepositions, the changes in declension and conjugation – are dropped, because there are no means of representing them; just as in a primitive language without any grammar, only the raw material of thought is expressed and abstract terms are taken back to the concrete ones that are at their basis. What is left over after this may well appear disconnected. (20)

What disappears here? The rational capacity to signify in the field of speech, which distances my body from reality, in order to let appear the sensible capacity to signify more proximate to the level of the flesh, which brings it closer. This is not to say that the signification of the subtler links disappears: they express themselves in a different mode, like a primitive language might. The general is dissolved into the particular, words give way to images, to sentiments, and to visions. Almost the thing itself, in its well-rounded presence without words and without mediation. The congealed and constituted articulations become relaxed; the relations return to the sensible and significant source that generates them, so the ego thinks, without 'paying the price' of words. This sensible language is not something I understand: for the official ego the image is what it presents in its sensible reference, in its material quasi-presence. This is why the subject who wakes up does not understand: *I* do not understand it, since I understand only what the representation, which responds to the repressive order, gave me to understand. Hence the 'technical' explanations that Freud gives to make us understand the 'theory' of dreams. Because in real life the predominance of the empirical, of the sensible present, of the 'material', is equivalent – in its immediate and unreflected signification – to the domination of the 'sensible images' and 'visual scenes' of the dream: they too give us the 'reality' of its most direct, most 'real' existence, although also most abstract for the person who is awake. And yet, the real too is surrounded by a halo of ideality, like the dream itself. But we do not know it: if we are in reality! As we are habituated to and distanced from the signifying power that rises up from the sensible, we do not understand our dreams: they are a hieroglyph. And, moreover, Freud tells us, 'dreams are not in themselves social utterances, not a means of giving information' (9). We talk to ourselves: it is a communication of the interior with the interior. It is the most proper and for this reason the least social: we communicate *subsequently* what the word denominated.

The dream was an illegible symptom of the imbalance of our 'normal' relation with reality. Because we read it, while awake, in another system. As in any transaction both parties obtain what is theirs: the id its satisfaction (but hallucinated); the ego its ability to sleep (but without lucidity).

Thus, both in the dream and in the symptom it is a question of an alternation, of day and night, of wakefulness and dreaming, of normal conduct and the irruption of the symptom. But in this game of alternations what is covered up is a transition that is halted, the promotion of a new signification, of a new possible order that remained frustrated in the separation. Here there appear two opposed systems, and each one has reason on its side in its own domain. In one case, the reason of sense; in the other, the reason of knowledge. One, the image, and the other, representation. In both, the transaction appears as a two-faced Janus: while the ego sleeps in the transaction with the rationality of the official ego (and taking the sensible of the recalled image of the dream as what its obvious everyday presence tells us); the id senses its realisation with the sensible wisdom of an affective corporeity. Each one sees what it can see, hears what its reason dictates to it, and feels what its feeling enabled in it as a potential sense, a sensible acuity; sensitised to feel what moves it.

Thus, between the known order and the sensed order, what installs itself is a transition that has been detained and converted in an alternation, which still awaits comprehension. Also put into place are sickness and contradiction.

3   The Conversion of the External into the Internal

We said that Freud is trying to understand the most subjective foundation that organises and in general frustrates a 'true' action in reality. Hence his interest in capturing the subtle link by which appearance filters itself into the latter and transforms it. The mechanism for obtaining such an appearance of a link between the internal and the external – to overcome with one leap the distance between desire and its satisfaction – is basically the conversion of the external into the internal. What does this conversion mean? It *simulates* a congruence, it *resolves* the incompatibility by means of the imaginary, but above all it *eludes a distance*: the distance of the subjective realm from reality. The mechanism for converting the external into the internal, and vice-versa, assumes that the fundamental problem of all genuine action is resolved: the elaborate work of rendering the imaginary adequate with regard to the real, the transformation of the subjective desire, by including it in the categories of social time and space, the search for a real object that implies both the transformation of oneself – coming from the dissociating alternation – and the transformation of the world. This problem of the passage, or the transition, which is none other than the problem of the real distance between the subject and the world, is what sickness and dreams have in common: to elaborate a transaction in which the internal is transformed into the external and the external into the internal. But not the individual sickness and dream: Freud – this is our goal – will show us how in the broader collective social relations, in the institutions and in history, this transaction also imposes itself, turned into social categories and forms of effective and material domination, with which power seeks in its own way to elude another distance: the one which opens up between people as class struggle, as the collective process that allows the broaching of a historical field for the real elaboration of unsatisfied desire.

If in the sick person there is a short circuit between the internal and the external, between the subjective and the objective, that which makes itself apparent in this way and reveals itself to us at the same time creates *the false agreement between the subjective and the objective* in the normal person. It opens up the contradiction, articulated as agreement, between the human being and the system of production, and it shows us on another level that which Marx, in the phenomenon of commodity fetishism, signalled as the necessary overcoming in order to convert the conventional way of seeing, determined by the social and objective form of the commodity as 'natural', into the true historical way of seeing. And this is what interested both Marx as well as Freud: to understand in what way the human subject appears as the place where the historical dialectic, at the same time that it produces the human being, also is interrupted.

This is why Freud begins his analysis of the splitting of psychic personality there where this distance appears internalised and congealed as division, with the symptom:

> Psychoanalysis ... began its work on what is, of all the contents of the mind, most foreign to the ego – on symptoms. Symptoms are derived from the repressed, they are, as it were, its representatives before the ego; but the repressed is foreign territory to the ego – internal foreign territory – just as reality (if you will forgive the unusual expression) is external foreign territory. (57)

There are, as seen from the ego that I am, two foreign territories for Freud: one internal and the other external. This distinction is fundamental. The symptom is the representative of the repressed closest to the ego, he told us, but this repressed is foreign to the ego. Strange, distant, and alien within the maximum proximity: the maximum distance at the heart of the self. The ego delimits what is proper in the subject and rejects what is proper but negated as if it were alien: it is not in the subject. Thus there are two exteriors to the ego for Freud: *the external that is inside and the external that is outside.*

But there is a genesis to the external foreign territory (reality and its history) just as there is a genesis of the internal foreign territory (one's own impulses that have been negated). To say internal foreign territory means: the external that is inside. And to say external foreign territory means: the external that is outside. Because, we ask ourselves, *how* can something strange to me have come to be in me? How could the external become internal and appear as determining for me inside my own self?

Let us think of Freud's conception of the instincts or drives not only at the level of psychic organisation but also at the level of biological organisation, and we will find the process that led to the understanding of the existence of this internal foreign territory against the backdrop of whose organisation it was formed. Freud already showed us this 'exterior that is inside' as specific to the biological instinct. The animal instinct too is the external that is inside and organises itself and differentiates itself from the external that is outside, from which it derives. The exterior that is inside includes, from the biological point of view, the instincts. *But in the biological realm the external that is inside is not an interior foreign territory*, in the way it will be for the human being by way of culture or civilisation.

Let us recall what Freud says in 'Instincts and Their Vicissitudes':

> External stimuli impose only the single task of withdrawing from them; this is accomplished by muscular movements, one of which eventually achieves that aim and thereafter, being the expedient movement, becomes a hereditary disposition ... There is naturally nothing to prevent our supposing that the instincts themselves are, at least in part, *precipitates of the effects of external stimulation, which in the course of phylogenesis have brought about modifications in the living substance*. (SE 14: 120, emphasis added)

We therefore must recognize a double genesis in the human subject: one biological and the other cultural, but with both being superimposed and sometimes undifferentiated.

1. *Biological genesis* of the relation organism-environment:
   a) *The 'natural' exterior that is inside*: precipitate of phylogenetic adaptations. 'Internal territory', but not foreign.
   b) *The 'natural' exterior that is outside*: nature, which stimulates the organism and to which the latter finds itself adapted. 'External territory', but not foreign.

This is, then, the biological organisation with which each child, by birth, would be endowed. But, as opposed to the animal, the 'natural exterior that is inside' will prolong itself as the id, through the development of its biological organism as human and cultural organism. That which in the relation animal-environment links the external with the internal is an adequation constituted by the phylogenetic development from which the animal adaptation results. But what in nature links the animal *becomes delinked and separated* in the human being because of the cultural genesis. And for this reason 'the exterior that is outside' is not only the external territory as it is for the animal: it is the territory that is opposed, *foreign*, which opens up the external that is inside – and this is what is important and hidden – as *foreign* external territory: *the foreign is as much outside as inside the self*.

2. *Cultural genesis* of the relation human being-world:
   a) *The cultural exterior that is inside*: determines the 'internal foreign territory' (Freud); it limits it from within culture *as if* it were alien to it and to me, a domain that is strange and irreducible to the coherence of the ego. It will be the id.
   b) *The cultural exterior that is outside*: 'external foreign territory' (Freud). This is the field of culture that, as social productive organisation, conforms the 'internal foreign territory' (the id) as incoherent with the external: it is the conventional repressive reality that will be internalised as super-ego.

If we consider these two modes of organisation, the biological and the psychic, which open up the relation of the individual to the external world, we see only *two* domains appear in the human being (and this is because from the point of view of the ego, which is the place that is not conscious of itself as such, there would be only two domains): the internal foreign territory and the external foreign territory. But in reality there are three: there is the ego, operating as mediator between the two. And the third term does not appear because the ego is unconscious of itself and of its being, *it thinks it is beyond and outside* of the external and the internal domains that delimit it, as if it were the natural place of a point of view that nothing supports, or that *supports itself*: *it lacks the distance with regard to itself in order to apprehend itself, relative to the 'external foreign territory', as a third term*. The ego, in its pretence of being *absolute*, believes itself to be the originary place of all distance from the non-distance and from non-time. In the animal there is no internal distance: it is 'the external that is inside'. In order for there to be an internal distance in the animal it would have to be able to say: I. In the animal, being is confused with corporeality without distance, but in the human being, by way of the ego or I, this is not the case. And yet the human being lives this internal distance *as natural*.

The exterior that is inside the biological instinct did not come about as the result of an adequation in the individual history of the human being, but in the phylogenesis of the species. This is its incarnated and corporeal point of departure. But it is on this biological model that *subsequently* the historical exterior is experienced that is inside, that which was in fact incorporated and constituted during the maturation of the individual in civilisation. And this second exterior that is inside or, in Freud's words, this 'interior *foreign* territory' *will have for the individual who lives it the same character of being immediate, natural and typical that the first natural exterior had from which it developed*. Civilisation and the foreign as such appear to be as natural as its own body, as if it were not repression that opened up this place within the self. The culture of convention and repression produces this result: it hides this internal foreign territory inside oneself as if its character of foreignness, of the separation of oneself from the self opened up by civilisation, did not stem from it and had been ratified as a radical and absolute distance at the heart of one's own subjectivity. But then, if this distance that removes us within ourselves from our own lived corporeality as foreign, 'internal foreign territory', is not accepted, how can we elaborate in each case the relation to this 'external foreign territory', to the world of culture or civilisation that is outside of me, the worldly field to which I refer? What is it in me that passes and must find satisfaction in the external world, if what is the most proper to me is strange for my own self? The internal foreign territory already reveals its meaning: I am colonised in my own being, given that there the external foreign territory delimited the areas of the proper as that which ought not to be such: as not-I. Thus, in this way of continuing to confront the proper as alien and strange, as if 'naturally' it were in me, we find the foundation of every cultural subjection, both in normality and in psychosis and neurosis: both in 'health' and in 'sickness'.

With regard to the opening of this subjective field in the human being, Freud refers to the latter's need for a 'protective shield':

> But the protective shield exists only in regard to external stimuli, not in regard to internal instinctual demands. ('Inhibitions, Symptoms, and Anxiety', SE 20: 94)

Clearly, the biological setup in the animal did not require this. Since in the animal there is congruence between the internal and the external, this device is biologically unnecessary. The animal is one and congruent with the schematism of its corporeality.

The world of culture or civilisation, by contrast, introduces the need to repress one's impulses and produces an 'internal foreign territory', which is not and should not be ours, even though it is. This introduces an absolutely new fact with respect to the nonhuman biological realm: it requires, therefore, a 'protective shield' against itself. That is to say, a protective device that from within ourselves protects us from what is most proper in us. But in reality this new protective device is the one with which the repressive culture protects us from ourselves within ourselves.

At first it would seem that this mechanism is a defence put up against those internal impulses that surge forth and, thus, it is the self who defends itself against them. But what is fundamental about this defence mechanism is the fact that it is 'they' that are the intolerable impulses. If we must defend ourselves against *them* it is because they are not ours: they are not me. Against the internal stimuli there would be no defence possible from the strictly biological point of view: one necessarily would have to give them satisfaction. The animal *is* its impulses: how could it oppose itself to them if its very being depends on them? Only the human being has to do this, but then it creates this mechanism, this protective device against itself. Thus a repressive dialectic is opened up at the heart of the apparent unity of the subject. Not being able to create a passage from the internal to the external, unable to give it satisfaction, it has recourse to an elementary scheme: *it transforms the internal in external*. It treats the psychic determination as if it were not such, that is to say, as if it were *external and material*. It thus obtains the identity of reality. The external has been made internal (but I do not know it: without history and without consciousness); the form of the other was incorporated into oneself as a directly material signification. The meaning that each impulse and each rejection thus acquires appears as a 'natural' condition of its very existence, as if it had not been produced, as it really was, from the outside. Following this same mechanism, I transform my signifying materiality, the psychic content, and project it onto the exterior world, which thus receives it and *therein directly materialises itself, but without transformation*. Reality is the receptacle of my fantasy in which at last I can dominate it, treating it as something exterior.

The human being thus reacts to the internal stimuli in the same way as to the external ones: by having recourse to the same mechanisms that it uses against the latter. It treats what is proper to it, the repressed, as external, only now by using the same primary mechanisms on the basis of which this conversion of the internal into the external took place. It supersedes the subjective with the objective. But this treatment of the internal as external is the result of having previously internalised the external as internal: of having constituted an 'internal foreign territory' as if its strangeness for me did not come from the outside.

This mechanism, which constitutes the new 'protective device', against the internal, which in reality is against oneself, is the foundation of the sick, abnormal solution. But it is also, in its objectively social corroboration of a repressive culture, a normal mechanism. This means that the 'sane' persons are sick with 'reality', that their reality is stabilised, that they cannot comprehend how fantasy determines reality because in them fantasy has been made adequate to the repressive reality and forms a system with it.

> ... they equate reality of thought with external actuality, and wishes with their fulfilment ... ('Formulations on the Two Principles of Mental Functioning', SE 12: 225)

Thus, at the very heart of the subject, as seen from the point of view of science and keeping the focus on the ego, two fields of relations open up: with the external foreign territory – reality – and with the internal foreign territory – one's own repressed impulses. But, as we are seeing, this internal foreign territory is such only for the ego. Foreign to the ego, its foreignness is different from the foreignness that on the other hand reality presents for it: it is its negation and they are contradictory. The foreign nature of the internal territory that confronts the foreign nature, for the ego, of the exterior reality, appears as opposed and contradictory: the ego is required for the exterior reality, but it is harassed by the 'internal foreign territory'. It thus looks upon the 'internal foreign territory' as though its sense of being foreign did not come from outside but from within its own self: it is strange because it is not me.

Already we are seeing the problem. The external that is inside (the instinctual) also comes from the outside and it is not, as I think, strange: it was produced by the whole process of nature, like my body. These impulses are subsequently organised and become determined in their orientation toward the objects and in their integration into the ego – therefore also in their possible transition to reality – by the world of culture or civilisation. Insofar as they are negatively determined by culture, they are in disagreement with it. The animal does not ask itself about the *agreement* with nature. And it is 'natural' for it not to do so: its instincts necessarily prolong themselves in nature. But the human being, and this is what surprises us and strikes us as strange, does not ask itself about the *disagreement* that now is included in its own body. This is the capital problem: *the disagreement between the ego and the id appears as the unconscious foundation of the agreement between the ego and reality.* The disagreement with the 'internal foreign territory' is necessary in order for the human subject to be in agreement with the 'external foreign territory'. It so happens that the disagreement appears as 'natural': it is in the order of nature, it is strange to me. All that predominates is the agreement – the articulation – on which my individual life is based. The internal foreign territory is what I have that is 'natural', as opposed to culture. Thus the internal foreign territory appears as 'nature' vis-à-vis the external foreign territory, which appears as 'spirit'. What has happened in this transformation? What we already know: the absolutisation of culture or civilisation implies, at the same time, the animalisation of one's own body for what it contains in terms of residual precipitates in its confrontation with repression. It was difficult, as we saw, to ask ourselves about the disagreement. But we also do not ask ourselves about the agreement: 'we agree' to subject ourselves to the external foreign territory, on which our lives are based. Except that – and therein lies the drama of submission that enables us for life – the proximity of the internal foreignness, which is so profoundly sunk into ourselves, turns out to be an embarrassing compromise: how, if it is strange to me, is it inside of me?

Freud clearly develops this problem – that of the strangeness inside me – in 'Negation':

> It is, we see, once more a question of *external* and *internal*. What is unreal, merely a presentation and subjective, is only internal; what is real is also there *outside*. ('Negation', SE 19: 237)

What has happened? Well, the extension toward reality has happened within the agreement. What is mine is that which is capable of extending itself towards the outside and *also* exists in the exterior world: it is the real. But whatever in me does not agree with the external is 'only internal', it has nothing to do with the external. It appears only as subjective, not real, imaginary: not-I. A hiatus thus opens up within the subject itself: that which does not verify the agreement with the external configures, since it is mine, the repressed. It is that which is denominated from the outside as the nonobjective, the nonreal, the merely imaginary: it has no domain in the social reality to verify itself and is condemned to the abysses of subjectivity, fantasy, and dreams. What happens is that at the same time, because of the genesis that unfolds from childhood onward, there are two genetic processes that converge on a single unity. One is the process that comes from far away, from biology, and the other from nearby, from within the world of culture or civilisation. The inside in the child, which comes from nature ('the primitive enjoying ego') and the inside that coincides with its outside ('definitive realist ego'). But the child does not know it. The child develops a quasi-biological form in its first relation with a world that is already cultural, and this form in its simplicity (the good is inside, the bad is outside) extends itself as a form of organisation *also* in culture. The 'primitive enjoying ego', which is pure affect without intellect, under the dominance of the oral phase, has recourse to a digestive logical form: to swallow or to spit out. The transition to reality, which already amounts to the reality of culture, implies on the contrary its determination by the cultural signification and its slow introduction in the universe of adult signs. But for this it needs to have access to negation: the 'no' sign. This 'no', Freud says, is the sign of *homemade* which signals beyond all doubt its origin in repression. But it does not know how to decipher the sign system that within it determines the interpretation and adequation of the good and the bad that defines it.

The new exterior that appears as 'new' for science is not so for the subject. For the latter it is what extends itself, like a continuum, from the first system to the second without understanding the transition nor incorporating its structural meaning: it sees the cultural with the same scheme of immediate natural vision. This implies the prolongation of the sensible determination, in the subject-object relation, into the new domain where the relation is no longer the same, for already the meaning of the object, as well as the meaning of the subject itself, has been determined by the system of production. But this determination by the cultural system is analogous, for the ego, to the sensible determination of nature: it is analogous to its mere material existence, which naturally confuses itself with its signification as if the latter emerged from the object itself. As if the cultural signification resided in its sheer empirical presence, without needing to be deciphered. Hence the accord: they are both, the subject as well as the object, regulated in conformity with the laws of society, they operate under its dominance: 'they know not what they do', as Marx says.

We may affirm that the specificity of the repressive cultural system consists in hiding, and hemming in, this 'internal foreign domain'; as if its signification of foreignness, with which the subject confronts it from within itself, did not come from the world of culture. Only for the science of psychoanalysis, or for Marx, for example, does this process appears to be capable of being disentangled. And this discovery would define the specific essence of the human being as historical being: to be able to insert oneself at last in the cultural reality by elaborating on each occasion the new adequation, the distance that the system proposes for the human subject, after the prior clearing of the interior distance that initially separated it from itself.

4   The Historical Distance in the Subject

Thus, if the symptom in sickness is 'the representative of the repressed close to the ego', psychoanalysis discovered that what the symptom expresses is a transaction by means of which one reaches all the way to 'the unconscious, to the instinctual life, to sexuality'. That is to say, it reaches an 'interior territory', the internal foreign territory. Who was it that denied the internal its citizenship card and declared it 'foreign territory'? Who proclaimed the truth of the rights of subjectivity only for the ego?

Freud started out from the symptom, not from the ego: he started out from what is most alien to the ego. The symptom does not derive from the official ego: it comes from what is repressed, clandestine, alien to the ego in the individual. It comes from the residual, unassimilated individual. But he also did not start out from the 'external foreign territory': rather, he began with what is foreign in oneself. And against what was this domain aimed? Toward which aspects of oneself? Nothing less than toward the unconscious, the life of drives, and sexuality: toward the brute being that is present in one. The not-known, the 'natural', the foundation of sensible life, sexuality: such was the domain that had been left by the wayside as foreign to the ego from which Freud started out. He started out from the humiliated and offended aspects of our own being: that of the repressed flesh.

But who was the humiliating party here? The foreign territory, perhaps? No. The 'resistant, repelling, and repressing' instance that thus subjected me coincided with the ego of traditional psychology. The ego as stated in this psychology, which confounded itself with the self as the most proper, was in reality the repressor. This is why Freud, who came from the marginalised zones of official psychology, was able to reach what was colonised in the subject: the internal colonies of oneself.

> But at last the point was reached when it was possible for us to divert our attention from the repressed to the repressing forces, and we faced this ego, which had seemed so self-evident, with the secure expectation that here once again we should find things for which we could not have been prepared. It was not easy, however, to find a first approach. (57–8)

What was it for which we could not have been prepared? The fact that the ego might be the repressing force. Precisely as Rimbaud said: *Je est un autre*. But not just any other: the other as enemy. The ego was not pure self-sameness, it was not one: I was an other. I was the other inside myself. Do we realise the profundity and magnitude of this discovery? Not only a whole new domain was being integrated into the conventional subject, incorporating the discarded aspects of bourgeois culture as foreign to oneself. But at the same time something much more important was being discovered: the fact that the ego itself was the one exerting the function of repressor inside me. That if the symptom was the representative of the repressed close to the ego, I on the other hand was the representative of the repressing force at the very heart of my own individuality.

For this reason Freud momentarily leaves the external foreign territory so as to analyse the dominant interior domain: the one whose domain is one's own self, who possesses its own internal colony. The ego thus is not sameness, I am not one: I am other. That is to say, one is determined by the form of the other, and the other with whom we become confused expresses our own ego. And yet there exists and remains in the human being an *interior distance* that Freud brings out, through which one's very own sameness obliquely shapes itself, concealed and disdained, in the direction of reality. But for this to become clear we first had to come to this understanding through the dream and through sickness.

As we will see, this internal distance opened up at the heart of the subject itself is the one that becomes consolidated as absolute in the fetishised notion of interiority. The exterior dialectic human being-world contains not just two terms: there exists an interior dialectic that must be included as well and to the exterior distance subject-object we have to add the internal distance subject-ego. This is what is fundamental for Freud as much as for Marx: *the dialectical structure that is internal to one's own subjectivity as a historical distance opened up by culture at the heart of the subject itself.*

If I were one, as a totality without fissures or distance, I would not be able to take myself as object: there would be no reflection, no return of oneself to the self. But it so happens that in this reflecting within the apparent unity of the one, in which I do not leave my self, the other who enables this already made an entrance: the distance between I myself and me is in reality a distance between the I and the other. In the 'I think', there is implicit an act of humiliation and renouncement: the act of reflection is an act of genuflection. The I must curve itself, lower its back in reflection, in order to take itself as object: in reality, rather than taking itself it is taken. But this power was already present in my biological corporeality, only without the mediation and without the distance introduced by the world of civilisation. If the body can make one hand take the other, one gripping and the other being gripped – one the subject, the other the object for the first, and all this within oneself as one body – it is because this instrumental power of dissociation signals, within the realm of corporeality itself, an apprehending totality capable of taking one part of itself against the backdrop of the organic totality, of the apprehending power, which is the body. This distance opened up as power within the body itself only expresses one modality that transforms itself qualitatively when we move on to the cultural distance: there where it is the I that takes itself as object. Now the apprehending capacity opens up on a new terrain: we have to take the I as object, 'our very *own* ego'.

> We wish to make the ego the matter of our enquiry, our very own ego. But is that possible? After all, the ego is in its very essence a subject; how can it be made into an object? Well, there is no doubt that it can be. (58)

Let us retain the expression: 'our very own ego'. Freud, as a scientist, does not speak about the ego of the other: he speaks of this object that he himself is, and he seeks to make everyone reflect on oneself as object of analysis. *This is a fundamental limit-case of science: subject and object coincide in the unity of the act of knowledge.* Both appear united, forming part of the same experiment of knowing. The point is precisely to discover the exteriority within the interiority: to discover in our own ego the distance that allows me to make myself into the object. It is one's own subjectivity that is at stake in the act of knowledge: an I myself with its own body.

What matters is this interior distance, which we must discover in our own ego as the capacity for apprehension and discernment. It shows that *I am not the whole subject*, that one exceeds the ego: that there is an excess of oneself in one's own individuality. That there is an 'inner wealth', in a brute state, not yet monetised, an internal foreign territory to be conquered.

> The ego can take itself as an object, can treat itself like other objects, can observe itself, criticize itself, and do Heaven knows what with itself. In this, one part of the ego is setting itself over against the rest. So the ego can be split; it splits itself during a number of its functions – temporarily at least. Its parts can come together again afterwards. (58)

This capacity should not surprise us: 'all this is nothing new', Freud tells us. But only in moving to the pathological cases does the habitual show itself to us with a different signification: in what they show in terms of heightened or definitive separation. Pathology, with its 'power of amplification and concretion', renders things extreme: the mental patient makes a clean break – with health – and opts for sanity.[2]

---

2 Translator's note: *cortar por lo sano* reads as a pun combining both the idea of a clean break and the choice for health and normality.

> Where it points to a breach or a rent, there may normally be an articulation present. (58–59)

The mental patient becomes disjointed, separates the articulated, and fractures the unified. This means that the sick person, in becoming disarticulated, emphasises and puts into relief the lines of demarcation, union, connection, and articulation of the compact ego. It is the drama of rupture: the mental patient tragically confronts the links of the compromise that the normal persons accept so as to install themselves in them, either because he cuts them off or because they are broken into pieces in him.

> If we throw a crystal to the floor, it breaks; but not into haphazard pieces. It comes apart along its lines of cleavage into fragments whose boundaries, though they were invisible, were predetermined by the crystal's structure. Mental patients are split and broken structures of this same kind. (59)

Mental patients thus have shattered themselves into pieces against reality: they are the ones who took seriously that which the alternation of sleep and wakefulness separated and they have ended up in the real affirmation of that which wakeful life postponed and invalidated. The sick persons are those who assumed the expression of the 'internal foreign territory' in themselves: they speak from the place of the colonised, but in terms of their own reason.

> They have turned away from external reality, but for that very reason they know more about internal, psychical reality and can reveal a number of things to us that would otherwise be inaccessible to us. (59)

Mental patients 'know' more than we do. We adhere too closely, without distance, to the external reality that dominates us, too centred as we are on our own ego for us to be able to understand the process that rendered us adequate to this reality and subjected us. The mental patient is a rebel for whom our normality is our insanity: how do we not know everything that makes life impossible for them? How are we installed, without tension, in the fundamental drama of the origin, as if we had given up already, turning a deaf ear to the voices that clamour for our perdition and request that we give in, without further ado, to their power? What happens is that for us, the normal ones, the sick persons are 'maniacs': they always insist, and so much, with the same thing! The sick persons repeat themselves.

> We describe one group of these patients as suffering from delusions of being observed. They complain to us that perpetually, and down to their most intimate actions, they are being molested by the observation of unknown powers – presumably persons – and that in hallucinations they hear these persons reporting the outcome of their observation: 'now he's going to say this, now he's dressing to go out' and so on. ... it presupposes that people distrust them, and expect to catch them carrying out forbidden actions for which they would be punished. (59)

In them the flesh speaks with its sensible, indelible record, embedded in the corporeal memory that, unperturbed, returns time and again to wake up an inaugural knowledge in which the relived affect maintains and brings back to us the unified signification of the first presence, now imaginary, which organised it. Knowledge here did not reach the abstract generality of the law sanctioned by the super-ego: the being that norms my body is still present in the flesh, and looks at me without compassion and judges me without commiseration. We are living under the gaze of that for which there is no appeal, that which we cannot call by its name because it has no name: there is only its terrifying sensible presence inhabiting our own body. Thus immersed without distance in the reality of the external world in which we are free, what other authority do we recognise besides the one that consciousness dictates to us? We are the owners of our own deeds: the rationality of the individual moral consciousness is the only criterion that sets the rules for us.

> How would it be if these insane people were right, if in each of us there is present in his ego an agency like this which observes and threatens to punish, and which in them has merely become sharply divided from their ego and mistakenly displaced into external reality? (59)

The sick persons not only 'know' what we do not know, they also possess a rationality that we do not have. In them there is only an error, but in us there is a non-knowledge. In them there is present a point of departure that we have removed, purely and simply, from the field of our reflection. And there is more truth there than we suppose. The mental patients look for the origin of their drama where it really is: in the external world, precisely in that eternal world from which we, installed without distance, reproach them for their insanity and deny their knowledge for being illogical. We, on the other hand, have separated our subjective contents from the external world and we do not believe in ghosts: the real is there, tangible, in its actual presence, overflowing in the plenitude of its visible and sensible materiality.

What is the error of the sick person? Basically only one: to elude the real transition. What happens is that the sick person treats the internal *directly* as external. The internal means: the interior, subjective survival of persons and relations that were internalised. They really came to us from the external world, onto which the mental patients now once more project them. But their actual reality, which they hallucinate, is only psychical: they no longer exist or have no more function as such, *now*. There is truth in signalling, as they do, their origin, their provenance, which is excluded in us. There is error, by contrast, in signalling their temporal subsistence. But it counted before and the mental patient does not live in the objective time that forgot this origin, which in the 'normal' discovery remains unknown. The sick person actualises these contents and once more situates them in the outside, in an attempt to recuperate *a lost agreement with reality* that might integrate that which the normal person, in the official solution, forgot and put to the side. In so doing the mental patient becomes unhinged but at the same time discovers that which in us is sutured as internal-internal, as if it had not come from the outside the way it actually did. If our official and 'normal' reason has no memory of the origin and hides it, the reason of the mental patient has the memory of the body without apparent reason but certain of whatever is inscribed in it, which remains as its undeniable and fundamental truth: the effective presence of the other in its own self. The normal person hides the historical 'before' that shapes its subjectivity henceforth radically separated from the outside, it treats the internal as though it had not come from the external world, and finds pleasure in the inexplicable accord in which the authorised subjective side coincides with the objective side. The sick person, on the contrary, discovers the 'before' that made up its subjectivity and searches anew, now in the outside, for what determines it. The 'sane' person is a 'normal' subject who lives in the present concealing its past and its origin; the 'sick' person is an 'abnormal' subject who lives its past as if it were its timeless present, and thus makes them both simultaneous. The material present for the 'sane'; the historical past for the 'sick'. Each one carries a partial modality of the truth, which neither of them reaches organically. But the sick person brings what it lacks into the empirical realm of everyday facts without distance: the personal origin of the whole process. But it does so badly: it treats it as if the felt truth of the sensible and significant impression were not linked to the objective determination of historical time, which in turn is linked to the corporeality, and the latter to the significant materiality of the world.

And so what happens is that the mental patients are right in what they affirm; when someone talks to them from the outside, we the sane ones say no, that they are crazy: if outside – based on our arrogance and our secure power of verification – there is nobody, if nobody talks to us. Never before has our 'seeing to believe' been more certain. But they see and hear what we do not recall: they recuperate a signification tied to its origin that we have 'forgotten' and 'lost' in the body's cemetery. Because to us it is reason that talks: our moral consciousness talks to us and, thanks to Freud, the super-ego. But we do not realise it because, flesh without origin, consciousness without body, we believe that we ourselves constitute this normativity that rules over us: are we not the judge perhaps? Do we not tell the truth and tell it to ourselves in the interior monologue in which we decide the justice or injustice of a decision? But what in us is rationality without origin, which we impose on ourselves in the form of (moral) consciousness, in the mental patient discovers the sensible and meaningful presence, in its utterly undeniable materiality engraved on one's own, of the other who imposed it, and brings it back to reality *as if* it were present. And in fact it is: it is present in the sick person, just as it is in us, except that in us the original breach is articulated: it is an articulation, but without consciousness. We are the consciousness that is its result: we are the field opened up by the articulation. The presence of the other who, by way of identification, gave us order, opens up in us in the guise of consciousness, in a severe splitting. The precise and sensuous other became, by way of conversion, an impersonal other. This is why there is no real splitting of consciousness: what effectively exists is the distance opened up by the other in oneself, which constitutes the interior relation in which we subsequently appear as 'taking ourselves as object'. But let us be honest: one can never be the object for oneself; for this to occur there need to be two. The dialectic that opens the fundamental split in the subject, the interior distance, includes without saying a word the other who made it possible. It opens and shows this distance inaugurated by civilisation in the flesh of one's own, which opened itself up because previously some other opened up in us the distance of a difference, of a perspective, but at the same time of a gap that no one else will be able to close anymore. Yet this distance is precisely that which the subject ignores, since it is its presupposition.

5   The Unnameable Domain

> Even if conscience is something 'within us', yet it is not so from the first. In this it is a real contrast to sexual life, which is in fact there from the beginning of life and not only a later addition. (62)

We thus recognise that the foundation of this rational consciousness or conscience is not something originally given: its origin appears in the material presence hallucinated by the mental patient. It has the same functions, except that in us, the 'normal' ones, they are internalised and lived only as if they were irreducibly ours and originally given:

> There is scarcely anything else in us that we so regularly separate from our ego and so easily set over against it as precisely our conscience. ... I might simply say that the special agency which I am beginning to distinguish in the ego is conscience. But it is more prudent to keep the agency as something independent and to suppose that conscience is one of its functions and that self-observation, which is an essential preliminary to the judging activity of conscience, is another of them. And since when we recognize that something has a separate existence we give it a name of its own, from this time forward I will describe this agency in the ego as the 'super-ego'. (59–60)

And so that exterior foreign domain, which the ego recognised in the outside, now turns out to be laying there confusedly and without a name in one's own interior, regulating it from within but without being recognised as external. This domain was not named by civilisation: it was, then, a domain without the appeal of a name. The denomination introduced by Freud brings into consciousness and at last makes an object of self-observation that which precisely was the foundation of every relation of objectification that the ego exerts as a power of its own. This is why the super-ego cannot be reduced to moral conscience alone, which is just one of its functions. Its basic function, from which all the others are derived, is the subjective capacity to apprehend ourselves as object of our knowledge. But then this relation appears in inverted form: I take myself as object from the perspective of the other and within the distance that the other opened up. The super-ego, thus, is a foreign power; an external foreign domain which hides, concealing itself, what it really is: the irreducibly other in oneself. What here appears unconscious, because it is the foundation of consciousness, is the subverted relation between the interior and the exterior: being a representative of reality in the midst of one's own subjectivity. The true foreign territory, therefore, is not made up of our repressed impulses, but of our super-ego. And, as we will see, it is also the super-ego who determines the inversion with which we capture the other domain, that of our repressed impulses, which we consider as 'interior foreign territory'. It converts it into something foreign when it is, in contrast to the other, the most proper and perhaps the only thing that is effectively proper.

> Even if conscience is something 'within us', yet it is not so from the first. In this it is a real contrast to sexual life, which is in fact there from the beginning of life and not only a later addition. (62)

This clearly indicates the inversion that civilisation, by way of conscience, produces in us in opening ourselves up to life and closing ourselves to it at the same time. There is an originary internal-internal, sexual life, the corporeality that we did not create and that nature prolongs in us as its highest degree of organicity in the body. We are from one end to the other the sexuality that constitutes us. And there is the internal-internal internalised in the process of our own access to the world of culture or civilisation, which is the product of our having been ordered to do so from the outside, and which we nonetheless treat as if it were more internal to us than sexuality itself, while the latter, by contrast, is apprehended as foreign. Such a distance is what remains hidden in the new articulation that civilisation opened, and it is what the latter continues to conceal so as to convert its own solutions and its order into something 'natural', more imperative and true than the demands of the sexuated body in the unity of its unsublimatable biology.

There is thus a real transition from the parents to moral conscience, which is concealed. This is the 'abnormal' that presents itself as normal. And not only this: it is the condition of normality itself.

> But, as is well known, young children are amoral and possess no internal inhibitions against their impulses striving for pleasure. The part which is later taken on by the super-ego is played to begin with by an external power, by parental authority. ... It is only subsequently that the secondary situation develops (which we are all too ready to regard as the normal one), where the external restraint is internalised and the super-ego takes the place of the parental agency and observes, directs and threatens the ego in exactly the same way as earlier the parents did with the child. (62)

I would like to prolong this observation beyond the sphere of the family, to which conventional psychoanalysis circumscribes it. To bring out the aim of psychoanalysis as coinciding with the constitution of the only true knowledge: that of the search for a true agency. That is to say, to inscribe psychoanalysis in a theory that would prolong this affirmation to the point of extending it to the wider field of social activity wherein its true meaning is situated. If the subjective element is, as we believe it is, the kernel of historical truth, then we must demonstrate that this inversion of the process, this non-occurrence, this concealment of the origin already marks the presence, via the parents, of political and social power at the heart of the subject. But for this we will have to extend this presence of the parents, in the way Freud does, so as to include that which the adult typically does not include: the system of production as that which determines the rational form of the structure of the ego.

We saw that for the mental patient regression makes sensible the immediate presence of the power that formed it: the voice of the parents who are at the source of personal repression. As in dreams. the hallucination includes them as present in the actual reality of which they begin to be part for him. As adults, already installed in the rational consciousness opened up by the super-ego, we laugh at this hallucination: but there is nobody out there, the parents are no longer there, they are not the same persons, now we think every act and we decide, as a result, based on reason alone. In us the alien voice lost its sound and became the voiceless word: it speaks through our own voice. But just as the sick person becomes dislocated and eludes the true reality in which the parents prolong themselves by situating it in the actual reality, will it not be the case that we, in turn, elude it in the abstraction of a reality that no longer encounters the system from which it derives? Because the reality that knowledge reveals to us is the following: the rationality of our consciousness, the order of our ideology that subjectively rules over us, that which we have avoided 'all too readily' as normal, finds its secret in the knowledge of the historical system of production that made us who we are. This subjective determination thus has its precise field of rationality, which for reasons of principle is its foundation. And just as the mental patient eludes the reality present in hallucination, we also elude it in the fantasy of an individual independence that is lived in the interstices of social determinism.

For this reason, the most important here is the movement by which Freud defines for us the personal foundation that we must discover in order to reach this true rationality: that *there is no transition to the true rational structure if previously we have not understood the sensible foundation in which the rational prolongation of conscience finds support*. And this is so from within *our own* history.

> The super-ego, which thus takes over the power, function and even the methods of the parental agency, is however not merely its successor but actually the legitimate heir of its body. It proceeds directly out of it. (62)

We are not dealing with a juridical problem of *legal* succession, and thus with an inheritance that is only rational. It is the flesh that here takes place together with the form of the law, and the stepdaughter has the legal form but also a precise sensible content, without which, if it is not incorporated, the meaning of the law is lost in the abstraction of a body separated, at the origin, from its true origin. What is lost is the experience of the transition, and what takes its place is the gap: the personal duality.

This dualism between body and spirit, though innocent in its appearance, is fundamental for the determination of the being of the human subject. The point is not to dissolve this tension by thinking of the 'concept' of the body-spirit unity, or to install oneself simply in the combinatory of its structure. Can I not perhaps as a scientist – some people tell themselves who think in concepts – think the truth of reason in the truth of its concepts which, via an epistemological break, retain the form of the movement of the real? Listen to Freud: this being, he tells us, which thus inhibited *in itself* the prolongation of the sensual in the rational, is a diminished being. It disbarred being from itself in order to remain only in having: what it has are concepts. A being which, as we will see, stays limited to the development of an apparent difference in which the strict basis of resemblance, of identity, remains as its foundation. This is the grave conclusion at which the human being arrives who, for all that he knows does not know what is fundamental: he thinks without making space for the transformation of the sensible, without incorporating his own flesh in the process that *he thinks* he transforms.

> I cannot tell you as much as I should like about the metamorphosis of the parental relationship into the super-ego ... So you must be content with the sketch that follows. The basis of the process is what is called an 'identification' – that is to say, the assimilation of one ego to another one, as a result of which the first ego behaves like the second in certain respects, imitates it and in a sense takes it up into itself. Identification has been not unsuitably compared with the oral, cannibalistic incorporation of the other person. It is a very important form of attachment to someone else, probably the very first, and not the same thing as the choice of an object. The difference between the two can be expressed in some such way as this. If a boy identifies himself with his father, he wants to be like his father; if he makes him the object of his choice, he wants to have him, to possess him. In the first case his ego is altered on the model of his father; in the second case that is not necessary. (62–3)

My foundation is thus the signifying corporeality of the other who, by incorporation, opened in me the field of resemblance: being. But this being *like* the other is what determines all posterior having, every object choice. Being is followed by having, but it is the form of being of the other which will determine my having. It is because I enlivened my flesh with the sensible form of the other that subsequently I am capable of having. But I will have only within the limits of my being, which in reality will be those of the other. If it were not ... in order *not to be*: that is the point, to run the risk of not-being in the development of the difference of the other who gave me, in the beginning, his being as point of departure. This difference is, as we will see later, the most fatal and terrorising form in the access to reality of the human subject. I necessarily made me into the other in my own corporeality, and from there I am. This being which subsequently opens out to having sets the rules not only for my subsequent, derived conscience but it is, in my very own sensibility, norm and law: incarnated norm and rational law.

If I ignore this being that sits in the beginning, at my own foundation, as the basis for every possible relation with reality, that is, with my capacity for having, *the problem of having will not imply the problem of being*. My being will not be at play in the having – and so I can even have concepts – and I will not be able to distinguish the true source on the basis of which every relation with reality for me is determined. In my relation with the world – love, friendship, art, science, politics, etc. – I will have erased the fundamental problem. The displacement of the problem of being in order to exercise directly the voracity of having eludes the plenitude of its source of desire and, disdaining its foremost content, wants only whatever the other allows it to have: to turn into an object, without being the incarnated source of desire itself.

> Identification and object-choice are to a large extent independent of each other (63)

What the psychotic does, by returning to the 'reality' of the internal, is only the result of an external frustration, but of an external reality in which the obstacle is neither recognised nor confronted in its actual reality: in which the repressive system appears as absolutely dominant and where it is impossible to confront the frustration. The mechanism to which the psychotic has recourse, regressively, is a quasi-biological mechanism within the psychic realm: the conversion of the external into the internal, which is simultaneous with the conversion of the internal into the external.

> If one has lost an object or has been obliged to give it up, one often compensates oneself by identifying oneself with it and by setting it up once more in one's ego, so that here object-choice regresses, as it were, to identification. (63)

To regress to identification means to return to the point where being is confused with having. The normal mechanism, as we will see, is equivalent to this: being what we already are, we want to have, and by way of repression we reach our object, which in reality is also the object of the other. But since this object is outside, and our having is adapted to our being, we believe that it is us who, in our truest self-sameness, reach the object. But in the other we actually pursue the other who thus obsesses and delimits our having. Only the sick persons, with their breach, put into relief our articulation, which has already vanished into the density of the desirous body. The mental patients, refusing to admit the limitation that we admit, do not connect with reality and keep present the source of their desire. And they actualise it, in a regressive movement, toward the past, as if they could unravel the reality of time and return, by traversing it once more, to the encounter of the first presence. To return there where *being coincided with having*, where being was everything because it was from there that sprung our existence as similar to that of the other who was present in ourselves. Identification is the earliest generative impression; the form of the other draws the form of the object of my desire, but as the form of myself from where the act of desiring on its basis creates the possibility of desiring on my own. What is most proper to me is defined by what is alien at the origin. The process of identification, which in the world of civilisation converts my natural body into a cultural body through the other, internalises into the flesh a determination that is as imperious as that of natural instinct itself, because it enables the transition to the only possible reality: the reality that corresponds to the human form with which I identify myself.

6   Having Decanted into Being

Hence the regressive return: to go back to the domain of the first linkage, to the only basis where things were sure and unquestionable, where there existed an *exact* overlap of desire with the object, insofar as the object gave it being in the very act of having it. But – and this is the difference – still without distinction and without distance. The non-distance in the distance: such is the punctual origin which necessarily will open up more and more as time goes by, there where the necessary abandonment of the first object does not always mean that we accept the distance that every object, now different, brings with it. The distance is what is intolerable, but it is precisely the difference that now opens this distance. The initial non-distance was that of being and having, but within resemblance. The actual distance separates being from having, because it includes the difference, which opens the distance between the ego and the object. Whence the drama of the situation: in the adult reality the distance is erased in the distance and we believe that we return to the first unity. With this form of being we are assured in our having. But this having now takes place without distance and without difference. This is why, when the obstacle appears and this being no longer really serves the purpose of having, the point is once more to put into play the foundation from where we descend, which is being: within reality to develop the difference, to assume the historical distance and introduce the time of death into the very flesh of timeless desire. But this is not easy, because all difference is felt as the anxiety of death before the super-ego.

The relations that in the child are confused with identifications, being as they are really object relations, remain determining for having, as if I existed only in *this* having. I only am if I have that which coincides with my being and fulfils me: enclosing my being within itself.

> With his abandonment of the Oedipus complex a child must, as we can see, renounce ... the intense object-cathexes which he has deposited with his parents ... Identifications of this kind as precipitates of object-cathexes that have been given up. (64)

The process, thus, became inverted: *having became decanted into being*. The adequate relations to the child's external world were converted into a 'cultural' instinct, in the same way that the natural external stimuli became decanted into the life of instincts. Let us recall:

> There is naturally nothing to prevent our supposing that the instincts themselves are, at least in part, precipitates of the effects of external stimulation, which in the course of phylogenesis have brought about modifications in the living substance. ('Instincts and Their Vicissitudes', SE 14: 120)

The residues, sedimentations, or precipitates of abandoned object-cathexes – father, mother – play the same role as the other 'precipitates of the effects of external stimulation' of nature in the process of life. Both become converted into determinations of the body, into instincts. But the super-ego itself becomes converted into something as natural as the instinct, and subsequent experiences are unable to reach it:

> Identifications then come about with these later parents as well, and indeed they regularly make important contributions to the formation of

> character; but in that case they only affect the ego, they no longer influence the super-ego, which has been determined by the earliest parental imagos. ... Normally it departs more and more from the original parental figures; it becomes, so to say, more impersonal. (64)

The impersonal where the super-ego ends up was, in the beginning, all images: flesh organised by the vision of the other made into myself by identification. I-the other: this is the instinctive-cultural form, the origin of my dualism sutured without distance in the very act that articulates it in me.

The fact that this is not only a concept metaphysically expressed by the notion of the flesh, but that there is coincidence between the concept and the sensible matter that the concept organises; that this is not only a formulation at the level of thought, a rational model without coincidence with the empirical reality, but that the model and the structure in reality give structure to the flesh determined as personal being, all this is what Freud immediately makes clear:

> I hope you have already formed an impression that the hypothesis of the super-ego really describes a structural relation and is not merely a personification of some such abstraction as that of conscience. (64)

If the super-ego simply were the personification of an abstraction, it would be a metaphor. Its mystery would remain intact, as the mystery of moral consciousness remains intact at the conventional level. When Freud says that he 'describes a structural relation' he is saying that it is a structure that personifies, that structures a person, flesh in which form and content coincide, because the first organises the second. The 'structural relation' makes this clear: it is 'structure' and 'event' (relation or circumstance) at the origin itself; it is signifying rationality lived in the sensible, it is structure embodied in the flesh. The super-ego, then, is not a metaphor or an image that helps us to think of an abstraction: it is a real structure that gives us being, in our very own materiality that thus is organised, in what we are: a place opened up by the form of the other in ourselves. Moral conscience, on other hand, is in fact the 'personification' of an abstraction: the result of going from the personal of parents to the impersonal of abstraction. But the moral consciousness does not know it: the transition from the sensible relation to the rational signification remains hidden. In its origin the personal of the other determines, as structural situation, my own person. And this is what the recuperation of the 'structural relation' can give back to us so that we may include it into the concept, whose origin lies in the real representation of a link that has already been dissolved. Marx teaches us the same lesson when he says that the commodity adopts a particular form in exchange, the 'form' of money:

> Money is not a symbol, just as the existence of a use-value in the form of a commodity is no symbol.[3]

This much is clear: money, gold, in its very existence would seem to 'symbolise' the other, that which is not money: the value of every commodity. But in reality money itself has value, and serves as equivalent, only in the extent to which a relation of production – a 'structural relation' – produced it as value. Money, gold, also expresses a 'structural relation': the social relations that in effect produced it. It is not an expressive function that it fulfils and in which it exhausts itself: if it expresses anything it is because in it are objectified, as general abstract labour, the determinate relations of individuals united in the process of production that turns it into value, and of which it is the result. Its appearance as mere symbol is the result of the concealment of the real relations that produced it. And this goes for the super-ego as well:

> One more important function remains to be mentioned which we attribute to this super-ego. It is also the vehicle of the ego ideal by which the ego measures itself, which it emulates, and whose demand for ever greater perfection it strives to fulfill. There is no doubt that this ego ideal is the precipitate of the old picture of the parents. (64–5)

This sedimented, residual character of one's own 'ideal' is what is lost in rationality without depth: the leftover residue conceals the representation linked to the flesh of what conglomerates and retains it together with the corporeal memory. The ego does not appear for itself as determined and orientated by this residue of its past. In the erasure of its precipitated, sedimented being, what is concealed is its determination closer to the sensible, the dialectic of effective and real relations that transformed it into the place from which a biological form, converted into a cultural form, is able to say: I. What is concealed is the one-to-one struggle of reason, which has a human form because it had, from the origin, a sensible form. The super-ego also has nothing symbolic about it: and there is nothing symbolic in the fact that in a human body, the place of the ego, the social form of the super-ego appears. The super-ego does not express

---

3 Marx 1959, p. 288.

only the structure, nor is the human being only its bearer: it is the flesh really structured by the others in the process of its access to being human.

It is therefore in the originary hand-to-hand combat with the other where the final dependence of the master and slave, or the dominant and the dominated, is organised. This dependence is set deep in our very own being as if it were not a difference elaborated in a transition but an absolute difference. For it conceals the first resemblance from which it took off: the dependence of the child's body as opposed to the adult's body.

> The sense of inferiority has strong erotic roots. A child feels inferior if he notices that he is not loved, and so does an adult. (65)

The child *feels* it, but does not *know* it. *To be* here means *to be defective*, for not being the way the other wants us to be. At the origin, if I am not the way the other wants me to be, I do not have the other. This is the complementarity, in the initial dialectic, where having and being are confused. In order to have I must be what the object is. *Object and subject are confused, at the origin, in one and the same object.* And inasmuch as they configure, at their sensible existence, a structure, they determine in me the personified replica of this confusion that I am. To be different is to be guilty and inferior: not having for not being like the other.

> Altogether, it is hard to separate the sense of inferiority and the sense of guilt. It would perhaps be right to regard the former as the erotic complement to the moral sense of inferiority. (66)

In the adult, to be is to be guilty: the most personal is being regulated, as the offender, before the most impersonal, the super-ego. But in the child being guilty is a person-to-person relationship, in a hand-to-hand combat in which, later on, in the adult, the body of the other became impersonal form, other, mere rational structure. I was left alone with my body without knowing against what to struggle, against which obstacle to fight, what flesh to confront. But it is the erotic bond that tied my inferiority to the other's superiority, it is for having made it into my object in myself by swallowing it that subsequently another feeling will lean on this, prolonging itself from the first feeling: the feeling of guilt. What at bottom is a libidinal relation, a relation of feeling to feeling, here appears – through repression – as a logical and purely rational deduction: I *deduce* that I am guilty, I *deduce* that I am inferior. The reason of my conscience is the geometrical order of a flesh that has lost the origin.

At the origin of this confusion, but also in the subsequent domain, the transition from the biological to the cultural is present, though in a confused way:

> But let us return to the super-ego. We have allotted it the functions of self-observation, of conscience and of [maintaining] the ideal. It follows from what we have said about its origin that it presupposes an immensely important biological fact and a fateful psychological one: namely, the human child's long dependence on its parents and the Oedipus complex, both of which, again, are intimately interconnected. (66)

What I am: self-observation; *what I must do*: moral consciousness; *what I must be*: ego-ideal. All my being, then, with the two extremes that define action integrated into it: knowledge, the objective, and the norms that regulate it are determined from the outside, surrounded by culture, all the while concealing their genesis. These mechanisms reduplicate in oneself the capacity for taking them as object: as object of knowledge, of the norm, and of the ends pursued in action. This structure is precisely the one that determines my transition to reality: I am real in the actualisation of this relation that objectifies me. And this 'higher side' that exists in myself is the aspiration towards which what is most proper to me strives. Thus the external foreign domain, which appears in the ego as one of its extremes when it gazes outward, only gives me an appearance of reality: I, in truth, am nothing if not a result, one of the two poles of its being-real. I am this exteriority internalised, the subjective moment of the external reality that produced me as *its* subject, the appearance of the nearest in what is most alien: I.

But we already know what influence the Oedipus complex exerts: it is precisely the production of conscience as guilty conscience, with the consciousness of the drama that determined it. Dependency lies at the foundation of the fantasised solution, where in my insufficiency I regressed to the oral phase of identification, and I became the other: I the father, he the child. And I did to him what he pretended to do to me: I annihilated him. But I gave him, after the murder, the force of survival within myself. Yet the consciousness that results from this knows nothing about that which gave origin to it as moral consciousness. This is why the higher side to which I strive is from now on not my aspiration but his.

> ... it is, in short, as much as we have been able to grasp psychologically of what is described as the higher side of human life. Since it itself goes back to the influence of parents, educators and so on, we learn still more of its significance if we turn to those who are its sources. ... They have forgotten

> the difficulties of their own childhood and they are glad to be able now to identify themselves fully with their own parents who in the past laid such severe restrictions upon them. (66–7)

What happens is that this later identification is the only one that brings back the precise object to fill the precise void of an absence for which we felt guilty. What remains forgotten, together with the difficulties of one's own childhood, is the revenge that we so cruelly exert against the most hated and most beloved being: all those severe restrictions, seen in retrospect, were very much deserved. In this way the biological and the cultural coincide in the determination of a biological insufficiency and an infantile dependency: riding on top of the dependency of biology is the cultural dependency.

And so as to leave no doubts about this social character of the super-ego and its historical determination, which the psychoanalysts usually reject, the explicit reference to a previous work, *Group Psychology and Analysis of the Ego*, clarifies the import of Freud's formulation:

> If we possessed more applications of this kind, the hypothesis of the super-ego would lose its last touch of strangeness for us, and we should become completely free of the embarrassment that still comes over us when, accustomed as we are to the atmosphere of the underworld, we move in the more superficial, higher strata of the mental apparatus. (68)

And so, then, we began with the ego, and not with the ego in general, but with our very own ego. But here we end up with the super-ego. We began with one and end up in the other. The endpoint we thus reach has been converted into the real beginning of the analysis of the ego. From this point, discovered as the true beginning – once our own ego has been decentred – the analysis of the ego can truly begin for science.

7   Repression, Texture of the Ego

As we have seen so far, it is a question of knowing how to transition to reality and recuperate the historical distance opened up in the midst of the psychic apparatus. This distance, which is the unconscious distancing that takes place at the heart of my own ego, of what is most proper to me, must become objectified in a distance that is really exterior: it must encounter the historical and objective structure that gave rise to it. But Freud tells us that it is precisely this transition repressed in the ego that must make this encounter possible: the only light we have at our disposal to open for us the path toward reality. It so happens that I myself resist moving on to reality, *but I know nothing of this resistance.* Which means, Freud tells us, that our own resistances remain unconscious.

What does it mean to say that the resistances of the ego (and of the super-ego) are unconscious? It means that the ego does not make the act of repressing into an object of knowledge because it does not distinguish itself: *in its very texture the ego is repression.* Consciousness appears against the backdrop of this texture, which is already ordered as form and repressive reason. The point is not, therefore, for me to take myself as object: to take myself as object would mean *to distance me from myself* in order to apprehend the foundation that constitutes me. But this is precisely what I cannot do: the subjective distance – between super-ego and ego – is what cannot be seen, because it is the foundation of the resemblance that gives me being.

For this reason, because it is the texture of consciousness, this 'dynamic' unconscious is 'permanently unconscious', Freud tell us. It is the foundation of the subject, but the subject knows nothing about it. What matters is that the unconscious is not only the repressed: the unconscious is also the repressor. The contact between the ego and the id is unconscious in both: *they coincide in the unconscious.*

> ... his resistance was unconscious too, just as unconscious as the repressed, at the lifting of which we were working. (68)

Here were two types of unconscious: the unconscious resistance of the ego, and the unconscious repressed of the id. And we ask ourselves, astonished, on the basis of this reflexive and objective consciousness that each of us is: how is it that reason does not face up to the consequences? No longer the reason of the repressed, which has given no reason that the unconscious repressed is included in the id, but the reason of the one resisting, that is to say the ego. Thus appears a distance that the ego cannot close: it is that which in the ego resists being thought, its very own repressed foundation.

There is thus an unconscious that seeks to rise up, opening itself to the reality of satisfaction (the repressed impulses) and there is a repressing unconscious that resists allowing this passage to become realised (the ego):

> We must rather attribute to the repressed a strong upward drive, an impulsion to break through into consciousness. The resistance can only be a manifestation of the ego, which originally put the repression into force and now wishes to maintain it. (68)

That original moment refers to the dawn of childhood: it enforced the repression while confronting an external relation, for fear of losing the love of the other. Now, as adult, thanks to consciousness, it represses itself. The ego is 'obedient to its commands', the commands of the super-ego: the delegated emissary in oneself. Thus the ego is the texture embroidered onto the lace canvas of the form of the other in me: negative links that in their moment did not have any consciousness in which to become decanted as thoughtful relations and were left behind as carnal structures, sensible and affective chains: values. Therefore, when the conscious signification is revealed in analysis, without our knowing why and surprising us with this order inscribed in the body as though it came from afar, there emerge 'distressing feelings': what hurts is the meaning that the psychoanalysts restore for us. The 'distressing feeling' is language still without consciousness, and, in the schematism of conduct, it operates as signal: a sensible call of attention that a danger is become actualised, a package of felt relations that act as language and affectively dramatise the wake of a situation that once was, as if we were no more than a bit of flesh ordered and always repeatable in that first order that gave it its form. The language of a body in danger, based on which all other language is always secondary and all other language is verified, in order to be true, in that first one. To think here means to link and weave together the threads that the affective and unconscious texture organises; every linkage that falls outside its scope hurts: it falls back on the living flesh, not integrated, residual. And this contact of the ego, extended to the point of brushing up against the repressed, is only felt but not known: felt as pain, consciousness 'knows nothing about' the repression it exerts. The repression that who or what exerts? Me? But I don't know it. I cannot know it because that which I cannot make into the object of my knowledge is precisely the very texture of the ego. I am resistance. If the ego took itself to this point as object, it would imply that it falls within the power that we recognise in it: that of knowing its foundation. But its own foundation is repression: I am repression. Here we have a fundamental consequence for any theory of knowledge and for any action in reality: what I cannot take as object is precisely the foundation of my being. I am in the extent to which I resist. This is why the thinking that weaves together the texture of the ego stops short before the repressed:

> The objective sign of this resistance is that his associations fail or depart widely from the topic that is being dealt with. He may also recognize the resistance subjectively by the fact that he has distressing feelings when he approaches the topic. But this last sign may also be absent. We then say to the patient that we infer from his behaviour that he is now in a state of resistance; and he replies that he knows nothing of that, and is only

> aware that his associations have become more difficult. It turns out that we were right; but in that case his resistance was unconscious too, just as unconscious as the repressed, at the lifting of which we were working. (68)

Thinking, by falling outside of the texture, touches upon the living flesh of the excluded, of the non-integrated, of the repressed, and only feels it: it feels the pain and the anxiety of what in its moment, in the original weaving of the texture, it lived as danger. This is why it does not know but only feels. But sometimes it does not even feel. Yet this not-knowing means not being able to encompass with thought that positive element of one's own that struggles to rise up: we only feel the negative side of pain, which the promised pleasure produced in its disappointed transition to reality. This is why it cannot produce new associations, name the unnamed. Consciousness does not gain access to new meanings except the ones that the official order tolerates. On the one hand, consciousness has no adequate words or logical links to express the repressed: in its very structure it is repression. But, on the other hand, what it must name did not reach consciousness either as representation or as image because the id has no words or signs: it only encounters, and not always, the sign of pain that it produces in the repressed flesh, the flesh that speaks painfully in the anxiety that consciousness awakens as the risk of death and not-being, if it dared to be. The unconscious of the ego's consciousness are shadows, and dark ones to boot: its own light is black.

But what is the meaning of this coincidence between the unconscious of the repressed and the unconscious of the repressor? What effect does it produce to know that both are unconscious?

> .... resistance was unconscious too, just as unconscious as the repressed, at the lifting of which we were working. (68)

We already saw this. The repressed is unconscious, and for a reason: it does not have the official words at its disposal. But the unconscious resistance comes from the ego. It does have the words, but does not know how to articulate them or use them to apprehend its own unthinkable foundation: it is 'unconscious resistance'. Everything therefore transpires as if nobody knew what it really matters to know: consciousness, the ego, does not have consciousness of this confrontation, of this mute drama that unfolds in the subject. To the unconscious repressed which struggles to rise up, the unconscious resistance opposes itself: it fights among the blind who need not see each other because the sensible surface of each one of them links up sense by sense with the surface of the other. Strange coincidence in which the same differentiates itself as other from itself, without which there could not be any unconscious point of contact. This is why they are not the same: there is one that is originary, true, and another that is the usurper. The unconscious, repressed instinctive element is originary, and not only cultural: it is raw being. But the unconscious resistance is only cultural. Since both are unconscious, they do not have the same meaning and do not occupy the same 'place' in the psychic apparatus, in spite of this common quality that fuses them into the same. It is necessary therefore to differentiate them by their origin, by their mode of appearing in the body, and by the position they occupy in the latter. Without a theory that integrates the history of the psychic apparatus in the body we cannot understand this basic fact: the difference between the unconscious repressed and the unconscious repressor. On the descriptive level, then, the difference between both types of the unconscious does not appear to be clearly established. Because of their functions, we know what they both are. But we do not know how they came to be: here the origin may give meaning and help disentangle more adequately their function.

From this 'descriptive' analysis of the unconscious Freud will move on to the 'dynamic' comprehension of the process, as a new level of access (and recapitulation) toward the distinction between both types of unconscious. But it is only upon reaching a final level of analysis, the 'topological' one, that we will be able to understand a distinction that neither of the first two, the descriptive or the dynamic, managed to explain. None of them is capable of accounting for the constitutive dialectic of the outside and the inside, of the exterior and the interior. Neither one of the first two but only the topological analysis will be able to integrate the historical organisation into the structure of the psychic apparatus, showing how it emerges in the biological corporeality of a subject who is making the transition from the natural to the cultural.

8   The Substantial Unconscious

In order to develop this distinction Freud must endow the *repressed unconscious* with an originary substantiality that does not correspond to the *unconscious repressor*, that is to say, to the resistance that the ego exerts against its own unconscious impulses. Resistance is the external repression internalised within the ego: the ego, turned repression as delegate of the other in oneself, resists. Against whom? Against itself.

Let us observe how unconscious resistance is an impediment for thinking: resistance to the becoming conscious of the unconscious. What thus becomes dislocated in the ego is the functional coherence of its own thinking apparatus, for whose efficiency apparently it was convoked. The morality of the consciousness that consisted, in its own implacable logic, in thinking the truth and nothing but the truth, comes undone and breaks its own laws: those of thinking the true.

At the level of consciousness Freud describes:

> 'Failure' of his *spontaneous* associations (which do not follow the straight line, that of the authorised logic)
> 'Departure' from the topic being dealt with (refusal to keep present the object of knowledge that the analyst proposes as the principal one, eluding it in the unconscious, taking it out of focus)
> 'I know nothing', says his consciousness (he ignores what he is told in the interpretation).

At the level of the body: affective repercussion of that which consciousness does not recognise.

The result is as follows:

> At the level of knowledge: 'I know nothing'.
> At the level of feeling: 'distressing feelings'.

The communication of one consciousness to another, which proceeds on the terrain of knowledge, answers us: 'I know nothing', and feels an affect that becomes autonomous from knowledge. But who does not know?

I do not know. Thus the I or ego, before the interior drama, remains silent. From this crucial opposition, in which the being or nonbeing of those who suffer is fought out, I in my conscious clairvoyance, on which I base my power, know nothing. At most I feel, but it is an insignificant feeling: I do not know of what my discontent is the discontent. But even though all this is unconscious, we must not confuse ourselves: not all is the *same* unconscious. It is not, therefore, the quality of being unconscious that can help us understand the problem. If all the repressed as well as the resistance are unconscious, they are the same in one sense, but different in another. To say that all is unconscious is a general affirmation, which is still abstract, merely descriptive of a quality whose support we still ignore, and which penetrates into the *system that is productive of unconscious subjectivity*. The problem that Freud poses here is that of the origin:

> ... from what part of his mind does an unconscious resistance like this arise? (68)

And he adds:

> The beginner in psychoanalysis will be ready at once with the answer: it is, of course, the resistance of the unconscious. (68)

In this way, following the answer of the beginner, the unconscious would be homogeneous, everything unconscious would enter into one and the same undifferentiated substance, but there would be no differences in the unconscious in function of the 'part' of psychic life from which it stems. This beginner's answer would be the trap of ambiguity that consciousness itself creates so as to hide, in its process of approaching the truth, its dependent structure. This is why what we must disentangle is the qualitative difference of the unconscious itself. Not everything unconscious has the same meaning, or occupies the same place:

> If it means that the resistance arises from the repressed, we must rejoin: certainly not! We must rather attribute to the repressed a strong upward drive, an impulsion to break through into consciousness. The resistance can only be a manifestation of the ego ... (68)

We already see: what the consciousness of the ego refused to make conscious was its own unconscious foundation, its resistance to include in knowledge, which is its function, the unconscious repressed. The unconscious repressed cannot reach consciousness because consciousness is, in its very foundation, *unconscious resistance against the true exercise of its conscious function*.

The sharp separation that consciousness offers to us, when it thinks of the unconscious as that which is its opposite and radically heterogeneous to it, is precisely the trap of non-dialectical thought which looks for support, credulously, in a result without asking itself about its origin and genesis. Let us therefore reiterate: the foundation of consciousness is unconscious. Even more: the unconscious foundation of consciousness determines it not to think of that which repression condemns. The unconscious foundation of consciousness resists its own exercise of the power that nonetheless would appear to be proper to it.

In order to specify the meaning of the unconscious that is at issue, then, we must determine 'from what part of his mind an unconscious resistance like this arises', the place where it finds support, from where it emerges and comes to us, how *it came to be* resistance. We must distinguish therefore the unconscious of the one who pretends not to know (the ego) and the one who, because it is repressed, never reached consciousness: the internal foreign domain. There is an unconscious that was never tied to the light, and another that comes from it. There are two origins that need to be differentiated. There is the origin of the unconscious of the ego, which is the prolongation of the other turned super-ego in oneself and which opens the field of resemblance as absolute limit. And there is the origin of the unconscious repressed, that which in us, as carnal knowledge, cannot make the passage into culture. There is one that is unconscious in its own right, and another that is unconscious due to cultural repression. To believe that consciousness has no origin: that is the foundation of the ego's resistance and its limits. To have believed the enemy, to have believed what 'its' consciousness tells it, without realising that it is the other that speaks in it: without realising that in that case the sick person was right. Consciousness and the ego are here spiritualists. They believe in pure ideas, in the ethereal support of the meanings that are thought: they do not know that they are the consciousness and the ego of a divided body, and that this division and this separation, which is precisely the unthinkable for consciousness, is its point of departure. The ego fell into the trap of the separation of an ideal consciousness, as if it were not the attribute of a body, because consciousness itself, its own ego, establishes the body as antagonistic to consciousness, as its most intimate enemy: 'interior foreign territory'. This is the trap of dualism that is incorporated into the foundation of consciousness, introducing into the subject itself the scission that the system produces throughout the whole field of reality: the commodity form that regulates, in its physical-metaphysical form, one's own subjective organisation.

This is a paradoxical situation! I, who am pure reason, I resist myself to understand the foundation of the reason that I exercise: to put into relief my own presuppositions. But how could I know this if I did not have consciousness then, when it was formed, if precisely consciousness is based on it? The unconscious foundation means culture without consciousness, for it is the negative side that identification engraved in us: in order for me to be. Thus, the ego's foundation is as unconscious as nature itself. But this is not a content of the ego that is unknown to it, like the repressed. Here what is not known is a function, a capacity for negative action on the basis of which the function of our ego, in certain portions of it, is produced.

> Since we have come to assume a special agency in the ego, the super-ego, which represents demands of a restrictive and rejecting character, we may say that repression is the work of this super-ego and that it is carried out either by itself or by the ego in obedience to its orders. If then we are met by the case of the resistance in analysis not being conscious to the patient, this means either that in quite important situations the super-

> ego and the ego can operate unconsciously, or – and this would be still more important – that portions of both of them, the ego and the super-ego themselves, are unconscious. In both cases we have to reckon with the disagreeable discovery that on the one hand (super-) ego and conscious and on the other hand repressed and unconscious are far from coinciding. (69)

What are these determinate 'portions' of the super-ego and the ego that are unconscious? We already saw: those that constitute their foundation and provide the support for the presumption that the function they fulfil is absolute. What matters to moral consciousness? To test the truth of the norm and to verify the accord with the law. What matters to the function of knowledge of the conscious ego? To test the limits and coherence of its personality and include the satisfaction of its desire – by means of the object – into reality. Precisely in the exercise of these essential functions the consciousness of its own foundation remains unconscious. Therefore, upon reaching the kernel of the ego and the super-ego, the conventional differences that previously separated the conscious from the unconscious, the repressed from the tolerated, disappear. 'Disagreeable discovery', says Freud. Do we realise the magnitude of the endpoint that we have reached? The basic categories of habitual thinking become inverted and contradict the common belief: the foundation of consciousness is unconscious; the repressed is consciousness itself; clairvoyance is in reality darkness. The ego, who is – so we believe – conscious, actually is not: the ego is unconscious in its very being as consciousness. The repressed is not merely the unconscious: it is part of consciousness itself, it is its point of affirmation and its foundation, which evidently I ignore. With these affirmations Freud accomplishes the most dramatic and irrefutable critique of bourgeois individualism and of the conventional conception on which traditional Western humanism is based.

At this point Freud feels the impact the reader will have felt, and as in analysis itself but now turned into pedagogy before the reader, he gives us time to breathe and reflect upon the depression that we will have felt before the magnitude of the conclusion he has reached:

> And here, Ladies and Gentlemen, I feel that I must make a pause to take breath – which you too will welcome as a relief – and, before I go on, to apologize to you. (69)

These excuses before the blood of the narcissistic wound inflicted upon us are part of the very same process of the understanding that is being developed: it is the ego that bleeds because of this wound. But since it is so painful, Freud tells us, let us be consistent and let us not have recourse merely to the habitual consoling belief. This result at which we have arrived is the fruit of a painful scientific experience, in which once again the rationality of what is affirmed rises forth only from the qualitative and sensible transformation of the human being who was capable of this thinking: it was the fruit of an irreducible praxis.

> Yet we have been obliged to recognize and express as our conviction that no one has a right to join in a discussion of psycho-analysis who has not had particular experiences which can only be obtained by being analysed oneself. (69)

This is why Freud started out from 'our very own ego': he did not borrow his object from the concept. He did not start from the abstract ego as a loan borrowed from the ego in general. The conceptual ego only discovers its truth from the experience it has of the limits of the embodied ego: from what is irreducibly one's own, because the discovery here is part of a personal relation that puts us to the test. It is, then, against the backdrop of a precise body and a precise flesh and a precise history from where the most rational and most finely theoretical affirmation – the foundation of rationality – can be accomplished, as its necessary presupposition:

> When I gave you my lectures fifteen years ago I tried to spare you certain speculative portions of our theory; but it is precisely from them that are derived the new acquisitions of which I must speak to you to-day. (69)

The new acquisition, the central theoretical point Freud reached, is the one already mentioned, and on which he repeatedly insists as the central node of his argument:

> Ego and conscious, repressed and unconscious do not coincide. (70)

Were the ego to coincide with the conscious, as we habitually imagine for ourselves, it would be pure translucency: it would be transparent to itself. The foundation of consciousness would be ideal, and we would be able to imagine it for ourselves as a purely spiritual capacity. It would mean, moreover, to confuse the unconscious with the irrational and the passive; to separate the flesh from the spirit. It would mean giving to the unconscious an irrationality that ignores the reason that structures it in its substantial texture, in its very being as matter endowed with meaning (significations not reached by consciousness), it would leave it cordoned off as radically opaque and irreducible to reason. But if the foundation of rationality is itself unconscious, and the repressed does not coincide with the unconscious, that arrogant ego who would be diminished as a result is that of a depressed consciousness: a consciousness that has lost its idealism, that must recognise its spurious origin, that makes vows of poverty not only in matters of knowledge but also about its very own being. What is at stake is not *having* knowledge: it is *being*. A consciousness that recognises, then, the unconscious basis in which it finds support, situated as it is in something other, beyond its own self-sufficiency. Whose power is a dependent power. It is only starting out from this depressed consciousness, which introduced deep doubts about itself and yet, in spite of everything, was really guided by the truth, that Freud will be able to set off on his path to show us its foundation. The theoretical analysis must continue the differentiation of the unconscious on the basis of a new consciousness.

9   The Flesh of Consciousness: Paths

If the interpretation is adequate, Freud is now going to emphasise a perspective that shows the body as the place of this debate. Here the ordering structures of the subject find support, qua systems, in forms of organisation that have the flesh as the place ('topographical' understanding) of their meaning.

Indeed, the 'descriptive' level from which Freud departed is an approach that allows for deductive inferences. It has the existence of a 'supposition': in order for this or that to happen we must suppose, as being part of its reality, something that nonetheless does not immediately appear in it:

> The oldest and best meaning of the word 'unconscious' is the descriptive one; we call a psychical process unconscious whose existence we are obliged to assume – for some such reason as that *we infer it from its effects* – but of which we know nothing. In that case we have the same relation to it as we have to a psychical process in another person, except that it is in fact one of our own. If we want to be still more correct, we shall modify our assertion by saying that we call a process unconscious if we are obliged to assume that it is being activated *at the moment*, though *at the moment* we know nothing about it. (70, first emphasis added)

This supposition, that of an underlying and active determination underneath the present moment, is merely theoretical: its objectivity is only external, a strange presence within the proper, the efficient cause that operates on the system from its outside, as if it did not make up the system from within it: 'we have the same relation to it as we have to a psychical process in another person', he tells us. The only difference is that 'it is in fact one of our own'. But this distance that reifies the efficacy of the unconscious in oneself, as external, is precisely an interior or immanent distance, which psychoanalysis tries to understand. If we are the unconscious, the unconscious is not a 'thing', an 'exterior object' in the midst of subjectivity: it is, by contrast, the very element of psychic life.

But on this 'descriptive' level the unconscious includes, almost indistinctly, *everything not actually present in consciousness*, and therefore also what is latent. What is latent can come back to consciousness. The description of the unconscious here does not provide us as yet with the different levels in the way of being of the unconscious: the latent, Freud writes, 'can easily become conscious again'. The conflicted and repressive quality that gives shape to the unconscious does not yet appear here. The portrayal of the truly unconscious only becomes more profound when we move to include it in the affective meaning of a dramatic situation, therefore at the 'dynamic' level. We already indicated as much: Freud's orientation aims toward the discovery of a substantial unconscious.

> This qualification makes us reflect that the majority of conscious processes are conscious only for a short time; very soon they become latent, but can easily become conscious again. We might also say that they had become unconscious, if it were at all certain that in the condition of latency they are still something psychical. So far we should have learnt nothing new; nor should we have acquired the right to introduce the concept of an unconscious into psychology. But then comes the new observation that we were already able to make in parapraxes. (70)

And so we must move on to the contradictory expression of an effective mode of conduct, in order to see the opening of the distance between the apparent meaning and the real meaning of parapraxis, which in this way shows us, in the relation opened up by the distance, the specific activity of the unconscious. But here it is no longer the deductive inference that sets it down as its supposition: here there is the evidence of the unconscious provided by the *expression* of the subject which brings the implicit to the surface with the intention of signifying beyond the conscious itself, contradictorily:

> In order to explain a slip of the tongue, for instance, we find ourselves obliged to assume that the intention to make a particular remark was present in the subject. We infer it with certainty from the interference

with his remark which has occurred; but the intention did not put itself through and was thus unconscious. If, when we subsequently put it before the speaker, he recognises it as one familiar to him, then it was only temporarily unconscious to him; but if he repudiates it as something foreign to him, then it was permanently unconscious. (70–1)

At the dynamic level the real existence of unconscious processes allows us to go into greater depths. Not everything latent at the descriptive level bears the same inscription in the subject's psychic structure:

> From this experience we retrospectively obtain the right also to pronounce as something unconscious what had been described as latent. A consideration of these dynamic relations permits us now to distinguish two kinds of unconscious – one which is easily, under frequently occurring circumstances, transformed into something conscious, and another with which this transformation is difficult and takes place only subject to a considerable expenditure of effort or possibly never at all. (71)

Thus emerges the distinction between the preconscious and the unconscious: that which can come into consciousness and that which never reaches it. The difference lies in the fact that one is *temporarily* unconscious, which means that it is a void of meaning between two full meanings: a link that is not present but whose coherence it suffices to introduce into the field of conscious meanings, with which consciousness can reckon as being compatible with it. We are in a single system. But the unconscious supposes two contradictory systems. This dynamic difference does not yet reach the foundation of the unconscious: it still refers to *its mode of appearing or not appearing*, and brings out the contraposition of 'forces' in struggle. But we still ignore what is at stake in these different modes, and even though the distinction between the conscious, preconscious and unconscious already draws a complex psychic field, the deduction still remains at the level of expressive reality. But of what is expression the expression? Expression puts into relief levels of organisation in the very corporeality of the psychological subject, and as long as these levels of organisation that prolong the sensible in the psychic have not appeared, it will not be possible to reach the true signification and reality of the unconscious. This outline necessarily involves a return to the domain from where the psychic life is organised, the problem of genesis at the most concrete level of its reality: from the biological corporeality up to the point where we reach its cultural transformation. Because the dynamic element only increases the descriptive level, but it does not go beyond toward the dramatic and substantial reality of the unconscious. And even though the dynamic level brings out the underlying 'forces' that exert their effects on conduct, only the 'topographical' level can manage to give an account of the fundamental structure of the conflict:

> You will admit, I hope, that so far that is not too bad and allows of convenient handling. Yes, but unluckily the work of psycho-analysis has found itself compelled to use the word 'unconscious' in yet another, third, sense, and this may, to be sure, have led to confusion. Under the new and powerful impression of there being an extensive and important field of mental life which is normally withdrawn from the ego's knowledge so that the processes occurring in it have to be regarded as unconscious in the truly dynamic sense, we have come to understand the term 'unconscious' in a topographical or systematic sense as well; we have come to speak of a 'system' of the preconscious and a 'system' of the unconscious, of a conflict between the ego and the system of the unconscious, and have used the word more and more to denote a mental province rather than a quality of what is mental. (71)

Here the distinction is no longer temporal, as in the descriptive unconscious, but spatial: topographical. And this recourse to the psychic organisation of the material spatiality of the organism in its topographical structure will make it possible to account for the fundamental distinction previously indicated by Freud: that 'portions' of the ego are also unconscious. Only in this way can we justify *the interior distance opened up in the subjective psychic organisation, as the place of a historical process in which the exterior became internalised without memory*. The topographical thus actualises the material, spatial place of a psychic organisation that preserves the origin, the genesis – engraved in its unfolding – of the psychic functions and capacities constituted in the process of its formation, as levels that can be actualised anew. How could the psychic be a province, a place, without being present anywhere as organisation?

The point is therefore to differentiate an unconscious of the ego and of the super-ego, separating it from *another*, which we no longer have the right, Freud tells us, to call 'unconscious' in the same manner. In what lies the distinction between one and the other? In that the unconscious of the ego and of the super-ego correspond to different 'mental provinces', and in that the interior foreign domain, which is unconscious, must be separated from that, internalised, which has its origin in the exterior foreign domain from which it results, and which *may be* unconscious. The unconscious aspect of the first is not exhausted by the fact that it does not reach consciousness: it has a material determination, which constitutes it as essentially different.

> Portions of the ego and super-ego being unconscious without possessing the same primitive and irrational characteristics. (75)

And so we see that there is a logical gradation that leads from the description, through the dynamic level, all the way to the topographical analysis, and it is in the latter where the meaning of the unconscious reaches its major difference and becomes concrete. From the descriptive and external end all the way to the opposite extreme, which is topographical and immanent, what reveals itself as necessary for our understanding is the gradual insertion of signification into the flesh: the quest for the corporeal seat, the spatial place where the ideality of the structure supposes the encounter of its field of insertion with the sensible materiality of an organism. There is thus a gradual descent from the foundation of the power of the ego and its slow restriction, as the degree to which the field of the subject broadens out. There is a slow return to the foundation, in the subject, of the roots of psychic significations decanted into corporeal articulations, where the memory of the flesh left engraved in the human being the path of its cultural development.

In reaching the topographical understanding of the psychic apparatus, the materiality of the unconscious encounters at last its seat:

> We perceive that we have no right to name the mental region that is foreign to the ego 'the unconscious system', since the characteristic of being unconscious is not restricted to it. (72)

Freud must therefore reject the unconscious as the mere negative of consciousness, as if it was only the ego that conferred its existence. There is an unconscious alien to the ego, but its existence is not defined solely by the quality of being unconscious: it has its own positivity and its own quality that is irreducible to the ego. With this what is Freud pursuing? To render independent a 'mental region' and recognise its proper status and reality, situating it where it really is: beyond the restricted limits that the ego attempts to give it from within its own partiality as its negative. If the ego is not the whole subject, if it is only the internalisation of a domain of interior translucency opened up in one by the exterior domain, which cuts us in two, how can we continue defining the unconscious on its basis? The reality of the unconscious is not conferred on it by the ego: it is not the repressor who must determine the effective reality of the repressed. It is necessary to let emerge the positive field of reality that the repressor manages to delimit and mark off. It is necessary to understand from the reality of the repressed that excess of being that the ego cannot create, because it is anterior to it. If we recall that the ego is the order, prolonged in the materiality of a body, of an exterior foreign domain which thus becomes internalised and assumes the monopoly of the subject's whole reality, how then can we define the unconscious that is repressed on the basis of that which it puts to the side, if I do not understand the content and form of that which thus is relegated? What autonomous reality does the ego have to accomplish this, if not for the installation that located it in the midst of a materiality where, internalised within it from the outside, it is only from this outside that it continues to seek understanding?

> Very well; we will no longer use the term 'unconscious' in the systematic sense and we will give what we have hitherto so described a better name and one no longer open to misunderstanding. Following a verbal usage of Nietzsche's and taking up a suggestion by Georg Groddeck, we will in the future call it the 'id'. This impersonal pronoun seems particularly well suited for expressing the main characteristic of this province of the mind – the fact of its being alien to the ego. The super-ego, the ego and the id – these, then, are the three realms, regions, provinces, into which we divide an individual's mental apparatus, and with the mutual relations of which we shall be concerned in what follows. (72)

The id, pro-noun and im-personal: that from which something will be named or given a noun, impersonal foundation of a person. The id designates here that primordial magma from where everything psychic, formed by culture, ends up and is kept. The id is the substantial foundation, the biological organicity that is already included in the psychic order of the human flesh that makes the transition towards the world of civilisation mediated by the ego that, as the place of order, it imposes. Where was the impersonal id, the not yet personalised, nature encapsulated without proper connection to the external world, there culture, in the form of the ego, personifies: 'Where id was, the ego shall come'. This is the primordial mystery of the individual being: its emergence, from the anonymous abyss of nature, which acquires human form.

But how can we decide what is the human being? How can we escape the conventional form with which each one thinks of him or herself, given that this one is not such, but it is rather the other who determines what I am? How can I take myself as object if this relation, which is an interior distance, was opened by the other, and making myself an object is equivalent to continuing to look at myself with the other's own eyes, hence eyes alien to me? It is a question of seeing that which the other in me cannot see, that which precisely the other pushed away from my being as invisible and insensible. And yet, it is from here that we will have to recuperate for the ego that excess of being that the ego represses. Because I am that, too, though in an obscure way. As its reverse side, repression draws up the form of the repressed that it tries to detain. But the content of what the ego represses is what I put there, that negated sameness with whose materiality the repressing force raised bit by bit its fortification and with what is most proper to oneself laid the foundation of its alien power. This return to the foundation, which is always inescapably present in each one of us, marks the interior distance in the process of gaining access to our being, the transition from the sensibility of a human body that came to life, but a life of culture, the primeval magma that each one of us is in the flesh as an extension of living matter. And thus it marks the emergence of what is relative to nature in this presumed absolute that each of us, as person, believes to be. This ordering logic that gives form to the body at the same time conceals, in its very order, the vital impulse of that which thus was ordered. This is our access to being and in principle we must accept it as such:

> At first we are inclined greatly to reduce the value of the criterion of being conscious since it has shown itself so untrustworthy. But we should be doing it an injustice. As may be said of our life, it is not worth much, but it is all we have. (70)

Conventional consciousness, as we saw, is the field of ideology. It is deceiving, venal, and prone to cover up things. But even though ideology means concealment, it is at the same time the field of the possible opening onto the real of culture: it is the very element from which subsequently there can be true knowledge, because previously the lived articulation with reality is opened up in us. Now, we saw, ours is a depressed consciousness, which knows that it is deceiving and dependent. And based on this we must be careful to try to give a name to whatever it contradictorily attempts to contain. This effort on Freud's part to think what is irreducible to thought but lies at the foundation of thought itself, defines a radical mode of thinking. It is an effort to think in the substance of enlivened matter that which gives us life and of which we are the result. It is the dark ground of being that is to be thought: 'the dark, inaccessible part of our personality'. They are the shadows that are still present as the anonymous background of this particular being that civilisation organised as the ego. It is the attempt to apprehend the original insertion of our individuality in the general phenomenon of life, the cultural non-being anterior to all culture, the being in the raw from where we derive and that thought, culture, and biology conceal. It is what exists within ourselves and terrifies us, because it is not death and the negation of life considered as the end of the days we still have left to go, but the actual subterraneous presence of the primeval nature that is pure obscurity present in being itself, at once living and mortal.

Let us signal first the place occupied by the id in the psychic apparatus:

> To the oldest of these psychical provinces or agencies we give the name of id. It contains everything that is inherited, that is present at birth, that is laid down in the constitution – above all, therefore, the instincts, which originate from the somatic organisation and which find a first psychical expression here [in the id] in forms unknown to us. (*An Outline of Psycho-Analysis*, SE 22: 145)

And in a note, Freud adds:

> This oldest portion of the psychical apparatus remains the most important throughout life; moreover, the investigations of psychoanalysis started with it. (*An Outline of Psycho-Analysis*, SE 22: 145 n. 2)

It is worth transcribing in its entirety the description with which thought attempts to gain access to the unthought, to that which does not think in us and only lives, so as to capture the effort to comprehend the meaning of the shadows that sustain us, the shadows that we are.

10 'Where It Was ...' (Where Was the Anonymous)

> You will not expect me to have much to tell you that is new about the id apart from its new name. It is the dark, inaccessible part of our personality; what little we know of it we have learnt from our study of the dream-work and of the construction of neurotic symptoms, and most of that is of a negative character and can be described only as a contrast to the ego. We approach the id with analogies: we call it a chaos, a cauldron full of seething excitations. We picture it as being open at its end to somatic influences, and as there taking up into itself instinctual needs which find their psychical expression in it, but we cannot say in what substratum. It is filled with energy reaching it from the instincts, but it has no organisation, produces no collective will, but only a striving to bring about the satisfaction of the instinctual needs subject to the observance of the pleasure principle. The logical laws of thought do not apply in the id, and this is true above all of the law of contradiction. Contrary impulses exist side by side, without cancelling each other out or diminishing each other:

at the most they may converge to form compromises under the dominating economic pressure towards the discharge of energy. There is nothing in the id that could be compared with negation; and we perceive with surprise an exception to the philosophical theorem that space and time are necessary forms of our mental acts. There is nothing in the id that corresponds to the idea of time; there is no recognition of the passage of time, and – a thing that is most remarkable and awaits consideration in philosophical thought – no alteration in its mental processes is produced by the passage of time. Wishful impulses which have never passed beyond the id, but impressions, too, which have been sunk into the id by repression, are virtually immortal; after the passage of decades they behave as though they had just occurred. They can only be recognised as belonging to the past, can only lose their importance and be deprived of their cathexis of energy, when they have been made conscious by the work of analysis, and it is on this that the therapeutic effect of analytic treatment rests to no small extent. (73–4)

Let us highlight: this non-ego is not a void, but a fullness. Seen from the ego, which prolongs the recognised official order, this plenitude is incomprehensible 'chaos': 'cauldron full of seething excitations'. But we are not indifferent or neutral in the description that we offer: this fullness, this negation of the ego on which our personality rests as on a volcano, stimulates us in a most lively manner. Stimulates whom? The ego, this same ego that I now am thinking. The id is only the psychic form by means of which the repressed thinks with the categories of the repressor that which the repressor rendered inferior, unrecognised, devalued, and disqualified, but which nonetheless 'burns'. We think of this diversity with the inadequate means we have at our disposal, because from this unity that names it the ego finds its 'psychical expression' therein: the seething impulses traverse the cultural zone that welcomes them, and they penetrate in it with the forms that were given to us in order to frame its stimuli and satisfy them in reality. The stimuli come from the 'instinctual needs': they call out with all their force to pass into reality. The id has no organisation for our eyes; we also do not understand how the prolongation works in the order of those satisfactions that the repressive reality tolerates. But it rises up from our flesh, which nonetheless, by the sheer fact of its existence, must somehow have order and structure. But these impulses cannot be realised, given that this boiling cauldron has no escape in and of itself, nor is it directly linked to the reality of the external world: the ego is its security valve. This is why those impulses that live in the id are life encapsulated: 'a small piece of living substance', Freud says. Since the id is the foundation where the cultural element finds its seat and personality is organised – the ego, let us recall the expression, is 'the cortical layer by which a small piece of living substance is surrounded' – it is anterior ('older') and denser than it. It is what exists before, and subsists after culture or civilisation brings it into existence in its own way: by way of repression. For this reason the norms of the pleasure principle already indicate the order of its organisation; they bring back a forgotten vital wisdom, forms of an anterior agreement now repeated in the weightless space of its being a small piece without a land but of which our culture does not necessarily keep any memory. There is a logic, that of pleasure, and this logic opposed to the cultural one is illogical for the ego. This is why in the id there is no validity to the 'logical laws' that govern us with the help of thinking, and least of all the 'law of contradiction'. We treat the id wanting to think of it with the same categories with which the early Lucien Lévy-Bruhl treated 'primitive' societies: as illogical. But if the id were *directly* related to the external world, if this life were not life encapsulated, locked in by the mediating layer of culture and the psychic apparatus, it would be regulated and articulated with some other reality, that of which the id in its structure brings us the recollection of a vital link that once was, but now no longer is. Because now what is there, its life, is only the life of shadows: it has no eyes and no proper touch open to the reality of the external world. It is some older life now retained, developed before but now compressed into the narrow passage through which, via the ego, it reaches a reality that it ignores. The logic of the id is a sensible logic, in which the associations and coalescences that are produced are the result of the carnal homogeneity that links them to one and the same body: all of them come together in the unity of life contained, just as they did earlier with culture. But since now they cannot prolong and order themselves for themselves, they are the fissures that encounter, in any way they can, some small crevice to escape – taking advantage of the equivocations that the order of the ego and repression impose on them. The repressed that returns and falls back in the id returns home like faceless children that nevertheless, in their representations, carry with them the tenuous presence of the light of the external world toward the interior of the shadows of life condemned to the infinitude of a repetition that is indistinguishable from death: they leave behind the verbal trail that will allow, from within the darkness, to distinguish the thread of light that opens an exit toward the forbidden external world. All the means are good to emerge, to rise up to reality: at last to give oneself a prolongation in the materiality of objects, impetuously opening oneself up to the external world.

What does all this mean, if not that the life of the id is confused with death itself for the ego? Its 'cauldron' is felt as the place of decomposition, dissolution, indiscriminate fusion, without control, hence threat of death and supreme disorder. Does not the life of the ego reside precisely in being an order, a regulated transition toward reality? In truth the id is not death: it is life, yes, but so 'mad', so unhinged, that it can lead to death. Because if death, insofar as we think of it, appears to us at the endpoint of life as the final disorganisation and the return to the inorganic, the id by contrast would appear to be this *actual* backdrop of death, which is no longer thought of as future, but as present in each of us as the contradictory and endearing foundation of what we are now. Whence the disjunction: either confront the risk of dissolution with which this dense and thick disorder threatens us, this foundation of life in the raw, actual and present, and open ourselves up to it, but then death is no longer thought of as future but felt as actual, coming from the flesh; or else postpone the dissolution toward the future, toward the 'true' death of the official ego, who in time counts and accomplishes its stages of birth, childhood, adolescence, adulthood, and only in the end death, the one that still gives us some time to breathe, which is the death that culture has delimited and marked off, but not the actual death, death so far away for me that I have to think of it in the temporal order as that future to which we are in truth condemned, but not for now. And so I put it off, separate myself from the id, which is anxiety of death in its actual presence – which is the risk of being in some other way – and the objective time introduces between the *now* that terrorises me and the *later* that consoles me a separation that is felt to be infinite and interminable. The time of the *thought* of death as belonging to the future, dislodging it from the life of the id, brings us to the feeling of infinitude, and thus takes advantage of the timelessness of the id in order to negate it. We do not realise that the postponement is based on the negation of the id, on the ground of its irreducible presence, but that is what we do. A death that is known is worth more than a terror still to know. We do not realise that in order to elude the id we nevertheless have to look for support in the feeling of its being 'pure' life, but abstracted as an eternity that nothing will disturb, now shorn of its 'seething sensations'. Life cooled off, the one that we have left as residue. We lean on a volcano that only in the final eruption will become visible: when it already will have devoured us and we are no longer. This final evidence is of no use: the instant of the collapse that borders on non-being, because it will be evidence produced while we are falling into the abyss, when there will be no more life to make use of. It is the feeling of life, of tepid and sensible life, which serves as the continuously repeated support, in the imaginary, for the idea of eternity – immobility – that the ego adds to it. What is tepid is the transition: it is the coldness of the limit that the ego imposes on the boiling sensations of the id. That is apparently the normal transition, but it does not escape the dilemma that the id poses for us. Either fusing with the id, residing in the id, making oneself into the welcoming eruption of what we negate but which already is there, overcoming the terror that more so than real death is difference felt as mortal. Or else confronting death as something external to oneself, but then detaining the id by detaining life, and making it present in the guise of the repetition of whatever is consolidated and ordered by the world of culture or civilisation, remaining in the resemblance of a common order. There is no other way out. Either joining the anonymity of the id, or else subjecting oneself to the anonymity of an ego that under the appearance of a name and a surname is an ego made according to the measure of the other: *appellation contrôlée*.

The whole 'understanding' of the id takes place, interestingly enough, from within the ego. Its rational judgment is already complicit with the super-ego that regulates it: it thinks against the background of the feeling of guilt. This is why what we *know* about the id, Freud tells us, has a 'negative character': that is its official representation, the 'common criminal' into which every guerrilla fighter becomes transformed. We do not have, in our culture, ways to give a positive name to the id, since its repressive existence always necessarily is supported by the negation of that which sustains it and gives it being. For ourselves the id is inaccessible; the most profound and proximate as the most remote: we are separated within ourselves from our own foundation. The cultural distance has, then, the appearance of a breach or rent when we think of it, and yet it lives thanks to its being articulated. Because to live the reality of the breach – like the mental patient – is not the same as to think of it with the help of concepts. And so the interior foreign domain is not a metaphor: we are our own colonisers, colonisers of our own virgin lands. 'We approach the id', Freud says, 'with analogies', taken from the external world: the image of the cauldron evokes the idea of the diabolical, of what is cooking, 'vital substance' in a state of boiling. The metaphor brings us a part of the truth, and a lot of repression of its meaning. It is not the devil cooking in the cauldron, but it is life producing life in the element of life. It is this life that cooks up life that we cannot tolerate: we cannot admit the organicity that produced the reality of the species and of everything that lives on this earth as being and still debating itself within us. It is the horror of being part of the substance of life still present in our cultural individuality. Civilisation has not dared to think in depth about this life's being, outside of the concepts of the biological 'science' that makes it alien and objective. Freud, by contrast, wants us to think of life at the level where it boils within us: how nature lives, feels, organises, burns, inside *oneself*. This is why the id is not the concept of 'nature' but its 'psychical representative': it is the attempt to think lived and felt nature as flesh, as foundation, and as sustenance of our own being that cannot be sublimated. This way of thinking the unthought does not mean therefore only the extension of a mere concept: it implies an eruption to overflow the limits that the life of culture and civilisation – the ego – introduced in ourselves in order to remove it as something strange and remote, all the while bringing it closer. It is not 'science' augmenting its rational concept alone, but it includes in rationality the daring attempt to look into the face of God, who previously made us blind, and who could not even be called by his name: this 'we give the name of id', says Freud. It is the inorganic already present in the midst of the organic, not outside of it: it is the prior organic element from which we proceed, which persists in us, and which the idealism of culture believed it had negated.

This way of filling with positivity that which only emerges with a negative character for the ego seems to be Freud's attempt: to look for the foundation from where civilisation found its organisation in us and which every human being who is born as a child necessarily goes back to cover up once more, in order to be. To let emerge the positivity of that which, precisely for being the presupposition of our existence, we may think of as 'negative', even inexistent, for such indeed is its persistence and reality: it persists, in spite of us, as the very foundation from which the very act of negation takes off. Hence when Freud is telling us that 'there is nothing in the id that could be compared with negation', in reality he is saying: it is, thus, pure positivity without repressive thinking, without culture, and without the categories of before and after, without succession. Indifferent to time, it only lives. But not without succession: it has no consciousness of its succeeding. *It succeeds* without lines of demarcation telling it what must happen and anticipating the development of 'something' that lies in the absolute density of its being as pure life process. It is, therefore, seen from the ego, eternity in the act: the finite rejoined with the infinite. This is why 'there is nothing in the id that corresponds to the *idea* of time', by which Freud means to tell us that it lies outside of time: it is time itself fused with the matter of its being as process. 'There is no *recognition* of the passage of time', which means, once again, that there is no course of time: it courses but without projecting, in the way the ego orders us to, the rationality of abstraction that sketches out the having-to-be of human phenomena without attending to the being that, for its part, is infinitely richer in the plenitude of the density that moves life, without forms to contain it: without repression.

> Space may be the projection of the extension of the psychical apparatus. No other derivation is probable. Instead of Kant's *a priori* determinants of our psychical apparatus. Psyche is extended; knows nothing about it. ('Findings, ideas, problems', SE 23: 299).

And when Freud tells us that 'wishful impulses which have been sunk into the id by repression, are virtually immortal; after the passage of decades they behave as though they had just occurred', he is telling us that their immortality is the 'virtual' immortality of life, which may not have been welcomed by the ego, which may not be totally developed, which may be repressed, but which all the same remains as the *foundation of being* because it is the condition of existence of the very thing that negates it. The immortality of brute 'nature' which lies like 'a kernel of lived matter' in the subject is beyond sublimation, even though the ego 'sublimates' it. And therein lies one of the substantial foundations of the Freudian dialectic: what civilisation represses is repressed *being* which returns to the substantiality of being in order to continue as retained, insofar as it is repressed, and maintained as the foundation that has not yet been elaborated but is always present. The id has, in its unawareness of time, more time than the ego: it can wait, because it lives the temporality of nature. The repressed of the id is the movement of return by means of which whatever of the id passed, or wanted to pass, into reality returns to the origin but with a cultural signification that determines and conforms it as 'negated'. But it does not stay alone: 'the repressed merges into the remainder of the id', it includes itself anew into the force of all of life and once again begins to cook in the cauldron until a new boiling point. But Freud does not say 'eternity': he says 'virtually immortal'. In other words, he says that the virtual immortality is what the cultural death of repression cannot annihilate: this is why negation is not foreclosure. It continues to love like life itself, returning to that which must be elaborated and which persists as foundation. This is the cauldron where the repressed once more boils up and unites itself with the substantiality of life that is part of it. Everything that is proper is once again assimilated and kept in its midst. Life says 'yes' to everything that it produces and which returns to it; it has no black and white children: they are all naturalised children, those whom civilisation negated. 'There is nothing in the id that could be compared with negation': this means, there is no thought dialectic, symbolic field, rational separation. There is still the dialectic in the fullness of the materiality of life itself, which nothing can disdain because it is a whole without fissures, without void, and without negation.

But this 'virtual' immortality has its history. It was reduced to nature by culture, dislodged from our own being as foreign: it was fused back into the interior inorganic, as if the negation that was imposed on it implied – this is the limit after all of the official 'intelligence services' – its destruction. 'Ideas cannot be killed', said someone who is dead already. But they can be refuted, they can be negated and disappear. The dialectic of being negates the false opposition: civilisation or barbarism. The id says, in its own way, 'barbarism', against a civilisation that keeps alive the ideas in order to kill the body. What cannot be killed is the life that persists as life, in spite of the ideas that negate it. Hence, the denied and repressed aspect of the idealist dialectic of the negation of the flesh does not disappear, it does not die: it returns to its foundation and remains, always tense, irreducible: 'virtually immortal'. *Virtually*: that is to say, until it comes back and emerges in reality. As long as it remains repressed this extension of life cannot disappear: it is part of the dialectic of the flesh and of being, because it is the substance of life. Dislodged by the idealist dialectic that thinks in terms of 'psychology', without the support of the materiality that organises it, the negated returns to be included and retained: it comes back to be in its own way. And stubbornly, as is only suited, it will attempt to emerge by all possible means. If it did not, life would not be life: my body would die without opening itself up to reality. 'Virtually immortal': 'after the passage of decades they behave as though they had just occurred': they belong to the time of individual life ('decades', not centuries) and exhaust it in their push to emerge: to put their life at stake in the time of their own personal existence. They were born as soon as the child gained access to its adult being, and they remain thus, as they are, in spite of the continuous negation and the continuous repression. Until when? Until knowledge and the new collective experience that is entailed by the real lifting of repression, hence a new cultural order, give them access at last to the reality of history in which they become integrated, starting from the individual body. 'They can only be recognised as belonging to the past', Freud continues to indicate so that we may understand. Which means: they come to be included as having been produced by time. But they are known only once they are 'deprived of their cathexis of energy', known belatedly, and badly: all the weight of the ego's reason fell on them. Thus the id becomes historicised in the ego: it recognises its past being from which it derives, its material historical determination, that which it put to the side, but when it was too late. There is a temporal distance between one and oneself, which is irreducible, unreachable forever: there is a *before* that will never appear as a *now*.

> Again and again I have had the impression that we have made too little theoretical use of this fact, established beyond any doubt, of the unalterability by time of the repressed. This seems to offer an approach to the most profound discoveries. Nor, unfortunately, have I myself made any progress here. (74)

This fact *established beyond any doubt*, that of *the inalterability by time of the repressed*, is fundamental in the dialectic of historical reality, in the unfolding of the truth of the human subject. *The repressed is maintained*, the repressed lives the life of shadows, but it *always* returns. That which repression suppresses survives in the foundation of the human being. Here we have a radical optimism, founded on a fact 'established beyond any doubt': that which struggles to integrate itself is indestructible for the repressor, unless it is life itself that is suppressed. And here there is no other possibility of conviction, no demagoguery, no will, no moral imperative, nor any human determination to be able to do this or that:

> The id of course knows no judgments of value: no good and evil, no morality. The economic or, if you prefer, the quantitative factor, which is intimately linked to the pleasure principle, dominates all its processes. Instinctual cathexes seeking discharge – that, in our view, is all there is in the id. It even seems that the energy of these instinctual impulses is in a state different from that in the other regions of the mind, far more mobile and capable of discharge; otherwise the displacements and condensations would not occur which are characteristic of the id and which so completely disregard the quality of what is cathected – what in the ego we should call an idea. We would give much to understand more about these things! (74–5)

Already we see: there is no human norm reached by civilisation that can, with its order and its legality, impede the emergence of the id. The id is beyond Good and Evil in search of another good and another evil, for any order that condemns it to persist without satisfaction cannot be good. The id does not let itself be seduced by civilisation or by the qualities that the latter has managed to produce. These qualities, the ones that appear as representations to the ego, that immobilise the id, are only the qualities and conscious representations of an order that denies it: the impulses of the id cannot be exchanged for words. It is energy that is not yet bounded to culture, and its mobility only has one polar north: to reach pleasure. Any reality that pushes it to the side cannot be accepted as real by the id, and cannot be continued. *The obstinacy of the flesh is, for our own good, the only certainty of a true logic: that of pleasure prolonged in the non-repressive reality.* The id knows nothing: it does not let itself be persuaded therefore by the principle of contradiction, which is the principle of dissociation. The contradictory terms that thought separates, opposes, and rigidifies, as if in these logical representations and in these qualities that it orders thought were the substantial reality of carnal life that organises itself – these terms in reality write on water: they are inscribed in the materiality of a process that they do not manage to encompass or understand, and it is the indestructible truth of the id that undoes all 'logic' that pretends to stop this truth. Except the logic that counts on *it*.

So much for the description Freud offers of the id. But he already had indicated: 'where it was ...'

11   '... I Shall Be' (the Anonymous That Civilisation Denominates)

Let us begin by seeing how the ego can be understood as coming from the id:

> We can best arrive at the characteristics of the actual ego, in so far as it can be distinguished from the id and from the super-ego, by examining its relation to the outermost superficial portion of the mental apparatus, which we describe as the system Pcpt.-Cs [perceptual-conscious]. This system is turned towards the external world, it is the medium for the perceptions arising thence, and during its functioning the phenomenon of consciousness arises in it. It is the sense-organ of the entire apparatus; moreover it is receptive not only to excitations from outside but also to those arising from the interior of the mind. (75)

The ego: 'sense-organ'. Organ, yes, but new: cultural. This corresponds to what Marx, referring to the new capacities that civilisation produces in the corporeality of a subject, called 'common organs' because of their form. Common, that is to say, collective; because of their form: that is to say, cultural. In the same way, what Freud must make us understand is how this new cultural sense organ is constituted from within the flesh. Let us recapitulate. The ego is a 'prolongation' of the id and the super-ego: paradoxically, a 'prolongation' of the conjunction of the external and the internal. It is 'the outermost superficial portion of the mental apparatus', which is to say: it is the surface of greatest contact with the inside and the outside. But this surface is turned towards the external world: it is the limit between the id and the world. If it is a limit, it is directed both towards the outside – seen from the mental apparatus – and towards the inside – seen from the external world and the super-ego. It is thanks to this limit situation that the ego can take itself as object and, therefore, necessarily, *as though it saw itself from the outside, since it is a limit that appears from its point of view, but as though it were outside of itself*. That is, outside the id. *During* this function, Freud says, consciousness is born. Consciousness is not a static field, given punctually all at once, but the temporal and historical act of a function that develops between the internal and the external: of the perceptual function which ends in consciousness and in motility, hence sensibly supported by the external as well as the internal world. Of interest here is the reflexive activity of the ego, which as limit in relation to the exterior world is defined by that which the external world inscribes in it as the reverse side of its very being as the id: its being for the others. Not without risk, it limits itself to the exterior: the limit is at the same time a contact, and the contact is at the same time a transformation. But this transformation is the determination of the limit which, coming with the impulses from the inside, encounters the external outside itself as a way of limiting, as containment: more so than limiting, the internal here is limited. One's own extended corporeality believes that it is precisely this limit since one is doing the limiting. But this being that limits is in reality delimited by the external pressure that marks the limits of the world in one's own body: only thus *is there* a one, coming from the mere *there is*. The limiting function of this sensorial ego is only the result of the delimiting pressure, felt in oneself as the limits of the proper, made up of the external world and its objects. Towards the outside, it is as though the internal were doing the perceiving; but when it is a question of perceiving the internal, which is as though it were oneself who perceived, in reality it is the form of the external which delimits in one the perception of the internal. How, otherwise, would we perceive our own internality, if it were not by the difference with the exterior, that is to say, from the meaning that from the outside limits the internal and makes it so that *there is* an internality for one?

> We need scarcely look for a justification of the view that the ego is that portion of the id which was modified by the proximity and influence of the external world, which is adapted for the reception of stimuli and as a protective shield against stimuli, comparable to the cortical layer by which a small piece of living substance is surrounded. (75)

But this being of the limit, which is the cortical layer, inscribes in it the form of the transition in both directions: from the internal towards the external, but also from the external towards the internal. The living substance palpitates inside, and only lives by being protected by the hardness – though ductile, mobile, and ubiquitous – of this differentiated shield.

> ... the surface turned towards the external world will from its very situation be differentiated and will serve as an organ for receiving stimuli. (*Beyond the Pleasure Principle*, SE 17: 26)

Its situation, that is, the *place* it occupies, creates the differentiation. The ego emerges as the place of a perspective. For this is how the ego shields the interior life.

> The relation to the external world has become the decisive factor for the ego; it has taken on the task of representing the external world to the id – fortunately for the id, which could not escape destruction if, in its blind efforts for the satisfaction of its instincts, it disregarded that supreme external power. (75)

The ego, which thus differentiates itself, is nonetheless an extension of the id: the id externalised, hardened, which confronts the reality of the external world and had to cover itself in order to last. But this limit-function of being a limit subsequently keeps it from discerning *of what it is the limit*: whether it is the limit of the exterior or of the interior. If it is the limit of the exterior world, then it must comply with the latter and strictly determine the internal. If, on the other hand, it is the limit of the internal impulses, of living substance, then it must confront the external and keep the latter from determining it as unable to pass over into reality. This is the ambiguity of the ego that thus constitutes itself: its being-limit, depending on the point of view, in the inside or on the outside. And yet, *the ego begins by being the limit of the internal; limit towards the outside*.

> In accomplishing this function, the ego must observe the external world, must lay down an accurate picture of it in the memory-traces of its perceptions, and by its exercise of the function of 'reality-testing' must put aside whatever in this picture of the external world is an addition derived from internal sources of excitation. (75)

This means that the ego is prone to confusion. The internal prolongs itself towards the external, and the limit being sought after becomes confused. What lends itself to this confusion? From the inside come the sensible significations, qualities, energies, impulses that seek to be discharged and satisfied: the boiling sensations. The internal speaks the language of the sensible. But from the outside, the qualities speak the language of representations. The external *represents*, the internal *senses*.

> The ego controls the approaches to motility under the id's orders; but between a need and an action it has interposed a postponement in the form of the activity of thought, during which it makes use of the mnemic residues of experience. (75–6)

Between the (internal) need and the act (relation with the external) there appears the postponement, the detention introduced by the mental elaboration: the translation, the adequate correspondence between the felt signification and the rational, ordered, delimited organisation of the civilisational world. In this way the proper internal to the ego gains access to being in the extent to which the exterior gives it a name. Thus, the transition from the internal to the external is the search for an accord, an encounter, a reconciliation: of how what exists in one system can inscribe itself into another. But, reciprocally, of how the cultural inscribes itself in the materiality of the biological.

But the id 'has to be ego': the emergence of the ego implies already the necessary determination of the id by its mediation. If the ego is the mediator between the internal and the external, we have seen that this mediation sketches out in the id the meaning that culture confers upon that which is boiling in it: it engraves as if negatively the possibility that civilisation, previously or simultaneously, engraved in the ego:

> In that way it has dethroned the pleasure principle which dominates the course of events in the id without any restriction and has replaced it by the reality principle, which promises more certainty and greater success. (76)

But this promise and this extortion, which the repressive reality presents, is something that only the ego could know and understand: the id *knows nothing, it only feels* pleasure and displeasure. The id irreparably continues to feel the margin of dissatisfaction that culture produces in it for reasons of what it represses. And what culture represses is determined by whatever it tolerates. The id will try to carve out a path, in the midst of this tolerance, by way of condensation and displacement: by the affective logic of the primary processes. This constant presence of that which seeks to rise up, in order for life to be possible, must necessarily find satisfaction in some way. The cauldron boils or explodes. Hence, even though civilisation is repression, it cannot for this reason avoid being at the same time and in some way – that is, in an ideological way – satisfaction. If there is a field for repression it is because first of all there is a field for satisfaction. And the repressive world of culture or civilisation uses the irrepressible satisfaction in order to repress. But the unconscious of the id insists: it seeps through the interstices in which the instincts that were prolonged into reality nonetheless move life forward, the miserable life of the tolerated in which our life is spent. In its own way: with the logic that allows for the repression or the infraction of mental illness. The insistence of the unconscious of the id and the apparent unreason that moves it, which is contradictory with the logic of the exterior cultural system, lends itself to this repression: it is illogical, it is unreasonable, it runs counter to the logical principles of Western reason. And in truth it has only those representations which, from within reality, are given to it in order to translate what is opposed to it. It must use the language of the enemy in order to transmit its own message. It is condemned to transmogrify itself in the form of the repressor in order to pass into reality. The instincts and *their vicissitudes*: the instincts 'sublimated', 'consumed', 'repressed'. So many forms to negate that which nonetheless tries to emerge via the path of that which already emerged, but now following the eruptive logic that is proper to it. Even so, we could say, this illogical logic of the unconscious of the id is the logic of the flesh and, as such, it cannot be destroyed, unless it is satisfied. Or unless it dies because it cannot find satisfaction. If the cultural logic and its links that facilitate the transition are denied to it, this logic incarnated in the sensibility of the affects then proceeds with representations that *do not start out* from the flesh, representations that only appear in the flesh, in the image, and in affective value. And this is how they appear: as well as they can, in neurosis or in madness. Or, if we want it to be me, but in another way, they will appear in the work of transforming culture, understood as contradictory system of production, where the impulses discovered in their collective force trace before the libido paths that confer on it another rationality and another satisfaction.

> But what distinguishes the ego from the id quite especially is a tendency to synthesis in its contents, to a combination and unification in its mental processes which are totally lacking in the id. When presently we come to deal with the instincts in mental life we shall, I hope, succeed in tracing this essential characteristic of the ego back to its source. It alone produces the high degree of organisation which the ego needs for its best achievements. The ego develops from perceiving the instincts to controlling them; but this last is only achieved by the [psychical] representative of the instinct being allotted its proper place in a considerable assemblage, by its being taken up into a coherent context. To adopt a popular mode of speaking, we might say that the ego stands for reason and good sense while the id stands for the untamed passions. (76)

How could the id have the capacity of the ego, if it is precisely impeded in the transition to reality? The order of the ego is one with the system of reality, and the synthesis that is proper to it does no more than reflect the order of the exterior system of production that determined it qua ego. The synthesis of consciousness excludes the proper and complete inclusion of the impulses of the id: they are illogical for the ego. But qua encapsulated instincts, living matter encrusted within the ego, they only have, literally, their 'blind' but 'untamed' passion. They are that which cannot be negated because they remain as life's foundation. In order for there to be synthesis there must be articulation, expansion, development, exchange, which is precisely what the id cannot do without negating the organicity without reason – without reason for consciousness – that is proper to it. Only the ego differentiating itself can do this: but this order of the ego does not appear all of a sudden. Only the unprecedented encounter of the id with the object of its satisfaction opens the place where the ego has to be. Thus, what later appears as order and reason of the ego comes from the most exterior but is lived as the most proper. Because it is the reflection of the order of the world, which nonetheless finds inside of itself, in the initial push of the id, the maternal form that regulates the flesh and organises it primarily as first object of its pleasure. But there not all the impulses had been developed yet; there was a 'hallucinated' coincidence between the object of the id and that of reality. The mother, as a resembling totality, coincides fully with the initial desire. The rational external synthesis, which is one that consciousness reaches only later, links up in the ego because it appears to the id as the prolongation of the sensible and sensed other, the first object now retained only in the ego, which offers itself anew as object for the id. But this beginning ego, which began by prolonging and projecting towards the external reality the form of its first object as the north pole of every quest and the nostalgia in every disappointment, finds support only in this impulse of the id that thus began by sucking, impetuously and unstoppably, the milk of alien life: but it was the mother who in the liquid warmth taken from her body extended herself towards the child. Thus, when the ego constitutes itself, it is the crossover between the internal and the external, the lake in whose surface all the subterraneous currencies flow together. This place for the interlacing of felt significations is already, without knowing it, the interlacing of reasons, of the flesh that orders itself in the form of the other that thus organises the place where the ego emerges and is born. The miracle that inaugurates the site from where something can say 'I' is that of the identification with what is similar: the place that another opened in one. It is from the sensible identity with the similar that later, in logic, the abstract 'identity of opposites' finds its prolongation. *Consciousness is always born in a second birth, which necessarily ignores the first one that truly gave it being.* Its being-conscious depends on one's being by the unity of the other who was inscribed in the id so that there might be an I. But this obligatory form – which already is order and 'reason', matrix of all future syntheses prolonging themselves into the world, origin of all difference and similitude – captures the instinctual element from which it arose with that form that cultural representation provided it with. And it is on this external path that from now on the 'vicissitudes' of the instincts will depend: whether or not they are recognised as capable of being prolonged in life, whether they are integrated or not into the unity of official consciousness, whether they prolong themselves as motility.

But this ordered, measured, and reflexive character of the ego, in which its positivity resides, quickly gives way to a negative function in which it finds support:

> So far we have allowed ourselves to be impressed by the merits and capabilities of the ego; it is now time to consider the other side as well. (76)

How does this other side appear? It is precisely the concept of limit and its ambiguity – not knowing whose limit it is, whether of the inside or the outside – which now leads Freud to consider the ego from the inside: limit of a flesh prolonged in reality, limit of the id.

> The ego is after all only a portion of the id, a portion that has been expediently modified by the proximity of the external world with its threat of danger. From a dynamic point of view it is weak, it has borrowed its energies from the id, and we are not entirely without insight into the methods – we might call them dodges – by which it extracts further amounts of energy from the id. One such method, for instance, is by identifying itself with actual or abandoned objects. The object-cathexes spring from the instinctual demands of the id. The ego has in the first instance to take note of them. But by identifying itself with the object it recommends itself to the id in place of the object and seeks to divert the id's libido on to itself. We have already seen that in the course of its life the ego takes into itself a large number of precipitates like this of former object-cathexes. The ego must on the whole carry out the id's intentions, it fulfils its task by finding out the circumstances in which those intentions can best be achieved. ... There is one portion of the id from which the ego has separated itself by resistances due to repression. But the repression is not carried over into the id: the repressed merges into the remainder of the id. (76–7)

We saw that the ego is a limit. As such, it senses the id, but it also feels the dangers of the exterior world. It is the only one that, precisely for being a limit, may sense both at the same time: the internal and the external. Since the ego is almost nothing, only a residual limit, its force comes to it from that which it contains in its expansion: from the id. But its force is its weakness in the face of the exterior world. If it folds and adapts itself to this force that is its own, it puts itself in danger, and the limit is surpassed: the destruction of the id with which reality would respond would mean its own destruction. It believes it is on the other side, but it senses this is not the case. Therefore, it must take charge of this force which *does not know* what it wants, but which it feels and seeks out, sure of its object, because originally the exterior object determined it as that oriented force in which its essence as pure impulse consists: impulse towards the object that gave it its form. But the ego qua limit is feeling which prolonged itself in representation and in reason: therein lies its superiority. It has recourse to a dodge: it simulates the accord that led to the previous satisfaction, the kept or abandoned objects that as residues constitute precisely the ego. This is the recourse; if it became ego it is because in the beginning it identified itself with the exterior objects of the world, it made itself one with the other within oneself so as to form the limit and recognise reality in what it turned into the reverse side of that side which was engraved forever in the flesh: because it circumvented the object and assimilated it. The ego thus contains 'precipitates' of old object-cathexes, from that period when the ego coincided point for point with them, because they coincided in the unity of a single flesh, and the id thus found its real satisfaction. This satisfaction, which is the basis of the synthesis that the exterior world engraved in the ego like the matrix of a distance that nothing will be able to close any longer, persists in it, and actualises it to trick the id: it offers itself as object, as if it were the 'first object' redivivus. It took its being-other seriously, that is, the extent to which its being was given to it by the form for which it substituted itself. Because it registered these forms, they remained written in blood in the ego: they did so as per the exact measure of the exterior reality. The ego thus awakens once again, in its hardened crust, that which condensed itself in order to give it its form. But this now returns so as to denote itself and distend itself until it opens up the slight texture that became compacted, which is enlivened and becomes aggrandised to the point of acquiring the phantasmatic form of that which previously was a real contact and now only an illusion: primary object, total object. This copy of the first object and this phantasmagoria that the ego enlivens in its limit-being are the precipitates of a bygone world, a world that therefore no longer exists, but which become animated and aggrandised when the world as it is now tolerates the satisfaction that the id demands. The ego, which opens up the objective temporal dimension, lacks a future for the id: it only knows the repetition of the past as actual in the present. It would be necessary to change the world! Between the force of the contradictory world, whose logic gave order to the ego who for this reason cannot think of it as different, on the one hand,

and, on the other, the chaos that surges forth in it as dislocation from within the impulses, for many there is no choice: it is necessary to dominate the id. The ego is the representative, qua limit, of the exterior world. The ego is repression. I am, for myself, the repressor.

But whom is the ego fooling with this trick? The ego is spiritualist: it does not believe in its own flesh that takes it so seriously. By repressing, the ego forgets; by forgetting, it suppresses; and by suppressing, it thinks that the fooled impulse disappeared. But the ego is fooling itself, not its carnal foundation, because while the ego represses, the repressed represses the id: the id, which is substantial life, welcomes it and fuses itself with the leftover of the id. It increases its own force and its power, which, as such, is 'virtually immortal'.

Thus the ego, qua limit, is both recto and verso, depending on how you look at it: limit of the id or of the exterior world and of the super-ego. A poor and always dependent thing, the ego.

> The poor ego has things even worse: it serves three severe masters and does what it can to bring their claims and demands into harmony with one another. ... Its three tyrannical masters are the external world, the super-ego and the id. When we follow the ego's efforts to satisfy them simultaneously – or rather, to obey them simultaneously – we cannot feel any regret at having personified this ego and having set it up as a separate organism.

Let us dwell for a moment on the notion of 'having personified this ego ... as a separate organism': the ego lives in the appearance of being 'somebody'. This is the lived experience of personification with which each one assumes the splitting that takes place within oneself: the power of taking oneself as object. This capacity, which ignores its own power, which is alien power, opens in oneself the fissure between part and whole within one and the same. Here is a part, and the most servile part to boot, which presents itself *as if it were the whole person*. Thus the most proper in the midst of the subject that Freud is in the process of showing to us, is the most alien for the ego. This relation with the most proximate and the most faraway, as if it were hell itself, is only such for the ego: it complicates its life to be a body, to be one. How does the ego manage to appear as that which in reality it is not? Let us read about its behaviour:

> With the id: loyal servant, it remains in harmony with it, recommends itself to it as an object and attracts the libido to itself.
> With reality: it cloaks the unconscious commands of the id with its preconscious rationalisations, conceals the id's conflicts with reality; it

professes with diplomatic disingenuousness to be taking notice of reality, even when the id remained rigid and unyielding.

With the super-ego: observed at every step, the latter lays down definite standards for its conduct, without taking account of its difficulties from the direction of the id and the external world, and, if those standards are not obeyed, punishes it with tense feelings of inferiority and of guilt. (77–8)

And when 'it is hard pressed, it reacts by generating anxiety', anxiety of consciousness and neurotic anxiety.

Thus, this personification is what I am. I, who take myself to be a person, a human being coherent with bourgeois and even revolutionary humanism, I am nothing more than this poor thing that presents itself as dignified and with pretensions of being different, 'period'. But already the ancients knew this: persona is mask. Or, as in French, *personne* can be, indifferently, a fullness and a void: something and nobody.

Freud, in disentangling the false and unstable equilibrium with which we edify ourselves, is not talking here only of the mental patient: he is talking of us. Let us recall: he spoke of 'our very own ego'. He speaks of our appearance that presents itself as full, that breaks and conceals the dialectic that gave origin to it and which, in order to be recognised as 'person', remains halted. Concealing the commitment that mobilises us: servile, rationalising, dishonest, rigid and inflexible, observed, punished, submissive lawbreaker, rendered inferior and guilty. Who can say anything more about themselves when they describe not only one of their own acts but the very essence, the foundation, and the structure of their own personality? Who, beyond certain modes of conduct that stand outside the norm, can affirm about themselves that this is not what they are in the very foundation of their personality? Who can negate the trap that we are as we live and that, nevertheless, in reading this, we put at a distance – again the scientific gaze, the level of the concept without a subject – as if it were only an object that we observe in the manner of having but not in terms of being?

Hence the only problem for a theory of agency: how to act in truth?

For Freud it was a matter of the task that defines the general aim of any individual cure:

– strengthen the ego
– make it independent of the super-ego
– widen its field of perception
– develop its organisation so as to allow it to appropriate new aspects of the id.

In other words, the ego must cease being only a hardened crust: it must recuperate its origin, penetrate in the id, let oneself be inundated by it, facilitate more impulses so that they may pass into reality, and thus broaden reality, its perception and its organisation. In this way the organisation of the ego is not a problem that is only individual: it corresponds to the organisation of the world to 'widen its field of perception', discern and see that which habitually remains clouded and invisible. The true sight and thought are at the service of the id.

But is this possible in the conduct that is merely individual? If it is a matter of transforming an interior distance into an exterior distance and opening up the historical power to discern the real, this task by definition cannot be an individual task but must be collective, historical. Let us put to the test this interrogation in the analyses in which Freud himself confronts the broadest structure that determines the individual conduct: civilisation and the masses.

PART 2

The External Distance

∴

The tradition *of all dead generations weighs like a nightmare on the brains of the living.*
      MARX

CHAPTER 2

Civilisation and Its Discontents

1 The Historical Categories, Foundation of the Psychic Apparatus[1]

1 *Affective Consolation and Discernment*

The political revolution, like the scientific one, implies discernment. This is why the task was always, like now, to increase the human subject's capacity for discerning the rationality of the world that needs to be modified and include this discernment in the perception. To discern the structure that organises the real in order to be able to comprehend the path that leads to true and effective action; this unwavering objective is also the aim of Freudian psychoanalysis. But since obtaining a new objective always implies confronting an old obstacle, its discovery is for this reason at the same time a combat. This is why, as opposed to the psychoanalysts who manage an aseptic theoretical field that is alien both to history and to politics, Freud always starts from a theoretical field that encounters its application in historical practice, and not only in the consulting room.

Hence Freud's tenacious effort to make comprehensible, within the subject, the rationality sedimented in an affectivity that is already an unconscious order, which for this reason cannot be apprehended with the rational categories that the historical system, which in this way makes itself felt, provides him with. In the beginning of *Civilisation and Its Discontents* the problem is posed all of sudden in terms of a radical confrontation: between the demand for the affective consolation of a lack of discernment, whose basic model, but not the only one, is religion, or else the discernment that prolongs itself in the real, confronts anxiety, and combines the truth of reason with the felt truth of the flesh.

What would be, under the pretext of widening the domain of reality, the most emphatic affirmation that would precisely impede its discernment? How can we conceive of the most profound remoteness of reality in the very act of affirming its maximum proximity?

For Freud, the most emphatic demand for the non-discernment of reality is the one that Romain Rolland proposes: to give human beings the pretence of

---

[1] All references and page numbers in this chapter, unless otherwise indicated, are from Sigmund Freud, *Civilisation and its Discontents* [1930], in *The Standard Edition of the Complete Psychological Works of Sigmund Freud*, Volume XXI (1927–1931): *The Future of an Illusion, Civilisation and its Discontents, and Other Works*, pp. 57–146.

reaching a relation to the world that is only felt, as if it were already contained in them and, therefore, resolved at once. Where the relation with the totality would not be something to be conquered but something already given. The 'oceanic feeling' that Rolland proposes appears as a 'transcendental feeling':

> One of these exceptional few calls himself my friend in his letters to me. I had sent him my small book that treats religion as an illusion, and he answered that he entirely agreed with my judgment upon religion, but that he was sorry I had not properly appreciated the true source of religious sentiments. This, he says, consists in a peculiar feeling, which he himself is never without, which he finds confirmed by many others, and which he may suppose is present in millions of people. It is a feeling which he would like to call a sensation of 'eternity', a feeling as of something limitless, unbounded – as it were, 'oceanic'. This feeling, he adds, is a purely subjective fact, not an article of faith ... That is to say, it is a feeling of an indissoluble bond, of being one with the external world as a whole. (64–5)

In this way the meaning of the external world would be present, by way of feeling, in the subject. The elaboration of this extension towards the totality, the task of discerning the meaning of the world, would disappear: the external would be revealed in the internal. But this solution, which Rolland takes for granted, is precisely that which the discriminating activity of science, in its struggle against ideology, tries to develop. For this was precisely the basic criticism of psychoanalysis in its opposition to bourgeois psychology: the solidification of the subject and of its contents implies, on the other end, the solidification of the corresponding world. Or, to put it differently: to suppose that immanence to the whole in each and every human being means to conceal the process by which civilisation internalised in the human being this presumed affective capacity to apprehend the totality.

> The idea of men's receiving an intimation of their connection with the world around them through an immediate feeling which is from the outset directed to that purpose sounds so strange and fits in so badly with the fabric of our psychology ... (65)

Indeed, psychoanalysis brought out the cultural constitution of the subject and its most intimate contents as the results of a laborious process, not exempt from vicissitudes, of gradual extension toward the exterior world. This is precisely its conquest: there is no aspect of the subjective realm that has not been determined by the external world, whether past or present. The taste for spiritualist intimacy thus lost one of the deepest seats of its power: the one that asserted itself in the subjugated individuals themselves. Psychoanalysis thus came to discover the external source of the latter's presumed subjective and innermost essence: the determination of its self-sameness originated by the system of production.

How can we then give up this discernment, so arduously obtained in scientific thought? Romain Rolland, with his affirmation, continued within the ideology of the system: by taking for granted a subjective knowledge of the totality, present in the intimacy of the subject, he affirmed implicitly the immobility of the exterior world, whose rationality and determination ended up being camouflaged. The absolute affirmation of the exterior world was a subjective, ahistorical function, which did not go through the work of constituting it in common. Thus the immobility of the external world, in its unquestioned order, relies on the immobility of the subject. The order of the world finds its affirmation in the subjective order. Indeed, in the act of returning to itself in search of what is most proper and indubitable about it, the subject turns into the confirmation of the world that produced it in the mode of submission, dependency, and concealment. This is the basic trap of the affective and intimate intuition: by rigorously defining the omnipotence of one's own powers and constituting them as capable of giving itself a priori the feeling of the totality, it defines at the same time the impotence and limitations imposed by the system in the face of an exalted power so as to impede the recognition of the limits, of the effort, and the work of extending them painstakingly in reality. Hence, parallel to the pretence of absoluteness of the omnipotent subject, there corresponds the pretence of the absolute and immobile nature of the system of production that subjugated the subject. Let us distrust the feeling of our self-sameness: it is an ideological determination.

> Normally, there is nothing of which we are more certain than the feeling of our self, of our own ego. This ego appears to us as something autonomous and unitary, marked off distinctly from everything else. That such an appearance is deceptive, and that on the contrary the ego is continued inwards, without any sharp delimitation, into an unconscious mental entity which we designate as the id and for which it serves as a kind of façade – this was a discovery first made by psycho-analytic research ... (65–6)

Normally, Freud says. Let us understand: in the conditions of our historically defined system of production. Marx already had made this clear:

> Only in the eighteenth century, in 'civil society', do the various forms of social connectedness confront the individual as a mere means towards his private purposes, as external necessity. But the epoch which produces this standpoint, that of the isolated individual, is also precisely that of the hitherto most developed social (from this standpoint, general) relations. The human being is in the most literal sense a *zoon politikon*, not merely a gregarious animal, but an animal which can individuate itself only in the midst of society.[2]

Marx tells us: the social relations determine the strictly personal subjectivity. But he adds: in bourgeois society, the more these social relations develop and objectify themselves, the more they become concealed and disappear from consciousness, which nonetheless came to be individual consciousness only by having internalised those relations into what is most proper. In the same way Freud tells us, coming from the isolated subject: 'such an appearance', that of the separated ego, 'is deceptive'. The limits of the ego are not immutable. To break the limits of the ego meant to explode the narcissistic delimitation with which bourgeois civilisation besieged every human being and to show that in its two extremes there is a world that prolongs itself from which it had been separated. Inwards and outwards: the walls surrounding the ego gave in and laid bare the weakness of its foundations:

> Inwards:
> The ego is continued inwards, without any sharp delimitation, into an unconscious mental entity which we designate as the id and for which it serves as a kind of façade. (66)

> Outwards:
> The boundary lines between the ego and the external world become uncertain or in which they are actually drawn incorrectly. (66)

But this prolongation of the apparent ego, who loses its façade, is not a new delimitation discovered as purely rational. It is the limits of the corporeality of the subject itself, which links up with the materiality of the external world, that break apart and reveal themselves as reciprocally confused:

> The boundary lines between the ego and the external world become uncertain: There are cases in which parts of a person's own body, even

---

2 Marx 1973, p. 84.

portions of his own mental life – his perceptions, thoughts and feelings – appear alien to him and as not belonging to his ego; there are other cases in which he ascribes to the external world things that clearly originate in his own ego and that ought to be acknowledged by it. (66)

Thus the human being is the place of an active exchange with the external world and with other human beings, an exchange that constitutes the foundation of their ego. Not only in the sexual relationship does one body penetrate another body overflowing the limits of its skin. Also perceptions, thoughts, and feelings lose the strict property that defined them and nobody knows *whose perceptions, thoughts, and feelings they are, to whom they belong*: I and the other are confused in these limits, breaking with the sharp division of being and having. Whence the conclusion on the basis of which Freud will take on his analysis:

the boundaries of the ego are not constant. (66)

We see, then, the difference that separates Freud from Romain Rolland: to give oneself, as the latter pretended, a felt totality of the world as essential complement of the ego, the 'oceanic feeling' that already is present in the subject as the *Whole-in-one*, implies to affirm as its foundation the independence and unity of the ego 'clearly demarcated from all the rest'. The appearance of a felt exterior totality thus eludes, and considers solved, the conquest of the external world in which the ego should prolong itself without limitation. To the impossibility of opening up qua object the field of the qualitative human world in which the material ego effectively prolongs itself, which impossibility defines the specificity of bourgeois repression, the felt totality of the world comes to add its subjective consolation, with its illusion of not needing any of it: *of already having reached it, and without going out of oneself*. But at the same time it means to install oneself in the dualism of feeling and reason as incompatible and contradictory with one another.

Scientific thought, which is not content with illusions, must pierce this appearance so as to reach the foundation, but it must also explain *the necessity of this appearance* in the individuality that the capitalist system produces, since it is complementary to a contradictory human system. But for this it must discern and make us understand how a subject emerges who makes the absence of discernment into its solution when faced with the contradictory reality that produced it as incapable of confronting this reality. And Freud will do so by trying to understand the genesis of this illusion.

2   *Subjective Genesis of the Apparent Unity of the Ego*

The problem: how is the separation and difference constituted between the internal and the external, which makes possible this congealment of the ego through a false differentiation? Freud here goes back to the development of his paper on 'Negation', which briefly summarises the transition from the primary to the secondary process, the appearance of a rational and subjective field in the midst of a corporeality that emerges as being solely sensible. It is a question, then, of 'reconstructing' the appearance of a symbolic field within the body. The material place from where someone will be able to *say*: I.

First moment of the ego: the primitive pleasure ego. The ego, Freud says, undergoes a 'disengagement from the general mass of sensations' (67). The point of departure is the primary indiscriminateness between the internal and the external: 'An infant at the breast does not as yet distinguish his ego from the external world' (66–7). But, regulating itself according to the logical-biological principle of pleasure-displeasure, the result of this initial discrimination consists in expelling from itself everything that would be contrary to it and retaining only that which pleases it. The mechanism is simple enough:

> A tendency arises to separate from the ego everything that can become a source of such unpleasure, to throw it outside and to create a pure pleasure-ego which is confronted by a strange and threatening 'outside'. (67)

This compact ego, pure affectivity without reason, which found support in pleasure in order to begin the act of discerning, culminates in a contradiction: the indices to which it has recourse – the affective discernment – do not correspond to its effective relations to the exterior reality:

> Some of the things that one is unwilling to give up, because they give pleasure, are nevertheless not ego but object; and some sufferings that one seeks to expel turn out to be inseparable from the ego in virtue of their internal origin. (67)

The affective discernment of pleasure-displeasure was therefore complementary to the affirmation of a hallucinatory field in which the external pleasure object was part of the ego itself. I held inside all that is good; and I expelled, as not-I, all the bad: everything was, as source of pleasure, in oneself. But via this path one does not reach reality.

Second moment of the ego: definitive realist ego. The process of rendering oneself adequate to reality thus implies a transformation: 'The boundaries of this primitive pleasure-ego cannot escape rectification through experience' (67). The procedure for learning is the following:

> ... through a deliberate direction of one's sensory activities and through suitable muscular action, one can differentiate between what is internal – what belongs to the ego – and what is external – what emanates from the outer world. In this way one makes the first step towards the introduction of the reality principle which is to dominate future development. (67)

What is fundamental here? The fact that the field of fantasy becomes verified, via muscular action, on the basis of our corporeality apprehended as linked to the materiality of the external world:

> ... some sources of excitation, which he will later recognize as his own bodily organs. (67)

It is precisely this 'later' moment of recognition and discernment that permits the apparition of the reality principle.

But this muscular action, deliberately directed, is nothing but that which later prolongs itself as thought. Rationality and the order of the exterior system to which the ego seeks to make itself adequate, is nothing more than the prolongation of this *practical* end through which the primitive pleasure-ego develops itself without transition. This internalised practice is the order of the external world delimited in one's own flesh, it is theory that does not know itself, symbolic field that appears as if it were the prolongation of one's own body. This is why its finality, even when it is a form of thought, is not the truth but accommodation:

> This differentiation, of course, serves the practical purpose of enabling one to defend oneself against sensations of unpleasure which one actually feels or with which one is threatened. (68)

It is here that there appears, inverted beyond repair, this equivocal genesis of the cultural as if it were biological: the capacity for discernment relies on the non-discernment of the process on which it is based. It does not distinguish the fact that the nucleus of indistinctness from which one starts as if it were the most proper already contains the form that the external world decanted in oneself. It does not realise that its thinking is neither ideal nor true, but practical: it ignores the lived presuppositions on which it depends. It does not understand that in the external world that the ego now confronts it only encounters as adequate to itself that which the form of the other imprinted in us as compatible. This leads to the treatment of what is most proper to oneself as if it were something alien and for that reason external to the ego, though of a type of exteriority that is different from that of the exterior world:

> In order to fend off certain unpleasurable excitations arising from within, the ego can use no other methods than those which it uses against unpleasure coming from without, and this is the starting-point of important pathological disturbances. (68)

What to do with that which emerges in one as need for satisfaction but which in the face of repression and the cultural order implies a danger? Treat it, with biological logic, as though it were external. The result is that, taking as the only reality the one we *practically* learned to know, we internalize at the same time a repressive order of the world whose historical genesis we do not understand, and in whose ignorance civilisation keeps us.

Thus, the struggle against the internal element, which is treated as if it were alien, results from the first indifferentiation and indiscrimination, which goes on to become the form of confronting any difference proper to oneself that civilisation does not tolerate: to struggle against oneself, as if the most proper of our own impulses were the most foreign, without realising that the real combat would have to take place against the repressive outside.

We are in a situation of not knowing what the flesh concealed because it does not know but only feels, namely, that the order within oneself first existed outside of oneself, that it comes from there and must be elucidated there. That between the biological logic of the body and the cultural logic of the system of production in which we prolong ourselves as if there were a continuum, there is in reality a leap, a breach, which subjectively ended up being sutured in the case of the so-called normal human being. And that this appearance of one's original emergence as adequate to civilisation and congruent with it hides a transition that the normal person ignores, the neurotic defuses, the mad person lives like an unbridgeable abyss, and Freud reveals in its truth. But to bring this out means to disentangle the true rationality of history that makes us its subjects: to decentre subjectivity in our greatest depth and from within the infantile feeling of being absolute in order to confront our existence as relative to the social system that produced us.

This decentring, and its illusion, is clearly demonstrated in a sentence in which Freud shows the difference between these two forms of conceiving of the point of access to reality from within the ego:

> In this way, then, the ego detaches itself from the external world. Or, to put it more correctly, originally the ego includes everything, later it separates off an external world from itself. (68)

1st form. Seen from the point of view of the scientist's decentred gaze: 'the ego detaches itself from the external world', the cultural world that produced it in a portion of animated matter qua individual. 'It disengages itself from the mass of sensations' (67).

2d form. Seen from the point of view of 'normal' subjectivity: 'originally the ego includes everything, later it separates off an external world from itself'. Here the process becomes inverted and the external world appears as an extension of the subject itself, a renewed encounter with the internal *too* in the external element.

Whence the fundamental conclusion at which Freud finally arrives:

> Our present ego-feeling is, therefore, only a shrunken residue of a much more inclusive – indeed, an all-embracing – feeling which corresponded to a more intimate bond between the ego and the world about it. If we may assume that there are many people in whose mental life this primary ego-feeling has persisted to a greater or less degree, it would exist in them side by side with the narrower and more sharply demarcated ego-feeling of maturity, like a kind of counterpart to it. (68)

In this way the 'normal' ego, which is the product of a civilisation that does not provide it with the knowledge of a contradictory system, would only have two types of totality in which to situate itself:

First, the *felt totality* of universal scope, which, as Freud explains to us, results from an intimate, purely sensible communion with the surrounding world. But this quasi-biological feeling does not correspond to the reality of an organised social system, but rather to an infantile illusion. *It is therefore an inadequate feeling.*

Second, the *known totality*. The structure of the repressive system determined the limits of the adult ego, 'shrunken residue', hardened, with 'narrower and more sharply demarcated' limits. Civilisation's repressive rationality forms a system here with the mental categories by means of which our own ego thinks both itself and reality: we are in the sphere of ideology. The true structure of the system of production, the broadest sphere to which the ego is linked, remains unknown. *This is therefore an inadequate rationality.*

Conclusion: both the *feeling of the whole* and the *knowledge of the whole*, which coexist side by side, are inadequate for a true comprehension of reality. But it is between these two rationalities that the 'normal' ego is debating: there exists no third possibility for it. The impossibilities and the failures, which result from this type of restricted individuality, do not find an opening in a reality known in its truth and felt in its affective prolongation towards other subjected beings. Bourgeois individualism, which opens onto a past affective certitude, or a present rational appearance, makes it impossible to find within this actual totality, in which the 'normal' person ends up, the integrating prolongation of that other, infantile totality – of communion with the surrounding world – which was present at the origin. Both totalities appear as opposed to one another. And since there is no other real totality possible in which this infantile feeling might continue and find fulfillment, because the actual order of dissociation of the individual is radically incongruent with that feeling, what consolation is there left? Only to oppose the present indiscriminate totality, in which we dissolve ourselves, with the return to the warmth of the first affective indiscrimination. To abolish the order of adult reason so as to return to the consolation that was preserved, as an unfulfilled yearning, in the body.

> In that case, the ideational contents appropriate to it would be precisely those of limitlessness and of a bond with the universe – the same ideas with which my friend elucidated the 'oceanic' feeling. (68)

The felt totality, the 'oceanic feeling', appears as the subjective, imaginary refuge in the face of the historical impossibility of thinking and constructing another field of totality. But this impossibility, which is the impossibility of the repressive system, is based on the restricted limits of the ego which, terrified by what historically lies on the other side, prefers the infantile refuge of the infinity that lies on this side.

3   *The Subjective Dialectic: The Psychic as Nucleus of Historical Truth*

Freud must therefore explain the existence of these two fields of the totality in the subject as the result of not being able to confront, in the extension of adult life, the contradictions of the present system. With this he inaugurates a conception of the psychical realm as a subjective field in which the dialectic of culture and civilisation becomes internalised and worked out. Freud will discover the specificity of the psychic like Marx discovered the specificity of the historical.

To say that the felt totality, the oceanic feeling, corresponds to a real totality and can be included in the actuality of historical reason, such would be Romain Rolland's confusion: to seal the subjective past in the subject as if it were effectively present. In other words: to hide the interior distance, the history of its own psychic life, of its own individual access to civilisation, and not to introduce the historical temporality in the genesis of its own contents.

> But have we a right to assume the survival of something that was originally there, alongside of what was later derived from it? (68)

If we accept the persistence of the primitive *together with* the actual, then there exists a temporal distance within subjectivity. Which, if admitted, would amount to saying: *the field of the psychic is historical*. But also that *the comprehension of this distance must be included in the subject as a condition of its thinking the truth*. Here we have a material historicity, which preserves in the unity of the subject the memory of the forms through which it gained access to the life of civilisation. In the psychic element there remains carved the path that the body traversed in its gradual access to the final and adult form of the subject. These forms, in which the moments of access to civilisation were encapsulated, were experiences of conquest of a growing organisation, moments of transitory equilibrium, which *sometimes* were integrated later on. And these are the forms of equilibrium that signal the internalised dialectic, incorporated into the flesh. The transformation of the subject is correlated with the constitution of the reality to which it gains access. And this path remains engraved in the subject:

> In the realm of the mind, on the other hand, what is primitive is so commonly preserved alongside of the transformed version which has arisen from it that it is unnecessary to give instances as evidence. ... Since we overcame the error of supposing that the forgetting we are familiar with signified a destruction of the memory-trace – that is, its annihilation – we have been inclined to take the opposite view, that in mental life nothing which has once been formed can perish – that everything is somehow preserved and that in suitable circumstances (when, for instance, regression goes back far enough) it can once more be brought to light. (68–9)

This way of highlighting the specificity of the psychic phenomenon, which does not appear in any other level of material organisation, opens the field for the development of the rationality of the world in the midst of the subject and, therefore, the possibility of discovering how the historical dialectic is internalised in the human being. The regressive actualisation of the past in the present is the index of the unintegrated remnant, the evident symptom of a false terminal integration. This conservation, which is the foundation for the comprehension of the psychic phenomenon in psychoanalysis, shows us the work of civilisation in the element of life, the foundation of what must be integrated in order for it to be able to appear as true civilisation. And, at the same time, it shows us the level of corporeal materiality that cannot be sublimated, and whose biological truth must necessarily develop itself, without interruption, into the truth of history. The putting to the test of civilisation becomes evident in this transition in which the negated element remains, insistent and persistent, in its delayed existence, as the meaning that is always present and that nothing can erase because it affirms itself in the materiality of a body. The cultural forms are synthesised in the body, following the path of biological maturation, but the body can become disintegrated into those forms as well. This is what Freud signals, 'the preservation of the primitive alongside of the transformed version which has arisen from it', and in this 'alongside', he shows us the juxtaposition, but not the integration. Whence the persistence:

> When this happens it is usually in consequence of a divergence in development: one portion (in the quantitative sense) of an attitude or instinctual impulse has remained unaltered, while another portion has undergone further development. (68–9)

In the psychic element considered as disembodied spirit, negation meant foreclosure and annihilation: like the object that children lose, it disappears from the world. Thus the negated or forgotten in the psychic realm would disappear forever. But in the psychic life in which the civilisational meanings and functions are generated in the process of corporeal maturation, each negation signals a rupture in development, but also its preservation. Whence the novelty of Freud's explanation: to recognise this bifurcation that repression imposes in the course of development means to accept the persistence in the subject of diversely organised fields. From the point of view of the genetic process two successive and distanced organisations, which correspond to contradictory links and solutions, can become actualised in the subject as though they already had simultaneous validity. The succession that produced them is not included in their lived meaning, nor is their adequacy or inadequacy in the present.

This is why both appear *alongside* one another, even though they are different: the past *alongside* the present, without discovering the separation that really constitutes them. But if they can remain near one another it is because from the form of actual reality in which both coexist without difficulty, the successive coherence of historical time was stripped away and the contradiction disappears together with the necessity to integrate into the present that which from times immemorial clamours for its inclusion without ever reaching it. In this way, not only the primitive is preserved *alongside* what has evolved from it; in the discontinuity what has evolved also shows its partial and fragmented character. But at the same time it reveals the ignorance and the concealment of this fragmentation that constitutes it.

There where the 'normal' person lives the *simultaneity* of two forms that do not become integrated – on the one hand, the individual dissolution at the level of the social relation; on the other, the regressive consolation, the fusion with the whole in the oceanic feeling – the dialectic, which is *succession* present as process, appears denied. For the integrative succession implies a final form in which both successive moments are included in a new guise. And it is the impossibility of this new form that determines the simultaneity of the disintegrated elements, the return of the primitive *alongside* the evolved. What happens is that instead of apprehending these forms as temporal succession, as contradictory and unintegrated, they are lived in simultaneity as if both of them could be affirmed as true: this is religion, which promises the spiritual community, side by side with a social system in which the effective integration of human beings is impossible. Succession, which is dialectical, introduces the temporal meaning of the development of world history in the development of one's own subjectivity. Simultaneity, which affirms both conjointly – being as they are contradictory – introduces instead the timeless absolutisation of solidified forms, without origin in reality: forms whose genesis is ignored and which for this reason become validated in the imagination. From this perspective, the 'oceanic feeling' becomes clearer:

> Thus we are perfectly willing to acknowledge that the 'oceanic' feeling exists in many people, and we are inclined to trace it back to an early phase of ego-feeling. (72)

If we go back to situate this feeling in the course of the adult's psychic development, which would correspond to a need for paternal protection in the child that no subsequent social reality can satisfy, the oceanic feeling appears as a regression in the face of a frustration: before the impotence of satisfying our deepest desires in reality, repressed by the system of production. And instead of breaking with this cultural narcissism to which bourgeois individualism condemns us, that is, the individualism of this well-rounded and restricted ego satisfied in its separation, we only dare to return to an illusion: to 'the restoration of limitless narcissism' (72). That is to say, the illusion of a primitive pleasure-ego that gave itself the illusion that it 'separates off an external world from itself' (67).

> I can imagine that the oceanic feeling became connected with religion later on. The 'oneness with the universe' which constitutes its ideational content sounds like a first attempt at a religious consolation, as though it were another way of disclaiming the danger which the ego recognises as threatening it from the external world. (72)

Outwards to discern the meaning of the reality of the external world thus necessarily implies inwards to discern the process that was incorporated into the ego as access to the world of civilisation. It means therefore to recuperate in this interior distance, materialised in one's own body, the successive dialectic of the disintegrating integration that led us to the appearance of an absolute ego. Faced with the flatness of the psychic realm envisioned as simultaneous, with the ideational contents and concepts as mere thought-relations that are not based on anything, it is necessary to rediscover and vindicate the density of successive forms of feeling and thinking that the flesh, in its progressive maturation, organised as moments of a development that is at the same time sensible and meaningful. And to understand that it is the history of the system of production which introduces itself, as a determination that comes from the universal, in the nascent history of a body that comes to life qua ego.

11   Techniques to Elude the Reality of the External World

Among the techniques to elude the reality of the world, religion provides the 'common man' with the most complete solution: acceptance of his painful finitude, to which he accommodates himself, in order to yearn for salvation in the fond infinity that is hoped for. The moral lesson is easily understandable: let us accept the limits of reality, since we will be saved in the beyond.

> ... the system of doctrines and promises which on the one hand explains to him the riddles of this world with enviable completeness, and, on the other, assures him that a careful Providence will watch over his life and will compensate him in a future existence for any frustrations he suffers here. (74)

But there where religion is not enough, for the people who are not common, there exist other 'techniques' that allow us to elude the suffering that reality has in store for us. But these 'techniques' will have to possess an efficacy similar to religion, since their aim is the same for all: the quest for happiness without pain.

Life, as we find it, is too hard for us; it brings us too many pains, disappointments and impossible tasks. In order to bear it we cannot dispense with palliative measures. (75)

Freud mentions three kinds:
1. Powerful distractions, whose model is scientific activity.
2. Substitutive satisfactions, illusory or imaginary, whose model is art.
3. Intoxicating substances, which make us insensitive to misery, since they modify the sensibility of our organs and make us feel pleasure only from internal stimuli, independently from external ones.

In order to confront the problem of the relation to reality, Freud begins by rejecting the question about 'the purpose of human life' (75). There never was and perhaps never is any answer, he tells us, to this question: one has 'a right to dismiss the question, for it seems to derive from the human presumptuousness'. This presumptuousness, which consists in looking for a purpose for human life created alongside with life itself, would be the product of religious thinking, which conceives of history as having a meaning external to it. It would mean to introduce an abstract conception of 'man' separated from the real field in which this purpose is created. The fact that life has no object means that its object is life itself, that it does not go beyond itself and must be created from within it. There is nothing in existence that prepares all that precedes as a process in which its ultimate aim would be man. Human life is life transforming itself in the element of life, and there is nothing outside of it that transcends, as its purpose, this existence.

We can think that the three forms of eluding the external world (art, science, and narcotics) are such because there is no proper purpose present in them: they are disillusionments in the transition to the reality principle. The reality principle suggests the *persistence* of the pleasure principle in the ways of confronting reality: it still regulates itself according to infantile models. This is why religion appears as the basis for all these options, supposing not only the idea of Providence but also Providence itself prolonged from the infantile father onward:

> The common man cannot imagine this Providence otherwise than in the figure of an enormously exalted father. Only such a being can understand the needs of the children of men and be softened by their prayers and placated by the signs of their remorse. (74)

And all the solutions that result from not confronting reality would be based on the disillusion of the abandonment of the father and the ineffectiveness of religion: there would be nothing to do. If the meaning of the world, transcendent and derived from religion, consists in giving 'man' a purpose in function of the super-ego that orders 'what you ought to be, or else, you won't be anything', then lacking this purpose, any other meaning is inexistent. The answers whose models Freud takes up are all regressive: intoxication, which is the answer before the anxiety of birth; art, which searches for a passive consolation in fantasy; and science, which prolongs knowledge beyond the anxiety over reality without mobilising the body. None of them is situated in the creative movement of life, none of them can withstand the uncertainty of a purpose that would be different from what is already known, the repetition of the same – anthropomorphism – as the only mode of existence. Outside the form of man already constituted, or advanced on the basis of the ego ideal, which is the narcissistic prolongation of the first, there is no other form of humanity: there also is no other form of happiness. This is why,

> Once again, only religion can answer the question of the purpose of life. (76)

For it is religion that encloses individual narcissism in collective and civilisational narcissism, and maintains the infantile illusion as for Romain Rolland, predetermining the meaning of all subsequent and future reality. Anthropocentrism-narcissism-religion-super-ego-resemblance: that is the series. Anthropocentrism, then, affirms the human being as transcendent creature with a predetermined end. It removes it from the movement which, from the cosmos and nature, produces itself as human history, immanent and without other purpose or end than those that this history itself creates in its development by going back to the origin: starting from the instincts of life and death.

1 *The Separation of Pleasure and Pain*

This explains the subsequent analyses that Freud formulates for himself, descriptively, against the backdrop of this civilisation completely steeped in Christianity:

> We will therefore turn to the less ambitious question of what men themselves show by their behaviour to be the purpose and intention of their lives. What do they demand of life and wish to achieve in it? The answer to this can hardly be in doubt. They strive after happiness; they want to become happy and to remain so. This endeavour has two sides, a positive and a negative aim. It aims, on the one hand, at an absence of pain

and unpleasure, and, on the other, at the experiencing of strong feelings of pleasure. In its narrower sense the word 'happiness' only relates to the last. In conformity with this *dichotomy* in his aims, man's activity develops in two directions, according as it seeks to realize – in the main, or even exclusively – the one or the other of these aims. (76, emphasis added)

Here the entire problem is already formulated. The *duality* of the objective implies the presence of a *separation between pain and pleasure*; therefore, the lack of integration of the pursued goal – happiness – in a contradictory field of reality in which the quest for the second is linked to the conditions of reality of the first. Or, in other words, a situation in which the pursuit of happiness does not require its inscription in a structured field of reality, which might link pleasure to its obstacle and its removal. This indicates, on the one hand, the *punctual* meaning of pleasure, reduced to its mere sensoriality without meaning, without being articulated with the determinations that prolong the body in civilisation. This is why this affirmation of punctual pleasure – and its correlate, punctual pain – also indicates the existence of a *nondiscernment of the real world* in which our body prolongs itself. Here we encounter the felt totality of Rolland as the basis of an abstract, indiscriminate totality, which is the correlate of this *punctual* and *separate* presence of pleasure and pain. This means that in the consciousness of those who pursue happiness as their goal there is no inclusion of the structure of the system that determines it in the insignificant persecution of pleasure and the insignificant avoidance of pain. The discerning of the world as determining its pleasure and its pain is so far removed from the discrimination of pleasure and pain themselves in one's empirical body that it is reduced to mere sensation without meaning. The description that Freud offers us here is thus the description of the happiness that bourgeois individualism strives to obtain:

> As we see, what decides the purpose of life is simply the programme of the pleasure principle. ... and yet its programme is at loggerheads with the whole world, with the macrocosm as much as with the microcosm. (76)

This is the individual and narcissistic solution to the contradiction that the system confronts us with. Here the individual is already determined by the reality principle, but continues to search for happiness in the programme of the pleasure principle. What happens is that the reality principle of our system does not include the human being, nor does it contain itself, as determined by the totality of the phenomena of nature from where humanity emerges and on the basis of which it continues to reproduce itself. The reality of the whole only prolongs itself as 'oceanic feeling', as oneness with the universe. This is why Freud says of this programme:

> There is no possibility at all of its being carried through; all the regulations of the universe run counter to it. One feels inclined to say that the intention that man should be 'happy' is not included in the plan of 'Creation'. (76)

It is this precise sense of happiness, in which the mere sensible satisfaction is split off from its insertion into the framework of reality, which appears to be embattled: this purpose of individual happiness would run counter to the plan of Creation because it does not take this plan into account. Happiness here is merely narcissistic subjectivism, only regressively realisable. To achieve such happiness one necessarily evades reality, in the fantasy that produces it as ideal. But to situate happiness means to situate the human being in the face of the basic determinations, or the limit-situations as we would say today, without which neither pleasure nor pain can be understood. Only starting from their inclusion in this field of reality, which is the necessary foundation of every lived relation, can we understand, perhaps, the meaning of pleasure and pain and, therefore, the individualistic ideal of happiness. Freud does so by highlighting the connection that links pleasure to pain, enjoyment to suffering, for this is an irreducible condition of our insertion into the real world. These limits would be *the limits that cannot be sublimated and remain as coordinates of every relation with reality*:

1. One's own body: condemned to decay and dissolution.
2. The external world: overwhelming and merciless destructive forces.
3. The relations with other human beings, perhaps the source of greatest pain. This level could be compared, for being 'fatefully inevitable', to the previous two.

So these limits are inevitable, they cannot be sublimated: we will have to go all in with our body. They delimit the contours of every action and every project, as well as of every analysis. Once again we find proof in Freud of the testing of limits, the courage experienced as presence of the truth for a thinking that *confronts the pain of thinking the limits without which thinking is the evasion of pain*. This means: any conception of happiness that does not necessarily contain the transformation of these three relations, and the recognition of their limits, will not be a true conception. And we will see that Freud here leads himself in the direction of the analysis of civilisation and of its discontents, by highlighting the possibility of avoiding the risk that the relation to other human beings turns into a destiny 'any less fatefully inevitable than the suffering which comes from elsewhere' (77). That is to say, he will emphasise the possibility of transforming *that relation in which the limits depend on us*.

Freud will thus proceed to analyse those solutions that are situated in the *separation between pleasure and pain* and that attempt to have an impact on only one of these extremes. They are all, therefore, transactions for eluding reality. This separation between pleasure and pain produces, under the guidance of the pleasure principle, the annulment of pleasure itself, which acquires meaning only as non-pain: non-pain here becomes equivalent to pleasure. The outlook which is fixated on *avoiding suffering in order to reach a pleasure without pain* must previously dominate pain in order for pleasure, as such, to become possible. It will be condemned to trying to avoid pain, which thus will become converted in quasi-pleasure. *Non-pain will here be pleasure*. But in that case the conduct regulated by the pleasure principle remains subject to not being able to feel it and having to dedicate all its life to avoiding the pain of confronting reality, against whose backdrop all pleasure appears.

> It is no wonder if, under the pressure of these possibilities of suffering, men are accustomed to moderate their claims to happiness – just as the pleasure principle itself, indeed, under the influence of the external world, changed into the more modest reality principle – if *a man thinks himself happy merely to have escaped unhappiness* or to have survived his suffering, and if in general the task of avoiding suffering pushes that of obtaining pleasure into the background. (77, emphasis added)

Let us note: the reality principle is the principle of a repressive reality dominated by human relations as confrontation and destiny. But let us also note that the problem thus presented is between *a pleasure without reality or a reality without pleasure*. This confrontation takes shape when reality previously defines pleasure as incapable of becoming real. And when it leaves for it only the small refuge of its own sensibility without reason or relation, looking for pleasure only within the limits where the interstices of the system tolerate the narcissistic pleasure that in no way affects or disturbs the process of production. *Narcissistic pleasure is thus the complement that the system gives to itself for its own imperturbability*.

Freud's analysis situates itself in the need to search for pleasure within a 'reality' that would not be defined as unmovable nor understood as natural like the other limits: those of the external world and one's own body. It therefore situates the search for reality in the removal of the obstacle and as a result in the pleasure that only risk and confrontation bring out. The pleasure, in other words, that in order to be able to emerge must shake up the limits to which the system restricts it.

We must therefore inscribe the 'methods for the avoidance of suffering' within this *quest for non-pain* as a substitute for the pleasure that in this way becomes displaced. Their focus is not on the quest for pleasure but on the sources of displeasure, in order to avoid them. But this avoidance means to elude the ground of pain that is tied to pleasure. The avoidance of displeasure must therefore preserve the positive side of the relation that is being avoided so as not to suffer. But this positivity, once it is reached, is no longer the same. All of life will be organised on the basis of the sole aim from which all the others are derived: to avoid pain.

2   *Techniques to Avoid Suffering*

1. Chemical intoxication: it is a question of transforming the dispositions of the organism so as to feel pleasurable sensations and avoid disagreeable impulses. Thus the weight of reality can be evaded.
2. Mastery of the internal sources of our needs: killing off the instincts. Life is abandoned so as to gain absolute repose. But instead of annihilating them, the instincts can only be tamed: 'In that case, the controlling elements are the higher psychical agencies, which have subjected themselves to the reality principle' (79). The limitation of pleasure, incomparably less intense than the satisfaction of the untamed instinctual impulse.
3. Displacement of the libido: 'shifting the instinctual aims in such a way that they cannot come up against frustration from the external world' (79). Sublimation is the installation in the dualism of soul and body, of instincts and spirit.

> In this, sublimation of the instincts lends its assistance. One gains the most if one can sufficiently heighten the yield of pleasure from the sources of psychical and intellectual work. *When that is so, fate can do little against one.* (78, emphasis added)

In this technique for eluding the suffering of the external world we can situate the artist and the scientist. But these solutions are derivations of the separating dualism. This is why Freud here says of art as much as of science:

> At present we can only say figuratively that such satisfactions seem 'finer and higher'. But their intensity is mild as compared with that derived from the sating of crude and primary instinctual impulses; it does not convulse our physical being. (79–80)

It is within this dualism that we can pose the problem of the truth of science and art. There would be an art and a science that also physically move us, and there would be an art and a science that are nothing more than a ruse so as not to confront reality: art and science as either true or false. Here we see how the condition for the exercise of an intellectual function is predetermined by the meaning that the latter has for the subject: in the way it has recourse to art or to science in order to activate its own repressed contents that newly put themselves into play, in action, searching for the discriminate pleasure.

In this way true science and art appear in the service of pleasure prolonging itself in reality to announce a possibility or discern an obstacle that is opposed to its transition. There is, then, a science and an art against the backdrop of instinctual satisfaction, which seeks out its path toward reality that it must discern in order to facilitate satisfaction, and this is the art or the science that is moving or 'exciting'. And there is an art and a science based on the 'sublimation' of the instincts, as techniques for eluding reality, which no matter how much they think and no matter how much they imagine only prolong terror into a reality that they do not confront and that they imagine and think precisely so as not to confront it. For true art and science put into play the totality of the subject: the latter makes the transition from the sensible instinctual impulses, which move the body with their recognised peremptoriness, toward a reality in which they search, by way of knowledge or imagination – which is only another form of knowing – to open up a transformative passage. The thinking of science and the imagining of art consist in including within the instincts the presence of the obstacle that links pleasure to pain. We are no longer in a division that separates pleasure without pain and which, for this very reason, is no more than the sad quest for non-pain. The problem of science in other words is also a personal problem, in which the entire subject must make itself capable of discovery, because it is in this discernment that the meaning of science once again reveals itself in its original foundation. Freud here once again comes across the critique against scientism and, prolonging it, we could say the critique of the scientism that is psychoanalytical as well as Marxist. What will be the greatest trap to elude reality? That which in the act of eluding reality believes that it is really confronting reality. Let us listen to the artistic skills of its seduction: Is truth perhaps not objective in and of itself – the scientists whisper to us, tranquilising – and all the more so in that it refers to the true and decentred knowledge, without subject, of the objective structures? This is precisely the trap: once again, in the name of true knowledge, to have dislodged that which is present in Marx as well as in Freud: the thinking of theory implies the thinking of the exact obstacle that is opposed to the subject's transition, together with the others, to a reality in which it would reinscribe once more the unsatisfied desire. This is why the removal of the 'epistemological obstacle', as it would be said in the fashionable jargon, is not enough: this criterion still remains at the level of science as mere technique for eluding reality. For reality is not only the reality of the knowledge of the external world in its rational filaments: it is the new relation in which a subject develops the concept until it finds the materiality of the precise obstacle, because this process is nothing but the prolongation of the intent to unite the flesh with the idea in which it can prolong the satisfaction of its impulses. Thus, if the lifting of the 'epistemological obstacle' is not based on the removal of the 'psychological obstacle', which drags along with it the truth of the proposal in the way that Freud shows us, then this knowledge, even in its presumed 'truth', is nothing more than a new turn of the screw in the technical innovations for eluding reality in the moment of affirming the real as what is most precious. This is not surprising: these techniques detect the danger and they approach this result in order to conceal it once again. In this way the scientific discovery that they enunciate, rather than prolonging and actualising the density of its truth, is discovered in an ambivalent form as what is most beloved, but at the same time as what is most dangerous: its embrace is nothing more than a fatal embrace which, beneath its declaration of love, only attempts to drown it out so that it may not live and make itself present with the flickering clairvoyance of the light that it sheds.

Thus we see how in science, converted into a technique for not suffering, truth is a means to cover up reality more so than to reach it. Truth is detected only with the purpose of annulling its purpose because *truth is precisely the obstacle* in need of vanquishing. And the mechanism, at the level of the specificity of 'theoretical practice', consists precisely in giving as criteria for oneself only the sublimated impulses: in giving oneself only the abstract field of thinking consciousness. Once this right to affirmation is acquired, one has taken away from science everything that rooted it in the blood of the subject who puts its situated and determinate truth at stake, in order to appear as its opposite: as the one who *detains the truth of truth* and who, for this very reason, is the only one who can annul its true content in the name of truth. Of this same truth in which it claims to find support but which, in reality, is there to destroy it.

This process in the case of science is, Freud tells us, clearly a cover-up:

> While this procedure already clearly shows an intention of making oneself independent of the external world by seeking satisfaction in internal, psychical processes, ... (80)

This rational satisfaction of reason as a means for eluding reality is even more pronounced in the case of art:

> In it, the connection with reality is still further loosened; satisfaction is obtained from illusions, which are recognised as such without the discrepancy between them and reality being allowed to interfere with enjoyment. The region from which these illusions arise is the life of the imagination; at the time when the development of the sense of reality took place, this region was expressly exempted from the demands of reality-testing and was set apart for the purpose of fulfilling wishes which were difficult to carry out. At the head of these satisfactions through phantasy stands the enjoyment of works of art – an enjoyment which, by the agency of the artist, is made accessible even to those who are not themselves creative. (80–1)

Freud is speaking here of the one who enjoys the work of art, not of the creator. The difference with the scientist once again sends us back to the nuance that we indicated earlier: the 'man of science' *thinks* that he is active due to the fact that he *exercises* this knowledge discovered by others, the true creators. But his exercise is similar to the one who enjoys the work of art without creating it: this serves the purpose of eluding reality, we said, in the very act of exercising the true result on which it is based, introducing the speculative and repetitive activity of a theory, which thus functions, like a cushion, between them and the world. What is more, in function of the social service that this activity may present, a 'technical' service covered up behind the designation of 'science', it finds its place in the reality that it fears, and in this way finds itself compensated for. This rationality of the 'scientist' remains within the reason governed by the super-ego, which conceals the carnal origin of this development that earlier found its point of departure in the sensible form of the father. Reason here ignores the repressive sensibility that gives it its organisation. And the one who enjoys the work of art enacts an imaginary field of sensibility that also remained defined by repression as though it did not have its origin in reality, as a subjective-subjective field radically opposed to it.

These two 'techniques', science and art, united in the 'technique' of narcotics, are not the only ones. Art is also a 'mild narcosis' and science, perhaps a rational and more continuous narcosis. But in the series of techniques for eluding reality there is that more radical and energetic one which 'regards reality as the sole enemy and as the source of all suffering' (81). The individual delusion (hermit) and the collective delusion (religion) are only the two extremes of this same transformation.

A special importance attaches to the case in which this attempt to procure a certainty of happiness and a protection against suffering through a delusional remoulding of reality is made by a considerable number of people in common. The religions of mankind must be classed among the mass-delusions of this kind. No one, needless to say, who shares a delusion ever recognises it as such. (81)

Another technique, also fruitless, to ward off suffering and reach happiness is to make love the centre of all things, 'which looks for all satisfaction in loving and being loved' (82). This is, once again, as in the previous forms, an attempt to apply a model that relies on a unitary and organic relation of the life instincts and the death instincts, there where pleasure is united to pain, but only in order deceptively to prolong it toward reality in the illusion of realising pleasure, when in actual fact, on the contrary, this technique also negates it. These techniques are thus ways of separating the positive from the negative, as in the false dialectic that Hegel showed to us, and they elude the terrifying presence of finitude by splitting it off from the infinitude in which the negativity of death would remain excluded. This technique

> locates satisfaction in internal mental processes, making use, in so doing, of the displaceability of the libido of which we have already spoken. But it does not turn away from the external world; on the contrary, it clings to the objects belonging to that world and obtains happiness from an emotional relationship to them. (82)

How could it do this by remaining within reality?

> Nor is it content to aim at an avoidance of un-pleasure – a goal, as we might call it, of weary resignation; it passes this by without heed and holds fast to the original, passionate striving for a positive fulfilment of happiness. (82)

But this passion, which separates itself from the reality of the object in order to concentrate on itself, comes back once more, in the loss of the object, from the illusion to the changing and frustrating reality so as to restart from the beginning, with another object, and then another, and another, this relation in which the object is not seen in its reality but only as a receptacle so as to be able to project on it one's love. Time and again frustrated.

But this technique of love, Freud tells us, is not exhausted in this description. In the next chapter we will see its fullest social consequence. It is not the real other whom we love: it is the other as object-support for a narcissistic passion that projects on every other the illusion of an indiscriminate love. What disappears is the unitary and organic form of love, sexual love, which is its starting model and contains the reality of the other and the time and the flesh and the rhythm of sex and the sensible presence of the different other.

And the same dissociation can be found in those who put the happiness of life in 'the enjoyment of beauty' (82). It is a vital orientation sundered from the origin where, once again, the presence of the sexuated body as the ground of all beauty disappears. We appreciate and we contemplate only the derived forms in which the effective and real presence of the subject who 'enjoyed' vanishes as the announcement of an effective, dodged, and feared relationship.

> All that seems certain is its derivation from the field of sexual feeling. The love of beauty seems a perfect example of an impulse inhibited in its aim. 'Beauty' and 'attraction' are originally attributes of the sexual object. It is worth remarking that the genitals themselves, the sight of which is always exciting, are nevertheless hardly ever judged to be beautiful; the quality of beauty seems, instead, to attach to certain secondary sexual characters. (83)

By way of conclusion to the various 'techniques' considered here, Freud closes his analysis by indicating the unsolvable contradictions that the search of happiness stumbles up against within the framework of the narcissistic individualism that flees the discernment of reality.

Thus, various oppositions reach their culmination:

> life and death
> pleasure and pain
> physical and spiritual
> individual and real world
> sensible and rational
> personal history and world history
> form and content
> anthropocentrism and the real universe (freezing of a determinate form of being human as absolute)
> immanence and transcendence

3   Substitution of Pleasure by Non-pain

All these 'techniques' – which Freud describes as proper to a civilisation in which only these social models are facilitated for the human being – do not constitute individual but cultural solutions. And all the cultural models find their general contradiction in this last formulation from Freud, which is not the one he presents to us but the description of the limits that he comes up against on the basis of the description, for those who pursue 'happiness' as their objective:

> The programme of becoming happy, which the pleasure principle imposes on us, cannot be fulfilled; yet we must not – indeed, we cannot – give up our efforts to bring it nearer to fulfilment by some means or other. (83)

Let us understand: the individualistic happiness that the pleasure principle *imposes on us* is unrealisable *as such*. But this imposition navigates life itself: it is Eros announcing itself in civilisation and demanding to be prolonged in it. This is why, *no matter how much we want to*, no matter how much we only dedicate ourselves to avoid suffering – we must not and cannot abandon the efforts to come closer, *by some means or other*, to its realisation. All the previous solutions, we saw, only pursue the pleasure principle without reality; this is *why they gave in, frustrated, to the reality principle without pleasure*. Its relation to pleasure was only so as to have recourse to all the forms of primary processes to satisfy it. They had the infantile form of pleasure, which consists in giving oneself a hallucinated object, *instead of its real adult content*. They had a hallucinated relation to pleasure, and a relation of effective submission to reality. Pleasure was only the halo present as non-pain, which was its objective. In this way the narcissistic happiness says it pursues pleasure, but its reality is that it pursues only the possibility of non-pain. All these techniques in search of happiness are techniques that sought after the suppression of pain, and in this they found pleasure: the substitute pleasure for not suffering. And Freud shows us, in its failures, that *it is unrealisable in its current conditions*. But also that we must not give up on pleasure, whose *model* is the sexual relationship: the one in which the pain of the death instinct is overcome in the pleasure of the life instinct that uses death and violence, in the real time of life, in its favour. Freud talks to us about a historical pleasure that faces up to the conditions of reality and reaches its happiness – its happiness tastes like death – within the limits of this only life marked off between birth and death.

But Freud tells us at the same time that the 'reduced happiness' with which we console ourselves also does not have any possibility of arriving:

> By none of these paths can we attain all that we desire. Happiness, in the reduced sense in which we recognize it as possible, is a problem of the

economics of the individual's libido. There is no golden rule which applies to everyone: every man must find out for himself in what particular fashion he can be saved. (83)

Is this clear? This *reduced* happiness, which distances itself from the conditions that define the historical reality of the human being and gives itself a partial object as if this were possible, is the unreachable happiness: Never 'can we attain all that we desire'. And this same kind of happiness is an individual problem, which remains restricted to the limits of one's own body. Private libidinal economy, as private as the capitalist economy: it depends only on how much *one's own body* has to offer to give itself the individual illusion of obtaining such happiness. But if for Freud the problem of happiness is a social problem, then here by contrast the norm is the strictest individualism: 'every man must find out for himself in what particular fashion he can be saved'. Science and knowledge, which is concerned with all of us, cannot do anything here once it has signalled the essential impossibility of pretending to obtain this happiness without reality. And the advice with regard to the private libidinal economy, in the interpretation that we propose of the capitalist investment, is not far removed from Freud, when he offers the sarcastic counsel:

> Just as a cautious business-man avoids tying up all his capital in one concern, so, perhaps, worldly wisdom will advise us not to look for the whole of our satisfaction from a single aspiration. Its success is never certain, (84)

And it will depend not on a collective but on a purely individual action:

> for that depends on the convergence of many factors, perhaps on none more than on the capacity of the psychical constitution to adapt its function to the environment and then to exploit that environment for a yield of pleasure. (84)

The problem is presented on the basis of the social determination, but the solution here is only individual. Those who come into this world with a libido that does not let itself be tamed by these escape routes, which the wisdom of civilisation teaches us as being compatible with the non-modification of its own limits, are condemned to sickness and to death:

> A person who is born with a specially unfavourable instinctual constitution, and who has not properly undergone the transformation and

rearrangement of his libidinal components which is indispensable for later achievements, will find it hard to obtain happiness from his external situation, especially if he is faced with tasks of some difficulty. (84)

This different libidinal constitution indicates the impossibility of sublimating and inhibiting the aims of the instincts that demand their urgent satisfaction. For this transition, the 'external situation' presents as the only ways out either adaptation to the repressive reality or else sickness:

> As a last technique of living, which will at least bring him substitutive satisfactions, he is offered that of a flight into neurotic illness. (84)

Let us pay attention to what Freud is saying: only neurotics preserve the pleasure that they did not wish to abandon as the aim of their selection; only they maintain present the objective of life. But their solution to obtain pleasure *continues to be individual* and, therefore, condemned to 'substitutive satisfactions': they only have their own body as field of transformation.

> The man who sees his pursuit of happiness come to nothing in later years can still find consolation in the yield of pleasure of chronic intoxication; or he can embark on the desperate attempt at rebellion seen in a psychosis. (84)

Intoxication and madness: the two terms of *rebellion in despair*, discovered too late when the subject is already of mature age and unable to exercise violence against the system but rather, finally, against itself. Thus, illness for Freud is inscribed as a solution that does not confront its opposite in the normality of life but in the revolution. 'Normality' is, like destiny, the collective illness that the social and unlivable models offer to the dependent individuality as a way of investing in it for *all of life*: the point is to administer, in the interstices of the system, one's individual capital, one's individual quantum of life, one's amount of libido, in order not to suffer.

These paths, which Freud indicated and studied, are apparently 'free': free to choose how to elude suffering, not how to obtain pleasure. And as far as pleasure is concerned, there is only the freedom that presents itself in the choice of illness: the field of the imaginary as the only refuge. This is why Freud says:

> Religion restricts this play of choice and adaptation, since it imposes equally on everyone its own path to the acquisition of happiness and protection from suffering. Its technique consists in depressing the value of

life and distorting the picture of the real world in a delusional manner – which presupposes an intimidation of the intelligence. At this price, by forcibly fixing them in a state of psychical infantilism and by drawing them into a mass-delusion, religion succeeds in sparing many people an individual neurosis. But hardly anything more. (84–5)

This 'play of choice and adaptation', we already saw before: variations of individual freedom, the bourgeois freedom to choose within adaptation. But this liberalism, even when it is separated from the Church and from religion, remains within the framework of the nondiscernment of the system of production that rigidly rules over each individual. Religion is its counterpart: that is why it appears as collective neurosis as opposed to individual neurosis. Hence the alternative: either the appearance of collective, 'social' normality, which repression and absolute submission provide for us, or the fall into neurosis and madness when the response remains within the framework of the individual solution and without opening itself up, as we will see in *Group Psychology and the Analysis of the Ego*, to another form of collectivity, which is the revolutionary task. Thus, the opposition between collective and individual neurosis leaves no other way out, and the previously analysed forms are all inscribed as variations of one and the same blindness: the nondiscernment of the system that produces both the individuals and the categories of the totality in which they appear as determining the framework of meaning of their relation to the world. The 'intimidation of the intelligence' was already present in all the individual 'techniques' for eluding suffering that reality produces: science, art, narcotics. All of them supposed the permanence in the separation of the pleasure principle and the reality principle, aimed solely at considering happiness as the absence of pain. And the culmination of this collective abandonment is religion, where suffering is already presented as supreme value: in religion the reality principle is the principle of pain. The inversion is complete.

> Even religion cannot keep its promise. If the believer finally sees himself obliged to speak of God's 'inscrutable decrees', he is admitting that *all that is left to him as a last possible consolation and source of pleasure in his suffering is an unconditional submission*. (85, emphasis added)

Thus is solved the problem in which the opposition between pleasure and pain culminates in its logic and its necessity: those who in order not to suffer decided to stop inscribing pleasure in reality had to preserve it in the realm of fantasy in order to dedicate themselves in reality to non-pain. And if this logic is prolonged as the abandonment of desire in order to obtain the absolute security of non-suffering, then suffering paradoxically becomes converted into the supreme value. *To suffer so as not to suffer*: such is the endpoint of this logic, which began by eluding pain, separating it from pleasure. And it thus concludes in the enjoyment of pain, which at the end of the day is the culmination of submission, the only guarantee for not having to confront reality. Subjugation, which was present at the beginning of the repressive reality principle and which at least provided us with the enjoyment of love, now returns in unconditional submission as the source of enjoyment and consolation: in the name of all it had to suffer.

Let us follow its trajectory. It began by wanting to elude the suffering that pleasure, as objective, could entail for it: it prefers the promised security, prolonged on the basis of the infantile scheme. In a movement of accommodation, compensated for in the realm of the imaginary by means of a scission, it separated pain from pleasure and made non-suffering into its objective. And the breach opened up wider and wider, insofar as by withdrawing pleasure from the field of reality, it had to continue inscribing it in an imaginary field in which, regressively – all the good is inside – nothing will ever be changed. And if all the bad is outside, as the primitive pleasure-ego affirms in its biological digestive logic, reality was precisely that which had to be avoided and devalued. The pleasure of security continued, nice and warm sheltered from within, from the form of the other whose love we ratified in each act of avoidance. Religion represents the culmination of this process, this series of gradual separation (from which others, those who put it at their service, take advantage). And thus the body, which did not wish to die or suffer, remains in unconditional submission to the reality that in effect dominates it, subjugated to continuous suffering, which in this inverted dialectic is the objective stamp and verification of the certainty of its triumph and of its pleasure, situated in the beyond, which it has reserved for itself by having subordinated itself.

III Analysis of the Real Obstacle

Discernment and concealment: those were the lines of demarcation that structured the development in the preceding chapters. In the next one, Freud confronts the problem of the meaning of civilisation, and of the impositions suffered by each human being who, thanks to civilisation, makes the transition from nature to culture. He starts once more from the recognition of the three sources of human suffering:

> ... the superior power of nature, the feebleness of our own bodies and the inadequacy of the regulations which adjust the mutual relationships of human beings in the family, the state and society. (86)

The point is to recognise the effective presence of the obstacle and the forms of confronting it, *in the way civilisation indeed had to do* in order to be what it is: culture or civilisation, that is to say, the distancing of nature in the midst of nature itself, and the increase of human relationships. And the emphasis falls from the start on that sector where suffering is the result of human beings themselves and therefore could be avoided: the 'social origin'. And so Freud says:

> And yet, when we consider how unsuccessful we have been in precisely this field of prevention of suffering, a suspicion dawns on us that here, too, a piece of unconquerable nature may lie behind – this time a piece of our own psychical constitution. (86)

What unconquerable nature are we speaking of here? Not that of 'natural nature', but a very peculiar one: that of our own *culturalised nature*, as we saw before, and thus the goal is to understand this determinism in a different way. Our psychic constitution can be conceived, as we saw, by ratifying its *appearance* ('normal' transition from the primary to the secondary process, without decentring). But it can also be understood in a historical process of formation, so as *to include within culture itself the knowledge of a transition that has been 'naturalised'* and for this reason put at the service of a minority of people against others. Freud in other words is not telling us that there exists a field of unconquerable nature against which there is nothing to be done. In fact, he maintains the exact opposite and writes against the conception of a 'sector' of 'natural' nature in the human being, which he will show precisely to be the product of this hidden transition.

From there he moves on to consider the hostility against culture or civilisation in those forms that maintain precisely the separation, *within culture*, between culture and nature: the dualist systems which, at the same time as they impose their norms and criteria, present culture itself as negative, facilitating a return to 'conditions' of a 'more primitive life'. This is the paradoxical form that according to Freud is adopted by that 'spiritual' power which sits at the basis of the dominant Western civilisation:

> How has it happened that so many people have come to take up this strange attitude of hostility to civilisation? (87)

And among the factors that must have intervened in this evaluation he indicates a penultimate and a final one. The penultimate is as follows:

> ... a factor of this kind hostile to civilisation must already have been at work in the victory of Christendom over the heathen religions. For it was very closely related to the low estimation put upon earthly life by the Christian doctrine. (87)

This is then the contradictory form of a civilisation that denies itself in the depreciation of the life that it is supposed to render possible, validate, and organise. The dualism of the scission, which separated nature and culture in the midst of culture itself, and presented the latter as contrary to nature, invalidates its own finality.

And in terms of the final factor that intervenes in the depreciation of civilisation, Freud situates the knowledge that the human being acquires about the illness produced by this very same civilisation: neurosis.

> The last occasion is especially familiar to us. It arose when people came to know about the mechanism of the neuroses, which threaten to undermine the modicum of happiness enjoyed by civilised men. It was discovered that a person becomes neurotic because he cannot tolerate the amount of frustration which society imposes on him in the service of its cultural ideals (87)

But, as we can see, Freud here signals as an anti-civilisational factor the psychoanalytical understanding of neurosis that remains within the Christian dualism of the scission: this understanding *fails to understand mental illness as the evidence of the contradiction within the whole dualist cultural structure that leads to illness as the only way out*. Indeed: we already saw what was 'the modicum of happiness': that of individualism, which ruling over its personal libidinal economy, that remnant of corporeality not yet invested that the social form left for it, sought after the interstitial satisfactions that would not disturb the system: where what dominated was the transformation of pleasure into non-pain. However, those who cannot bear giving up on pleasure, but also do not manage to situate it in the necessary transformation of the whole world of culture or civilisation that thus condemns them, fall into neurosis. The latter then appears as the only way out allowed by the system for individual rebellions. And this fall into individual illness is not seen, in conventional psychoanalysis, as a proof that would render invalid the dualist solution of our civilisation. By maintaining themselves in a single conception of culture or civilisation as necessarily repressive, conventional psychoanalysts only see a way out in the return to nature and in the negation of all culture. Without realising that it is precisely *this culture*, lived as the *only* form of culture, which dictates to them, from their own absolutised subjugation, the false solution with the categories that produce illness. In this way we should point out that Freud does not speak of a 'natural determinism', or of an 'unconquerable nature', as if it were a question of maintaining the false opposition of nature-culture. Freud here is showing that the unconquerable nature persists as that corporeality negated by a civilisation which, up on high, proclaims its contempt for the earthly life but, down below, takes advantage of this life for being the unsublimatable and inevitable foundation that culture must transform and prolong. Freud's position is not a dualism: it is precisely the negation of this dualism. Between the below of nature and the beyond of culture, Freud shows us, in the discovery of neurosis, the need for a validation of culture conceived of as the prolongation of pleasure in reality. But at the same time he clearly indicates his position against a form of psychoanalysis that would maintain itself within the dualism, *pretending to salvage this remnant of individual happiness from within the contradiction of civilisation*, without putting the whole system up as bond. The struggle of psychoanalysis, as a science, is the theoretical and scientific struggle against a form of dominant culture and, as we will see, against a whole system of production.

What are the disappointments that civilisation produces in us? Precisely the fact that the mastery of nature would not have increased the amount of pleasurable satisfaction. Because this is a spiritualist civilisation, which does not scorn, in actual fact, the earthly realm.

> Men are proud of those achievements, and have a right to be. But they seem to have observed that this newly-won power over space and time, this subjugation of the forces of nature, which is the fulfillment of a longing that goes back thousands of years, has not increased the amount of pleasurable satisfaction which they may expect from life and has not made them feel happier. From the recognition of this fact we ought to be content to conclude that power over nature is not the only precondition of human happiness ...; we ought not to infer from it that technical progress is without value for the economics of our happiness. (87–88)

Once the opposition between technical progress and happiness is presented as a false one, the point is to analyse the conception of civilisation of which this opposition is the product, and why. Freud thus maintains the presence of pleasure, 'which we may expect from life', *within the realm of civilisation and technology*.

1   *The Prolongation of Corporeality in Cultural Production*

Let us have a look at the definition of civilisation that Freud gives us:

> ... the word 'civilisation' describes the whole sum of the achievements and the regulations which distinguish our lives from those of our animal ancestors and which serve two purposes – namely to protect men against nature and to adjust their mutual relations. (89)

It is a question both of the *transition* from nature to culture, which each human being continues to repeat, and of the historical *distance* that this passage represents, and in which the *achievements* and *institutions* become incorporated into the subject so as to constitute the latter, transforming it into a cultural being. Here we see that the deepest, most abyssal subjective element is determined by the historical: by production and institutions.

But immediately Freud goes on to *understand* these achievements and regulations, against the dualist conception, as a *prolongation of the organicity of nature and of human corporeality in the organicity of culture or civilisation*. The definition of civilisation here knows nothing of the abstract separation, which power proclaims as its ideal, between the spiritual and the material: it is from within the materiality of human transformations that Freud reads spirituality.

> We recognize as cultural all activities and resources which are useful to men for making the earth serviceable to them, for protecting them against the violence of the forces of nature, and so on. (89)

The meaning of culture can be read in the human needs that it comes to satisfy, and shows us this *prolongation of corporeality in cultural production*. Let us quote explicitly:
- 'With every *tool* man is perfecting his own *organs*';
- '*motor power* places gigantic forces at his disposal, which, like his *muscles*, he can employ in any direction';
- 'by means of *spectacles* he corrects *defects* in the lens of *his own eye*';
- 'by means of *the microscope* he overcomes the limits of visibility set by the structure of his *retina*';
- 'in the photographic *camera* he has created an instrument which retains the fleeting visual impressions';
- 'a *gramophone disc* retains the equally fleeting *auditory* ones';
- '*materialisations* of the power he possesses of recollection, his *memory*';
- '*the dwelling-house* was a substitute for the *mother*'s womb' (91, emphasis added).

We thus see how culture and technology are inscribed in the organicity of the natural body, which prolongs itself in the element of nature itself, transformed by modern industry. And what thus becomes prolonged is the unsatisfied desire, for which all these transformations in the reality of work in common seek to provide the new sphere of pleasure, even though pleasure, as we saw, has disappeared in this production:

> These things that, by his science and technology, man has brought about on this earth, on which he first appeared as a feeble animal organism and on which each individual of his species must once more make its entry ('oh inch of nature!') as a helpless suckling – these things do not only sound like a fairy tale, they are an actual fulfillment of every – or of almost every – fairy-tale wish. (91)

But it is precisely this distance from nature to culture, not assumed as a process whose meaning would always have to be present in determining the relation of domination, which here emerges anew:

> Man has, as it were, become a kind of prosthetic God. When he puts on all his auxiliary organs he is truly magnificent; but those organs have not grown on to him and they still give him much trouble at times. (91–92)

This non-prolongation of the human being's organic corporeality in the rationality of technology opens up a breach specific to our civilisation. Hence the sphere of mere usefulness, which circumscribes and determines the character of capitalist production and which becomes evident in the way in which culture or civilisation is *measured*:

> We recognize, then, that countries have attained a high level of civilisation if we find that in them everything which can assist in the exploitation of the earth by man and in his protection against the forces of nature – everything, in short, which is of use to him – is attended to and effectively carried out. (92)

Our civilisation, first defined in terms of the sovereignty of the spiritual, reveals that in its productive reality it is governed only by the rule of utility. In the face of the predominance of the useful, worshipped as the highest value – at the same time as the farthest removed from pleasure – to what is the most elevated and noble reduced, for example, beauty? Removed and reduced to being nothing more than something useless:

> We soon observe that this useless thing which we expect civilisation to value is beauty. (92)

Thus from Freud's description we see the specific features of civilisation emerge, but also the contradictory character and the different emphasis put on the values its proposes:
– the useful (production) opposed to the useless (beauty)
– technology (production) opposed to the organic (the body)
– order (regulations) opposed to disorder (revolution)
– cleanliness (civilisation) opposed to filthiness (barbarism).
Not only usefulness separated from beauty, which is then considered useless, predominates in our civilisation. There is also order and cleanliness. The latter is something strange: not because humans should not consider cleanliness a value but because of the indignant opposition to the dirtiness *from which it derives*. Barbarism is the dirty, the foul-smelling: civilisation is the clean. Freud calls this distancing 'organic repression' (99 n. 1).

> Dirtiness of any kind seems to us incompatible with civilisation. (93)

Here Freud is trying to indicate the cut and the concealment of the visceral, vital, and organic character of the human being, which distances humans from their own materiality, in a process that conceals its foundation.

This same cut is the one that appears in terms of order as diametrically opposed to disorder.

> Order is a kind of compulsion to repeat which, when a regulation has been laid down once and for all, decides when, where and how a thing shall be done, so that in every similar circumstance one is spared hesitation and indecision. (93)

Order does not appear as a cultural accomplishment over and above a previous order, but rather as a fixation. As the death drive within civilisation, it interrupts the process that produces new orderings and new solutions, in the extent to which each order pretends to install itself, 'once and for all', as an absolute form. Thus human beings, on the basis of 'utility' and 'saving' as the greatest value, abdicate precisely the power that led them to their cultural achievements.

All of these developments are forms of distancing: distancing of the useful as opposed to the beautiful; distancing of technology as opposed to the body; of order as opposed to creation; of cleanliness as opposed to life.

And, on top of this, as the crowning example of all these real abandonments, Freud traces the description of civilisation:

> No feature, however, seems better to characterize civilisation than its esteem and encouragement of man's higher mental activities – his intellectual, scientific and artistic achievements – and the leading role that it assigns to ideas in human life. Foremost among those ideas are the religious systems, on whose complicated structure I have endeavoured to throw light elsewhere. Next come the speculations of philosophy; and finally what might be called man's 'ideals' – his ideas of a possible perfection of individuals, or of peoples or of the whole of humanity, and the demands he sets up on the basis of such ideas. (94)

Of particular interest to us here is the fact that these superior activities are based on the previous ones, which are considered inferior within the value system of civilisation.

But the ideological character of this evaluation and this cultivation jumps to the eye: we saw that they correspond to the modes of concealing reality that Freud analysed in science, art, religion, and philosophy. They are part of the same system together with the other activities, and here the superior element repeats the dualism mentioned before: they also do not emerge from the body but are also, like the other activities, 'prostheses'. It is not by accident that they are 'only developed by a minority' (94). And it is not surprising that, in view of these elites given over to the superior activities as opposed to the masses dedicated to technical work, Freud immediately moves on to the analysis of the social relations that crown this edifice of civilisation. He quickly traces a genealogy and its present culmination:

> Human life in common is only made possible when a majority comes together which is stronger than any separate individual and which remains united against all separate individuals. The power of this community is then set up as 'right' in opposition to the power of the individual, which is condemned as 'brute force'. This replacement of the power of the individual by the power of a community constitutes the decisive step of civilisation. The essence of it lies in the fact that the members of the community restrict themselves in their possibilities of satisfaction, whereas the individual knew no such restrictions. (95)

This process of transition from nature to culture and civilisation, which Freud will analyse in greater detail in another chapter, is *the transition from the natural individuality to the cultural community*, in which individuality, now cultural, finds itself restricted. These cultural individuals, already installed in history, continue to be dominated by terror, the threat of which persists in the recollection of the castrating father of the primal horde. The rule of law, which inhibits the development of individuality, is only the regulating super-ego that against the backdrop of the dead father continues to determine the dissatisfaction of the individual instinctual impulses in civilisation. Here already, at the beginning of civilisation, there opens up the repressive dissociation. What was negated at the individual level is the fundamental aspect of the historic event: the collective rebellion of the brothers and the murder they committed. What ended up being affirmed, without memory, was only the subjugated individuality. Civilisation, in its appearance without origin, begins as the opposition of the collective and the individual, so much so that here individuality would no longer be natural but cultural. The emergence of the instinctual impulses reawakens the first repression of the act that is meant to be forgotten: the act of having killed the father. And those impetuous desires in the individual are 'condemned as brute force': as if they awakened in the human being a content anterior to civilisation, when in reality they are present, being debated and put to the test as part of civilisation itself. Because it still continues to rule by way of negating the form of the natural father, whose powerful instincts were the only ones satisfied. Equality thus is the result of concealment and terror before the appearance of any difference that might break the security of the obtained order. The ghost of the dead father haunts civilisation: the latter is the concealment of the murder of the natural individuality with which it began.

> The further course of cultural development seems to tend towards making the law no longer an expression of the will of a small community – a caste or a stratum of the population or a racial group – which, in its turn, behaves like a violent individual towards other, and perhaps more numerous, collections of people. (95)

The super-ego is here, qua law, a collective super-ego. As a social class, caste, or tribe, it appears 'like a violent individual': they are all regulated by the same form, which makes the collective into an aggressive individuality towards others. And, above all, against 'other, and perhaps more numerous, collections of people', in whom the impulses demand, collectively, to be satisfied. But this order of law and right is the one that comes to be prolonged: as the restrictive form of the emergence of difference towards all spheres of culture. The masses or collections of people too are ordered within this imposed form by the powerful groups who use repression to obtain their ends: work, technology, order, and cleanliness. The world of culture and civilisation thus enters, even in its more collective development, into the order of repetition and the predominance of the death instinct. Because we must not forget what Freud already knew: that the artificial masses or groups are halted in function of a relation where the predominance of the individual form repeats within civilisation the dependency that previously was natural.

> The final outcome should be a rule of law to which all – except those who are not capable of entering a community – have contributed by a sacrifice of their instincts, and which leaves no one – again with the same exception – at the mercy of brute force. (95)

This culmination seals the previous analysis. Those individuals adjusted for life in community are those in whom repression triumphed. The mad and the neurotic, the rebels, and the artists fall outside the order of integration: they are the ones who do not submit themselves to the collective repression and clamour for an individual satisfaction of their impulses. In them, that which civilisation represses but also provokes appears as if it were 'brute force', and Freud insists: 'again with the same exception'. Woe unto those who do not limit themselves: they cannot remain in the community and are expelled. But Freud is also once again showing us a path: the way out is not individual at the level of civilisation. If we went back to the coherence of the origin, present in the rebellion of the fraternal alliance, he would have to say: for the dominated group, in which the unsatisfied impulses emerge spontaneously and dissolve the existing order, it must be possible to transform the whole cultural order of civilisation, all the orders previously analysed on the basis of the scission and dualism, in material production as well as in ideology, in order to make a new form of culture appear. But this is only suggested in Freud's text by way of interpretation, not expressed in any direct form. Here he only gives us, in a few lines, the synthesis of this complex process that will be developed further down.

The problem, then, is the opposition individual-collectivity in the midst of civilisation's cultural order. In the previous chapters we saw that the presumption of individuality – the ego neatly defined in opposition to the external world – was only an appearance: a delimitation imposed by the system of production which at the same time as it granted us the presumption of the most absolute individuality surrounded us and limited us and rigidly defined a relation with reality that was restricted and contained. Thus was ruptured the dialectic that links individuals with the domain of the world that determined them. This rupture is what matters here; but this continuity was already present, though limited in its development, in the individuality of the primal horde. Civilisation, from the moment Christianity placed the greatest emphasis on the person and his or her interior depth, appears as a halting and an inhibiting of this historical dialectic that should have been facilitated in the human being:

> The liberty of the individual is no gift of civilisation. It was greatest before there was any civilisation, though then, it is true, it had for the most part no value, since the individual was scarcely in a position to defend it. (95)

It was precisely the rebellion against the only powerful natural individual – the primordial father – in whom this maximum individual liberty manifested itself, which led to civilisation through the fraternal alliance. This new domain, where the value of individual liberty created the necessity of collective organisation in order to obtain it, is what at the end of the day appears as its maximum negation under the illusion of its achievement.

Here is where Freud's question becomes radical: there are transformations that are compatible with this civilisation, and others that by contrast inscribe themselves as radically opposed to it, negating it. Such negation, which implies the complete transformation of its repressive foundation, is seen from the point of view of civilisation as the negation of *all civilisation* pure and simple. Freud makes this observation from within the order of civilisation that he is describing, where there are only two options allowed by the system in place. But this is not Freud's own position, as we will see further along:

> What makes itself felt in a human community as a desire for freedom may be their revolt against some existing injustice, and so may prove favorable to a further development of civilisation; it may remain compatible with civilisation. But it may also spring from the remains of their original personality, which is still untamed by civilisation and may thus become the basis in them of hostility to civilisation. The urge for freedom, therefore, is directed against particular forms and demands of civilisation or against civilisation altogether. (96)

We already saw before that the negation of culture as the mere return to nature was the solution of Christianity and of that type of psychoanalysis which kept itself within the Christian dualism. But Freud shows us here with the utmost clarity the option that appears within the cultural system that does not question the basis of its split foundation: *either reformism or nihilism*. Either changes within the same cultural order of civilisation, or else the negation of all culture and all civilisation. But we can already see where the analysis is aiming: towards the radical transformation of the very foundation on which Western and Christian civilisation is based, which is to say, necessarily, towards the revolution. On the basis of this contained and disdained force of human individuality, of those impulses that could not be subjugated by the dualistic culture, on the basis of this unity that through one's own corporeality keeps present the unsublimatable aspect of pleasure and of the impulses, the need arises for the radical questioning of the productive system. The problem phrased in terms of reformism, nihilism, or revolution, is here clearly laid out. The individual claim is only the moment of the emergence of a false culture that is being tested, in terms of the system of production, in the human beings who produce it. But to break this false alternative, Freud must show that this individuality that is opposed to the collective rose up as individuality from within the collective itself, and that it is only by going back to a modification that also would have to be collective that the quest for individual freedom regains its true meaning as well as its true historical process of transformation: the one that takes up the problem again on the basis of the fraternal alliance, renewed once more.

This is why it is not strange that what Freud goes on to analyse would be the first and most basic 'techniques', on the basis of which the dualistic culture imposes its repression, and that he would thus reveal the effective obstacle that any revolutionary process must confront, even in the midst of the individuality of human beings who rebel against the system.

> The development of civilisation appears to us as a peculiar process which mankind undergoes, and in which several things strike us as familiar. We may characterize this process with reference to the changes which it brings about in the familiar instinctual dispositions of human beings, to satisfy which is, after all, the economic task of our lives. (96)

These changes that civilisation imposes suppose a gradation in the transformation of the instincts or drives, whose order of depth and, thus, of access to the consciousness of the transformation they have undergone, decreases from the most profound and almost indistinguishable (the used up instincts), via the sublimated instincts, to the most superficial level (the unsatisfied instincts). These are the only instinctual dispositions, in actual fact, in which the dissatisfaction caused becomes visible to all. The same happens as in the capitalist process: production, the foundation on the basis of which the exploitation of surplus value is organised, is hidden. Only the circulation of commodities, the most superficial level of the economic process, is evident to all. But that is not where the secret of exploitation lies.

2 Analysis of the Cultural 'Techniques' of Adaptation: The Instinctual Renunciations

1st Cultural Technique: 'Instincts Used Up'

These instincts are so profoundly transformed by history that their original direction appears to be completely replaced by a cultural finality. But at the same time, there also exists no possibility for reviving their original meaning. This is the level where culture is most profoundly felt as 'natural': the level of impulses 'used up' in such a manner that nothing will be able to restore them or reanimate them.

This transformation shaped us forever in what we are and was converted into an unmodifiable 'destiny': an essential trait. But the extraordinary aspect here is that these personal traits at the same time lay the foundation for the domination of social forms. What constitutes the basis of the repressive culture and its system of production here turns out to be the foundation most proper to human beings themselves, that which determines their most intimate and personal mode of being.

> A few of these instincts are *used up* in such a manner that something appears in their place which, in an individual, we describe as a character-trait. (96, emphasis added)

Used up means: they prolong themselves in personal qualities in which some instinct became inverted; nothing is left of it that might pursue its own ends outside of this inversion. Here every instinct or drive is transformed by culture. Its root cannot be seen: it is an unchangeable character trait, where the cultural response forms a single body with the subject. But we should stress Freud's affirmation: 'something appears in their place which, *in an individual*, we describe as a character-trait'. In the isolated individual it stands out, it *seems* to be something personal, *its* character; in reality, as we will see, it is a social and collective determination.

Indeed, the character-traits that Freud indicates are those that correspond to the anal eroticism, where the interest in the function of excretion by reason of its corporeal organs and products transforms itself into the sense of saving, order, and cleanliness.

What does Freud show? That the external cultural distance disappears in the ignorance of an interior distance: the transition from nature to culture is completed in the subjugated subject. The articulation hides the history of its own body, which only the breach of madness allows us to catch a glimpse of. *And precisely these essential traits, which lay the foundation for the subject's personality, are the ones that coincide with the fundamental traits of civilisation described by Freud.* The subject, in its most profound subjective modality, in the very essence of its being, coincides with the culture in which it was produced, but to which it was also essentially adapted. The structure of the subject shows its analogy with the structure of civilisation:

> Now we have seen that order and cleanliness are important requirements of civilisation, although their vital necessity is not very apparent, any more than their suitability as sources of enjoyment. At this point we cannot fail to be struck by the similarity between the process of civilisation and the libidinal development of the individual. (97)

This means: civilisation conforms the body *by analogy*, it imprints its form onto the instincts, and this form is analogous, in its libidinal structure, to the form with which civilisation organises material life.

The cultural transformation here leaves no residue in the body: it appears *as if* culture were natural. Only when it is exacerbated does it jump out as a character-trait. The anal conduct, which is the pivot where being is articulated with having, prolongs itself, as we have seen, in the habit of hoarding (money), the sense of order and cleanliness. They are, then, behaviours of repetition (order) and rational organisation of the world that cling to such traits (practices and theories derived from them), but together with a form of *having* from which the index of the human form has disappeared.

2d Cultural Technique: The Instincts Displaced. Sublimation

> Other instincts [besides anal erotism] are induced to displace the conditions for their satisfaction, to lead them into other paths. In most cases this process coincides with that of the *sublimation* (of instinctual aims) with which we are familiar, but in some it can be differentiated from it. Sublimation of instinct is an especially conspicuous feature of cultural development; it is what makes it possible for higher psychical activities, scientific, artistic or ideological, to play such an important part in civilised life. (97)

Let us recall that Freud, in the previous chapter, showed that science, art, and philosophy were cunning devices to elude the reality of the external world.

> In this, sublimation of the instincts lends its assistance. One gains the most if one can sufficiently heighten the yield of pleasure from the sources of psychical and intellectual work. When that is so, fate can do little against one. (79)

We might suppose therefore that there is a science and an art that are the products of sublimation, which displaces the conditions for the satisfaction of the instincts. There is also pleasure in the substitution of the impulse: pleasure in work itself, that is to say, in productivity. Pleasure in work is here therefore pleasure in avoiding pain: if we work well, 'fate can do little against one'. There would be a science developed in order not to confront the obstacle that the instinctive impulse encounters in reality. The recourse to sublimation deviates *both the subjective impulse and the objective means* that culture produced in order to face the obstacle that places itself between the satisfaction and the object. Now not even the means for confronting the difficulty appears in its true meaning: from means it turns into the end, and we find enjoyment and pleasure in its secondary exercise. This is, clearly, the scientism that we analysed earlier.

In this way sublimation, though 'an especially conspicuous feature of cultural development', covers up the true meaning of culture or civilisation: it produces the scission between the spiritual and the material, and the distance is maintained between one process and the other. This is why Freud told us earlier:

> At present we can only say figuratively that such satisfactions seem 'finer and higher'. But their intensity is mild as compared with that derived from the sating of crude and primary instinctual impulses; it does not convulse our physical being. (79–80)

And this is so because, as Freud indicates in another work, these impulses that are developed in the activity of sublimation are precisely those that have not been integrated in the definitive form of genitality. They are, then, the impulses that have not been elaborated, those that culture left without integration:

> The forces that can be employed for cultural activities are thus to a great extent obtained through the suppression of what are known as the perverse elements of sexual excitation. ("'Civilised' Sexual Morality and Modern Nervous Illness', SE 9: 189)

These are the sexual energies that remain linked to the ego, thanks to which the libido desexualises itself and comes to be used by the ego in the service of its own apparent coherence: in the service of 'the unity, or tendency to unity, which is particularly characteristic of the ego' (*The Ego and the Id*, SE 19: 45). Sublimation, as Laplanche and Pontalis also indicate, 'depends to a high degree on the narcissistic dimension of the ego, and consequently the object of sublimated activity may be expected to display the same appearance of a beautiful whole which Freud here assigns to the ego'.[3]

This 'technique', taken up by civilisation as if its creative character depended on it, is put into question by Freud:

> If one were to yield to a first impression, one would say that sublimation is a vicissitude which has been forced upon the instincts entirely by civilisation. But it would be wiser to reflect upon this a little longer. (97)

> *3d Cultural Technique*: The Instincts Unsatisfied. Cultural Frustration

On the surface this seems to be the most general mechanism, as it is also the one most evident to all.

> ... it is impossible to overlook the extent to which civilisation is built up upon a renunciation of instinct, how much it presupposes precisely the non-satisfaction (by suppression, repression or some other means?) of powerful instincts. This 'cultural frustration' dominates the large field of social relationships between human beings. As we already know, it is the cause of the hostility against which all civilisations have to struggle. (97)

Civilisation frustrates, but it frustrates precisely that which it also excites. Frustration happens with regard to that which was present in all of us as needing to reach its satisfaction: the unsatisfied desire. It is precisely 'the degree' to which civilisation actually makes frustration necessary that we must understand. The question that returns here once more is the one that Freud formulated from the very beginning: Must civilisation *necessarily* be frustrating? And Freud looks for the answer in 'the large field of social relationships between human beings', that is to say, in *that historical obstacle which depends on human beings themselves*. Here it is neither the external world nor one's own body that is present: what becomes evident here is the degree to which human beings historically have elaborated the need for frustration as that which characterises the world

---

3 Laplanche and Pontalis 1973, p. 433.

of culture or civilisation. And the implicit counter-question appears: Must all civilisation be frustrating? Or are we making an essential condition out of what is only the result of *one* civilisation, precisely the one that turned its form of the human into the absolute, that is to say, an *anthropomorphic civilisation or culture*, which is to say, *ours*?

But here lies 'the cause of the hostility against which all civilisations have to struggle' (97), as if all civilisation actually presupposed this. We already saw, however, the origin of this hostility: Christianity and the discovery of neurosis. Freud is telling us, then, that this cultural frustration is such only for a culture in which the dualism, the separation of body and spirit, constitutes the essence of its whole process: this is its 'prior condition'. And he tells us that this culture will find it impossible to offer a self-critique as long as these presuppositions, which condition the life of human beings in the vast field of their relationships, are not also brought to the fore and transformed. These presuppositions must be analysed by putting civilisation in relation to the historical origin: the transition from nature, which appears as a hidden presupposition.

And the understanding of the first two mechanisms, of the instincts *used up and sublimated*, must serve as the foundation for analysing the last ones: the instincts *unsatisfied*, the frustration that did not include them as part of what civilisation elaborated and on the basis of which its power actually is built. These, then, are the levels where the essence of the human being affirms itself as if they were natural instincts. They constitute the place where culture *used up and sublimated nature*, and they must be understood first in order for us later, starting from this understanding, to analyse the frustration and discontent present in civilisation:

> It is not easy to understand how it can become possible to deprive an instinct of satisfaction. ... But if we want to know what value can be attributed to our view that the development of civilisation is a special process, *comparable to the normal maturation of the individual*, we must clearly attack another problem. We must ask ourselves to *what influences the development of civilisation owes its origin*, how it arose, and by what its course has been determined. (97–97, emphasis added)

Thus the nonrepressive cultural form implies a process whose historical meaning must not be excluded from the human being who makes the transition. In the normal maturation of the individual there must be present a general condition that civilisation, as a collective process, presupposes. History is not a process centred on *one* subject, on *one* human form considered to be absolute: whence the refusal to understand its meaning on the basis of an anthropocentrism that situated the human being as *separated and defined in its essence* as absolute.

IV   The Historical Foundation of the Lack of Discernment

1   *From the Negation of Originary Violence to Christian Love*

To be able to discern reality: this is the personal capacity that was undercut in the subject as a result of its indiscriminate access to civilisation. The collective lack of discernment, which is historical and characteristic of the adult, is based on the individual lack of discernment, which is unconscious and infantile, characteristic of the child that gains access to culture, whereby the first ratifies the second in an agreement that makes a destiny out of a transition that needs to be understood.

This transition in need of understanding, which must be included in the content that culture elaborates and in the forms of order with which it is organised, is what Freud wants to return to the subject in order to think the latter's relation to civilisation.

To explain this Freud proposes an original situation in the transition from nature to culture. There, in contrast to the present, sexual love appears united to work, not separated from it. He begins from the attempt to understand how the process of separation between the two, in which Western civilisation culminates, must have had its beginning in an *equivocal transition*. The adult world of civilisation or culture in which we find ourselves shows, as its endpoint, the culmination of a development that *prolonged and emphasised to the extreme limit this initial equivocalness* that the historical process would have had to rectify.

Freud starts from the *primitive* or *primordial* human beings whose communitarian unity was the natural family. The relations among families were collaborative. In this way, after the family, collaborative work constitutes the other great achievement of human beings: the fact that their neighbour would work *with them or against them*. Non-collaboration implied war; collaboration, friendship. This was the field in which relations were defined *beyond the family*, prolonging the decision of permanence between the sexes alongside the permanence working the earth. From pastoral nomadism to settled communities: the settlement of the family on the land presupposes the settlement in the relations of collaboration with others. The transition from intermittency to permanence in the relations among the sexes, which takes place in function of the evolution of sexual satisfaction, also prolongs itself in the relationship among human beings through cooperative work.

> After primal man had discovered that it lay in his own hands, literally, to improve his lot on earth by working, it cannot have been a matter of indifference to him whether another man worked with or against him. The other man acquired the value for him of a fellow-worker, with whom it was useful to live together. (99)

The relation with other human beings is one of *usefulness* in function of work, and collaboration occurs for the sake of production. With regard to the relation to women, on the other hand, the transition from intermittency to permanence has other motives, where the presence of the other appears especially in the couple:

> One may suppose that the founding of families was connected with the fact that a moment came when the need for genital satisfaction no longer made its appearance like a guest who drops in suddenly, and, after his departure, is heard of no more for a long time, but instead took up its quarters as a permanent lodger. When this happened, the male acquired a motive for keeping the female, or, speaking more generally, his sexual objects, near him; while the female, who did not want to be separated from her helpless young, was obliged, in their interests, to remain with the stronger male. (99)

However, neither work in collaboration (usefulness) nor the permanence of the family (genitality) exhaustively defines civilisation. They only put us on the 'threshold of human civilisation'. This is why Freud adds:

> In this primitive family one essential feature of civilisation is still lacking. The arbitrary will of its head, the father, was unrestricted. (99–100)

Here a second historical creation appears, which is specific and fundamental. Without it, the origin of civilisation would be incomprehensible, for it 'led from this family to the succeeding stage of communal life': the one that goes from the primitive horde to the fraternal alliance (100). As we will see in the chapter devoted to *Group Psychology and the Analysis of the Ego*, this transition means not only to move from one community to another, from the horde to the alliance, but also to pass from the quasi-natural individuality – the head and father of unlimited power – to the cultural individuality. In this way cultural individuality emerges only as the result of a new communal relationship. It is no longer the usefulness of work that ties human beings together, but the liberation from the dominion that the omnipotent father exerted over all of them.

Freud signals this as the *essential element* in the transition from the primitive to the civilised human being. The fundamental relationship on the basis of which work develops, as well as the possibility of the cultural couple, is the product of this fraternal alliance. Here the dominated sons give death to the despot in the form of a new cooperation, no longer referred only to work, since it implies the transition from being dominated to being free, from being natural individuals to being cultural individuals. Before, genital satisfaction was for the few; now it is for all; before, the product of labour was for the omnipotent chief-father; now the product is for all.

This transition, Freud tells us, implies that one maintains within civilisation, as the form that regulates the existence of human beings amongst themselves, the rigid precepts of the murdered father, whose death the sons, out of guilt, could not confront and integrate as the foundation of their subsequent relationships. The transition meant the death of the most hated and the most beloved being, and it is this permanence as the installation of the super-ego that determines the field of consciousness and the relationships that are thought and regulated among human beings. By negating the foundation – by negating the murder – that gave them their origin and opened them onto a new freedom, by denying the violence and death at the origin of their new relations of pleasure and satisfaction, they prolonged in the world of culture and civilisation the split form that, now in the midst of satisfaction, kept being imposed on them and corresponded to repression, non-satisfaction, and domination. The new pleasure thus was split from the pain on which it was based: it veiled its historical advent as pleasure and cultural love, whose meaning depends on a precise sense of pain and hatred.

> The taboo-observances were the first 'right' or 'law'. (101)

Thus, the paternal prohibition is prolonged, thanks to the super-ego, in the order of law and shows the persistence in culture of the repressive power against which precisely it was set up in order to count as civilisation. What is negated by culture turns into its unconscious foundation, and continues to rule over the new field with the categories of the old one:

> The communal life of human beings had, therefore, a two-fold foundation: the compulsion to work, which was created by external necessity, and the power of love, which made the man unwilling to be deprived of his sexual object – the woman – and made the woman unwilling to be deprived of the part of herself which had been separated off from her – her child. (101)

What was revealed as *the only foundation*, the fraternal alliance against the paternal power in order to reach genital satisfaction in that first collaboration in which the brothers discovered their being subjected in common, now appears once again dissociated: acquiring 'a two-fold foundation', Freud's text says literally. *On one side*, work; *on the other*, love. By covering up the murder, the violence as origin, they cover up at the same time the foundation of civilisation and they internalise and prolong in it the previous separation. The separation between the natural legality (predominance of the natural individual as chief-father) and the cultural legality (the rule of law) is the result of the historical concealment of the *violent* and collective passage from nature to culture. And as a result it preserves, in this new form, the separation that is not integrative but dissociative, between
– cooperation (fraternal alliance) and useful work;
– culture and nature;
– pleasure and pain;
– individual and collective;
– historical order and absolutised rule of law.

Thus, in the very transition from nature to culture a separation is produced by hiding the meaning of the process from those who are part thereof as its continuation. There is a meaning present at the origin, a foundation on which this passage is based: it inaugurates the human significance of history. This signification is repressed, and this repressed implies the dissociation of the instincts in their cultural prolongation. This is why we interrogate the past on the basis of the present.

> Eros and Ananke [Love and Necessity] have become the parents of human civilisation too. The first result of civilisation was that even a fairly large number of people were now able to live together in a community. And since these two great powers were co-operating in this, one might expect that the further development of civilisation would proceed smoothly towards an even better control over the external world and towards a further extension of the number of people included in the community. Nor is it easy to understand how this civilisation could act upon its participants otherwise than to make them happy. (101)

It is not easy to understand our present unhappiness, but some things we already know. Cooperation remained, like before the transition, as if only usefulness united us. Genital satisfaction remained, like before the transition, as the satisfaction that does not come from the collective and only corresponds to an individual decision: that of the powerful male. The new relations, which are already cultural, since they produced this essential fact which is the 'band of brothers', remain inscribed as they were before, as natural and individual. Their collective sense continues to be unconscious.

But this separation was not without consequences. To hide the origin meant to hide the transition as the violent prolongation from the natural to the cultural: to elevate onto the *absolute* the significations that from the body were elaborated towards reality. It meant not being able to account for the origin of norms or for the logical order in which consciousness, extending itself, was able to think. In this way the aspiration to happiness of the members seemed to have found the ideal solution: genital satisfaction and mastery over nature. Except that the cultural logic also proceeds in the element of material truth, and the historical truth must adapt itself to this. Happiness was sought after without consideration of what necessarily was found at its origin, and this point of departure constitutes its truth, both in its painful and in its pleasurable aspects. But this initial truth, by being hidden, implies the parallel concealment of the extension of consciousness and its norms in the midst of the legal order. The repressed is kept, Freud tells us, and it is in the element of memory that the truth of the body and of human relationships is elaborated. There is no elaboration of the truth of the external world if in this process we do not prolong the truth of the historical process that constituted us as subjects. Because what we hid is dynamically present, preserved in the kind of identification with which we proceed to give life to it, based on the initial upsurge. And that which we thus preserve lives off our lives: the pain that we deny outwards, the pain of that being whom we loved so much, continues to talk to us, with its full voice, from within: we could not bear for it to die completely and in exchange for its life we finally gave it ours.

2   *From Violence to Pleasure*

This pain of the historical origin that we do not wish to suffer will nevertheless determine the strict historical meaning of our pleasure. Here the contradiction explodes: we must continue to pursue an unreachable individual form of happiness, because we hid the presence of the fraternal alliance, the violent transition to reality, which made it possible to reach genital pleasure. We forgot, or never knew, that the conquest of maximum pleasure was linked to the production of maximum pain: that of the collective murder of the father who was opposed to our life. And it is this dead father who hides, together with the pain, the key to gain access to the cultural reality in which we search in vain, once again, for pleasure without pain. And this is why, as we saw, it ends up only in the search for non-pain.

From this analysis we can infer that *what is essentially repressed is the violent collective determination, the fraternal alliance, which necessarily lies at the origin of my individual existence*. This is why happiness can appear as if it were a personal affair: because the social signification of my most individual relation is hidden.

And Freud continues his relentless description by showing how genital sexuality, though it is the prototype of all happiness, does not for this reason allow us to reach happiness itself. We said it before: sexuality contains, in the adult, the social significance of its exercise. We will have a chance to see, in *Group Psychology*, the problem with the 'normal', narcissistic way of falling in love. But here Freud once again places it necessarily at our point of departure:

> We said there that man's discovery that sexual (genital) love afforded him the strongest experiences of satisfaction, and in fact provided him with the prototype of all happiness, must have suggested to him that he should continue to seek the satisfaction of happiness in his life along the path of sexual relations and that he should make genital erotism the central point of his life. (101)

This means that the form of sexual love is the unsublimatable ground from where all pleasure derives as from its most profound source. Here the form of the human requires the form of the other in the most exalted fusion of the flesh. This one-to-one coincidence is that from which all cultural meaning is derived, if we know how to find the origin of all difference and the source of all enjoyment there where this sexual enjoyment itself is already social enjoyment: opened up in the field that the others draw for us.

But this form, while being the most pleasurable, is at the same time the most dangerous:

> ... doing so he made himself dependent in a most dangerous way on a portion of the external world, namely, his chosen love-object (101)

Only before the chosen love-object? In a manner of speaking: the love object implies, in its presence, the persistent presence of the dead father against the backdrop of whom our pleasure is perennially inscribed. Guilt increases in the face of his power, which we bring back to life in the activation of desire, and this dependence on the object becomes aggrandised: the risk of losing the love object is linked to the impotence of truly approximating it, of including it completely in our pleasure. There is a distance that we want to cross in the most profound proximity to the sexual couple. But this distance is a distance that only loosens, develops and extends itself into the field of the world in which the norms of the super-ego prolong themselves. The sphere of the couple depicts the field of a mirage whose hallucinated counterpart is the 'oceanic feeling' of being-one-with-the-whole. Being one with the whole becomes confused with being-one-with-the-one: narcissism. Pleasure is a middle term, which stops just there where the source of pain comes back to life, provoked by the presence of the other whom we had to kill in order to obtain pleasure:

> ... and exposed himself to extreme suffering if he should be rejected by that object or should lose it through unfaithfulness or death. (101)

Unfaithfulness and death. This is what, as a son, he was to the father, and which led him to kill him: unfaithful and murderous. Like that of the son, all love would appear to be unfaithful and murderous. And all love renders gigantic, on the outside, one's own guilt, on the inside.

Thus the love for the other sex appears against the backdrop of the death of the father. The prototype of all happiness is overrun by pain: what its flesh promises is the unreachable pleasure, because at the source of its pleasure there is pain. All love comes close to incest, they say, but since one actually is a lawbreaker, all love comes close to murder. And all love finds death again there where it pretended to have eluded it: because at the origin of the unsatisfied desire there is the negation of the father, which interposes itself, as an enormous NO. So there are two paths: either to enjoy the alternation of nocturnal and clandestine pleasure, and finding the daily pain of work with which we pay for the social right to infraction, or else to reach a transaction on the basis of the super-ego's conscience blown out of proportion to the point of intolerable guilt – to dilute the flesh as the object of love and ratify in the spirit the life that the dead father continues to live in each one of us, in spite of the fact that as real flesh and body he lost his life – because of us. Thus, universal love becomes diluted into indiscrimination, the sensible presence that saves us the guilt of a death which, with this cunning, becomes converted via conscience into life. The life that we suppress outwards in reality, we restore in the memory of the dead father in our deepest intimacy.

> A small minority are enabled by their constitution to find happiness, in spite of everything, along the path of love. But far-reaching mental changes in the function of love are necessary before this can happen. These people make themselves independent of their object's acquiescence by displacing what they mainly value from being loved on to loving; they protect themselves against the loss of the object by directing their

love, not to single objects but to all men alike; and they avoid the uncertainties and disappointments of genital love by turning away from its sexual aims and transforming the instinct into an impulse with an *inhibited aim*. (101–2, emphasis in the original)

This form of love coincides with the form in which the primordial father loved his children, there where the cultural individuality did not yet exist: with 'equal love', for 'all men alike'. The father's love did not discriminate: it was a natural love. But he dominated with his love, because he jealously kept the women for himself. This new love of the guilty son encounters and fulfils the two impositions of the father: equal love, like he wanted, but without sex, as he prohibited. The son can *be* the same as the father (affectively) but he cannot *have* the same as the father (the phallus and the woman). Only thanks to this dematerialisation, this devitalisation, and this desexualisation can the son save himself, in the relation of submission to the one whom he nevertheless assassinated: denying his own impulse.

Here the truth lies in the corporeal feeling and texture whose only content is the mental field left to the subject by an external reality that has been subjectivised as spirit and negated as matter. In the loving spiritualism there is only the materiality of affect, and the field of one's own body. It is necessary to mark off the body as index of all external signification. The body, in its qualitative power of discernment, ceases to be the index of the world. But then what is left in it is what was left behind as absolute: the father, culture, teachers – the super-ego.

Consider the solution: 'These people make themselves independent of their object's acquiescence'. Of the two poles in the relation, the subject and the object, only one remains: the object vanishes into indetermination, into the absence of any quality. There is no more extreme in the world in which my relationship becomes verified, because I fill it with my fantasy. I myself as subject and object: one as regulator of all, part and whole at the same time. The experience of 'being loved', as a bad experience, is not assumed as such in the real vicissitudes of the world: it is converted, separated from the precise and situated presence of the incarnated other, into *universally good*. The hatred of the object comes to be converted into the love of all objects alike. But the only flesh that senses that a unique object is one's own covers with its sensibility its own form – and that of the other, which was contained in oneself. One's own is the only salvific flesh: the only qualitative attribute. What is determined by a precise hatred, which is not assumed, passes over in this negation into the abstract universality of love for all. And the deviation of the sexual aim is the rubric that comes to seal this disincarnation: 'a state of evenly suspended, steadfast, affectionate feeling', outside of time and space, mere mental domain.

But, Freud tells us, this love 'derives' from genital love: precisely from that which this new love pretends to negate. It is not a love that would stem from a presumed 'spiritual' capacity; it is a love that lost its flesh:

> What they bring about in themselves in this way is a state of evenly suspended, steadfast, affectionate feeling, which has little external resemblance any more to the stormy agitations of genital love, from which it is nevertheless derived. (102)

The external resemblance disappears: the procession moves inwards, it is internal. In this way the 'love of humanity' can be the result of a good or bad sublimation. Bad, if it depends on an impulse inhibited in its aim. Good, if it *maintains* the impulse. Wherein lies the difference? In the fact that the libidinal prolongation, by passing from one concrete relation to other much broader ones, maintains in this transition the *real* character of the object to which love aims. Love then ceases to be 'universal'. Even more: there is no actual love of humanity. There exists a precise love for precise beings, from where its signification prolongs itself to the point of encompassing, in the kind of rationality that thereby is discovered, the social rationality, that of the system on which this precise love or hatred is based. Thus, we not only have a theoretical formalism in the rationality that unfolds itself from the body all the way to include civilisation as the field of totality. The libidinal body, which the world of culture or civilisation contradictorily orders in its being as sentient flesh, is the content of every form of thought, of every abstraction. Rationality extends itself starting from this matrix of every relation that is the sexual relationship all the way to encompass the class struggle. Freud himself signals as much in *Group Psychology*: there are groups that deserve to be repudiated, artificial groups with whom it is a mistake or a falsehood to identify, like the Church or the bourgeois army. And there are groups who are the vehicles of the meaning of history, like the revolutionary masses. This is the sense of the popular as opposed to the official privileged groups. There is thus in Freud a dialectic at the core of history through which the body circulates, preserving the material significations that emerge from it. And there is another dialectic through which the 'spirit' circulates, but spirit defined in the official sense, which is based on the domination of the body of others.

This domination, as we see, is not an individual technique. It is a social technique that we discover, which means that the subjective transformation implies as its correlate the necessary objective verification, in the others, of my truth, presented as the highest. What began as a way of eluding the pain of the assassin, and the collective guilt for having killed the father, was in reality an act of cowardice and oriented by the search for pleasure: pleasure without pain. Why would it not extend itself to all of reality, prolonging this deceptive transaction, which at bottom searches for the infinitude of enjoyment against all, given that it already exerted this pain against the one it loved the most? Let us not fool ourselves, Freud tells us: in the most spiritualist and saintly attitude what presents itself of necessity as its most fundamental meaning is the pleasure to which everything is sacrificed. *The problem*, which this time is already social, *is to know upon whom objectively speaking the pain that thus is being eluded bounces back.*

3 *Christian Love, Technique for Suffering*
Let us take a closer look. Freud has the following to say about the official, Christian or Western love:

> Perhaps St. Francis of Assisi went furthest in thus exploiting love for the benefit of an inner feeling of happiness. Moreover, what we have recognised as one of the techniques for fulfilling the pleasure principle has often been brought into connection with religion (102)

With the appearance of this type of love, as with every discovery, the individual case gives way to a collective use. Love, as we saw already, appears as a personal discovery: thanks to it, St. Francis manages to reach only 'an inner feeling of happiness'. This is no more than a 'technique' and one to be 'exploited': it does not prolong itself from the body outward. Here love is no more than a prosthesis, albeit a 'spiritual' one. But at the same time as it pours out over *all the living*, it does so only in order to annul their differences: in order to annul the living as differentiated source of stimuli, and killing it in the very same moment when it proclaims and in its fatal embrace swears by its love. If life is precisely difference, then this 'technique' of conceptual love annuls all the articulations of the organicity of the world and of human beings.

> ... the distinction between the ego and objects or between objects themselves is neglected (102)

And this 'individual form' is proclaimed, qua ethical norm, as the regulative form that ought to determine all social conduct:

> According to one ethical view, whose deeper motivation will become clear to us presently, this readiness for a universal love of mankind and the world represents the highest standpoint which man can reach. (102)

In reality what is obtained through this attitude, which civilisation considers 'the highest standpoint'? The most despicable and false of all relations to the world and to others. The subjective salvation, from the moment it reaches what is apparently the highest, most just, most absolute, and most loving totality, shows at the same time its determination for the most abject, the most unjust, the most relative, and the most odious:

> A love that does *not discriminate* seems to me to forfeit a part of its own value, by *doing an injustice to its object*; and secondly, not all men are worthy of love. (102, emphasis added).

In the act of being more just and more loving toward the object, I commit before this same object my act of greatest injustice: I do not see it in its difference relative to reality. I use it, as prolongation of my technique, to procure my *sensation* of subjective happiness without giving any importance to its material qualitative significance as situated in the real world. It is the support for my need for which it does not really function as other.

But if we say with Freud that not all human beings are worthy of being loved, *then hatred is, as much as love, a discriminating index of the rationality of the world and of reality*. Here the problem, as we will see, is the role played by social models that act as mediators between the family and the social system, as an *alternation between the clandestine and the tolerated*. Let us retain therefore these characteristics, which are the results of love for spiritual humanity:
- nondiscernment of the other as other
- nondiscernment of the objects among themselves
- nondiscernment of the material and qualitative structure of reality
- nondiscernment of the different realms of social reality.

It is not surprising that Freud, after describing this model of love that is desexualised, undiscerned, and unjust, goes back to trying to understand *what happened historically with the original family that inaugurated history*: that of the fraternal alliance.

> The love which founded the family continues to operate in civilisation both in its original form, in which it does not renounce direct sexual satisfaction, and in its modified form as aim-inhibited affection. In each, it continues to carry on its function of binding together considerable numbers of people, and it does so in a more intensive fashion than can be effected through the interest of work in common. (102)

The family is *now situated* as a minimal community vis-à-vis another global community: that of work governed by utility. The community of the family, contradictory of the community of work. The first regulated by the form of genital sexual love; the second regulated only by usefulness, from which the presence of the other, as another being with needs, disappears into the relations of labour. On the basis of the family, which finds support in the form of genital love, a relation extends itself that tends to unite the other human beings as 'aim-inhibited affection', from which the body of the other as real and distinct presence disappears so as to appear in its mere existence as 'labour power'. Freud thus once again encounters the duplicity of our system of production: personal relations among persons, but only within the bosom of the family; impersonal relations among human beings as mere bearers of labour power, but in that social organisation in which only utility unites them. Yet the important thing to note is that *there happened a historical separation between the aim-inhibited affection and the aim-inhibited instinct.*

> Love with an inhibited aim was in fact originally fully sensual love, and it is so still in man's unconscious. (102–3)

In the family the libidinal conflict or bodily encounter of the life instinct Eros continues, which when it turns into 'aim-inhibited affection' does not suspend its signification against the backdrop of the sexuated plenitude of the body of the other: it only substitutes it with another sexuated being in which the love relation thus constituted is prolonged. This is why its function, which is that of binding together the greatest number of people (a *considerable* number of people, says Freud), is the one that should prolong itself in all the other cultural relations in which human beings, from the family onward, become included. But *at the origin* that which now is separated was also what was united in the relations of work in the fraternal alliance, since the work relations prolonged the relations among the brothers who had conquered sexuality. The brotherhood in labour prolonged the brotherhood of those who, separating themselves from the natural individuality, discovered themselves as brothers in the cultural collectivity that conferred on them a new individuality, the product of that originary and inaugural act in common of history.

But now this is no longer the case: in the work of capitalist society the dissociation between body and spirit typical of Christianity culminates in the form of technology, but technology as encompassing all orders of life: *techniques* in the spiritual domination of humanity and *techniques* in the material domination of production. Thus we see how the technique of subjective domination for eluding reality without confronting death appears as a technique of collective domination of unsatisfied subjectivities, subjects who are condemned, in the perseverance of work, to nonsatisfaction. And these subjectivities form part of the ones that become activated in the control of the relations of work, from which the significant body of the other disappeared as meaningful to production. Just as in the family the human-form is maintained, but individualistically, so too in the relations of production the commodity-form predominates, but socially. The clash of bodies which in Marx is prolonged in the 'common body' of the community and inorganic nature, appears disguised when it is capital that predominates. Here the definitive rupture becomes consolidated, in the separation between work and love, of the primitive unity of love united to production. The first historical production is the production of human beings in the fraternal alliance, that is, the first historical production appears as a *production of men as brothers*. This first act of historical production included within it both the relations of genital love and the relations of labour over nature, *and from this act every relation to reality took its meaning*. Insofar as it expressed the cultural surplus that the human being had to create in order to prolong, for all, that which in the relations of natural dominion appeared only as scarcity or lack: lack of genital satisfaction, in the dominion of the most powerful natural individual, the father; lack of satisfaction in the production of goods and, therefore, in the dominion over nature. Thus, it becomes clear that among the three types of relations that Freud distinguishes vis-à-vis reality, *it is the relations of human beings among themselves that give meaning to all the other relations that appear to confront humanity: with one's own body and with external nature*.

There occurred, then, a historical rupture. This was the creation of a contradiction, which distorted the initial setup:

> But in the course of development the relation of love to civilisation loses its unambiguity. On the one hand love comes into opposition to the interests of civilisation; on the other, civilisation threatens love with substantial restrictions. (103)

The beginning of civilisation presented love and work in the unicity of a fraternal relationship: sexual love prolonged itself in affectionate feelings, without concealing its origin. But the seeds of dissolution were present for those in whom guilt, in the unconscious, impeded this unity in which pleasure, even though it was linked to the reality of the obstacle, concealed in its superficial pain that more profound pain from whence it came: from the killing of the father. This false solution formed by 'a small minority', *which distanced itself as much from work as from the opposite sex*, was subsequently used by the dominant classes, *which did not distance themselves from the results of labour or from the pleasures of women*. It was thus converted into the system of domination to subtract that portion of materiality which, as an immediately collective surplus tied to the others through work, allowed the brothers now once again dominated to remain without guilt in the genital satisfaction only within the family. Such indeed is the individualistic solution of those who, against the backdrop of the real existence of the historical community, *pretend as though they were outside the community while remaining inside of it*. And this becomes the model for solutions in which the initial contradiction is not confronted but merely avoided in the technical quest for a desexualisation. This is how, as we saw, the form of the natural father once again comes to constitute a regulating model for cultural relations. But even though the model of the solution – the ascetic saint – involves an individual transaction which totally sacrifices the body in order to gratify itself in the spirit, for the majority of those who maintain the reality of the system of production this model can only appear as an objective transaction and not only a subjective one, as happens with the saint. *The objective transaction, in which pleasure is reconciled without the pain that engendered it, is work*. Work would be the mediator between the partial satisfaction of genitality within the family and the sacrifice, which we have to make, out of the guilt for still having held on to this enjoyment. And it is in this socially obligatory act, the act of production, where the law of the ancestral father is recognised as absolute, while being only historical. Except that now this law works in the service of the dominant system of production. Just as the subjective transaction of St. Francis reaches already, in one fell swoop, the infinitude of his belonging to the kingdom of the Father and makes himself, in his image and resemblance, like him (a psychosis which is necessarily individual), this descending model only in the realm of labour reaches the transaction between the subjective and the objective (collective neurosis) which still keeps it in reality, albeit contradictorily. It is indeed here that the men who did not renounce the enjoyment in genitality (in the family) pay with their labour for the infraction that the system conceded to them, as if its law had come from the Father himself. In the realm of labour the Father becomes the objective transaction of subjective terror, and society, which prolongs this terror, authorises in common this 'technical' solution of the contradiction.

4   *The Concealment of the Contradiction between Love and Work*
In the place of the unity between love and work, which in terms of satisfaction stemmed from a determining collective act (the fraternal alliance), now the dissolution of this unity produces as result a *contradiction between love and work*, but this conflict is not legible as such insofar as we are taught this lesson only *as if it were a contradiction between love and civilisation*. Freud's first theory

of the drives is based on this contradiction. Love and work, inasmuch as they are separated, do not appear in our civilisation as contradictory: for it is precisely their separation that constitutes the foundation recognised as 'normal'. All that appears is the contradiction, whose meaning is lost in the lack of discernment, as love and civilisation: as the necessary unhappiness to which all culture or civilisation perforce must lead us. This is why Freud at the beginning said that Christianity is inscribed in the anti-civilisational current: it rejects precisely that which previously it destroyed. And it rejects this with the argument that its result, which is unhappiness, is something essential to this earthly life, given that it is this earthly life itself that produces us as unhappy beings. Freud's struggle is titanic: he must confront the most powerful power that for centuries insidiously – every sickness is insidious – organised civilisation, and he must do so by recognising and discerning, by undoing the hardened crust of the impossibility to think that which civilisation itself segregated in order to keep it under its control.

But civilisation can do so because this meaning, though split, subsists in the unconscious and in the earthliness of sexuality which, in this case effectively, cannot be eradicated. Unsublimated sexuality is the matrix of all cultural life. At the extreme end of its negation it can only reach a negotiation. It must allow life to engender life, humans to engender humans: for man and woman to remain as the originary meaning in which the repressed emerges in return, bringing back its forgotten but never destroyed truth-content. This meaning subsists and prolongs itself between the system of production and the human forms of relationship. Here Freud shows two extremes, both of which remain associated because both continue to be present as the form of every cultural equation: *human beings will always maintain the form of man-woman, of sexual life, as the prototype of all happiness*. But by imbricating itself with the global system of civilisation, this relation appears negated, though also utilised in order to keep it in place. Religion shows most fully *this transition from the personal to the civilisational as a passage in which we must leave the sexuated body as index both of the transition and of the truth of the transition*. This body, which they leave to us only in the clandestine life of love regulated within the individual couple; this body whose excessive libido does not find a human form in which to prolong itself, given that the relations of fraternity have been excluded; *this body which is thus abandoned is the one that consumes itself in the labour ordered in the capitalist system of production as form of domination*. This discord introduces, as in any transaction, the impossibility of fully loving one another in the sexual form and by impeding the transition to its discernible inclusion in the social structure that produced us: the love of humanity.

We therefore must be clear in signalling a central distinction in Freud:

- 'impulse inhibited in its aim' (p. 48): the most dramatic example of which is the Christian love for all, from which sexual corporeality has been excluded;
- 'affection inhibited in its aim' (p. 48): the love which gives up on taking the mother or the father as genital love object but continues to subsist as impulse and subsequently gives itself another sexual object. Here we have the transition and development of the libido: the primordial object, man or woman, remains. The nurturing Woman or the protective Man both continue in the form of the apposition.

But here it is important to retain the difference: in the '*affection* inhibited in its aim', the impulse is not negated but transformed, its mode of satisfaction is culturally organised and its object changed. By contrast, in the case of 'the *impulse* inhibited in its aim', the impulse itself, the instinctual push, is halted, held back, denied.

Thus, the libido that can develop itself in the family, and only in the family or else in friendships, as '*affection* inhibited in its aim', in the passage to the utilitarian relations of production in the workplace turns into '*impulse* inhibited in its aim'. The sexuated confrontation of bodies, the libido which has the form of the 'human', cannot extend itself in the domain of work. This means:

> Both – fully sensual love and aim-inhibited love – extend outside the family and create new bonds with people who before were strangers. (103)

The others do not appear as others in whom the 'humanity' of the family relations would extend themselves and encompass them as similar and different at the same time. They are only abstractions of human beings, merely empty forms from which all precise discernment has vanished. It is the prevalence of the abstract domain of love which, toward the lower end, corresponds to the domain of abstract and undifferentiated labour, in which the other is for me only qualitative wealth reduced to being a commodity, object of buying and selling in the service of absolutely selfish interests in which the transaction and economic exchange always imply the *opposition and utilisation of the other* for one's own benefit. Just as in love, they 'became independent from the consent of the object', so too in work they became independent from the consent of the worker. Christianity thus depicts the universal form of all negation: the social 'independence' with regard to the 'object', whatever form it may take, is in each case derived from this conception which constitutes the ideological base of all the others.

What began at the origin as the uniting of families amongst one another, which produced civilisation and the broader forms of association, culminates

CIVILISATION AND ITS DISCONTENTS 169

in the capitalist system as the opposition between the family and the system of production. This is a real opposition, though it seems *apparent* at first:

> This rift between them [civilisation and love] seems unavoidable. The reason for it is not immediately recognizable. It expresses itself at first as a conflict between the family and the larger community to which the individual belongs. (103)

This appearance takes shape from within the family that is already determined by the system of production that generated it as though the family were in contradiction with the system. But it is *its* family. And that which remains contradictory in it – namely, Eros, which aims 'to bring people together into large unities' – does not seem to discover the contradiction of the system that produced it, nor the internal meaning contained in its own family organisation:

> But the family will not give the individual up. (103)

Clearly, the individual of the family is precisely the one who repressed and ignores his collective origin, which made possible the formation of the family as the domain of genital enjoyment: the fraternal alliance. The individual is produced by the family as opposed to the larger society, in spite of having been determined by the latter from the origin. This origin is present in the transition from the primitive horde to the fraternal alliance, but is hidden in the end. This is why Freud can say:

> The mode of life in common which is phylogenetically the older, and which is the only one that exists in childhood, will not let itself be superseded by the cultural mode of life which has been acquired later. (103)

This means that the current capitalist family lives its organisation as if it were originary, as when it was the dominant social form at the origin of history. But what it does not comprehend is the development that from the familiar form of production led to the capitalist system of production. This form of the family is no longer the same: its meaning now appears only against the backdrop of the broader system that determines it, whose form is completely different from the one that would correspond to the family. But since we are all born into this form, with the family being the widest domain as seen from childhood, the need for the system to hide its meaning becomes confused with the appearance thanks to which the child gains access to the world of civilisation. The result is evident: in the false opposition that thus is created, the *mainten-*

ance of the family and of the forms derived from it *against* civilisation leads to an impasse and a state of ineffectiveness: combating the system is like combating oneself. This contradiction keeps the opposition always necessarily intact on a superficial level. As individuals who came from the bourgeois family, we are the firmest supporters of the system by maintaining ourselves as one of the *true* poles of a false contradiction.

The conception of work in turn impacts the life of sexuality; the impulses inhibited in their aim are a necessity of the system of production that prolongs itself from within the family. But this happens not only with the prohibition of incest, which would correspond to the affection inhibited in its aim, but also with the very drive of sexual love itself:

> ... the economic structure of the society also influences the amount of sexual freedom that remains. Here, as we already know, civilisation is obeying the laws of economic necessity, since a large amount of the psychical energy which it uses for its own purposes has to be withdrawn from sexuality. (104)

If we recall a quote from the *Introductory Lectures on Psycho-analysis*, we will see that this energy is diverted in the direction of work:

> The motive of human society is in the last resort an economic one; since it does not possess enough provisions to keep its members alive unless they work, it must restrict the number of its members and divert their energies from sexual activity to work. (*Introductory Lectures on Psychoanalysis*, SE 16: 312)

However, for Freud, it is not just any work, but the specific work of the capitalist system, which opens up the class struggle and the domination of one class over the other. It does so first in the mode of imposing repression:

> In this respect civilisation behaves towards sexuality as a people or a stratum of its population does which has subjected another one to its exploitation. (104)

But the strict rigour of our system has reached an endpoint in history:

> Fear of a revolt by the suppressed elements drives it to stricter precautionary measures. A high-water mark in such a development has been reached in our Western European civilisation. (104)

Thus, what began as unity between work and love ends up being an opposition in which we have witnessed the development, at its terminal endpoint, of a compromise between pleasure and pain. And we see the direction where Freud's explanation is heading: to show how guilt is instrumentalised in order to grant us a form of pleasure which, in its petty satisfaction within the family, leaves work as the social domain in which to purge the guilty satisfaction. The whole process, which tends to exclude pleasure from pain by separating it from its prolongation in reality, leads to duplicity in the form of our social organisation. The sphere of pleasure, opened up in the family but restricted to an individuality without history, hides its contradictory relation with global society. It is as if in the latter the pain of work and the domination of impersonal relations were not a necessary consequence that appears determined from within the family itself, produced by this very same system. And it hides the fact that this residual pleasure, which the family still maintains as its own, also runs the risk of being subtracted from it, or at least reduced to a technique of production in the service of the system as well:

> Present-day civilisation makes it plain that it will only permit sexual relationships on the basis of a solitary, indissoluble bond between one man and one woman, and that it does not like sexuality as a source of pleasure in its own right and is only prepared to tolerate it because there is so far no substitute for it as a means of propagating the human race. (105)

The amorous relationship is reduced within the system to an instrument without pleasure for the reproduction of the individuals. This is the terminal instrumentalisation of the system: from the point of view of our civilisation the capacity for love, which extends itself in the sexual act in the production of children, is reduced exclusively to the technical reproduction of human beings adapted to the production process.

v   The Negation of Aggressiveness

1   *The Couple, Double Individuality*

For Freud the contradiction between civilisation and sexuality appears as a contradiction between two fields, both of which are social:

1. The minimal field of the couple: a relation of two people from which any third is excluded.
2. The maximal field of global society, in which the largest possible number of people find themselves integrated.

In both fields we find Eros. But in the former, its goal is 'making one out of more than one' (108). There is thus an activity of Eros which, in the couple, seems to tend only towards the union of two already existent beings into one; and there is another function of Eros, whereby in the institutions, as we read earlier, 'life in common is ... made possible when a majority comes together' (95). We see how here, too, the meaning of Eros depends on the totality for which it strives: either a collective totality, in which the individual is part of the collective, or the totality of the couple, but fused into one.

One form of Eros encounters the collective extension of the historical process; the *same* Eros, which means the return to a fusion in which individuality is dissolved in the couple, requires by contrast an indiscriminate totality and a return to the destruction of historical individuality: it is opposed both to the collective and to the historical.

> When a love-relationship is at its height there is no room left for any interest in the environment; a pair of lovers are sufficient to themselves, and do not even need the child they have in common to make them happy. In no other case does Eros so clearly betray the core of its being, its purpose of making one out of more than one; but when it has achieved this in the proverbial way through the love of two human beings, it refuses to go further. (108, translation modified)

But this libido, which thus coils up inside the couple, is a libido halted in one moment of its cultural development:

> We have treated the difficulty of cultural development as a general difficulty of development by tracing it to the inertia of the libido, to its disinclination to give up an old position for a new one. (108)

In this way we have an opposition between Eros and Eros, as two moments of its development: the Eros halted in the couple, which does not 'give up an old position for a new one', and the Eros which extends itself in 'an even better control over the external world and towards a further extension of the number of people included in the community'. There is an intensive Eros and an extensive Eros.

Coming from the intensive Eros, that of the couple, we can imagine, as Freud does, a solution to the contradiction:

> So far, we can quite well imagine a cultural community consisting of double individuals like this, who, libidinally satisfied in themselves, are

connected with one another through the bonds of common work and common interests. If this were so, civilisation would not have to withdraw any energy from sexuality. But this desirable state of things does not, and never did, exist. (108)

The conclusion is obvious: this state of things does not, and never did, exist, because the couple is already, insofar as it is cultural, the result of the historical community that alone made it possible. But the couple acts *as if* this community that gave it existence – and continues to do so – did not exist as determining it as such. They join the others without extending their libido until they include them as part of this 'double individuality'. The double individuality is a form of narcissism for two, reflecting mirrors lost in the infinity of their complementary mutual reflections. History and the current system that made possible and produced this love are excluded. Therefore, if the others were not necessary for the love relation, when would the others appear as necessary? Only *afterwards*: for work, in a mere relation of utility. But we already saw that the very access to the form of man or woman implies the presence of the others in the process of production, in the process of producing them historically as human beings who conquered, by way of the fraternal alliance against the dominating father, the right to genitality. As a result this imaginary solution remains caught in the solipsistic illusion of narcissism. What is specific to civilisation is, from its origin and essentially, the inclusion of the others in oneself, the extension of consciousness as a quality of the body, the opening of a world of meaning that is part of our very own subjectivity. One already is, as we saw, the others. But if the origin of the process is not reanimated in each birth, bringing into relief the renewed fraternal alliance that must time and again remove the historical obstacle, the emergence within the family provides the human being, once again, with the pretence of his *individuality without other*, since he carries his own father, like his ancestors did with the primordial father, deep within himself. In the couple this individuality without others, and therefore without the cultural field and without the system of production, in the fusion with the other, man or woman, only returns really to that other, which underlies oneself as being-one-with-the-whole. For this reason, if beyond the couple we discover this necessity of the others as merely utilitarian, we encounter the others *too late*, only in the apparently 'external' relations of production. The latter, then, will mean production of things, of goods, but not of human beings. And the libidinal bond will be considered only as rational and merely instrumental.

But this rationality, discovered in an instrumental 'technique' for the production of things or commodities, will not appear as determined by the rational structure of the system of production, which is *at the same time producer of human beings and goods*. In this way, the rationality that produces human beings is eradicated.

> But this desirable state of things does not, and never did, exist. Reality shows us that civilisation is not content with the ties we have so far allowed it. It aims at binding the members of the community together in a libidinal way as well and employs every means to that end. It favours every path by which strong identifications can be established between the members of the community, and it summons up aim-inhibited libido [labour, productivity] on the largest scale so as to strengthen the communal bond by relations of friendship. In order for these aims to be fulfilled, a restriction upon sexual life is unavoidable. (108–9)

This passage is particularly revealing, important, and synthetic. Where does civilisation come from with its pretension to bind people together? It comes from the dominant form in the rationality of its productive system, the organisation of social work. But in the capitalist system it is not the human form but the commodity form that is the dominant form of wealth: wage labour, without quality. We do not need Freud to think in these terms, but we can find a clear indication of the *quantitative* element, which here appears as determining of the social bond, when he speaks of 'aim-inhibited libido on the largest scale', or 'the maximum quantity of aim-inhibited libido'. Qualitative work, which prolongs itself from the moment of its being put into place, does not appear here: the powerful identifications that the system requires to strengthen its organisation and create the appearance of community, juxtaposed with its real inexistence, are based upon instinctual repression and divert the aim of the impulses whose organic form of unity they would only be able to find in the collective process, as the prolongation of the sexuated form. But if we start with the conventional form of sexuation (the 'double individual', without others), this is neither visible nor comprehensible, because the model that structures it from within, based upon the transition from nature to culture realised in the family, is a model that stems from the system itself. In this way the paths of the libido, contained at the level of the personal relationship that thus is repressed as though it were contradictory with the social form, once they are delinked from this human form *no longer have any human model on which to base their prolongation in the world of culture or civilisation*. The available models are models of repression, containment, and scission. The body made available through repression is the body needed by the system as mere force applied to its system, which negates the very human being that thus must sacrifice and subject itself to it. The repressive model, which acts as super-ego, prolongs itself in civilisation through unliveable forms, which reaffirm in their domination the dependence and mediation that they enable for their inclusion in the existing institutions. From 'the dead father' all that remains is the skeletal form of the ego-ideal, the form of subjection and split rationality which, within the subject itself, prepares the repressed flesh as sacrificeable body, ready to adhere and submit itself to a power that in its extreme magnitude, in its widest rationality, is congruent with the repressive rationality that left the father decanted inside one's own body. Because this body is thought, in its maximal imaginary unfolding, as 'double individuality', that is to say, as a *non-significant but empirical synthesis*, in which *the effusive bond of the two means fusion separated from the whole that nonetheless determined it*. This affect without rationality, this pure spontaneity raised up from within narcissism, that is, from the extreme individuality which surprises itself in the act of loving the other but can do so only by withdrawing from the world, is nothing but a form of the primordial bond that appears exalted in the romantic love relationship that survives in capitalist society. In the very form in which bourgeois love is lived we already find the form of alienation adapted to the system that produced this love. In its maximal sexual exaltation this love does not receive its incarnated sense from the world of culture or civilisation that produced it: it lives itself, naively, in the radical separation from culture, as if it were opposed to this world, as the clandestine moment ratified or not by the given institutions. This is a regulated pseudo-clandestine life, which objectively talks to us in the language of maximum proximity and maximum exclusion of all that is not the two of us. Meanwhile, in reality and objectively speaking, this kind of love was already determined by the system from before, as a bond foreseen by this system, as a body invested by fractions, as an overcoming of repression, even as it plays within the limits of the latter and gives itself the illusion of an absolute bond. We feel the fusion with the part of the libido that the system left us as a personal form: *whatever we do not put into love* (and soon enough time betrays the illusion) *we must put up externally as a loveless body in the service of its system of production.*

This containment of the libido, which organises itself in the form of the deviation of the aims of the impulses, could not develop its differences from the others. It would have had to initiate its similitude based on the form of its appositionality, and not from within narcissism: what it was, is, or would like to be. With what can we supplement this lack of real presence of the others that we cannot invest with our libido, since the path of its prolongation is prohibited? With a diluted perception, which does not discern the effective quality of the other: we cannot animate the others with our own body. This is why Freud says that this repressive civilisation offers only a substitute in which we can put the body that they subtract: work, the army, the Church. We have to simulate the prolongation, but by sublimating it: by referring it, for its meaning, to an institutional form that conceals the system on which it nonetheless depends:

> It favours every path by which strong identifications can be established between the members of the community, and it summons up aim-inhibited libido on the largest scale so as to strengthen the communal bond by relations of friendship. (109)

Who are those members with whom there is such a strong identification? We will see in group psychology: they are the models of the system, directed by the artificial groups or masses, which install the human subject in a relation of terrorised adhesion that is the prolongation of the form of the father that prepares the submission to the chain of every power and every form of security. This form of libido inhibited in our subjectivity is the libido that did not integrate itself in any unitary way in the form of the other, which the primordial other inhibited and prohibited from passing over and integrating itself in the unity of our own cultural body. Thus, what remains of this libido after the sexual investment in the heterogeneity of the other, which only the sexual difference opens up, is the homogeneous libido that narcissism invests in a social model (the general, the priest, the bourgeois leader), which merely covers over the internal other who lies within us. It does not extend itself toward the real other, but only toward the imaginary other for which the real other appears as a support.

2   *The Holy Trinity*

Thus, 'sublimated' love discovers an abstract field that is its 'adult theory'. This is necessarily an abstract totality of love, in which the qualitative difference is inscribed as indifferent to the signification of the other. This theory of a type of love congruent with the 'two are one' has its necessary correlate in the mystery of 'one is three', the Holy Trinity: the One who contains the other two. The loving narcissism of the restricted and clandestine couple is based, as its foundation, on Christian love, the 'love of all human beings'. Thus, to the illusion of a love reduced to its empirical signification, in the bodily encounter experienced as the unification that erases every limit and every difference, there corresponds, at the other extreme, a love of pure form, abstract universality in which all would be included – except now only as mere forms that no different human body inhabits. The rationality and meaning that we could not embody in the love of the couple, in the sexuality that did not extend itself to include the effective difference and meaningful field of the world that produced it as loving human body, this rationality subsequently appears from the outside, but cleared of all sensible footing, dematerialised. And it does so from within a system of production that cannot show the sensible difference and exploitation on which it is based: the same exploitation that subtracts from the body as mere quantity, as labour power, as mere material identity. This concealment of the rationality of the real that the system of production also produces, this negation of the legibility of the true meaning on which it is based – the exploitation of one class by another, the domination that it exerts on the body of the others for its own benefit – continues to be based in a privileged way on the primary subjection in which the father, as model or form of the system of production of human subjects in the bosom of the family, continues to produce narcissistic individuals subjected to the laws of the system in the very form of being human.

'What necessity pushed civilisation to opt for this path?' Freud asks himself. And he believes to have found the answer in the precept: 'Thou shalt love thy neighbour as thyself'. And placing himself outside-within the system, he begins to ask the question from within the contradiction of the bourgeois subject:

> My love is something valuable to me which I ought not to throw away without reflection. It imposes duties on me for whose fulfilment I must be ready to make sacrifices. If I love someone, he must deserve it in some way. ... He deserves it if he is so like me in important ways that I can love myself in him; and he deserves it if he is so much more perfect than myself that I can love my ideal of my own self in him. ... But if he is a stranger to me and if he cannot attract me by any worth of his own or any significance that he may already have acquired for my emotional life, it will be hard for me to love him. Indeed, I should be wrong to do so, for my love is valued by all my own people as a sign of my preferring them, and it is an injustice to them if I put a stranger on a par with them. But if I am to love him (with this universal love) merely because he, too, is an inhabitant of this earth, like an insect, an earth-worm or a grass-snake, then I fear that only a small modicum of my love will fall to his share – not by any possibility as much as, by the judgement of my reason, I am entitled to retain for myself. What is the point of a precept enunciated with so much solemnity if its fulfilment cannot be recommended as reasonable? (109–10)

Here the opposition is between the real features of narcissistic individualism, which this system produces, and the contradictory precept that nonetheless the same system ideally imposes on this kind of subject. The categories with which the bourgeois subject, always sensible, confronts the precept are obvious here: the expenditure that 'throws away' love; the 'sacrifice' it imposes on him in the face of constitutive egotism. He could only love the other if he were 'the same as him' (narcissism), that is to say, to love himself in the other, or if he were that which 'the ego ideal' presents to him as what must be loved. If all difference was always excluded, why should he now love the one who is different, the one who is a 'stranger' to 'his own worth'? What is just and unjust revolves only around what is proper to the self and finds therein the norm of its individual conduct. The love for one's own is a preference in which justice and injustice find their basis: 'It is an injustice to them if I put a stranger on a par with them'. But if he is asked to love them like he loves every living being, erasing every limit, with only the general limit that he knows, then the empirical, insignificant anthropocentrism turns out to be impotent to love all the others, one by one. There is a 'quantity' of love, and the model of the family, without extending the meaning of the libido nor going beyond the empirical presence of those who are near to oneself, finds no other form of gaining proximity or having any incidence on the others, to demonstrate one's love, except the same sensible and insignificant love that only the meeting of two bodies permits. And moreover, bourgeois and individualistic reason is on its side: 'to nobody can such a precept be recommended as reasonable'.

Here we see once again with great clarity the scission between the sensible and the rational, which finds contradictory support in two different totalities. There is an individual realm of the sensible, whose rationality is strictly determined by the relations of production, where narcissism reigns as the normal form of connection with reality. But the overcoming of this lived situation, which the moral precept of religion proposes us to reach, does not explain the true contradiction of the system that produces narcissists. It only presents the norm as an imposition that is impossible to fulfil, against which the empirical affirmation continues to be valid. There is no transition from the empirical and real organisation to the rationality without sensibility that religion demands. To the material structure in which human beings find themselves situated is opposed an ideal totality devoid of matter, whose rationality is not prolonged from within the corporeality of human beings but as the complete, trenchant, and impossible negation of their individual organisation. When the 'moral' norms demand that we open ourselves up, beyond the family, to the broader connection with reality, all that appears is this reason without sensibility. Opposed to the individualistic discernment there is only the affective indiscriminateness of a formal and general rationality. Between the particularity of narcissism and the generality of love for all there is no transition: there is only opposition.

But this is an opposition from both extremes. From the sensible side, since the impossible is asked of me: to love the others as I love myself, that is, within the empirical and sensible coincidence, in similitude. And the bourgeois narcissist denounces this, for good reason, as absurd. From the rational side, I am asked at the same time to dissolve all difference, therefore I am asked to stop exercising the anthropocentrism on which difference – bourgeois man as essence – is founded.

But between these two extremes there is another rational understanding that begins to take shape by putting into relief the effective structure of human relationships that must be transformed. This is the rationality that religion conceals and that the bourgeois subject experiences as fact, for whose understanding the rationality offered to him by religion is of no help, let alone of any comprehensive help. And it is understandable why this moral system, which dissolves the sense of reality, installs itself at the heart of the subjectivities of the capitalist system of production. It is in order to avoid the exercise of power of those who are subjected to it; it is to avoid the violence that the true rationality, were it understood, would unleash. It is to keep the just hatred from aiming outward, toward its true source, the aggressiveness that in narcissism we effectively aim inward:

> Not merely is this stranger in general unworthy of my love; I must honestly confess that he has more claim to my hostility and even my hatred. He seems not to have the least trace of love for me and shows me not the slightest consideration. If it will do him any good he has no hesitation in injuring me, nor does he ask himself whether the amount of advantage he gains bears any proportion to the extent of the harm he does to me. (110)

When we negate the indifferentiation that general love proclaims, hatred appears, but it is a situated and just hatred. What kind of signification, what order of the world do we discover to be the basis of this hatred? Now we see that it is in the capitalist system of production where this individual form of being is based on the qualitative reduction of the others to the merely quantitative magnitude of their abstract utility. If we adequately prolong this rationality that emerges, as an index, in this act of hatred, we will find the rationality that produces it: the system that produces human subjects and becomes evident through relations that are now *labour* relations.

The impulse of qualitative love traverses the immediate significations and from there prolongs itself toward the other: the other appears from within a quality that signifies a reciprocity and a confrontation, but not from an external law which, abstractly overcoming this quality in a negation that annihilates it, would attempt to replace the *determinate and situated affect* with the moral obligation:

> If he behaves differently, if he shows me consideration and forbearance as a stranger, I am ready to treat him in the same way, in any case and quite apart from any precept. (110)

In this way, against the abstract legality of amorous indiscriminateness, there is a more profound rationality to be constituted, which is on the path toward the organic rationality of the body, but which the existing system of production inhibits, distorts, and manages to use in its own favour. And it does so, as we saw, through a false rationality, which is external, quantitative, and imposed by the law. For we can infer that Freud does not separate the logic of libidinal organisation from the logic of the cultural or civilisational system. We already saw how illness distorted the dialectic of the inside and the outside, of the individual and the external world. This same distortion is now the one Freud faces, after having departed as he did from the problem of integrating the individual in the world. We saw how the patient must, through psychoanalysis, converge towards reality and undo the false significations in which his or her body contradictorily had installed itself, so as to discern within these significations their link with the external world that produced them. In an analogous manner, here too the point is to reaffirm the qualitative and significant links with reality in order to give them meaning in function of this very field. The qualitative indices are the points of insertion into reality, the precise points on the basis of which we must begin to undo the contradiction and the false rationality that in conventional consciousness continue to negate us from within ourselves.

3   *Logical Absurdity as the Result of Affective Indiscrimination*

We saw that in the 'love thy neighbour as thyself' there was hidden, implicitly, a decision of indiscrimination: to love the neighbour with indifference for the subject's qualities. But where this decision reveals its meaning as leading not only to general love but to an explicit decision to serve a slave morality, as Nietzsche said, is in a second formulation of this precept:

> And there is a second commandment, which seems to me even more incomprehensible and arouses still stronger opposition in me. It is 'Love thine enemies'. If I think it over, however, I see that I am wrong in treating it as a greater imposition. At bottom it is the same thing. (110)

To punctual love there corresponds a punctual enemy. But the structure that produces enemies and in which they acquire meaning disappears from this depiction just as much as it disappears in the objective world of being-one-with-the-whole. We are no longer in the mere abstraction of generality: we are now in a higher degree in the precise dissolution of significations that, from within hatred or love, prolong themselves with certainty to designate their object. But in front of the object, the commandment orders me to hold still: either to love it genitally or to destroy and annul it. The further precision that the act of discernment had acquired thus ends up being dissolved, and precisely in front of the one who is opposed to my existence. I must love the one who hates me, destroys me, negates me. The amorous generality proposed to me is an ascent toward my integration within an abstract totality from which the historical differences vanish. Or, rather: I have to erase these differences as indices of the signification of my reality and that of the others. To love the enemy is purely and simply the destruction of the historical dialectic: the contradiction is dissolved in abstract love. This does not take away the fact that it continues to produce material effects in reality. But the contradictory qualities, which inscribe their logic in the sensible materiality of human relations, are not for this reason abolished. Who could impose on me my own destruction?

> I think I can now hear a dignified voice admonishing me: 'It is precisely because your neighbour is not worthy of love, and is on the contrary your enemy, that you should love him as yourself'. I then understand that the case is one like that of *Credo quia absurdum*. (111)

We already understand who or what it is that continues to impose on us, from within ourselves, our own destruction: the super-ego. Let us recall when we also had to bend before an absurd imposition, whose incoherence forced us to abandon our own coherence which from the body prolonged itself as affirmation of our virile member: the threat of castration accepted as real. It was the omnipotent voice of the absolute which made us accept, though absurd from our point of view, the reality of the threat and made us doubt whether the girl 'would end up growing one': she was, in her lack of penis, the certainty itself of the threat and its fulfilment.

Now we see the prolongation of this logic, which from the initial absurdity prolongs itself objectively all the way to the final absurdity. The dissolution of the contradiction appears here as constitutive of my point of insertion in the structure of the productive system. *I believe because it is absurd*: point of entanglement where the subjective and objective meet in the meaninglessness, that is, the irrational convergence affirmed as the only truth, and *because of this* accepted. Not without reason did Freud say about religion that it supposes as its prior condition the 'intimidation of the intelligence' (84). Here resides the dissolution of the dialectic, at the very moment when it confronts failure turned into success through submission: *I believe*. And the contradictory result I arrived at converts this logical error, in which the contradiction explodes, in the point of support from which the sensibility of an arrested body gives in to and loves the contradictory reality that rationality reveals to it precisely for this reason: *because it is absurd*. Just as the child, due to the fear of castration, abandoned the infantile theory in order to substitute it with the repressive theory. What do we find here? That reason already had been abandoned in the very form of living sexual love, in which the other appeared as mere empirical presence, devoid of reason, except the one projected on it as ego ideal, in the fusion of the one into the other: the absolute of double individuality. To the absurdity of sex without reason there coherently corresponds the absurdity of a society without reason:

> As a result, their neighbour is for them not only a potential helper or sexual object, but also someone who tempts them to satisfy their aggressiveness on him, to exploit his capacity for work without compensation, to use him sexually without his consent, to seize his possessions, to humiliate him, to cause him pain, to torture and to kill him. (111)

This description corresponds *exactly* to the relations of domination of our capitalist system of production: 'the appropriation of alien labour without exchange, but with the semblance of exchange' (Marx, *Grundrisse*); the subjection of women; class dependency; colonialism and the wars of extermination.

Against the backdrop of the false solutions that are being proposed, this whole description tends to emphasise the eminent presence of aggressiveness among human beings. But the problem is the following: if there exists a *general*, indiscriminate form of aggression, to which that *general* kind of love previously analysed would come to give an answer, what is the origin of these aggressive tendencies? Can they be overcome? Is there a fundamental pessimism in Freud, and must the human being continue forever to oscillate between the tendencies to destruction and the formalism of impotent norms? At first it would indeed appear to be the case, and it is good to accept this *appearance* in order to understand it, because it is also what imposes itself, albeit contradictorily, on a certain level within us as being present in Freud:

> The existence of this inclination to aggression, which we can detect in ourselves and justly assume to be present in others, is the factor which

disturbs our relations with our neighbour and which forces civilisation into such a high expenditure [of energy]. (112)

But let us take into account the fact that in Freud there is a theory of the drives not inhibited in their aims, a theory of the fusion and defusion of the life and death drives, from whose unity life is born and develops itself as tension towards the obstacle that aggressiveness helps to overcome. Aggressiveness works in the service of life. There exists a normal form of this fusion, which is the sexual relationship. There is also a conception of culture or civilisation, as we saw, in which the drives are separate and do not become integrated into the sexuated form but as such, in their separation, are aimed merely toward the relations of utility in the production of labour. It is not possible, therefore, to understand this affirmation in Freud if we do not at the same time place it against the backdrop of this civilisational, Western and Christian solution, onto which it projects itself and against which it is aimed:

> In consequence of this primary mutual hostility of human beings, civilised society is perpetually threatened with disintegration. The interest of work in common would not hold it together; instinctual passions are stronger than reasonable interests. (112)

Let us clarify: the community of work is produced on the basis of instincts or drives inhibited in their aim, which were excluded, in the preparatory stages of the development of the libido, from the organic integration into the sexual form as the matrix and prototype of all specifically human relationships. They are, in other words, drives not integrated into the organic rationality of the human form. These 'instinctual passions', therefore, remain in the margins of this rationality and, in their form of social integration, they stand in opposition to it. Freud, then, does not mean to say that in his essence 'man', because of his instincts or drives, is necessarily hostile to the others: this would be to talk of a natural instinct in the midst of a cultural or civilisational determination that necessarily transfigured them. 'Instinctual passion' is then the passion of a body that civilisation organised in the mode of negative spontaneity, given that these instincts were disintegrated in the human form and only integrated in the production of things. How could we recuperate these instinctual passions that were repressed, disintegrated, and cut off from the human form in which they should prolong themselves in the unitary search for satisfaction? And what would be their paths if the passionate materiality of the world, love and hate, have been removed as criteria of aggressiveness? Thus the qualitative contents of one's own body, which in their contradictory organisation struggle to carve out a path towards the material reality, find that the moral consciousness, the ideology that the system imposes on it from the inside, but in the organisation of the productive relations of labour from the outside, structures them against the body. The work in which the instincts prolong themselves only *turns back on us the aggression that the system*, as lack of retribution and humiliation, *imposes on us against ourselves*, in the objectivisation of an impulse that failed in its means and in its object-aim. The rationality of this system sucks the power of its labour force from the instinct: organising it in the production without compensation, without enjoyment, without integration. But the corporeal drives, which are thus subtracted, overflow the limits imposed on them and appear in their lack of satisfaction as violence and aggressiveness. And it is not this rationality of the system of production of commodities that could explain the meaning of the violence that thus is generated. *It is precisely this residual violence of the drives consumed in labour that the moral precepts pretend to orient and direct*, and that the institutions pretend to integrate in the simulation of libidinal bonds by way of those 'powerful identifications', in which the totality of the libido that has been subtracted and not integrated gives itself the supplementary presence of an exterior object that renders it immobile: models, leaders, institutions.

In this way, therefore, if the 'rational interests' of the community of work, in the system where the appropriation of labour without equivalent is dominant, are congruent only with the rationality of the commodity form but not with the organic form of the human being, *the most powerful 'instinctual passions' that appear in aggressive forms are the ones that we must retain as the index of a passion that struggles*, in its own way, *not to give in to frustration*. All of civilisation, in the form of its moral precepts, has failed to elaborate the indices to read in them the meaning of the aggressiveness that it provokes, but precisely in order to conceal them. *Aggressiveness, then, would be in human conduct the appearance of an integrative force whose power of discernment finds itself at the farthest distance from becoming integrated into the capacity for discernment of the human being's psychic apparatus.*

It is, however, this residual aggressiveness that civilisation must simulate as if it were integrated, in order to avoid the aggression:

> Hence, therefore, the use of methods intended to incite people into identifications and aim-inhibited relationships of love. (112)

That is to say, relationships of love without love: the corporeal filaments that once again come back to resuscitate within the human subject the initial similitude of what the other tolerated and left available as homosexual libido. There would be an attempt to return to *the origin of the containment of aggressiveness*, by looking for support in the primary and necessary repression of the Oedipal complex in order to reincorporate, from this point onward, every new relation of dependence and submission. The conflict is not, as might have seemed to be the case, between nature and culture, or between body and reason. The conflict is between civilised body and repressive reason.

If this is indeed the case, Freud's conclusion should not be surprising to us:

> The time comes when each one of us has to give up as illusions the expectations which, in his youth, he pinned upon his fellow-men (112)

This pessimism is not Freud's: it belongs to the civilisation that Freud rejects.

4 *Economist Communism as Solution to Repressive Culture*

Having formulated the contradiction of bourgeois culture, whose analysis will be extended throughout the entire book, Freud moves on to consider the communist solution. Wherein consists his critique? Communism, in the interpretation that Freud offers to us, would suppose that the human being is good by nature:

> According to them, man is wholly good and is well-disposed to his neighbour; but the institution of private property has corrupted his nature. ... If private property were abolished, all wealth held in common, and everyone allowed to share in the enjoyment of it, ill-will and hostility would disappear among men. Since everyone's needs would be satisfied, no one would have any reason to regard another as his enemy; all would willingly undertake the work that was necessary. (113)

It is evident that this critique does not apply to Marx but only to what Marx called 'crude communism' in the *Manuscripts*, that is to say, a conception of communism which continues to be based on a bourgeois form of thinking about human relationships, still dominated by the commodity-form, without understanding the radical qualitative transformation suggested by the modification of the system of production under communism. It would seem that Freud reads the economic level as if in the field of relations of production the most refined psychological determinations were not also at stake. Rather, we think that Freud here signals a deficit in the political Marxism of his time: insofar as it does not point in the direction of a profound and radical reform of the human subject but only remained limited to the transformations of the economic system. His criticism would seem aimed against the economistic conception of communism, or against Stalinism, which on the other hand was prevalent at the time (1930):

> Aggressiveness was not created by property. It reigned almost without limit in primitive times, when property was still very scanty, and it already shows itself in the nursery almost before property has given up its primal, anal form; it forms the basis of every relation of affection and love among people (with the single exception, perhaps, of the mother's relation to her male child). (113)

There is an anteriority of the instinct of aggression with regard to capitalist private property. The aggressive drive is merely derived from the death drive when it confronts the obstacle that opposes itself to life, when therefore aggressiveness works in the service of life, not separated from it. It appears outwards when the child, having lost the sense of property in its anal form referred to its own excrements as part of itself that it either gives or retains, opens itself to the world of adult communication in which property 'changes in substance': it is no longer what is one's own that one gives, but now the things given or taken are exterior to oneself, goods and money. The child always confronts the other in a relation of opposition or love, and it maintains or contains itself within the limits of the loved ones: only to them does the child give its excrements as a gift. Now, inexplicably, it must give and appreciate that which no longer has the form of the human: money. But retention appears here in its contradictory form; not only must the child retain its faeces, it also must retain the aggressiveness in the name of love. The aggressive impulses are the result of this containment, for the sake of love of the other: *only love, but without aggression*. In the child the aggressiveness is held back, and it is understood that the child must give up on it in the service of love: not the love the child feels toward the other, but the love that the other feels toward the child: *it is the other who does not tolerate aggressiveness in conjunction with love*. The other is always, at the origin, Manichean.

Aggressiveness thus turns into the obverse of love, but it is always present as that which one had to renounce in one's fusion with the life drive. But in the child this aggressiveness only finds those objects that are the nearest within its limited horizon: aggression in truth has no meaning, no signification with regard to the field of culture or civilisation. The contained aggressiveness is a consequence *not of private property but of the necessary containment that the appropriation of the other imposes on the child*. The appropriation of the other implies the retention of aggressiveness. It is from this point of view that Freud understands the dialectic that later, coming from the child, prolongs itself in private property. The first property, coming from the form of infanthood, before it appears mediated through objects, money, gold, and commodities, is *the appropriation of the other as the meaning of every relation with reality*. Therefore, all aggressiveness, and above all that which appears *afterwards* in the economic domain of property, has its first origin that must be put into relief in order to understand what is at stake when aggression appears later on: the fact that the problem at issue in all human property is in reality, once again, the appropriation of the other. The subjection to the other once again appears as the fundamental problem when the real but contained differences, for the sake of which aggressiveness was preserved, appear directed not against the true obstacle but against its semblance: only against the property of goods. The workers must produce *objects without love*, exchange values: they must produce 'indiscriminately'. But it is the power of discriminating or discerning the obstacle on the altar of the dependency created by love – which meant submission to the other – that aggressiveness must include within itself. To abolish property, Freud tells us, is for this very reason insufficient: the problem is broader, more profound, and through the property of things concerns the problem of the appropriation of human subjects. Therefore, once property is destroyed, the aggressiveness will not be abolished for this reason: it will always be present as that unreduced margin which the other imposes as indiscriminate subjection, as the nucleus where its being announces the impossibility of all difference that would negate it, because similitude is the absolute.

We already saw the solution that Freud reveals as part of our civilisation: the presence of the other as similar disappears when we move on to the relations of work starting from the sexual relationship in the couple, where the only difference tolerated – but always within the similitude imposed by the ego-ideal – is the sexual difference. And the cut that is introduced here defines the impossibility of organically prolonging this dialectic that the nonintegration of the drives, partialised by civilisation, interrupts. Thus was produced the opening of two contradictory fields: genitality, reserved for the human form, ends up being limited to the relationship within the couple. And the remainder of the nonintegrated libido extends itself in the relations of work, in which the form of the other as similar would convey only the biological energy. It becomes clear that, since the initial similitude is a class similarity, property appears as a social domain that determines the confrontation among different subjects. The contained aggressiveness unfurls there where difference appears in the mere having without being, as purely quantitative difference, of a libido that ignores the meaning of the aggression that in this way has been held back. And the aggressiveness that has been held back is pure indiscriminateness which, for the sake of an absolute love, finds outside itself, as the prolongation of this transcendence, the world's quantitative domain and the class differences, as the radically other.

Thus the contained aggression, which was part of the unified process of the life and death drives, appears on the one hand as separating itself from the domain of life, which has as its sole domain that of the relation of 'double individuality' in sexual love, and on the other hand as extending the aggressiveness, now without love, without the support of the human form, towards the domain of the economy and work.

These initial similitudes, which *later* find support in private property, after one's self has been produced as property of the other, prolong themselves in others, wherever the dominant classes recognise themselves in their way of positioning *death outside*, in the differences among classes, pretending to *conserve life only within one's own class*. Indiscriminate aggression, separated from its origin in love, appears prolonged in civilisation as the diffusion of the life and death drives: for some, life – for the similar ones; for the others, death – for those who are different. Once again, we see hatred and love, life and death, clearly marking off, with their cultural or civilisational solutions, the discontent. For this reason, even though private property is one of the objective forms in which this profound imbalance presents itself in the productive process of human beings, its abolition does not entail, in and of itself, this transformation:

> In abolishing private property we deprive the human love of aggression of one of its instruments, certainly a strong one, though certainly not the strongest. (113)

Whence Freud's critique of the partial solutions, which do not integrate the universal field of human subjectivity, and which appear therefore as apparent solutions: they pretend to have reached the predominance of love when they suppress the forms of economic domination. But if the problem is not confronted at its root, and if the community continues to be merely a community of work – no matter if the means of production now are communal property – all that will have been obtained is an apparent human community. In such a community the inhibited aggression, not included in the development of differences and the negation of the other as absolute other, will maintain the nucleus of dependence and indiscriminateness towards the true obstacles, in the midst of which the subjects are liberated only from one of the instruments of domination but not from all the others that continue to subject them.

Freud wants to tell us that we will continue to maintain ourselves within the narcissistic form of individuality, although now, instead of being a 'double individuality', as in the couple, it is a 'collective individuality', as in the groups or masses.

The rationality for understanding and the mode of confronting the enemy could find guidance in the economic determination, in politics, and perhaps up to a point it reaches success in discerning him. But in the long run the lack of foundation of the economic and political activity in the liberation of the human form, which regulates the meaning of the struggle – the human being conceived as an organic form without scission on the basis of which what we put up in the struggle is not mere biology without meaning, mere body without signification, mere labour – will deform the meaning of all politics and of the whole economic process. Any process that tends to abolish private property tends in essence to make possible the appropriation of human beings amongst themselves. It is not by chance if this emphasis on the human form, as regulator of the process, was what Ernesto Che Guevara explicitly placed at the centre of his analyses of the relations of production in opposition to socialist systems such as the Soviet or Czechoslovakian, where the human form disappears in favour of the sole production of goods: substituting one form of the property of things for another.

The meaning of this solution resides, once more, in the collective process:

> Over and above the tasks of restricting the instincts, which we are prepared for, there forces itself on our notice the danger of a state of things which might be termed 'the psychological poverty of groups'. This danger is most threatening where the bonds of a society are chiefly constituted by the identification of its members with one another, while individuals of the leader type do not acquire the importance that should fall to them in the formation of a group. The present cultural state of America would give us a good opportunity for studying the damage to civilisation which is thus to be feared. (115–16)

This problem of the mass or group will be studied in detail in the final part of this book. For now suffice it here to signal how the social cohesiveness does not discriminate between the forces that determine it and replaces these real forces, from which objectively the meaning of dependence can be read off, with psychological bonds of identification in which the purely psychic similitude conceals the other kind, which is fundamental. Only the apparition of new models of human subjectivity would make this transformation possible, undoing the trap present at the heart of each ego. This enabling of the power of the masses for the transformation of civilisation is a constant in Freud's thinking. The risk is the permanence of the group in a situation of submission to a conventional bourgeois leader, but its liberation appears through a revolutionary leader (see the scheme on pages 370–71).

vi   Out of Hunger Not Being Capable of Love

> I should be glad to seize the point if it were to appear that the recognition of a special, independent aggressive instinct means an alteration of the psycho-analytic theory of the instincts. (117)

Uncomfortable position, that of Freud: against the conception of Christian love, to recognise the need to discriminate on the basis of hate and to recuperate aggressiveness as an index of the real; and against the disingenuous conception of a certain economistic Communism, to vindicate the idea that aggressiveness is something profoundly inherent in the human condition, which the mere suppression of private property does not solve. Does this mean that Freud has recourse to 'the recognition of a special, independent aggressive instinct'? If this were his position, it would entail a modification of the psychoanalytic theory of the instincts or drives. 'We shall see, however, that this is not so', he says: there is no aggressive instinct, unique and special, 'it is merely a matter of bringing into sharper focus a turn of thought arrived at long ago and of following out its consequences' (117).

In the transition from one theoretical conception to another, mediating between the first theory of the instincts proposed by Freud and the one he is now going to expose to us by 'following out its consequences', we will see the ideological importance of the 'turn': its effective independence from the ideological categories that the repressive system provided, in order to think their integration from within this system.

Freud begins by describing his first theory of the instincts and its intuitive origin:

> ... that theory was so indispensable to the whole structure that something had to be put in its place. In what was at first my utter perplexity, I took as my starting-point a saying of the poet-philosopher, Schiller, that 'hunger and love are what moves the world'. (117)

1   Contradiction among the Instincts

Freud began by distinguishing two structuring axes in the human subject, two instincts, but opposed to one another: the instincts for the *conservation of the individual* (hunger) and the instincts *conservative of the species* (love).

All the instincts, as we see, are conservative, but from the beginning they tend towards the conservation of *two extremes* presented as opposed to one another and contradictory: individual and species, part and whole.

> Thus, to begin with, ego-instincts and object-instincts confronted each other. (117)

This opposition, which constitutes the drama of the instincts in the first theory, could be formulated in the following disjunction: *out of hunger not being capable of love*. Or, put differently: if I dedicate myself to the conservation of the whole species, out of love, this implies that I have to renounce the conservation of my individuality, out of hunger. From the very beginning of the first theory of the instincts there appears the description of a social and historical situation – the opposition individual/collective – projected, as if it were natural, onto the essence of human individuality. As if this contradiction, which appears in the midst of a system of production – the capitalist one – were merely the repetition of an organisation that has come about from within nature as unmovable: as instinctual.

In this way the notion of the body and its fluidity in the cathexis of objects appeared only in the second kind of instincts – in the instincts of love and of the conservation of the species – but not in the ego-instincts. Thus appeared an instinct of the ego, without a body in movement, without a sensible subject. The first theory of the instincts was not, therefore, dialectical, because it was fully installed within a conventional description taken to be scientific: the acceptance, as essential for the psychic life, of an opposition between the objective and the subjective, the individual and the species. It thus reproduced, at the centre of the subject, the ideological opposition that the contradictory civilisation of capitalism presented as if it were a universal destiny, whereas it was only the destiny of *its* civilisation. This is not to say that this opposition did not exist, or that it did not appear in reality. But there was a distance to be understood and a contradiction to be confronted.

How did Freud discover this inadequacy of his first theory of the instincts? When he had to explain the violence that a subject exerts on another: sadism. Thus he understood that there was a passage from the instincts of the ego to the instincts of the libido; that the ego-instincts prolonged themselves contradictorily in the object-instincts:

> One of these object-instincts, the sadistic instinct, stood out from the rest, it is true, in that its aim was so very far from being loving. Moreover it was obviously in some respects attached to the ego-instincts: it could not hide its close affinity with instincts of mastery which have no libidinal purpose. (117)

This discrepancy was only such for a conception that separated hatred from love. It was necessary to include hatred in love, the other's pain in individual pleasure; to break the first simplicity and to make the ego appear as engaged in this affective dialectic that links the individual to the species:

> But these discrepancies were got over; after all, sadism was clearly a part of sexual life, in the activities of which affection could be replaced by cruelty. (117–18)

This much is clear: if love is played out with two, why not also play with cruelty? The conception of love, in this opposition, also maintains the possibility of justifying cruelty directed outwards as a somewhat exaggerated exacerbation, perhaps of this same component that was also present in love, though kept within its correct limits:

> Neurosis was regarded as the outcome of a struggle between the interest of self-preservation and the demands of the libido, a struggle in which the ego had been victorious but at the price of severe sufferings and renunciations. (118)

Thus, the neurotic, in the first theory, was the one who had not *given in* to reality: it was the extreme individualist. But the system's conventional reality continued to have the better of the ego. The individual's interests in the case of the neurotic were dominant compared to those of society. Sickness would reveal, in this mere loss of reality, the predominance of 'egotistic' interests. Sufferings and renunciations were its double punishment.

2   Contradiction between the Instincts and the Productive System

This is where we are at, Freud tells us, with the first theory of the drives or instincts. But something important, the announced *theoretical turn*, becomes apparent:

> Every analyst will admit that even today this view has not the sound of a long-discarded error. Nevertheless, alterations in it became essential,

as our enquiries advanced from the repressed to the repressing forces, from the object-instincts to the ego. The decisive step forward was the introduction of the concept of narcissism – that is to say, the discovery that the ego itself is cathected with libido, that the ego, indeed, is the libido's original home, and remains to some extent its headquarters. This narcissistic libido turns towards objects, and thus becomes object-libido; and it can change back into narcissistic libido once more. (118)

As we saw in the first part, this turning back from the repressed to the repressor requires us to understand that the ego was already determined from the outside, by the forces of civilisation; that the part was determined, in its most narrow individuality, as ego, by the interest of conservation of the 'species' – except that this species is not a natural but a cultural species. Thus, the repression of the system was organising the individual in depth: *the conservation instincts of the 'normal' ego were determined, as opposites, by the conservation instincts of the species.* The process therefore had to be inverted so as to understand the ego of the narcissistic individual according to the mode in which a civilisation inhibits its organic extension outwards as well as inwards, towards itself. *The opposition between ego-instincts and the species was an opposition determined by the system of production,* in the extent to which civilisation subjected the ego to its repressive dependency.

But the conception of the ego also changes in another sense: the ego, originally, is a libidinal ego, a corporeal ego. The adult ego is the surface, which looks to the outside, of that corporeal ego which had identified itself with its objects, which in order to become acculturated, had made itself similar to the other. And only by way of this adult ego, tailor-made on the model of the repressor, the libido orients itself towards the world. The ego-instincts are conservative because they contain, by identification, the objects thanks to which the so-called 'conservation instincts of the species' permit life in a state of correspondence that from the external world retains only the authorised object relations. And we thus understand that the ego's libido, converted in object-libido, may change back into narcissistic libido: when the impossibility of finding satisfaction of the unsatisfied desire on the outside, makes it go back, in a regressive solution, to the search for the first object, on the inside: there where the ego offers itself as object to the id.

Neurosis or psychosis, then, could not be explained by the predominance of the 'ego-instincts' against the 'libidinal instincts', or object-instincts, or instincts for the preservation of the species, such as appeared to be the case in the first theory. The ego's return to itself was a return within the subjective form that the 'species', in this case civilisation, had organised as the locus of a contradictory subjectivity where both the transition towards reality – towards objects – and its failure – return to the subject – were determined by civilisation itself. Where, therefore, civilisation was already present in the very form of the ego. The separation between the ego-instincts and the object-instincts maintains the separation subject-world at the heart of individuality. Civilisation was already active in the organisation of the libido itself.

> This narcissistic libido turns towards objects, and thus becomes object-libido; and it can change back into narcissistic libido once more. (118)

This transformation was not a return to the ego's instincts, but towards an ego determined by the other: toward a cultural 'instinct' or 'drive'.

By contrast, what now appeared to be at risk was the concept of libido, hence the understanding of the cultural or civilisational corporeality that comes from nature:

> Since the ego-instincts, too, were libidinal, it seemed for a time inevitable that we should make libido coincide with instinctual energy in general, as C.G. Jung had already advocated earlier. (118)

If this were true, the drama of civilisation in human conduct that Freud pretended to understand would dissolve itself once again in the homogeneity of nature. And yet, it was to be supposed that the debate which Freud found prolonged in culture came from nature itself: that from the biological this opposite disposition constituted itself as the foundation of a cultural opposition, which would serve as its basis. But above all it was to be supposed that in the realm of culture or civilisation this debate acquired a different meaning. Culture or civilisation merely prolonged a process that lay at the origin of life itself as opposition, but a basic opposition: life and death. And that only by understanding them could we confront this determinism distorted in the form of a repressive culture. We cannot elude the confrontation with aggressiveness by going back to nature, since it is also present there; but nor can we do so by preaching the *inborn goodness* of the human being, since culture or civilisation must recognise the true foundation on which it is founded. And nor does it suffice to *elude nature* by means of a spiritualism that fears the pain that it implicitly conveys, escaping into the different 'techniques' for not confronting reality. Libido is not, therefore, a 'general instinctual energy': it entails an opposition that continues to be fought over in history.

> Nevertheless, there still remained in me a kind of conviction, for which I was not as yet able to find reasons, that the instincts could not all be of the same kind. (118)

To abandon the first particular opposition, which only corresponds to a contradictory system of production – either hunger or love – did not mean to dissolve this opposition by having recourse to the generality of an 'instinctual energy'. It was necessary to find a universal foundation from which the particular oppositions – both those present in nature and those produced in history – would turn out to be understandable. The first opposition between the individual and civilisation gives way now to two fundamental instincts or drives: the instincts of life and death.

> Starting from speculations on the beginning of life and from biological parallels, I drew the conclusion that, besides the instinct to preserve living substance and to join it into ever larger units, there must exist another, contrary instinct seeking to dissolve those units and to bring them back to their primaeval, inorganic state. That is to say, as well as Eros there was an instinct of death. The phenomena of life could be explained from the concurrent or mutually opposing action of these two instincts. (118–19)

Concurrent and opposing action, that is, interaction and antagonism: no longer mere opposition but agreement to make life possible, life which as such is summoned to death. Life as the equilibrium that this unity makes possible, which dissolves itself in the inorganic, once the equilibrium gives in to one of the two terms:

> It might be assumed that the death instinct operated silently within the organism towards its dissolution, but that, of course, was no proof. A more fruitful idea was that a portion of the instinct is diverted towards the external world and comes to light as an instinct of aggressiveness and destructiveness. In this way *the instinct itself could be pressed into the service of Eros*, in that the organism was destroying some other thing, whether animate or inanimate, instead of destroying its own self. (119 emphasis added)

This text is fundamental in the turn that Freud introduces. Aggressiveness finds its meaning by incorporating itself into every process that increases life, and recognising the specificity that each organised, or organic, level acquires as a function of the obstacles that are opposed to its development, whether vegetative, animal or cultural. Individual aggressiveness has meaning not in opposition to the species or civilisation: it is part of the development of the system to which each individual belongs. And in its confrontation with the external world it attacks and violates the obstacle that stands in its way: the death instinct or drive, as long as there is interaction and equilibrium, works in the service of life. If we move from the natural obstacle to the cultural obstacle this can be clearly situated: *in the contradictory system of production in which the obstacle for life appears in the death that one class imposes upon another.* Eros manifests itself in the field of historical struggle through the access given to all human beings to the establishment of noncontradictory relationships among themselves. Destruction and aggression acquire here a very precise meaning: the death which does not destroy the organism must be projected outwards. But it will depend on how the organism, in this case the human being, conceives of its relationship with the structure of which it is part, so that the meaning of destruction, of the death that it expels outwards, implies a true or false solution:

– neurosis: aggressiveness, making it impossible to recognise the real obstacle on the outside, turns back against oneself, in a regressive conduct in which the totality is contained within one's own individuality. Being-one-with-the-whole.
– the 'normal' solution: situated within bourgeois individualist narcissism, death and aggressiveness are directed against everything that opposes itself to one's own life. This corresponds to the society of free competition, in which class determinations make one's satisfaction appear as the only meaning of the individual. The other is within oneself, regulating one's proper form. And the nondevelopment of difference and of the discernment of one's own origin, at most, takes the form of a 'double individuality' as the only domain for the prolongation of Eros. For the others: aggressiveness and death.
– the revolutionary solution: death and aggressiveness acquire a different meaning if they are understood as determining life in the world of culture or civilisation in function of a discerned totality of human beings. I cannot love all of them; there are those whom I must hate because they inhibit the life of the other, subtracting their labour without compensation, sexually taking advantage of them, condemning them to violence and death. This was clear to Freud: violence is fair against the obstacle placed before us by those who take away life and condemn us to failure, frustration, and death. Meaning as revealed in science – the analysis of the dominant mode of production of human subjects under capitalism – signals with great precision the sense of

cultural death: to confront those who, in order to maintain their own life as privilege, do not hesitate to condemn the others to death and split within themselves life from death, just as before they separated joy from pain. For them, life; for the others, death.

This implies a 'beyond the pleasure principle', but not in the destructive repetition of oneself, or in the imaginary repetition of an impossible real act converted into symbolic satisfaction, or the traumatic repetition that plays itself out in the subjective field. It implies situating the origin of human death, and then situating with regard to the latter the only death to which in the final instance we will succumb, the real death, the absolute master, as Hegel used to say, the death that the historical master uses in his favour. We must distinguish two deaths that in this way appear conflated: the death that comes from the hand of the one who uses death in his favour, as a privilege that class power confers on him as the reverse side of life; and, on the other hand, the other death, the one that we can make recede to a certain point, by way of cultural creation. But in truth there is only one: the death that the system imposes on us.

In this way, there are two forms of the inorganic: there is *the inorganic of nature*, to which we necessarily return. But there is *the inorganic of culture or civilisation*, of the system of production, which is the cultural emissary of death, and which installs among human beings the inorganicity that one class of them, in order to salvage their own life and their own privilege, delegates and projects onto the others.

Freud, already from the beginning of this work, showed how *the inorganic of culture* became transparent in the indiscriminateness of the real: religion, conventional science, art, ideology, and philosophy, labour as mere quantitative utility. These modalities impeded the understanding of the obstacle that was opposed to the development of life, and they were therefore processes of historical dissociation between the life and the death instincts. Thus, they worked in the service of death – for the repetition of already constituted forms – against life. Here, at this point of Freud's work, we find at last its true meaning: how all these activities depend on death aimed against oneself as well as on death directed against the others.

3   *The Discernment of Aggressiveness*

In this way, then, there exists no aggressiveness in the pure state, no aggressive instinct that would be unique and independent: everything in the human being is determined by the system of production and must be read at the level of human signification in which the instincts or drives appear organised and ordered. There is, therefore, a *precise rationality* to be discovered in the life drive and in the death drive. Death without content, the anxiety of death, the one that Freud analysed in *The Ego and the Id*, death without obstacle, was the absolute domination of the super-ego in oneself. Not in the face of the real obstacle: in the face of an ego that was nothing, because it was haunted and enabled by the form of the other, who was everything. The destruction of narcissism and its normal form, bourgeois individualism, means to open up the human subject within a domain of historical significations where the limits acquire their precise meaning: destruction, violence, and aggressiveness directed against the real obstacles that are opposed to the development of social life. But the system, which conceals itself within ourselves, does not give us any choice between its destruction and our own:

> Conversely, any restriction of this aggressiveness directed outwards would be bound to increase the self-destruction, which is in any case proceeding. (119)

What is the difference between the inorganic of nature and the inorganic of culture or civilisation? In the animal, as we saw, the conservation of individual life is already immediately, in and of itself, conservation of the life of the species. In the animal, individual aggressiveness against the obstacle that is opposed to its life, the aggressive instinct used in favour of its own subsistence, is already, immediately, the implicit preservation of the species. This is not the case with the human being. All individual conduct inscribes itself within a structure in which aggressiveness appears determined, from within the ego itself, by the system of production. Except that in the subject of bourgeois individualism the individual conduct is lived as if it were natural. The dissociation of the life and death instincts is already inscribed in the libidinal development and structure of the narcissistic ego. And the latter encounters its corroboration in the structure of the system. This is why, if we do not situate the individual conduct as class struggle prolonging the psychic realm within the structure of the system of production, it becomes impossible to read the dissociation of the instincts or drives within the framework of their true meaning. Because in the case of the 'normal' integration of the ego, the 'double individuality' would seem to preserve love in the sphere of the family, and death inscribes itself also as externally 'normal', in the process of labour or in its subsistence for a privileged class. Here the diffusion of the instincts cannot be interpreted adequately at the personal level: it is 'normal' for aggressiveness to reign in the relations of production. Indeed, is there not much talk of an 'aggressive' economic behaviour? And in this impersonal domain death does not show itself with the precise features of the face of the others who, nevertheless, receive it. Death only acquires precise features in a theoretical reading, when we understand that the system turns death outwards, against the others, as an imposition of the normal functioning of the system itself.

In illness, where the individual assumes him or herself as part and whole at the same time, and aggressiveness is turned inwards against oneself, the diffusion appears to be clear and the amalgamation is clearly revealed as destructive. What happens is that *the effects are visible within the unity of the very subject*: it makes itself 'conspicuous and tangible', says Freud.

> In sadism, long since known to us as a component instinct of sexuality, we should have before us a particularly strong alloy of this kind between trends of love and the destructive instinct; while its counterpart, masochism, would be a union between destructiveness directed inwards and sexuality – a union which makes what is otherwise an imperceptible trend into a conspicuous and tangible one. (119)

The problem appears when we prolong the aggressiveness outside the sexual behaviour in which it becomes legible, and we pursue the aggressive tendencies beyond the framework of the bi-personal and sexual relationship:

> I can no longer understand how we can have overlooked the ubiquity of non-erotic aggressivity and destructiveness and can have failed to give it its due place in our interpretation of life. (The desire for destruction when it is directed inwards mostly eludes our perception, of course, unless it is tinged with erotism.) (120)

This is the aggressiveness that we must disentangle on the basis of its effects within the system of production, effects which only the human being would appear to show: the tendency toward evil. And we have to look for this tendency in the logic that, prolonging itself from the first identification, extends itself as senseless evil, as rational necessity of evil-doing, starting from the very form of the desexualised super-ego. How are evilness and aggressiveness determined, for example, as rational opposition and destruction of all difference that, captured logically, would exceed and oppose itself to the ideal of the ego?

Indeed, Freud tells us enigmatically:

> The name 'libido' can once more be used to denote the manifestations of the power of Eros in order to distinguish them from the energy of the death instinct. (121)

And in a footnote he adds:

> Our present point of view can be roughly expressed in the statement that libido has a share in every instinctual manifestation, but that not everything in that manifestation is libido. (n. 1)

Thus the libido, in its increment towards life, conveys in spite of itself the instinct of death. The libido nourishes death, whose orientation it nonetheless receives here from the instinct of destruction. It is destructiveness that makes use of the libido, subtracting a quantum of energy aimed at another end: opposed to itself. In the realm of civilisation this orientation can only appear on the basis of an organising model of life that orients it from within itself, in an indivisible amalgam that is visible only in its results: that which life did not form as being capable of passing into reality, appears as opposed to and destructive of life itself. But if the death instinct uses the life instinct, then it is *life that opposes itself to life*. It is life retained, subtracted as a disabled charge, which attacks life, the one that did in fact pass through and developed further. *It is aggression against oneself at the foundation of the psychic structure of the subject.*

> It must be confessed that we have much greater difficulty in grasping that [death] instinct; we can only suspect it, as it were, as something in the background behind Eros, and it escapes detection unless its presence is betrayed by its being alloyed with Eros. (121)

'Something in the background', a residue or remnant hidden behind Eros: the death instinct, therefore, is not something originary but a *result*. If it is a residue and a remnant, this is because it remained as something not integrated: that which in the development of the libido was not integrated in the external world, not oriented toward the production of more life, but which remained contained. But who contains this residue? Whose residue is it? It is the form of the other that determined our own by way of identification and incorporation: it is the human form of the other that organises and represses our own, in the flesh itself, which struggles to carve out a path towards life. Death and destructiveness are the other in oneself, in what we possess in terms of originary and absolute repression. In the animal there is no aggressiveness preserved against itself, as the residue of unemployed and contained charges: life and death come into play in the absolute externality of the animal's individuality confronting nature. And it kills or dies. Only in the human being does aggressiveness remain, as instinctual diffusion and seed of death, at the very origin of its emergence into cultural existence. Death is a residue; it is the undeveloped difference from the other, which the other inhibits in its development, as absolute impossibility of developing it except in the form of similitude with the one who creates the opening onto life. This is the originary contradiction: the one who opens us up to life at the same time closes us off from it and plants the seed of death that time will bring to fruition, together with life, as the destruction and annihilation of oneself.

Man dies from his internal conflicts.

This is the cultural genesis, which includes and transforms the biological genesis. For the life and death of culture are based on the life and death of nature, on a prior process that is prolonged in culture. This is why, on the other hand, death and aggressiveness are at the same time the residue of that which life had to vanquish in culture in order to come into being. If life is the tension organised towards integration by means of new syntheses, it cannot fail to be at the same time the preserved disintegration of prior syntheses that were opposed to this process of growth. Every new tension that opens itself to life preserves, as its remnant, the result of the prior battles, the aggressiveness now contained towards objects against which, by way of identification, the living being fought: against that which it had to make its own so as to distinguish it in its specificity for itself, so as to be able to negate it afterwards as alien and incompatible. Just as the ego is the residue of old object cathexes, so too the instincts or drives, in nature, are the residue of old stimulating relationships with the external environment that remained, as already contained aggressiveness, together with the new adaptations that no longer require aggressiveness in order to triumph. They remain only as arabesques, contained gestures of an experience which has passed but which no longer has to be repeated because it is part of the individual baggage that the species transfers onto it. Thus, every new adequate relationship with reality, which ended up being incorporated into the wisdom of the flesh as the conquered result of an adaptation (which supposed aggression against the obstacle, confrontation with death, and, finally, the maintenance of life), by actualising itself in the automatism of the life drive – which is conservation – also actualises, as if in a whisper, its residue contained inwards of an aggressiveness that we no longer have to exert outwards. But every repetition, even an adequately adapted one, qua instinct or drive, has in human history another result: it naturalises culture and holds it back. Because in history the new adaptation is inaugurated as absolutely actual and unrepeatable in the newly gained access to another model of cultural life which, made present as absolute in the father, inhibits the creation of that which the peculiarity of cultural life requires: the development of difference.

And here the two aspects come together: that which the instincts or drives have in common, in both the animal and the human being, but also and at the same time that in which they are different. In human history every access signals the opening onto a field where Eros does not biologically reproduce the same thing. It does so through complex and contradictory social structures, in which each generation implies submerging the individual in the difficult system of a distinct and determinate contradiction, which is the challenge that the world of culture or civilisation presents.

From this follows the narcissistic pleasure that Freud assigns to the destructive fury, which is also punctual, as is all simple pleasure: it is at the service of sameness and not of difference.

> But even where it [the death instinct] emerges without any sexual purpose, in the blindest fury of destructiveness, we cannot fail to recognize that the satisfaction of the instinct is accompanied by an extraordinarily high degree of narcissistic enjoyment, owing to its presenting the ego with a fulfilment of the latter's old wishes for omnipotence. (121)

In relation to this absolute other, we are the result of a task that is already finished: I myself as absolute, the definitive endpoint of an ego who only affirms himself in the repetition of himself. It is here that the residual aggressiveness fails to integrate itself in the new demands that derive from the new obstacles and the new differences: the aggressiveness remains as contained, just as I remained contained within the limits of the other. The 'blindest fury of destructiveness' fails to see what it destroys: *it destroys what I am not*. Only what is different must be destroyed, only similitude must be saved. This much is clear: the narcissistic pleasure of the destructive fury obtains its meaning only against the backdrop of a totality subjectivised as absolute, the permanence of the Father, the alien form regulating one's own: the super-ego. What the blind fury does not see is that which the ego does not discriminate. Therefore, if death is the remnant that is hidden behind Eros, not alloyed with it, but left behind as an unassimilated result, then it is clear that to a form of Eros, to an arrested form of libido that takes itself narcissistically as its own object, there corresponds a death instinct that cannot unfold itself except against the backdrop of its own arrested form.

And we ask ourselves: who or what nourishes the death instinct? The death instinct nourished itself with life held back, with the contained id that thus appears, though it is life, as its obverse: as that which life cannot prolong without destroying itself. Thus the meaning of life is determined by the meaning of death. The synthesis that the ego, qua cultural model, prolongs in its conduct, is the one that determines the meaning of death for the person:

> What distinguishes the ego from the id quite especially is a tendency to synthesis in its contents, to a combination and unification in its mental processes which are totally lacking in the id. (*New Introductory Lectures on Psycho-Analysis*, SE 22: 76)

But we saw that:
1. the synthesis of the ego, as prolongation of the rationality of the super-ego, was the result of a civilisational process that gave order to the body as a function of historical models;
2. the rationality, the order, or the synthesis that the ego prolongs, and the libido which in this way organises itself – negative and positive – works as a function of the system of production that determines this personal and subjective order as coherent with the objective order in its conventional normality. And this is true both in what it excites and in what it represses;
3. therefore, the lines of meaning in which death, or the destructive instinct, is inscribed, are determined by the cultural form in which Eros is prolonged;
4. what in the individual appears as a debate between life instinct and death instinct, is nothing but the interiorisation of a form of culture or civilisation that determines its different modes of manifestation and the orientation of aggressiveness, both inwards and against oneself: against any appearance of difference that casts doubt on the system;
5. the individualistic point of departure, which at the most prolongs the libido only with the human form within the double individuality, lacks the capacity for rational and libidinal synthesis, which would inscribe one's own body within the true structure of the system, and would prolong the aggressiveness present in it, following the lines of meaning that would allow it to discern the true obstacle.

Thus, precisely at the most touchy moment of one's existence, as we saw, in the fury of destructiveness or the loving embrace, the presence of the flesh of this other whom one must enjoy or make suffer, the body is merely halted and detained within the limits of its sensible presence, without rational signification: it ignores the rationality and order which nonetheless binds it both in hatred and in love. Hatred-love, rising up and coming from the inside, ends up being deposited, as a seed, from the outside: and so it grows now, almost autonomous, as if it came from the very essence of our own being.

But let us not fool ourselves: at the moment of maximum aggressiveness, what appears is only aggressiveness exalted to the point of simulation:

> The instinct of destruction, moderated and tamed, and, as it were, inhibited in its aim, must, when it is directed towards objects, provide the ego with the satisfaction of its vital needs and with control over nature. (121)

Here the destructive instinct lost its essential orientation and meaning: the removal of the precise obstacle that is opposed to life in civilisation. It only remains, tamed, moderated, *almost* inhibited in its aim: which is to say, without throwing into doubt or attacking the form of the other that halts the expansion of our own. The death and destructive instincts are exercised only in the restricted form, in the field of control over nature, in relation to inanimate objects, but this form ceases to include within its dialectic the removal of the human obstacles that are opposed to life. And maintaining itself, as narcissistic form, within the limits of the other who remained within oneself without prolongation in a rational understanding, all that is left of it is either the personal and institutional aggressiveness towards what is different, for the sole reason of being different, or the destruction of nature. 'Vital needs': mere reproduction of a body, without a cultural subject; 'control over nature': mere omnipotence over things.

4   *Aggressiveness in the Service of Life*

It is as if Freud's recourse here were to awaken once again the instinct of death and destructiveness and to consecrate it as an impulse in need of being reanimated once more, not inhibited in its aim, in order to determine its meaning at last with the true death and the true life. And the truth of aggressiveness and of life is the truth of its system of production, since it is an instinct that sits astride life as promoted by Eros, which is already cultural, and the aggressiveness that accompanies it is also, necessarily, aggressiveness against the cultural obstacle. It is as if Freud invited the irruption, within history, of that force contained and tamed in the systems of control, and sought to reawaken once more the true death, the one that is present in the mute background of Eros. And it is mute because the realm of culture or civilisation *does not name* the true aggressiveness in the human subject, it does not give humans the words that would include this aggressiveness in a coherent way into their lives. This is why Freud goes back to awaken death so as to situate it in the rational and historical meaning of life, as if only life, in the epiphany of its synthesis and its action of producing life, could make available to us a precise death that erases the terror of its unspoken word, of its drowned scream, and that because of this, for giving us speech, kills us silently from within. If death is the residue of previous struggles that were in fact actual and cannot be reanimated, these struggles within the subject can only actualise ghosts that once were real presences but that, without continuity in reality, remained as forces of destruction that are not welcomed in any objective or exterior world, except our own body.

Thus, death must be spoken out, it must be expressed, it must be represented, it must abandon its drowned voice that speaks to us in an incomprehensible language: that of the terror of the super-ego, which aims it against ourselves if we dare to develop our differences. It is as if Freud told us that we must go back to resuscitate death, to reveal it as a force united to life beyond the dream state and placid lullaby of love that religion proclaims in the call 'to love each other', or in the couple that in a 'double individuality' only takes upon itself the animal determination of its shared psychosis: to treat the other's body as mere materiality without signification, without basis in the world and without announcing the transformation that nonetheless must surge up from one's own pleasure so as to animate the bodily encounter with its universal meaning.

We can understand, then, Freud's affirmation:

> The inclination to aggression is an original, self-subsisting instinctual disposition in man, and I return to my view that it constitutes the greatest impediment to civilisation. (122)

It is a disposition: as such, it is undetermined in its means and in its object. It is original or inborn: it is tied to life itself, as the foundation that accompanies it. But it is *self-subsisting*: it appears as if it were natural, even though it is the product of a collective process, as remnant and residue. And what is still more serious: the fact that it is self-subsisting means that *it is not integrated into the drives of Eros*. It is a separated aggressive drive, made independent of life: it works on its own account. Thus, the aggressive tendency considered as the greatest impediment to civilisation is not given in terms of its human meaning, which would correspond to a definite form of Eros vis-à-vis the precise cultural or civilisational obstacle. It is precisely its *self-subsistent* or *autonomous* character, the cultural fact that aggressiveness and death would appear delimited only within the exact limits of the form of narcissistic individuality, the one which interprets aggressiveness and death only as the negation of its own individual being, as if it were a matter of corporeal death and did not undo the trap of the primary process which still continues to determine us. It cannot interpret the rational signification of aggressiveness because it cannot rationally discern its own foundation: the origin of its own aggressiveness, which has been postponed.

This is why the repressive civilisation, which increases the level of individuation, is at the same time a process that *erases the cultural meaning of death and aggressiveness by emphasising the experience of personal and individual death*. What sense could there be in autonomous aggressiveness, delinked from the indices of reality towards which the instincts prolong themselves that are not inhibited in their aim but integrated in their objects? Death in the free state, death alone, as if it were pure death: that it is its self-subsistence.

> At one point in the course of this enquiry [p. 96] I was led to the idea that civilisation was a special process which mankind undergoes, and I am still under the influence of that idea. I may now add that civilisation is a process in the service of Eros, whose purpose is to combine single human individuals, and after that families, then races, peoples and nations, into one great unity, the unity of mankind. Why this has to happen, we do not know; the work of Eros is precisely this. These collections of men are to be libidinally bound to one another. Necessity alone, the advantages of work in common, will not hold them together. But man's natural aggressive instinct, the hostility of each against all and of all against each, opposes this programme of civilisation. This aggressive instinct is the derivative and the main representative of the death instinct which we have found alongside of Eros and which shares world-dominion with it. (122)

Here we clearly see, in its generality, the meaning of civilisation. Freud characterises it in terms of its universality incarnated in noncontradictory personal relationships, the rigour and coherence of whose logic can be read in the flesh of human subjects: in the libidinal bond through which the human form, the reciprocal presence of human beings, would prolong itself. 'To combine single human individuals, and after that families, then races, peoples and nations'. But for this to happen it would be necessary to integrate them from within the flesh: there where our humanity circulates from where all the other bonds derive and are produced, but whose pre-eminent presence is the only one capable of giving meaning to all other relationships. The problem is the integration and presence in the collective of the individual form, transformed by way of the collective creation that is present in its very individual existence, albeit brought to a halt by the repressive civilisation: 'These collections of men are to be libidinally bound to one another. Necessity alone, the advantages of work in common, will not hold them together'. But this requires the return from the level of individualistic and narcissistic disintegration and separation to the discovery of a common power. It is necessary to discover the collective character of violence now reduced exclusively to its irrational and individual presence, which like death lays contained in the depths of the individual as an unintegrated remnant: as if it were a matter of a natural death and not of a cultural precipitate that must be reanimated and historically situated. The aggressiveness that now is contained, the nucleus of individual death, is actually social and only in the social obstacle can it once again develop its potentiality in connection to life and to individual development. Only its reanimation can tilt the force of life libidinally towards the revolutionary transformation of reality: when the individual death is uncovered as social failure. This is why death in Freud's eyes is linked to aggressiveness: it is not mere death, it is an active death, it is the drive towards destructiveness that kills in order to live. And that only dies from not being able to reanimate the breath of Eros that traverses life: when it is life arrested, like the individual life that closes in on itself and delinks itself from the totality that produced it.

> But man's natural aggressive instinct, the hostility of each against all and of all against each, opposes this programme of civilisation. This aggressive instinct is the derivative and the main representative of the death instinct which we have found alongside of Eros and which shares world-dominion with it. (122)

The diffusion of the death instinct *in society at large* is what makes aggressiveness appear, insofar as it is the 'representative' and 'derivative' of the death instinct, as mere aggressiveness. It is no longer death itself as linked to the meaning that life confers upon it in the development of history. Aggressiveness is not the death instinct: it is its 'representative' and 'derivative', already organised as such psychically by civilisation, split off from its origin. It is the initial relationship of part to part, individual to individual, which plays itself out in the birth to life as civilisation's authorisation to be able to live. It is aggressiveness against the other, as we saw, but tamed or contained: directed against that which the other did not tolerate in oneself. Contained aggressiveness keeps on the threshold of life itself the meaning that links it to the human form of the other as that which must be vanquished: as model which later, in adult life, prolongs and inscribes itself in the institutions. Life arrested at the origin prolongs itself until its end: it holds, we said, the seed of individual death, insofar as its power is kept within the limits of one's own body.

We thus find that the death instinct can only be read in terms of the structure in which it acquires sense: as a function of how the obstacles to civilisation convert it into a destructive as opposed to an integrative element. From the personal point of view, acting only as 'the main representative' of the psyche, it is already rendered inoperative: it only finds its efficacy in the vanquishing of whatever is opposed to it in the maintenance of its merely individual life. It is, therefore, in the class struggle, as we will see in *Group Psychology*, where the debate about violence and aggressiveness acquires its meaning, once again as a function of the instinct of life and the instinct of death, fused in their historical work thus brought back to light.

> And now, I think, the meaning of the evolution of civilisation is no longer obscure to us. It must present the struggle between Eros and Death, between the instinct of life and the instinct of destruction, as it works itself out in the human species. This struggle is what all life essentially consists of, and the evolution of civilisation may therefore be simply described as the struggle for life of the human species. And it is this battle of the giants that our nurse-maids try to appease with their lullaby about Heaven. (122)

The struggle between Eros and death changes in the case of the *human* species; here it acquires its specific character. And if this struggle is 'what all life essentially consists of', the analysis must disentangle, in the class struggle, the carriers of life and of death, those who in the diffusion of the instincts pretend to demarcate death from themselves and project it, in life, onto the others. It is moving to see how Freud places this struggle at the beginning of life itself, which already is the life of culture or civilisation, which the infant lives and which the nurse-maids, in the absence of the mother, unknowingly pretend to appease with their lullabies when they already announce, from the cradle onward, the songs of war.

And it is in these terms that Freud reveals to us the most general meaning of the 'evolution' of culture or civilisation, its progressive sense: as a struggle for life, understood in the sense of Eros, universality understood at the level of the flesh integrated into the others against the bad death, against the death that the human forms of production generate and which condemns all the others to illness, frustration, and aggressiveness against themselves. The contradictory civilisation of the capitalist system exploits for its own benefit this self-subsisting nucleus of aggressiveness and death which, of necessity, signals the transition of the child into civilisation. What was born by force as individual and absolute prolongs itself as such in the collective and relative element of its historical institutions. Instead of confronting the death that the others impose on us, they hide it in the guise of terror and fear, and turn it against themselves. But they do this not against the real obstacle that, by way of the super-ego, prolongs itself in the institutions of power. This is Freud's way of saying that the forms of control in civilisation, all of them, contain death without assuming it, while at the same time, because of the activity in which we engage, we pretend to confront it. Science, which controls nature without human form; religion, which teaches us the illusion of saving us from death in exchange for life paid upfront; art, which with the imagination evades the domain of reality that nevertheless consumes us; love, which in the fullest proximity remains, alone, in front of a body arrested within the only tolerated form of difference: sexual difference; productive labour, which uses our force in order to maintain us, but at the expense of maintaining a system in which lack of satisfaction and privilege conceal the hunger that is opposed to love, and which in order to put an end to hunger kills in us the very form of the other with whom nevertheless we suffer in common from a similar dependency. All these forms are haunted by death, which is held back in the face of the obstacle and works inside of us to dissolve and separate our power from the collective power that confronts it. We do not know how to exercise violence, how to put it in the service of life, how to awaken it and unite it not only to genital love but to also prolong it in Eros, which goes further: in the presence of the brother, sister, or father who is present, albeit hidden, in every dominated other.

In this way, then, there is a rationality of destruction. Let us follow Freud's guiding thread from the beginning of this chapter.

VII   The Halting of Aggressiveness Due to Guilt

1   *On How to Liberate Once More the Contained Aggressiveness*

We were led to the following problem: how can we rescue the positive impulse of the death drive, tilting it towards the ends of life, uniting it with the cause of life in order to destroy the obstacle that opposes itself to its unfolding? We saw that the instincts of life and of death obtained precise meaning as a function of a social field that needed to be objectively defined. And this objectivity appeared when we let ourselves be guided by the rationality that the system of production, revealed in its truth, presented to us: the discernment which allowed us to interpret the coherence or incoherence of the relationships among human subjects on the basis of the broader structure in which these modes of conduct are inscribed as extensions of Eros. For this purpose we can count on Marx's scientific interpretation of capitalist society. His conclusions converge, I think, with the ones Freud proposes and they are even, I would say, complementary.

Marx saw that the function of social science was to organise the 'aggressiveness' of the dominated class and that violence is necessary in order to eliminate the death that historically is imposed on this class in the negation of its own life, so that social life implies social death. But not like that death which 'naturally' comes only at its end, but insofar as death is the constant risk to confront life, which means the obstacles that are opposed to our plenitude in life.

Freud, as we saw, also endeavours to understand the problem of aggressiveness, of the instinct of death as disintegrative of that which cannot develop itself, of that which remains arrested or held back: that which does not possess the tension towards a new form. At the same time instinct of aggressiveness, drive, impulse towards ... – which in the animal is defined by an adaptation that is more or less fixed beforehand – in the human being appears as variable in terms of its means and the ends it pursues. 'Instincts and their vicissitudes ...' Where do they lead in the end? There are no fixed objectives, and those that do appear take shape against the backdrop of a structure that at a given moment gives meaning to the drive. This variability, this continuous inscription of desire in a field of human signification, this confrontation with death as the limit marked by what is already constituted must be present, therefore, in the development of the aggressive impulse.

In this chapter we will verify our first affirmation: that *it is necessary to incorporate, in the psychic apparatus, the historical sense of the process of one's own formation in order to reach a true mode of conduct.* The debate of the historical struggle is present in the nucleus of every conduct as its foundation. And it appears clearly wherever an attempt is made to remove the obstacle that is opposed to the unfolding of life, that is to say, the unfolding of Eros. In this way we will see that the access to civilisation and the submission to power that this access invites are not merely a spontaneous adaptation and recognition, in the child, of the external reality to which it turns itself over. The point is not for the child to give in, as weak, to the strongest, and from there to derive later the recognition of the power and force of the system which, as adult, will extend itself over him or her. The child engages in a struggle to the death, and from this struggle will result his or her life: as adaptation, neurosis, madness, or rebellion. But what will interest us is to show how Freud includes the collective determination of the historical process in this advent of civilisation that each child, individually and solitarily, initiates. In the matrix of this individual conduct there already is at play a collective process that the child ignores and civilisation conceals.

Freud is able to develop the problem of the evolution of the individual only by asking himself which methods civilisation uses to 'inhibit the aggressiveness which opposes it', that is to say, the aggressiveness that rebels against the lack of satisfaction of desire. He will try to verify how this 'method' of control enters into the constitution of the model of psychic organisation of the subject:

> What means does civilisation employ in order to inhibit the aggressiveness which opposes it, to make it harmless, to get rid of it, perhaps? We have already become acquainted with a few of these methods, but not yet with the one that appears to be the most important. This we can study in the history of the development of the individual. What happens in him to render his desire for aggression innocuous? Something very remarkable, which we should never have guessed and which is nevertheless quite obvious. His aggressiveness is introjected, internalised; it is, in point of fact, sent back to where it came from – that is, it is directed towards his own ego. There it is taken over by a portion of the ego, which sets itself over against the rest of the ego as super-ego, and which now, in the form of 'conscience', is ready to put into action against the ego the same harsh aggressiveness that the ego would have liked to satisfy upon other, extraneous individuals. (123)

Thus, that which is most ignored, 'which we should never have guessed', is precisely the most active: that which makes our 'desire for aggression' innocuous. On the other hand, as we have seen, there would be no desires that in their transition to reality would not require this aggressiveness to reach their satisfaction. This is why, in our society, *to render innocuous the aggressive desires amounts to rendering innocuous our desires pure and simple.*

This 'quite obvious' process that happens but which we ignore consists in the fact that 'aggressiveness is sent back to where it came from'. Where does this aggressiveness come from? From the 'place' enabled by civilisation, in which the subject affirms his or her being as being for another who, precisely because of this emergence that makes me possible, disappears as other. Instead of aggressiveness being exercised outwards, in an objective manner, the subject returns to a subjective doubling whose result consists in the fact that the primordial other who is present in oneself, as phantasmatic super-ego, attacks the ego that it made possible. In this way 'regressive' behaviour is the normal foundation of the moral conscience: the more the ego attempts to reach the truth of its intimate relationship with the external object, the more there is an actualisation in it of the structure of the primary process which is the persistent model of its adult reaction. Instead of encountering externally the collective historical process that through adequate aggression allows human beings to satisfy their desire and to share it, the subject remains, from childhood onward, determined by the form of his or her original emergence: from the infantile helplessness, when the other was present in me as the form of all satisfaction as well as of all prohibition. What has happened? In my individual access to civilisation I began by incorporating the other in me, I conflated myself with the other. Unable to attack the other on the outside, I returned to the behaviour of the primary process in order to attack the other from within. This inversion, which the repressive system consolidates, has a result in the life of the adult that makes it the basis of its system: it 'puts into action against the ego the same harsh aggressiveness that the ego would have liked to satisfy upon other, extraneous individuals'. The same harsh aggressiveness: the greater the reaction against those who confront us and attack us, the harsher will be the aggressiveness against oneself.

> The tension between the harsh super-ego and the ego that is subjected to it, is called by us the sense of guilt; It expresses itself as a need for punishment. Civilisation, therefore, obtains mastery over the individual's dangerous desire for aggression by weakening and disarming it and by setting up an agency within him to watch over it, like a garrison in a conquered city. (123–24)

2   *The Sense of Guilt, Fundamental Method in the Service of the System*

Who could ask for more? That the enemy may use the same force of response that his aggression provokes, but not against him but against the subject of aggression itself. That the more aggressiveness the repressor awakens, the more the dominated subjugate themselves. This infernal machine is set up within our very own self: it is the normal 'psychic apparatus' that each one of us, on our own, sets off. And it explodes precisely in the contact with the obstacle that is opposed to the satisfaction of our desire: when we were nearest to reaching it.

It is at this point that Freud will try to understand the evolution of the individual so as to verify how this method of control enters into the constitution of the nucleus of the psychic organisation of the subject:

> What means does civilisation employ in order to inhibit the aggressiveness which opposes it, to make it harmless, to get rid of it, perhaps? …. This we can study in the history of the development of the individual. (123)

But in that case, as we will observe, the understanding of the evolutionary process will depend on the scientific presuppositions from which one departs. Either we consider the origin of the sense of guilt by explaining its formation as a merely individual fact, or we include in this understanding the historical sense that determines it. The sense of guilt is a cultural 'method' of control, Freud tells us, and it can be understood by extending its domain in the direction of the scientific 'method'. Here it will also be revealed that this scientific method, which serves to know the sense of guilt, keeps intact the concealment of reality that determines its rational mode of understanding. By this we mean to say that the sense of guilt, as 'method' of cultural control, will determine at the same time the limitation of the scientific method if it does not previously transform the control that the repressive culture exercises in the dominated ego of the scientist. Only the overcoming of the domination that the sense of guilt exercises over us will enable us to acquire the appropriate method for its comprehension. If not, the 'method' of knowledge too, starting from its foundation, which is the guilty conscience, will be at the service of the repressive cultural 'method', covering up its meaning and sharing its finality.

Civilisation, as we already saw, indeed has recourse to several 'methods' for concealing reality. Among them, together with narcotics, were art and science. But the most important 'method' of control *from which all the others derive*, Freud tells us, is this sentiment of guilt that universally becomes part of all human beings, regardless of what are subsequently the modalities for the cover-up and reinforcement to which we have recourse.

> We have already become acquainted with a few of these methods, but not yet with the one that appears to be the most important. (123)

And so it is here that we come full circle: the foundation of the scientific 'method' is based on the 'method' of cultural repression, and *the elucidation of an affective subjection seems to condition the exercise of the power of reason*. Not just any 'thinking consciousness' can, therefore, know *in truth* based simply on the fact of its power to exercise its rational capacity. This presupposes, previously, the liberation of the affective ties and determinations that constrain it to not be able even to perceive adequately the foundation of the real. Whence the importance that the sense of guilt has for Freud as a 'method' of control, the 'most important' method of cultural subjection.

Every sentiment, we know, is the affective repercussion of a link between humans and the world. But the feeling of guilt, Freud will tell us, is not an affective relation between the internal and the external, between the human being and the external world. It appears as an 'internal tension', which plays itself out in the domain opened up in subjectivity by civilisation. The sense of guilt, in other words, is a feeling between the internal and the internal, between the subject and the internalised civilisation. It is, at the same time, the primeval nucleus of its historical determination: between ego and super-ego. But it is also a subjective tearing apart, which is experienced as if it were a tension between life and death: between the cultural life authorised by civilisation and the mortal rupture of these limits. To ask oneself scientifically about the formation of this sentiment in the evolutionary history of the individual therefore comes down to the following presentation: how did the 'internal tension' manage to produce itself from the outside and become autonomous from the outside that produced it? But even if we understand that civilisation produced it, this does not mean that the problem is solved: whether or not this question reaches its true answer will depend on how we conceive of the historical reality of the world of culture or civilisation.

In general terms, then, we may say that there was no internalisation, in the psychic apparatus, of the comprehension of the process that produced it. The symbolic order that organises us, as moral conscience, had its origin in the sensible human form of the other who, by redoubled identification, gave us being. We were part and whole at the same time: the good was inside, the bad outside. But in reality, in the form of the other, what was also organising us, from within ourselves, was the obligatory form of all satisfaction. We remain attached to the sensible other whose order, in a muffled way, rules over us with its model of being which delimits within us the contours of our own flesh. When we are already adults, the debate continues in this interior domain where the seminal similitude with the other that enabled us for life opens itself up as merely subjective difference in the consciousness of the ego. In this way, the adult relation 'individual-external world' is transformed, by way of regression, in a relation of individual to individual. 'The aggressiveness is sent back to the place from where it proceeded', Freud tells us. In search of the origin, but *inwards*. Yet outwards there is only the infantile fantasy of the origin as the inverted form of every true relationship. The contained aggressiveness, instead of prolonging itself towards the system of production in search of the foundation of the obstacle that stirs it up, returns to its subjective form, in which I was one-with-the-whole. From the history of the world, now as adults, we regress to the individual history such as it presents itself in the equivocal genesis of the psychic apparatus, which validates its appearance as if it were real. The problem is therefore *the foundation and the ratification of this appearance as the absolute origin of reality*. The one that leads to the situation in which the human being, at the root of every confrontation that requires the exercise of discerned violence, *never has reason on its side: it may have feeling, but it is the feeling of guilt*, and without reason.

3 *Genesis of the Feeling of Guilt*

Freud begins by recognising that psychoanalysis in this regard has an opinion that is different from that of other psychologists, and aims at the foundation of good and bad: the psychological genesis implies the genesis of values that form the basis for human conduct. What appears thus are two *actual* forms of this feeling, which when they are considered genetically would correspond to two successive forms of its final formation:

1. The guilt felt as a result of the *realisation* of an act.
2. The guilt experienced merely because of the *intention* to realise such an act.

That which was realised, or which one had the intention of realising, defines what is bad, the sinful. 'Both cases, however, presuppose that one had already recognised that what is bad is reprehensible' (124).

But the capacity for this recognition is not natural but historically acquired:

> We may reject the existence of an original, as it were natural, capacity to distinguish good from bad. (124)

Between what the individual wants and what the norm regulates there is often a contradiction: the bad thing is not always 'what is injurious or dangerous to the ego'. It must be, therefore, injurious and dangerous for others:

> Here, therefore, there is an extraneous influence at work, and it is this that decides what is to be called good or bad. Since a person's own feelings would not have led him along this path, he must have had a motive for submitting to this extraneous influence. (124)

Freud will distinguish two methods to explain the genesis of the sense of guilt: *the chronological sequence* and another, which we could call *the dialectical sequence*.

a   Analysis of the Apparent Form: The Chronological Sequence

The chronological sequence, as we will see, is based only on the linear causality. From the evolution of the individual it only considers the temporal course as the successive index of an uninterrupted progress, but it ignores the dialectical sequence and the succession of forms that are engendered therein. And this happens because it does not refer the structure of the psychic apparatus to broader forms on which it depends, in this case the historical form on whose basis it becomes meaningful and organises itself in the first place. *It ignores, therefore, the discontinuity that civilisation introduces into subjectivity precisely as the rupturing of the apparently continuous sequence.* And this continuous sequence in time, which consciousness retains, hides precisely the discontinuity of the rupture, the drama of a confrontation that will persist – unconscious –

as the foundation of a rationality from which violence has been barred. This apparent understanding forms a system with the persistent reign of the sense of guilt.

First phase of the sense of guilt: The discernment between the good and the bad begins as the result of an affective inadequacy with regard to the other, and the fear of the loss of its love will be the index of its agreement:

> Such a motive [for discernment] is easily discovered in his helplessness and his dependence on other people, and it can best be designated as fear of loss of love. ... At the beginning, therefore, what is bad is whatever causes one to be threatened with loss of love. For fear of that loss, one must avoid it. This, too, is the reason why it makes little difference whether one has already done the bad thing or only intends to do it. In either case the danger only sets in if and when the authority discovers it, and in either case the authority would behave in the same way. (124)

In this first phase it is the relation with the external other which determines the orientation of one's conduct. Originally the good and the bad only make sense as a function of being loved, or not, by the other. We love the one who is at the same time, in his or her very presence, the order that regulates our relation and makes it compatible with reality. The law of the loved object is confused with the object of love itself: originally, there is no separation between being and norm. Love is what determines, in the eye-to-eye and body-to-body encounter with the other, the adequacy with regard to reality. Because as yet there exists no radical incongruence between the internal and the external: between myself and the real other. The opposition is not yet deadly. We read the meaning of our act in the external world, the subjective in the objective, even though this objectivity is dominated by the real, concrete, and visible person who rules over us. Here there is not yet any law: the other decides face to face, for each one of its reactions, the form of my act. It is the norm incarnated, whose meaningful contours are beginning to reveal themselves in the affective coherence that my empirical relationship, one sense at a time, in one gaze after another, is showing to me:

> At this stage the sense of guilt is clearly only a fear of loss of love, 'social' anxiety. (125)

That is to say, anxiety that is not only psychic but objective, controllable, verifiable, and enabling my adequate relation with reality. It is a regulating sense that does not put into doubt the object of its love, given that every movement counts or will count on its agreement: the child will always end up giving in to love. It is rather fear and not anxiety: the basic relationship on the grounds of which this adequacy is elaborated is more profound and more firmly rooted. The other is already present in oneself, and the point is to verify out there this unquestioned warm feeling of possession in here.

Second phase of the sense of guilt: This phase signals the transition from external to internal adaptation:

> A great change takes place only when the authority is internalised through the establishment of a super-ego. The phenomena of conscience then reach a higher stage. Actually, it is not until now that we should speak of conscience or a sense of guilt. At this point, too, the fear of being found out comes to an end; the distinction, moreover, between doing something bad and wishing to do it disappears entirely, since nothing can be hidden from the super-ego, not even thoughts. (125)

This 'great change' indicates the transition from the relative and sensible form of affective regulation to the rational and absolute law. More profoundly, it introduces the reduplication into the subject: I am one before the law, which is also present in oneself. Here the intention prevails over the realisation of the act. To think or imagine the satisfaction of the forbidden is already an infraction. Descriptively, this implies that one continues to be ruled by the form of the other, but now ratified on a different level: its corporeal and determinate form disappears so as to appear only in the reason of the super-ego, as an instance of our conscience. But this new imposition of the law in its absolute foundation no longer comes only from the father: it is inserted and acts as a pivotal mainspring in the repressive reality that civilisation exercises on the ego. The paternal authority, that corporeal other which was normative for my body with its form that determined the contours of my own and thus gives form to sensibility as signification, disappears and becomes the rational substructure or fine print. In the mere rationality of the law the origin disappears and the clash of bodies conceals itself. This is why it is not the normativity of consciousness that determines the beginning of moral conduct. The tables of the law are not drawn up by a pure spirit: there is no Law without the flesh. As the foundation of its persistence, the father provides it with this waste product, this subjected being that civilisation later includes, through a long apprenticeship, into the system of production. But here everything is already played out: in this second step we prolong and internalise, via the moral conscience, the form of the rational system that from the outside continues to expand and universalise the field of multiple dependencies, of allowed connections, and of moral regulations. And so what is most external finds support in what is most internal: in the other who affectively subsists and becomes blown out of proportion as the felt foundation, which now appears to be absolute, of my individuality. The extension of my rational capacity, which brings the invisible closer and renders it visible, coherent, and systematised, is based on this absolute transparency of my being in which the other expands his power to see, like an extraneous eye in the depths of my own flesh. My rational knowledge is prolonged only on the basis of his absolute sight, which knows it all and watches over it all: I am wholly transparent to the law that brings order to my relationship with the real.

This is why Freud says in this second phase:

> ... it is not until now that we should speak of conscience or a sense of guilt. (125)

Moral conscience is the rationality of the law as absolute law. The sense of guilt is the felt foundation of my desire as infraction. In this way *sentiment and reason* are conjoined for an identical social purpose of dependency. The previous empirical verification here undergoes a radical transformation: *all of a sudden* we capture the certainty of an absolute and, therefore, also universal law. It would seem that it is from the sense of being guilty for desiring what the law represses that the law's well-foundedness is validated. The adult law would thus continue the infantile sense of dependency, and we move from the affective submission to the rational submission. It would seem that we reach a new level both in feeling and in reasoning, and that both – affect and reason – have progressed in this social expansion that requires them. But this is not actually the case:

> It is true that the seriousness of the situation from a real point of view has passed away, for the new authority, the super-ego, has no motive that we know of for ill-treating the ego, with which it is intimately bound up; but genetic influence, which leads to the survival of what is past and has been surmounted, makes itself felt in the fact that fundamentally things remain as they were at the beginning. (125)

This new level, with its seeming autonomy, only reproduces the form of the first dependency, though now elevated to the absolute. The internalised rational structure only prolongs the infantile dependency, and replaces the sensible form of the father with the rationality of the moral norms of the system of production that finds support in the persistence, now fetishised, of the first. It is no longer the father with whom I measured each act in function of his love: it is the Father, the form of forms, who manifests himself only in a comprehensible, rational, and known form, as penal code of order, *without origin*. In the second phase of the chronological genesis as apprehended by scientific reason, the origin it discovers is not the one that the guilty conscience knows: for the latter, its origin is confused with ours and is inseparable from it.

> ... genetic influence, which leads to the survival of what is past and has been surmounted. (125)

This means that the form given through identification, the absolute access to being, continues to be the hidden genesis of the ego and the super-ego. Thus the result of civilisation, which is based on the universal validity of its law, appears to hide the historical genesis of its production. In the same way the access of the child to civilisation, by way of its parents, hides the development that from the first identification onward elevated it to the human form as similar. But it is on the basis of this infantile feeling that the adult's rational infraction finds its repercussion. The rationality of conscience does not *truly* expand the signification of my body and its possible prolongation, just as it also does not open up the signification of the world.

> The super-ego torments the sinful ego with the same feeling of anxiety and is on the watch for opportunities of getting it punished by the external world. (125)

Conscience torments the sinful ego with 'the *same* feeling of anxiety', that is to say, the same infantile affectivity, now no longer of fear – given that there is no visible form of the other as obstacle or as object of my love – but of anxiety. But it is no longer 'social anxiety', but rather anxiety before the super-ego, which equals the anxiety of death. The basis for the anxiety before the super-ego is the terror before the loss of life, as opposed to the previous fear, which was only fear of the loss of love.

But something has happened in this transition from the first phase to the second, which the chronological sequence does not manage to explain:

> At this second stage of development, the conscience exhibits a peculiarity which was absent from the first stage and which is no longer easy to account for. For the more virtuous a man is, the more severe and dis-

> trustful is his behaviour, so that ultimately it is precisely those people who have carried saintliness furthest who reproach themselves with the worst sinfulness. (125–6)

This paradox shows us a lack of meaning in the seemingly direct and immediate passage from the first phase to the second. If there was nothing more to it than the continuous prolongation of a transition, the imposition of the law in the human being would be clear as water: prolongation of the external power into the interior. It would suffice to show that the rationality of the law does nothing more than prolong, all the while forgetting its genesis, its foundation in submission out of love. And, disentangling the reason of conscience, it would suffice to ratify the power of the father in the power of the system, now accepted. But then submission would not have to provoke the sense of guilt: the best ones would be those freed from guilt and the subjugated ones would live in the end the reencounter of the love of the father with the benevolence of the law of the system.

Things do not happen like this. Observance of the law paradoxically culminates in self-destruction.

> This means that virtue forfeits some part of its promised reward; the docile and continent ego does not enjoy the trust of its mentor, and strives in vain, it would seem, to acquire it. (126)

In this second phase, then, the decisive aspect in the sense of guilt would be *the need of punishment*. In the first phase the external punishment was the result of the external non-adaptation to the requirements of the loved one. Here, with moral conscience, the internalisation of the law into the subjective elements also delegates the need for punishment, which no longer comes from the outside but from the inside, from within ourselves.

Summarising, Freud tells us:

> Thus we know of two origins of the sense of guilt: one arising from fear of an authority, and the other, later on, arising from fear of the super-ego. The first insists upon a renunciation of instinctual satisfactions; the second, as well as doing this, presses for punishment, since the continuance of the forbidden wishes cannot be concealed from the super-ego. We have also learned how the severity of the super-ego – the demands of conscience – is to be understood. It is simply a continuation of the severity of the external authority. (127)

Thus it would seem possible to understand the sense of guilt as the direct result of the renunciation of the instincts, and the chronological description of the sequence, rather than two origins, would give us a single continuous transition in which only the internalisation of external power would be the relevant difference. First there would be the external authority, and later the authority internalised in the form of moral conscience.

The sequence, in other words, would be as follows:

a. 'Originally': the 'renunciation of instinct was the result of fear of an external authority' (127). There really is, then, renunciation of satisfaction for fear of the loss of love.
b. 'Fear of the super-ego': here renunciation is not enough: 'the wish persists and cannot be concealed from the super-ego' (127). Need for punishment. The sense of guilt arises therefore in spite of the renunciation achieved outwards, because previously there was transgression inwards.

The sequence of this process, Freud insists, would be the following:

> 'First', instinctual renunciation owing to fear of aggression by the external authority;
> 'After that', the exterior authority (the super-ego) is erected, with instinctual renunciation owing to fear of the moral conscience.

There would be, as we see, a succession of fears and dreads: *fear* for the exterior aggression and, then, *fear* for the moral conscience. Here, in this second situation, 'bad intentions are equated with bad actions' (128).

> The aggressiveness of conscience keeps up the aggressiveness of the authority. (128)

Thus far the chronological sequence, which tries to show us the genesis of the sense of guilt, only shows us that the human being, as offender of the moral law, would always be the true culprit for violating the law and, as a consequence, the need for punishment would be the adequate response to the sense of guilt. The transition from child to adult would only be the emphasising of the responsibility that the autonomy of the psychic development would make possible. The feeling of guilt, as the consequence of this positive acquisition of the moral conscience, regulates more fully our adequate relationship to reality. We no longer need to be supervised by the other: civilisation internalises the law of the system in order to make us more independent as autonomous individualities. Each one watches over him or herself. The infantile submissiveness is prolonged directly in adult submission, and the need for punishment signals always its single direction: from the outside inwards, in the first case; from the inside inwards, in the second. *But always against oneself.* In this process the law is not put into doubt, nor is its foundation. *The question of the true or false origin of the law historically would not have any place in the science of psychology.*

All this would seem to be very clear if it were not for the fact that Freud, as we saw, asks himself about two important phenomena that the chronological sequence attempts in vain to account for:
– The chronological sequence does not explain the reinforcement of the moral conscience under the influence of external adversities (visible, external, and comprehensible), which would much rather weaken it: all the bad things I have coming to me are well deserved.
– The chronological sequence does not explain the intensity of conscience in the best and most docile beings, precisely those that should feel the least guilty.

This is the paradox of moral conscience: it punishes the just more than the sinners.

> We have already explained both these peculiarities of conscience, but we probably still have an impression that those explanations *do not go to the bottom of the matter*, and leave a residue still unexplained. And here at last an idea comes in which belongs entirely to psycho-analysis and which is foreign to people's ordinary way of thinking. This idea is of a sort which enables us to understand why the subject-matter was bound to seem so confused and obscure to us. (128)

With this new idea, which he goes on to state, Freud adds to the linearity of the chronological sequence the dramatic discontinuity of the historical dialectic in the understanding of the sense of guilt.

b   Analysis of the Real Form: The Dialectical Sequence

The chronological sequence contained the reality of the external world, but not its historical meaning. What was contained was the transition from the sensible to the rational dimension of conscience, but not the historical understanding of this rationality. What was contained was the experience of the individual, but the latter did not find itself determined in its subjectivity by the collective forms. In short and to use a language that we will have to justify in what follows: the moral conscience was not determined by the class struggle.

The chronological sequence as previously described gives us real moments of affirmation, but the sense that links them is not fully understood. In reality the causal transition from the 'first' to the 'after that' is nothing of the kind: the second is neither 'continuous' with nor 'perpetuates' the first. There is, between one and the other, a cut and an inversion. The process, Freud thus postulates, would be the following:

> For it tells us that conscience (or more correctly, the anxiety which later becomes conscience) is indeed the cause of instinctual renunciation to begin with, but that later the relationship is reversed. Every renunciation of instinct now becomes a dynamic source of conscience and every fresh renunciation increases the latter's severity and intolerance. (128)

We already see that the sense of guilt in this case neither continues nor perpetuates the same fear of authority. And the first foundation of the original renunciation is also not fear, but anxiety. The renunciation owing to anxiety – pure anxiety – is the foundation of the fear, and the 'dynamic source' of moral conscience. Why is every new renunciation a 'dynamic source'? Because by renouncing the instinct owing to anxiety, that is to say, by anticipating the result of satisfaction in function of a prior catastrophic situation, its possible realisation is lived as a confrontation with death. The first 'dynamic source' of the sense of guilt is the anxiety of death that forms the backdrop for every subsequent satisfaction. When there is renunciation, the game is already over: there was an actualisation, via the 'dynamic source', of the anxiety of death.

In order to explain the sense of guilt, the sequence takes us behind fear toward the external authority. The fear of the loss of love leads us, in the first phase, to a traumatic situation, to the first drama of the child who is born: into the anxiety of birth. Let us recall its meaning. The anxiety of birth was an adequate response in the transition toward autonomy coming from the warm depths of the mother's womb: the affective commotion, which was *only internal*, produced a chemical reaction. And this response was successful: it made life possible. In the wake of this first anxiety – the first 'interior tension' – the first fear is later produced: the fear before the external authority. We will see that something is covered up from one phase to the next, which must be deciphered, but it has to do with the drama of the origin of the human being. But not only with its individual origin in birth, in the second phase this individual origin is also united with the historical origin. Because this first anxiety, which led to a purely subjective transformation, will be the reanimated base of the moral conscience later on. The limit-situations of the transition, first from birth to life and then from birth to culture or civilisation in the form of man or woman, depict two crucial situations in the development – anxiety of birth and castration anxiety in the Oedipal complex – which truly define the drama in question and give meaning to the sequence.

Here it so happens that what was considered the *cause* in the chronological sequence is much rather converted into the *effect* in the dialectical sequence: it is not moral conscience that determines the instinctual renunciation but the instinctual renunciation that is the foundation of moral conscience. Freud in other words does not remain at the level of affirming moral conscience as the foundation of human conduct, but he shows us that moral conscience is a secondary effect, the result of a prior process on which it is based. In the *apparent* relations of linear causality and chronology it seemed as though our conduct were determined by moral conscience. In the relations that psychoanalysis discovers, those in which the dialectical sequence is dominant, the apparent determination of our conduct reveals at last its secret: *it is the renunciation of satisfaction that turns into the dynamic source of moral conscience and, therefore, of its existence*. It is because we give up on and renounce desire that there is moral conscience. The focus of the problem thus varies: it is no longer a question of explaining that guilt arises because, in reaching pleasure, we transgress the prohibition of moral conscience. No: the point is to understand *how it is possible that humans renounce their satisfaction*. Something more fundamental must have happened in the child for renunciation to become the foundation and reinforcement of moral conscience.

This then would be the dialectical sequence:

> If we could only bring it better into harmony with what we already know about the history of the origin of conscience, we should be tempted to defend the paradoxical statement that conscience is the result of instinctual renunciation, or that *instinctual renunciation* (imposed on us from without) *creates conscience*, which then demands further instinctual renunciation. (128–29, emphasis added)

In other words, the problem leads us to the foundation of the renunciation of satisfaction. And to invert the usual comprehension of the problem: it is not, as is commonly believed, that moral conscience would produce instinctual renunciation, but the other way around, it is instinctual renunciation that creates moral conscience. Therein consists, basically, the inversion that is invisible in the merely chronological sequence. The latter sticks to the conventional representation of repressive culture, which affirms that moral conscience is the unquestioned determining instance of instinctual renunciation. In the chronological sequence the logical law of science sticks to the uncritical validation of the moral law as its presupposition. What happens is that in this compliance with the law, *guilt does not appear to constitute the foundation that validates the law*. The law would impose itself all by itself in its objective function: its power is obeyed as absolute. Whence the fundamental character of the question for the science of history: how could guilt have converted itself into the foundation of the law? Once guilt is destroyed, the absolute foundation of the law, and its power, would disappear: the system could not continue to rely on us in order to submit ourselves. In other words, the chronological explanation, which is consistent with the apparent rationality of the system, does not understand the subjective drama, which in the wake of a prior renunciation led to the installation of the moral conscience. And it is this process that Freud is going to try to show more clearly with the example of the basic instinctual renunciation of every human being, the one which we might call 'the renunciation of all renunciations': the renunciation of aggressiveness.

The renunciation of aggressiveness. According to the understanding derived from the chronological sequence, the amount of aggressiveness that we inhibit and direct against ourselves, inasmuch as we are guilty for desiring, is intrinsic to the super-ego, and not the result of a renunciation on the part of the subject. The amount of aggressiveness is equal to the amount of aggression of the external authority that has been internalised: we receive that aggression which the system determines that we deserve. The aggressiveness that the super-ego aims against ourselves is 'a continuance of the severity of the external authority and therefore has nothing to do with renunciation' (129).

By contrast, according to the dialectical sequence:

> The effect of instinctual renunciation on the conscience then is that every piece of aggression whose satisfaction the subject gives up is taken over by the super-ego and increases the latter's aggressiveness (against the ego). (129)

The distinction is important: whereas in the chronological sequence the aggressiveness that we receive *continues* the external aggressiveness of the system, for the dialectical sequence the aggressiveness of the super-ego is nothing but the aggressiveness of the subject itself, but aimed back against itself. For the latter, in other words, there would be 'a different derivation for this first instalment of the super-ego's aggressivity' (129).

The aggressivity that we receive, then, is in truth the aggressivity that we give up. Why do we give up on being aggressive? And herein resides the problem: if in effect the power of external aggression, in the way we feel it, were always to lead to death, its force would be invincible. And this is precisely the point for Freud: to explain that the omnipotence of this power that is exercised and felt at the level of subjectivity does not correspond to the reality of the repressive power, and that it is this attribution, which is felt as though it were the prolongation of the external power, that seals with fire the relation of submission: due to the anxiety of death, should we dare to confront it. In this way the 'scientific' rationality, which affirms and justifies the super-ego's aggressiveness as the prolongation of the external aggressiveness that has been internalised, continues in its explanation to ratify as absolute the external power. If it is true that the process is inverted, and the aggressiveness felt as though it emanated from the super-ego is in reality the subject's own aggressiveness, then the conventional chronological explanation not only makes moral conscience absolute; it converts an absolutised subjective feeling into an objective power that is absolute and real. The official explanation, with its chronological reasoning, ratifies a subjective appearance and thus it, too, fulfils an ideological function of justifying submission.

And so, the first charge of aggressiveness with which our own super-ego is invested, that 'military garrison in a conquered city', is nothing but our own aggressiveness that we were not able to exert against the external authority and that we now direct, as though it was alien to us, against ourselves. This is the important aspect of which the chronological explanation could not give an account: *the super-ego's aggressiveness that condemns us to punishment is nourished with our own aggressiveness that we renounce.* Thus the child not only gives up on the satisfaction that is forbidden to it; it also gives up, in this very act, on the aggressiveness that the repressive force awakens. But there is more, as we see: the child ends up directing this aggressiveness against itself, for being guilty of desiring. Not only 'no' to satisfaction; but also 'no' to aggressivity.

In this way, then, if we accept the genesis of moral conscience simply as if it were an introjection of the external authority on the path that leads to the internalisation and formation of rational norms, which coincides with the conventional understanding of normal consciousness, the moral conscience would be first, and the instinctual renunciation would come secondarily. But, as we saw, the paradoxical thesis introduced by Freud, the inversion, proposes that we begin from the opposite end: with the renunciation of aggressiveness as the foundation of moral conscience. The linearity of the chronological progress does not account for the drama of a confrontation that, after exerting it, led us to give up on aggressiveness.

> But the discrepancy is removed if we postulate a different derivation for this first instalment of the super-ego's aggressivity. A considerable amount of aggressiveness must be developed in the child against the authority which prevents him from having his first, but none the less his most important, satisfactions, whatever the kind of instinctual depriva-

tion that is demanded of him may be; but he is obliged to renounce the satisfaction of this revengeful aggressiveness. He finds his way out of this economically difficult situation with the help of familiar mechanisms. (129)

4   Rebellion and Guilt

Thus the origin of conscience must be situated on another terrain, prior to its implementation, prior to its apparition. It is not enough to give an account of moral conscience; it is necessary at the same time to understand that its foundation is linked to and based on the renunciation of aggressiveness: that *conscience is already, from its very origin, a conscience that has given up, because it is a guilty conscience*. The capacity of being conscious in the human being is inscribed within the development of Eros, and to the complexity of historical social life there corresponds, in the psychic organisation, the acquisition of the capacity to understand the structure of the real, to confront the obstacle, and to satisfy the desire. But here we precisely come upon the fundamental moment of this formation, when this essential capacity by a sleight of hand is made to vanish and when, as a result, *the exercise of the death drive is deviated from its orientation toward life and toward the obstacles of the external world so as to be flipped over as the death we deserve against the subject itself: for having dared to desire*. It is here that the fundamental drama reveals itself in which this subjugated conscience finds support: the ego who is subjected by the system thereafter is not a vanquished subject but, on the contrary, a guilty subject. And we will see why this subject is guilty: guilty for having vanquished in the imaginary that oppressor whom the subject also dearly loved. Submission here comes afterwards, from the guilt of being an assassin.

Civilisation does not triumph over the child because, subjected from birth, the latter would prolong and extend this submission into adulthood. The child is a rebel and an aggressor and a victor; only the remorse over its triumph leads to the guilt that subsequently bends and subjects the child. It is because the child has a deeply moral gut feeling and pays with its guilt for the imaginary murder that the adult's morality, which is the true assassin, takes power over this noble sense and with its judgment ratifies an imaginary situation as if it were real.

What happens, then, is that the child – as opposed to how the adult sees the child from his or her alienated optic – did not let itself be vanquished nor did it give in so easily to the repression that was imposed on it. And in order to confront the obstacle the child has recourse to an old artifice, in which its infantile power resides:

> By means of identification he takes the un-attackable authority into himself. The authority now turns into his super-ego and enters into possession of all the aggressiveness which a child would have liked to exercise against it. (129)

'It takes into himself by means of identification': this is the most regressive identification, the oral type. The other, who confronts the child with his incommensurable power, is incorporated: he enters into the child and becomes part of its own body. What else could it do to defeat the other, helpless as it is, if not acquire also a similar power? We once again confront the drama that developed in increasing exteriority (renouncing the instinct out of fear of the loss of love, but not renouncing one's penis) only now within one's own subjectivity, where the other once again becomes part of oneself: oneself as attacked and attacker. This drama, which now leads to such a drastic solution, is the threat of castration that produces the outcome of the Oedipus complex. Challenged to confront him, the child identifies with the father in order in this way to turn over the situation in its favour. But this subjective revenge is its condemnation: the child identifies with the aggressor and with the repressor. From there the logic of development cannot overcome the character of reflection and remains, from the very beginning, framed in the terms that the other imposes on it:

> The child's ego has to content itself with the unhappy role of the authority – the father – who has been thus degraded. (129)

Imaginary power in the face of a real power: such is the basic asymmetry of the confrontation. Freud tells us, in synthesis, anticipating the result:

> The authority [with which the child identifies by incorporating it] now turns into his super-ego (129).

But this transformation is not sudden: the mere identification does not suffice. Something happens within this subjectivised relationship, which makes it possible for this authority to enter into the possession of all the aggressiveness of the child. It does so because previously the child exercised this aggressiveness in its own way, against the external authority:

> Here, as so often, the [real] situation is reversed: 'If I were the father and you were the child, I should treat you badly'. (129)

Everything hinges on this 'as if': 'If I, the child, were the father; and you, the father, were the child', what would I do? I would only impose one form of justice: that of reversing the situation by turning the good into the bad and the bad into the good, *for me*. I, the child (made into the father) would treat the father (made into the child) badly. I follow his example, except now in my favour. And with all the aggressive fervour provoked in me by the fear of losing my very own being for reasons of my desire, I attack the one who, after giving life to me, does not hesitate to sacrifice me so as to preserve, without sharing, his own pleasure. The dilemma in other words is the following: either stop desiring and abandon what I most love, or else maintain the desire and confront the obstacle. *Here then we see the basic, though also extreme, form of all human desire*. And it is from the denouement of this basic form adopted by the drama of desire in search of satisfaction from where the way of confronting all subsequent desire will become implanted in the depths of the human subject. Poor satisfaction, that of this ego turned inside out, who fell in the trap of its own impotence, but who *could not do anything less than fall in this trap*. The foundation of the law here finds its seat also, in the child, in a bloody fact: the father runs through its veins.

This form of exercising justice does not increase the access to reality: it takes advantage, as we saw, of a cunning artifice, which it reaches regressively in the return to an infantile power.

> The relationship between the super-ego and the ego is a return, distorted by a wish, of the real relationships between the ego, as yet undivided, and an external object. That is typical, too. (129)

It is the result of this return, of this subjective triumph, which produces *afterwards* the conversion of the father into the super-ego. If previously there had not been this subjective drama of infantile revenge, the father would not be transformed into the super-ego. But there also would be no access to historical reality. The question, then, becomes: how does the super-ego obtain its absolute power, and how does it appropriate the child's aggressiveness?

Let us keep in mind the guiding thread: thus far there is only, first, the subjective aggressivity of the child against the internalised object. And this allows us to understand and solve the problem with regard to the charge of aggressiveness of which the super-ego *afterwards* takes possession. After what? For now Freud tells us:

> But the essential difference [from the old real relationships between the ego, which is still undivided, and the external object] is that the original

> severity of the super-ego does not – or does not so much – represent the severity which one has experienced from it [the object], or which one attributes to it; it represents rather one's own aggressiveness towards it. (129–30)

Clearly, the aggressiveness is the one we exercise, as the result of identification, against the subjectivised object. But with this aggressiveness we still do not have the complete picture of the process: the most important thing is still missing. And the most important thing is *the definitive renunciation of all subsequent aggressiveness owing to the sense of guilt*. But which aggressiveness is Freud referring to? Evidently, not the aggressiveness aimed outwards, which the child already had renounced before, but the aggressiveness inwards, which *for the child, though, is as real as the other*. It is from here, on the basis of what has happened or will happen here, that conscience is produced. What comes first, as we already saw, is not moral conscience. What interests us here is its foundation, which necessarily will remain unconscious.

> If this is correct, we may assert truly that in the beginning conscience arises through the suppression of an aggressive impulse, and that it is subsequently reinforced by fresh suppressions of the same kind. (130)

What matters is this mechanism by which the victor turns out to be, by the same token, the vanquished. Because he was the victor he turns out to be the vanquished. Such is the mechanism: the winner loses. And who wins, we might say, after losing, is the least moral one: the winner is the brute force without love, *only because the vanquished, the father, is loved by the victor*. The weakness of the victor is *his love*. Now already without hatred: without reality index. And the vanquished returns, in reality, to the exercise of its power without love. It is not strange that bourgeois justice and Christianity should preach love, especially to those who are subjected: they reanimate the bottom feeling of culpability of this first historical act that made them, forever, absolutely guilty. Consciousness, and not only moral conscience, begins with a crime.

> ... in the beginning conscience [therefore not only moral conscience but also consciousness] arises through the suppression of an aggressive impulse ... (130)

That is to say: after having exercised this aggressiveness. It is in the moment after the crime when conscience appears. It is through the suppression of an aggression that the child effectively (for the child itself), by means of a regression, exercises against the father, there where only love and hatred were dominant, but successively. In this act, the exercise of hatred is followed by love, and the absolute vigour of the first is followed, but now forever, by the absolute validity of the second: infinite love reigning against the backdrop of guilt and completely removing the hatred that preceded it. There was no law as yet: the child applied an empirical criterion. But it is here, in the face of the intolerable consequences of that necessary and effective action, that the law all of sudden erupts. What was negated absolutely by hatred, in a second moment is affirmed as absolutely valid: only out of love. What happens is that the alternating affirmation of love and hatred is followed by remorse. And the hatred that searches for its invincible power in the infinitude opened up through regression – when in reality it possesses no such thing – gives way to the love that is situated in this infinity: by maintaining alive forever after the one in whom we incorporate ourselves in the first place to torment and kill him. The other resuscitates from among the dead, now invincible, so as to subject us in our need to be ourselves the ones who continuously give him his life, which thus nourishes itself with ours.

In this way the aggressiveness that we renounce is not just any aggressiveness: it is the aggression against the true oppressor, against the most beloved one who broke, without reciprocity, the law of love and threatened us with castration. It is this drama, which plays itself out in the subjectivity of the child, that turns into the foundation of conscience, in the internal distance opened up by the presence of the other. Conscience is, initially, a battleground. And later, with the help of metaphysics, it pretends to be pure conscience! Conscience is an internalised battlefield, the space of a confrontation in which the dramatic form of dependency and liberation is depicted: aggressiveness, death, and remorse as the foundation of all signification. The drama of the crucifixion is the drama of the resurrection of the father made child. It is the inverted replica of the Oedipus complex, which validates as real its imaginary foundation. The holy spirit, which for the Christian opens up the domain of conscience as unconscious and pure, is the result of this confrontation between the child made into the father and the father made into the child, whereby the holy trinity is resolved in the absolute maintenance of guilt and the absolute affirmation of a spirit purified of the crime that absolves us. It is the maintenance, at the same time, of two affirmations: we were effectively guilty; we will effectively be absolved of our guilt. But on one condition: never to desire anymore.

5 *Collective Violence Not Assumed at the Origin of Guilt*

This is the drama that was not included in the first conception of the sense of guilt, and of which the chronological sequence in its linearity and externality could not give an account. It concealed that which Hegel knew already from his youthful Christianity: that the origin of conscience is a struggle to death between *master* and *slave*, just like that, *in the singular*. But it is not only the individual Oedipal situation that Freud includes here in order to give meaning to the sense of guilt. What really defines the historical meaning of this subjective drama is another fundamental fact, without whose understanding the sense of the Oedipal drama would play itself out in the margins of history: *the really effectuated transition, at the origin of human history, from the primitive horde to the fraternal alliance*. The individual Oedipus lacks meaning, in the conduct of the human being, if we separate it from the historical Oedipus. Only, therefore, if we include in the transition to individual culture the historical transition from the primitive horde to the fraternal alliance does the true significance of the individual drama become clear to us:

> Thus, if one shifts over from individual to phylogenetic development, the differences between the two theories of the genesis of conscience are still further diminished. (131)

Thus the process presents itself as included in a historical understanding:

> [M]an's sense of guilt springs from the Oedipus complex and was acquired at the killing of the father by the brothers banded together. On that occasion an act of aggression was not suppressed but carried out; but it was the same act of aggression whose suppression in the child is supposed to be the source of his sense of guilt. (131)

The Oedipus complex that plays itself out individually in the child has its origin in a collective historical process: the fraternal alliance. There the Oedipus complex was acquired after the collective killing of the father: this is the *real and historical origin* of the Oedipus complex that each child repeats later on as it individually accesses it. It is this originary collective sense that remains covered up in the child. The Oedipus complex would be the result of the universal form of access to independence, and supposes the exercise of power against the one who opposes the autonomy of the human being, that is, against the one who opposes the initiation of life in the conquest of the right to the satisfaction of desire. Civilisation repeats in each child this drama of the transition, and in each father there reappears the function of the primordial father in the threat of castration and the prohibition to satisfy one's desire. In both cases, as Freud says, it is a question of 'the same act of aggression' (131).

Thus, there is an adult, real, and primary origin of the historical super-ego (the originary Oedipus complex in the transition from the primitive horde to the fraternal alliance), which is the consequence of a collective act that was really carried out; and there is an individual super-ego (the infantile Oedipus complex), which plays itself out in the 'as if' – for us – of an apparent act. In this way to every guilty child civilisation owes a real assassination that the child did not carry out but which is attributed to it. To each child is due a fundamental act of aggression that it effectively must realise, a violence that it really must exercise, but of which, precisely for having believed and imagined that it exercised it, the child is deprived forever. And it is this violence of which, now that it already is an adult, it is deprived, that it would have to exercise against the existing power which, through the historical system of production, prolongs the domination of the father into the domination of the oppressive classes. To each child the repressive culture owes a death, the one it did not execute, but for whose guilt it pays with its life as if it really had executed it. To each human being is owed a fundamental violence, which effectively marks its real transition from nature to culture, its recuperated participation from individual behaviour into the collective fraternal alliance, once again renewed. *And without exercising this violence, Freud would tell us, there can be no true access to civilisation.* Only the violence of the break with the repressive power effectively gives birth to us as human subjects after this false introduction into the world of culture or civilisation. History begins, for every human being, in the child – with a false move.

Before civilisation, at the dawn of history, there was no Oedipus complex: the historical and cultural field had not yet been opened within which the possibility of individuation and conscience would be produced. The field of culture or civilisation exists because the children of the horde came together and in the fraternal alliance put the oppressor to death and gave rise to the first human collectivity. Because there is culture, because there is language, because human beings create the child as human child and because the access implies the shared domain for the satisfaction of desire, for this reason there is the Oedipus complex: because the child wants to be recognised, from the origin, as similar. But in this equivocal and unequal initiation, the similitude is lost so as to make room for difference: between masters and slaves, between rulers and subjects, between judges and culprits. The child must once again reconquer, in the drama of each new transition, that which the people in the fraternal alliance produced – even though they subsequently covered up the meaning of their act and, out of guilt, erased it from history.

And so the Oedipus complex exists because at the origin of history there was the rebellion of the brothers who banded together against the repressive father. And the Oedipus complex is unresolved because civilisation does not preserve, in its current form, the recognised presence of that first renewed historical fact in which each child – now made into the father due to the renewed prolongation in each revolution as the fraternal alliance – would have to reserve for each new-comer its place in the alliance. But in our repressive civilisation there no longer exists any fraternal alliance: *the current system is the system of the dominant horde in the field of capitalist civilisation*. The fraternal alliance must be rediscovered among brothers – among class brothers. What began as fraternal alliance against the father continues and prolongs itself as class struggle in the historico-capitalist system.

Let us continue the analysis. The child is born in a field opened up by the historical Oedipus complex: that of a civilisation which also internalised the dead father who continues to regulate it and dictates his norms to it. The actual child makes its transition towards reality as if there had not already been a historical transition: as if this drama of its own passage had not transitioned through civilisation in its development. What happens is that the current system of production, which persists in the ancestral concealment of submission, neither actualises nor validates the fraternal alliance on which its origin is based. This is why the current civilisation cannot give it its support: it makes it drop, in a tragic coincidence, from the individual history into the collective history as if both were equal and admitted only an individual solution. But the initial obstacle to civilisation, which required the exercise of violence against the father, marks the distance from the current civilisation and the asymmetry between the transition of the child and the transition of history: between an individual fact and a collective fact. Civilisation drops the child in the field of historical concealment, where its necessary infantile non-knowledge is coupled with the adult's cover-up. There is no effective transition from the I to the we, because the child falls directly into the individualistic separation that comes after the fraternal alliance, where the sons who are already remorseful for their father's death preserve the dead father inside themselves and thus objectively conceal the crime: the dead one lives on with the life of those who conceal the fact of their having assassinated him. The coincidence is not by chance: both history and child share the same need. The premature child prematurely confronts that which the adults, at the beginning of history, confronted in due time. But only in the class struggle does the necessity of this confrontation now continue the renewed alliance of the brothers, no longer against the father but against the oppressive system.

In the historical origin there was a *real guilt*. The latter derives from the fact that the children have really carried out the maximum violence against the oppressive father: that of collectively putting him to death. Let us retain this affirmation: the guilt at the origin is the result of a collective deed. The remorse, subsequent to the act, led to an individual solution: each one kept, at the level of the imaginary, the dead father who thus was converted into the field of conscience and super-ego. The individual solution to a collective fact leads to the concealment of the formation of the individual conscience at the origin. But the same is true for the child: its individual transition to civilisation, its access to conscience, is produced in the collective domain that the child ignores, but not in the same way as it was ignored at the origin of history and in the development of adult history. Because the first fact was a historical event, not of the child but of the adult: the rebellion of the sons against the effectively castrating father. In their case castration was a real threat exercised by an adult power against the subjected adult sons, and the violent reaction was an adequate response to the violence to which they were being subjected. The real violence was confronted with a real violence: effectively greater than that of the father.

In the individual origin of the child, by contrast, there is real guilt for an imaginary fact: the fact of having 'imagined', by way of identification, that one killed the father individually in one's subjectivity. Really to have killed the father means: that which affectively was present in him that belonged to the father was destroyed by the violence felt by the child. In the process of incorporation, truth is on the side of feelings: to feel is already the truth of what is felt. And the truth is that *I felt that I martyred him*. The felt memory of his martyrdom, which invaded with all my hatred the triumphant feeling of my flesh, will forever be present as an unavowable proof – not even I know it – of my fundamental evilness, of my infinite aggressiveness and my condemnation. In the infantile origin the guilt is individual guilt for an imagined individual fact. Or, which is the same thing: every child repeats in its infantile fantasy the historical assassination of the father. The ambivalence of love and hatred refers not only to an external being, but to a being that, by identification, is contained within one's own individuality. Here, the threat of castration also lacks reality, and it only acquires a symbolic reality that no father exerts anymore. But castration is here, in the final instance, something similar and equally grave: it means leaving outside of life the necessary aggressiveness to prolong the satisfaction of desire in reality. The child keeps his penis, yes, but he loses his object. Not only his material, empirical object, but the human sense of the object. And he loses himself: he becomes tailor-made for the system of production and returns to integrate, bland and submissive, the primitive horde, the quasi-biological individuality of the capitalist form. There civilisation reserves him his wife: supremely good-natured, she is not like the primitive father who withheld the women. But here in the current system of production, it is no longer sexual difference alone that is at stake: the penis is a symbol, not this piece of flesh, and the Phallus is its truth.

6 *To Return the Aggression out of Guilt*

This transition, which is necessary but resolved at the level of fantasy as the only negation available to the child to face up to the omnipotent paternal power, is the basis for the repressive forms of civilisation. Each civilisation introduces the child to the system, but what was its inaugural collective triumph in the beginning of human history, and the subsequent guilt, begins in the child with its individual conduct and fantasised act of aggression. In this scheme civilisation, identified in its artificial function with the function of the primordial father, manages to invert the collective violence of the origin in its favour: it dissolves the collective into the individual and converts the infantile transition into a true form of access. The sons, in the fraternal alliance, were not capable of confronting the inaugural pain of their freedom, and they hid, out of guilt, the aggressive violence of the origin: the identification with the dead father. The subjective affirmation that followed meant conceding back to him, now in this life extended inward, the aggressive and castrating power of which the collective historical deed had deprived him for good.

This origin now prolongs itself in a two-fold manner. On the one hand, it circulates throughout global society, in the structure of its productive process in which the power of the father acquires the function of its new historical reality. On the other hand, this origin circulates in personal individuality, in the structure of its psychic apparatus, because of the necessary confrontation that we just analysed. These constitute in a way two parallel and complementary series. *What had its origin in a single fact subsequently in our civilisation culminates and splits into two:* there is *one* history for the personal emergence of the child, and *another* history for the system of production. Lacking an explanation for the historical determination that traverses with one and the same structure both origins and gives them a common form, the separation between the individual and the collective, the psychological and the historical, only knows the miracle of a correspondence between the two to explore an adequate relationships whose true foundation remains concealed. The locus of 'forgetting', or of the cover-up, lies in the civilisation and not in the individual. The two series hide the fact that it is the same debate that is at stake and participates in the same sense: the renewed transition from the primitive horde to the fraternal alliance in each individual access to the human world.

In the first case, before the Oedipus complex, the child behaves like the son of the primitive horde: it effectively gives up on that which the father prohibits. In the second case, by contrast, after the Oedipus complex, the child and the adult act in the cultural wake opened up historically by the fraternal alliance. But they do not know this. Because without collectively having killed the father, they move on to become individuals in the field opened up by this historical or archaic fact, which prolongs itself in our current society. Together with repression, they acquire the capacity of being conscious, except on a level where consciousness no longer is conscious of being the field historically opened up, at the origin, by the internalisation of the dead father, preserved out of guilt. The fraternal alliance now circulates among the class allies against the power of the dominant classes. Only here could the foundation of the law of conscience be disentangled; only here could the collective power against the system be reunited; only here could the feeling of guilt discover the infantile reason for its necessary confrontation, and the dead father would reveal itself as brother within one and the same system. Here, in the contradictions of our current civilisation, one lives under the subjective domination of the father and the objective domination of the power of the dominant classes, which are nothing but one and the same power divided into two. One lives under the control of the vanquishing father because, finally and objectively, *the system vanquished the father and the father vanquished the son*. This model of transition of the child into culture is analogous to the originary historical transition, which necessarily continues to produce itself on the two levels, individual and collective. As adults, we do not enter into the dominion of the fraternal alliance but into that of the primitive horde in the repressive civilisation of the capitalist system.

7 *Abstract Heritage or Historical Heritage?*

In Freud, there are thus two origins for the moral conscience of the human subject, which are convergent and must be elucidated together, given the ambiguity of their framing:

1. There is an archaic, phylogenetic origin of guilt, the drama of the transition from nature to culture, where the children really had to put the father to death. This origin would be present, as an archaic heritage, in the child, reinforcing its own drama.
2. There is an actual and individual, ontogenetic origin of guilt, the drama of the transition from nature to culture that each human being repeats at birth, and in which the fantasy of the death of the father also turns out to be affirmed as access to civilisation. This is the process that was already analysed by Freud. Both, according to him, would be convergent. Thus the super-ego is constituted by three factors:

- phylogenetic factors (archaic heritage);
- innate constitutional factors (biology);
- environmental influences from the real surroundings (current mode of production).

All of Freud's theory as developed so far would seem to reinforce the third factor, when he says:

> ... the original severity of the super-ego does not – or does not so much – represent the severity which one has experienced from it [the object], or which one attributes to it; it represents rather one's own aggressiveness towards it. If this is correct, we may assert truly that in the beginning conscience arises through the suppression of an aggressive impulse, and that it is subsequently reinforced by fresh suppressions of the same kind. (129–30)

Freud writes against the exaggeration of cultural dependency, which finds support in the fact that 'A child who has been very leniently brought up can acquire a very strict conscience' (130):

> But it would also be wrong to exaggerate this independence; it is not difficult to convince oneself that severity of upbringing does also exert a strong influence on the formation of the child's super-ego. What it amounts to is that in the formation of the super-ego and the emergence of a conscience innate constitutional factors and influences from the real environment act in combination. (130)

And in a footnote he adds, giving strength to this conception:

> Apart from a constitutional factor which may be supposed to be present, it can be said, therefore, that a severe conscience arises from the joint operation of two factors: the frustration of instinct, which unleashes aggressiveness, and the experience of being loved, which turns the aggressiveness inwards and hands it over to the super-ego. (130 n. 2)

As far as Freud's affirmation of the phylogenetic heritage is concerned, this appears when he adds:

> It can also be asserted that when a child reacts to his first great instinctual frustrations with excessively strong aggressiveness and with a correspondingly severe super-ego, he is following a phylogenetic model and is

going beyond the response that would be currently justified; for the father of prehistoric times was undoubtedly terrible, and an extreme amount of aggressiveness may be attributed to him. (131)

Between both positions, the ontogenetic and the phylogenetic, one of which explains the aggressiveness of moral conscience from its current structure and the other from the archaic heritage, Freud opts for an intermediate path:

> We cannot get away from the assumption that man's sense of guilt springs from the Oedipus complex and was acquired at the killing of the father by the brothers banded together. On that occasion an act of aggression was not suppressed but carried out; but it was the same act of aggression whose suppression in the child is supposed to be the source of his sense of guilt. (131)

Indeed, the child, in order to 'follow a phylogenetic model', must not have received it necessarily by heritage. This possibility, such as Freud himself presents it in the Oedipus complex, allowed us to affirm the following hypothesis: the drama of the transition from nature to culture continues to develop itself at the most profound level of human beings, in the most subjective elements of their existence. But this rather more individual access is at the same time totally social and actual: the very transformation produced by this transition engraves forever in the child the form of a universal drama, whose distance between the historical origin in which we include ourselves and the endpoint that we constitute is present and internalised as the basic historical dimension in each individual; its access to being human among humans. And this access to the universal form is, nonetheless, necessarily particularised in each system: with the specific characteristics of the civilisation to which one belongs and which defines the content and meaning one has.

This double determination, the archaic and the actual, has a different meaning when looked at from the point of view of the scientific analysis, which affirms that the subject is the necessary site of the historical debate.

1. *Original Oedipus*: beginning of civilisation. Transition from the primitive horde to the fraternal alliance.

> We cannot get away from the assumption that *humankind*'s sense of guilt springs from the Oedipus complex and was acquired *at the killing* of the father by the brothers banded together. *On that occasion an act of aggression was not suppressed but carried out* .... (131, emphasis added)

2. *Individual Oedipus*: the one that each one lives as personal drama in the bosom of the family:

> ... it was the *same act of aggression* whose suppression in the child is supposed to be the source of his sense of guilt. (131)

Thus the original Oedipus appears, in the individual access, presenting the basic drama of access to civilisation realised by the first humans, but which each human being, subsequently, repeats. It is here, then, that the historical-collective-originary and the actual-individual become united. And it is precisely here where Freud will develop the difference in access that, thanks to Oedipus, brings us together in a common access, except that now this is lost on us *because in the necessarily individual access of the child the collective reality of history was not included*. But this historical origin is not restored to us due to the course of civilisation: civilisation does not straighten this inverted process by means of which we gain access to it.

Whence the question that might be asked by an interlocutor with both feet planted in reality:

> So it makes no difference whether one kills one's father or not – one gets a feeling of guilt in either case! ... it would be a case of something happening which everyone expects to happen – namely, of a person feeling guilty because he really has done something which cannot be justified. (131)

Here, at the conventional level, what is missing is the adequate discrimination between reality and fantasy, and the sense of truth conveyed in the latter. It so happens that the interlocutor with his feet planted in reality ignores – because this remains unconscious for him – that the foundation of his thinking and of his moral conscience is his own drama of transition, his own Oedipus denied.

8 The Pain of Truth

Freud, then, must go back to rediscover, starting out from the conventional level of customary modes of conduct, that prior unconscious level, which constitutes their foundation. He will once again distinguish two modalities in the feeling of guilt.

1. *Remorse*: the feeling of guilt after really having committed a misdeed. This relates only to a deed that has been done. But this feeling 'presupposes that a *conscience* – the readiness to feel guilty – was already in existence before the deed took place' (131).

> Remorse of this sort can, therefore, never help us to discover the origin of conscience and of the sense of guilt in general. (131)

Here the satisfaction of an instinctual need could momentarily vanquish the limited energy of conscience and, once reached, by way of remorse go back to validating the power that for a brief moment it had opposed. Psychoanalysis cannot remain at this conventional and disingenuous level, which does not reach the essence of the moral act and whose only ambition is to not feel guilty for breaking the law. We must go to the source of remorse, which is precisely what this feeling of remorse hides without allowing it to come out, because once the infraction has been effectuated, it once again finds itself in a condition *as if its action had left intact the power against which it rebelled.*

> Psycho-analysis is thus justified in excluding from the present discussion the case of a sense of guilt due to remorse, however frequently such cases occur and however great their practical importance. (132)

We already know what is hidden: the feeling of guilt, which comes from remorse, conceals the basic Guilt which caused there to be, for the human being, a realm of culture or civilisation. Freud thus recuperates the domain of the imaginary, of desire, in which *fantasy determines reality as cultural reality*. The 'normal' human being sticks to 'reality', to the remorse that follows after the realisation of the act. But in this he does not have knowledge of his own act as stemming from another primordial Act, which serves as its foundation: the foundation of the law of his conscience.

Here there appears a second conception of remorse which, different from the actual one that is dominant in our culture, is linked not to an act of satisfaction and infraction subsequent to the moral conscience, but produces itself there where no moral conscience exists as of yet: the remorse for having killed the primordial father at the beginning of history, as a collective deed.

And so we would have:

1. An originary remorse (the killing of the primordial father), which is not based on any moral conscience, but on the very field of the presence of the other in which the meaning of the deed was verified.
2. A secondary (cultural) remorse, which is based on the moral conscience, but delinked from its foundation in the historical experience.

Only by uniting both processes of genesis – the originary history of the collective transition from nature to culture with the individual history of the same transition that repeats itself in every human being – can we comprehend the signification of our moral conduct and the sense of guilt on which our repressive civilisation is based. *Individual history, for the comprehension of its true meaning, presupposes the comprehension of the historical logic of the human being's access to civilisation.* This is the only logic, moreover, capable of helping us set right the equivocal transition that we have analysed before.

Thus, in the originary drama there lies hidden the structural meaning of the foundation of every human being: there where event (the murder) and structure (the transition from natural individuality to cultural individuation through the fraternal alliance) constitute the originary point from which all human rationality was produced. In the relation of individual to individual (between father and son), the mediating third was a collective being: the fraternal alliance. This initial moment is crucial because it is from this first opposition that, in the ambiguity of love and hatred toward the father, the point of insertion of the cultural dialectic takes shape – that is, of the type of reason that finds support in the flesh of the other but at the same time in the common body sketched out by the brothers, as a necessary process for one's own coming-into-being. But this necessarily implies, at its origin, both the engenderment of differences starting from new similarities and the exercise of negation. The primordial human being faced a situation that was dramatic beyond comparison, in which *the meaning and the origin were present and engendered at the same time.* In the ambivalence the real affirmation of one of its moments (one's own individuality on the path to conquer, in a new reality, the right to pleasure) implied at the origin the real negation of the other (his assassination at the hands of the fraternal alliance). But this is the starting point for the creation of the properly human level.

> This remorse [the originary or primordial one, which did not yet presuppose a moral conscience or a super-ego] was the result of the primordial ambivalence of feeling towards the father. His sons hated him, but they loved him, too. After their hatred had been satisfied by their act of aggression, their love came to the fore in their remorse for the deed. It set up the super-ego by identification with the father; it gave that agency the father's power, as though as a punishment for the deed of aggression they had carried out against him, and it created the restrictions which were intended to prevent a repetition of the deed. (132)

Thus, in its origin, in the 'remorse for the deed' that was collective and historical, the super-ego that emerges out of identification is the identity with its negated opposite, now internalised. There is not yet a symbolic plane here, since we are at the beginning of conscience in its sensible foundation. It is the form of the other, by identification subsequent to an act, that creates the psychic domain in which the negated is rescued with one signification that previously was postponed (love) by the real pre-eminence of the other (hatred). Thus the first internalised form that sketches out the domain of an ideality continues to be the form of the father, the form of one's own origin, but also the meaning of the real obstacle that it had to confront. Here, however, the conscience that thus emerges does not preserve the truth of the event. This internalisation retains only one of the extremes of the fundamental ambiguity, namely, love, as present in the wake of the act, which was the moment subsequent to the exercise of hatred. But in the form of remorse, this next moment seeks to rescue as actual that which was negated. Now it puts up front that which in the act was split as an appropriate response to the violence of the other, and which made it necessary to make one signification (hatred) prevail over the other (love) in order to initiate life, which is the life of human history. It is this act of remorse that lies at the origin of human conscience, of morality, of the super-ego, and of the domain for the elaboration of truth: where it would have to reintegrate and preserve, once disappeared, that which the act had separated. For Freud, at the foundation of conscience, there is no separation between ethics and truth: in its origin the truth is determined by the restitution of the truth of the other. In the same way that for Marx *the truth is the norm*. And there is truth, though painful, in the beginning of history: the children had to kill the father. But the meaning of this truth consists in the fact that it is based in the pain of the signification that has been maintained. This is the power of the spirit, as Hegel would say, 'the magical power that transforms the negative into being'. The beginning of the relation to the world implies, at the beginning of history, the confrontation with the father as obstacle to one's own life, and his being put to death. There is no historical process that does not imply sacrificing, in the creation of a new synthesis, that which is opposed to it, in spite of its also being loved. In its beginning the truth of the human being is initiated with the objective act of aggression, following a sustained prior aggressiveness that was aimed against it. There is, afterwards, guilt and terror in thinking, because the negation carried out in thought, when it is true, actualises the origin of the negation of the other, now phantasmatic but real in its origin, on which our transition to being human is based.

9   *The Relegated Origin*

At first the opposite of one's self is the other. But that other with which, after the crime, and because of the crime, we identify. The crime opens up the domain of identification, hence the domain where the other engraves his meaning, the affirmation of his life that we deny him, in oneself. The one and the other thus initiate their dialectic: in a first moment, the father was everything and I was nothing. But a nothing determined by the father. The negation of the father, his collective assassination, implied already that this nothing determined by him would acquire being. But this being was already a 'magical power' previously inexistent in nature: it contained that from which one proceeded *in oneself*. Fate was sealed. If in the beginning there was the word, it was the word incarnated in the flesh: it was the father who kept speaking in oneself *as in the moment prior* to the historic deed. We gave him the life he had lost in ourselves: we gave him our being so that it may continue to be the sense of what we inaugurated against him, because in order to live we dared to put him to death. But this death, that of the Dead father, from now on haunts us forever. Thus, *the origin appears within us, as prior to our own origin*. And as partial, since it retains only one of its significations as fundamental: love.

But civilisation for Freud was *a decision of forgetfulness*. This forgetting of the traumatic situation par excellence constitutes human evil converted, by way of concealment, into the direct foundation of the Good as absolute.

However, between this historical origin and the actual endpoint in which we find ourselves there is a similarity and a difference. *The obstacle that Freud places at the beginning of history*, which continues to be an obstacle at its endpoint, *in the end does not have the same structure as at the beginning*. In the actual endpoint it presupposes the capacity to see and assume the act of aggression not against the phantasm of the primordial father who subsists in each human being, but which has the form into which the external obstacle was developed in history to the point of acquiring the dominant form of the system of production. *What began as having the form of the human-father ends up having the form of the social system that dominates us*. Whence the need to destroy the form of thinking, the obstacle, only with the form of the human: the capitalist is an incarnation of the system. Now he is not the obstacle: we must not aim the act of aggressiveness against this subject, but against the meaning that from within the system determines him as model. But this structural meaning reawakens and reintroduces into the human being the rationality that from the father is prolonged in the system, and from there once again determines the meaning of each human being.

This is what lends itself to equivocation: the infantile categories are, basically, the ones that regulate the process of the first transition. Indeed: in the subject who, collectively, killed his father, the 'family' form was the social form in which he found himself included. What is hidden, and what is different, is the framing of the solution: the collective way out in the fraternal alliance. And the act of really having put the father to death.

Let us consider the emergence of conscience in the historical transition. This conscience emerges, necessarily, before the categories of objective thinking are produced, since the latter is the product of a process of differentiation and historical creation that is posterior. Therefore, conscience here appears only with the forms of relationality and organisation that still correspond to the primary process. In the act of killing the one whom we loved we expelled outwards what we hated, but we retained inwards, via identification, what we loved: the dead father. But the dead father 'lives' in us as being ourselves made other and henceforth, with its internalised form, ruling over our relations with the external world. Except that, though the deed was real, he now, in the concealment that follows from the pain and remorse for his death, also appears erased for the conscience that thus develops. Conscience erases its origin in this other, as if it lacked any genesis. Because to reanimate the origin would imply, for this first man alone, to remit himself to that first act of his killing. In this way in the beginning of history itself there opens up *an anteriority to history, as if the super-ego that thus inaugurates it were its absolute beginning, and not a secondary moment of a real event that conscience does not know, even though it constitutes its foundation.* Consciousness appears as an absolute foundation, devoid of presuppositions. This absolutisation of the relative – relative to our own historical and collective act – is the result of remorse, and at the same time opens into two separate fields a development that distances love from hate, and situates it in two distinct contexts, just as it opens an infinite distance, a hiatus, between reality and fantasy. By not assuming the ambivalent meaning of its own act in conscience, and by not accepting the consequences of a choice decided by violence so as to enable one's own life for enjoyment, we believe we give to the father the life that we took from him with our own body. Apparently, the solution seems happy: we put the real death outside, and we reserve the imagined life inside. Except that it is our own life, which subsists, and not the life of the other, which we take away, that serves as the foundation for this solution. But this life of the other that we incorporate also internalises its signification, the one against which we fight and which continues to live together with him: the reason why we put him to death. Thus, the death that we imposed on him and that, qua collective violence exercised outwards, we conceal in the negation of the act, will appear as violence exercised inwards. He will continue to maintain his incorruptible meaning: ruling over our own flesh with his prior violence, with his individual repressive form. We will not know it on the outside, because the word of our civilisation hides it, and death will appear as silence: *mute*, like the id itself, conflating itself with our being. But at the same time the collective origin of individual conscience appears hidden. We internalise what we negate, but we cease to include the new historical capacity, on which the real negation was based: the fraternal alliance, which lies at the foundation of individual conscience.

And yet this first act continues to be at play, though now in the imaginary, in each new individual who gains access to history:

> And since the inclination to aggressiveness against the father was repeated in the following generations, the sense of guilt, too, persisted, and it was reinforced once more by every piece of aggressiveness that was suppressed and carried over to the super-ego. (132)

Only the first inaugural act of history was remorse: the others were already merely the internal drama, the *feeling* of guilt.

We now must compare this historical access to civilisation with the access that each child and each human being renews when they enter into it. The first historical act, the killing, was a real deed; the act of the child plays itself out on the imaginary level: it is not a real death (the first one was a collective act, that of the child an individual one; the first was carried out by an adult body, the second by a child's body).

However, in the child, whose primary process is analogous to the psychic process of the first human, the imaginary effect of the suspended action is similar to the real effect of the action carried out in a form close to the primary process. Human history emphasised the development and formation, starting from this cultural and collective deed, of the secondary process, which is symbolic and rational. But in the child this historical transition from the primary to the secondary process, in which it reaches the most rational and complex categories of civilisation, takes place inside the child itself. The foundation of conscience, in the child, is unconscious, but for another reason: it does not have the necessary categories to retain that process of confrontation with the father, which led it to internalise the act of aggressiveness. But it also does not have knowledge of the real process that produced in it the categories that it acquires. The historically developed categories, now for reasons to do with repression, also do not keep present in their process the aggressive and collective origin that lies at their foundation. Thus the current social reality ends up ratifying in the child the presumption of its imaginary access. The absolutisation of social power, once again, as power of the fathers of the primitive horde, and their control over the human beings they dominate, comes to validate and verify the subjective process that the child, helpless and dependent, had elaborated. In its form, coming from the child, the process would seem to be analogous and its figure symmetrical. But not so coming from the scientific knowledge that historical materialism developed in order to explain to us the truth of history.

And here, once again, the question arises: Must Freud, to explain the force with which the repression of the super-ego imposes itself, necessarily postulate an archaic, phylogenetic heritage? Must the incommensurable force with which its omnipotence appears and nourishes itself necessarily be ascribed to the force attributed by heritage to the primordial father? On the contrary, we postulate that this hypothesis is not very economical: that the force which Freud encounters in the analysis of adults would not require such a hypothesis if he emphasised, as he should, the force of the system in which the child is created.

10 The Historical Heritage Present in the Current Structure

If the archaic heritage results from an archaic historical *situation*, the aggressiveness of this first relation was provoked by the system of which the brothers initially were part. The subsequent dialectic therefore cannot do less than pursue this first form as the one which, in its modes of social organisation, contains the violence provoked by domination. But this first collective transition, Freud explains, did not produce guilt: it produced remorse. The feeling of guilt is posterior to the institution of the super-ego, and already implies the negation of the real deed. If indeed, as Freud tells us, the dead father continued to regulate the relation with the outside world. But by internalising the dead father as super-ego, what disappeared from human consciousness was *the real and determinate situation* that led to his killing. To the absoluteness of its ideal normativity there corresponds the negation of every real category of time and space. But the meaning of truth of the moral conscience then does not contain the true process that produced its advent. The violence denied to the father, exercised outwards, now appears internalised. This violence without reason, which is authorised only by sentiment, is also absolute violence: absolutely deserved. What thus appears is the meaning of reality together with the violence that the obstacles in reality require in order to prolong life. *This excluded violence also excludes the meaning of the organisation of reality that produces the guilty subject*. Historical objectivity does not give us back this violence in its capacity of origin and foundation of the subjective violence: the fact that its origin is linked to the collectivity of brothers in order to liberate themselves from subjection. But through the successive historical forms it is only this content that develops and attempts to understand itself. There was a historical sense that split off from the subjective sense, to which it was related and which was its consequence. Therefore, the reference to the archaic subjective heritage, which would survive in each human being, would also necessarily correspond to *an archaic heritage of productive systems*, of the external reality that produces it, and *the latter survives in the structure of each productive system*. The historical forms of production posterior to the fraternal alliance *prolonged the violence of the father in the specific articulations of each system as the form of domination and repression over the others*. The aggressiveness contained on the inside, which organises us, finds its *determinate* complementarity in the activity contained on the outside, in the contemporary productive system of this same subjectivity. So there is no explanatory return to the guilt at the heart of the subject's subjectivity, as is the proposition of those who find support in the archaic heritage: such is not, in our view, Freud's thesis, which is much more nuanced. This return takes us back to the origin of subjectivity, but of a historical subjectivity which, even as it goes back to rediscover its origin in the archaic heritage, must always necessarily as Freud would say, rediscover this meaning present and actualised as confrontation, which continues the original one in the current system of production. And, upon returning from this comparison, we come back with two complementary forms: that archaic subjectivity, which there corresponds to an historical objectivity, would have to incorporate into the current subjectivity no longer just the archaic form of the ancestral family but the current form of objectivity of its system of production, for it is this system that constitutes the domain of its meaning and its truth. And this is all the more so when the process that leads from the child to the adult contains already, in its very structure, the basic foundational drama that every historical process presents. The reactivation of the process of the child's formation, then, would be a propaedeutic for every possible history.

Once again, then, the subjective aggressiveness finds its secret in the domain of objectivity where the new fathers and the new powers, now properly understood, must find the exact measure of the act of aggression towards the outside that puts an end to them. If there exists an archaic, phylogenetic heritage, at the individual level, there also exists an archaic, phylogenetic heritage at the level of the system of production. If the first subject, in the transition of the child, is an individual one, the second is a collective subject.

This can be clearly inferred from Freud's affirmation:

> This conflict [the eternal struggle between Eros and the instinct of destruction or death] is set going as soon as men are faced with the task of living together. So long as the community assumes no other form than that of the family, the conflict is bound to express itself in the Oedipus complex, to establish the conscience and to create the first sense of guilt. When an attempt is made to widen the community, the same conflict is continued in forms which are dependent on the past; and it is strengthened and results in a further intensification of the sense of guilt. Since civilisation obeys an internal erotic impulsion which causes human beings to unite in a closely-knit group, it can only achieve this aim through

> an ever-increasing reinforcement of the sense of guilt. What began in relation to the father is completed in relation to the group. (132–33)

In our view this is one of the most important consequences that lead us to understand the profundity of Freud's thinking in relation to the problems of history. It clearly shows where the individual conflicts culminate in Freud, and where according to him the solution is to be situated. To the family form there organically corresponds a form that is adequate to include oneself in the drama of civilisation: the Oedipus complex. But at the level of the group or mass, that is to say, at the level of collective social organisations *where it is not the family form but the capitalist system that is dominant, the form of the Oedipus complex no longer is adequate to it*. Now to the group there corresponds the specific form of the system of production that determines the family. Which means: *with the categories that we apply to the analysis of the family there can be no comprehension of the human drama that opens up on the basis of the capitalist system of production*. The latter creates an opening to other categories, which respond to the structure of its global social system, of which the family is only one internal and partial form, dependent on and determined by it. The false integration of the individual in the historical process would stem from the fact of continuing to live and think the integration into the group with the categories that belong to the family form, and furthermore in inverted form. This rationality, in all its simplicity, hides how the subjective content that corresponds to it is abstract:

> When an attempt is made to widen the community, the *same conflict* is continued in forms which are dependent on the past; and it is strengthened and results in a further intensification of the sense of guilt. (132–33)

To the infraction vis-à-vis the father there correspond multiple infractions and repressions that the social system imposes, but which are not understood within the context of this new structure: *they continue to produce meaning on the basis of the previous structure*. While it is not the same conflict but another, it is understood and lived as though it were the same. What is more, because of the mechanism that Freud already analysed as the product of an inversion, each internal violence unleashes the guilt that makes it well-deserved: the sense of guilt is strengthened and intensified.

However, there is only one path of return: to broaden the family until we reach the social system that produced us. To disentangle the system that determined us as part thereof. To move from the family, as Freud says, in order to understand it in relation to the group or mass:

> What began in relation to the father is completed in relation to the group. (133)

This beginning that thus is completed integrates both the individual and the historical level: the first human began with the family and concluded in the group; each one of us repeated, starting out from the bourgeois family, the same process. There is a historical unity between the meaning of the individual access and the social development: both are traversed by their insertion into the truth of the collective history.

But this is what Freud tells us cannot be thought because the psychic structure, and the content that it organises in this way, does not allow the rational understanding of the system to be incorporated, as signifying the social, into the body that thus is affectively determined by the sense of guilt. The unconscious feeling of guilt will be the sensible background, made into an unlimited power, which will always oppose itself from within ourselves to the necessary force that we will have to oppose to that which the new rationality discovers: the violence that the system exerts against us. The scientific rationality, no matter how much it broadens the comprehension of the domain of the world and allows one to integrate it in oneself as the reason of all that exists, will always encounter this unconscious feeling, which is the foundation of conscience itself, as its support and its limit. Unless … unless in the material domain of the system of production, besides the presence of the enemy's force, which has been zigzagging in history from the castrating *Ur*-father onward, we also encounter the primitive fraternal alliance in the development of the contemporary group or mass. To our eyes the imaginary father always appears naked, and always less frightening, in the objective form of the repressive system. But at the same time we can also see the real force that is opposed to him, and which we can finally think of as a continuity in which our dominated body prolongs itself and finds support. It will no longer be the anxiety of death, which is the anxiety before the super-ego, anxiety before the nothing. It will be a precise fear, for which we will have to stir up the precise force that may oppose and vanquish it:

> Since civilisation obeys an internal erotic impulsion which causes human beings to unite in a closely-knit group, it can only achieve this aim through an ever-increasing reinforcement of the sense of guilt. (133)

But what is 'fatal' about this 'fatal inevitability of the sense of guilt' (132)? Everything depends, as we will see, on how the transition from the family to the mass or group continues to produce itself according to the models imposed by the artificial group, whose system is prolonged in the leader, general, or priest, for example, in congruence with the form of the super-ego. But for Freud in *Group Psychology and the Analysis of the Ego* another path out had opened up: that of a new model, which would unravel the mirage in which human beings were kept by the social form of a system in which the collective relations continued to be paternalistic, still dominated by the Oedipus complex. The power of the others that in the revolutionary mass was confused with mine and extended itself in the common force; the form of the other who, by identification with the leader, in the new model of organisation, objectified the archaic element and situated it in the present life; the meaning of the system which extended my drama and took it out of the realm of the absolute and towards history: all this is nothing less than the path toward the 'defatalisation' of guilt. Or, at least, it is the only possible path that opens up in history if we want to assume knowledge and transformation as the capacity of control over reality, which depends on us – exactly as Freud himself conceived of it.

And yet, it would appear that Freud is pessimistic with regard to this solution, which inscribes itself in the direction of his analyses. When he says, for example:

> If civilisation is a necessary course of development from the family to humanity as a whole, then – as a result of the inborn conflict arising from ambivalence, of the eternal struggle between the trends of love and death – there is inextricably bound up with it an increase of the sense of guilt, which will perhaps reach heights that the individual finds hard to tolerate. (133)

Perhaps the last sentence shows us the path to follow: if things continue in this way, without dissolving the system of guilt and, on the contrary, ratifying it all the more in the extent to which the aggressiveness preserved and aimed against oneself becomes greater, then, yes, it will be 'hard to tolerate' for the individual. What emerged as collective remorse is difficult to tolerate as individual guilt. The 'individualistic', narcissistic subject will find it hard to tolerate *this* civilisation whose historical development led to this result. But Freud had shown us the deviation in which we had fallen as a consequence of the splitting, which was also historical, between the instinctual renunciation that this civilisation imposed on us and the ratification produced by the system as it strengthened our first emergence. Only if we gain access to the discovery of the collective drama and the collective force at play in civilisation might this intolerability disappear.

The individual, by definition, cannot destroy him or herself. Guilt has a degree of intolerability, and this is found in the death that the individual gives to him or herself: it is tolerable as long as it makes possible his or her individual life. But the origin, the conflict arising from ambivalence, of 'the eternal struggle between the trends of love and death', precisely because it is eternal, for this very same reason cannot be hidden from humans for good by any system. Death is at the service of life – until life is incapable of sustaining itself in the face of the external world and its own conflicts. But death itself, Paul Ricœur tells us, can be sublimated – and he says so as a believer. It can be, yes, as long as it does not *effectively* lead to death, because death can be sublimated *only as long as we are alive*. As long as its presence does not make itself visible in life's everydayness. Why? Because the sublimated death finds support in the imaginary death, in the infinity opened up by the persistence of the superego. But the real death, which the human being imposes, no longer admits any sublimation: it comes with the precise obstacle that produces it. Here too the problem is economical (quantitative): it 'will perhaps reach heights that the individual finds hard to tolerate' (133). This means that as long as the system produces the human subject as adequate for it, and the act of aggression can be deviated inwards, the internalised cop will fulfil his function. This is true as long as the narcissistic subject remains. But when this limit is exceeded, when the amount of guilt is nothing but the amount of an immense aggressiveness that shows us the real obstacle and for which we discover the objective power with which to confront it, the dilemma once again becomes the following, as Marx says quoting George Sand:

> It is only in an order of things in which there are no more classes and class antagonisms that *social evolutions* will cease to be *political revolutions*. Till then, on the eve of every general reshuffling of society, the last word of social science will always be:
> 'Le combat ou la mort: la lutte sanguinaire ou le néant. C'est ainsi que la question est invinciblement posée'. [From George Sand's novel *Jean Ziska*: 'Combat or Death: bloody struggle or extinction. It is thus that the question is inexorably put'.]

Indeed, we should keep in mind that, when Freud speaks of 'an ever-increasing reinforcement of the sense of guilt', in reality he is saying: ever-increasing reinforcement of the aggressiveness that the system of production directs against the individual. The act of aggression against oneself, which comes from the outside, when it is not confronted translates itself, in the inverted form engraved in the resolution of the Oedipus complex, into guilt for having dared to confront this aggression in the imaginary. But to confront it in the form of the power that we attribute to the father, not of the social power, which is its true objective sense. The more the system dominates us, the more it frustrates us and condemns us to submission, and the more, Freud says, there is an increase not of reaction but of guilt. It is as if Freud were telling us: Until when are you going to swallow the aggressiveness *individually*? Until when are you not going to discern that the system no longer responds to the form of the Oedipus complex, that the thing is not the family, that we are not in the family *but in the artificial group*?

> So long as the community assumes no other form than that of the family, the conflict is bound to express itself in the Oedipus complex [...] What began in relation to the father is completed in relation to the group. (132–33)

VIII Ideology, the Concealment of Guilt's True Content

We had seen that Freud situated the origin of guilt in a social deed: the rebellion of the brothers and the killing of the father in the beginning of history. But, as an archaic heritage, the form of this first human experience would be prolonged in each and all human beings and would actualise itself anew in their own drama of the transition from nature to culture. The fundamental insight, therefore, is the following: if the original remorse is the consequence of the act of aggression against the real obstacle, the exact meaning of the actual guilt can only become objectified in the current situation of repression that the system of production generates.

Let us clarify: the first historical deed necessarily produces its 'archaic heritage' not only in the individual memory but it also appears, objectified and waiting to be disentangled, in the relations of production where this first paternal power continues, only now in the guise of another form of oppression. There is an objective, external relation between this first objective power, the primordial father of the primitive horde, and the current objective power of the capitalist system of production. In the same way that, Freud shows us, there is a relation between the first archaic form of the real assassination which continues and renews itself, in each childhood, as imaginary assassination. Just as the child's memory does not retain the true structure that led it to the sense of guilt, and as such the inverted process must be disentangled and put the right side up, so too with the system of production: people enable the signification of their structure at the level of ideology and capture the meaning that circulates in the relations of production that receive their order from it. But this objective signification is also to be disentangled and revealed in the collective advent of the process that orders the productive forces: here too the perspective must be decentred and put the right side up. At both extreme ends: in the individual case and in that of the objective structure of the system of production, *the collective creation, qua origin and actual foundation, is invisible*. There exists an 'implicit' memory of the structure of the productive system, since its rationality also implies a regressive anteriority provided by the historical presuppositions on which it is based and whence it proceeds. This memory that is to be disentangled only appears before the question about its origin: what are, for example, Marx asks, the presuppositions of the division between wage labour and capital on which our system of production is founded? What are, for Freud, the presuppositions of the sense of guilt and of the fact that human beings aim the act of aggression against themselves and not against the obstacle that does violence to them?

Whereas Freud starts from the 'father of the primitive horde', is it not strange that, when they come to the actual father, psychoanalysts only actualise one part of Freud's phrase, 'father', but not 'primitive horde', which determines it, and as a result they do not go from 'primitive horde' to 'capitalist relations of production'? The social determination of the father, which Freud underlines, disappears in the individualistic father, without society, of bourgeois psychoanalysis.

1   *Oedipus and History*

Yet psychoanalysis gives itself this first archaic location, the family, as the sole field of modification and meaning. The primitive family of the horde now is succeeded by the complex system of capitalist industrial society, and the system of relations that regulates the latter is, for us, the class struggle and the imperialist dependency that effectively order everything in a ferocious and bloody dependency. In the face of this power, which determines the massive repressive of millions of people, how does the individual drama of guilt open up? It is as if this field that gives meaning to the repression, which is the one that historically continues the oppression and violence of the horde's primordial father, did not exist. Conventional psychoanalysis continues, at the most, within the framework of the holy family as its only frame of meaning. But Freud already showed: 'What began in relation to the father is completed in relation to the masses'. How then can we undo the guilt, the dependency, and the submission, without confronting what Freud indicates: the fact that the real obstacle, which gives meaning to the individual behaviour, necessarily encompasses the collective problem, and signals its relation with global society? Thus the cure would necessarily have to open itself up to the field of political action, which is the one that determines the field of the social 'cure' at the level of the group or mass. At the level of the family, *before* there would have been a cure, in the epoch of the primitive *Ur*-father and the horde, but not now. *Thus psychoanalysis now turns out to be a technique adapted to an archaic but not a current illness: in reality it cures what we no longer are, and situates us in a world that no longer is.*

Oedipus is – everyone repeats this – a crucial moment in the development of the human being. But, Freud tells us, its triangular form does not account for the real structure of the historical drama that fiercely determines the adult's individuality. It is a crucial moment of the subject's development, but one that has been halted, without prolonging itself in the historical system of production that, with global society, determines the specific mode of resolution of the Oedipal drama. If we started out from Oedipus as the basic form of all human access to civilisation, the truly determining instance, which is the system of production, would appear as extrinsic and, in reality, determined and accidental. Oedipus, as such, is a form of universal access, but the mode of its resolution will depend in each case on the historical system that fiercely and necessarily determines each subjectivity in relation to the community in which it is included. Analysing an Oedipus without situating him in the field in which, as adults, we include ourselves – the mass or group – what is analysed is an essence of the human without situating it as a concrete human being: we find ourselves before an abstraction of man in which the psychoanalysts, as we saw, abstract in the first place from themselves, owing to the demand of their ideology and their dependency on the structure that determines them both. Whence the first criticism formulated against Freud, which was puzzling to many: 'Oedipus would not be universal', for example, 'because in other societies it is the maternal uncle who occupies the place of the father'. This meant consolidating that necessary form of passage from the perspective of bourgeois ethnocentrism: it privileged bourgeois civilisation as the only dramatic one. It meant not seeing how each culture or civilisation determines the form of the Oedipus: that Oedipus would be, at most, a necessary propaedeutic for every form of society and that all characters are already social models that in one and the same form determine their prolongation in all the domains of reality.

That fundamental act of aggression that determined the sense of guilt is the one that immediately links up with the system. Freud says in a footnote:

> ... the education of young people ... does not prepare them for the aggressiveness of which they are destined to become the objects. In sending the young out into life with such a false psychological orientation, education is behaving as though one were to equip people starting on a Polar expedition with summer clothing and maps of the Italian Lakes. (134)

The young people who enter into a system that determined them, do not receive the rational knowledge of the structure that nonetheless regulates them. This too is part of the 'psychological orientation': the psychic apparatus would necessarily have to integrate the 'map' of the capitalist system of production and the true historical genesis of its own psychic organisation as a collective process that links us to the history of the advent of civilisation by way of violence. But no: they only give us the depth psychology that opens onto the profundities of a ratified narcissism, or they give us the 'map' of the family form or of the level of exchange between offer and demand and of competition as the only possible form. Does not conventional psychoanalysis prolong the infantile 'map' into the truth of the adult's scientific geography? Neither the 'family' form, as we already saw, nor the form of the 'Oedipus complex' in isolation, is the 'map' that will allow us to comprehend the structure that produces the violence with an eye on confronting it. Thus, power, as well as the conventional psychoanalyst who is its accomplice, conceals in every new arrival and in every patient the secret that could destroy them. Because Freud here is not thinking about sexual repression: his 'maps' do not give us the geography of the mountains and crests and crevices of the human body. He goes beyond them so as to reach the ideology of the system, in which sexuality is only *one* aspect (and now apparently a liberated one) of a more profound repression:

> That the education of young people at the present day conceals from them the part which sexuality will play in their lives is not the only reproach which we are obliged to make against it. (134)

The point is not sexual education in which the boy or girl might discover the rationality of a complementation, organ by organ. At issue is the sexual *function*, what we analysed as the mode in which civilisation organises sexuality and orients it in the direction of work. Freud tends to show that there is a necessary congruence between the education that the system gives us and the inverted structure of the child's reaction in the resolution of the Oedipus complex. This is why it is not possible truly to think of a relation to reality with an affectivity that continues to feel as if it is in an infantile stage. *It is not possible to have one's affect in Oedipus and one's thought in the system of production.* There is a mobility in consciousness just as there is, necessarily, a mobility in the affective bonds, felt significations that follow the bends of this thinking and mobilise the body. Without this there is no true thinking for Freud. Therefore, to think is to think continuously of the adequate relation to reality, and the subjective modification that we experience in this process is the putting to the test of the global system in the extent to which it determined us. Thus, in the rational thinking that makes the invisible visible, subjective thought rediscovers a field of meaning in which what becomes sensible is also the insensible, that which until now we did not feel or, extending ourselves, could not feel. If the thought of the reality of the social system did not extend the affective signification restricted to the family form in which we remain, how could we mobilise ourselves in reality, if our body remains insensible to this thought? How could we animate in a different way the reality in which we live if our affective capacity does not extend itself to encompass this domain of reality that, before, was foreign to us? This is why there exists an extension of the body in the act of thinking. There exists, as Freud would say, an extension and a flexibility of the libido. On what basis does signification signify? What is the fundamental signifier of every signified? Not the mere sound that serves as its support, but the mobility of the body that becomes sound in its flesh and conveys this meaning. It is the body that mobilises itself, it is the flesh that signifies itself.

2 *The Unconscious Foundation of Guilt*

Freud indicates to us 'the sense of guilt as the most important problem in the development of civilisation' (134). And he adds:

> Anything that still sounds strange about this statement, which is the final conclusion of our investigation, can probably be traced to the quite peculiar relationship – as yet completely unexplained – which the sense of guilt has to our consciousness. (134)

The central problem, then, is the relation – as yet unexplained – between the felt signification and the known signification. 'Normally', consciousness at the conventional level is 'the' psychical: given that consciousness would be pure transparency in terms of what it expresses, there would be a relation of adequacy between feeling and thinking. Consciousness thinks what the body feels or senses: there would be no conflict in the subject's proper organisation. Whence the typical but inappropriate substitution, in which to have consciousness and to have feelings would be equivalent.

> In the common case of remorse, which we regard as normal, this feeling makes itself clearly enough perceptible to consciousness. Indeed, we are accustomed to speak of a 'consciousness of guilt' instead of a 'sense of guilt'. (134–35)

At the 'normal' level what the feeling or sentiment signifies affectively, the consciousness apprehends clearly. Feeling equals consciousness. Affective signification is completely transparent to consciousness. There is no opacity between feeling and thinking. There is no need for an intellectual process to decipher its meaning: there is full adequation between the affective and the rational.

This adequation, all Freud's discoveries point to this, is only an appearance. Because in reality what consciousness gives us, as we saw, is the product of a repression that succeeded. We only become conscious of that which the system determines as thinkable. The external rationality is introduced as delimiting the field of the sensible, the form of feeling of the body which thereby is given its order. But if this is true, that means that the zones of obscurity, for the 'normal' consciousness, are excluded for good from consciousness as that which is incompatible with the ruling rationality. Every excess or surplus of sensible signification is excluded or relegated: it does not gain access to consciousness and, for this reason, it is as if, for the subject, it did not exist. *There are unconscious feelings*. There is opposition between feeling and thinking:

> Our study of the neuroses, to which, after all, we owe the most valuable pointers to an understanding of normal conditions, brings us up against some contradictions. (135)

It is precisely this opposition or inadequacy between the affective and the rational that is revealed in illness, that excess of felt signification which the consciousness does not apprehend. There is an unbridgeable distance between felt significations and known significations. It happens, for example, that in obsessive neurosis, 'the sense of guilt makes itself noisily heard in consciousness': consciousness apprehends this excess only qualitatively, as intensity, not as variation of the rational signification. But this intensity is *obstruction* of the conscious activity: 'it hardly allows anything else to appear alongside of it' (135). There is a disorder, which the sense of guilt introduces in the apparent order that consciousness produces. It so happens, as we have seen, that consciousness cannot think its own foundation. And precisely the sense of guilt was that starting point from which conscience and the super-ego were developed. The foundation of reason is affective, but consciousness wants to know nothing about it.

> But in most other cases and forms of neurosis it remains completely unconscious, without on that account producing any less important effects. Our patients do not believe us when we attribute an 'unconscious sense of guilt' to them. (135)

Here the largest hiatus appears: the sensible, the affective, that which the body feels and which it determines starting from the flesh in its basic schematism with reality, is what consciousness does not know. Thus the patients, to paraphrase Marx, 'feel it but they do not know it'. This is the extreme limit of the inadequacy between the sensible and the rational on which all civilisation is founded. And it forms a system with the extreme limit of the normal adequation between the two, there where humans *only feel what they know*. The normal adequation ignores – and it could not be otherwise – the basic inadequation on which it rests, the one that explodes in the neurotic. Consciousness does not possess the adequate categories to integrate discordant significations, or to inhabit affective significations that are contradictory with the system. This should not surprise us: the categories of consciousness – which are those of the super-ego – are the categories of the system of production. But this could not be understood either by the sick person or by the normal person. This is why Freud tells us:

> Our patients do not believe us when we attribute an 'unconscious sense of guilt' to them. In order to make ourselves at all intelligible to them, we tell them of an unconscious need for punishment, in which the sense of guilt finds expression. (135)

As we saw, there is no transition from the basic affective significations to consciousness: they are on separate planes. The feeling wants to be thought by consciousness in the case of the obsessive persons, but consciousness cannot do so: *it does not know how*. This is why the patients cannot believe what Freud tells them: this incredulity is precisely their illness. But in that case let us see what Freud does: he gives them back a connection in which the unconscious feeling links up not with something conscious – which is precisely what they cannot do – but with another unconscious feeling. The conscious explanation – but this time it is Freud's, not their own – only serves as mediator between the affective and the affective, the unconscious and the unconscious: guilt and punishment. This linkage is the one that the logic of the unconscious affect lives, but that the logic of consciousness does not apprehend as a 'coherent' link. From where does Freud obtain this organic, rectifying logic, which allows him to understand and feel what the patient does not know but feels? He gets it from his understanding of the process of civilisation that formed the patient as adequate to the system, as produced for submission, squared in his pretensions of escape with the rationality lived in the form of Oedipus, not the rationality of the understood system of production.

3   *The Logic of Consciousness and the Need for Punishment*

The patient thus understands the relation that unites affect with affect: guilt with punishment. But in this feeling there is no understanding, because in order to placate the guilt the affective logic demands to be punished. This logic of guilt, which searches outside for the punishment to placate the anxiety, shows us – as illness – what the normal person does continuously to avoid anxiety from appearing in the first place: to bend oneself to the order of the world so as to avoid punishment. The normal person lives the adequation not as anxiety but as pleasure: the pleasure of submission. On the outside he does not find his punishment but his being: he affirms himself as one in the security of the negation of difference, in making himself into that which the other solicits him to be. But this is what the sick subjects – in whom repression failed – cannot do: since they broke the law and maintain the presence of the instinctive impulses that strive to find satisfaction in reality, they encounter in this reality the constant presence of repression. But the repression is not only outside: it is already inside, as we have seen, organising their affectivity in the form of guilt and punishment. Since they cannot verify the meaning of affectivity in the world, all they have left are the objects of hallucination or the splitting of the self in which the external is played as the internal. Since the sick persons are lawbreakers from the beginning, but lawbreakers who double down, in fear and trembling, on the infraction, the case is judged from the origin: to be is to be guilty. Guilty of what? Of having dared to desire. For having found satisfaction inwards they must realise certain acts outwards: they must seek punishment. *To the imaginary infraction there corresponds a real punishment.* They thus 'feel it as a tormenting uneasiness, a kind of anxiety, if they are prevented from carrying out certain actions' (135).

If the guilty subjects find their punishment outside, this shows where we must look for the meaning of what they do without knowing: to bend themselves, to give themselves up to the system that from their parents they internalised in themselves. The cop whom they internalised as super-ego came from an outside that was much earlier, anterior to the current outside. But they found, without knowing it, the real cop of the real system, tormenting and punishing them. They took their fantasies of enjoyment for reality; so they believe they really killed the father. They do not understand that this dead father outlives himself not inside but outside: in the current prolongation of that first oppressive system of the primal father, whom they ignore, but who subsists now as power of the capitalist – and sometimes socialist – system of production. For accepting the fantasy of having killed the father (but inside) they really submit themselves to the system of oppression, which continues and gives real life to the father (but outside).

> Here perhaps we may be glad to have it pointed out that the sense of guilt is at bottom nothing else but a topographical variety of anxiety; in its later phases it coincides completely with *fear of the super-ego*. (135, emphasis added)

This ratifies what Freud said before. It means that the sense of guilt was formed *before* the rational consciousness appeared. Before being super-ego and determining the thinking and rational ego, there was an order inscribed in the body. There, in the bodily struggle with the other, we did to him inside that which he threatened us with outside. The knowledge of the guilt does nothing except find support in the being-guilty of the flesh and ratify with its rationality that which the flesh – the infant's cultural body – already was. In the anxiety of this mortal confrontation fear *subsequently* finds support: the precise flesh of the other who, by identification, delimited my own extends itself afterwards, not towards the world so as to locate in the first father the father of the adult, but inwards, towards the super-ego.

> Consequently it is very conceivable that the sense of guilt produced by civilisation is not perceived as such either, and remains to a large extent unconscious, or appears as a sort of *malaise*, a dissatisfaction, for which people seek other motivations. (135–36)

Unconsciousness here equals negation carried out by civilisation so as to conceal the rational structure of guilt. If this is not perceived as such, it is because the rationality that civilisation offers as the only possible one is in agreement with that of the super-ego. For the domain of reality means, necessarily, the impossibility of the satisfaction of desire and, above all, of the adequate transformation of infantile desire into adult desire. This reinforcement of the rationality of one's consciousness is the reinforcement of that reason which 'civilisation produces': the historical system of production. Whence the malaise: feeling of guilt constantly placated by submission, but at the same time discontent of a constantly renewed situation, and what is worse, one unable to comprehend the true motives of its discontent. There is no cultural reason that gives us back this knowledge: 'a sort of *malaise*, a dissatisfaction, for which people seek other motivations'.

With what kind of reason could we think of the true motives of our discontent, if we think of it with the rationality that the oppressive system provides: with the rationality that only has the triangular form of the Oedipus – father, mother, child and, finally, the holy spirit who resolves this trinity into a unity? The family is constituted on the basis of the repression of incest and the threat of castration: this is precisely what is unthought in the family. With the 'family' form, we saw, we cannot think the 'system of production' form. And this is the 'spiritual' way out that the systems of oppression provide us with:

> Religions, at any rate, have never overlooked the part played in civilisation by a sense of guilt. Furthermore – a point which I failed to appreciate elsewhere – they claim to redeem mankind from this sense of guilt, which they call sin. [...] in Christianity, this redemption is achieved – by the sacrificial death of a single person, who in this manner takes upon himself a guilt that is common to everyone (136)

How can we think of the system, the reasons for the guilt, if we are given a social model only to *feel*, and, furthermore, to feel that we are guilty? In this way the unconscious feeling of guilt searches for the sense of punishment and offers us, in the body of the other who suffered for the guilt of all, the incarnated reason, which in the suffering body, lacerated and guilty, is made the model of reality that ratifies our own. Christ continues to speak to us, with his guilty and punished flesh, from unconscious to unconscious, body to body, in mute form, in the same way that from inside the flesh the dead father continues to talk to us with his body, which silently coincides with ours. Both speak in the way death speaks: without words.

Thus in religion we find only a symbolic way out for a symbolic situation, but not a real way out for a real situation: it gives us the form of the father but not that of the system of production, in which there no longer is a guilty man but a whole structure to be disentangled. But in the Christ who purged our sins – what are they? we do not know – we all find only the objective analogy of a subjective fantasy. *Christ is part of the same system as the infantile fantasy, but not of the historical reality*. And he continues in reality with the repressive logic, via the Church, which conceals and sustains the true origin of repression. In its essence Christianity is always pro-government: including when it protects the 'poor' it is saving the sinners. In this way, if someone paid for our sins, this payment itself seals the unconscious truth of the assassination, the verification of the fantasy that is implicit in the acceptance of Christian salvation. We are for good reason and forever guilty. If there is redemption, it is because previously we accepted the guilt that redeems itself of its acts. But the unconscious murder persists, unanalysed and accepted, as foundation and point of departure of our being. Thus, the impulse of life is halted in the human being from the very origin onwards: in its impetus to live, it is confused with death. The objective guilt is ratified with the subjective guilt, and to the form of the super-ego is opposed that other 'objectivity', which corresponds to it, because it presents itself to us as extending the reason of the super-ego, which is the normative rationality, until it finds reason itself made not into the historical system but into the 'invisible head' – Christ – outside. In addition to the repressive model on the inside, we are offered the model of the acceptance of guilt on the outside. To the absolutisation of the form of the father, by identification, is added this model of the son made into the father, who coincides exactly with the fantasy of the child: 'If I were the father and you the child ...', you would suffer what I suffered. Thus, the religion of the father turned into the religion of the son. The father, who is in the heavens, transformed himself on earth into the son, and suffered and died for us: for each one of the sons made into the fathers. In the same way, but in inverted form, the child had made itself into the father.

We see then that the 'discontent' of civilisation is an illness – a contradiction – of certain civilisations. We cannot conceive of the true cause of the discontent, because we cannot even understand its motivations. The discontent situates these motivations in the subjectivity of the subject. It is not that they are not there, but they are ill-situated. The discontent is subjective, narcissistic, individual. We cannot feel or know the meaning of discontent, in spite of the fact that it is given in each one of us. But the problem, as we saw, is not that we cannot think. The problem is that we feel ourselves to be guilty if we dare to think and act outside the moulds that were given to us for thinking and doing only that which the historical system of production allowed.

IX   Transformation of the Fundamental Bourgeois Categories

And so we have arrived at an important conclusion: the foundation of consciousness lies in being guilty. Therefore, the foundation of consciousness is the sense of guilt. Therefore, rationality is supported by feeling as its base. This means that at the base of consciousness we find, as point of departure, a form of organisation: the dual form of submission. From there derives later all thinking, all action, all feeling and, by extension, all linking and all perception of reality. Look at the distance there is between thinking in consciousness as a neutral reflective and rational activity and that which is its truth but which consciousness ignores. Keep in mind at the same time that this function of consciousness, derived from the super-ego, always concludes with the need for punishment. The necessity of this ordering logic is built, as organising principle, not on the need for logical principles that epistemology reveals to us: the 'necessity' of linkages that regulate it inevitably lead to the 'necessity' of punishment as the conclusion to every deduction. The logical rigour of consciousness is based on this necessity of punishment, because its affective foundation is the terror of the super-ego: 'Anxiety is always present somewhere or other behind every symptom' (135).

The internalised drama, whose form constitutes the foundation of consciousness, is a relation between a tyrant – the super-ego – who finds enjoyment in making people suffer and producing them pain and a masochist – the ego – who finds enjoyment in pain and takes pleasure in suffering. This connection, on which the logic of consciousness rests, is an erotic attachment:

> The fear of this critical agency (a fear which is at the bottom of the whole relationship), the need for punishment, is an instinctual manifestation on the part of the ego, which has become masochistic under the influence of a sadistic super-ego; it is a portion, that is to say, of the instinct towards internal destruction present in the ego, employed for forming an erotic attachment to the super-ego. (136)

1 The Movement of Guilt

The feeling of guilt is a topographical variety of anxiety, Freud tells us, which in its later stages coincides with the fear of the super-ego.

This means: remaining without the other as foundation = not being = anxiety of death. After which Freud explains various terms, of which we will retain two:

Sense of guilt: this is the *perception* that the ego has of being watched over (by the super-ego), it is the *assessment* of the tension between its own strivings and the demands of the super-ego.

Need for punishment: this stems from the ego's appreciation, which because of this perception and assessment leads the ego to awaken the anxiety that lies *beneath all these relations*.

With this Freud wants to say that all these relations that the ego apprehends are relations that before did not operate between the ego and the super-ego but between the child and the father. But what does the ego do? The ego has become masochistic (instead of carrying out the act of aggression outwards, the ego aims it against itself) as a consequence of the sadistic super-ego (which merely prolongs the threat of destruction that the father exercised against the child). As we see, the problem of the successive inscriptions of reality into the psychic apparatus always depends, first, on the scheme of the anxiety of birth, second, on the anxiety for the loss of love, and, finally, the anxiety of the super-ego. All these are *anxieties of death*, which regressively rehabilitate the first model of reaction before the catastrophe: before life sensed as the risk of death and reaction *inwards* which led, in the anxiety of birth, to salvation and to life.

We observe that there is a gradation and that because it is not comprehensively rooted in the origin of the anxiety of birth, on the one hand, and the anxiety over the rebellion against the primal father, on the other, we are kept from discerning its meaningful sense. Both origins must be brought into presence at the same time: the historical origin of civilisation and the individual origin, in order to account for the feeling of guilt such as it appears in the human subject. Both configure two modes of unconsciousness, but the unconsciousness of the individual anxiety of birth meets up again later on and fuses with the anxiety before the threat of castration, which in turn meets up again with the historical process.

Individual genesis: The analysis starts from the sense of guilt, which is anterior to the consciousness of guilt. But in reality the mechanism is as follows:

– anxiety of birth
  ↓
– feeling of guilt (remorse). The deed is carried out.
  ↓
– consciousness of guilt (super-ego). No need to carry out the act.

Freud will show us that what appears in conduct as immediate and direct, the feeling of guilt, is not such at all: it is mediated by the anxiety of birth but, above all, by the first identification with the other that engraved in oneself the form of the whole posterior process.

If in the descent from the *consciousness* of guilt – thought and rational – we reach the *feeling* of guilt, the latter appears as the *direct and immediate expression of the fear before the external authority*, as the *recognition of the tension* between the ego and that authority. It is the *direct derivative of the conflict* between the need for parental love and the urge towards instinctual satisfaction, whose inhibition generates the inclination to aggressiveness.

And in the next step Freud states: the *superimposition* of these two strata, namely,
– feeling of guilt (external, real, direct, etc.)
– consciousness of guilt (internal, ego and super-ego, sadistic-masochist),
has hampered our insight into the relations of moral conscience. Why did it make this insight difficult for us?

It made it difficult for us because *remorse* was what was felt *after really having* carried out *the act*. Conscience appears as if it were anterior to the act. But it is not.

Freud himself says:

> Remorse is a general term for the ego's reaction in a case of sense of guilt. It contains, in little altered form, the sensory material of the anxiety which is operating behind the sense of guilt; it is itself a punishment and can include the need for punishment. Thus remorse, too, can be older than conscience. (137)

That is to say, it suffices to reanimate the feeling of the loss of love: it is not necessary for conscience to exist. But this anxiety is linked to the anxiety of birth, and not to the development of difference. Remorse equals punishment. Here it is as though the father punished the child from within: it is also the reactivation of a real anterior relation.

All this is in relation to the *genesis in the individual*. At the endpoint of this process the individual thus contains all the blocked possibilities:
- if one does it: remorse (first stage)
- if one does not do it: consciousness of guilt (second stage). *Whether or not I do it, I will always be guilty and punished.*

Let us see what happens in the process of *historical genesis*. The latter, apparently, must be integrated into the first, individual one, in order to discern the meaning of the whole process.

In the *historical genesis* there is also a *before* and an *after* which determines the meaning of the act:
- *a before*: the transition from the horde to the alliance, once the murder has been committed. Therefore, realisation of the act of aggression. Remorse.
- *an after*: moral conscience, institution of the super-ego.

Before, the feeling of guilt coincided with remorse. This is why Freud warns us 'that the term "remorse" should be reserved for the reaction after an act of aggression has actually been carried out' (137).

But let us immediately indicate the connection with remorse in the child and the adult. Here, in the historical origin, it is an inaugural act of rebellion, where the instinct of life confronts death on the outside and imposes it on the other in order for oneself to live: the attacked confronts the attacker and ambivalently, out of love, maintains him alive in his interior. But this life, as we have seen before, *subsequently turns into death*. This beginning in history *does not coincide* with the beginning in the child, which experienced the anxiety of birth as a reaction inwards and not outwards, and was successful in doing so. In this way the two are asymmetrical: one is born into the life of civilisation, towards the outside, by exercising a real collective act of aggression. The child, defenceless, is born into cultural life, but by exercising aggressiveness against itself, against its own obstacle on the inside, as the most solitary and isolated act. Afterwards, in order to live, the child identifies with the other. But the other with whom it identifies is not, as in the previous case, the complicit brother. It is the dominator: the father. That is to say, the same father who, in reality, is only a slave who does not know it. The poor father, humiliated and servile, is naively the omnipotent primordial father for the child.

Let us continue with what Freud says about the historical transition. Subsequent to the fraternal alliance, the brothers changed this relation due to the incorporation of the dead father, now turned super-ego.

> Before this [the institution of the super-ego], the sense of guilt coincided with remorse ... After this, owing to the omniscience of the super-ego, the difference between an aggression intended and an aggression carried out lost its force. Henceforward a sense of guilt could be produced not only by an act of violence that is actually carried out (as all the world knows), but also by one that is merely intended (as psycho-analysis has discovered). Irrespectively of this alteration in the psychological situation, the conflict arising from ambivalence – the conflict between the two primal instincts – leaves the same result behind. (137)

This is the important thing that needs to be disentangled: there was *a loss of the historical meaning* of the act of the human subject in relation to reality and to the obstacles to be confronted. The perception was altered, because it took on the form of the father in all its extension, as the model of reality and ideal of the ego. Now, whether or not we carry out the act, we will always be guilty. But, what is more, the relation with the world was split into one level of appearance and another one of reality.

Indeed: remorse, with its punishment, gives us the illusion of having satisfied the desire as if it were following a deed that was really carried out. But in reality this is not the case; we are always guilty for bringing into reality that which the father prohibited: sexuality as developed in reality in the form of the libido, and here the libido is always narcissistic, without sexual difference. But it gives the illusion of realising an act like the previous one, the act of the first human who opened up history, while in reality what he does is ratify the closure, the Law and the prohibition. It is not possible to go beyond the prohibition, except in the repetition of one and the same act, which leaves the law intact. What ended up dominating is the super-ego as the ceiling of each and every relation.

2 *Aggression against the Self*

In this way we reach a coincidence between the individual and the historical:

> Irrespectively of this alteration in the psychological situation, the conflict arising from ambivalence – the conflict between the two primal instincts – *leaves the same result behind*. (137, emphasis added)

What is this same result? The one we are seeing: the diffusion of the instincts of life and death make it so that death, aggressiveness, becomes directed against oneself, inwards, so that life may prolong itself outwards, already distorted, but without being able to stand up to the obstacle that is opposed to it, and for this reason unable to develop itself as life. The originary ambivalence, hatred and love, separated from their originary sense – killing the father in order to live or, in general terms, face up to the obstacle in order to render life possible – kept on separating the affective from the rational. That is to say, it did not prolong affectivity for it to acquire signification as a function of the reality that determined it. Affectivity was not constituted as an index of reality whose meaning stemmed from the discriminated understanding of the obstacle and of the other human beings. Affectivity was separated, qua felt repercussion in the body, from the historical system in which it was produced. And by internalising the interpersonal drama, as a merely subjective drama, it expelled it from collective reality and from history. This affectivity without reason will henceforth determine a rationality that ignores its foundation in affectivity, which already is an unconscious rational order. If the heart has its reasons that reason does not understand, it is not because, as we saw, the heart would not have any rationality: it is just that it is capable of connecting reason with the heart, and the heart with the world.[4]

This is why Freud cast doubts on whether the reality confronted by the adult in remorse is a clearly discerned reality. If we think that remorse, as he said, is consecutive to an actual deed, we could say that all remorse in civilisation necessarily would have to be conscious. But no:

> It might be thought that a sense of guilt arising from remorse for an evil *deed* must always be conscious, whereas a sense of guilt arising from the perception of an evil *impulse* may remain unconscious. But the answer is not so simple as that. (137)

---

4 *Translator's note*: The reader should remember that in Spanish, the word for 'heart', *corazón*, allows for a wordplay on 'reason', or *razón*, which is not available in English.

And, in effect, both are unconscious, because both are rooted in an affective structure that distorts the relation with reality in function of an anterior process, which is ignored. Even in the attempt to maintain the love relation with another adult it cannot realise that this other is already a relation of love played out on the basis of its pre-existence as a model due to the primary identification. The other is silently present in oneself, enabling the form of one's own flesh as identical with that of the other. The other need not be present as superego: my own urges are modelled, in their form of appearing, on this anterior relation that habilitated me for life. Outwards now there is re-cognition, re-discovery of what the other wants or not: the primary identification, without distance and without consciousness of the hiatus, connected me with reality. I made the transition from not-being to being, conflating myself with the other: making myself other in order to be one.

In this way we cannot say that the affective *feeling* of guilt differs at bottom from the rational *consciousness* of being guilty:

> ... what remained as the essential and common factor was that in each case we were dealing with an aggressiveness which had been displaced inwards. (138)

Let us read this as follows: we are dealing with an aggressiveness *outwards* which has been displaced inwards. But let us recall Freud's earlier quote:

> Henceforward a sense of guilt could be produced not only by an act of violence that is actually carried out (as all the world knows), but also by one that is merely intended (as psycho-analysis has discovered). (137)

That is to say, psychoanalysis has discovered something that only science knows, but 'all the world' – those who live the malaise and discontent of civilisation – does not. 'All the world' only apprehends 'the reaction after an act of aggression has actually been carried out'. But this is precisely what is *inverted* in the individual: when the human being is attacked from the outside, as is customary in the civilisation that represses the satisfaction of desire, this act of aggression, which begins *from the outside inwards*, is perceived as if it were the response to 'the reaction after an act of aggression has actually been carried out', *from the inside outwards*, which is one's own act of aggression carried out against the father, and which constitutes the guilty and original foundation of our civilised being. The system attacks, but we always have it coming: this external act of aggression is, for the subject, the answer for the guilt of internally having broken the fundamental Law. Thus every external act of aggression that we suffer comes to seal and validate the crime with its punishment. To an imaginary act there corresponds a real act. But to set right the inversion does not imply only that we locate the real father outside: it implies that we recognize the contradictory cultural system, with its institutions and its relations of production, in which the concealment at the origin of history is prolonged. And this concealment consisted in hiding the collective origin of the real deed that gave us access to cultural individuality and adult enjoyment. To the concealment and the individual subjective inversion, which condemned us to narcissism and individualism without others, there corresponds a social organisation in which the others to whom I find myself connected in the relations of production are opposed to me as other culprits or attackers, for good reason.

How can we engage in the combat outwards if the power that we experience subjectively, in its omnipotence and its omniscience, is the truth of the repressive process, the very presence of Power in oneself? In the face of this power, which is present in us, what can the poor and dependent ego do when in horror it discovers that everything one thinks is already known to the other? Not even thinking is possible, let alone rebelling in thought. Much less with a body that this ego must mobilise, because every act is repressed from within. But this is the historical description, Freud says, meaning: it is the story that the ego tells to itself and the parents repeat and the system teaches.

But Freud produces the theory of this empirical, directly lived history, which has no consciousness of its own process. The theory of psychoanalysis says: 'it [the aggressive energy] consists, on the contrary, of one's own aggressive energy which has not been used and which one now directs against that inhibiting authority' (138). This much is clear: the energy is one's own, it is the body's response that mobilises itself in order to confront the obstacle.

Except that instead of confronting the obstacle on the outside, it confronts a representation of this external power – an imaginary and subjective presence. By attacking the other I attack myself within me and I use the force of the obstacle in order to negate myself. The energy that the ego experiences is always greater than the real energy of the object: the latter, which would be the condition of its success, is the condition of its failure when the ego turns it against itself.

At issue, as we already saw, is the death drive which, instead of including itself and alloying itself with the life drive that extends itself into the reality of the historical system of production, attacks the subjectivised obstacle in the image of its primary dependency: the first attacker. And so Freud tells us that we must search for the origin of guilt in a real act of aggression, following a decentring: the child lived the reality of an act of aggression, but this was imaginary. To this imaginary aggression, however, there corresponds the historical situation of a real act of aggression in which the child effectively attacked the father. But this truth of the child's fantasied aggression is not present in its subjectivity: it is present in the theoretical understanding, which is necessarily theoretical, of the system of production in which the primary violence of the primitive horde is hidden in the actual masses, as if they were not the result of the fraternal alliance but the reproduction, I repeat, of the natural primitive horde, now in the space of civilisation. What the external collective power ignores about itself on the outside forms a single coherent system with what the child ignores about itself on the inside. Neither of the two knows how to comprehend the origin of the act of aggression and the real presence of the obstacle. But there is no possibility in civilisation to undo the correlated inversion of this process in the subjective element of the narcissistic individual and in the objective element of the collective system of production, except in a convergence whereby the meaning of the one is included in the other and produces a mutual transformation. There is no possibility to recuperate the external power without a prior understanding of the collective origin of historical power. There can be no discovery of the capacity adequately to direct the individual aggression if the latter is not understood as being part of a necessary collective act of aggression in response to an external aggression. But for this it is necessary to decentre the lived signification on which our perception of reality is based, the one which in its very foundation finds itself in inverted form.

Guilt always has its origin in history: whether it is displaced into a history that *would have been real* (the killing of the primordial father), which *was real* from the imaginary perspective of the child (the killing of the father) or which *is real* from the perspective of the repressive system. But then to search in history for the comprehension of guilt means to understand, with the help of science, three real structures that at the same time must be put the right side up, or rectified from their inversion:

– the presupposed structure of the origin of history;
– the structure of the origin of oneself in the family;
– the structure of the current system of production.

These three structures converge and begin to indicate three necessary decentrings, which reciprocally require one another if we want to disentangle the meaning of the sense of guilt. There can be no comprehension of the subjective organisation without moving, as an organically necessary moment, to the understanding of the objective organisation of aggressiveness of the historical system. There is no truth in individual history if its meaning is not discovered as a function of universal history.

For no matter how much in the individual analysis we recognise subjective guilt as a psychological mechanism, but without integrating the other two structures against whose backdrop it appears, this guilt continues to be reduced to an insignificant guilt: it does not signify against the backdrop of the current system that requires it. It will perhaps make itself independent from the real presence of the father, but not from the institutions and relations of production that control it and in the direction of which the narcissistic libido prolongs itself. It will perhaps make itself independent from the empirical father, but not from the social model that the father represents.

3 *From Individual Desire to Shared Need*

'The secret of organic life in general' prolongs itself, according to Freud, in civilisation. The meaning of civilisation is woven into the canvas of life, and the rationality that guides it cannot be antagonistic to it.

> We can only be satisfied, therefore, if we assert that the process of civilisation is a modification which the vital process experiences under the influence of a task that is set it by Eros and instigated by Ananke – by the exigencies of reality; and that this task is one of uniting separate individuals into a community bound together by libidinal ties. (139)

At the level of nature there is no opposition between the species and the individuals of which it is comprised: the meaning of the latter is integrated into the limits as predetermined by the species. In civilisation this objective pursued by Eros becomes more complex, whether we look at it from the perspective of the individual or of the social structure:

> ... in the one case the integration of a separate individual into a human group, and in the other case the creation of a unified group out of many individuals. (140)

What happens, as we saw, is that civilisation would seem to posit an irreducible opposition between the finalities pursued by both processes:

> In the developmental process of the individual, the programme of the pleasure principle, which consists in finding the satisfaction of happiness, is retained as the main aim. Integration in, or adaptation to, a human community appears as a scarcely avoidable condition which must be fulfilled before this aim of happiness can be achieved. If it could be done without that condition, it would perhaps be preferable. To put it in other words, the development of the individual seems to us to be a product of the interaction between two urges, the urge towards happiness, which we usually

call 'egoistic', and the urge towards union with others in the community, which we call 'altruistic'. Neither of these descriptions goes much below the surface. (140)

Once again, then, we see an opposition appear which is not essential but produced as such by civilisation itself. The individual 'happiness' corresponded to the narcissistic individuality, which ignores its individual being as produced by the collective historical deed. And posing the problem from this point of view implies, contradictorily, placing the obstacle *there where it is and is not* impeding happiness. *There where the obstacle is not*: because only thanks to civilisation did individual happiness appear as possible, and therefore its true quest implies that we stress the conditions of civilisation; *there where the obstacle is*: because it is precisely this historical system of civilisation that impedes, at the same time, the resolution of the antagonism. If not, what does it mean to say that 'if it could be done without that condition [the necessity of integration in a community], it would perhaps be preferable'? Only the perspective of an individualism, which repressed, or ignored, the collective process that made it possible.

This opposition maintains the false contradiction: the subjective in opposition to the objective, the individual to the community, pleasure to reality. And it prolongs itself, as we have seen: the body opposed to consciousness, the mass or group opposed to the individual, labour opposed to sexuality. And also in the ethical opposition framed as egoism versus altruism, that of a legal requirement in which the farthest extreme for the individual, the collective, is presented as the necessary and most valuable sacrifice to which, nonetheless, individuality must be summoned. The falsity of the opposition ends up affirming a moral conscience of which the contradictory demand is the foundation. Thus the problem ends up being framed between a required adaptation and an individualism that relegates this adaptation; but to accept this framing of the contradictory disjunction is already an adaptation.

How can we elude this false opposition? By decentring the subject? This cultural demand appears as the sacrifice that the individual must make to civilisation, to achieve the coincidence between the individual objectives and the cultural ones of civilisation: 'adaptation to the community' (140).

4   *The Necessary Inclusion of the Subject in History*

In reality these oppositions are superficial because they do not take into account the sense of the collective structure that is present in individuality. This means that the existence of the collectivity is not external to its parts but immanent to them. The drama that develops within the structure includes each one of its members, as well as their movement, as an essential moment of its process:

> Just as a planet revolves around a central body as well as rotating on its own axis, so the human individual takes part in the course of development of mankind *at the same time as he pursues his own path in life*. (141, emphasis added)

The rotation of the earth on its own axis is a movement that is part of the movement around the central star. The movement of each celestial body here is not incompatible with the movement of the system, but rather contains it as one moment of its existence.

> But to our dull eyes the play of forces in the heavens seems fixed in a never-changing order (141)

This fixed and never-changing order is external to the drama; it contains nothing but the apparent rationality that regulates it: the gaze of our dull eyes.

> ... in the field of organic life we can still see how the forces contend with one another, and how the effects of the conflict are continually changing. So, also, the two urges, the one towards personal happiness and the other towards union with other human beings must struggle with each other in every individual; and so, also, the two processes of individual and of cultural development must stand in hostile opposition to each other and mutually dispute the ground. (141)

Thus, moving back from the physical to the biological, the rationality becomes more precise and makes itself more evident. It is as though in the extent to which the organic comes closer to our own flesh, the rationality of the universe in its proximity became more comprehensible. But this is only an optic effect of the methodology: it is because we are at the same time the locus of the dispute and of the drama. In each individual the same confrontation plays itself out, the evolution of the cosmic order, which in the human being finds the domain of its development. Civilisation is the domain in which the meaning of the human being is disputed and towards which the cosmic order converges. But does the opposition that is in dispute in the individual meet up again, in its evolution, with the evolution of civilisation? Does the prolongation of the dispute between life and death correspond, in the individual, to life and death as disputed in history? Or, in other words, do the individual life and death have the same meaning as the life and death that traverse civilisation? Freud's answer is no:

> But this struggle between the individual and society is not a derivative of the contradiction – probably an irreconcilable one – between the primal instincts of Eros and death. It is a dispute within the economics of the libido, comparable to the contest concerning the distribution of libido between ego and objects (141)

This means that the opposition internal to subjectivity neither corresponds to nor agrees with the opposition that civilisation proposes in terms of its ends. Whereas in the subjective realm, in the narcissistic individuality, the opposition appears thus:

> ... the main accent falls mostly on the egoistic urge (or the urge towards happiness); while the other urge, which may be described as a 'cultural' one, is usually content with the role of imposing restrictions. (140)

As a result, the 'egoistic' element is the happiness that the ego strives after; the 'altruistic' are the restrictions imposed by the super-ego. This is why Freud says 'the other urge, which may be described as a 'cultural' one': it seems as though it were the whole world of culture or civilisation that thus determines me subjectively, whereas it is only the cultural dependency of the super-ego which appears as if it were the truth of the structure.

By contrast, the opposition in the objective domain of culture or civilisation presents itself as framed in different terms:

> But in the process of civilisation things are different. Here by far the most important thing is the aim of creating a unity out of the individual human beings. It is true that the aim of happiness is still there, but it is pushed into the background. It almost seems as if the creation of a great human community would be most successful if no attention had to be paid to the happiness of the individual. (140)

Thus we see that civilisation, defined on the conventional level, which corresponds in its development to the capitalist system of production, does not contain as its finality the integration of the individual and his or her needs. The finality of the system of production is autonomous with regard to the happiness of the individual, and they pursue different and antagonistic ends. This signals the culmination of a contradictory civilisation and, for us, of a contradictory system of production. Freud thus reaches the same conclusions as Marx.

> The developmental process of the individual can thus be expected to have special features of its own which are not reproduced in the process of human civilisation. It is only in so far as the first of these processes has union with the community as its aim that it need coincide with the second process. (140–41)

Adaptation or exclusion: this is the option that our civilisation proposes to the individual. This is why now there is such interest in turning to the analysis of those 'special features' that characterise the individual and are not reproduced in the process of human civilisation. Because the question then would be the following: is there an essential antagonism between the individual and civilisation? Does the human being necessarily pursue goals that civilisation, in spite of having generated them, will deny?

We see that the humanity internalised a drama that does not correspond to the one that plays itself out and continues in civilisation: the individual's confrontation is false because its subjective terms do not correspond to the true dilemma that civilisation objectively proposes.

And this is so because what civilisation inscribed as drama in the human being is a false drama:

> But this struggle between the individual and society is not a derivative of the contradiction – probably an irreconcilable one – between the primal instincts of Eros and death. It is a dispute within the economics of the libido, comparable to the contest concerning the distribution of libido between ego and objects (141)

That the struggle between the individual and society is not a derivative of the antagonism between Eros and Death means that civilisation, in the affective structure and consciousness of humanity, does not transpose the true formulation by which the coordinates of history would at the same time be the coordinates of the subject: *for the opposition Eros-Death civilisation substitutes the opposition ego – super-ego*. And, Freud tells us, this second opposition is 'comparable' to the opposition ego-objects. This new opposition between ego and objects, which refers to the distribution of the libido, for the subject would not imply the opposition Eros-Death: it is a secondary opposition. It conceals the foundation that includes both the collective and the individual in a common process.

We must explain this substitution, on which the false oppositions between the individual and the collective are based. If we recall the individual subjective structure as a function of the topographical description of the id, the ego, and the super-ego, we will immediately understand that the ego was the seat of anxiety: of the limits that the ego encountered in its transition toward reality. Freud had already indicated what happened with the sense of guilt and the libido:

> When an instinctual trend undergoes repression, its libidinal elements are turned into symptoms, and its aggressive components into a sense of guilt. (139)

This means that the libido, owing to the terror and the feeling of death of the ego, cannot invest the objects of the external world denied by the super-ego. And the symptom expresses the place where the object-libido is going to end up: to invest a substitute form, an ideal or perhaps hallucinated object, but always a subjective one. The aggressiveness, which the instinct of life would have to orient toward the obstacle that opposes itself in the world to satisfaction, is here also turned back to the subjective element, converted into masochism, against the subject itself. Thus neither libido nor aggressiveness – with the help of Eros – can come to integrate themselves into the course of meaning that, in the repressive system, would allow the subject to confront the frustration in reality. This is what the universal drama has come to for the subject: at the subjective level the adaptation is inscribed in the organisation of the psychic apparatus. And adaptation here implies aiming against oneself the act of aggression that the dialectic of civilisation, Eros and death, requires to be elaborated necessarily on the outside. To put death inside, to put oneself to death, because this is what the anxiety of the super-ego announces before every possible satisfaction. For eluding the death that we must confront outside, we put ourselves to death. But both deaths are not the same: the system threatens with Death at every confrontation, as if it were indeed the absolute master who is hidden behind every possible satisfaction. If the act of aggression that the ego exercises against the father was not the one that the father exercised but the one that we 'attributed to him', it is this same force intensified to the point of absoluteness that closes in on every act of one's own. But in truth this is not where the force of the system lies. It is the one that we attribute to it, immersed as we are in narcissism.

The subjective conflict, as opposed to the cultural one, is the evasion of death, the evasion of the true drama in the infinity of the narcissistic individual. For fear of death we elude life. This is why Freud can read the meaning of the cultural structure in the mode in which the individual, as part of this civilisation, eludes precisely the drama of its being a part, and a mortal one at that. But this economy of the individual libido is regulated, as we also have tried to show, by the capitalist system of production in which the individual's needs are concentrated on the production of commodities from which is excluded the human form, both that of the producer and that of the consumer in whom they are realised. The object libido encounters a world of objects-things and objects-persons, but delibidinalised: the libido is consumed in the internal struggle, in the production of transactions.

To preserve life for oneself, so as not to risk death, in reality implies putting death also outside: to inscribe one's own objective behaviour in the triumph of the forces of repetition that arrest life.

5 *Civilisation in Dispute within Ourselves*

This is, then, the false option: either individual pleasure or else submission and adaptation. Either fantasy or reality. Either egoism or altruism. This is why Freud goes back to formulate once more the renewed opposition between Eros and death, starting from the foundation inscribed in nature – the one which from the cosmos presents itself to every human being in the rotation around his or her own axis at the same time as one rotates along the axis of civilisation. Thus the discovery of one's own drama necessarily opens out onto the drama of the cultural system in which the opposition appears framed because we, each one of us, already came framed from within the domain that produced us as individuals congruent with the system: from the domain of the contradictory civilisation, from the capitalist system of production.

> ... the human individual takes part in the course of development of mankind *at the same time* as he pursues his own path in life (141)

At the same time: a time *homogenous* with our participation therein.

This fact of *being ourselves the place of the dispute of civilisation* implies that we make the psychological reach an ontological level. And, therefore, to formulate from this level what is 'sickness' or 'health' means to link the subjective logic to the objective logic of the historical process, to remove sickness from the narrow limits of a destiny outside of the social in order to include it as an index of the forms of normality. An index of the false escape routes, but at least an index of a dispute assumed in the sick person to reach the extreme limit of the false presentation that civilisation created in us to dispute our access to satisfaction. Either adaptation or madness. Either to accept this most miserable form of life in order to protect ourselves from death, or else to confront the death that the system imposes on those who dare to transgress its limits, both subjectively and objectively.

This immanence in oneself of the historical dispute means that, whatever is the historical form that we might consider, every civilisation acquires meaning in its mode of producing human beings: enabling them as the locus where the logic of history is verified in one's own subjectivity. It means that the human form will always be the index of truth of the system; the index of an imbalance that screams out in sickness with its mute language – for in it death speaks with itself – but in the 'normal' person keeps silent and hides itself in repeated language, and in the revolutionary comes to transform, at the risk of one's own life, the system that produces human subjects with the discovery of a collective power that previously had been dispersed.

Whence the image of the revolutionary as the medical doctor of civilisation. Revolutionaries are not those defective beings who preferred pain to pleasure, as some psychoanalysts think. On the contrary, they are those beings in whom the subjective drama of their own transition to reality prolonged itself to the point of finding its exact measure in the objective death that the system imposes on us. They are the ones who truly dared to prolong the father. And forgiving him his life inwards, in the development of their own difference, they unravelled the trap in their own flesh, in order to confront the system that produced them both: father and child, assuming for themselves the pain and frustration of both, but prolonging this form of the father to the point of rediscovering from there the contradiction of the system productive of human subjects. They are the ones who truly dared to prolong the rationality of the flesh in the libido that meets up again with the common form of the bodies that are dominated but at the same time creators of the reality that dominates them. Extending and putting into play their libido to the extreme limit of the tension, until 'the absolute disruption', which implies not only confronting the hallucinating anxiety of death before the super-ego but the death itself of the system of production. They are the ones who dared to maintain the act of aggression and aim it toward the precise point of the system that generates violence; they are the ones who knew how to stir up the objective force among the brothers of a fraternal alliance once again renewed and opposed to the super-ego's omnipotence. To stir up death in the service of Eros, to include death in the sense of life as destruction of the obstacle, of that primordial father turned into repression today: CIA, police, army, electric baton, torturer.

6   *The Destruction of the Models of Subjection*

This is why Freud's analysis of 'the discontent in civilisation' culminates with the models of human beings who mobilise history. The rational meaning of a system of production enables one to understand the contradictions that, beyond the appearance, account for the process that reproduces the system, and, by understanding this, to organise an action that strives to transform it. But since every system of production is a system of production of human subjects, the meaning of history will find expression in the form of the human being, and this will be the most certain index of all rationality: whether coming back from the system or from nature. Every cultural formation or civilisation always implies the validity of certain human models: they continue and retain the transformative work that converts into collective appropriation something that came into being through the integrative effort of which the accumulated sediments are legible in those who preceded us.

Here Freud rediscovers the convergence between the collective and the individual in the collective models of the super-ego, which are determining with regard to each individual super-ego. Again, the collective and historical determination acquires pre-eminence with regard to the individual determination, which would not exist in the strict sense. Let us not forget the sentence from *Group Psychology and the Analysis of the Ego*: 'From the very first individual psychology, in this extended but entirely justifiable sense of the words, is at the same time social psychology as well' (SE 18: 69).

> The analogy between the process of civilisation and the path of individual development may be extended in an important respect. It can be asserted that the community, too, evolves a super-ego under whose influence cultural development proceeds. It would be a tempting task for anyone who has a knowledge of human civilisations to follow out this analogy in detail. I will confine myself to bringing forward a few striking points. The super-ego of an epoch of civilisation has an origin similar to that of an individual. It is based on the impression left behind by the personalities of great leaders – men of overwhelming force of mind or men in whom one of the human impulsions has found its strongest and purest, and therefore often its most one-sided, expression. (141)

Necessary to retain here is the dependency that is established between the individual super-ego and the social super-ego; the first is nothing but a result of the second, the subjective clearly signals its foundation in the social framework that produces and exalts the unique forms of human beings compatible with the system. Thus the system expresses itself through models of life that prolong it and determine the valid forms of being human. It is here that the true dispute over the human form finds its social meaning on the basis of the understanding of the structure. It is here, in other words, where the origin of the individual super-ego objectivises itself and discovers the possibility of being analysed as a power generated by humanity in the process of civilisation. At last, then, a super-ego that organises itself in history and not in subjective and unconscious existence: the super-ego of someone who visibly was an I. The relation between the system of production and the system of personalised qualities here becomes evident both in regard to what is repressed in it and in regard to what it contains as possibility. If there exists a collective super-ego, and the 'great leaders' are those who have been concentrating it, albeit unilaterally, this begins to show in an inescapable way that it was the mode of confronting reality that stirred up these forms of being, whether to preserve them or to transform them. This is why there are models of covering up and there are models of discovery. There are levels of true or false existence of the collective super-egos. Here the models give dramatic form, like the Olympian gods, to the vicissitudes of humankind: they express the contradictions in the human form of gaining access to reality. Basically speaking, then, there are models of two kinds: those congruent with the system, which in their time were creators of an historical way out and yet continue to preserve themselves beyond their time and the system that generated them, as if they were still valid answers even though in reality they are not (the figure of Christ, for example). But there are others, current ones, which assumed their time and the necessity of their one-sidedness like those qualities they had to conquer because they were the foundation of all the others (the figure of Che, for example). Which means, for the latter type, that they assumed their own time without having true models at their disposal; that they had to confront the creation of new forms of being human in which the then-current and determinate necessity would find expression. About these it would be possible to say that they are not super-ego figures, because they lack the absolute character that the others acquire: the character of inhuman remoteness and normativity. But, nevertheless, they become part of the consciousness of human beings, as forms that regulate the objective meaning of their acts. With this we would like to underscore the political character that here, in Freud, the collective super-ego assumes. If every form of the human is nothing but the form in which the historical system becomes in its contradiction, if in each human being the contradiction of the system is internalised without the possibility of an escape except in the form of submission, neurosis, or madness, Freud here shows us that the only historical possibility for a cure is the confrontation with the cultural models, too, which regulate the forms of being an individual as the only possible forms of humanity. 'You will be what you must be or, if not, you will be nothing' is the very slogan of repression, which from the father's mouth to the fatherland, continues to be disseminated to all the children who inhabit it.

There are, then, official models of the super-ego and revolutionary models of the super-ego. This is what happens with certain models:

> ... these figures were – often enough, even if not always – mocked and maltreated by others and even despatched in a cruel fashion. In the same way, indeed, the primal father did not attain divinity until long after he had met his death by violence. (141–42)

Following the case of Che Guevara, we clearly see how his conduct appears, qua index of a cultural contradiction, sharpened by him to the extreme limit of confrontation. But we also see that it is not *all* civilisation which 'despatched him in a cruel fashion': his confrontation as an individual is included, qua model, in the contradictory rationality of the system and he is the one who stirs up the form of being human that is adequate to the obstacle so that it may prolong itself, through his mediation, in the others as common form of confrontation and struggle. The father continues in this son who confronts him, no longer from within, in his fantasy, but in this prolongation in the capitalist system of production. And this model opens to others the meaning of the conflict and shows the historical characters of the drama, in which each one necessarily must include oneself. He who dared paid with his own life for the confrontation. But at the same time he forced the historical power to show itself as cultural form for the imposition of death, to show its weakness and with that its relativity. The temporality of power, thus dislodged from the subjective domain of fantasy, turns the subjective inversion right side up again. The power of the system is itself a mortal power and, as such, dying: it lost the infinity that we assigned to it. He who dared wanted to stir up the collective confrontation with his individual example: he wanted to prolong the libido of the dominated and the humiliated, make them understand and feel that the power that oppresses them inwards is our force that we must use against the outside obstacle. But his model, as the terminal model that depicts the limit form of all current confrontation, also delimits with extreme precision the historical dimension of the obstacle as well as the rationality and force that must be incorporated in order to discern and defeat it. The repression demonstrated its rationality organised in history, made into the repressive system of production. It showed its institutions, its organisation, its calculation, its alliances and its material support: it showed its human character. This discovery, in the fright of its death and its cruelty, is the inverse of the discovery of each individual super-ego: it transforms the absolute into the relative, metaphysical death into historical death. It is no longer the figure of Christ that reigns in our epoch, even though the repressive system still pretends to base itself on this model as the false way out of a remote era, which for this reason, even in its one-sidedness, still remains in power. Every new cultural model that inscribes itself by breaking the determination of the current system implicitly carries with it, in its sheer existence, the critique of all previous models and puts them to the test to see whether they are verified in their truth or in their falsity.

7 The Return to the Collective Experience as Foundation

But it is interesting to show here that Freud is not ambiguous, he does not lend himself to a psychoanalytical interpretation that would offer the possibility of escaping from this discovery. He says so with total clarity:

> Here, indeed, we come across the remarkable circumstance that the mental processes concerned are actually more familiar to us and more accessible to consciousness as they are seen in the group than they can be in the individual man. In him, when tension arises, it is only the aggressiveness of the super-ego which, in the form of reproaches, makes itself noisily heard; its actual demands often remain unconscious in the background. If we bring them to conscious knowledge, we find that they coincide with the precepts of the prevailing cultural super-ego. At this point the two processes, that of the cultural development of the group and that of the cultural development of the individual, are, as it were, always interlocked. For that reason some of the manifestations and properties of the super-ego can be more easily detected in its behaviour in the cultural community than in the separate individual. (142)

The individual categories, therefore, are not able to capture a phenomenon whose reason lies in the collective. This is why the individual consciousness must be extended beyond the forms with which it thinks of itself so as to reach outside of itself. In the individual the process that produced him or her does not show its root but hides it: what makes itself 'noisily heard' is the aggressiveness of the super-ego. The super-ego screams at us from the inside and deafens us: its mode of manifesting itself in consciousness is by invalidating it with its 'reproaches', moral conscience dictating and judging without appeal. By contrast, the truth, the 'actual demands', which also should show the right to domination that they exercise, those do not appear: they 'remain unconscious in the background'. But now when the scientist brings these demands to 'conscious knowledge', what happens? What happens is that which the repression covers up: that they coincide with the precepts of the prevailing cultural super-ego. What a coincidence for the conventional psychoanalyst, this super-ego on which both the patient and the doctor depend! In reality, as we already saw before, there is no coincidence but the production of the subjective element by the objective domain of the cultural formation, the production of the individual super-ego through the mediation of the collective super-ego. This coincidence shows a common rationality, which organises the individual as well as society. But this can only be read, qua reason, in the collective forms that produce it. Here, once more, the structure of the system is determining with respect to the structure of the individual. And the fact that the super-ego can be 'more easily' read from this perspective means that here, in the collective, in the productive structure that recognises the super-ego as the model of the person congruent with its own stability, is where the 'demands that remain unconscious in the background' find their meaning. The individual super-ego prolongs itself as collective super-ego when the individual becomes integrated in the group or mass as part of the system's institutions; for example, the Church or the army. The collective super-ego can only be read at the level of the institutions; it is, therefore, a direct function of the dominant structure.

If this is the case, the sickness of the individual subject signals the precise domain of its dispute: the domain of the contradiction of the system, where the need to break down the individual limits that led to the illness at last meets up again with the reason and force, the aggressive energies adequate for the conscious knowledge of the obstacle that is opposed to them: to the system of production which, via the institutions, promotes, extends, and validates the collective super-ego as the only form of being – whether possible or real – in *this* reality. Here it will no longer be one's own body that is the domain with which the force of the other nourishes itself: it will become perceptible and consciously known that the power of the repressive system rests on, and objectively uses to its own advantage, the forces of the masses, the forces of production organised by a rationality that its subjects ignore, tailor-made as they are for the system.

Thus, what at the level of the individual consciousness is invisible and inaudible becomes visible in the return to the collective phenomenon. And here it is no longer the super-ego who screams: the situation becomes inverted. Those who vociferate, those who scream, those who make themselves noisily heard, are the same ones who as individuals in the subjective realm were merely yelled at. But then this social being must be analysed with the appropriate categories, which are neither the categories of subjectivity nor those of the individual consciousness. It so happens, though, that the authority of the medical doctor feeds off the authority of the collective super-ego, on which he depends for his insertion in the strictly marked social division of labour. All the pathologies of the non-integrated libido, which enter the transaction in the one-sidedness of those organisations that are pathological but congruent with the system and are exalted as 'personalities' up to the category of untouchable models and regulators – models of purity, of sacrifice, of prudish enjoyment, of altruistic force and personal abandon, of order, etc. – are those which appear in the great men and official heroes: in the founding fathers and the patron saints. But they also appear in the 'subjugated' models that are disseminated in chain form on the radio, on television, in the newspapers, magazines, and schools. Models of triumphant and rewarded individuals who repeat ad infinitum one and the same form of subjection and detention of life – under the appearance of its fulfilment.

Thus, these are the human forms with which the contradictory system attempts to perpetuate the arbitrariness of its structure by producing men who are 'essentially' adequate to it. But in fact this arbitrariness sees itself redoubled by the normativity that, in the guise of moral canons, is imposed on each of its members. The ethical norms constitute the rationality of the system in the guise of imperatives, mediating (and reinforcing) the familiar rationality by extending themselves to all the domains of reality in which the individual, as adult, prolongs him or herself. The ethical norms are the forms that regulate one's adaptation to the system; they prolong models of being human into models of conscience with which an attempt is made to put a halt to all conscious doubt and indecision. The norm justifies rationally, in its very being as absolute and imperative reason, the submissive adequation before the injustice on which the system is based:

> The cultural super-ego has developed its ideals and set up its demands. Among the latter, those which deal with the relations of human beings to one another are comprised under the heading of ethics. (142)

For the relations of human beings with things and with nature, there is science qua 'technique of control'. For the relations of human beings to one another, as another 'technique' that obliges one to elude reality, there is ethics.

> People have at all times set the greatest value on ethics, as though they expected that it in particular would produce especially important results. And it does in fact deal with a subject which can easily be recognised as the sorest spot in every civilisation. Ethics is thus to be regarded as a therapeutic attempt – as an endeavour to achieve, by means of a command of the super-ego, something which has so far not been achieved by means of any other cultural activities. (142)

In this way we see what the conventional psychoanalysts do not see in their individual task. Whereas they cure individuals, the system 'cures' collectively. The official cure knows what it does: it is collective. It tries to accomplish this through the imposition of norms that ratify a material dependency in which human beings already find themselves subjected. That is why we have to ask: this repressive surplus that plugs up the interstices of the individual super-ego, how could this be counteracted by psychoanalysis in the individual cure which, as if this were not already bad enough, does not get involved at all with the system that produces illness in the first place? And how would it have to do this if, in the final instance, the same ethical norms regulate the activity of the psychoanalyst, basically the inexorable law of the fundamental norm: the strict and absolute requirement of paying the fees? The law of money, at the very heart of psychoanalysis itself, runs counter to the fundamental norm of 'free association', which is *the law that orders one not to respect the law*, whereas the first, contradictorily, orders one absolutely to comply with the law in the form of 'honorariums'.

But, above all, let us ask ourselves: who tries to impede and put a halt to the 'therapeutic attempt' of the repressive system?

> As we already know, the problem before us is how to get rid of the greatest hindrance to civilisation – namely, the constitutional inclination of human beings to be aggressive towards one another; and for that very reason we are especially interested in what is probably the most recent of the cultural commands of the super-ego, the commandment to love one's neighbour as oneself. (142)

We had seen this already: the 'constitutional inclination of human beings to be aggressive towards one another' was the result of the collective dissociation of the act of aggression from its historical sense in the face of the precise obstacle. Whence 'the most recent' character of the command: the greater the violence of the system against its members, the greater must be the attempt to control the individual violence which is left to each and every one as the only path forward. Thus the unsublimatable libido of the individual economy also explodes inwards: the act of aggression returns to its own way and the system, which apparently managed to deviate it away from its own course, cannot avoid that it breaks out in utter meaninglessness in the opposition of one person to another. The addressees of this precept are not the ones in charge of the aggression, the owners of power continuously exercised: the addressees of the norm of love are the dominated. This is why the domain of the norm is exercised from within the religious form, where personal relations reign that in the form of the family conceal the system. Religion speaks from person to person in order for them to submit themselves: it is a 'personalist' submission. Therefore, the violence for which an attempt at containment is made is the violence of the attacked.

We ask ourselves: will it be possible to remedy this 'social illness' with the individual cure, or, on the contrary, is the exact measure of the cure the capacity to stir up an act of aggression adequate to the repressive power? The fact that the analysis remains at the level of the individual super-ego is neither effective nor sufficient to counteract this real force of the collective super-ego, which is rooted in the real power of economic, police, and military repression. Rather, this analysis is complicit with the system; it remains, like religion, determined by the family form, and therefore inscribed within the concealment of the structure that produces it. The analysis of the individual super-ego, once completed, creates independence from the paternal fantasy, but not from the collective super-ego that is based on the real force of the system of production. Here appears the limit of the psychoanalytic cure, its confessed impotence. The analysis of the individual, the individual 'cure', necessarily opens out onto the collective 'cure' if it pretends to be coherent as a science and a therapy: it opens out onto the revolution.

If, as we have seen, the act of aggression that repression produces in the individual is not that of the repressive father, nor that which the child attributes to him, but that of the system, then the individual force – which in the first case would appear to be comparable – reveals in their difference – individual and collective – the necessary failure of the individual energy in confronting the energy of the system. No individual cure can solve this conflict, insofar as its opposition demands a confrontation of forces of comparable magnitudes, which would have to be congruent with the level at which repression develops. Therefore, this necessarily requires that we read the process at the level of the social opposition that the system entails: it demands a reading at the level of the class struggle. Only here does the 'cure' acquire its true meaning, and the individual therapy reencounters, as its foundation, the social revolution. If individual psychology is social psychology, then individual therapy cannot elude the individual compromise with the collective truth on which it depends.

This conclusion, which Freud is in part discovering and which we in part are prolonging as a necessary extension of his theory, nevertheless reencounters the limits. The limits of the non-comprehension of the productive processes such as they arise from the relations of production.

And in spite of the fact that Freud reaches all the way to the threshold of the need to make the transition to another form of society, he nevertheless stops short because of his spontaneous class concepts. He continues to think as a scientific therapist, without comprehending the necessarily political character of the transformation.

> And as regards the therapeutic application of our knowledge, what would be the use of the most correct analysis of social neuroses, since no one possesses authority to impose such a therapy upon the group? (144)

Here, in this domain, the therapists are the revolutionaries, the ones who before the group or mass reach the necessary 'authority' to impose the corresponding transformation. (This is what we will see in *Group Psychology and the Analysis of the Ego*.) It is as if Freud thought about and addressed himself here to a person, to a culture that would function like an individual being who represses, imposes, and proposes. What is left of the analysis of labour, of sexuality, of the artificial groups, of the fraternal alliance? It is as though the exposition had changed interlocutors and sought to direct itself to someone who would represent, as a person, what is only a productive system that possesses other categories for it to be explained and understood.

> It [the cultural super-ego], too, does not trouble itself enough about the facts of the mental constitution of human beings. It issues a command and does not ask whether it is possible for people to obey it. On the contrary, it assumes that a man's ego is psychologically capable of anything that is required of it, that his ego has unlimited mastery over his id. This is a mistake; and even in what are known as normal people the id cannot be controlled beyond certain limits. (143)

That the super-ego 'does not trouble itself enough'; that it 'issues commands'; that it 'does not ask'; that it 'assumes'; that 'it is a mistake': all these are just manners of speech. The capitalist system of production and the men who control it do not ask themselves if they can issue commands, given that all means are good to disarm the aggressive power of the masses they dominate. But beyond this attributed intentionality, what is left thereof in the manner of expository rhetoric, in the dramatisation of the opposition as a game of equivocal and mistaken intentions? One conclusion that interests us: the corporeality of the human being whose libido was thus organised, the nature that culture transformed, does not admit just any cultural form that one might want to impose on it. Even when repressed, human beings have their limits, which do not depend on their will in order to become intolerable. This limit entails a putting to the test of every repressive system and announces a basic optimism present in the long run in Freud. The control of culture may pretend to achieve a total submission, but it cannot go 'beyond certain limits'. And every attempt at control is an attempt to exceed oneself in the power achieved over other human beings, because the system presupposes ever greater increments of repression to maintain itself as such: that is its unsustainable contradiction. Because the matrix, the id, around which the individual and narcissistic ego is formed, does not tolerate repression beyond a certain limit: the id is united, despite the individualism to the materiality of collective nature which is its unsublimatable foundation. We think that this limit is the non-destruction of life, but of a life that civilisation itself comes to define in the field of control of the last form that has been reached: capitalism. What happens if these limits are exceeded? What happens in our system:

> If more is demanded of a man, a revolt will be produced in him or a neurosis, or he will be made unhappy. (143)

It is clear what are the ways out:
  For those who do not give in to the repression:
- subjective way out: neurosis;
- objective way out: rebellion.

For those who give in to the repression:
- the only way out, both subjective and objective: accommodation, unhappiness.

We thus see that the only historical and scientific way out in order to destroy the repression is rebellion. But not rebellion understood as a subterfuge to elude reality. The individual revolt that turns into the collective revolution is the only one that confronts the repressive reality at the level of the objective system: it is the only one that confronts the foundation of the official collective super-ego. We can say: *neurosis* does not manage to distinguish the existence of a collective super-ego that results from the system of production, and remains under the terror of the super-ego, as individual – lawbreaker and guilty in the imaginary realisation – who is prolonged in the confirmation of the collective. *Normality*, the kind that makes us feel the malaise or discontent, is the reality that accepts as absolute both the individual and the collective super-ego and submits itself to its norms both outside and inside. Only *rebellion* is an attempt to confront, subjectively as well as objectively, the foundation of the individual and collective super-ego in the reality of the system.

This is what we will try to understand in *Group Psychology and the Analysis of the Ego*.

CHAPTER 3

Group Psychology and the Analysis of the Ego

> It is not the *unity* of living and active humanity with the natural, inorganic conditions of their metabolic exchange with nature, and hence their appropriation of nature, which requires explanation or is the result of a historic process, but rather the *separation* between these inorganic conditions of human existence and this active existence, a separation which is completely posited only in the relation of wage labour and capital.
>
> MARX, *Grundrisse*
>
> ⋰

1   Introduction[1]

Le Bon writes: 'Group psychology'; Freud adds: 'and the analysis of the ego'.[2] What kind of complementation does Freud indicate with this addition? *To introduce the problem of the subject into the historical process.*

This is why the quotations that follow require some justification, especially because they do not come from Freud but from Le Bon, the author whom Freud analyses in the opening pages of his book. Ours are quotations from a political Le Bon that Freud does not include in his text. For the traditional science of psychology Le Bon belongs to the opening of a new field of knowledge: social psychology. Because of his influence, he is perhaps the first social psychologist in the strict sense and, as such, Freud only retains from Le Bon the opening of this new field. But what does not appear in the 'objective' science is Le Bon's

---

1 All references and page numbers in this chapter, unless otherwise indicated, are from Freud 1921.
2 *Translator's note*: the original French title of Gustave Le Bon's essay is *Psychologie des foules*, quite inexplicably rendered in English as *The Crowd: A Study of the Popular Mind*. In German, the title is translated as *Psychologie der Massen* and in Spanish, as *Psicología de las masas*, which more neatly corresponds to the first part of Freud's title, *Massenpsychologie und Ichanalyse*, translated in Spanish as *Psicología de las masas y análisis del yo*, thus allowing Rozitchner to see the second half of the title as a clear and direct extension of the first.

psychology as political psychology. Le Bon is a thinker from the right, at the vanguard of European fascism and Nazism. This meaning of his work is excluded from the 'science', so as to keep only its rational framework, its conceptual contribution completely cut loose from the precise moment of the historical struggle in which this knowledge became serviceable. Whence its validity: it comes to the aid of the right. This is why Le Bon, who constitutes the foundation of contemporary social psychology, shows the origin that now, among us, is covered up in the final developments of this science.

But Le Bon's inclusion here obeys another aim. Freud, in his *Group Psychology and the Analysis of the Ego, situates himself in the midst of this concealment.* He picks up on Le Bon's theory, but *he excludes from his exposition all the explicit references to politics and to the historical sense that in Le Bon's book are overwhelming.* This gave rise to those 'naive' readings which, projecting their class categories, have been above all the work of psychoanalysts. Like any reading, this one too can be taken as a projective test and, in this case, be returned to the analysts as a diagnostic of their class insertion. Because Freud, who also retained only Le Bon's theoretical core, the strict basis of his rational explanation, does what they do not dare: with his analysis he accomplishes, nonetheless, the scientific destruction of the social psychology of the bourgeoisie and of the bourgeois individuality integrated in its institutions. This is why we think that it was the *complete content* of this text from Le Bon that *necessarily* formed the point of departure of Freud's critical analysis. Our aim then is *to include the text that Freud read but excluded* from his theoretical development. Because this excluded text too is present in Freud's theoretical combat, which therefore is political, as we will try to show.

And thus the question that immediately arises is: why did Freud not include this? Cowardice? Cunning trick of someone who knows the limits of the society in which psychoanalysis develops and does not want *directly* to take on the combat but instead battles it out exclusively on his own terrain? It is not my goal to offer an analysis of Freud's motivations and strategies: his work suffices for us. But what we do have to retain is that his *Group Psychology and the Analysis of the Ego* is, we think, the most demolishing reply, even in its partiality and from within the field of psychology, to the conceptions of fascism and of the social organisation of capitalism. Just as it is also the opening onto the comprehension of the meaning of any truly revolutionary process *whose concern continues to be the human being.*

This knowledge is not limited to the psychoanalysts: the lack of interest and understanding demonstrated in their reading signals historically that its discovery is inscribed in another field: in the field of revolutionary struggle. Its problem is not the individual cure alone, but the social 'cure': the transformation of the system of production of subjected human beings. What began as individual psychology ended as social psychology: '*From the very first individual psychology, in this extended but entirely justifiable sense of the words, is at the same time social psychology as well*'.

1   *Le Bon by Himself: His Political Thinking*[3]

>   History tells us, that from the moment when the moral forces on which a civilisation rested have lost their strength, its final dissolution is brought about by those unconscious and brutal crowds known, justifiably enough, as barbarians. Civilisations as yet have only been created and directed by a small intellectual aristocracy, never crowds. Crowds are only powerful for destruction. ... When the structure of a civilisation is rotten, it is always the masses that bring about its downfall. It is at such a juncture that their chief mission is plainly visible, and that for a while the philosophy of number seems the only philosophy of history. (18–19)

>   A knowledge of the psychology of crowds is to-day the last resource of the statesman who wishes not to govern them – that is becoming a very difficult matter – but at any rate not to be too much governed by them. (21)

---

3   Le Bon's book, published for the first time in 1895, by the time Freud makes it into the point of departure of his analysis, had reached its 28th edition in France. In Argentina Ramos Mejía uses it as the basis for writing, in 1899, *Las multitudes argentinas* (The Argentine Masses or Multitudes).
    This 'object' of study proliferated after the Russian Revolution (Spengler, Scheler, Simmel, Ortega y Gasset, Heidegger, among others). It was translated into multiple languages, which indicates the vitality of its description and of its practical consequences for the bourgeoisie: into English, German, Spanish, Italian, Danish, Swedish, Russian, Polish, Czech, Turkish, Japanese, etc.
    Le Bon is part of the 'vitalist' current that from Count Gobineau onward has expanded throughout aristocratic Europe, in crisis after the French Revolution, a theory based on racial preeminence whose practical consequence was German Nazism and, at present, the racism of the USA both in its own country and in the countries it has subjected.
    Of this theory Lukács says that it is 'an attempt philosophically to solve from the standpoint of the imperialist bourgeoisie and its parasitic intelligentsia the questions raised by social evolution, by the class struggle's new forms'. See Lukács 1981, p. 404. *Translator's note*: All quotations from Le Bon are drawn from Le Bon 1914. However, in order to adapt the vocabulary more closely to the translations used by Rozitchner, the reader should always keep in mind that Le Bon's term *foule*, translated as 'crowd' in the official English translation, in Spanish has been rendered most often as *masa* ('mass') and sometimes as *muchedumbre* ('multitude').

It will be remarked that among the special characteristics of crowds there are several – such as impulsiveness, irritability, incapacity to reason, the absence of judgment and of the critical spirit, the exaggeration of the sentiments, and others besides – which are almost always observed in beings belonging to inferior forms of evolution – in women, savages, and children, for instance. (40)

It is difficult to understand history, and popular revolutions in particular, if one does not take sufficiently into account the profoundly conservative instincts of crowds. They may be desirous, it is true, of changing the names of their institutions, and to obtain these changes they accomplish at times even violent revolutions, but the essence of these institutions is too much the expression of the hereditary needs of the race for them not invariably to abide by it. (62)

A crowd may be guilty of murder, incendiarism, and every kind of crime, but it is also capable of very lofty acts of devotion, sacrifice, and disinterestedness, of acts much loftier indeed than those of which the isolated individual is capable. [...] The crowds that go on strike do so far more in obedience to an order than to obtain an increase of the slender salary with which they make shift. (64–65)

We should not complain too much that crowds are more especially guided by unconscious considerations and are not given to reasoning. Had they, in certain cases, reasoned and consulted their immediate interests, it is possible that no civilisation would have grown up on our planet and humanity would have had no history. (66)

It cannot absolutely be said that crowds do not reason and are not to be influenced by reasoning. ... The inferior reasoning of crowds is based, just as is reasoning of a high order, on the association of ideas, but between the ideas associated by crowds there are only apparent bonds of analogy or succession. The mode of reasoning of crowds resembles that of the Esquimaux who, knowing from experience that ice, a transparent body, melts in the mouth, concludes that glass, also a transparent body, should also melt in the mouth; or that of the savage who imagines that by eating the heart of a courageous foe he acquires his bravery; or of the workman who, having been exploited by one employer of labour, immediately concludes that all employers exploit their men. (73–74)

… the powerlessness of crowds to reason aright prevents them displaying any trace of the critical spirit, prevents them, that is, from being capable of discerning truth from error, or of forming a precise judgment on any matter. (74)

Institutions and laws are the outward manifestation of our character, the expression of its needs. (7)

… nothing is more fatal to a people than the mania for great reforms, however excellent these reforms may appear theoretically. (6–7)

The entry of the popular classes into political life – that is to say, in reality, their progressive transformation into governing classes – is one of the most striking characteristics of our epoch of transition. (15)

The masses are founding syndicates before which the authorities capitulate one after the other; they are also founding labour unions, which in spite of all economic laws tend to regulate the conditions of labour and wages. They return to assemblies in which the Government is vested, representatives utterly lacking initiative and independence, and reduced most often to nothing else than the spokesmen of the committees that have chosen them. (16)

To-day the claims of the masses are becoming more and more sharply defined, and amount to nothing less than a determination to utterly destroy society as it now exists, with a view to making it hark back to that primitive communism which was the normal condition of all human groups before the dawn of civilisation. Limitations of the hours of labour, the nationalisation of mines, railways, factories, and the soil, the equal distribution of all products, the elimination of all the upper classes for the benefit of the popular classes, &c., such are these claims. (16–17)

The writers who enjoy the favour of our middle classes … display profound alarm at this new power which they see growing … These new converts forget that it is too late. (17)

Universal symptoms, visible in all nations, show us the rapid growth of the power of crowds, and do not admit of our supposing that it is destined to cease growing at an early date. Whatever fate it may reserve for us, we shall have to submit to it. (18)

All reasoning against it is a mere vain war of words. Certainly it is possible that the advent to power of the masses marks one of the last stages of Western civilisation, a complete return to those periods of confused anarchy which seem always destined to precede the birth of every new society. But may this result be prevented? (18)

It is tradition that guides men, and more especially so when they are in a crowd. The changes they can effect in their traditions with any ease, merely bear, as I have often repeated, upon name and outward forms. (93)

The ideal for a people is in consequence to preserve the institutions of the past, merely changing them insensibly and little by little. (94)

Institutions and governments are the product of the race. They are not the creators of an epoch, but are created by it. Peoples are not governed in accordance with their caprices of the moment, but as their character determines that they shall be governed. ... Moreover, it is in no way in the power of a people to really change its institutions. Undoubtedly, at the cost of violent revolutions, it can change their name, but in their essence they remain unmodified. (97–98)

It is illusions and words that have influenced the mind of the crowd, and especially words – words which are as powerful as they are chimerical, and whose astonishing sway we shall shortly demonstrate. (101)

Foremost among the dominant ideas of the present epoch is to be found the notion that instruction is capable of considerably changing men, and has for its unfailing consequence to improve them and even to make them equal. ... On this point, however, as on many others, democratic ideas are in profound disagreement with the results of psychology and experience. (102)

... the worst enemies of society, the anarchists, are recruited among the prize-winners of schools ... criminality is particularly on the increase among young persons, for whom, as is known, gratuitous and obligatory schooling has – in France – replaced apprenticeship. ... I have myself shown, in a work published some time ago, that the French system of education transforms the majority of those who have undergone it into enemies of society, and recruits numerous disciples for the worst forms of socialism. (102–3)

Were this education merely useless, one might confine one's self to expressing compassion for the unhappy children who, instead of making needful studies at the primary school, are instructed in the genealogy of the sons of Clotaire, the conflicts between Neustria and Austrasia, or zoological classifications. But the system presents a far more serious danger. It gives those who have been submitted to it a violent dislike to the state of life in which they were born, and an intense desire to escape from it. The working man no longer wishes to remain a working man, or the peasant to continue a peasant, while the most humble members of the middle classes admit of no possible career for their sons except that of State-paid functionaries. [...] At the bottom of the social ladder the system creates an army of proletarians discontented with their lot and always ready to revolt (104–5).

The number of the chosen [for work] being restricted, that of the discontented is perforce immense. The latter are ready for any revolution, whoever be its chiefs and whatever the goal they aim at. The acquisition of knowledge for which no use can be found is a sure method of driving a man to revolt. (106)

... the mass of the indifferent and the neutral has become progressively an army of the discontented ready to obey all the suggestions of utopians and rhetoricians. It is in the schoolroom that socialists and anarchists are found nowadays, and that the way is being paved for the approaching period of decadence for the Latin peoples. (113–14)

Thus, when crowds have come, as the result of political upheavals or changes of belief, to acquire a profound antipathy for the images evoked by certain words, the first duty of the true statesman is to change the words without, of course, laying hands on the things themselves, the latter being too intimately bound up with the inherited constitution to be transformed. (121)

The philosophers of the last century devoted themselves with fervour to the destruction of the religious, political, and social illusions on which our forefathers had lived for a long tale of centuries. By destroying them they have dried up the springs of hope and resignation. Behind the immolated chimeras they came face to face with the blind and silent forces of nature, which are inexorable to weakness and ignore pity. (125)

Not truth, but error has always been the chief factor in the evolution of nations, and the reason why socialism is so powerful to-day is that it constitutes the last illusion that is still vital. In spite of all scientific demonstrations it continues on the increase. Its principal strength lies in the fact that it is championed by minds sufficiently ignorant of things as they are in reality to venture boldly to promise mankind happiness. (125)

The most gigantic of these experiments was the French Revolution. To find out that a society is not to be refashioned from top to bottom in accordance with the dictates of pure reason, it was necessary that several millions of men should be massacred and that Europe should be profoundly disturbed for a period of twenty years. (126–127)

To bring home conviction to crowds it is necessary first of all to thoroughly comprehend the sentiments by which they are animated, to pretend to share these sentiments, then to endeavour to modify them by calling up, by means of rudimentary associations, certain eminently suggestive notions ... (128–29)

In the case of human crowds the chief is often nothing more than a ringleader or agitator, but as such he plays a considerable part. ... A crowd is a servile flock that is incapable of ever doing without a master. The leader has most often started as one of the led. He has himself been hypnotised by the idea, whose apostle he has since become. It has taken possession of him to such a degree that everything outside it vanishes, and that every contrary opinion appears to him an error or a superstition. [...] They are especially recruited from the ranks of those morbidly nervous, excitable, half-deranged persons who are bordering on madness. ... They sacrifice their personal interest, their family – everything. The very instinct of self-preservation is entirely obliterated in them, and so much so that often the only recompense they solicit is that of martyrdom. ... The leaders of crowds wield a very despotic authority, and this despotism indeed is a condition of their obtaining a following. It has often been remarked how easily they extort obedience, although without any means of backing up their authority, from the most turbulent section of the working classes. They fix the hours of labour and the rate of wages, and they decree strikes, which are begun and ended at the hour they ordain. (134–35, 137)

> Ideas, sentiments, emotions, and beliefs possess in crowds a contagious power as intense as that of microbes. This phenomenon is very natural, since it is observed even in animals when they are together in number. Should a horse in a stable take to biting his manger the other horses in the stable will imitate him. A panic that has seized on a few sheep will soon extend to the whole flock. (143)

This is, then, the political content of Le Bon's book that Freud did not explicitly include in his. Let us keep this in mind in our reading of *Group Psychology and the Analysis of the Ego* in order to extend its affirmations and analyses, and bring out this latent presence that necessarily must have been present in Freud's thinking.

2 On How Freud Amplifies Subjectivity to the Point of Including the Social Field

Freud in his first lines exposes the limited and abstract nature of traditional individual psychology:

> It is true that individual psychology is concerned with the individual man and explores the paths by which he seeks to find satisfaction for his instinctual impulses (69)

The individual man: this object that the scientist adopts directly from reality such as it *appears* to him, is the same Robinson Crusoe of classical political economy that Marx criticised among the presuppositions of that science. The object of traditional individual psychology, then, is an object defined from within the rational field of bourgeois ideology, with which the investigator himself forms a coherent system.

However, psychoanalysis had already shown that in the subjectivity of depth psychology the social determination was also found to be present:

> In the individual's mental life someone else is invariably involved, as a model, as an object, as a helper, as an opponent; and so from the very first individual psychology, in this extended but entirely justifiable sense of the words, is at the same time social psychology as well. (69)

And yet, will this social determination really be present in psychoanalysis in the individuality that it analyses? Freud tells us no: until his time the maximum of collectivity that psychoanalysis had reached was certainly not the broader social structure. It was, and still is, a collective domain *limited* in its maximal extension *to the family*:

> The relations of an individual to his parents and to his brothers and sisters, to the object of his love, and to his physician – in fact all the relations which have hitherto been the chief subject of psycho-analytic research – may claim to be considered as social phenomena (69)

'All the relations which have *hitherto* been the chief subject of psycho-analytic research'. Hitherto but not after what I am about to say, Freud would seem to be telling us. Which means: the individual patient included the family in his intimacy and arrived at the doctor's place as the *maximal extension*, outwards, in his demand for help and for a cure. The psychoanalytic doctor 'hitherto' had remained confined to this field that the illness allowed him to reach *within the limits of the ill person himself*. But this field that science discovered *was therefore delimited by the categories of the illness, and not by the categories of science*. And yet Freud had discovered the 'other' within the most subjective determination. But this 'other', though appearing in the individual origin as parents or siblings or friends, is already the result of the social other – the system of production – that will have to be included in the *signification* acquired by that which is nearest to us as the index and model of the social structure.

The problem is thus the following: how to include the determination of the social structure in the sensible presence of the individual? Thus far science, psychology or sociology, had latched on to the *empirical presence* of its object, to its directly material existence. Psychology was individual because its object was 'an' individual; sociology was collective because its object was 'a large number' of individuals.

> The individual in the relations which have already been mentioned – to his parents and to his brothers and sisters, to the person he is in love with, to his friend, and to his physician – comes under the influence of only a single person, or of a very small number of persons, each one of whom has become enormously important to him. (70)

Individuality, as a one-to-one relationship, excluded therefore the social and collective determination. The determination by the structure was not included in the science because, for the scientist, it was not *materially* present, embodied in the individual field. And it could not be: it is a relation between isolated terms.

Reciprocally, the same thing happened in collective or group psychology with the individual subjectivity:

> Now in speaking of social or group psychology it has become usual to leave these relations on one side and to isolate as the subject of inquiry the influencing of an individual by a large number of people simultaneously, people with whom he is connected by something, though otherwise they may in many respects be strangers to him. (70)

Simultaneous influence in the collective realm: it had to be bodily present in the same field. In the same way that depth psychology is defined by verticality, collective or group psychology is defined by horizontality. Time for the depth psychology of the isolated individual; space for the simultaneity of collective psychology.

The individualities come together even though they are strangers to one another (collective), they become separated even though they are near (individual); in this transition from the personalised individual relations to the impersonal social relations we can locate the contradiction between the individual and the social.

Where then should we start in order to negate this false opposition? Precisely from the case of *extreme subjectivism*, narcissism, which will permit us to confront the opposition posited by psychology between social phenomena and individual processes. In the beginning Freud thus must face up to two problems: he must consider that

1. The scientific object that is 'the individual' corresponds not only to individual psychology but also to social psychology. 'Narcissism' is nothing but an extreme case of individual psychology, and therefore, as we will see, of social psychology as well.
2. Psychology is social not because it refers to the fact that 'a large number of persons' or the 'influencing by a large number of people simultaneously' necessarily intervene. This means that what matters is not necessarily the relation of the individual to the totality either *one by one* (psychology) or *all at once* (sociology), but the *mediations* that are produced between the totality of the social and the individual, and, at the extreme limit, with *'one' who expresses, signifies, or represents the whole*. What interests Freud here is the *symbolic* field that the social opens up in the individual human form.

Whence the three levels of organisation in which these relations manifest themselves:

a. narcissism or autism: where the individual eludes the influence of other persons or dispenses with them entirely.
b. partial relations to the whole: where the individual appears actually in relation to his or her parents, the person who is the object of his or her love, or his or her doctor;

c. relations with the broader social forms: tribe, people, social class, caste or institution (group, mass, or collectivity).

All these relations correspond, as we will see, to both collective and individual psychology. All of them can be analysed from the point of view of the subject as well as from the social system. Thus, in the most isolated individual there is already present, necessarily, the social form that determines his or her subjectivity.

We see that the problem that presents itself involves the solution of the equation individual-society:

– the individual, no matter how isolated (narcissism), is determined in his or her individual existence by the social structure;
– the social totality, no matter how numerous, is in turn necessarily determined by the relation individual-individual.

From the very beginning, then, Freud's layout of the problem becomes radical; if the social determines the most subjective element, it destroys one of the most stubborn separations of science and bourgeois individualism, which, on the other hand, is the basis for the opposition between individual and society, between the subjective and the objective, and, therefore, the opposition between nature and culture. If Freud rejects the 'scientific' explanation that presents the social as a 'natural' determination as if it were an 'instinct' – *herd instinct, group mind* – that arises in the human being independently from the historical experiences that create social relations, he does so because social psychology does not grasp the moment of the objective elaboration within the subjective. Whence his refusal to accept numbers as criteria of the collective: 'the influencing of an individual by a large number of people simultaneously'. Freud justly indicates the very presupposition on which the conventional perception of the object of psychology is based: the fact of having ignored the subjective moment of collective organisation, of having considered the human being as a mere 'support' of these social relations.

3   *Society and the Individual as Invariants*

Freud tasks himself with understanding the interdependency in which both individual psychology and social psychology find themselves. If *individuality* was studied in psychology without reference to the totality, it was because this social totality was supposed to be noncontradictory, unmovable, invariable. If *the social* was analysed in sociology without reference to the individual it was because this individual, solidified as essential in his or her human form, was also not subject to analysis and instead was posited as invariable too. Each one moved around in its own field all the while finding support, as a limit, in the invariability of the other. This separation was ideological and led, both in traditional social psychology and in individual psychology, to consider as social being and therefore as true individual only that 'man' who is *inserted without contradiction* into the *stable* social organisations of the bourgeoisie.

But Freud already had understood this. That which social psychology *dispenses with* is what psychoanalysis had revealed to him: that the social was already present in the relations of person to person, individual to individual. We might say: the human form, as elementary form, disappears in the analysis of the collective processes of social psychology. Had it not been the case, perhaps, that psychoanalysis itself remained circumscribed only to the domain delimited by the patient, that of the family or the doctor, but *excluded*, as stranger, the social totality and the broader forms on which the family depends? Just as group psychology was barred from individual psychology, so too individual psychology was not included in group psychology. This separation, which was prolonged in the realm of science, was already the index of a contradiction that came from the cultural formation or civilisation itself. In science there thus continued a decision of concealment.

> ... it has become usual to leave these relations on one side (70)

What does social psychology leave on one side? The relations in which the individual is subjected to the influence of 'a single person': that falls outside its domain. But these relations are precisely the place where the other acts 'as a model, as an object, as a helper, as an opponent' (69), where the social is also supremely present. What social psychology excludes is the field where the social, in the individual form of the other, is decisively determining for the formation of the subject. Thus social psychology reaches its object *too late*, when all has been consummated already, when the social has been etched with fire into the form of the individual. What is hidden in social psychology is what psychoanalysis reveals: the moment in which the social, considered as a whole, is mediated in the part, in the individual. As this moment of cultural determination is concealed, the individual who is *later* found by sociology would appear 'naturally', without historical genesis, conformed as a cell adequate to *this* stabilised form of society. This is why the social whole hidden in the process of subjective formation is encountered later on as if were absolute, because it conceals the source from which the individual was formed: that which in the other, 'as a model, as an object, as a helper, as an opponent', even in his or her very individuality, is social and historical – the structural signifier of the whole.

How does Freud explain this concealment that occurs in social psychology? If it is 'usual' for sociologists to dispense with the individual relations, it is because they conceive of the forms of sociability themselves as absolute.

Group psychology is therefore concerned with the individual man as a *member* of a race, of a nation, of a caste, of a profession, of an institution, or as a *component part* of a crowd of people who have been organised into a group at some particular time for some definite purpose. When once natural continuity has been severed in this way, if a breach is thus made between things which are by nature interconnected, it is easy to regard the phenomena that appear under these special conditions as being expressions of a special instinct that is not further reducible – the social instinct ('herd instinct', 'group mind'), which does not come to light in any other situations. (70)

Here we already see formulated the transition from *member* of a stable organisation to *component part* of a spontaneous and disorganised group or mass. The 'presupposition' of social psychology is that one stops being a *member* (a person normally integrated) of a people, social class, etc. and becomes a *component part* (a merely biological, disintegrated individual) of a crowd or multitude when the limits of stable society are transgressed. Whence the disjunction: either one is a member or one is an element; either a human being or a biological form. 'Once natural continuity has been severed', Freud says: once the organic relation is broken that linked one as 'natural' member, without historical genesis, to the bourgeois social forms, there occurs a lapse into nature. It is as if in this passage, in which the stable social forms break down, the social element too disappeared in the multitudes and from their dissolution a natural tendency to associate emerged. But then this tendency would no longer be social and historical but purely animal-like: the herd instinct. Thus the scientific analysis presupposes as its point of departure a value judgment: the fall into the inferno of animality no sooner than we abandon the exact limits that bourgeois society traces for us in order to exist. Either we are integrated members of this society and therefore persons with total dignity; or we are, separating ourselves, component parts of the mass and therefore lose the dignity of personhood so as to descend to the rank of animal individuality. Both for individual psychology and for social psychology the scientific problem appears in this point of friction where the social forms and the individual forms explode and dissolve themselves in the 'abnormality' of the mass.

Freud traces the beginning of this view as follows:

1. 'The social instinct may not be a primitive one and insusceptible of dissection' (70) and as a consequence it has a historical genesis that must be reconstructed;
2. 'It may be possible to discover the beginnings of its development in a narrower circle, such as that of the family' (70).

Thus the dilemma of traditional psychology disappears, which situated us either in the totality of the current *stable* society or in the descent into the totality of current nature. And it does so because it conceals the genesis of the social in the child and maintains itself at the level of empirical appearance. Coming *from the individual* (the child), the family will appear as the *maximal initial totality*. But at the same time, coming from science, the family reveals itself only as a still current *minimal totality* that contains the determinations of the *larger social totality* that constituted it (global society or, for us, system of production), with regard to which all individual conduct must be understood.

From this we can infer:

1. For Freud, the analysis of the social individual must be referred to the minimal social totality that produced it (the family).
2. This minimal social unit must be understood as a function of the broader social forms that in turn determine it and situate it historically (nation, social class, caste, institutions, mass or collectivity).
3. The contradictory structure of individuality must be understood as a function of the contradictory structure of the social, mediated through the family.
4. Every individual cure is inseparable from the transformation of the social totality that produced the individual illness.

Whence the need, expressed but not fulfilled by Freud, of taking on 'the mere classification of the different forms of group formation and the description of the mental phenomena produced by them' (70). One of our – secondary – aims will be precisely to ask ourselves why conventional psychoanalysis and analysts have left to one side this necessary reference of the subject to 'forms of group formation' as Freud suggests, all of them in turn understood within global society, and why these would not have to be integrated in the scientific conception and the elaboration of the cure, as if this social field did not determine the meaning of the individual conduct and its conflicts.

It is not strange that Freud would begin his study precisely with the problem of the masses, the one problem that constitutes the crucial point of the contemporary historical process; and it is not strange either that the bourgeois psychoanalyst would have abandoned this. Freud does so, we believe, because this problem contains the foundation of the basic ideological categories of bourgeois thought, which forms the necessary counterpart of humanist individualism with which the conventional psychoanalyst interprets himself and the others.

4 'The Barbarians Are Coming': Critique of the Bourgeois Conceptions of the Mass: The Collective Mind according to Le Bon

We already have reminded ourselves of the political and ideological sense of Le Bon's theses. We also have shown the view with which Freud will try to go against the traditional conceptions of social psychology. Now we must demonstrate that Freud *effectively*, by pointing at the theoretical aspects in Le Bon, is criticising the political and ideological signification implicit in them.

The first problem that Le Bon faces is to understand the transformation undergone by the individual when he or she becomes incorporated into a transient collective form, such as the spontaneous mass or group. This is the crucial problem for Le Bon: 'Le Bon – Freud says – is principally concerned with typical transient group formations' (118–19). The mass or group is an especially appropriate case for analysis, because only here does the individual reorganise him or herself in a way that is incomprehensible to individual psychology, and the analysis comes upon this case precisely when it thinks it is done with its task of comprehending the subjective realm:

> If a psychology, concerned with exploring the predispositions, the instinctual impulses, the motives and the aims of an individual man down to his actions and his relations with those who are nearest to him, had *completely achieved its task*, and had cleared up the whole of these matters with their interconnections, it would then suddenly find itself confronted by a new task which would lie before it unachieved. It would be obliged to explain the surprising fact that under a certain condition *this individual, whom it had come to understand, thought, felt and acted in quite a different way from what would have been expected.* (72, emphasis added)

Before being incorporated into the mass or group everything in the individual was understandable for psychology. Afterwards, everything remains to be explained. Freud is telling us, in in other words, that the individuality understood in this way was always such as a function of the necessary belonging of the individual to certain social forms with which it formed a body (family, institutions, social class, etc.), but that *within these forms considered stable there was nothing contradictory* between the belonging of the individual and the social organisations in which he or she was integrated. Thus all social forms appeared as *invariants* in the analysis of the variations of the individual. All except one, which ruins everything by revealing a contradiction that psychology cannot absorb: the new subjective phenomena that occur when the individual begins to form part of a spontaneous group or mass. Here already traditional psychology does not manage to explain the *whole* individual, since there is something inexplicable for it: *this individual thinks, feels, and acts in an unexpected way*. Traditional psychology cannot explain this *excess* or *surplus* that the individual's participation in the spontaneous mass or group reveals inside this same individuality.

It is therefore understandable that, for the analysis of this new phenomenon, everything depends on a decision: the decision to transform the social invariant into a variable, to understand the mass as the result of a contradiction produced at the heart of bourgeois structures, which thus would cease to appear as absolute and immovable forms. This is why this change in orientation now causes Freud's gaze to turn not towards the individual but towards the social, and specifically towards this particular phenomenon – the group or mass – that produced such a dislocation in the individual. This is why he asks himself:

> What, then, is a 'group'? How does it acquire the capacity for exercising such a decisive influence over the mental life of the individual? And what is the nature of the mental change which it forces upon the individual? (72)

Le Bon, as a social psychologist, confirms this dissolution of the implicit agreement between the individual and the stable society. He describes the separation, but does not question the absolute and balanced character of global society. He only starts from the individual when the latter incorporates him or herself into that other new social form – the mass – defined from the very beginning as negative. Neither the new individual nor the new collective form is the result of the contradiction of the society in which they emerge.

Le Bon says:

> The most striking peculiarity presented by a psychological group is the following. Whoever be the individuals that compose it, however like or unlike be their mode of life, their occupations, their character, or their intelligence, the fact that they have been transformed into a group puts them in possession of a sort of collective mind which makes them feel, think, and act in a manner quite different from that in which each individual of them would feel, think, and act were he in a state of isolation. (73)

He comes from isolation and arrives in the group, I come from the isolated part and reach the collective. By not questioning the global society in which this phenomenon is included, the opposition continues to be between the thinking, feeling, and acting of an *isolated* individual in the spontaneous *group*. And it is the dissolution of the bourgeois individual form that produces this collective 'new being': the psychological group or mass. For Le Bon the psychological crowd is 'a provisional being formed of heterogeneous elements, which for a moment are combined' (73).

But Freud immediately intersperses, signalling the possible *new rationality* to which this bond gives rise in the new collective being:

> If the individuals in the group are combined into a unity, there must surely be something to unite them, and this bond might be precisely the thing that is characteristic of a group. But Le Bon does not answer this question ... (73)

This observation is of capital importance for the turn that Freud introduces in the analysis, because it will transform a *psychological* explanation into an understanding that extends its conventional limits so as to include in the science of psychology the *historical significance that the psychic element acquires in the social process*.

To understand this 'excess' or 'surplus' that suddenly appears in human beings, owing to their participation in the group or mass: that is what we must disentangle. Either it is, as Freud phrases it, the manifestation of 'something' new that binds them together and therefore it is a process of collective creation, or, as Le Bon thinks, it is the mere emergency of a common quasi-natural content that makes them fall back on an anterior level of civilisation. This problem poses itself as a function of the authors' different conceptions of the 'unconscious'.

Le Bon finds underneath the consciousness of the cultural individual an unconscious 'substratum' that erupts with his or her inclusion in the mass:

> This substratum consists of the innumerable common characteristics handed down from generation to generation, which constitute the genius of a race. Behind the avowed causes of our acts there undoubtedly lie secret causes that we do not avow, but behind these secret causes there are many others more secret still, of which we ourselves are ignorant. (74)

Le Bon's unconscious forms a residue: that which led to civilisation but did not culminate in it. Only when it is linked to the final forms of official civilisation does this genius of the race verify itself as true; otherwise it remains like a quasi-natural push, without orientation and destructive. This type of unconscious is thus, in each individual, the 'nature' that civilisation did not elaborate, but on the basis of which the individuality was produced. Each individual thus encapsulates his or her belonging to a previous totality that civilisation covers up and modifies: this modification adopted by civilisation is the individual.

But Freud does not accept this conception of the unconscious:

> Le Bon – says Freud – thinks that the particular acquirements of individuals become obliterated in a group, and that in this way their distinctiveness vanishes. The racial unconscious emerges; what is heterogeneous is submerged in what is homogeneous. As we should say, the mental superstructure, the development of which in individuals shows such dissimilarities, is removed, and the unconscious foundations, which are similar in everyone, stand exposed to view. (74)

From this let us retain the following: for Le Bon the differentiated part, the individual, becomes dissolved in the ancestral totality, where the social organisation vanishes in tandem with the cultural differentiation. *There is a collective unconscious for Le Bon but, as we will see, there is no individual unconscious*. The totality that emerges in the group or mass is not composed of cultural individuals. The cultural diversity that was the starting point – which appeared as the result of its integration in the stable and traditional social forms – lets emerge in the group the quasi-biological base that has not yet been acculturated, as the formation of the group were a process of cultural entropy, the return to an inorganic state prior to the social individuality. But for Freud such a conception of the unconscious cannot be sustained. If in the group or mass, for him, 'there must surely be something to unite them', the cultural individuality persists all along with them. This is why the negation of the group produces in the individual not a negation and dissolution of all civilisation but *the negation of a determinate form of cultural individuation*. This is the novelty: the group or mass produces a new social totality and, as a consequence, a new form of individuality.

What Freud indicates in the group is the emergence of *another level of individuality*. The ideological signification of this opposition between Le Bon and Freud is obvious. If to the cultural individual we oppose, as Le Bon does, a quasi-biological residual totality in the process of access to civilisation, then this common base which thus subsists and into which each individual, by his or her participation in the group, becomes dissolved, is entirely negative: it is disorder opposed to order, the instinctive opposed to civilisation, evil as opposed to the good. The only valid social forms are those compatible with these forms of individuality. But Freud does not share this exclusion outside the field of history that Le Bon applies to the unconscious. The opposition between culture and quasi-nature disappears so as to transform itself into a relation that continues to be viewed as culture-culture, namely, *as two forms of being cultural contrasted in the midst of one and the same contradictory cultural formation*. This means that in the group or mass there is no return to 'an average character' of individuals in a group, as Le Bon affirms, that is to say, to a collectivity without personal individuation. What disappears in the group is nothing but a *certain form of individuality* ready to be dissolved into the contradictory cultural system. The spontaneous mass or group thus appears as a *new social form that is not recognised by bourgeois society* as compatible with it. To the meaninglessness of the spontaneous mass that Le Bon presents to us, Freud opposes the meaning that in the group bonds the individuals amongst themselves: 'there must surely be something to unite them'. And this bond that the group creates and in which the cultural individual remains present cannot be thought of as a rational bond by the bourgeoisie, since the latter thinks only of the socially acceptable bonds: those forms of social relations compatible with its own.

This is the price that bourgeois rationality makes the masses pay that oppose themselves to it: dissolution of the individual, who is something less than a human being; dissolution of the cultural forms of society, which thus return to a purely animalistic conglomeration.

What is missing from Le Bon's description is the notion of *repression*. This is precisely the basis for the presumption of his civilisation's absoluteness. And it is this notion of repression that will allow Freud to show that in the mass or group there is *another form of individuality* that is produced. This other form arises when, as a result of the collective action, that which is repressed by the official culture in the isolated individuals acquires the force and the power sufficient to gain access to reality. This means that once what repression tied up is unleashed, the individual does not become submerged once again in the primeval magma where the residues of the labour of civilisation would be preserved in their undifferentiated state. On the contrary, there opens up a sphere of particularity and of cultural difference as well, but one that the official culture cannot accept as its own. Le Bon does not understand that his civilisation, consolidated as stable and absolute, is a repressive culture. And that repression is present as the foundation of bourgeois individuality.

This is why, over and against the appearance of 'new characteristics' in the individual dissolved by the group (anonymity, irresponsibility, lack of control) according to Le Bon, Freud opposes another conception:

> From our point of view we need not attribute so much importance to the appearance of new characteristics. For us it would be enough to say that in a group the individual is brought under conditions which allow him to throw off the repressions of his unconscious instinctual impulses.

> The apparently new characteristics which he then displays are in fact *the manifestations of this unconscious*, in which all that is evil in the human mind is contained as a predisposition. (74, emphasis added)

The 'new characteristics', then, are not new at all: they were present, though repressed, in the subject.

Thus, compared to Le Bon's distinction, for whom there exist only two levels – the unconscious of the mind of the race, which is quasi-natural, and the official cultural consciousness in which the former consistently prolongs itself – Freud introduces an intermediate level between the two: *the cultural unconscious, repressed by civilisation itself in each individual*. This cultural unconscious, in which is contained that which Le Bon remitted outside the field of culture and of the individual, contains in each human being the contradictory nucleus that the official culture cannot recognise as proper. In Le Bon's ideology the unconscious, common to all, hides the historical transition from nature to culture of which every human being partakes who emerges therein. But at the same time it shows us the limits that repression introduces in the investigator himself. There is a repressed transition in the man of science himself whose social emergence, inasmuch as he introduces the disorder into the order of his privileged class, is understood by him as destruction pure and simple of civilisation and of humanity. This is why Le Bon can say that in the mass or crowd there appears anonymity, irresponsibility, excess; outside the forms distilled as proper by the bourgeoisie, any other social emergence that would contradict it is asocial, chaos. But Freud, as we saw, asked himself about the problem that Le Bon could not conceptualise:

> If the individuals in the group are combined into a unity, there must surely be something to unite them, and this bond might be precisely the thing that is characteristic of a group. But Le Bon does not answer this question (73)

There exists, therefore, rationality and order also in this new unity. There is a social meaning to be disentangled in this sphere of apparent meaninglessness in which bourgeois individuality is dissolved. To ask about *the bond* then means to conceive of the nucleus of meaning that organises the group and which remains covered up in Le Bon's analysis. *The logic of the social bond*: such is the problem that Freud must explain.

This 'something to unite them', which Le Bon does not understand, is the repressed human content that the spontaneous masses convey. Because he misrecognises this, the affective bond that Le Bon assigns to them refers to a form of biological relation: contagion or suggestion. If Freud rejects this modality of the bond between the members of the group or mass, it is because he maintains that in them this bond is, on the contrary, eminently cultural, the product of a new social process. This 'something to unite them' is the vehicle of new contents that the usual affective relations and social bonds are unable to contain.

5   *Critique of the Bourgeois Conception of 'the Tie That Binds Human Beings among Themselves' in the Group*

Philosophers and researchers from the right have analysed the phenomenon of the mass with the limited categories of their class. They thus have transferred to the field of the sciences the rejection and horror inspired in them by the inhumanity that they themselves, as a class, produce. This is why the psychic resources that they assign to the people of the mass correspond to this diminished vision. This is the case of Le Bon, who has recourse to 'mental contagion' and to 'hypnosis' in order to explain the bond that ties them together and in this way to justify the lack of a 'spiritual' content in their relations, so different from his own. But Freud already knew the moral sense of hypnosis: in a therapeutic treatment that he attended, he could not bear that the doctor would impose on the patient the acceptance of suggestion:

> When a patient who showed himself unamenable was met with the shout: 'What are you doing? Vous vous contre-suggestionnez', I said to myself that this was an evident injustice and an act of violence. For the man certainly had a right to counter-suggestions if people were trying to subdue him with suggestions. (89)

If even in the patient there exists, as we see, a rejection of suggestion, how much more so would the group, in the explosion of its impulses, reject as well, like the patient, the contagion and the suggestion. Already for the suggestion to be accepted there previously must exist *something* that leads to its acceptance or, on the contrary, to its rejection. There is thus an agreement manifested in this bond, and it is *to the content of this agreement* that the analysis is directed. But Le Bon has recourse to contagion and suggestion precisely to *cover up* the cultural significance of this agreement. If the bond that Freud is after appears to Le Bon as mere contagion or suggestion, the explanation is purely psychic. It is a bond that presupposes by definition the depersonalisation of the suggested person, in whom *nothing new is created* but, on the contrary, in the quasi-biological passivity of the subject *the created is unmade* so as to return to a prior form of individuality. In the person of the mass, all essentially human qualities having been lost, there would appear an inferior form of individuality, which manifests itself in the fact that 'new qualities' appear, those that civilisation inhibited.

What are the 'new qualities' that Le Bon sees appear in the man of the mass? The first, and the most important, is his *power*, his 'invincible power'. Freud summarises Le Bon's affirmation as follows:

> ... the individual forming part of a group acquires, solely from numerical considerations, a sentiment of invincible power which allows him to yield to instincts which, had he been alone, he would perforce have kept under restraint. He will be the less disposed to check himself, from the consideration that, a group being anonymous and in consequence irresponsible, the sentiment of responsibility which always controls individuals disappears entirely. (74)

This power of the man in the mass or crowd, then, is anonymous, instinctive, collective, irresponsible, and unstoppable. As this power is deprived of all sense of orientation, being only natural, it is the 'mental contagion' – second cause – which defines the orientation of the mass according to Le Bon. By means of contagion, interlocked with hypnotism, in which the individual is interpellated in his passivity and dependency, the latter returns from Christian and Western civilisation to the animality of the mass without culture. And it is in this sphere thus constituted where the collective interest replaces and overpowers the personal interest. Le Bon says:

> In a group every sentiment and act is contagious, and contagious to such a degree that an individual readily sacrifices his personal interest to the collective interest. This is an aptitude very contrary to his nature, and of which a man is scarcely capable, except when he makes part of a group. (qtd. 75)

The personal interest is part of the essence of the human being; the collective interest runs counter to it, is opposed to it, and belongs to the sphere of the diminished and animalistic relation that is actualised in the mass. This would be the meaning of the negative, but terrifying power that emerges from it: in the mass a *natural power* is actualised that runs counter to the *power of culture*. It is then a struggle among powers in which the class struggle disappears only to appear as subjection of the human being to nature. The dominant class thus gives itself the good conscience of its privilege and its repression, by considering the totality of human beings who are opposed to it as mere animality to be tamed. What has been lost, then, is the cultural and historical meaning revealed in the conquest of power in the masses.

'Science' is good for anything in the powerful hands of the bourgeoisie. Since contagion depends on suggestion, and suggestion refers to hypnosis, the latter does nothing else but 'paralyze the cerebral life of the hypnotised subject'. The person forming part of the group or mass is compared no more and no less than to a *brainless subject*: this is the endpoint of the degradation that the collective belonging to the mass produces in the person who abandons the bourgeois forms of being:

> We see, then, that the disappearance of the conscious personality, the predominance of the unconscious personality, the turning by means of suggestion and contagion of feelings and ideas in an identical direction, the tendency to immediately transform the suggested ideas into acts; these, we see, are the principal characteristics of the individual forming part of a group. He is no longer himself, but has become an automaton who has ceased to be guided by his will. (qtd. 76)

This is how Le Bon sums up his conclusions. The ideas, suggested and contaminated, meet up with the impersonal animal force that moves them. But Freud, as we had indicated, resists this dissolution, this annihilation of the historical signification of the masses. 'There must be *something* to tie them'. This something, we saw, signals *the permanence of personality* in the bond. Thus the predominance of the human form in the midst of the collective organisation of the mass is one of the boundary markers that Freud will maintain throughout his analyses: individual psychology is *at the same time* social psychology. There exists no human group in which the analysis can do without the human form that it conveys as its model. This is why for Freud this something which appears in the mass as giving meaning to the bond that Le Bon leaves to one side, is precisely *another human being*. The understanding of the mass-form is inseparable from the understanding of the form of the human.

> We may perhaps best interpret his statement – says Freud about Le Bon – if we connect the contagion with the effects of the individual members of the group on one another, while we point to another source for those manifestations of suggestion in the group which he regards as similar to the phenomena of hypnotic influence. But to what source? We cannot avoid being struck with a sense of deficiency when we notice that one of the chief elements of the comparison, namely *the person who is to replace the hypnotist in the case of the group*, is not mentioned in Le Bon's exposition. (76–77)

In leaving to the side the form of the human conveyed by the mass as its model, what Le Bon left out was precisely *the only thing* that would allow him to recognise the *historical and situated signification*, the experimentation with the form of the human present in collective processes. Thus, what Freud is suggesting is to include the rational and historical content that the spontaneous group conveys as opposed to the traditional forms of social organisation: the historical power that is generated in them. With regard to Le Bon's distinctions, Freud is telling us that this new power is a cultural power, which confronts the current power; and that the relation which unites them amongst themselves is a social relation, determined by the form of the other who, emerging from within the contradictory situation, gives it meaning: the leader. Introducing this dimension into the analysis of the group or mass requires that the purely psychologist reading include the historical sense into the psychological, the social into the individual.

However, we ask ourselves: how can we introduce the historical in the individual, and vice-versa? For this, Freud must previously dismantle the structure in which Le Bon halts, fixates, and immobilises this process: the conception of subjectivity, his mode of conceiving of the relation of the individual to the rationality that is active in and traverses history.

6   *The Destruction of the Person in the Group*

When Le Bon had recourse to hypnosis to explain the reciprocal influencing among members of the group or mass, he did not limit himself to just *comparing* a collective relation with an individual one. Instead, Freud tells us, he established a true *identity* between the two. In this identification between the individual and the collective resides, in part, the concealment of the specificity of the collective phenomenon. Le Bon could not discern, as we saw, the 'other source' in which the collective expresses itself in the form of the leader, and it is 'this influence of "fascination" which remains plunged in obscurity' (77). Once again: the person of the leader appears for Freud here as significant of a collective system. By identifying hypnotist and leader – which means reducing the collective to the individual – what is concealed is the character of 'model' assumed by 'the person who is to replace the hypnotist in the case of the group' (76–77). Le Bon could not understand the signification of the person who guides the mass as the model of a new social form. Beyond the form of the person conveyed by his own system, and furthermore only for the collective forms that are likewise proper to his theory, there is no possibility of creation.

Le Bon says, as cited by Freud:

Moreover, by the mere fact that he forms part of an organised group, a man descends several rungs in the ladder of civilisation. Isolated, he may be a cultivated individual; in a crowd, he is a barbarian – that is, a creature acting by instinct. He possesses the spontaneity, the violence, the ferocity, and also the enthusiasm and heroism of primitive beings. (qtd. 77)

But Le Bon will not be satisfied with identifying an individual function (the hypnotic relation) with a collective function (the one that binds the person of the mass with the leader). He also produces a second identity: the one that assimilates the individual of the mass with the primitive person and the child. But what for Le Bon is an *identity* for Freud is an *analogy*.

And yet both Le Bon and Freud look for support to a *description* of the phenomenon of the mass from which very different conclusions will be drawn. Freud starts out from Le Bon's description and accepts it, just as he accepts his interpretation. Let us see then, by transcribing it, the description that Le Bon offers of the mass and let us read in what way both interpretations differ. Le Bon describes and Freud transcribes:

> A group is impulsive, changeable and irritable. It is led almost exclusively by the unconscious. The impulses which a group obeys may according to circumstances be generous or cruel, heroic or cowardly, but they are always so imperious that no personal interest, not even that of self-preservation, can make itself felt. Nothing about it is premeditated. Though it may desire things passionately, yet this is never so for long, for it is incapable of perseverance. It cannot tolerate any delay between its desire and the fulfilment of what it desires. It has a sense of omnipotence; the notion of impossibility disappears for the individual in a group.
>
> A group is extraordinarily credulous and open to influence, it has no critical faculty, and the improbable does not exist for it. It thinks in images, which call one another up by association (just as they arise with individuals in states of free imagination), and whose agreement with reality is never checked by any reasonable agency. The feelings of a group are always very simple and very exaggerated. So that a group knows neither doubt nor uncertainty.
>
> It goes directly to extremes; if a suspicion is expressed, it is instantly changed into an incontrovertible certainty; a trace of antipathy is turned into furious hatred.
>
> Inclined as it itself is to all extremes, a group can only be excited by an excessive stimulus. Anyone who wishes to produce an effect upon it needs no logical adjustment in his arguments; he must paint in the most

> forcible colours, he must exaggerate, and he must repeat the same thing again and again.
>
> Since a group is in no doubt as to what constitutes truth or error, and is conscious, moreover, of its own great strength, it is as intolerant as it is obedient to authority. It respects force and can only be slightly influenced by kindness, which it regards merely as a form of weakness. What it demands of its heroes is strength, or even violence. It wants to be ruled and oppressed. that the primary dream-thoughts are not acquainted with doubt and uncertainty as critical processes. (qtd. 78)

All these phenomena, in which rationality breaks down and affectivity becomes dominant by disrupting and dissolving the given order, have long been familiar to Freud. He compares them with his discoveries in the psychology of neurosis, with the conception he had to develop about primitive people and children, and about the dream of the 'normal' person. But does this 'similarity with the mental life of primitive people and of children' hold the same value for Freud as for Le Bon? Is his approach also a reduction, as in Le Bon, of the person of the crowd to primitive people and children? Or is there something present in the debate of so-called primitives and children – 'savages', says Le Bon – that the identity established by Le Bon refuses to recognise? For the scientific ethnocentrism of Western civilisation, are primitives not the evidence of a historical distance that historically has already been overcome, namely, the one that separates Westerners and Christians for good from the barbarism in which others remain stuck, just as it separates them today from the peoples of the Third World, who in this view are also situated in prehistory? Primitives, masses, and children: three distances from the origin concealed in the normal person, moments in the process of the advent of Western civilisation that the bourgeoisie tries to keep away, because in all three there emerges the presence of a historical transition which is always present in Western civilisation but which it cannot recognise without at the same time destroying its own.

> It will be remarked that among the special characteristics of crowds there are several – such as impulsiveness, irritability, incapacity to reason, the absence of judgment and of the critical spirit, the exaggeration of the sentiments, and others besides – which are almost always observed in beings belonging to inferior forms of evolution – in women, savages, and children, for instance. (Le Bon, *The Crowd*, 40).

Le Bon freezes savages, women, children, and crowds as inferior forms of organisation that disappear forever once the final order of civilisation has been reached. Freud, by contrast, considers them as permanent moments that put into relief the *foundation* and the *transition*, always actual and always repeated in the development both of the human subject and of social organisations, forms in which the unfinished cultural elaboration still keeps present that which repression did not finish integrating. Whereas for Le Bon this permanence is proof of inferiority, which serves to validate in an absolute way one's own closed and superior forms, for Freud by contrast it is evidence of the false equilibrium of the apparently superior, which cuts short and does not prolong that from which it proceeds, but rather demarcates and represses it. What interests Freud is the questioning of the already elaborated, the already consolidated; to see emerge the persistent obstinacy with which the repressed attempts to reassert its claims so as to dislocate the official order.

This is why the analogy makes sense for Freud. The group thinks *like* one thinks in the dream: abstracting from doubts and uncertainties due to the action of censorship: 'the primary dream-thoughts are not acquainted with doubt and uncertainty as critical processes' (78 n. 1). The group acts *like* primitive people: the notion of the impossible, which holds people back in stable social formations, breaks down. The omnipotence of the group includes the feeling of an unlimited power. And the group feels *like* the child: 'the same extreme and unmeasured intensification of every emotion is also a feature of the affective life of children' (78 n. 2). But the people of the group or mass are not primitive, they are not asleep, nor are they children. The analogy does not turn into an identity for Freud. What is of interest in the analogy are the functions of destruction and reconstruction, of integration and disintegration; of repression and the emergence of the repressed. The permanent demarcation of the contents that civilisation cannot accept, and the stubborn persistence of their emergence: what interests Freud is to understand how these repressed cultural contents, which are not elaborated, come to be integrated into reality and find a path toward consciousness.

We saw this before: Le Bon thinks from the point of view of the repressor; Freud thinks from the standpoint of the repressed. This is why Freud can bring out what the other conceals. Thus what in Le Bon appears as the destruction of personality due to a person's integration into the group or crowd, in Freud is understood as the moment of the collective questioning of traditional social forms: contents repressed by civilisation but that the group attempts to integrate and develop.

7 *But It Is Only the Bourgeois Person That Is Destroyed*

In the spontaneous mass or group what disappears is a separation consolidated in the bourgeois personality, while a different modality of the link to reality is produced. Something is diminished and something is intensified:

1. '*lowering in intellectual ability*' and in conscious linkages (77);
2. 'extreme and unmeasured *intensification of every emotion*' (78 n. 2);
3. 'a sense of *omnipotence*' (77, emphasis added).

The incorporation into the group or mass destroys the dualism of the 'isolated' individual: the flesh subjugated to an order imposed on it by consciousness. The body, in bourgeois individualism, is halted in its sensible extension: it *feels* or *senses* only within fixed limits. But it also *thinks* within the limits that consciousness imposes on it. Finally, it *acts* in the field indicated by the division of labour. If, in the group or mass, individuals '*think, feel, and act in an unexpected way*', this is because they exceed the materiality that previously was restricted to the limits of their own skin, just as they transgress the rationality that their consciousness fixated for them. It is here that bourgeois individuality disappears as a limit: limit in one's consciousness, limit in one's body. Intensification of the affects: the body turns into the index of felt identifications; diminishing of intellectual activity and of conscious bonds: consciousness overflows the rational categories to which it had been subjected. And feeling of power: the individual corporeality extends itself, by including into its limited force the unlimited force of the others with whom it converges.

This extension of affectivity and corporeal sensibility; this diminishing of the official rational compulsion and this feeling of omnipotence, which express the destruction of the social order subjectivised into the person as repressive order; this cannot but be seen by Le Bon as the destruction pure and simple of humanity. If only suggestion, hypnotism, and contagion are the mental functions that develop in the individual who merges with the mass or crowd, for Le Bon this means that the personal organisation and its most civilised forms end up being annulled. From his point of view, as we saw, there is a return to a mindless animal-like form of activity. But the solution may allow for another answer if, extending conventional rationality to the point of encompassing the rational structure of the productive system and extending the body to the point of encompassing thereby the materiality of the system, we understand the rupture of the subjective order – which is produced in the individual who becomes part of a group or mass – as a new organisation that is produced, by way of the group, in relation to the existing social order. If we understand, therefore, that the subject of the mass gains access to a new organisation of individuality as a function of a new collective historical experience.

And this concealment in Le Bon is the result of his class ideology, which is *inverted*, in that the thought relations and the (ideal) contents of consciousness are not determined by the material bond that human beings sustain in the midst of a given productive system. The ideal determines and regulates the materiality of the relations. Consciousness, therefore, is not the domain in which the latter reproduce and complement, on the symbolic level, the order of the real. In Freud, by contrast, this inverted process is put back on its feet: consciousness is a quality of the body, and the body, via the libido, extends itself in the direction of the world. To Le Bon's dualism, Freud opposes a historical materialist monism, which determines the affective and rational qualities of the subject. Besides, he already knew this clearly: for Freud, repression maintains and consolidates the scission between the affective and the rational, the intellectual activity separated from affectivity.

The dualism in Le Bon, in other words, presupposes the separation between body and soul. At the level of the soul there exists, for the individual consciousness, a logical order, which impedes thinking of the contradictions that the system presents. Validated as rational are only those bonds and those forms that are compatible with the contradictory system of production. All thinking that transgresses these limits is irrational. At the level of the body: this rationality implies, as its complement, the acceptance of the narrowing of the field of material relations and of the affective repercussions that it experiences in its relation with the world.

Therefore, in bourgeois dualism there is a *false extension of consciousness*, which integrates the ideology of the system and keeps it from thinking reality. But, concomitantly, there is a *restriction of the body*, of the link it sustains with the world, which is limited to the miserly forms that the system tolerates. Thus, for spiritualism, the broadening of consciousness as the field of ideality is not verified in an extension of the field of material relations to which the body is linked. This coupling opens up and institutes a hiatus between thinking and being in each subject.

In this way the social forms, which here correspond to the social division of labour under capitalism, as they become internalised subjectively go on to delimit partial areas of belonging, as is the case for social classes or the institutions that frame us, or the modalities of the relations that close or open us onto others. The domain of the movement of the class delimits the domain of the movement and expansion of the individual body. Consciousness merely reflects, in the subjective realm, the objective order that has been halted. The rationality of the system is the complement of the rationality of the individual consciousness, providing the appearance of congruence between the two series. The individual's unfolding, regulated by his or her individual consciousness that thus has been subjugated, encompasses exclusively those zones of reality that coincide with this consciousness. It is in the system of production where both the subjective individualities and the diverse 'forms of group formation' find their true rational meaning, and that is the invariant on which, as we saw, Le Bon's social psychology is based.

And it is precisely the transformation of this invariant structure that is announced as a possibility in the group or mass. The mass is the field in which a social experience is inaugurated that is 'aberrant' from the official point of view, since in it two dissociated and contrasting extremes are united: the affective and the rational, the isolated individuality and the collective experience, and it announces the putting to the test of the coherence of the whole system. But if it is put to the test this is because the *implicit agreement*, which is contained in the forms of bourgeois individuality and restricted to the field of the subjective, is here succeeded by a *collective and objective verification* that transforms the limits both rational and sensible that give it its organisation. The collective experience that rises up in the mass or group opens the possibility of a radical modification of the person.

8   The Removal of the Obstacle, Aim of the Mass

This is why, if we explain the transformation undergone by the individual in the group or mass, such as Le Bon describes it, from this new perspective that Freud introduces, its meaning is radically changed. What meaning is acquired by the '*lowering in intellectual ability*' and in the conscious linkages in the person who becomes part of a group or mass?

At the level of consciousness there appears a negation (suspension) of the bourgeois logic. Let us go back to Le Bon's description: 'it has no critical faculty'; its 'agreement with reality is never checked by any reasonable agency'; it is 'in no doubt as to what constitutes truth or error, and is conscious, moreover, of its own great strength'; 'anyone who wishes to produce an effect upon it needs no logical adjustment in his arguments'; 'the most contradictory ideas can exist side by side and tolerate each other, without any conflict arising from the logical contradiction between them'; 'reason and arguments are incapable of combating certain words and formulas'; 'it thinks in images, which call one another up by association'.

We thus see that Le Bon's description of the lack of rationality in the mass is only the expression of a disappointment and a state of impotence: that of not being able to continue dominating the individual consciousness of people who gain access to this new experience where the rational limits are broken. Evidently, it is the negation of one logic, of one order, but not of *all logic* and *all reason*, even though we also cannot say that because of this negation we would have obtained the fullness of another logic. It only shows the moment of suspension of the official logic in the subjectivity of the repressed subject. And it is this logic that the individual of the mass, within the collective experience, rejects. What Le Bon interprets as if it were the negation of all reason at bottom is only the negation of his own logic considered the only one.

But if this transformation is produced in consciousness, how can we understand the second transformation, the 'extreme and unmeasured intensification of every emotion'? What happens is that in the collective experience the corporeal limits are broken in which bourgeois individuality maintained itself.

At the level of the body, therefore, there simultaneously occurs in the person in the crowd an extension of individual corporeality up to the point of encompassing the mass as its common body, and thus the incorporated feeling of a new collective power, which breaks the delimitation in which individualism was maintained.

Le Bon's description shows this: 'The impulses which a group obeys ... are always so imperious that no personal interest, not even that of self-preservation, can make itself felt'; 'It cannot tolerate any delay between its desire and the fulfilment of what it desires'; 'It has a sense of omnipotence'; 'The feelings of a group are always very simple and very exaggerated'; 'a trace of antipathy is turned into furious hatred'; 'What it demands of its heroes is strength, or even violence'; 'individual inhibitions fall away'; 'all the cruel, brutal and destructive instincts, which lie dormant in individuals as relics of a primitive epoch, are stirred up to find free gratification'; 'personal interest ... is very rarely prominent'; 'They constantly give what is unreal precedence over what is real; they are almost as strongly influenced by what is untrue as by what is true' (78–80).

Thus, what hurts the most is the disappearance of the obstacle that the system, with the aid of consciousness, introduced between desire and satisfaction. And what becomes evident in this 'affective' aspect of the destruction of bourgeois personality is the transformation of consciousness, previously separated from the body, as a function of the *felt* experience, where the body is turned into a *significant index* of reality through the new bond that the experience of the group reveals. The body is extended to the point of integrating powers and capacities of verification of which, as a function of the repressive logic, it had been deprived or which had been inhibited. The body is extended to the point of including in one's own individuality the force and significations that the new collective experience provides it with, once the separating dissociation in each one has been dissolved by the collective experience. And the indices on which the body now bases itself, in their immediate expression, are no longer only *known* rational indices. What is incorporated is a form of knowledge despised by the bourgeoisie but faithfully kept and taken up by the body, which now prolongs itself and produces itself in a different way: the *felt rationality*, in a new congruence which is verified in the common agreement starting from the individual. This felt rationality, though incipient, begins to break down the limits of bourgeois rationality by breaking with the limits of one's own individuality. This is a phenomenon concomitant with the discovery of one's own force, which is also the discovery of a common force that previously was ignored and dispersed. And it implies first of all a change in meaning of the real: the 'unreality' of the mass is not just any unreal, in this case the domain of subjective 'fantasy', the cemetery of impossibilities that have been abandoned forever and in parallel accompany each individual life. The 'unreal' indicated by Le Bon, which he contrasts with the sole reality, that of his class, is in the mass the emergence of a new real power, which incorporates in the collective field this excess that previously was repressed, that the imagination maintained at the level of the body, and that searches for its verification in the realm of objectivity. And it is this imaginary stirred up by the real as a possibility which the bourgeoisie sees only as an illusion, incapable of giving it sensible consistency without negating the dominion over the material reality that it retains, as private property and capital. 'The illusion – says Le Bon – born of an unfulfilled wish'. Unfulfilled, but seeking and intuiting where to find its fulfilment.

This unfulfilled desire, relegated by the official mode of thinking outside of reality as illusion, will be our sole index of truth and of every project. Let us also retain this in theory, because it is what the subject of the mass brings closer to us, and because it shows us an unsuspected possibility for those who remain in the restricted and professional individuality of the bourgeoisie. And let us keep this as an index of our own analysis, of this rationality of which the spontaneous group has a presentiment on the basis of an experience that is irreducible to individual thought, and which guides its body in the common experience, fissuring reality and searching for a new form, a new order that science must prolong by prolonging what the group itself began. With good reason this index is of capital importance for Freud: because from the first group, from the primitive horde which begins history by transforming itself in fraternal alliance, to the current masses that are driving Western reason insane, Freud saw in them the emergence of a new historical signification, which necessarily had to be incorporated into the depth of the subject. 'Depth' psychology has its roots in the depth of collective history. And it emerges from it by showing that the limits of individual neurosis, restricted to the subjective field in the vain and endlessly repeated search for health, encounters at last the possibility of an objective verification when it transcends the limits within which the bourgeois solutions of individualism condemned it to persevere as 'unfulfilled wish', but forever after.[4]

'The unfulfilled wish': such is, then, the common lack both for individual subjectivity (neurosis) and for the subjects who are integrated collectively (the mass). And it is likewise the unifying nexus between individual psychology and collective psychology. But why does this transition take place? What new dimension of reality opens up for the unsatisfied desire when the mass inscribes it in an objective historical conjuncture, but one which psychoanalysis in its clinical experience did not reveal? What is the meaning of this prolongation from the doctor's office all the way to the social struggles that take place in the streets? Is this a mere extrapolation of the omnipotence of psychoanalysis projecting its individual categories onto social and collective phenomena? But it so happens that if individual psychology is already social psychology, and vice-versa, this does not mean that for this reason the social element present but implicit in the individual is identical to the social element that, now explicit, gathers its effective collective forces and inscribes them *directly* in the system. *The mass is thus the place where the implicit other becomes 'actualised'*. The problem therefore is that of the verification of the unfulfilled desire in the context of the collective reality. The inscription of the unsatisfied desire in this way reveals two domains: on the one hand, the search for satisfaction is regulated by the pleasure principle (the primitive pleasure ego) that prolongs itself in the absolute character of its own subjectivity; on the other hand, this first figure was followed by the creation of an exterior field of reality, which thereafter appeared as the effective and social condition of all satisfaction: the transition to the definitive ego who is realistic and, let us add, conventional and well-adapted. In both cases, in that of neurosis and that of the spontaneous mass or group, the problem is the same: the passage from the unfulfilled wish to the satisfaction in reality. But what does 'reality' mean here? Everybody believes they are in it, even the psychotic person. And so we ask ourselves: is there an individual subjectivity and a collective subjectivity? Does the collective imaginary that appears in the mass possess a real power of

---

[4] Freud had already described this capacity and disposition of the sick person, in contrast to the 'normal' person adapted without contradiction to official reality, to assimilate the new rationality, similar to what happens in the subject of the revolutionary mass: 'the certainty and appositeness of his interpretations are a surprise to the doctor, and the latter can only take note with satisfaction that here is a patient who readily accepts all the psychological novelties which are apt to provoke the most bitter contradiction among healthy people in the outside world' (*Introductory Lectures on Psycho-analysis*, SE 16: 440).

which the individual neurotic is dispossessed, and therefore do the solutions point in the direction of distinct possibilities in each case? Or do they all lead to the same failure and the same frustration?

> We have pointed out that this predominance of the life of phantasy and of the illusion born of an unfulfilled wish is the ruling factor in the psychology of neuroses. We have found that what neurotics are guided by is not ordinary objective reality but psychological reality. ... Indeed, just as in dreams and in hypnosis, in the mental operations of a group the function for testing the reality of things falls into the background in comparison with the strength of wishful impulses with their affective cathexis. (80)

If the frame of reality in which individual psychology is inscribed prolongs itself to the point of including the social frame of collective psychology, this means that the function for testing the reality of things, which falls into the background in both cases, is not the same. The frame of reality is not the same in the individual neurotics, restricted to their subjectivity without verification, and in that of the mass or group, whose verification opens itself up to historical action. The problem consists in discerning how the function of testing the reality of things falls away in both cases, and which 'objective reality' it is that in each case fails either to prove it right or to give it satisfaction.

9 The Human Form as Model of Transformation

In Le Bon reductionism consists precisely in reducing the reality in which the phenomena analysed inscribe themselves:

1. he reduces and identifies the subject of the mass with children and primitive people;
2. he reduces and identifies the mass or group with the flock, without attending to the model who leads it, the 'leader of crowds': the human form that regulates the group.

Freud is able to recognise in Le Bon's descriptions the similarities and analogies, but what he cannot do, and this is his criticism, is ignore the specific character of each phenomenon. And what is irreducibly specific to the group or mass is precisely its inscription within a reality in which it exercises its effects. If Le Bon reduces the subject of the group to the primitive person or to the child or to the flock, in this reduction he leaves to one side the historical and situated signification of the group. If Le Bon ignores the role of the 'leader of crowds', he leaves to one side the cultural model and project of action incarnated by the latter. And, in the final instance, what this entails is the concealment of the criteria of reality in regard to which the human phenomena define themselves.

Freud, by contrast, does not identify but *compares* this scission that is produced in the group with that which is produced in neurosis. Speaking of the child, he indicates how two ambivalent attitudes are combined, without either one disturbing the other in its origin. If a conflict arises, one of the feelings of the child's ambivalence is displaced onto a substitute object. Freud here attends to the form, to the structure of the displacement, and points in the direction of the discovery of a logical law of the substitutions and transactions that take place in the face of the conflict, but without losing sight of the domain of reality that thus organises itself or of the specificity of the one organising it. Thus also in the case of adult neurotics, in whom, 'suddenly', we are told, a conflict is produced between the affective charge and the ego. Here too there is opposition between the affective and the intellectual, as happens in the group. But the 'suddenly' that produces the separation in individual neurosis and in the group or mass is completely different. The 'intensification of the affective cathexis' in the 'suddenly' of the neurotic individual is different from the objective and historical conditions that in the mass produce 'suddenly' the simultaneous convergence of subjectivities who in order to accomplish this must have something in common. There is analogy but not identity in this new ordering of reality. There can be no reduction of one phenomenon to the other without losing the specificity of each; they inscribe their *effects*, their failures and their successes, in different levels of reality. In the mass or group there exists a common and simultaneous character of the individuals – 'there must be something to tie them' – and this something in common that ties them together is already, in its convergence, a social content *that objectifies itself in a collective act*, which goes from implicit to explicit. What is more: it could not be common if it were not social, if in this convergence it did not put at stake something that only the real collective experience could provide: the common cultural form in which the individual difference, previously subjective, is undone and turns into a collective objective similitude. Thus the unconscious wish searches outwards, in a collective experience, in a 'common body', what before was restricted to the sole domain of individual fantasy and one's own body. With this we do not want to say that we would be reaching the non-contradictory reality and the satisfaction of desire: we only say that here there appears a different field of reality in which desire inscribes itself, and that this difference must be retained.

This is why Freud, as we saw, attempts to discern the meaning of the group's activity as a function of how it transforms the repressive reality and in the model of the subject – leader or chief – whom the mass considers as model of satisfaction. There is a point that for Freud will remain constant in the analysis of the collective processes: the form of the other, of this other who was present in individual psychology and also regulated the collective formations. Whence the criticism of Le Bon:

> What Le Bon says on the subject of leaders of groups is less exhaustive, and does not enable us to make out an underlying principle so clearly. (80–81)

That is to say, Le Bon does not include the organisation imposed by the leader, whose meaning would allow us to understand the direction in which the mass thus reorganised is heading:

> He thinks that as soon as living beings are gathered together in certain numbers, no matter whether they are a herd of animals or a collection of human beings, they place themselves instinctively under the authority of a chief. A group is an obedient herd, which could never live without a master. It has such a thirst for obedience that it submits instinctively to anyone who appoints himself its master. (81)

Freud unravels the reductionist argument by putting into relief the *signification* of the model of humanity, of the form of the human, conveyed by the leader, and the relation of the latter with the unfulfilled desire in proposing a form that makes satisfaction possible:

> Although in this way the needs of a group – says Freud – carry it half-way to meet the leader, yet he too must fit in with it in his personal qualities. He must himself be held in fascination by a strong faith (in an idea) in order to awaken the group's faith. (81)

Thus appears the rationality that links the mass to the leader: strong faith in an idea. Whence the role of ideology in the process of adhesion. Union, therefore, of affectivity (faith) in rationality (idea), once again unified in the leader of multitudes.

Freud is relentless in his continuation of this orientation:

> Moreover, he [Le Bon] ascribes both to the ideas and to the leaders a mysterious and irresistible power, which he calls 'prestige'. Prestige is a sort of domination exercised over us by an individual, a work or an idea. It entirely paralyses our critical faculty, and fills us with wonderment and respect. The sentiment provoked is inexplicable, like all sentiments, but it would appear to be of the same kind as the 'fascination' in hypnosis. (81, cf. Le Bon, *The Crowd*, 148, trans. modified)

Thus culminates in the recourse to 'prestige', the destruction of the new rationality and the new affectivity that ties human beings together due to their entering a group or mass. That is to say, the new form of feeling and thinking that is suggested starting from the model with whom the mass identifies: the leader of crowds. For Le Bon there is neither truth in the ideas nor truth in the feeling. But above all the body is erased as signifier of reality: 'The sentiment provoked is inexplicable, like all sentiments'. Where would reason in history circulate if the domain of affectivity, of human materiality, became irreducible to reason, if it is not understood as 'felt rationality'? The 'model' of the human being ceases to be what Freud signalled in the beginning: 'the other as model, as object, as helper, as adversary'. We return to the other's merely empirical, insignificant presence. The human form of the other does not signify another link with reality and another possible opening. All that is left, in this irrationalism, is prestige as the inexplicable aura that surrounds its attraction. The meaning of the bond with reality that this model opens up remains covered over and there is no more effort to interpret its objective consequences: in the mode in which the group makes its transition, in a new form of collectivity, towards the terrain of history. This is why Freud complains in lapidary style:

> All prestige, however, is also dependent upon success, and is lost in the event of failure. (81, cf. Le Bon 1914, p. 159)

The meaning acquired by the model for Freud always operates as a function of the effective transition to reality: in its practical putting to the test. Therefore, it depends on how the leader of crowds opens the possibility of satisfying that which the subject conglomerated around him had in common: the unfulfilled desire. This convergence on the human model that the group or mass assumes as its own – to make the passage from fantasy to reality – is one of the fundamental elements for the understanding of this collective experience:

> Le Bon does not give the impression of having succeeded in bringing the function of the leader and the importance of prestige completely into harmony with his brilliantly executed picture of the group mind. (81)

11   Critique of the Bourgeois Conceptions of the Group (Continuation)

> We will howl with the wolves.
> MCDOUGALL

1   On How the Only Possibility Granted to the Group Is to Return to the Same Form of Repressive Organisation from Which It Pretends to Distance Itself

A major difference separates Freud's conception from *all* those which hitherto, in official science, had analysed the phenomenon of the groups or masses: the *creation* of new cultural contents produced by the latter. Freud once again signals the points of agreement with Le Bon, the emergence in the individuals of the mass of *separate functions* – affect and consciousness – which in the official institutions find themselves unified. He agrees with Le Bon, he reiterates, in 'the emphasis which it lays upon unconscious mental life' (81); but not with the meaning acquired according to Le Bon by the collective inhibition of the intellectual function and the intensification of affectivity in the crowd or multitude. The question, then, becomes once again the following: whether this separation is *the destruction of a terminal equilibrium* or, on the contrary, *the evidence of a disequilibrium that remits the dialectic of creation* – the sensible and the rational – to the only domain where new cultural syntheses may continue to elaborate themselves: in the collective domain. Therefore, the *value judgment* expressed by the scientist with regard to these psychic functions will be the determining factor. This is why Freud signals his difference with regard to Le Bon as well as with so many other ideologues:

> Everything that he says to the detriment and depreciation of the manifestations of the group mind had already been said by others before him with equal distinctness and equal hostility, and has been repeated in unison by thinkers, statesmen and writers since the earliest periods of literature. (82)

If the value judgment changes, the perception of the phenomenon of the group also changes. And, concomitantly, the meaning assigned to these apparently separate functions that arise in the group also changes. If the group or mass was shown in its negative sense, now we will see appear, with reference to one and the same scientific object, its positive aspect which remained invisible or, at best, merely accidental:

> There is no doubt that all the phenomena of the group mind which have just been mentioned have been correctly observed, but it is also possible to distinguish other manifestations of group formation, which operate in a precisely opposite sense, and from which a much higher opinion of the group mind must necessarily follow. (82)

The group dissolves the individual, said Le Bon. But it makes appear qualities of which the isolated individual is incapable, says Freud. The significance of the phenomenon varies, and it does so by turning some of Le Bon's descriptions back against himself:

> Le Bon himself was prepared to admit that in certain circumstances the morals of a group can be higher than those of the individuals that compose it, and that only collectivities are capable of a high degree of unselfishness and devotion. 'While with isolated individuals personal interest is almost the only motive force, with groups it is very rarely prominent'. Other writers adduce the fact that it is only society which prescribes any ethical standards at all for the individual, while he as a rule fails in one way or another to come up to its high demands. Or they point out that in exceptional circumstances there may arise in communities the phenomenon of enthusiasm, which has made the most splendid group achievements possible. (82–3, cf. Le Bon, *The Crowd*, 65).

All this with regard to the affective function, the display of sensibility. But in the intellectual aspect, too, the mass or group demonstrates its capacity to create rationality:

> But even the group mind is capable of creative genius in the field of intelligence, as is shown above all by language itself, as well as by folk-song, folklore and the like. It remains an open question, moreover, how much the individual thinker or writer owes to the stimulation of the group in which he lives, and whether he does more than perfect a mental work in which the others have had a simultaneous share. (83)

This affirmation on Freud's part meets up with that of Marx: the activity of the 'social brain'. And breaking with the limits of individuality, it enters the human field that produces it precisely when it appears most particularised and differentiated from the latter. There is no strictly individual creation, in spite of the fact that the individual, as isolated unity, expresses it. Individuals – the component parts of this group or mass – in particularising themselves as individuals give expression to that which collective activity communicates to them on another level of their connection to it, and the artist or thinker appropriates the meanings elaborated by a collective process in which the other subjects have participated simultaneously. With this assertion *Freud at once establishes the collective character of the most individual creation*. He unifies the most outstanding and elevated aspect of spiritual creation – art and thought – that expresses itself through the transformation of the sensible and the rational, the two moments commonly dissociated in bourgeois society at the level of individual activity. The elaboration of affectivity, which expresses itself in the sensible element of artistic expression, and that of rationality, which expresses itself in the work of thought, find their domain of unification and of creation in the collective labour of the mass or group. It is in the group where the affective and rational activity elaborates new links and new forms that expressed themselves in synthesised form at the individual level. Thus 'simultaneity', which defines the collective as mere numerical coexistence in traditional social psychology, here shows the collective work that was covered up: 'a mental work in which the others have had a simultaneous share'. *Thus Freud establishes the creative preeminence of the group's collective activity with respect to that of its individual members.*

The most particular and emphatic individuation – the poet or the thinker – is the result of the most profound participation in collective elaboration. This is why Freud could speak in *Civilisation and its Discontents* of an ideology and an art that cover up the relations with reality – mere 'technology' – and of a true art and thought that express and confront the conflicts presented by civilisation. Bourgeois individuality separates itself from this creative domain, because by turning into a personal and private privilege that which is a collective result, it covers up its debt together with its source and condemns itself to remain ineffectual. The *stabilised separation* between the sensible and the rational, between thinking and feeling, which this individuality shows, expresses only its separation from the collective domain that serves as its foundation. It does not link sensibility to the sensibility of that common body in which it should prolong itself because this is where it comes from; and for this reason it does not link the rationality of its consciousness with the domain that produces the relations that made it possible as a subjective domain of thought.

Every form of the individual, both in its creativity and its sickness, expresses the result of 'a mental work in which the others have had a simultaneous share'. But if this is indeed the case, is it *the same* collectivity, taken as a whole, that produces both the positive and the negative?

> In face of these completely contradictory accounts, it looks as though the work of group psychology were bound to come to an ineffectual end. (83)

But this appearance is erased only if we keep in mind the result at which Freud arrives: the observation that the stabilised bourgeois individuality is congruent with its stabilised class, whereas the individuality that dissolves itself emerges from the mass where the official bonds become disorganised. If this is true, then the society that psychology studies cannot be maintained as a *homogeneous whole* but must be conceived of as a *contradictory whole* in which different collective forms confront one another.

2   The Historical Meaning of the Group

We must therefore determine what is the meaning of the masses or groups within a contradictory social system.

> But it is easy to find a more hopeful escape from the dilemma. A number of very different structures have probably been merged under the term 'group' and may require to be distinguished. (83)

In this regard Freud fully finds himself in the midst of a crucial distinction:

> The assertions of Sighele, Le Bon and the rest relate to groups of a short-lived character, which some passing interest has hastily agglomerated out of various sorts of individuals. The characteristics of revolutionary groups, and especially those of the great French Revolution, have unmistakably influenced their descriptions. The opposite opinions owe their origin to the consideration of those stable groups or associations in which mankind pass their lives, and which are embodied in the institutions of society. Groups of the first kind stand in the same sort of relation to those of the second as a high but choppy sea to a ground swell. (83)

For the bourgeois psychologists 'good' groups are therefore the institutionalised ones; 'bad' groups, the revolutionary ones. Freud thus distinguishes the contradictory character of society expressed by the masses, as he understands their negative or positive meaning as a function of how they inscribe themselves within this contradictory society, either adapting themselves or opposing themselves to it. There would be two basic forms of groups or masses for Freud, which form the *extremes* of all collective formations:

1. The *institutionalised groups*, which form a body consistent with the global system, and are rendered immobile within a contradictory rationality.
2. The *revolutionary groups*, in which human beings finds themselves united by a common interest which can lead them to radically transform the system.

Between the two, as we will see, Freud situates the *spontaneous groups*.

In the first, institutionalised groups, 'mankind pass their lives', that is, they seal the indissoluble unity of the individual and the social institution. If these were the only groups that existed, it would seem that society already reached, in the process of civilisation, its definitive equilibrium. But the fact that it produces revolutionary masses incompatible with the system and the institutions, groups which constitute themselves in the convergence of common interests by erasing the constituted individual differences, signals precisely the existence of a contradiction that bourgeois social psychology could not assume without throwing into doubt its own social system as well as the researcher's own individuality. For Freud this difference between these two groups is radical:

> Groups of the first kind [the revolutionary masses] stand in the same sort of relation to those of the second [the masses consolidated in the system] as a high but choppy sea to a ground swell. (83)

Once these types of group or multitude are distinguished on the basis of the function they fulfil in the transformation of global society, Freud will shows us how an ideologue of the bourgeoisie – McDougall – solves the contradiction between 'good' and 'bad' groups or masses. McDougall starts from the same contradiction that Freud confronted, but by maintaining as 'invariants' the institutionalised groups. He resolves the conflict by introduction the factor of 'organisation'. This means that we will become witness to a verification of Freud's hypothesis about the meaning of the masses, as a function of how traditional social psychology considers the transition from the disorder to the order of the group to the institution, from revolution to restoration.

Even though McDougall affirms that the mass possesses no organisation at all, or only a rudimentary one, he 'admits – Freud tells us – that a crowd of human beings can hardly come together without possessing at all events the rudiments of an organisation, and that precisely in these simple groups some fundamental facts of collective psychology can be observed with special ease' (83–84). This is why Freud picks up on this 'confession' on McDougall's part, and summarises it for us as follows:

> Before the members of a random crowd of people can constitute something like a group in the psychological sense, a condition has to be fulfilled: these individuals must have something in common with one another, a common interest in an object, a similar emotional bias in some situation or other, and ('consequently', I should like to interpolate) 'some degree of reciprocal influence'. (qtd. 84)

Here the random character, in its apparent disorder, reveals a precise order. Except that McDougall does not know, from within his system, how to understand it. Something *in common*, a *common* interest in an object, a *similar* emotional bias in *some* situation or other, inscribed with precision in reality. But not only a common objective, there is also a similar interest in it. And a participation, which is not only a question of thought: it is a common objective *felt* as common, given a new dimension through collective embodied participation. And, moreover, there is the power that thus is multiplied through collaboration, by the reciprocal influence. But once again, starting out from this recognition, McDougall comes to the same results as Le Bon: the individuals by fusing in the mass lose the sentiment of their individual delimitation and become scattered. The mass is thus contrasted with the individual, as is to be expected. But we could say that what most surprises and terrifies the social researcher is this *multiplication of power that is produced in the accidental group*. This is the surprising effect that explodes as he describes with great distress in the case of the multitudes that are not integrated into the system, thanks to a renewed emphasis on affectivity.

McDougall writes:

> the emotional contagion ... is calculated automatically to arouse the same affect in the person who perceives them. [...] The individual loses his power of criticism, and lets himself slip into the same affect. [...] and thus the affective charge of the individuals becomes intensified by mutual interaction. (qtd. 84)

> This mechanism for the intensification of affect is favoured by some other influences which emanate from groups. A group impresses the individual as being an unlimited power and an insurmountable peril. For the moment it replaces the whole of human society, which is the wielder of authority, whose punishments the individual fears, and for whose sake he has submitted to so many inhibitions. (84–85)

But the tastiest effect is the terror provoked in the researcher himself, now uncertain of his own existence:

> It is clearly perilous for him to put himself in opposition to it, and it will be safer to follow the example of those around him and perhaps even 'howl with the wolves'. (85, trans. modified)

We can clearly see that the power emanates from an affective and corporeal bond among the individuals. The dissolution of individuality is the opening onto this new power which puts itself in opposition to 'all of human society', of whose integrity the group, excluded, would not be part as it rises up in revolt against the repressive authority. What becomes diluted here is the rational contention that, qua consciousness, refers the individuals to an institutionalised rationality that marks their limits as well as their affect. The same principle that we found in Le Bon, the contrast between affective irrationality and thought rationality, continues to be at play here. This is why Freud adds:

> The judgement with which McDougall sums up the psychological behaviour of a simple 'unorganised' group is no more friendly than that of Le Bon. Such a group 'is excessively emotional, impulsive, violent, fickle, inconsistent, irresolute and extreme in action, displaying only the coarser emotions and the less refined sentiments; extremely suggestible, careless in deliberation, hasty in judgement, incapable of any but the simpler and imperfect forms of reasoning; easily swayed and led, lacking in self-consciousness, devoid of self-respect and of sense of responsibility, and apt to be carried away by the consciousness of its own force, so that it tends to produce all the manifestations we have learnt to expect of any irresponsible and absolute power. Hence its behaviour is like that of an unruly child or an untutored passionate savage in a strange situation, rather than like that of its average member; and in the worst cases it is like that of a wild beast, rather than like that of human beings'. (qtd. 85)

But the importance of McDougall's contribution lies in understanding how the bourgeoisie conceives of the transformation of this social 'sickness'. In signalling its therapeutic dimension, the 'organisation' of the disorganised, he will bring out something crucial: something will become visible that was implicit in Le Bon, that is, how the social organisation is prolonged in the individual form and needs it for the existence of its system.

3   *Return to the Same*
The multitudes of 'superior organisation', the institutions, are McDougall's model. And sarcastically Freud says:

> we shall be particularly interested to learn in what this organisation consists, and by what factors it is produced. (86)

Freud's impatience is immediately satisfied; the conditions that McDougall establishes to go from disorganisation to organisation are those that recreate in the multitude the form of the human that the mass dissolved. That is to say, the goal is to reproduce in the group or mass once again the only form that the bourgeoisie can conceive: the subjected humanity of bourgeois individualism, precisely the one whom the group or mass, in its apparent disorganisation, reorganised.

> It seems to us that the condition which McDougall designates as the 'organisation' of a group can with more justification be described in another way. The problem consists in how to procure for the group precisely those features which were characteristic of the individual and which are extinguished in him by the formation of the group. (86)

That is to say, the point would be for the individual to return to

> ... his own continuity, his self-consciousness, his traditions and customs, his own particular functions and position, and [in which] he kept apart from his rivals. (86)

In other words, the point would be to recreate in the subject the same contradictory subjective domain that corresponds to the organisation of bourgeois capitalism. The organisation of the system of production descends and organises the head and body of the subject it needs: this is its answer to the presence of the revolutionary mass. It is necessary once more to implement the dissolution, the individualities separated from one another, and the rivalry that opposes them among themselves. And in order to achieve this, to maintain the same values, the same qualities that were one with the oppressive system: 'his self-consciousness', as restricted and contradictory rational domain; 'his own particular functions and position', as limited by the social division of capitalist labour; 'his traditions and customs', to become what the system demands from them in order to live in it. And, finally, as the foundation of the ensemble of producers separated from one another, which conceals the basic links that determine the relation among human beings: the separation in which he 'kept apart from his rivals', and which the revolutionary mass precisely attempts to destroy by producing new common objectives, new needs, new modalities of action and a new possible form of reality.

III   The Amplification of the Body beyond Dependency

Suggestion or Libido

Freud returns to the fundamental nucleus of the phenomenon of the spontaneous group or mass and insists on keeping it firmly present in our mind:

> We started from the fundamental fact that an individual in a group is subjected through its influence to what is often a profound alteration in his mental activity. His liability to affect becomes extraordinarily intensified, while his intellectual ability is markedly reduced, both processes being evidently in the direction of an approximation to the other individuals in the group; and this result can only be reached by the removal of those inhibitions upon his instincts which are peculiar to each individual, and by his resigning those expressions of his inclinations which are especially his own. (88)

The proposition already clearly shows the path on which Freud will continue. There occurs a modification in the individual who becomes part of the spontaneous group and this modification can be extremely profound: the totality of his or her person is at stake. Affective intensification, intellectual limitation. What emerges in the group? *Equality*, Freud tells us, which erases the personal differences. But what is the content of this equality? That which appears after the erasure of the peculiar inhibitions of each individual and the renunciation of the personal and individual expressions of his or her inclinations. What is erased as a result of the collective activity, in other words, is the personal or different element of each one: the different forms of inhibition and satisfaction. But that which 'personalises' me, which 'individualises' me, which differentiates me from the others, was precisely that which impeded satisfaction. Both the 'expressions of my inclinations which are especially my own', which *led me* to the objects, as well as the 'inhibitions upon the instincts which are peculiar to each individual', which *kept me* from approaching those objects, defined the strict limit with which civilisation demarcated the boundaries of my individuality. From the individual point of view they were 'personal' and 'peculiar' before my insertion in the group. Upon my collective participation the apparent difference is dissolved and the fundamental similitude is revealed: in reality we are equals. Which means: we are equally produced by the system insofar as it inhibits us and leads us, on the basis of need, to the impossibility of satisfaction. And this is what is discovered once we renounce and abandon the separation and presumption of personalisation. What is objectified as common, and, therefore, what discovers its source in the process of cultural production, appears in an indispensable experience: *after renouncing the pursuit of the search for satisfaction of the unfulfilled desire via the individual paths that civilisation* left imprinted in each human being as the only possible paths, but which lead to failure and to frustration.

This discovery of the *most personal* that previously was inhibited is precisely what is held to be the *most common*, and only collectively produced. What the group negates is what the individual, owing to the individualistic organisation of his personality, affirmed in himself as the prolongation of a repressive system. The rational organisation of the institutions is extended in one's own body as institution. In the group or mass a lived decentring of the subject takes place with regard to its individual subjective centring. The apparent perspective of the subject, centred on his or her consciousness as absolute, is followed by the decentring of the body that apprehends itself affectively as open and crisscrossed by the others in a common objective field. There is an individual decentring and a recentring, which converges on the collective in the group. Thus, to say that in the group there occurs an affective intensification means the opening of a body marked by its boundaries, the preeminence of lived signification from within the collective materiality, which finds in the body and the historical space discovered in this convergence the locus where new relations unfold that amplify and destroy the institution that encloses it. On the other hand, the limitation of intellectual activity means the postponement of the institutions turned consciousness. There is thus a felt opening onto the others, an overflowing power that previously was contained, which the body preserves and expands and which in the social forms that fenced it off delimits the strict domain of a new belonging, of a new effective equality, of a new and incipient common corporeality, discovered on the basis of the common unfulfilled need.

But if this feeling is not mere disorder but rather the possible beginning in the establishment of a new organisation, this means that the group continues and develops a dialectic that one attempted to bring to a halt and that now finds verification in the group. The participation of human beings in the system blurred the contours in the body of the field of possibilities that it could not satisfy. And these negated possibilities, which the institutions nonetheless aroused, are the ones that the body faithfully maintains and objectivises in the speechless domain that now the group, with its force, opens up: a determinate void. What the body posits and fills in the collective process is the void that the logic of official reason determines as that which ought not to be but whose negation nonetheless opened up as possible, because it was inscribed in reality as an impediment, as the inhibition of a really existing power of creation and satisfaction.

Thus is dissolved the false individuation and personalisation, which was the counterpart of social repression. The novelty, in order words, is the field of objectivisation that civilisation represses. From this perspective the solution of traditional psychologists hides the problem, because the organisation and institutionalisation they propose corresponds to a return to the dissolved unity. They do not integrate the new signification that erupts in the mass or group when it produces the rupture between the affective and the rational. And by not understanding *the rational element conveyed through affectivity*, that is to say, the reason that circulates in the new links that give rise to the collective materiality of converging bodies, they cannot understand the tension between the two contrasting domains of signification – the affective and the rational – in which the conflict and contradiction would become visible and would require a new form capable of integrating them.

1   Subjection as the Human Essence

The bond that, 'correcting it', the bourgeois 'organisation' could provide to the spontaneous group or mass means covering up the novelty of the phenomenon that it produces: the 'fundamental fact' of the separation between the affective and the rational of which Freud wants to give an account.

> It is clear that rational factors (such as the intimidation of the individual which has already been mentioned, that is, the action of his instinct of self-preservation) do not cover the observable phenomena. Beyond this what we are offered as an explanation by authorities on sociology and group psychology is always the same, even though it is given various names, and that is – the magic word 'suggestion'. (88)

From the 'official' perspective there is no rationality to explain the bond. Tarde, Le Bon and McDougall in the final instance refer back to suggestion. For them, in other words, this would be 'actually an irreducible, primitive phenomenon, a fundamental fact in the mental life of man' (89).

Suggestion is a key concept because it shows, as did the 'genius of a race', a synthesis projected onto the phenomenon rather than discovered in it. Suggestion would suppose a relation with the other in which dependency would exclude any possibility for reaction on the part of the subject in question. It is as if suggestion had touched upon the psychic foundation of slavery and dependency within the human being; as if the latter were part, qua function, of every individual. Suggestion would be the imposition of a bond of dependency not resisted but solicited by the subject. It would express a mode of basic psychic connection, irreducible and present in each subject of the group, in which the influence of the superior finds in the other, the inferior, the seat of his or her submission. In other words: suggestibility would be the nucleus that in the subaltern human beings fiercely determines their necessary adhesion to the superior who orients and leads them and to whom they remain essentially riveted.

What can Freud oppose to this conception? The lessons provided to him by a hospital patient, the most diminished of all diminished beings, because from the outset he accepts his dependency on the doctor as the one knows more about him than he himself. But there is *something* in the patient that resists: in sickness and in the voluntary relation of maximum dependency, there persists a domain that is irreducible to resistance and freedom. Thus the 'irreducible' and 'primitive', the 'fundamental fact' that appears in the relation among humans is not suggestion or dependency. The irreducible fact is the common power that expands life, albeit only in the imaginary: to oppose itself to subjection and to imposition when these appear to contradict the expansion of the subject. The resistance to restrictive violence, that is, the capacity to resist dependency, in Freud would be the irreducible phenomenon, which shows us the contradictory organisation of the psychic apparatus.

Bernheim, his teacher, upheld the thesis of suggestion as a primitive and irreducible fact. The dramatic resistance in the master-slave relation, covered up behind the appearance of the cure based on suggestion, is told by Freud himself as the basic lesson taught by the patient to his doctor, from 'subjugated' to 'dominator':

> Such, too, was the opinion of Bernheim, of whose astonishing arts I was a witness in the year 1889. But I can remember even then feeling a muffled hostility to this tyranny of suggestion. When a patient who showed himself unamenable was met with the shout: 'What are you doing? Vous vous contre-suggestionnez', I said to myself that this was an evident injustice and an act of violence. For the man certainly had a right to counter-suggestions if people were trying to subdue him with suggestions. Later on my resistance took the direction of protesting against the view that suggestion, which explained everything, was itself to be exempt from explanation. (89)

The trajectory of 'suggestion' in the 'scientific' explanation was prolonged from individual psychology to social psychology as an attempt to *justify* domination.

The dependency of the patient with respect to his doctor in the hospital is prolonged in the dependency of the subject in the group with respect to the leader of the crowds or masses. The same individual subjection that the doctor solicits from the patient is projected, qua form of relationality, in the submission of the subject of the group with regard to the latter's leader.

The bottom cause that ties together the subjects of the mass would only be the natural and irreducible vocation for dependency and submission of inferior beings, 'a fundamental fact' of human psychic life.

Thinking of it, I repeated the old conundrum: having kept away from it for some thirty years, I find there is no change in the situation. (89–90)

But now the context of the question has changed. It is not the individual relation but the collective relation – the creative process in history – that is at stake. What will be the consequences of this putting into doubt of suggestion in the passage from individual to social psychology?

The most important consequence would be the following: whereas the individual and humiliated patient, precisely as patient, only has his individual power to counteract this dependency that is being imposed on him, by contrast the group acquires the collective power that rediscovers the field of opposition of dominating and dominated as the effective terrain of struggle that would be verified in the collective power of the individuals who make up the group or mass. The individual impotence of the patient is followed by the collective omnipotence of the mass. That nucleus of terror which appeared in Le Bon as well as in McDougall faced with the fact of the spontaneous and, above all, the revolutionary mass – which Bernheim did not encounter – was the destructive emergence of the power of suggestion. Here we see that the mass or group, autosuggesting itself, should let itself be led by the 'illustrious' and 'free' men, qua 'true personalities', just as Bernheim pretended to dominate his patient through suggestion. But why is it that the masses do not let themselves be suggested by the good guys? Why do they only let themselves be suggested by the bad ones? If suggestion is what appears as the collective demand for control in the masses, if servitude is what they require, there is no other way out of the conundrum except to dominate the masses, to impose on them the slavery and dependency that the doctor imposed on his patient. Thus the scientist's rationality does not understand what happens in the body of the patient, *which resists in him*. What resists in the mass is the felt rationality postponed in the flesh, the historical and no longer individual truth of its repressed content.

This is why for its utter lack of precision and, above all, its inability to reveal its true and unavowable content, suggestion will 'soon come to designate any sort of influence whatever' (90).

Freud thus reopens the question once more by indicating wherein lies the central knot of incomprehension:

> But there has been no explanation of the nature of suggestion, that is, of the conditions under which *influence without adequate logical foundation* takes place. (90, emphasis added)

The lack of sufficient logical foundation does not pertain to the phenomenon being analysed; it pertains to the 'official' categories with which one pretends to understand it. The bond – 'there must be something to tie them together' – has an essence, it has a reason irreducible to the logic with which it is analysed: irreducible to that which is prolonged as rationality from within the repressive social institutions.

2   Resistance against Repression, Truth of the Foundation

But before we move on to the notion of libido, let us analyse Freud's criticism of suggestion. What does this rejection mean for him?

At its origin it was the discovery of the submission doctor-patient: to deny oneself a solution imposed *from the outside*, which in front of the patient continued to maintain the doctor as the one in charge of ordering his conduct, but without recognising or integrating the patient's fundamental imbalance, whose meaning and logic were being ignored. Suggestion was not the cure, in other words, because the patient was only reoriented – and this could only be transitory – in the new shortlived modality that the other – the doctor – imposed on him. The process did not consider the sick subject as the domain for the dispute and the contradictory convergence between two structures, as a function of its own problem: the logic of the contradiction was being avoided.

> ... total success turned out to be entirely dependent upon the patient's relation to the physician and thus resembled the effect of 'suggestion'. If that relation was disturbed, all the symptoms reappeared, just as though they had never been cleared up. ('Two Encyclopaedia Articles', SE 18: 237)

The patient thus required the permanent presence of the doctor, of a continuous suggestion. This impeded the emergence of the conflict, but not its existence. The doctor, through suggestion, from the outside imposed on his patient a form of organisation that signalled the predominance of one system over the other: the dominant one, the doctor, over the dominated, the patient. But the patient (or the mass) admits this strange rationality because it is rooted in the admission of another dominion already presupposed in the act of submitting himself to the cure: the dominion of (official) 'health', the norm and law with regard to its own (clandestine, persecuted, lacking, unfulfilled, and above all, *unreasonable*) sick being. The patient's rationality was, in suggestion, ignored by 'science'. This lack of recognition led to an imperative form of being cured, to a 'duty to be normal', which concealed the origin of the law. But above all it ignored the reason of the sickness.

'He had a right to counter-suggest himself', protests Freud. Meaning: the patient had the right to maintain and reaffirm his own order as opposed to the order that was being imposed on him. The illness, with its insuperable suffering, here enclosed more rational truth than the presumed cure; it showed that element that is always present and cannot be renounced, which overflowed the official solution, even if the patient did not know this. The patient made evident a lived contradiction. The doctor, by suggesting him, made him renounce this evidence, sacrificing one of its extremes: the unsatisfied desire. Freud had to discover the illness for himself so as to break the normal and official separation between health and sickness, to decentre his own professional 'objectivity' with respect to the system that had produced him as a doctor, by including himself in the object of knowledge and thus discovering a more profound rationality. However, in its passage to collective phenomena, could the bourgeoisie by any chance assume for itself, in its official presumed normality, the truth of the 'sick' mass that it lives off? Here, in the rebellious masses, the forms of social 'illness' are heavier, they are not resolved inside a hospital or a consultation room, and the indices of reality are readable only within an experience that is irreducible to individual culture: the class struggle.

This is why the theoretical superficiality was a scientific insufficiency, but at the same time an ideological limitation: a questioning that did not touch upon the foundation.

> Bernheim, with an unerring eye, based his theory of hypnotic phenomena on the thesis that everyone is in some way 'suggestible'. His suggestibility was nothing other than the tendency to transference, somewhat too narrowly conceived, so that it did not include negative transference. (*Introductory Lectures on Psycho-Analysis*, SE 16: 446)

This means that the theory of suggestion could not comprehend the counter-suggestion; the arrogant imposition of the master could not comprehend the deaf rebellion of the slave. The scientist's own self-affirmation that locked him up in his theory could not comprehend that what was coming from a patient, from the other system denied and diminished by the rationality of science, was the negative transference, the rejection of the imposition. To do so, it would have to doubt the doctor himself; to make itself, for a moment, into the other, and thus to assume the illness in itself.

> But Bernheim was never able to say what suggestion actually was and how it came about. For him it was a fundamental fact on whose origin he could throw no light. He did not know that his '*suggestibilité*' depended

on sexuality, on the activity of the libido. (*Introductory Lectures on Psycho-Analysis*, SE 16: 446)

Freud's criticism thus becomes understandable. The master does not have to explain the origin of the power he exercises over the slave: it is a 'fundamental fact'. But with this he leaves to one side the domain of the interpretation in which the phenomenon of 'suggestion' is produced: starting from the flesh made into human form by way of sexuality, body made culture by the mediation of the others.

It is important to dwell for a moment on the signification of this criticism of suggestion for Freud, since it signals one of the axes on which his conception of the human subject and truth is based. We will therefore quote some of his texts in which this difference appears clearly marked:

> Direct suggestion is suggestion aimed against the manifestation of the symptoms; it is a struggle between your authority and the motives for the illness. In this you do not concern yourself with these motives; you merely request the patient to suppress their manifestation in symptoms. (*Introductory Lectures on Psycho-Analysis*, SE 16: 448)

There are, then, two systems: the doctor's reason and the patient's reason. The doctor does not broaden the field of his rationality so as to include that of the patient, who he feels to be contradictory with his own. For lack of arriving at a new rationality in which his own reason would open itself to contain and comprehend the other's reason, that is, including his first exclusive and repressive reason as complementary to that of the patient, what the doctor does is impose from the outside his own rationality, making it impossible for the other reason to manifest itself. The doctor does not doubt his own reason, except that in this way he has to negate the reason of the sickness and, without understanding it, to repress it.

> ... without being able to learn anything of their sense and meaning. It was hackwork and not a scientific activity, and it recalled magic, incantations and hocus-pocus .... (*Introductory Lectures on Psycho-Analysis*, SE 16: 449)

> Hypnotic therapy seeks to hide something in psychic life, and to gloss it over; analytic therapy seeks to lay it bare and to remove it. The first method works cosmetically, the other surgically. *The first uses suggestion in order to prevent the appearance of the symptoms, it strengthens*

the repressions, but, apart from that, leaves all the processes that have led to the formation of the symptoms unaltered. Analytic treatment makes its impact further back towards the roots, where the conflicts are what gave rise to the symptoms, and uses suggestion in order to alter the outcome of those conflicts. Hypnotic treatment leaves the patient inert and unchanged, and for that reason, too, equally unable to resist any fresh occasion for falling ill. An analytic treatment demands from both doctor and patient the accomplishment of serious work, which is employed in lifting internal resistances. Through the overcoming of these resistances the patient's mental life is permanently changed, is raised to a high level of development and remains protected against fresh possibilities of falling ill. This work of overcoming resistances is the essential function of analytic treatment; *the patient has to accomplish it* and the doctor makes this possible for him with the help of suggestion operating in an *educative* sense. (*Introductory Lectures on Psycho-Analysis*, SE 16: 450–51, emphasis added)

Anyone who has himself carried out psycho-analyses will have been able to convince himself on countless occasions that it is impossible to make suggestions to a patient in that way. The doctor has no difficulty, of course, in making him a supporter of some particular theory and in thus making him share some possible error of his own. In this respect the patient is behaving like anyone else – like a pupil – but this *only affects his intelligence, not his illness*. After all, his conflicts will only be successfully solved and his resistances overcome if the anticipatory ideas he is given tally with what is real in him. Whatever in the doctor's conjectures is inaccurate drops out in the course of the analysis; it has to be withdrawn and replaced by something more correct. (*Introductory Lectures on Psycho-Analysis*, SE 16: 452).

Let us underline the important elements. In direct suggestion there is:
– Affirmation of one's own rationality without including the reason of the other.
– Magic, exorcism, hocus-pocus: ritual to keep the other at a far remove, as the field of irrationality complementary to the official rationality.
– Cover-up of the truth discovered by the other, which negates one's own. Glossing over: cosmetics.
– Suggestion prohibits, based on the – normal – authority, those symptoms that put into relief the contradiction of the system. It reinforces the repressions: it consolidates the illness.

- It maintains the patient in his or her passivity: it does not integrate him or her creatively into the reason of the structure that determines them. It remains subjected to the determinism that consciousness conceals and the body suffers.
- Suggestion operates on the intellect, on consciousness separated from the body by illness itself, but not on the totality of the subject. It operates on the strange field that illness and repression open up as their own: it works on the terrain of the enemy. The enemy is the illness, consciousness is the other in him.

In psychoanalytic work, by contrast, patient and doctor include themselves in the same contradictory system, and they elevate themselves to another structure from which the contradiction that led to the illness appears to be integrated in a rational form and an order that allows its resolution and its transformation. In the patient the order of the contradictory reality is included as a known and controllable order. The patients must transform themselves in their very own individual structure so as to gain access to that reason which the doctor, in his own process, did not reach. There is no communication of conscious knowledge, but rather the inescapable facilitation of an autonomous human place from where the relation with reality is produced through the subject.

3 *The Amplified Conception of Love*

What does Freud oppose to the logic of bourgeois consciousness, to the social bonds made official in institutions and ideas? Where does he go in search of the foundation and essence of human bonds? By having recourse to a key concept of psychoanalysis: *the notion of libido*, that is to say, a concept that allows us to understand reason made body, the flesh made signification of the world.

> Instead of this I shall make an attempt at using the concept of libido for the purpose of throwing light upon group psychology ... *Libido* is an expression taken from the theory of the emotions. We call by that name the energy, regarded as a quantitative magnitude (though not at present actually measurable), of those instincts which have to do with all that may be comprised under the word 'love'. (90)

In this way Freud moves from the concept of suggestion, which reveals the nucleus of a dependency constituted and consolidated by civilisation, and which therefore is a derived function, to the concept of love, which belongs to 'the theory of emotions' or affectivity.

> What would correspond to them is evidently *concealed* behind the shelter, the screen, of suggestion. (91–2, emphasis added)

Freud, then, is going to consider what happens with this affectivity that the mass or group amplifies in the individuals due to the diminution in their intellectual consciousness. But from suggestion he moves to love. How? We are allowed to ask ourselves: once again the same old hackneyed notion of love, the same recourse to sensibility as in all of the Christian West to impose submission and maintain dependency? But Freud tells us: ours is love in a 'wider' sense.

> The nucleus of what we mean by *love* naturally consists (and this is what is commonly called love, and what the poets sing of) in sexual love with sexual union as its aim. But *we do not separate* from this – what in any case has a share in the *name* 'love' – on the one hand, self-love, and on the other, love for parents and children, friendship and love for humanity in general, and also devotion to concrete objects and to abstract ideas. Our justification lies in the fact that psycho-analytic research has taught us that all these tendencies are an expression of the same instinctual impulses; in relations between the sexes these impulses force their way towards sexual union, but in other circumstances they are diverted from this aim or are prevented from reaching it, though always preserving enough of their original nature to keep their *identity* recognizable (as in such features as the longing for proximity, and self-sacrifice). (90–1)

We see clearly how 'love in this "wider" sense' is diametrically opposed to the Christian notion of love. In the face of the dualism of the scission, which separates the spirit from the body just as it separates the affective from the intellectual activity, Freud tells us that 'we do not separate'. Here he vindicates a notion of love that finds in the cultural body the matrix of every relation with reality. This conceptualisation implies, in its 'widening', an extension of one's own body so as to the reach what is remote, an extension of the visible so as to include the invisible, of the sensible so as to prolong itself into the rational. That is to say: the flesh is the very domain of the extension, and to extend the flesh entails *maintaining* it as the element where this extension is elaborated, by affirming it as flesh.

If we order Freud's affirmation, we will obtain the following progression:
↓ 1. sexual love
↓ 2. self-love
↓ 3. parental or filial love

↓ 4. friendship
↓ 5. love of humanity in general
↓ 6. love of concrete objects
↓ 7. love of abstract ideas.

Sexual love: the most intimate relation of entanglement of one body with another. Love of abstract ideas: the relation of one concept to another that needs to be disentangled. But, appearances notwithstanding, a *continuum* links them together: the body-to-body relation is present in the concept-to-concept.

By taking up the extreme end that starts from biological nature (the instincts) Freud extends this so as to include abstract thought (culture). By considering the integration of the human subject into culture or civilisation, he radicalises the problem and presents us with a philosophical interpretation that situates us all at once at the foundation of the human phenomenon. There is thus a transition from one's sensible body to the abstract ideas. There is a process that leads from the individual to the universal, from the separated sensible to the inclusive rational, from the parts to the whole. But this process includes, it does not separate sexual love. Is there anything more paradoxical for Christian spiritualism, for the abstract scientist who considers himself the support system of rationality, than this explosive approximation in which sex is allowed to emerge again, in which the treacherous form of the turgid and erect sexual organ appears as the synthetic index of a body whose contours had been blurred to the point of the pure form of a mathematical equation? Only a culture of scission and separation, only a system of production that subtracts the body from humanity (labour reduced to a commodity) could in its ideology keep separate the scientific rationality and the social order of its prolongation and verification in the shared corporeality. And insofar as the process was not explained by which the flesh becomes the spirit without ceasing to be flesh, without any explanation except that of 'all hitherto existing history', it was capable of consolidating its ideological dominion on the basis of the concealment of its origin. But, as we see, its origin negated by consciousness and knowledge, cannot suppress the body, which on the basis of affectivity expands itself and rises up in rebellion.

This is why the questions that must be asked would be the following:
– How does the body extend itself from its carnal form to encompass the reality of the world and the social institutions in which it participates?
– How do the most abstract significations insert themselves in the sensible corporeality?
– How is there a line of consistency that links feeling with thinking?
– How does the flesh, originally biological, become cultural signification?

- How does the conceptual theory prolong itself on the basis of the order of the sensible body?
- How is the incoherence or coherence of the world reflected in the sexual relationship, in the bodily relation with the other?

These, then, are the problems that Freud renews when in his interrogation of the truth of social structures (artificial groups, spontaneous groups, and revolutionary masses) he has recourse to the concept of love.

4   *The Concept of Libido: The Fluidification of the Body*

Around the concept of libido Freud traces the cultural path of the body: how it organises itself in function of the social system of production. As a biological form, which transforms itself into human form, human beings acquire a capacity that no living organism possesses: the capacity to extend itself to the point where, implied in its own form, there appears the relation with the field of significations covered under the totality of the human world. Or in other words: the process of turning itself into a historical subject. There is thus an extension of the body that is the basis for the extension of consciousness, which is not always – as repression proves – equivalent to it. It is the flesh of a human form that, by becoming significant, by developing itself as systematised, organised, cultural flesh entails the *felt congruence* with the cultural field of humanity and nature. By saying 'human form', what do we mean? We mean the cultural organisation that preserves the incarnation of the biological body as the matrix of every relationship. Here we have an essentially monist conception, which sustains a serious and for many disconcerting affirmation: the prolongation of rational thought, no matter how far it reaches in the realm of abstract ideas, maintains both in its beginning and at its endpoint the form of the cultural carnal body as meaning of all rationality. The form-of-the-body is our unsublimatable insertion in the dialectic of the historical process, but at the same time this cultural body is our truth-content: it opens us onto the possibility of some congruence with the meaning of historical truth. Human beings themselves, we said, are in their carnal structure 'true' or 'false'. We do not say therefore 'truth' as the formal conformity among concepts – I, qua 'theoretical consciousness', who pronounce them and formulate them in the domain of science, and others who – as theoretical consciousness in their own turn – understand, accept, or reject them. We mean 'truth' as congruent links of material and sensible relations, to which all rational signification is referred and in which it finally discovers its meaning. We do not mean therefore that the moment of truth is exhausted in that of a 'rational objective knowledge': there is always a beyond of the body, which the latter designates as its material foundation. As Marx said of the categories of political economy: 'the abstraction ... becomes true in practice': human beings organise their material relations in this rational form, so too with the categories of thought: they makes themselves into true relations in the extent to which they incarnate themselves as relations that unfold within the sensible materiality of the subjects in question. Here a kind of knowledge is posited in which the 'felt', affective equilibrium or disequilibrium is the synthetic expression of rationality, and that which gives it its embodied truth-content. 'Objective world', 'reality', for Marx as well as for Freud, designate the extreme domain to which this cultural body is referred, but which this body reproduces within itself, opens within itself as its own extension: the subjective domain of an embodied dialectic that includes the subject as a necessary moment, both in the constitution of social reality and in its extension and its truth. Thus, for Freud, we might say, in the flesh of each human being the truth of the cultural system is at stake, the truth of the historical order that produced this being as human. And it is in the direction of the discovery of this dialectic, which links the subjective with the objective, that the scientific work required by this human being aims.

If from the domain of material relations scientific knowledge extracts and constructs the formal structure that gives us its true knowledge – the concrete in thought – Freud here refers this first material domain which inaugurates all relations: the body that progressively becomes culturalised and on the basis of which it is possible for there to be history. Therefore he refers to the subjective genesis of the objective world: the possible progress that, from the ideological determination, might lead to reality. Or, as he shows in 'Negation', he tries to find the psychological foundation, based on one's own corporeality, of logical statements. The foundation of an affirmation or negation must be developed from the act of swallowing or spitting out. Therefore, Freud shows us the way in which the flesh gains access and incorporates itself into this historical production and, developing itself, becomes *significant* of this totality of belonging in *its* corporeal materiality itself. Thus sexuality, in its final corporeal synthesis aimed towards the other in whom the whole body, tense and needy to the absolute extreme of another human form that covers it, spasmodically unifies itself and this synthesis, which is felt as agreement or disagreement reached in the organism, shows us the originary location of all possible rational synthesis, the incarnated *a priori* of all rational coherence. This is why, when Freud says that the concept of libido expresses a *quantitative* concept he meant to say: significations for which a tangible and quantifiable matter serves as foundation. Here this means that it is the mobilisation of the body that is ordered through its sensitive or erogenous zones, which communicate the inside with the outside – mouth, penis, vagina, anus, lips, materialities that assimilate and expel each other, mucous substances that in their secretion fluidify the body to the point of enveloping the organ of the other, and therefore the other, in the maximum turgidity and erection that bring the proximity closer, that almost suck it in or adapt it, flesh on flesh, to its own form: the inside of one that, on the outside, prolongs itself in the inside of the other. Thus the body invests the signification of the other – of the cultural other – with its own flesh, and it is the materiality of the body that shapes the meaning of the agreement or the felt congruence: its 'reading' implies the metamorphosis of the flesh into signification.

But this form of the other that thus is incorporated is already a cultural *model*: meaningful organisation of the social relations that cross through it, to which it refers, and which place it at the centre of confluence of the determinations of the system of production. I already see Olga as presence, irradiating toward the world and signifying, with her corporeity, toward the world, toward me. But it is the system that converges toward her and constitutes her as presence for me, just as it constitutes me for her. I sense her, but my sensing is determined by the way in which she inscribes herself in the system in which I myself am inscribed. And yet, it is only her sensible presence, her gesture and her expression that I see and hear: but in me the agreement is thought without concepts, in me the compatibility is elaborated in which later on I participate and which overcomes me or fulfils me. I must read the signification that is elaborated in me like a text that would be alien to me, being as it is the nearest at the same time. The letter does not enter with blood: it comes out with blood. The signification, including rationality, circulates in me: it envelops me and requests me in a felt agreement for which, always, the proof arrives too late, either to disappoint or to ratify. In the body there occurs the genesis of the cultural agreement, the appearance of a symbolic capacity that starting from the anonymous, from the sensible that is proper to the individual form, opens up the vast field of universal relations in which the particular body inscribes the meaning of its acts. But in order to succeed in this, this body must follow a path in culture. This path of the body is the path of libido.

To extend the body? For idealism, which only sees relations in the form of 'thoughts', and whose counterpart is the empiricism that remains imprisoned within the limits of materiality defined by the clear-cut surface of one's own skin, this concept must appear disconcerting. How could the 'absolute' power of thought be based on a corporeality that would also be like thought itself, elastic, extendable, fluidifiable, even 'unctuous' and 'viscous', as Freud says?

We form part of the capitalist system of production in which the human being lives separately from his or her subjective being, conscious and subjected to the imposition of categories of thought that do not imply the consciousness of the extension of one's body in inorganic nature, which is the common body, but which is precisely private property of others or the strict limit of our own.

For us, this conception of Freud has the importance of the radical rupture. It invites us to think *the rational form with the material content; to think the structure with the body*, prolongation of the body in the corporeality of the other and the materiality of the world in which our most profound subjectivity, called abysmal 'depth', is imbricated. It invites us, in other words, to verify the formal truth as stated through the personal experience in the material and significant extension of the flesh. This return to the libido as sensible and significant domain in which the dialectic is at play, once again lays out the problem of a subjectivity which, in order to understand itself as power, must recuperate this capacity of the body that is covered up by ideology and dependency.

Thus Freud's discovery of one's own body as libidinally determined by the other is parallel to the discovery of Marx, of the human being necessarily linked to nature as common body, as the 'objective body of its subjectivity' that was whisked away. In both, the recuperation of the domain of objectivisation and material production is converted into the index for the reading of the rationality that has an 'organic' form, that is, a 'human' form.

IV   The Official Institutions Are Groups Congruent with the System

Church and Army as Models

Ideological thought, by taking its own institutions to be unchangeable, considers the spontaneous collective phenomena as aberrant forms of social relations, which in their nascent spontaneity are referred back to primitive and quasi-natural forms: the herd, the horde, the pack. But Freud will follow the reverse track. He will consider precisely those terminal forms, in which the official culture found stability, also as masses or groups, only now institutionalised, in order on their basis to understand the less organised masses or groups. In other words, he begins with the complex final organisations in order to understand the simple and initial ones. Freud seeks to introduce a genetic and regulating principle in the empirical dispersion of the many groups described in their external ordering by the different authors:

> We may recall from what we know of the morphology of groups that it is possible to distinguish very different kinds of groups and opposing lines in their development. ... But for reasons which remain to be explained we should like to lay particular stress upon a distinction to which writers on the subject have been inclined to give too little attention; I refer to that between leaderless groups and those with leaders. And, *in complete opposition to the usual practice*, we shall not choose a relatively simple

group formation as our point of departure, but shall begin with highly organised, lasting and artificial groups. (93, emphasis added)

Thus, the fundamental point is that Freud will begin his investigation with those 'groups' or 'masses' that traditional psychology does not consider groups: the Church and the army, as 'artificial groups'. That is to say, those stable and institutionalised collective organisations in which the individuals 'normally' find themselves integrated. These groups are collective forms of social organisation that compose a coherent body within the structure of global society. And it is not surprising that Freud would start precisely from these organisations, which are the mainstay of the capitalist social order: the Church, in which resides the most absolutised form of ideology; and the army, in which resides the armed repressive power. Ideological power and armed power: those are the points of departure in the analysis of collective formations.

The question that immediately arises is the following: if every group links human beings libidinally to one another through bonds of love, on the basis of what kind of organisation of the flesh turned human form does the existence of groups such as the Church and the army become possible? What kind of 'love' turns out to link human beings among themselves to form, in the Church, a so-called 'community of love'? What affective bond ties together the subjects who, as soldiers, become unified in the military institution?

It is of crucial importance to retain the distinction that Freud introduces among the groups considered in function of whether or not they are integrated into global society, in agreement or in opposition to it. The psychologists and sociologists who analysed them principally attended to those groups that were opposed to the system: they began from the invariability of the very groups in which they themselves as individuals were integrated.

These groups that are congruent with the system are the artificial groups. Their conservative character is revealed in the way each individual is integrated into them, and through these groups, into the productive system:

> A Church and an army are artificial groups – that is, a certain external force is employed to prevent them from disintegrating and to check alterations in their structure. As a rule a person is not consulted, or is given no choice, as to whether he wants to enter such a group; any attempt at leaving it is usually met with persecution or with severe punishment, or has quite definite conditions attached to it. (93)

The artificial group is a partial totality within a larger totality, which is global society. The 'external force' indicates precisely this character: it is the global system that determines, in its organisation, the compulsion to enter such groups. 'Prevent them from disintegrating' means: the permanence of the global system of production requires the army and the Church as moments that are organically constitutive of its own total unity. But this disaggregation that is preserved at the same time is the disequilibrium that is being repressed. We are part of such groups not by a free decision in which the individuals would enter as a function of an autonomous choice. On the contrary, the very fact of emerging within a cultural formation or civilisation determines us and obliges us to integrate ourselves into such artificial groups. And within these, the individual, who did not choose, also cannot escape or confront them: the severe punishment that accompanies separation shows the obligatory nature of our integration and permanence in the groups, if one were to dare extracting oneself from them. All of us thus with great precision find sketched out before us *the necessary social inscription of each individual in the repressive organisations of the system* for the simple fact of being, prior to becoming the object of analysis in individual or social psychology, the object of the system of production that determined us as *its* individual. What individual psychology does when it discovers that it is 'at the same time and from the start social psychology' is precisely discover also this direct social subjection at the most strictly individual level. Thus the individual of individual psychology, the one whom Freud may find laying down on his couch, for being 'psychoanalysed' within the confines of the solitary consulting room, is no less part of a society that fiercely and compulsively determines him or her as *its* form of being human. The determinations that weigh on these individuals and 'institutionalise' them *for belonging to the 'artificial' groups*, are also present in and determine their subjectivity when, momentarily, they separate themselves from them:

> ... certain facts, which are far more concealed in other cases, can be observed very clearly in those highly organised groups which are protected from dissolution in the manner that has been mentioned. (93)

This is why, extending these artificial groups or masses that Freud takes up only as *models of social organisation*, we cannot avoid encountering in them the fixed result of a process that in other groups shows us the lively and creative labour of a new organisation. Freud in other words is indicating to us a *logical gradation* in the organisation of collective processes, which can be read from two perspectives:

1. Within a determinate cultural formation, that of bourgeois capitalism, he shows us the stabilised, 'artificial' groups that are congruent with the system and, at the opposite end, the masses that, as a result of the disequi-

librium of the system, begin to organise themselves against the system itself, breaking with the constituted models (spontaneous and revolutionary groups or masses).

2. From the perspective of historical development he shows us the genesis of the artificial groups, which currently appear frozen or fixed, as the product of a previous process, of collective organisations that before were spontaneous and revolutionary and that have developed themselves during the evolution of various productive systems.

It is strange, and at the same time not strange, that many psychologists would reproduce the scission that Freud is going to reveal to us: to conceal that the psychological individual inscribes his or her conduct in reality *also*, and at the same time, as social individual. And that the patient in analysis is necessarily, *at the same time*, part of an organisation that prolongs outwards the same dispute of his or her individual truth in the social organisations – the different 'artificial' groups – to which he or she belongs. And that each social organisation therefore has its truth content: it inscribes itself within the historical process by allowing or inhibiting its development. But to achieve this, it is obvious that the psychoanalyst himself should begin at least by inscribing his consulting room and his activity in this peculiar type of artificial group, the psychoanalytical institution to which he belongs and whose congruence with the institutions of repressive power – given that it is inscribed within the field opened up and enabled by the social division of labour under capitalism – defines it too as an artificial group: coercive, rigid, rigorous, repressive, limiting. And that, moreover, the psychoanalysts also find themselves affiliated with other artificial groups that delimit and define their social insertion.

In the previous chapter we already saw how Freud has recourse to his 'widened' conception of love. In *Civilisation and its Discontents* he will specify even more what this 'widening' entails with reference to the social field, when he says:

> ... civilisation is a process in the service of Eros, whose purpose is to combine single human individuals, and after that families, then races, peoples and nations, into one great unity, the unity of mankind. (*Civilisation and Its Discontents*, SE 21: 122).

This diachronic aspect, which shows us the historical development of universality, adds to the determination of the current sense of social organisation: how collective activity halts or promotes this. But at the same time it shows us the access to history starting from personal history: individuals from within their corporeality open up links and capacities that gradually inscribe them in ever broader fields. With this Freud means that love, Eros, necessarily prolongs itself in political activity: in the preoccupation with integrating nations in the field of humankind, and this starting from the family. The 'political' meaning, in the sense of an inscription in collective processes that break with the models that fix the individual element in its place, necessarily will determine the true, 'healthy' conduct of the psychological individual, if we take seriously the 'widened' conception of love, and with this take seriously Freud himself. For this is one of the most important conclusions of his conception of the libido.

1   The Appearance of Integration

Let us observe, then, how these inferences derive from Freud's analysis of the 'artificial' groups whose models are the Church and the army. In these two models of conservative groups Freud is going to analyse the *appearance* and *simulation* of this integration of the individual into the field of development of the universality of Eros. This apparent amplification of the individual field, from the point of view of the bourgeois institutions, is in reality a containment. The individual remains stuck and fixated in a social structure of repetition that simulates affective bonds denied in the reality of the system. We should always keep in mind that the groups or masses are subordinated models of organisation, whose final meaning can be read in the global system of production.

But Freud does not begin his analysis as a sociologist; he starts from the individual and the latter's lived relation, in the 'artificial' group, with respect to the others. Freud will disentangle the phenomenon of the group as a psychoanalyst, looking to relocate the determinations of the social system in the individual, and based on the social illusion in which the later lives in it.

> In a Church (and we may with advantage take the Catholic Church as a type) as well as in an army, however different the two may be in other respects, the same illusion holds good of there being a head – in the Catholic Church Christ, in an army its Commander-in-Chief – who loves all the individuals in the group with an equal love. Everything depends upon this illusion; if it were to be dropped, then both Church and army would dissolve, so far as the external force permitted them to. (93–94)

We already observe in what consists the *illusion* in the Church: a collective organisation in which the individuals are not integrated in a real universality, but in an invisible personal symbol – Christ – who pretends to be universal, and toward whom all converge.

> He stands to the individual members of the group of believers in the relation of a kind elder brother; he is their substitute father. All the demands that are made upon the individual are derived from this love *of* Christ's. A democratic strain runs through the Church, for the very reason that before Christ everyone is equal, and that everyone has an equal share in his love. ... There is no doubt that the tie which unites each individual with Christ is also the cause of the tie which unites them with one another. (94, emphasis added)

This supposed extension of love, which presents itself as universal, is in reality a restriction. I, insofar as I am part of the community of love, do not love the other human beings for what they are, but because they are *of* the Christ. Christ is, in his love for me, the cause of my love for them. It is not the 'widened' love that from my precise corporeality discerns the precise sense of the other; it is not an affect that becomes amplified by opening one's own limits from within the difference that is being elaborated, but rather by leaping over the difference. I thus begin to participate in an affective totality, which abandoned the precise indices of the world and of the reality to which I belong as member of a system of production. Therefore, it is not even the same love that unites me with each one of them, because in themselves, in their individuality, they remain indiscriminate subjects. They are not the organic support of personal qualities that make them lovable for me. I love only Christ, and for the love that I suppose in him for everyone, hence also for me, I love them (in a manner of speaking): if I did not love them, Christ would not be able to love me, for I would cease to belong to the set of human beings defined in their infinite salvation by the fact of belonging to Christ. To love the other is not an effective affect: it is the passcode that defines me as being part of the ensemble of Christ's subjects. This coercive, external bond appears as if it were an internal determination, and the most profound one to boot. Christ as model of being introduces in me, in the midst of a capacity for affective and rational discernment, its inversion and negation: the need for indiscriminateness, which thus comes to be replaced with another unique index: the belonging to the Church as community of love. It is not, then, the signification read off from the sensible, as incarnated form of the other, or of the others, which leads me to unite myself to them: this 'something' which here unites me is the love-bond with the figure of Christ-the-father, on whom the genuine libidinal bond is projected from which all other bonds derive.

What can be obtained with this model of love? If Christ loves everyone with *equal* love, the affective prototype that regulates me does not imply the discernment of the other as loved one, but only as an abstract equality: he loves us in spite of difference, against difference. And he is, moreover, the only one who could read this difference. But precisely my incarnated difference in the face of the other is the foundation of my unfulfilled desire: this desire, which surges forth from the flesh, is sin which He knows how to read not from outside but from within myself. The 'democratic strain' that runs through the Church is the equality in the love He has for us, but it is an equality within a concealment: everyone hides their true being from the other. This is why, as substitution of the individual father prolonged in the collective father, the role played by Christ, as father of fathers, is the institutionalised consolidation of the superego as absolute and transcendent regulator of my individuality. Christ thus appears, outwardly, as ratifying the persistence of an infantile family relation of dependency in the order of broader social relations. But at the same time he validates, as an illusory absolute elevated to divinity, the illusion of infinity with which the child, absolutely dependent, idealised its paternal image. Thus the Christ, model of a repressive and artificial institution, serves so as not to develop the difference, within oneself, of the form of the other who determined our own: subjectively we are nothing but compliance with this other prolonged from the superego, via the father, toward the form of Christ. But at the same time we are submission of our flesh to the form of life, to the model of the phantasmatic other, who haunts us and inhibits in us all difference and all relation to the social reality that negates it. Religion enlivens death, but not the real death that the system gives us in life: it enlivens the 'anguish of death', without a face, so as to subject us to its archaic system of an equally imaginary salvation. This profound submission that religion, for the terror of death, demands from us is only terror before the superego: not before the real death that we receive in life, but before the death that appears as anxiety when we negate the other – the father enlarged and turned into the rational form of the superego – as foundation of our emergence into reality. Christ offers consolation for death, he loves us in spite of our defective being, just as our father loved us. But this consolation is possible only in the very same act in which the temptation appears to break the rule: to develop the opposition, the difference toward the outside, the discernment that habilitates my cultural body for a life of its own.

What is obtained with this libidinal relation from the point of view of the conservative social organisation? The dissolution in the human being of the real social determination so as to privilege the phantasmatic, subjective, archaic determination; the concealment of one's relation with the others as a function of the strict signification that each human being assumes in the system of production; the erasure of oneself as historical index, in accordance with the meaning that one's conduct acquires against the backdrop of the rationality of the system. Here is a community in which human beings find themselves linked, they believe, in their most intimate form of entanglement with the others, but with a feeling that corresponds to an infantile stage of their life, where one's own libidinal body had not yet been constituted as unitary form: where what reigned, as dependent flesh, as seminal resemblance, was the identification with the father. The body had not yet made the transition to the genital form; the child had not extended this corporeality so as to imbricate it in a unified way in the reality of precise historical time and space opened up from within its flesh, where the powers of the body would discover its own by extending itself so as to include in it the powers of the world. No: here the equality of love is only the return to an affect that requires us to replace the adult corporeality with the regressive form of an infantile body; the feeling of instantaneous and magical unity, which in the adult stage reduplicates this primal identity of a confused and dependent affect. Thus this community of the spirit, thanks to 'love', provides the model of an ideal collectivity, which presents itself as the model for every real community. Every subsequent insertion of the subject within the multiple levels of social reality will only prolong this other, inverted kind as its foundation.

The results are obvious:
– There is repression of the adult power of the body as social body, which prolongs itself and discovers its material power as collective power.
– Concomitantly, a real social organisation is supplanted by an imaginary totality – the kingdom of Christ – which appears as the foundation of the real collectivity to which we remain subjugated.
– The family form, as elementary institution, remains as the model – the Church, the Holy Family – of the global social form and in this way inhibits the comprehension of its true structure.
– I tie myself to the other subjects of the system for what we have in common: because we live the same subjection. The differences that separate us are erased: the real discernment opens out onto the terror of death. The others, my equals, are the only objective guarantors of my individual persistence: my exact accomplices because they are, exactly, under an *identical* terror. There is no discernment of the other as a function of the real differences: those of the class struggle.
– Thus is sealed the separation between rationality and affectivity. Faith renders up reason before the absolute reason of the other, as dictated by the doctors of the Church, dissolving in a sentiment of abstract love the precise rational signification of each affect that emerges as carnal index of a relation with the material world.

And this residue of individuality, which the bourgeoisie recognises as the 'true' individual, was the one that the 'men of science' opposed to the subject of the revolutionary masses, because in its poor personal and dependent being it confirmed the submission to the system.

Freud, starting from the 'amplified' conception of love, arrives at this false 'amplification' and reveals it as an *illusion*: the illusion of an equal love for all the members of the collectivity. This conception is the exact complement of a social form of organisation in which labour qua personal activity finds itself strictly determined as 'abstract general labour', and in which the precise form of the worker disappears so as to appear only in its generality, in its merely quantitative expression as exchange value. The disappearance of the cultural body as index of the qualitative difference of human beings among themselves, and of their developed particularity, corresponds to a form of productive organisation in which the particularisation of the worker is also annulled in its mere presence as 'labour power', in its quasi-biological nature. To the predominance of a 'purely' spiritual signification, of an abstract form of being human (whose precise content, made up of the system of production, is concealed), there corresponds an indiscriminateness of the qualitative corporeality of the human being, in which the body is reduced to quantitative labour power. Not without reason Freud complements this analysis of dependency, which is due to the abstract kind of love in the Church, with the analysis of the direct subjection of the body by material force in the bourgeois army. And I say bourgeois army because, in his own terms, it is one in which the subjects who are part of it do not integrate the rational *knowledge* of the force and violence that this warring community generates, as happens by contrast in any revolutionary army. The bourgeois army conceals the rationality that shows it to be the repressive force of the system of production. This is why, in his analysis, Freud does not think that these ideas determine the 'something' that ties human beings together in this group: this common 'something' is here, too, an illusion:

> An objection will justly be raised against this conception of the libidinal structure of an army on the ground that no place has been found in it for such ideas as those of one's country, of national glory, etc., which are of such importance in holding an army together. The answer is that ... such ideas are not indispensable to the existence of an army. We shall presently touch upon the possibility of a leading idea being substituted for a leader and upon the relations between the two. (94–95)

What happens is that in the bourgeois army the ideas of 'country' and 'national glory' are abstractions, which do not prolong the rationality of the individual into the rationality of the institution. There 'one's country' is the soil owned as private property by a few, and 'national glory' freezes values that are merely those of the dominant owner class. The army, as the exercise of power that one privilege class exerts over the majority of the population, cannot show the true rationality that rules over it: that of being the army of one class and, therefore, of having to use those same dominated men to exercise the power that keeps subjugating them. Even though the repressive power may have recourse to 'abstract ideas' such as national glory or country, these are for Freud inoperative as leading ideas due to their very emptiness, their unverifiable ideality. They are the ideal justification adequate to the lived reality of dependency, the only one that is certain.

This is why Freud rejects such ideas in the real analysis of the 'something in common' that ties human beings with one another in the army. And he will show us, once again, that what reunites them in their adhesion is the same scheme of regressive individuality that demands from the soldier an adhesion analogous to that which Christ requests, via the priest, of the faithful:

> The like [as of the Church] holds good of an army. The Commander-in-Chief is a father who loves all soldiers equally, and for that reason they are comrades among themselves. The army differs structurally from the Church in being built up of a series of such groups. Every captain is, as it were, the Commander-in-Chief and the father of his company, and so is every non-commissioned officer of his section. (94)

This difference is 'economic', in the sense of being materially quantifiable and legible. Whereas in the Church the dependency is internal, pertaining to 'knowledge' ('more knowledge and care about individuals may be attributed to Christ than to a human Commander-in-Chief'), to this dependency in the army is added the external one: the material dominion and effective utilisation of the individual force integrated into the common force. What unites and ties together, therefore, in both social institutions, is not the real signification that the institution acquires for the fact of working in the service of the maintaining of the global system, in which everyone fulfils a precise function. The individuals are no longer capable of discernment: neither in their body nor in their consciousness. In other words, it is not the explicit rationality, the ideology of these institutions, that might reveal to us the truth of the relation: neither the Church, with the abstract community in which faith exhausted reason; nor in the army, in which the direct subjection defeated the body. What in both institutions *unites* human beings with one another and with the leader is the 'libidinous structure', that is, a specific form of sensible, corporeal bond. And we have to ask ourselves, with Freud, in what consists this bond of union. To the indiscriminate totality of the world, the concealment of the rationality of the system in which human beings find themselves included, there corresponds, as we will see, an individuality in which one's own flesh, one's own body, appears itself as the site of a false dispute, of a false organisation, and – as a consequence – the impossibility of prolonging oneself toward reality. It is a body besieged by the historical system of production.

2 Individual Dependency, Foundation of the Collective Bond

> It is to be noticed that in these two artificial groups each individual is bound by libidinal ties on the one hand to the leader (Christ, the Commander-in-Chief) and on the other hand to the other members of the group. ... But we shall venture even now upon a mild reproach against earlier writers for not having sufficiently appreciated the importance of the leader in the psychology of the group, while our own choice of this as a first subject for investigation has brought us into a more favourable position. It would appear as though we were on the right road towards an explanation of the principal phenomenon of group psychology – the individual's lack of freedom in a group. If each individual is bound in two directions by such an intense emotional tie, we shall find no difficulty in attributing to that circumstance the alteration and limitation which have been observed in his personality. (95)

The individual, in other words, is 'bound in two directions by such an intense emotional tie' to two different centres: in the first place, to the person of the leader, individual to individual (individual psychology); in the second, tied collectively to the other as 'equal', but not personalised (collective psychology). This dissociation which shows the double and antagonistic belonging, first of master to slave (individual psychology) and then of slave to slave (collective psychology), is the foundation of the separation that bourgeois science encounters and analyses as essential to every human bond: the separation of the individual and the collective. What social psychology left to one side and what Freud introduces in the collective is the relation with the leader, the relation of individual dependency that psychologically shapes the other relations with human beings in the collective element. The sequence he establishes is illuminating: first, 'on the one hand to the leader' and, second, 'on the other hand to the other members of the group' (95). Thus the collective, which is the foundation of individuality, appears in inverted form: in reality *the individual determines the collective*. The organisation of the collective form, whose foundation lies in the system of production, is lost as determining index in the depths of the relations of personal dependency where the person of the leader – Christ or Commander-in-Chief – emerges as the whole of the one. Not as the symbol of the whole, but as if it were the whole itself. We see, then, that social psychology analysed an appearance and reached an illusion: that which ideology imposes on it as its order, but not its true structure. It is this concealment of the true structure that the bourgeois psychic organisation produces in each human being as adequate to the contradictory system, which limits one's personality and inhibits one's liberty. The relation between the individual and the collective, in the empirical integration, is still regulated by the relations of individual dependency.

Let us look at this in greater detail.

a. With respect to the leader: the libidinal bond that ties me to the leader signals the containment of my libido that covers it as an object homogeneous with the superego. The leader thus appears as the redoubling of the repression of my libido which, by covering this other as model of the social relation, only keeps me in narcissism. And narcissism is, under the semblance of a real object tie to the leader, the maintenance of the form of that originary other – the father – who is present in me as impediment of all development and all difference. Through the leader I do nothing else but take myself as object, for the leader is only a new incarnation, now from the outside, of that other which, within, has my body at its disposal as being already shaped from its very beginning by the form of the other.

b. With respect to ideology: the rationality of the 'community of love' or 'one's country' or 'the nation' is nothing but a legitimating appearance, congruent with the ideology of the system of production, which inhibits the emergence into consciousness of the truth of the social organisation that requires me as its subjugated self.

c. With respect to the others: the others are my fellow human beings, but similar to me in the abstract. Since all discerned relations were erased, due to the rule of my libido contained within the limits of narcissism, the other does not appear as a real other, understood and felt in his or her qualitative presence as a different other. The other is but the mirror image of my own being, which reduplicates and verifies in its submission the well-founded character of my submission. It is the dominated themselves who verify, outwards, the illusion of the one through the illusion of the other, and all of them within one and the same field of belief and submission. The illusory verification does not open out onto the meaning of the world, nor do we elaborate in reality, taking it as an index, the common disequilibrium in the presence of the others as equally subjugated. In the common submission there opens up the illusion of a common integration.

As we see, the disintegration of the individuals in the social structure is produced within *a semblance of true integration*. What does exist is the integration, unknown and subjected to the contradictory system, which circulates in the bodies and social relations, using them for its benefit and in its service. The leader is not the *significant index* of a reality that produced him as leader; the others are not for me those in whom we might read the meaning of the system that produced us as subjugated. The rationality of the ideas offered to me to think my insertion into the whole appear as opening out onto an abstract totality – formal equality as citizens of one's country, equality of love as believers in the Church. And all this under the dominion of terror and the anxiety of death, which appears in every personal attempt to separate oneself from them. But not as an objective terror before the precise obstacle; here the infantile terror before the super-ego, the anxiety before death, which is the anxiety before the development of difference, comes to inhibit *from within ourselves* any glimmer of independence and freedom.

What Freud puts into relief is the following: the subjective organisation, the libidinal development of the child through which civilisation becomes incorporated in the subject, determines its subsequent adaptation to the institutions. The latter find in this first infantile organisation the congruent form in which global society ratifies, in adaptation, the production of the family. This adaptation is not a chance occurrence; it will show us how the broader determinations of the system enter and organise everything that is produced in its sphere as compliant with it. In the case at hand, it shows us the family as producing human beings that are psychically adapted to the social forms in which, as adults, they prolong the infantile life that thus prepared them.

This family tie, Freud shows us, did not really open up the body towards the community: it inscribed in the body the social form as organisation of its individuality. Its individuality, in spite of the collective participation, continues to remain restricted to the limits of one's own body, without including the others, despite the appearance of being with them. In this way he shows us the lack of true integration in the social fact of integration itself. This means that in these forms of social organisation there is no creation for the individual; there is no effective domain in which individuality might develop its difference in the exchange with the others.

3   *The Dissolution and Verification of Dependency*

That this social integration is only illusion, that the field of reality is neither opened nor widened, is shown in the phenomenon of the dissolution of the artificial groups. Indeed, in the moment of crisis, in the distension of the bonds maintained by the submission to the model, that which truly unites them is laid bare and the illusion vanishes so as to give way to the crude emergence of the true disunity. The process of dissolution analysed by Freud is the panic that comes over the artificial groups or masses: the sudden de-totalisation of a totality. What is produced in this situation, once the tie to the leader is broken, is the crumbling of each individual with respect to the whole:

> A panic arises if a group of that kind becomes disintegrated. Its characteristics are that none of the orders given by superiors are any longer listened to, and that each individual is only solicitous on his own account, and without any consideration for the rest. The mutual ties have ceased to exist, and a gigantic and senseless fear is set free. (96)

If the collective participation appears as an increment in the individual power over reality, and this thanks to the development of the relations of reciprocity, precisely the phenomenon of panic lays bare its new appearance: the artificial group, in this case the army, was not an effective amplification of this power, but on the contrary a semblance of community. When the Commander-in-Chief is not present to regulate this relation that each one is incapable of discerning, panic breaks out:

> ... it is of the very essence of panic that it bears no relation to the danger that threatens, and often breaks out on the most trivial occasions. If an individual in panic fear begins to be solicitous only on his own account, he bears witness in so doing to the fact that the emotional ties, which have hitherto made the danger seem small to him, have ceased to exist. Now that he is by himself in facing the danger, he may surely think it greater. (96)

When they were together they did not see the danger (it 'made the danger seem small', Freud says). The usual explanation accounts for this dissolution and panic in terms of fear. But Freud inverts this line of questioning:

> The very question that needs explanation is why the fear has become so gigantic. ... it is of the very essence of panic that it bears no relation to the danger that threatens, and often breaks out on the most trivial occasions. (96)

Thus, in the moment of dissolution the meaning of the artificial collective organisation becomes evident: the fact of having been part of an enemy whole, from the point of view of integration into reality, and of having been part of an illusory whole, from the point of view of reciprocity. There is no effective domain of common reality that might be present in each; the collective experience was not a real opening in the midst of separated individuality. The dissolution returns them to the defenceless situation of invalid individuals, with their individual terrors, precisely the situation that found refuge in the artificial group, but was not modified by it.

> ... the mutual ties between the members of the group disappear, as a rule, at the same time as the tie with their leader. The group vanishes in dust, like a Prince Rupert's drop when its tail is broken off. (97)

Freud shows the analogy between this social process and neurosis. Neurosis is an individual solution in the face of a reality that is not assumed; the neurotic solution creates a domain of subjectivity in which symbolically the conflict that objective reality presents is resolved. Neurotic individuals subjectively provide themselves with an imaginary totality and at the same time situate themselves as part thereof: whole and part. Thus too in the artificial group, compliant with a social system whose disequilibrium is halted in it: the individual is provided with *a collective totality which, in its very reality, is imaginary*, in which the 'illusion' of being in effect part of a real whole also continues to base itself necessarily on the indiscriminateness of the material historical reality. The effective relations of production that produce individual life do not become part of the collective organisation; they are not integrated as content in the individual's 'psychic apparatus'. The effective participation in the social division of labour, its necessary tie to the system of production, remains hidden in this semblance of integration with which the institutions of domination once again unite, in their own way, what on another level they produce as dissolution. Indeed, the effective dialectic of this participation would have entailed gaining access to a historical world that would undo the infantile submission to an absolute and transcendent power so as to reencounter the effective reality of the repressive power. And this external sense would determine the union of the individuals of the group or mass with one another, because the reality of the objective danger is the irrefutable index of our true insertion into history. But this real obstacle is covered up in the artificial group, and its own power is used to maintain it.

> If we take the word 'panic' in the sense of collective fear, we can establish a far-reaching analogy. Fear in an individual is provoked either by the greatness of a danger or by the cessation of emotional ties (libidinal cathexes); the latter is the case of neurotic fear or anxiety. In just the same way panic arises either owing to an increase of the common danger or owing to the

disappearance of the emotional ties which hold the group together; and the latter case is analogous to that of neurotic anxiety. (97)

In the confrontation with the obstacle, then, two possibilities present themselves: one is that the fear arises before the real magnitude of the danger, which is the normal situation; the other that it is the resurgence of an ancient terror, and therefore that it is not in relation to the actual objective reality. This last scenario is what happens in neurosis and in the artificial group when the unity with the leader breaks apart. In both cases it is the repressed subjective organisation that, all of a sudden impotent, is undone: it had not internalised the real structure of the objective world that would permit, both in the neurotic person and in the group, an adequate response in the face of reality. Since there is a lack of adequacy between the subjective and the objective, the truth of the system cannot be assumed. And the return to an individual subjectivity, which neither transformed itself nor acquired the collective power adequate to the obstacle, as we see in the dissolution of the agreement, leaves one defenseless in the face of reality when the anxiety before death arises. The collective organisation in neurosis or in the group was on the order of an illusory union: it was not determined by the reality of the world that it had to confront. In the dissolution, therefore, the falsity of the agreement is verified as dispersal and illness: as return to an archaic form of organisation from which, as we now see, one had never escaped.

We thus see what significance the libido holds for Freud: it signals the extension of one's body, as cultural form conveyed by the flesh, into the world considered as our inorganic body. The neurotic anxiety was anxiety before the id: before the instinctual drives that had to be considered as something external to the ego. The neurotic cannot find out that his or her own id, his or her own flesh that is contained within the limits imposed from the outside, is part of an id that is also collective: the one that was discovered in common, in the spontaneous group, with the other human beings who were also subjugated to the same power in their corporeality that before was lived only as individual and at the same time as alien. How can I struggle, with the weak force of the impulses of my individual body, against the power of the system that all reality ratifies? The form of the human, reduced to the limits of one's individuality, does not widen itself to include the form of the social system. It remains only in the form of this other unique being, the father, as imaginary totality that does not include the conditions of social reality that produced it as transcendent and omnipotent other. In the adult stage, by contrast, there would exist the possibility of recognising the historical and objective sense of this dependency, in the discovery of one's own body extended, via the libido, all the way to include the material power of the others in the collective fraternal alliance. But this is what is impeded by the artificial social institutions to which we are introduced. In the capitalist system of production this extension of one's body, this common and cultural materiality, is covered up by the very form of the system. Because the common body, the inorganic nature into which we should prolong ourselves, is the private property of those who require our submission to continue having the usufruct of it as their own. The social forms, as we have seen, prolong and ratify the infantile dependency in the helplessness of the adult. There is no common force that might discover the signification of this system in the common danger, because in this pseudo-community the individual is prolonged in a double dependency, already analysed above: dependency on a totality of fellow beings who are similarly subjected, who do not organise their bond with the discovery of the repression that weighs on them; and on the form of the other – Christ or Commander-in-Chief – to whom each one individually continues to be tied, converted in an imaginary totality that prolongs the individual form of one's body in the image of the other exaggerated to the point of inclusion.

And in the same way that in the army, where the dissolution of the link produces the anxiety that leads to panic, there is a return to the individual and therefore ineffective weakness to confront the danger, so too when the dissolution of the religious group occurs the return is to the individuality from before its integration into the 'community of love'. From the army, the individuals return to their mere corporeality without collectivity, just as from the Church they return to their mere individuality without love.

> The phenomenon which accompanies the dissolution that is here supposed to overtake a religious group is not fear, for which the occasion is wanting. Instead of it ruthless and hostile impulses towards other people make their appearance, which, owing to the equal love of Christ, they had previously been unable to do. (98)

It was not the external reality that dispersed them ('the magnitude of the danger'); it was the false internal connection of the members with one another ('the dissolution of the emotional ties'). It is the illusion of a union in the artificial group that cannot confront the reality of the obstacle. Thus, too, in the Church: there occurs a return to the individual, the selfish and hostile form that the community of love in Christ was meant to conceal. The hostile and egoistic individual is present, without transformation, in the individual of the community of love. His or her overcoming was only an illusion, that of suddenly having reached, in love, by identification with Christ, the possibility of being *like* the model. But the model, as we saw, concealed the real likeness – the dependency – so as to give rise to the illusory likeness: the archaic undeveloped individuality persisted, though hidden.

> Therefore a religion, even if it calls itself the religion of love, must be hard and unloving to those who do not belong to it. (98)

v   The Discernment Repressed

1   *The Logic of Collective Bonds*

The contradiction of the artificial group – army and Church, taken as models – is expressed in the fact that, as we have seen, there are

> … emotional ties of two kinds. One of these, the tie with the leader, seems (at all events for these cases) to be more of a ruling factor than the other, which holds between the members of the group. (100)

This is its contradiction. In the midst of the collective an individual relation continues to predominate: the one that each and every one maintains with the leader. But we also had already seen that this privilege of the individual-leader relation is not generalisable for all members: the status of this privileged individuality puts it, within the collective, outside the collective. And we showed wherein resided the contradiction: in the fact that the interests of the whole had to be sacrificed in the name of the part. If there is contradiction, it is because, though invisible, there is a logic that regulates the process, and because this process *cannot be stopped* at any moment of its apparent equilibrium. The artificial group thus appears, in spite of its claim to durability and permanence, as a moment in the historical development whose endpoint is the revolution. The contradiction that becomes transparent in this double affective link is but the reproduction, at the level of the members of the artificial group, of a contradiction that the material domain of collective production necessarily contains as the place of evidence. Here the whole – the system – is replaced by the part: by the army general, or the priest, or Christ. And this is why the contradiction explodes both at the affective level and at the rational level. In the members of the artificial group the social structure, the true structure of the whole, is not present in individual consciousness. But this rational restriction is also a corporal restriction: the flesh of the subject cannot prolong itself coherently towards the others. The consequences for the development of the individual are clear: in the domain that reunites them collectively as similar fellow beings they cannot develop their individual qualitative differences. And this is because the development of differences implies the opening of a real domain of universality and personal exchange – which is, by definition, repressed in the artificial group.

There where reason should give us back the rational and conceptual signification of the system, an infantile form occupies its place that makes us once again feel the other as if he or she were all. Instead of broadening and prolonging the body towards the others and including in it the knowledge of this amplification, an archaic sentiment comes to occupy its place. It is this infantile affective form, which animates and gives meaning to the adult body, that comes to inhibit the development of the capacity to extend oneself towards the others. The thinking that complements it, and which the system offers, agrees in its absolute character with this absolute primordial sentiment.

The logic of history circulates in the truth of these bonds. Humankind has had to try to disentangle them, with great difficulty. This is why Freud is going to propose the existence of *a logical gradation in the development of the collective bonds that human beings develop in historical struggles*. The dialectic of collective psychology in Freud implicitly reencounters, as its motor, the confrontation of human subjects with the process that produces the material relations and, therefore, as class struggle.

This problem, taken up from the extreme end of individual psychology that is at the same time collective psychology, will give us the structure of the subject that this new perspective inaugurates: how to give oneself a true totality of human beings in which to inscribe the individual conduct? How does that adult social totality, which in its infantile origin presented the sensible father as *everything* for the child, acquire its rational signification? And all this without losing its centre in the sensible element from which it came, but now broadening itself out so as to include in it the system of production? The problem, viewed from the perspective of psychoanalysis, is thus that of the presence of the totality – the system – in the sensibility of the subject. But this implies, as we already saw in the notion of libido, a process of amplification in the midst of subjectivity, which Freud described as his 'concept of love in the "wider" sense'. And his monistic position consists in affirming that to the rational amplification of conscious subjectivity – the passage to thought which sends us back to the totality as known totality – there corresponds necessarily a parallel amplification of the individual body in its material relations with the world, with the system of production, as a relation lived from within the sexuated body. The extension of the thinking head, if it wishes to reach the truth, implies at the same time and necessarily the extension of the qualitative and sentient body. The problem, in other words, is as follows: *the presence, necessarily symbolic and conceptual, of the whole requires in its rational comprehension at the same time, and as an unavoidable condition, the sensible prolongation of the body, whose affective capacity would accompany and verify the rational extension.* This means to habilitate the flesh as the domain of the historical dialectic, in which to think means to think in the materiality of the body that is linked and determined by the materiality of the system of production.

This access of sexuated corporeality to signification, of the sensible to the rational, of perception to the concept, is what is at stake in the historical struggle of the masses. This is why the historical production of categories of thought, which traditional psychology ascribes only to consciousness, is the result of the collective historical action that by creating new material links among human beings is the foundation of those categories.

Wherein consists this *logical gradation* of collective organisations? Freud describes various morphological possibilities in the groups or masses:

> We should have to give our attention to the different kinds of groups, more or less stable, that arise spontaneously, and to study the conditions of their origin and of their dissolution. We should above all be concerned with the distinction between groups which have a leader and leaderless groups. We should consider whether groups with leaders may not be the more primitive and complete, whether in the others an idea, an abstraction, may not take the place of the leader (a state of things to which religious groups, with their invisible head, form a transitional stage), and whether a common tendency, a wish in which a number of people can have a share, may not in the same way serve as a substitute. (100)

Starting from the first relation of the child with the form of its first likeness, the father, we could establish the following gradation, which we will verify later on:

Amplified concept of love
Logical gradation of the integration of the individual into the collective processes

Real collective forms	'I'	Forms of symbolisation of the collective structure
Family (father, mother, siblings): institutionalised	'I' ↓	Parental couple
		Oedipus complex *Super-ego* (Disappearance of the

		real presence of the father in the rationality of the law).
Artificial group: Army (Institutionalised)	'I' ↓	*Commander-in-Chief*: Visible head (Empirical part as if it were the whole) Absolutised finitude.
Artificial group: Church (Institutionalised)	'I' ↓	*Christ*: Invisible head. (Celestial whole). Mediator between the finite and the infinite: Mediatised infinitude.
Group in search of an immediate benefit (Contractual relations. Exchange of private producers).	'I' ↓	*Idea or abstraction*: (Without shared libido). Finitude without others and predominance of things. Merely empirical presence of the others.
Spontaneous group: (Breakdown of the institutionalised relations).	'I' ↓	*Omnipotent leader:* (Substitutes with empirical presence for the ideal of the group). Predominance of things. Merely empirical presence of the others.
Revolutionary group: (Transforms the system of production and the artificial institutions).	'I' ↓	*'Tendency or desire shared by a large number of persons'*: Collective integration of the libido and true rationality. Revolutionary leader.

2   *Increasing Process of Substitution*

We see that the integrated and amplified solution that Freud sketches out necessarily brings with it – as its final, congruent, and true form – the creation of a human subjective domain that fulfils the following basic conditions of objectivity:

1. The individual, *as sexuated and sensible body*, participates in the totality of the material field from his or her desire shared and recognised by the others.
2. The individual, *as thinking consciousness*, reaches the known rationality of the system of production that determines him or her.

The historical process appears for Freud, as much as for Marx, as an amplification of the domain of universality that is not possible unless both extensions – sensible and rational – are being produced at the same time. The amplification of the relations of production, as development of the productive forces that define the movement of history, means at the same time the amplification of the categories of thought that integrate into consciousness the development of the relations produced in the material exchange.

And if Freud begins with the artificial groups – Church and army – he does so in order to put into relief a contradictory moment of this development: where to the attempt to steal away, for the benefit of one class of human beings over others, the wealth that is a product of collective labour and of the slow control of nature, there is added as a condition of this exploitation the concealment in consciousness of these material relations. Therefore, the separation between consciousness and body, which both individual psychology and social or collective psychology maintain in their character of conventional sciences, merely expresses the existence of a repressive phenomenon, the production of a type of human being adequate to the material and theoretical dominion exercised over them.

This is why the logical gradation sketched out by Freud is the outline of a dialectic in which, via the revolutionary group or mass, this integration necessarily is in the process of being produced.

In the army and the Church we saw wherein consisted the cunning logic to interrupt the dialectic of access to 'widened love'. In the artificial group, the meaning of history once again comes undone: the development of subjective desire, when it believes it extends itself towards its objective source, returns to the most subjective element. The adult desire, which is based on and prolongs itself from the father-form (sensible without consciousness), does not reach the signification that from this primal whole leads to the comprehension of its adult insertion into the totality of the system of production. Individual sexuality remains suspended: it does not prolong itself as libido into the collective so as to reach from the father-form to the system-form of production.

The leader of the army, who acts as synthesiser, turns the signifying power that the group provides for or requests from him into a personal power. He turns into a personal reality what was only the capacity for meaning present in him as the place towards which the collective relations, which are the truly creative ones, converge. This capacity for meaning is the one that the leader, by personifying this signification, usurps and conceals. He is, in his empirical presence and his separated corporeality, the whole itself, not the meaning of the whole. Herein lies the privilege of being the index of the system, dominating the system, which the leader uses to hide for his own benefit the collective force on which it is based. The meaning that emerges from the leader – to appear as if he were the whole – hides the collective and historical materiality on the basis of which he produces meaning, just as happens in the super-ego with the sensible identification with the father from which it derives: it hides its foundation in the collective whole of labour and of the relations of production. But that which is hidden, the material base that allows the leader to appear as significant, is precisely what is being exploited. In this process the emphasis placed on the absolute materiality of the leader as separated corporeality, to which the signification of being absolute remains sutured, implies the concealment of the materiality subtracted from us. If we confuse the individuality with the signification of the leader, and he is the whole while his material existence only the part, then in a reciprocal movement this same substitution reverts back and impacts our materiality. The materiality of the common body, as inorganic nature, ceases to acquire meaning against the backdrop of the productive relations that organize it: the rationality of the productive system is hidden from sight. To the material dependency, in which the individuals are inside the whole, is added as its necessary complement the fetishism of the other. Subjectivity thus is produced as adequate to the relations of domination.

This collective power that organises itself in the artificial groups appears as a continuous process of dematerialisation and detotalisation: in it, therefore, the merely empirical, sensible, and abstract presence of matter is predominant, together with the concealment and dispersion of relations. Coming from the relations of economic production, its collective force in the army appears to inscribe itself in the name of a false totality, 'country' or 'nation', which hides the differences and imbalances that constitute it. But this compartmentalisation of the subject in multiple references to various institutionalised groups in which society includes it, develops the apparent cultural particularisation of its individual being all the more, the more it de-subjectivises and de-materialises its insertion in the collective domain. And this suspension of the symbolic capacity of the adult, which leads him or her to signify without including the real bond that in the body is one with signification, suffers a new deviation or a new reinforcement in the domain of the religious group. Here, as the link among human beings, the relation is maintained with the other source that determines them: the father-form. But this new father makes his body vanish into thin air and hides even more profoundly the sensibility on which it is based: the father prolongs himself all the way to the father who is in the heavens, toward the celestial father, outside the human system. This transition, therefore, is not an amplification, but at the same time it simulates being one: it is the substitution of the absolute infantile power by an absolute adult power. To succeed, this institution that appears to determine my ties to reality from within consciousness and the body, must hide the libidinal development of my body and keep it as a suspended body. It must not prolong itself in the inorganic body of nature and with other human beings.

In the Church, Christ is no longer a power personified in flesh and bone, as is the commander in the army. Christ is a vanishing materiality, elevated into immateriality, finitude transformed in infinitude, located outside of time. This is why Freud says that in the transition of the group with leaders to the Church, there is an increased emphasis on rationality, as a domain of ideal relations, but there is perforce a detachment and distancing of materiality: Christ is the 'invisible head'. Pursuing its line of flight, the collective signification of the whole, previously personified in the army general, vanishes into thin air and escapes into the celestial ether where its corporeality is dissolved and all that remains is signification without matter: the terrestrial part expanded itself, via the mystery, into a celestial whole. To reach reason and think the whole, in consciousness, implies here that we abandon the body and the material relations as that which precisely gives food for thought. Christ in other words is an infinite materiality for which our body, by identification, serves as basis and support: He can live only from the negation of our own materiality and our own finitude. In Christ the materiality of the leader as 'head' goes up in smoke so as to become transmuted into a symbol: a head, yes, but 'invisible'. This invisible-visibility is a moment of the transition from symbol to sign, as human power elevated from the body, which thus conceals its historical source. We can move from the sensible to reason if previously we strip reason from the body – which already is not just the body of Christ but our own.

This is why the idea that is the quasi-body, or the invisible-head, fulfils a function in the artificial group: it strips the collective power of its material seat by dissolving the thought relations and separating them from the real domain that produced them, and it centres the body thus separated and negated on the celestial infinite: in individual but eternal salvation. Astronaut of ideas, each one thus loses his or her footing on earth – where power takes advantage of our collective power. Rationality opens out onto immaterial infinitude, not onto the finitude of historical time. And by sucking life out of us, it consoles us in the spirit and gives us eternal life – in exchange for the other one. The asexuated body of Christ realises the transmutation of sensible corporeality into the most absolute negation of materiality – converting it into something invisible. Its power is based on our disingenuousness: it is true that in the institution I do not *see* all the others, nor do I *see* the structure that determines me. The structures, like the others, are in this sense also 'invisible'. But this invisibility is not the heavenly invisibility that, by affirming me as merely empirical and separated body, they want to impose on me. For it is from my sensible seeing that the rational signification is prolonged, Freud says, and it is from my sexuated body that the relations with the common body are verified. The invisible is present in the visible, not outside of it, like the domain of human totality that only reason can integrate. Thus incarnated reason guarantees for us the existence of that which we cannot see but which, link after link, relation after relation, body after body, ties my proximate quality with the distant qualities of others. The human invisible does not open out onto the infinite but onto the signifying flesh: it is the capacity to make present the absent in the causal and material determination it exercises in the world.

3   *Dialectic of Resemblance and Difference: The Discernment Repressed*

In this way the true meaning of the world and the comprehension of its structure have gradually been dissolved. Therefore, the artificial groups have continued to constitute us as subjects in whom *the capacity has disappeared to discern the social obstacle that is opposed to life*. It follows that the thought relations, in order to be effective, must drag along with them their index of relations lived from within one's corporeality. If Freud retains the libidinal ties it is because of the meaning conveyed by the masses who revolt against repression, the spontaneous masses as conglomerates of human beings who feel the presence of the obstacle that is opposed to life, as well as the need for its overcoming. Not for nothing does Freud go back to describing the relations of affective ambivalence: in order to explain to us, on another level, how the capacity for discernment was inhibited in the artificial groups.

> ... every intimate emotional relation between two people which lasts for some time – marriage, friendship, the relations between parents and children – leaves a sediment of feelings of aversion and hostility, which only escapes perception as a result of repression. ... The same thing happens when men come together in larger units. (101)

'Sediment of feelings of aversion and hostility': product of the elaboration of lived relations to the point of reaching the adequate proximity – for example: the porcupines frozen stiff mentioned by Freud – for allowing love. In this process of reconciliation and integration, the alternating comings and goings that move within the polarity of 'love and hatred', as indices of integration or separation, are being elaborated. The organic model that Freud gave us was that of the sexual relation: there the instinct of life is tied to the death instinct, love to aggression. But aggressiveness is at the service of life: it levels out the obstacle and receives its meaning from how it makes life possible. Aggressiveness, then, is not repressed in love, but integrated. By contrast, the repressed – the internalised hatred, the feelings of hostility – this separated residue, as we saw, is what constitutes conscience and the super-ego: that signification which from my own experience cannot be integrated in it. It is the negative of the other as repressed foundation of my subsequent relation with him or her. It is the act of aggression turned inward, aimed against oneself for the sake of love. It is, then, *the repression of difference not elaborated with the other and expelled as index*. In other words, it is *difference without reason*, which consciousness does not integrate in its rationality, which is why we repress it inside ourselves. Because we are the ones who cannot give the reason of our desire and of the vicissitudes that mark off its path in reality. And this is because our reason is already, insofar as it is determined by the super-ego, the reason of the other.

After establishing the possibility of optimal contact thanks to the retention of aggression, Freud naively moves on to indicate the functioning of difference with others in terms of the aggressiveness that has been suspended, internalised, but *converted into external* aggression: placed not in the one who inhibits the development of difference due to the repression of aggressiveness, but in a *different other*. This different other shows the following particularity: that we oppose ourselves to him not because he would provoke in us a relation of opposition owing to what he signifies. No, the only thing the other does to deserve our hatred is *be different*. The content of difference is what interests us here. At issue is simply the global and indiscriminate form in which difference appears: as the equally indiscriminate negation of what is proper to us.

We are beginning to see the direction in which Freud is pointing: the repression of difference with respect to a close relation, in which the precise sense of love implies the discernment of a precise hatred or a hostility due to the sensible and concrete evidence the other's action has for me, this repression turns into *repression of the faculty of discernment* toward the nearby, but also and necessarily indiscriminateness with respect to the faraway. Since *I have no reason* to justify my hostility, because my reason is not mine but the reason of the other, I cede my reason to the affectivity of the other's love: out of love I give up my capacity for discernment. But the dialectic of significations elaborated in the flesh is obstinate: repression ignores it, pretends to expel it, but internalises it all the same, and the precise and situated hatred *persists as feeling without reason* in the midst of individuality. The felt hatred is not rooted in the rationality of the other, precisely that other who produces the repression of the hatred that it awakens: because it split off and extracted for itself only love, what to do with the hatred that is present in me? I keep it and aim it against myself, for having dared to transgress the commandment of the reason of the other: love thyself as thy neighbour ... Thus (indiscriminate) love toward the neighbour, which inhibits my reading in him or her the precise sense of his or her act, becomes transmuted into hatred against myself. Thus, reason orders us around. And its maximal order of command is the following: out of love 'you will not develop difference'; out of love, 'you will keep to resemblance'. You will hate in yourself that which differentiates you from me. The index of love is resemblance; the index of hatred, in this absolute dialectic, is difference. All that is different must be hated because it would contravene the law of love of the similar.

Whence Freud's affirmation, which when read only from the psychological, descriptive point of view would seem to be a fundamental law of human relations, against which there would be nothing to do:

> Every time two families become connected by a marriage, each of them thinks itself superior to or of better birth than the other. Of two neighbouring towns each is the other's most jealous rival .... We are no longer astonished that greater differences should lead to an almost insuperable repugnance, such as the Gallic people feel for the German, the Aryan for the Semite, and the white races for the coloured. (101)

Every time? If so, Freud would be justifying, he as a Jewish person, the hatred of the Aryan, the acceptance of a psychological law that orders the hatred of the other without reason. He would be justifying the hatred of the white person against the black person. But that is not Freud's affirmation: he does not pretend to establish an essential law of psychology. It is the description, at the level of individual and social illness, of a process whose secret he tries to put into relief precisely in order to explain the origin of indiscriminate hatred, the permanence of affect separated from reason. Or, in other words: in order to show the need to introduce discernment into affectivity, to unite *the true reason with the affective life*.

Freud is speaking of a rationality that prolongs itself from within the affective element without repression: a rationality that ties the precise affect to the rational order that discerns the organisation of the world and situates my affect in the domain of discernment of the real and, therefore, of history. If the reason that represses me is the reason of the other, because it does not contain the difference that surges forth from my affective experience, where will hatred and aggression have to find their seat? In the only rational index that the other left in me as capacity for discernment: against the rise of difference. Only in this way does hatred once again come up; only in this way does my affectivity without reason meet up again with reality. But the reality it encounters is *a reality that is likewise without reason*, except for one index: the fact that, for being different from me, it deserves my hatred and my violence.

4 *The Collectivity Can Also Be Narcissistic*

We have already analysed this subjective dialectic. What interests us now is its consequence for the domain of collective processes. This is the domain of groups, where the production of individuals in the midst of the family finds its consistency again in the midst of the social relations of production: in the artificial group:

1. The rationality of the social system, which produces our specific hatred, is not clearly discerned: the system of production does not reveal its true structure.
2. The system presents therefore a rationality based exclusively on the global difference – without contradiction – as its sole index: our nation *against* another nation; our country *against* another country.
3. And in mobilising the hatred that the contradiction within its own system generates, it uses this hatred, not against the system itself, but against another, different system.

This is why Freud immediately confronts the analysis of narcissism again:

> In the undisguised antipathies and aversions which people feel towards strangers with whom they have to do we may recognize the expression of self-love – of narcissism. This self-love works for the preservation of the individual, and behaves as though the occurrence of any divergence from his own particular lines of development involved a criticism of them and a demand for their alteration. We do not know why such sensitiveness should have been directed to just these details of differentiation; but it is unmistakable that in this whole connection men give evidence of a readiness for hatred, an aggressiveness, the source of which is unknown, and to which one is tempted to ascribe an elementary character. (102)

Now things are clearer: the behaviour revealed in the artificial groups is the product of a system that produces narcissistic subjects, that is, subjugated in their individuality to the absolute form of the other as if it were their own, where all development of differences is inhibited because of the anxiety before the superego, that is, the anxiety of death. Or, put differently, out of fear of being nothing if we dare to be, we remain without the affective foundation of the primeval other, who habilitated us for life. Which indicates, as its corollary, that we were unable to develop our relation with reality outside the box and the framework that, beginning with the father, the social institutions signal to us as being the only paths that can be traversed without risk. Thus the difference announced by the other with his or her *strange* presence does not awaken our own difference as a quality to be developed, as exchange, but as containment and death threat. The death we feel before the other's presence – to remain without the love of the other who sustains us – is the death we now deploy against the other who is different. This is why Freud states here with precision 'as though the occurrence of any divergence from his own particular lines of development involved a criticism of them and a demand for their alteration'. The qualitative and precise presence of the different other implicitly carries with it an invitation: let us transform our own qualities in the exchange. Here lies the true logic, though repressed, of the flesh and Eros, the qualitative dialectic of the transformation of human beings. But this attraction toward the different other is felt with the rationality of the superego that inhibits us: it implies its implicit criticism. How to dare to negate the reason of similitude? Does this mean that we are not right in excluding difference? Here the development of the qualitative aspect meets up with the limits that the rational critique, the moral conscience, imposes on us: the absolute reason of the superego cannot be criticised, because it would mean the loss of love and of its absolute character that sustains us. And it is this implicit criticism, felt as a signal of anxiety, which opens up in the subject the emergence of the contradiction between our sensibility and rationality, which leads us to project it against the other, for the simple fact of having dared to traverse our consciousness at all: the different other is the one that criticises me. In the fleeting moment in which the felt quality before the other awakens the desire to develop my own qualities, in this moment the contradiction with the rationality of our consciousness is revealed. In this imperceptible perception, but which had to be felt to awaken our reaction, this feeling is frightened of what it has dared to think and perceive. And the hatred that is thus aroused changes direction, following the orders of the superego: it orients itself in reality with the rational signification that the system imposed on it and, instead of aiming itself against the one who halts the development of difference, the thirst of life once more buries with all its violence the difference that attracted it, and kills it: for being different.

Thus the system has us as its firmest supporters. Each one demands it as what is most proper to us, as the maximum support, because each one is at the same time the most alien: having the form of the other as if it were one's own.

And this is why Freud adds:

> *We do not know* why such sensitiveness should have been directed to just these details of differentiation .... (102, emphasis added)

We do not know it: in a manner of speaking. We do not know it, but Freud does. We do not know it, because our rational consciousness does not possess the reason of its sensibility and of its affective attractions, because we think with the reason of the other. Science – psychoanalysis – knows it, but not we who find ourselves in the institutions that form a coherent system with our individuality.

> ... it is unmistakable that in this whole connection men give evidence of *a readiness* for hatred, an aggressiveness, the source of which is unknown, and to which *one is tempted to ascribe* an elementary character. (102, emphasis added)

It would be an equivocation to believe that Freud is here speaking about himself, when in reality he is telling us how *we* think. Freud is describing us to ourselves, which is why he says: at the conventional and psychological level the only thing we retain is the form of hatred without content, the sheer existence of an 'innate' hatred and aggressiveness, which in its generality would constitute the 'essence' of every human being. The kind that leads us to say, for example: there will always be wars, human beings will always hate each other, and 'to which *one is tempted to ascribe* an elementary character' (102, emphasis added). But the thought of this elementary character is a product of repression, which keeps us from seeing that it is only the *readiness* that is elementary in all of us, because hatred and aggressiveness are significant indices in each individual to the extent that they are both at the service of life. And thus it keeps us from seeing that the 'elementary' character signals the cultural and no longer natural transformation of an elementary affective discrimination that has already taken place: the affective discrimination in hatred or love. But this elementary fact is not the mere, or the pure, emergence of a biological capacity inscribed in the 'psychic apparatus'. Freud tells us that this elementary index is an index of cultural reality: how to discern the true meaning of the obstacle that rises up from within affectivity, from within the unity of the individual organism in the confrontation with life. But he is saying that in the realm of culture this affective index is defined by its integration in the domain of the discernment of the reality of the system. And that, in case they do not integrate the truth of the system into the domain of subjectivity, these indices function as if they were merely biological, that is to say, also devoid of reason. The rationality that the psychologist fails to discern in hatred or love with reference to the social system as their index demonstrates that his thinking is determined, qua science, by repression: he represses within himself the rational sense of reality. From that point of view hatred or love are elementary: affective units dislocated from the reality to which they signal, 'to which *one is tempted to ascribe* an elementary character' (122, emphasis added).

This whole explanation leads us once again to the problem of the artificial group. If narcissism, from the perspective of individual psychology, is a negative form of being an individual, here we see that in the group, as Freud tells us, one of the most important reactions of narcissism disappears, which is its intolerance:

> But when a group is formed the whole of this intolerance vanishes, temporarily or permanently, within the group. So long as a group formation persists or so far as it extends, individuals in the group behave as though they were uniform, tolerate the peculiarities of its other members, equate themselves with them, and have no feeling of aversion towards them. Such a limitation of narcissism can, according to our theoretical views, only be produced by one factor, a libidinal tie with other people. Love for oneself knows only one barrier – love for others, love for objects. (102)

Once again, what the artificial group shows us is the disappearance of intolerance *only* with regard to those who are included in the same institution. This does not entail therefore a moving beyond narcissism: it only shows the effect of narcissism within the collective, when it begins to work in the service of the repressive system. There occurs no transformation of the individuality and no extension of the qualitative capacities in the collective exchange: the collectivity implies the immobilisation of its members present within it.

The peculiarity is 'tolerated', not assimilated. The equality is merely formal: individuals in the group 'equate themselves' with other members (102). The qualitative signification of the other represses my affectivity: they 'have no feeling of aversion' (102). Thus, the qualitative signification ceases to signify; it becomes insignificant. This indiscriminateness with regard to the others in the group only reveals the rationality that runs through it: the fact that the form of the system and its meaning are not congruent with the qualitative relations that conform it. There is no agreement between the affective and the rational; the rationality of the system requires the sacrifice of the qualitative significations. This is why 'individuals in the group behave as though they were uniform' (102). What is this uniformity that defines them as though they were cut from the same cloth, given that as individuals they were not produced by the leader but each one of them by their own families? The cloth that seems to cut them so uniformly, in one case as much as in any other, is a model that requires the nondevelopment of difference and the permanence of similitude. This can only be a structure that determines the meaning of all other structures that depend on it: the social system of production. The result of this insertion into the traditional group is the formation of a *narcissistic institution*. Here it is the institution that appears as a collective individual. It is an 'individual' collective that continues to be subjected to its dependence on the leader who rules over it, since its members remain subjected, one by one, to him.

Thus, the apparent dissolution of individual narcissism in the traditional group works only in the service of the narcissism of the collective institution. Dissolving difference inwards, it becomes homogeneous – it does not tolerate difference outwards. Now the collective power, as a multiplied social force, is opposed to the development of all difference and all discernment in the social field.

Faced with this situation, are we going to vindicate the union with the others by emphasising that which the artificial groups conceal, namely, the community of class interests, so as to privilege the individual interests? Freud thus reencounters another historical kind of solution, in whose critique he will engage: the 'social contract'.

5   *Community of Interests: The Contractual Relation without Libido*

One possible solution, coming from the artificial group, would be a link, determined solely by reason: the 'community of interests', in which the human form is not predominant in the link; whence the return to the individual form in the satisfaction of needs. With regard to this, Freud also signals the impossibility of constituting a lasting human relationship in this way:

> The question will at once be raised whether community of interest in itself, without any addition of libido, must not necessarily lead to the toleration of other people and to considerateness for them. This objection may be met by the reply that nevertheless no lasting limitation of narcissism is effected in this way, since this tolerance does not persist longer than the immediate advantage gained from the other people's collaboration. (102)

Thus, there is always an excess at play in human relationships, and this excess is the form of the other as the backdrop against which all satisfaction becomes meaningful. Freud here once again indicates the inevitably human character of every need and every form of satisfaction. People cannot decide in favour of a partial collaboration in the existing work relationships, based exclusively on the rational contract that divides up the interests and momentarily combines them, as if it were nothing more than such an abstraction of their partial interest that determined their relation. The 'human' excess, the libido, once again transgresses the boundaries that are being imposed on it in this delimitation, and it exceeds them or annuls them. This limitation can appear only there where the traditional group used up the libido of the individual in its own institution, and only sets it free in the momentary association of work.

> The libido attaches itself to the satisfaction of the great vital needs, and chooses as its first objects the people who have a share in that process. And in the development of mankind as a whole, just as in individuals, love alone acts as the civilising factor in the sense that it brings a change from egoism to altruism. And this is true both of sexual love for women, with all the obligations which it involves of not harming the things that are dear to women, and also of desexualised, sublimated homosexual love for other men, which springs from work in common. (103)

This is the culmination of the process that Freud is showing to us in the development of the sexuated body as the matrix of all rational and social organisation. As we said, the form of the relation that a group is capable of developing in order to constitute a human totality is:
- neither the group dependent on a leader (homosexual love not sublimated but repressed, which takes a man as the supreme object-substitute for the dependency with respect to the father) – so not the army;
- nor the group dependent on an invisible head, in which homosexuality represses in its object even its real and carnal presence so as to render it invisible – so not the Church;
- nor the community of partial interests, in which the form of the other would not be determining the bond but instead privileges only a formal and juridical relationship: once the interest disappears, so does the bond that ties the individuals together – so not the independent producers.

We saw that the traditional and artificial groups were dominated by love, but not the 'wider' love: what dominates is Christian love, separated from its relation with sexual love. Therefore, what dominates is the repression of the flesh. This is why *both institutions*, Church and army, which owe their existence to one another and whose alliance has been secular, *express the dissociation at the heart of the system they sustain: on the one side, love, but abstract, in the Church; on the other, hatred, as effective violence, in the army*. These two forms of institutionalised artificial groups in other words are the expression of the system that is based on them and in this way they define the global incoherence that constitutes them.

We have to go back to the 'wider' conception of love, to the element of libido, in which signification circulates and which maintains the individual as not dissociated and the collective organisation, the social, as a congruent extension in which these effectively become realised. What is the point of departure? Again: the unsatisfied desire, which looks for its satisfaction from within the sexual body that has not been negated, until it reaches the common body in the community.

'The libido attaches itself to the satisfaction of the *great* vital needs', Freud says. The *great* vital needs are the ones that emerge as soon as the body developed its organisation through the different stages that amplify it to the point of including itself, as sexuated individual, in the world. The oral, anal, phallic, and genital stages were moments in a development of the individual's unity and the assumption in the body of its difference on the basis of a still indiscriminate similitude: on the basis of the oral conduct. At the beginning what was predominant was the incorporation and identification with the other, the similar, on the basis of which the immature body made its breakthrough in the field of culture or civilisation. The process of the body's becoming mature included in its development the cultural forms of relation. And to the organism's biological synthesis there corresponded the synthesis of civilisation, which culminated in the differentiated individual. In the realm of sexuality this biological power of establishing an autonomous relation to the world and to the different other, women for men, men for women, indicated the root and the matrix of all difference. On the basis of the radical difference that is prolonged in biology – man and woman – civilisation is able from there to extend every other difference. The assumed sexual difference is, from within our corporeality, the unfolding of every difference at the core of the similitude of the human. This is why Freud says that the libido finds support in the satisfaction of the great individual vital needs: it extends the body as prolongation of every differentiation and qualitative discernment towards the world, prolonging the discerning capacity of the flesh. If sexual difference is erased as the basis of all difference, then so is the capacity for discernment that prolongs itself from the flesh towards the world, from the sensible towards the rational, from nature to culture. The flesh, as sexuated body, maintains the irreducible presence of the historical origin of all human signification.

6   *The Matrix of All Difference*

But at the same time Freud showed us the diversion introduced by the negation of sexuality; the permanence of similitude without difference, there where the body did not acquire the capacity to develop its powers in reality:

> The libido [...] chooses as its first objects the people who have a share in that process [in the satisfaction of the great vital needs]. (103)

The 'great needs' of the infant, which are those of a still impotent body, choose their first object: the mother, the father, in the most absolute dependency, making themselves into that which the others are. On the basis of this similitude they set out on the path that will lead, in its sexual endpoint, to difference. But in this first moment we are still only in similitude. We now see why in the artificial groups the libidinal expansion disappears and what is privileged is a primitive bond with the director of multitudes: the dependence on the leader, the submission to Christ. In this relation, in which the difference does not come from the individual but is imposed by the other, the individuals in order to satisfy their 'great needs' remain tied to an infantile form of submission and dependency: they must submit to the system in order to satisfy their need. But in order to accomplish this, only one thing is demanded of them: that they do not develop their difference, that they do not actualise the discerning power of the body, which is present in them as sexuated beings. That they may develop the difference only in the field of a 'biological' sexuality, without prolonging it into the world of culture or civilisation as discerning power and seat of all discernment. And that they react against difference. Because all difference developed by some other is a threat for them: *it brings out the homosexual bond that ties them to the leader* in the flesh, even as consciousness, casting aside all sexuality, represses this. All difference awakens the master's threatening terror, which forms the basis for the undeveloped similitude of the subjected.

But by hiding the body as the place from where all discernment develops, I inhibit in myself the power to produce signification from within the sensible and on the basis of the qualitative differences that already exist, as material imbalances and privileges, in the social organisation. The artificial social organisation, in which there exists a predominance of differences without reason, establishes the rule of similitude at the level of a rationality unable to find its meaning in the sensible and the material.

And yet, despite this moment of predominance of the artificial groups or masses, Freud shows us the inevitable dialectic that circulates through history:

> And in the development of mankind as a whole, just as in individuals, love alone acts as the civilising factor in the sense that it brings a change from egoism to altruism. (103)

This should be read as *love in the widened sense*, which is based on sexual difference as the matrix of all discernment; culture or civilisation, which is based on the development of life that circulates through the materiality of bodies in the prolongation of nature. This is why there is no passage from egoism to altruism if the other as other who is both similar and different at the same time does not broaden his or her relation from within the flesh: broadening their desire until they share in mine. Not the permanence in the narcissism of the homosexual body, in which one is at the same time part and whole, having robbed it of its libidinal extension with others and with the world: this is the foundation of all egoism, the permanence in the undeveloped similitude of one's meager individual flesh. Instead, the development of difference to the point of including in oneself the effective difference presented by the other as qualitatively other; as truly similar recognised in his or her material and finite existence, which is required in its corporeal difference for the satisfaction of my need – like man and woman, different-and-similar, loved for their difference from within similitude. The distance that opens up between similitude and difference is the field in which the satisfaction of adult needs is inscribed; because they extend themselves from within the matrix of all satisfaction, in which the carnal form of the other covers my own in the meeting of two bodies as its highest object, similar and different at the same time. And thus, as the just measure of every relationship extended into reality from which every prolonged need receives its meaning.

This widened sense of love for Freud – love based on the development that takes its index from the real and sensible, material difference – is the one that prolongs itself in human labour, in the work in common that the capitalist system covers up. Once human beings are subjected to the determination that the military and religious powers bring to bear on them, inhibiting their body and their consciousness, the domain of labour uses those beings as those whose *surplus corporeality, not invested in human relationships, remains free for inhuman labour*, quantified and without quality, in which labour that lost its human form only assumes the form of technology: the form imposed by the machine. The horror of sexuality's materiality among the 'spiritualists' causes the rise of a materiality that is more brutal but for them more efficient: it allows them to increase the subtraction of the body of the other for their own benefit. Thus life subtracted from Eros follows its arc and appears, against the human being, as death and submission in the system of production, feeding itself precisely with the life it has subtracted.

Here we clearly see where Freud's analyses lead us: work in common is the final form of the relation that started in the sexual relationship. Hence, as the index of the truth or falsity of a given system, Freud here refers to the way in which the work relations appear to verify the development of the matrix of all difference: on the basis of the assumed sexual love. Therefore, the 'relations of production' no longer find their meaning solely in production understood as the mere production of things, in which the commodity or object form is determining. This production without libido is materiality without humanity: 'this tolerance does not persist longer than the immediate advantage gained from the other people's collaboration' (102). Only the sensible form of the other as different, maintained in the productive process, accounts for the truth or falsity of a given system of production. Both for Freud and for Marx production is not only production of things but from the beginning to the end, if it is meant to be human production, *production of subjects*.

> If therefore in groups narcissistic self-love is subject to limitations which do not operate outside them, that is cogent evidence that the essence of a group formation consists in new kinds of libidinal ties among the members of the group. (103)

The problem is therefore that of the *new* libidinal ties: that is to say, not those that the individuals develop – by way of Oedipus – in their individual relationships. We are dealing with ties of a different order, within the collectivity. Until now as we have seen in the artificial groups or masses, these ties were not new: they repeated the model of previous forms in the midst of the institution while *simulating novelty*.

> Our interest now leads us on to the pressing question as to what may be the nature of these ties which exist in groups. In the psycho-analytic study of neuroses we have hitherto been occupied almost exclusively with ties with objects made by love instincts which still pursue directly sexual aims. In groups there can evidently be no question of sexual aims of that kind. We are concerned here with love instincts which have been diverted from their original aims, though they do not operate with less energy on that account. Now, within the range of the usual sexual object-cathexis, we have already observed phenomena which represent a *diversion* of the instinct from its sexual aim. (103, emphasis added).

Thus appears the need to justify the affirmation of love in the widened sense: how the love instincts extend themselves to the others and make possible the development of civilisation. Does the amplification of love base itself on the diversion of instinctual aims? And if so, what class of diversion is the one that leads from the artificial mass to the spontaneous mass, and from the spontaneous mass to the revolutionary mass? Freud will try to understand the different pathological modalities of the diversion of instincts, prolonging the observations from individual psychology and using them as the basis for clarifying the essence of collective psychology.

> Now, within the range of the usual sexual object-cathexis, we have already observed phenomena which represent a diversion of the instinct from its sexual aim. We have described them as degrees of being in love, and have recognised that they involve a certain encroachment upon the ego. We shall now turn our attention more closely to these phenomena of being in love, in the firm expectation of finding in them conditions which can be transferred to the ties that exist in groups. But we should also like to know whether this kind of object-cathexis, as we know it in sexual life, represents the only manner of emotional tie with other people, or whether we must take other mechanisms of the sort into account. As a matter of fact we learn from psycho-analysis that there do exist other mechanisms for emotional ties, the so-called identifications, insufficiently-known processes and hard to describe .... (103–4)

VI   The Human Form as Index of the Coherence of the Social System

1   *Identification: Substitution of Being by Having*

Something peculiar happens with this chapter of Freud's text, which confirms the sense of our interpretation. Usually his analysis of identification is abstracted by conventional psychologists and, separated from the collective context in which it is situated in the book, the topic is considered as if it were only one more contribution to individual psychology. Its historical inscription, which includes this analysis in a progressive series that goes from the individual to the collective, is completely obliterated. Ideological negation thus is at its maximum level.

In reality, what does Freud propose to us with the analysis of identification? Identification is a universal phenomenon, which lies at the origin of our access to civilisation: the point of departure of what in his *Project* he called 'the complex of the neighbor'; that is to say, the equivocal initiation that may lead us to remain in mere similitude or to develop difference. Or, put differently: he shows us the first access to the *structure* of culture or civilisation, the leap that enables us to incorporate ourselves into civilisation by incorporating ourselves into the other. This is why Freud once again comes up against this problem when he questions the coherence of a given social structure in which the integrating 'parts', the human beings, appear from within their individual organisation as assuming the dialectic that ties them to the 'whole' of the social system. The social system can be coherent or incoherent, true or false. But the incoherence that is lived within the system implies that one makes oneself into the locus of a false organisation or, to use Freud's expression, it implies that subjectivity becomes the locus of 'error' ('the resultant compromise is *incorrect*, analogous to an error in thought', letter to Wilhelm Fliess, 30 May, 1896).[5] In identification Freud will show us how the fundamental relations, in order to be true or false, are based on the affirmation of the other as real presence, as true or imaginary other. The effective reality of the other, when it is recognised on the basis of the flesh of one's own that animates it, implies the affirmation of my own reality. This process does not unfold only at the level of ideas: its vehicle is the body. This is why the dialectic is nothing but the process that leads us to find a foothold in the truth that is at stake in the domain of the history of which we are the product. It is thus the form in which we determine ourselves as concrete subjects: where the meaning of the totality is present, determining the meaning of being a part thereof. But here, in the beginning, when Freud refers to the process of identification, what is at issue is the affirmation or negation of the dialectic, incorporated as true or false, based on the way in which from the moment of my first emergence onwards I am incorporated into the world of culture or civilisation. I am, as corporeal subject, a locus of the human inaugurated in the historical process in which the truth of the structure is also at play to the extent that I, as human being, put into play my singular existence as part thereof.

How do I gain access to this broader structure of which I am a part? This process of relating to the whole is already ongoing, as a point of entrance therein, beginning in the relationship with the parents. And we will see that the infant's drama of gaining access to – masculine or feminine – human identity is prolonged in the drama of gaining access to the adult form in the historical system of production. The infantile drama is the Oedipus complex, just as the adult drama is that of the contradictions of the system of production.

Freud reiterates the problem of identification in the following terms:

> Identification is known to psycho-analysis as the earliest expression of an emotional tie with another person. [...] A little boy will exhibit a special interest in his father; he would like to grow like him and be like him, and take his place everywhere. We may say simply that he takes his father as his ideal. [...] At the same time as this identification with his father, or a little later, the boy has begun to develop a true object-cathexis towards his mother according to the attachment [anaclitic] type. He then exhibits, therefore, two psychologically distinct ties: a straightforward sexual object-cathexis towards his mother and an identification

---

5 Freud 1896, p. 189.

> with his father which takes him as his model. The two subsist side by side for a time without any mutual influence or interference. In consequence of the irresistible advance towards a unification of mental life, they come together at last; and the normal Oedipus complex originates from their confluence. (105)
>
> Identification, in fact, is ambivalent from the very first; it can turn into an expression of tenderness as easily as into a wish for someone's removal. It behaves like a derivative of the first, oral phase of the organisation of the libido, in which the object that we long for and prize is assimilated by eating and is in that way annihilated as such. (105)

What this process shows us is the following: *how I have to be in order to have*. And the discovery is this: I must *be like* the other (model) in order to *have what the other has*. And the drama of the Oedipus complex could be summed up in this re-discovery, which is painful like no other: that even if I may *be like* the other, in reality *I am not the other*. And that, therefore, the object of my desire (the mother), which I made into my own, in reality is not mine but the object of the other (the father).

> 'Having' and 'being' in children. Children like expressing an object-relation by an identification: 'I am the object'. 'Having' is the later of the two; after loss of the object it relapses into 'being'. Example: the breast. 'The breast is a part of me, I am the breast'. Only later: 'I have it' – that is, 'I am not it' ... ('Findings, Ideas, Problems', SE 23: 299)

These categories of *being* and *having*, which are fundamental in the dialectic in which meaning is incarnated in a body, thus define from the very first the basic modality of any link with reality. And they grasp this in its originally determining moment: from the moment that any relation to reality, and to the objects of this reality, appears in this equivocal beginning in which *being is equivalent to being like the other*. This shows us the moment in which the rational meaning is articulated with its sensible base and, therefore, the possible hiatus between one and the other as well. But this *being as if one were the other* is not lived by the child, in the beginning, according to this matrix – 'as if' – which discerns the distance between the I and the other with whom I identified. In the beginning, *I am the other*. In the primary process I incorporated the other in me, and it is the other's form, internalised as my own, which enabled my body as similar to the other's. It is the assumption of this matrix as real difference – I am *like* the other but I am not the other – which leads to the resolution of the Oedipus complex: in which by being *like* the father, without being him, I can have objects *like* my mother, without having her. We see the difficulty that we must face in order for an autonomous being to come into existence, a being that by undoing the incipient sensible logic that opened up an external world for it – swallowing and spitting out – finds a way to acquire a power of its own based on the assumed autonomy of being one human among others.

What is important to understand is the transition that leads from this sensible logic of the primary process to the rational signification of the dialectical logic, which finally rediscovers its true link with reality. We must understand, therefore, how from this primary logic in which there is as yet no synthesised body that organises its meaning on the basis of its sexuated form we move to the logic in which the unity of the human form – a body centred on genitality with the meaning acquired through this access – reaches at last a form of being of its own, in which body and culture coincide in the reality of a social field where its secret resides.

From this follows the importance of being and having for any human logic. *Being* implies an organic human being, centre and locus enabled by culture in a body that transformed itself in the form of the human. *Having* is the power that this being can exert in the world and thus shows, in the relation with the first object, the mother, how these relations prolong themselves, from *one* cultural form to the whole of reality. But this first object for Freud is an 'object-person' (*Objektperson*), the form of forms, object of all objects. This is why the dénouement of the Oedipus complex is so important: it allows us to understand whether we have been able to cease being the inaugural other in order to be another similar to the other. Or, better yet, whether we have been able to be another different from the other.

Thus the process of psychic development once again refers us back to the logic of the whole and the parts, in which form and content constitute the determining moments of the quality of the relation. And this will allow us to understand the true and possible relations, once the true form and content of each part – each human being – has been determined in its relation to the other parts – to other human beings and to things – within the network of possible relations sketched out by the system of production. This will depend, then, on how this cell of the social structure – the human form – acquires the power to assume the full array of cultural determinations of the system. In the capitalist system, we know that all wealth is determined by the commodity-form, and the commodity is the elementary form that necessarily corresponds to the structure of the productive system. Similarly, the form of the human being that this system determines also necessarily presents, in the domain of psychology, an organised subjective form, which structurally corresponds to this basic form of objectification that is typical of the system.

Let us have a closer look at how this logic is organised, how it is diverted, and how it keeps the human being from exercising that power, which nonetheless from birth onwards it must conquer.

What is the distance between incorporating the object in the primary form of identification – taking it in – and relating to the object by recognising its independent material existence? The first is a magical act, based on an assimilatory biological activity, inadequately extended into the field dominated by symbolic relationships. The power of the body is not extended to the point of grafting itself onto the real conditions of the world and of the object. By swallowing the object I make it my own: the body here exercises only a *psychic power*, but reduced to its biological scheme on which, necessarily, it is based. The child believes that it is part and whole at the same time: we are in the realm of fantasy. The power of one's own body, not yet matured to the point of reaching its adult form in which it would really be able to exercise it, is a purely fantasied power, in which the symbolic becomes realised: it turns into the thing. Hallucination is its sphere of operation, the psychic medium of its reality. The effective reality of the separated object and of the world disappear as obstacle and as field of appropriation. It is not that they disappear: for the child they do not yet exist. Thus what this process allows us to understand is its persistence, *later on*, as form of relationality among adult human beings, there where the obstacle and reality, magnified to the point of becoming absolute obstacles, cause a regression to imaginary forms of relationality superimposed on top of the real ones. And this allows us to elude them in a form of satisfaction in which, once again, as in the case of fetishism, what comes to dominate is the trap of being part and whole at the same time. In other words, the distance between the form of identification in the oral stage and the adult forms of the relation with others and with objects is determined by the absence or discerned presence of the real world. At stake is thus the differentiation of a *real power* and an *imaginary power*. It is in the acquisition of this power and in the overcoming of this distance that the fate of the human being plays itself out.

2 *The Body as Locus of the Dialectic*

This is the problem at issue in Freud's analysis of identification. The adult's form of identification, such as it is revealed in sickness, shows us three basic modalities depending on the aim pursued by the sick person: I identify with *one* aspect of the other in order to *be or have all* of the other, or I identify with the *situation* in which the other is found.

Identification with *one* aspect, *one* attribute or *one* property of the other.

a) Identification in order *to be the other*: Here Freud gives the example of a neurotic symptom whereby the daughter, wanting to replace the mother in her relation with the father, *identifies herself*, in a hostile manner, *with the stubborn cough of the mother*.

> ... the symptom expresses her object-love towards her father, and brings about a realisation, under the influence of a sense of guilt, of her desire to take her mother's place: 'You wanted to be your mother, and now you are – anyhow so far as your sufferings are concerned'. This is the complete mechanism of the structure of a hysterical symptom. (106)

Here the symptom fulfils its function: it *signifies* the transaction between an imaginary power and an adult non-power. The adult power would imply something of which she is not capable: to recover the real form of the father with the corporeality of her own adult feminine form. But to do so she would have to confront the real form of the mother. Here, instead, the body regresses to a previous power, which still persists in her and actualises itself as if it were a present power, but without coinciding with the real structure of the present. The actual desire that persists is elaborated in an infantile imaginary corporeality. What is its mechanism? *One* aspect of the other, her cough, is abstracted from her, cut off from the other of which organically it is a part. One separates a partial aspect of the real organic support – its human form – in which it has as much corporeal reality as meaning. By having the other's cough I am *all*, the whole other. I make it my own: I give it my own body as support of that quality which, *by having it, gives me being*. In the real chain of human relationships the mother's cough *signifies* the sickness of her body. In the imaginary chain of unconscious transactions the mother's cough is separated from her real body and acquires, in its separateness, a new function, which is arbitrary from the point of view of real relations and only coherent from the point of view of primary relations. Thus the cough acquires another signification, but within a field of fantasy in which *there is no real body that might serve as its support*: there is the infantile body, regressively actualised in the adult as form of organisation, there where it had not yet reached the cultural and organic reality that the process of maturity turned into the real adult body.

This would bring us to interrogate the foundation of arbitrary significations in human relations. The order of signification, in order to be true, cannot disturb the basic dialectic of parts and whole in which these relations develop within the social structure. The true signifier here has the form of the human being, and it is on the basis of this form sustained as the nucleus of all meaning that each signification appears. And here, in the field of psychology, the form and content that give meaning to each signification – the form of the human being – are taken as the point of departure to verify every true or false relation to reality.

In this first case I identify with what I *would like to be*: by adopting, as we saw, just one feature of the other. Now let us look at a second case developed by Freud: the one in which I identify with what I *would like to have*.

b) Identification in order *to have the other*: We have seen how in these processes, in which the first identification cannot develop itself as difference on the basis of the organic constitution of the human form, whose social matrix finds its key in the resolution of the Oedipus complex, *the part is taken for the whole*. This structure is basically that of the fetishist structure. The mechanism implies that one eludes the reality of the world, by eluding the unified reality of one's own organisation: the real transformation of my natural body into a cultural body, which connects with and recuperates the biological synthesis in the synthesis of the world. A body which incorporated the signification of the cultural order into the flesh.

In the case that interests us now the daughter identifies with one part of the other not in order *to be* the other – the mother – but in order *to have* the whole other – the father. Here the symptom is the same as that of the beloved: the patient imitates this time the cough of the father.

> In that case we can only describe the state of things by saying that identification has appeared instead of object-choice, and that object-choice has regressed to identification. (106–7)

What has happened here? We are no longer dealing, as in the previous case, with wanting to be the other by identifying myself with one of the other's aspects. Here I *have* the other, as object of my desire, by being one aspect of the other.

> ... the ego assumes the characteristics of the object. It is noticeable that in these identifications the ego sometimes copies the person who is not loved and sometimes the one who is loved. It must also strike us that in both cases the identification is a partial and extremely limited one and only borrows a single trait from the person who is its object. (107)

In this way the adult *non-power* (to have on the outside) is replaced by an infantile *being* (to have on the inside). By identifying myself with a quality of the object, I have the whole object for myself. Once more what has been eluded? The real conditions, both of the being of the other and of my own being. Here, too, the quality is separated, by way of abstraction, from the organic support. If the other's quality is mine, this implies in reality that *I have to make the other into me* in order to have the other's qualities, in order to enjoy them. But since the other does not answer, or does not have to, I give life to his or her quality with my body: I give my subjectivity to a quality, which objectively speaking belongs to another. I am, therefore, *all and part at the same time*: in the unity of my own form, by way of a fantasy formation, the form of the other is coupled with my own. I go back once more to that place where the real world did not yet exist for the child, and the quasi-biological logic of the primary processes once again recuperates its predominance over and above the real dialectic that cannot be assumed.

> [...] under the conditions in which symptoms are constructed, that is, where there is repression and where the mechanisms of the unconscious are dominant, object-choice is turned back into identification (107)

In both cases, then, it is the exteriority of the ego with respect to the id, the consideration of its own instinctive impulses as alien and the subordination to the superego, which determines this escape or way out. The ego, by investing itself with the qualities of the external object, and thus being itself situated as external to the id, to its own flesh, *offers itself up to the id as its object*. Through repression the ego has distanced itself to such an extent from itself, from its own impulses, the abstracted signification has become reality, and the spirit has delinked itself from the body to such an extent, that it has managed to acquire the reality that the adult's own body, which was repressed, has lost. The distance that separates me from reality now opens itself up as interior distance, which I am able to close, at the level of fantasy.

c) Identification by placing oneself in the *situation* of the other. The third mechanism that Freud signals is the one in which 'the identification leaves entirely out of account any object-relation to the person who is being copied' (107).

This third mode of identification discovers a new regressive mechanism, but always against the backdrop of a real capacity that in this way becomes twisted. What is this real capacity? The others announce to me the meaning of the world, the possible relations that through their conduct they open up as possibilities also for me. The other appears as an index of the real structure of reality.

But in the case that Freud considers here, the function of announcing the structure of reality that the other would fulfil appears on the contrary as a reduction and an inhibition of its meaning.

I place myself in the other's position but am not tied to the other by way of libidinal bonds: here the function is more clearly cognitive.

> Supposing, for instance, that one of the girls in a boarding school has had a letter from someone with whom she is secretly in love which arouses her jealousy, and that she reacts to it with a fit of hysterics; then some of her friends who know about it will catch the fit, as we say, by psychic infection. The mechanism is that of identification based upon the possibility or desire of putting oneself in the same situation. The other girls would like to have a secret love affair too, and under the influence of a sense of guilt they also accept the suffering involved in it. [...] One ego has perceived a significant analogy with another upon one point [...]; an identification is thereupon constructed on this point, and, under the influence of the pathogenic situation, is displaced on to the symptom which the one ego has produced. The identification by means of the symptom has thus become the mark of a point of coincidence between the two egos which has to be kept repressed. (107, translation modified)

Just as in the previous cases the abstracted quality of the cough entered into the infantile atemporality and infinity of a halted subjective time, the same occurs when I identify myself with a situation: it takes it out of historical time, away from death and real suffering. It ceases to be the historical place, the index of the reality of the world, so as to coincide with an absolute instant with the other. Just as before, in the identification with the quality, the other disappeared as organic foundation, here what disappears is the concrete world that sustains the diversity of behaviours, the historical and precise reality that for each subject opens up in the present. I live the situation of the other *by analogy upon a single point*, not in its particular differentiated signification. What this 'psychic infection' produces is a generalisation, starting from what happens to one case, extended onto all the others. The form of the personal world as lived by the other is *the whole* form of the world. But the others do not live the same situation: they could live it, they fear it, but in reality it was not something that happened to them but to the other. What determines this generalisation of the situation? It is not the confrontation with reality and the verification, as part thereof, of difference, which for each case is distinct. What enables the generalisation is the aspect they have in common: the repression of unsatisfied desire. Repression here produces a link on an imaginary terrain, where the subjectivities erase the differences in the common form of repression that unites them, in which each one suffers, induced by the other, the same drama. Which is actually not the same, because what brings them closer and makes them appear as being 'the same' is exclusively the identification with the symptom, in 'a point of coincidence between the two egos' (107). But if the point of encounter has significance as an analogical index of reality, it is above all determining as an affective index of repression. They coincide in the repression, not in the real content. Or, put differently, what ties them to reality as something in common is the fact of repression: the common submission to a sense of 'I should not be living this reality', under whose influence they discern the common element of their different contents. What they have in common is thus the element of repression, the opposite of life, its necessary negation. There occurs a narrowing of the world: repression generalises for all what is feared by one. For this reason, even though 'the other girls would like to have a secret love affair too', or may desire to have one, this does not constitute the field of the dispute in which they might prolong the unsatisfied desire that seeks to open a path towards its object. The analysis of the real affective situation disappears once the common form of submission makes its sudden appearance.

What interests us in these three forms of identification that Freud describes would be the following:

1. Identification, in its first infantile form, was necessarily equivocal: it took the part for the whole when the child took itself as both part and whole. This form, in which signification proceeds without keeping present the effective reality that is signified, may prolong itself into the life of the adult and, as we will see, it can also be included in that of the 'normal' person.

    Prolonged in the adult, as we saw, this false form of the logical linkage breaks up the organic dialectic of reality in which the form of the human being, on the one hand, and the structure of the social system, on the other, determine a precise signification for each relation, by determining at the same time the precise material content that the logical connection necessarily must carry with it.

2. The relations of signification of the part – the individual – with regard to the whole – the system – become converted into a quasi-corporeal operation, in an imaginary relation of which ingestion serves as the model. The relation of the human being to the world from an external one turns into a relation in which oneself is the whole and the other, by identification, is only part of oneself. The rational capacity, which results from the amplification of the body in its material affirmation of objects, does not move beyond this primary form in which the signification of the other materialises itself only in my own corporeality. The world disappears as a totality

of relations that gives meaning to my actions. Since I cannot assume the qualitative and rational reality of the world in which I am one and the other is another, because repression inhibits the movement whereby I might unfold myself in it, I negate this reality. I negate it not at the level of reality, but I actualise an ancient modality of the relation, the one in which there was not yet any external reality for me: I was the totality in which every other was contained.

3. But this activity is also on the order of the 'as if': the transaction of the symptom is metaphorical. I continue to find support in the representation of the other, but as if this representation that animates me did not have this signification for me but instead provided me with the other's qualitative reality itself. The cough gives me the signification of the sick mother. But by having the cough in my body, I *am* my mother. I love my father, who coughs: the cough is one aspect of him that signifies him on the basis of this salient point. But when I myself cough, it is as if the very corporeality of my father were fully present, coughing, in me.

4. The important amplification of this mechanism that Freud analyses, and which consists in taking oneself as whole and part, comes in the third example: the one of putting oneself in the *situation* of the other. Here what becomes visible is how the dialectic of parts and whole, even when seemingly extending itself toward the external world, continues to prolong the falsity of one and the same scheme. Even though here I remain as other, what I *equate are the conditions of the world* lived by the other as though these were also mine. I am another different from the other, but his or her world is, by identification, analogous to mine. The structure of the world turns, by identification, into my own structure. The intervening factor here is also the repression that inhibits the real prolongation of my desire towards the world in order to give itself the object that would satisfy it. In this world I cannot be in order to have: my being is, like that of the other, by analogy with my own situation, perennially unsatisfied desire. Thus the real failure of the other, which becomes exacerbated to the point of the absolute in the expression of pain, also announces for me the same impossibility and the same negation.

3   *Identification as the Foundation of Collective Social Bonds*

All these are models of neurosis, of sickness, and the conventional psychoanalyst would not see in them anything other than a strictly individual phenomenon. But Freud prolongs this negation of the dialectic so as to include it in the logic of the social world. In all the cases analysed, what fails, via identification, is the real participation in the structure of the world. However, this very structure of real relations must also correspond to the existence of a repressive social system. What does this mean if not that the destruction of the capacity truly to connect with the real for the sick individual is isomorphic with the destruction of the capacity truly to connect with the real for the artificial masses? Freud, in the identification with *one* situation as if it were the total situation of the world, amplified the field of one-to-one identification and moved on from the one to the many. But immediately he added:

> The more important this commonality is, the more successful may this partial identification become, and it may thus represent the beginning of a new tie. We already begin to divine that the mutual tie between members of a group is in the nature of an identification of this kind, based upon an important emotional common quality; and we may suspect that this commonality lies in the nature of the tie with the leader. (108, translation modified)

It is thus the gradual amplification of the form of part-whole that we are interested in pursuing in Freud's analysis. Because this is the guiding thread for uniting the extremes that previously were separated, whether in mere individual psychology or in social psychology. Identification is the presence of the part in the whole as well as, reciprocally, the presence of the whole in the part. Identification is the unifying nexus, where the convergence of the social and the individual will be verified.

It is in this development that we can inscribe the gradual amplification of the individual phenomenon of identification so as to reach its decisive inscription in the collective processes. To accomplish this Freud will have to show how this twisted logic of parts and whole acquires two fundamental characteristics in the case of collective processes:

1. It turns into a *continuous* and not only transitory form of being and thinking.
2. It is extended to the point of determining the *entire* field of the reality of the common.

Continuous and simultaneous in time and space. Indeed: all these cases that have been analysed, as cases of pathology, presuppose that the real world continues to subsist as such. Hysteria, which is the domain from where Freud took these examples, makes them into *passing* moments within an apparently normal participation in reality; the hysterical fit marks an interruption in the 'normal' life of the patient and exists side by side with it. Thus, the irruption of the symptom introduces the discontinuity of the hysteric fit into the everyday continuum of normality. But if we wish to prolong the problem of individual sickness to the point of reaching the collective determination, we will have to show that there the problem is of a different variety: the continuous defines the predominance of the sick form as habitual mode of existence. This is why the existence of an artificial group or mass presents us with the problem of the *lasting, organised, and directed* subsistence of the concealment of the dialectic of whole and parts, stabilised in time and space as a lasting reality. When sickness ends up constituting the 'normal' form in the collective existence of human beings, the structure that both objectively and subjectively determines this phenomenon must for this reason be *persistent* in time: a lasting and continuous correspondence between subjective form and social structure.

This transition of sickness from discontinuous to continuous form is what interests us in Freud's development. This is what we want to follow. It is not surprising that Freud should move on to analyse the problem of identification in psychosis. In neurosis, as we saw, the conventional reality subsists *side by side with* the hysterical fantasy: there is an alternating passage from one to the other. In psychosis, by contrast, reality as a whole appears transformed in function of the sick subjective organisation. We suspect that in the artificial mass as well the nature of identification will have to be closer to psychosis than to neurosis. For in the artificial mass or group the objective social structure corroborates the subjective fantasy and keeps it from reading itself as sick subjectivity: the individual subjective element forms a system with the objectivity of the social structure.

4   *Homosexual Identification*

Up to now Freud in effect considered the extension of these identifications by taking only *one aspect, one quality*, or *one situation* of the other with whom those identifications took place. By moving on from a quality to a situation, the subjective was extended into the objective, but the level of participation too was extended: from the one-to-one relation, we went to the relation of one to the many. Now, by contrast, the identification he analyses is an *intermediate* situation between neurosis and psychosis: the one in which the subjective transformation implies the identification not with a quality or a situation of the other, but the *whole* sexual being of the *other*. In the sphere of identification, there thus occurs a gradual invasion of the other into the one, which is determining for the mode of conduct. The example Freud here analyses is homosexuality:

> ... after the end of puberty, the time comes for exchanging his mother for some other sexual object. Things take a sudden turn: the young man does not abandon his mother, but identifies himself with her; he transforms

himself into her, and now looks about for objects which can replace his ego for him, and on which he can bestow such love and care as he has experienced from his mother. (108)

What has happened here, as opposed to the other, neurotic identifications, is that the symptom does not express itself in a quality of the other taken as if it were the whole; here the individual has converted himself into the symptom: he is the whole other. He has turned himself, with his actual corporeality, into the other, and he lives himself wholly as if he were the other. Which means that he maintains a set of relations to the whole of reality as if he were that which he is not. The field of fantasy coincides with the field of reality as one body in relation to a whole other body, and not as one part to another part. The individual covers, in his inversion, the full world as his own fully inverted form. The masculine form of the human is lived, as corporeal form, as if it were the feminine form of the human.

> A striking thing about this identification is its ample scale; it remoulds the ego in one of its important features – in its sexual character – upon the model of what has hitherto been the object. In this process the object itself is renounced – whether entirely or in the sense of being preserved only in the unconscious is a question outside the present discussion. Identification with an object that is renounced or lost, as a substitute for that object – introjection of it into the ego (108–9)

It is worth underscoring the ample scale of identification in this case, the substitution of one's own external object in order to become oneself the external objet for others like him. But the difference that has not been developed towards reality in this way is considered as a problem only at the level of the sexual relationship with the world. The other, as model of the object, is in turn entirely summoned up with my own body: and I pursue my relation with the external world in such a way that it treats me just as I treated it. The psychic determination rules over matter to such an extent and acquires such pre-eminence that my whole corporeality serves as support for its signification. The signifier here is not my own body that would prolong itself as signified congruent with the form of the biological determination that it should prolong. The signified, which is that of the other, in this case comes to switch around my body, and without caring for its signifying materiality uses its flesh as support for an incompatible signification. This is the idealism of the (male) homosexual according to Freud: he renounced, for the sake of his object, the signification of his own flesh in order to signify, in the latter, the flesh of the other.

In this way, what Freud underscores in line with his development is the ample scale of this identification: 'A striking thing about this identification is its ample scale'.

In this case, in other words, the substitution of the object, by identification, sketches out an *analogical* dialectic that is much broader than in the cases of hysteria previously described. The relations of the part with the whole, and with the other parts (individual to individual) are preserved and realised. Except that in these bonds that mobilise our bodies, the material difference on which they are based is not the point of departure: the body functions here 'as if'. As if, being a man, he were a woman. 'As if' the spirit, the psychic element, determined matter with indifference to the difference – man, woman – that manifests itself therein. The signified is here, once again, cut off from the material signifier and the psychic determination avoids the dialectic of bodies. But it simulates it and acts accordingly in materiality.

5   *Melancholic Identification*

Another case of amplification, but this time a subjective one, is that of melancholia. In homosexuality the identification with the other makes me live as if I myself were the object of my desire, and I desire in reality in the way I would like the other to desire me. By contrast in melancholic identification the object of my desire does not allow me to live.

> Another such instance of introjection of the object has been provided by the analysis of melancholia, an affection which counts among the most notable of its exciting causes the real or emotional loss of a loved object. A leading characteristic of these cases is a cruel self-depreciation of the ego combined with relentless self-criticism and bitter self-reproaches. Analyses have shown that this disparagement and these reproaches apply at bottom to the object and represent the ego's revenge upon it. The shadow of the object has fallen upon the ego ... (109)

> But these melancholias also show us something else, which may be of importance for our later discussions. They show us the ego divided, fallen apart into two pieces, one of which rages against the second. This second piece is the one which has been altered by introjection and which contains the lost object. But the piece which behaves so cruelly is not unknown to us either. It comprises the conscience, a critical agency within the ego, which even in normal times takes up a critical attitude towards the ego, though never so relentlessly and so unjustifiably. (109)

With melancholia Freud brings us to a more complex situation: the antagonistic organisation with respect to the objective world, but now dramatised in my own subjectivity. Here we can already see that it is not only the introjected other, nor an alien situation assumed as my own, but something more complex and definitive: the existence, at the level of subjectivity, of the contradictory structure present for the human being in relation to a world that has been *entirely* internalised. The relation of the subject with an object in reality is thus framed from within the subject itself, even though split and inverted:

1. The ego, self-deprecated, criticises *itself* and reproaches *itself* (seen from the outside) *as if the subject were one*. This is the level of appearance of the sickness.
2. But, in truth, there exists a subjective dialectic that is invisible from the outside, from within the level of appearance, and which psychoanalysis reveals: in reality the ego criticises and reproaches not *itself* but the object. Because it so happens that the object is no longer outside but inside, introjected. Separated, subject and object are part of the subjective unity. Unable to take revenge against the other in reality, I take the other as the object of fantasy.
3. Thus, a divided ego makes its appearance. If in conventional reality I am one, in the melancholic process this apparent unity becomes dramatically split: one is two. One part of the self relentlessly attacks the other, *within oneself*. But let us look closer at this singular battle: the part that engages in self-criticism and self-reproach is not the part that corresponds to the introjected object. The part that combats the object within, in my own subjectivity, is the same that combats the object without, which since always cruelly attacked the ego. This regulatory aspect of the ego or 'I', this 'critical agency' located in the ego, shows us a splitting prior to this new instance, which constitutes the backdrop against which this subjective dialectic prolongs itself: it is the normal conscience 'which even in normal times takes up a critical attitude towards the ego, though never so relentlessly and so unjustifiably' (109). Here Freud brings to the fore the ego-ideal.
4. The ego-ideal against the ego, both confusing and separating themselves in one: I am both. But the internalised distance of the ego-ideal and the ego is only the form in which I am determined by the other: by the superego. Before the splitting of subjective-subjective, the relation was oriented toward the outside: subjective-objective. Thus what appears within the subject as an agency that the subject would have given to itself is only the form to which I must aspire, if I do not wish to stop being loved by the superego: by the father, who was real before, but now introjected, who

left in me the form of my current being as the only one possible. Thus the ego-ideal only prolongs as if it were mine what in reality belongs to the other. It is the foreign gaze that spies on me and criticises me, fulfilling as my own a set of functions that are alien and defined by the reality of the external world: self-observation, moral conscience, dream censorship, and repression.

5. The origin of these functions clearly shows the external determination (for psychoanalysis) but this is not recognised as such by the subject.

We have said that it [the ego-ideal] is the heir to the original narcissism in which the childish ego enjoyed self-sufficiency; it gradually gathers up from the influences of the environment the demands which that environment makes upon the ego and which the ego cannot always rise to; so that a man, when he cannot be satisfied with his ego itself, may nevertheless be able to find satisfaction in the ego ideal which has been differentiated out of the ego. (110)

Thus the subject returns to the most foreign as the most proper. And it is the ego-ideal that acts as if it were I, the true ego, who engages in the combat against the object. But the object, introjected on the model of the first object, is *oneself made object*. The ideal form of my being, which is that of the being of the other, and which only shows the non-being of what we really are, here occupies the highest point of my being. And therein consists the structure of this internal drama: I, who did not dare losing the object of my love on the outside, made myself by way of repression into this object: I introjected it. But I did so determined not by love for the object but determined by the ego-ideal: I could not stand the humiliation of being abandoned by it without renouncing my ideal – am I unworthy of its love? This renunciation is based on and actualises the terrifying fear of the first abandonment. Because not abandoning my ideal meant, in the final instance, not being able myself to be the other who determined this ideal for me as my own – if I wanted to enjoy his love. It is not out of love for the final object, but out of fidelity for the first object that I am unable to abandon my ideal without also abandoning myself: without ceasing to be. I cannot change my object, but the object that is thus internalised was, at the same time, the authorised object. The object of the narcissistic choice was a bond with *the other like me*; faraway or dead, how could I abandon this object without annihilating myself?

If in melancholia there is introjection of the object, it is because from the start the choice was narcissistic: because 'the object-choice has been effected on a narcissistic basis' ('Mourning and Melancholia', SE 14: 249) But at the same time we are interested in knowing that the aggressiveness we feel towards the object, toward the outside, is not directed in a movement of inversion towards the ego, inside, that is to say, towards the subject's own self. And what is even more surprising: there is enjoyment in this martyrdom:

> The self-tormenting in melancholia, which is without doubt enjoyable, signifies [...] a satisfaction of trends of sadism and hate which relate to an object, and which have been turned round upon the subject's own self ... ('Mourning and Melancholia', SE 14: 251)

This conversion of the external into the internal is the regulating principle of a false relation to reality, of the transformation of a real dialectic (whose form corresponds to the material content) into an imaginary dialectic (in which only the form of the objective world is preserved, but whose content is filled by fantasy in subjectivity). It replaces, in other words, the real signification of the object in the world with the 'psychic' reality, in which one's own body operates as 'world stage', by inscribing the object within itself. This impulse to destroy the object, which I did not dare exercise in the objective world, can go so far as to destroy oneself, based on the belief that one is two. And it is here that we could verify the de-fusing of the life drive and the death drive: in that one kills oneself *as if* one were the other. The initial *as if*, which constitutes an almost insensible solution, a quasi-metaphorical construction, here meets up with the terrible truth of its unforgiving subjective dialectic: one puts oneself to death as if one were the other. But one dies really in one's unique body, which for its part is in fact an unsublimatable unity, and thus goes back to inscribing oneself, against oneself, in the true dialectic, *but when one no longer exists.*

> ... no neurotic harbours thoughts of suicide which he has not turned back upon himself from murderous impulses against others. ('Mourning and Melancholia', SE 14: 252)

This tendency to kill oneself, which is the *necessary* corollary of a merely subjective confrontation with reality, is based on a *subjective simulacrum* that does not look for its verification in the reality in which the object exists or existed but in the unconscious fantasy, which is *not known*:

> In melancholia, accordingly, countless separate struggles are carried on over the object, in which hate and love contend with each other; the one seeks to detach the libido from the object, the other to maintain this

> position of the libido against the assault. The location of these separate struggles cannot be assigned to any system but the unconscious, the region of the memory-traces of *things* [...]. In mourning, too, the efforts to detach the libido are made in this same system; but in it nothing hinders these processes from proceeding along the normal path through the preconscious to consciousness. This path is blocked for the work of melancholia ... ('Mourning and Melancholia', SE 14: 256–257).

And Freud goes on to analyse this remoteness of reality:

> Thus everything to do with these struggles due to ambivalence remains withdrawn from consciousness, until the outcome characteristic of melancholia has set in. ('Mourning and Melancholia', SE 14: 257).

That is to say, we are in a situation where the lapsed object is none other than the subject who made of his or her ego the object of its libido, the object of the id. There is no exit towards reality because there has been no verification in reality, and the conflict was only internal.

Thus love cannot extend itself to the point of encompassing reality with its own corporeality: the other is only a part of the ego. With this Freud reveals the restrictions inherent in the human form, as determined by the repressive social system. How could the senses, 'social in their form', as Marx says, extend their own sensibility and become constituted in the human being as social senses, open to the signification of the structure? The narcissistic form of love is a social form of love, a social sense complementary to the system of production. And if consciousness is not extended toward the real, this is because the rationality in which it moves, and which it was given in order to think itself, cannot embrace more than the inverted subjective conflict in which it is debated – as if this history relative to the world that determined it had to be concealed in the absoluteness of its own origin, which like an unreachable secret lies in the cemetery of its own flesh.

> After this regression of the libido the process can become conscious, and it is represented to consciousness as a conflict between one part of the ego and the critical agency.
>
> What consciousness is aware of in the work of melancholia is thus not the essential part of it, nor is it even the part which we may credit with an influence in bringing the ailment to an end. ('Mourning and Melancholia', SE 14: 257)

This abstract loss that Freud brings to the fore in melancholia presents many analogies that we would like to retain in order to understand the subjectivity of the human being subjected to the mass or group of a repressive system. Fundamentally what interests us is this consequence with regard to the truth that the ailing subject reaches about his own reality: the consciousness of the drama it lives through. The ailing person, Freud says, 'knows *whom* he has lost but not *what* he has lost in him' ('Mourning and Melancholia', SE 14: 245). He does not situate the object in the real configuration that gives it its true meaning. He only focuses on his loss as empirical object, the materiality of his individuality (*whom* he has lost), but he does not take into account his psychic content: the foundation of the value he has for him (*what* he has lost). This is why 'the psychic existence of the object' continues, *unconscious*, and the melancholic subject does not see that his real loss has for him an 'ideal' signification that he does not know: 'there is a loss of a more ideal kind' (245). This is why Freud says:

> This would suggest that melancholia is in some way related to an object-loss which is withdrawn from consciousness, in contradistinction to mourning, in which there is nothing about the loss that is unconscious. ('Mourning and Melancholia', SE 14: 245)

What remains unconscious, for the melancholic, is the real content of the loss: The loss is unknown.

Thus the lack of signification that we subtracted from the real object on the outside remains inside as a merely psychic content, as if it were not the result of an original process in which, due to my relation with the primordial other, there were objects for me and this opened up the meaning of the world. But now this lack is lived as if it were only subjective: we are its unconscious support, only the result, without history. This form prolonged itself, when we were already adults, as the normal form of every objective relation. The materiality without outside meaning finds its signification without matter inside: mere psychic content. Perhaps this extreme point of dissociation, in which signification does not manage to recuperate its source in the reality of the external world, because originally it did not have it and could no know it, may adequately express the separation between the rational and the sensible, between signification and the material dialectic that produces it in the world.

This is why, in our opinion, Freud ends his chapter on identification in *Group Psychology* by trying to relocate the social determination that is the foundation of this scission:

> ... by way of functions we have ascribed to it [the ego ideal] self-observation, the moral conscience, the censorship of dreams, and the chief influence in repression. We have said that it is the heir to the original narcissism in which the childish ego enjoyed self-sufficiency; it gradually gathers up from the influences of the environment the demands which that environment makes upon the ego and which the ego cannot always rise to; so that a man, when he cannot be satisfied with his ego itself, may nevertheless be able to find satisfaction in the ego ideal which has been differentiated out of the ego. In delusions of observation, as we have further shown, the disintegration of this agency has become patent, and has thus revealed its origin in the influence of superior powers, and above all of parents. (110)

Clearly, in the decomposition of the 'ego ideal' there appears what sits at the origin, but concealed: the familiar repression, through which the model of the disappearing social system is filtered as external.

It is this internalisation of the real dialectic, turned into a merely subjective dialectic, in which the only materiality that serves as the basis for development is the individual materiality of one's own body, as part and whole at the same time, which Freud invites us to retain for his later analyses with reference to the masses:

> But these melancholias also show us something else, which may be of importance for our later discussions. They show us the ego divided, fallen apart into two pieces, one of which rages against the second. This second piece is the one which has been altered by introjection and which contains the lost object. (109)

The division and separation between the human being and the world, therefore, was a purely subjective separation: between me and myself.

VII   Being in Love and Hypnosis: From Individual Dependency to Social Dependency

In the previous chapter we saw the decomposition of the compact appearance of subjective individuality. Beyond the visible empirical relations that the stabilised subjects sketch out in their corporeal exteriority, we saw the appearance of relations in which the psychic content gained the upper hand over the carnal foundation and the real-material organisation of the world. The axiom proclaiming the impenetrability of bodies comes undone at the level of psychology: a body is penetrated, invaded, replaced by another. And yet, in parallel, the physical reality of the law that governs us is maintained: the other is at the same time outside of me, really other, already living next to me, whether he or she is at a far remove from me or becomes disaggregated as a lifeless body on the ground fusing once again with the inorganic. The reality of 'psychic life' explodes here in its contradiction with the reality of merely physical or biological existence. But in the spiritualism of the sick dialectic the 'psychic reality' is not the affirmed continuity of biological reality. On the contrary, it is opposed to it like the spirit to the body, as two antagonistic substances each of which, in its development, would necessarily imply the abstract negation and setting aside of the other. This destruction of the dialectic emerges in the case of illness. But it only becomes visible and understandable for someone who, like Freud, affirms a continuity and a process in which the biological is not negated but continued and affirmed in the psychic – in which, therefore, the psychic element emerges as a cultural particularisation *in* the medium of life itself. In other words, for someone for whom the cultural corporeality continues to be affirmed as the index of the congruence or incongruence of the truth or falsity of the historical elaboration. And it is the integration of the human body in the world that puts this to the test.

Thus, for psychology, identification is the matrix of all human exchange. What human beings exchange is the carnal and signifying form of the other on the basis of which each one gains access to historical existence. This coincidence of one with the other, this 'libidinal coupling' in which even Husserl had to locate the foundation of all eidetic signification, is the incarnated foundation from which all signification derives, no matter how far removed the cultural body that signifies it appears to be in its abstract ideality. This pairing and this covering of bodies is what defines and forms the base of every synthesis of consciousness.

But this dualism, which becomes evident in the 'decomposition' of the ego ideal, in mental illness, would this not also be the basis of contradictory societies, in particular for our case, in capitalism? Does this not become evident in the decomposition of the ideal – the formal principles of bourgeois egalitarianism – that governs these social processes? Are these not governed by the dualism of a scission that, by privileging the spiritual 'psychic reality', also maintains itself *alongside* a material organisation reduced to its merely empirical insignificance in the material processes of production, which nonetheless are the determining ones?

But before moving on to this analysis, Freud not only stays on the level of mental illness, he also has to bring out these same phenomena of identification – the ones that become visible in the fissure of mental illness – in the articulation of the 'normal' individuality. No longer just there where the object in its materiality is merely the imaginary or dispensable support – 'the *shadow of the object*' that falls over the ego – he also must bring out the modality that the object acquires when it is really affirmed, in its exteriority, in the love relationship: there where 'the object, so to speak, has consumed the ego' (113).

Let us then have a clearer look at this 'normal' phenomenon. We had already analysed the 'amplified notion of love', from self-love to the love of humanity. But in this chapter Freud is going to show us a minimal social process, the historical 'cell' on whose development it will depend, according to the system in which it is inscribed, whether it culminates in a form of artificial mass or in a revolutionary mass.

1   *From the Fleeting Moment to Permanence*
Freud is going to show us that there is a 'scale' within the reciprocal relations that the ego sustains with its object. This scale would express a vertical cut, in depth, with respect to that other, horizontal one in which we showed the transition that went from the relation with the father to the broader forms of collective organisation (see pages 370–71). The two are complementary to each other. This scale reveals the amplification (or restriction) in the sense of the 'libidinal investment' of the object, which thus would determine its inscription in the world as human object. It would show us the transition from the object's material presence to its conversion into a cultural object, animated by the signification that we project onto it. In this way, there is a transition from the abstract to the concrete, the appearance of basic categories around which the historical and cultural determination of the object becomes solidified. There is first a transition from the *fleeting* libidinal investment of the object that subsequently turns into a *lasting* one. And then we see the appearance of a new modality in the material relation, which incorporates into the object of desire the lasting signification of a continuous and sustained relationship. This affirmation of the object beyond the fleeting instant of satisfaction situates it in the time and space of a new domain of objectivity:

> In one class of cases being in love is nothing more than object-cathexis on the part of the sexual instincts with a view to directly sexual satisfaction, a cathexis which expires, moreover, when this aim has been reached; this is what is called common, sensual love. (111)

The body of the other here signifies only in the instant of desire and its signification is exhausted together with the punctual moment of satisfaction. Its presence almost signifies its naked and natural corporeity. This extreme, in which the signification of the empirical body of the other is exhausted in the instantaneous satisfaction, would show this *minimum* in the scale of possible relations in which a cultural body coincides in the requirement of the other as adequate for its desire.

> It was possible to calculate with certainty upon the revival of the need which had just expired; and this must no doubt have been the first motive for directing a lasting cathexis upon the sexual object and for 'loving' it in the passionless intervals as well. (111)

The presence, in the interval, of the previously lived relationship, the known persistence of desire in its absence, thus opens up in the bond with the other a *continuous* field of relations in which the first remains incorporated, beyond the instant of satisfaction, also in its persistent and continuous actuality. The object of my desire extends its existence beyond the punctual act of fleeting love, so as to become integrated in the quotidian reality of the interval, where its other aspects and qualities also remain incorporated that determine it in its being for me. In the persistent presence of the other, the instant of pleasure opens up the continuity that also links it to non-pleasure and even to moments of displeasure and suffering. Pleasure does not stay separated from non-pleasure, and desire incorporates the persistent signification of the other as necessary for my pleasure. There has occurred an amplification of the *minimum* in continuity.

This process refers to the development of culture or civilisation among adults, signalling to us the essence of its historico-cultural phylogenesis. But *within an already constituted civilisation*, as in the case of ours, there is another factor that intervenes in the individual transition, and here the genesis shows us the infantile genesis of this access that in the child leads from the atemporal to the temporal and culminates in the persistence of the other beyond the instant:

> To this must be added another factor derived from the very remarkable course of development which is pursued by the erotic life of man. In its first phase, which has usually come to an end by the time a child is five years old, he has found the first object for his love in one or other of his parents, and all of his sexual instincts with their demand for satisfaction have been united upon this object. The repression which then sets in compels him to renounce the greater number of these infantile sexual aims, and leaves behind a profound modification in his relation to his parents.

> The child still remains tied to his parents, but by instincts which must be described as being 'inhibited in their aim'. The emotions which he feels henceforward towards these objects of his love are characterised as 'affectionate'. It is well known that the earlier 'sensual' tendencies remain more or less strongly preserved in the unconscious, so that in a certain sense the whole of the original current continues to exist. (111)

The point of departure in the case of the child is not the reality of genital sexual satisfaction, as in the phylogenetic description, but *the fantasy of satisfaction*. There is as yet no real time and space in which to inscribe this relation: they are relationships in which the persistence of the object of desire is also fantasied. Hallucination makes it appear as present in oneself when the desire returns, without having to confront the conditions of its effective external reality. But the first great reality test that is the resolution of the Oedipus complex permits the effectuation of a great step forward in the transition toward the world of civilisation. The fantasy of satisfaction, projected onto the loved object, must recognise it in its persistent reality as object of the other's *real* sexual desire, in the face of which the illusory character of my own desire gives ground. And the appearance of the 'affectionate' feeling connects with the reality of the prolongation of this fantasy whose limitation is here verified. The 'sexual' tendencies that tied me to the object of my desire are preserved, and for them too, with the body's maturation in which the imaginary capacity of connecting corporeally and effectively with an object becomes real, a second verification must come into play in which those tendencies now actually do prolong themselves in a real other, beyond the constellation of family and incest.

2 From the Affectionate to the Earthly

This is why Freud promptly moves on to the 'reality test' that is offered to us in puberty. Here, with the awakening of a real power, the body must recognise the transformation of its infantile fantasy in the effective adult relation with the real object of its desire. The first fantasy now verifies itself in the real body of the other towards which converges the result of the first 'experience of reality' of the dénouement of the Oedipus complex – the 'affectionate feelings' – whereby the latter adds this: the satisfaction, at last, of the directly sexual aims that before it had to postpone and that in reality it could exercise only in its imagination, for lack of a mature body with which the child might actualise them. But this prolongation in the direction of reality does not always verify this increment:

> At puberty, as we know, there set in new and very strong impulsions towards directly sexual aims. In unfavourable cases they remain separate, in the form of a sensual current, from the 'affectionate' trends of feeling which persist. We then have before us a picture whose two aspects are typified with such delight by certain schools of literature. A man will show a sentimental enthusiasm for women whom he deeply respects but who do not excite him to sexual activities, and he will only be potent with other women whom he does not 'love' and thinks little of or even despises. More often, however, the adolescent succeeds in bringing about a certain degree of synthesis between the unsensual, heavenly love and the sensual, earthly love, and his relation to his sexual object is characterised by the interaction of uninhibited instincts and of instincts inhibited in their aim. The depth to which anyone is in love, as contrasted with his purely sensual desire, may be measured by the size of the share taken by the aim-inhibited instincts of affection. (112)

Thus in the midst of 'normal' love and, more precisely, in that state of 'romantic love' exalted in our culture ('typified with such delight by certain schools of literature', Freud says), a dissociation appears. What has happened? The first sexual tendencies, previously repressed, now *leap* toward reality *without passing* through the feelings of affection: repression was unable to maintain the contact between the repressed and the authorised; the affectionate bond with the parents did not prolong itself, carrying with it the body as a unit in the same affect. There was no transition from the instant of fantasied satisfaction to the lasting affectionate feeling of real satisfaction. This scission between the imaginary and the real, between the instant and the long term, will be prolonged in reality *later*, in the mature corporeality, as the separation between objects, in which the same tendency is condemned to an alternating and never satisfied oscillation, between a flesh without signification and a signification without flesh. But this relation with the originary other is the prototype, Freud told us, of every human relation and every form of happiness. This split scheme brings up two opposed temporalities, which contradictorily determine the link with the *whole* of reality. Where the spiritual signification and the persistent link of a sustained and accepted bond appear, there the flesh disappears as foundation together with the unitary satisfaction that comes tied to it. This temporality, the time of the affectionate and lasting feeling, is the time of official culture and of the social forms that this culture validates, just as in the beginning it validated the emergence of the tolerated realm in our own affectionate feeling: shorn of the determining unity of its sexual tendencies. There where desire appears prolonged in the body, only an element outside of the time and space of sociality prevails, and the object of desire must remove from itself any signification that would situate it in the cordoned off cultural order: it only lives in the fleeting life of clandestinity without signification. But the very lack of cultural signification is already a signification: it signifies its incoherence with regard to the repressive order. And there where the insufficiency of the body seems to validate the pure signification, there also is a body, albeit devalued: the support of significations that the flesh abhors and which, for this very reason, signifies its particular value – its value for repression.

These contradictory forms configure the categorial 'a priori' of time that will orient every subsequent relation with reality. And these categories signify that our most profound, most persistent desire must desist in giving itself a persistent object: it is condemned forever to the domain of the instantaneous and of the imaginary.

This is why Freud, once again, shows us two fields, in which the world of culture or civilisation inscribes the dualism in the individual:

1. Spiritual and asexual love: inscribed in the *real* time and space.
2. Sexual and earthly love: inscribed in the *imaginary* time and space.

This inversion should not surprise us. What is most proper to us is lived as the least real; what is most alien to us is lived as the most real. These categories are already, in their prolongation, *social* categories. This is the form that civilisation imposes on the qualitative body of the human subject, and what gives it its meaning.

But, the question then becomes: how is it possible to be in love and reconcile this opposition, if this opposition is necessarily present in love? Let us remember that the signification which finds its logical and rational link with the real is the one that is tied to the 'instincts inhibited in their aim', and, thus, to the state of sensible and affective insignificance. Meanwhile the unconscious, repressed signification, in contrast to the other, has no logical or rational area of deployment to which it might link the desire of the flesh: for this all it has are metaphorical relations and metonymical connections in which to pursue the development of its process. They are condemned not to be deciphered by the consciousness of their own subjectivity. They can only be acted out and lived in the fleeting drama of a guilty and transgressive instant.

If 'more often' than not there occurs a falling in love, does this mean that the multitude of 'normal' people live a true reality to which the split subject of the neurotic has no access? Does this mean, perhaps, that in their case the transition to reality was able to articulate itself without fissure? Because the problem lies in the fact that the 'normal' mass or group, which is the artificial mass, is in turn composed of 'normal' people. But Freud, as we saw, did not consider the artificial mass the highest point reached in the equilibrium but, on the contrary, the conjunction in which the imbalance of the institutionalised system formed split subjects that were adequate to its good functioning. The appearance of normality therefore must cover up an abnormality that is more difficult to detect. This is the reason why the analysis of being in love puts us on the track of this 'normal' subjective organisation, which nonetheless, due to its structure, prepares already the possible form of social dependency in the subject of the artificial mass.

Let us keep in mind that Freud begins with 'being in love' and thus not with simple sexual desire. He begins with the subject in whom the 'instincts inhibited in their aim' were integrated, as affectionate feelings, into sexuality. In other words he begins from that 'normal' case in which the equilibrium of civilisation produces *passion integrated into reason*: within the domain of permanence in which the fleeting instant would also find itself included.

> In connection with this question of being in love we have always been struck by the phenomenon of sexual overvaluation – the fact that the loved object enjoys a certain amount of freedom from criticism, and that all its characteristics are valued more highly than those of people who are not loved, or than its own were at a time when it itself was not loved. If the sensual impulses are more or less effectively repressed or set aside, the illusion is produced that the object has come to be sensually loved on account of its spiritual merits, whereas on the contrary these merits may really only have been lent to it by its sensual charm. (112)

What has happened is that a process of inversion has taken place *even in the case of the normal subject*. People *believe* they love the other for his or her qualitative and not merely sensual merits, they *believe* they are attracted because of a rational evaluation and not out of passion: they *believe* themselves to be passionate, in their noble heart, about the other's 'spiritual merits', which from the heaven of values would project their halo onto the flesh. This is the illusion, Freud tells us. In reality, he corrects himself, it is the sensual attraction that leads people to 'lend these merits' to the object of their love. In the end, this is the ruse of the vanquished flesh: the real attraction gives itself an ideal 'reason' to love the other. *It must give itself* this reason in order to justify its attraction. But, unfortunately, its judgment is false.

> The tendency which falsifies judgement in this respect is that of idealisation. But now it is easier for us to find our bearings. We see that the object is being treated in the same way as our own ego, so that when we are in love a considerable amount of narcissistic libido overflows on to the object. It is even obvious, in many forms of love-choice, that the object serves as a substitute for some unattained ego ideal of our own. (112)

What new trap is here set up around the solipsism of the ego? What apparent opening is Freud here trying to capture in the very moment of the greatest affective intensity aimed at the real and exterior object of my desire? In the final instance, he says: to love the other with our body, we must invest it with the other's rational form that prolongs itself through our own ego. At the very moment I love the other, I am loving in him only the form of the other, which precisely is not this other whom I have in front of me. The exaltation of my own impulses that converge toward their object need, by way of correlation, the exaltation of my own ideal, which is the ideal of the other, projected onto the object. Thus, there also is no verification, not even in the object of my love: the qualitative dissociation that the ideal imposes on me at the same time keeps me from letting the qualitative difference emerge that my impulses discover in the reality of my sensible and carnal affect. The other's difference and qualitative complementarity with me, that toward which my desire is inclined, this is *not perceived*: the object of my desire, in order to be loved, receives my own form, that of my own ego, which means only that I invest the object as if I wanted that which the other ordered me to do. And what did the other order? That I should not love from the flesh but with the affectionate feeling that is devoid of the body, or with the body repressed. In the moment of maximum fusion with the other, in which the unstoppable impulses of the id pass over into reality, I nevertheless continue to be its object. Only by way of this transaction can the id pass over into reality. What has happened? The fact that reality here always takes the form of the other, that love does not open me up to the real other with whom my differences can be developed on the basis of sexual difference, that I love from within the domain of similitude because I inhibited the essential difference. This transaction is the knot that ties together the two opposed extremes: rationality, turned into ideal, and therefore absolutised as transcendence; and the flesh, investing the form of the ego, whose rational and conscious norm continues to move always with the coherence of the repressive authority. This is why Freud can say, in *Civilisation and Its Discontents*, that the 'normal' couple in our cultural system is a 'double individuality': each one sees in the other not the other but their own ego. And in this appearance of coincidence the bodies continue to be unable to develop that rationality that from the flesh emerges as the sensible difference that prolongs itself in the direction of the world: the body remains imprisoned around an abstract sex without reason and without signification. For the realm of signification, which should opens itself to the form that the other, as person, presents in the world as human form, locks itself up in the repetition of the same: the longed-for father or mother repeat ad infinitum this game of reflections in the mirror whose shadows are all we see in the other.

3 *The Duration of the System, Foundation of Sexual Pleasure*

Thus the alternation *simulates* continuity: the exaltation of the body in the sexual embrace is the instant in which the infraction opens for me the transition towards the flesh of the other covered under my own in exact adequacy. This is the moment of sensuality. But this instant does not continue into the affectionate feeling in which it must find its prolongation. Instantaneity is followed by permanence, that is to say, the emergence of a new time opened up to everyday reality. But in this domain it is the form of the other that is predominant: what prevails is the superego. In this way we go back from the flesh to the everyday reality of affectionate feelings, towards the shared time and history. Here what predominates is a time without body, the ideality of the superego tracing the form of all life and all effective reality, to which we guiltily return and in which we submerge ourselves anew. What predominates is the objective time of the system of production, in which the superego prolongs itself in the affirmation of the collective superego, as models that are congruent with the system that produced us. Every system of production is a system for producing human subjects, and here we see how the system produces us, even in the conduct of maximum exaltation of the other as object of our most intimate and most particularised desire, as human beings adequate to the system itself. At the heart of the most personal act of loving the other, where the spasmodic synthesis of the body would also seem to be the synthesis of the world of culture or civilisation, we once again come across the fundamental dualism of the system as that which orients and gives form to the thin mesh in which everything is woven together: the infinity of a flesh without time, which tolerates only the instant of exaltation, and the finitude of an affectionate feeling where the regulated and uniform reality of the everyday introduces us, by way of guilt, into the field of human subjectivity.

Thus the indices of objective reality disappear as significations that I might verify from within my body. In the same way that the love object, in order to be loved, enjoyed a certain 'freedom from criticism', while 'all its characteristics are valued more highly', so too all affective perception that exalts itself in the direction of the world will happen only when we will have projected onto the object the ideality that deforms it while making it conform to the form of the superego. The rational form that comes from the ego ideal is exalted to the point of making it coincide, in a completely external coincidence, with the impulses of the id. The a priori categories of the ideality of the ego are thus filled up with the sensibility of the postponed body, which makes itself 'official'. The ego in other words performed its transaction: it satisfied the sexual impulses of the id, but by paying the price of subjecting itself as critical agency. It transforms the presence of the other by giving it the only form that makes it compatible with itself. But this ideality projected onto the other necessarily determines the ideality of every perception of reality.

What have we done at the same time? We have parcelled out our sensibility. The impulses that pass over into satisfaction are determined as 'narcissistic libido': I use my body to cover that which the love object has in common with me, and homosexuality filters itself into this form of the self, which is that of the other, now projected into the object of my desire. In the other, as object of my love, I love the other from whom I could neither separate nor differentiate myself. Because in reality what I discover in the other as exaltation of my love is this equivalence and this similitude that is the fruit of the exaltation provoked in me by what we have in common: whatever aspect of me there is in the other. Thus, the repressed impulses carve out a path for themselves, now that they are in part liberated, the floodgates having been opened that allow them to pass over into the corporeality of the other taken as object. But what thus happens is what repression repressed, halted, and conformed as hallucinatory object: the primordial other that was the object of my first love, which returns once more from the original introjection, now in projection. In the guise of the ego ideal that I project onto the other, it is the sensible form, held back and repressed, which once more with the mechanism of the primary process goes out in search of that first object, but now outwards and without pausing on the details: every other is good to the extent that it serves to project onto it, as unique and irreducible but in reality as mere support, a fantasy that uses the other's body to acquire the maximum certainty of its own absolute reality. It suffices that its form is approximate, man for woman, woman for man, and that is enough: the qualitative content is what I posit. The exaltation of sex erases the differences: at bottom they are equivalent, just as I am equivalent to the ego ideal.

Thus to the ideality of the ego there corresponds the idealisation of reality. As opposed to what happens in the pathological processes, this coincidence passes for being 'normal'; the subjective trap coincides with the objective world, and in this consolidation of appearance, in which the subjective covers so exactly the objective, there is no longer anything that betrays it. And whatever could be betrayed as being unsatisfying is explained on account of the necessary disillusionment that all love brings with it, insofar as time, far from being constructive, as they say, 'destroys everything': the continuity necessarily dissolves the first instant of passion. Thus the normal form of official love sends it back, exhausted, to the reality of the first mirage. But what could be denounced, the meaning of this transaction, is no longer readable at the level of the relation of the 'couple', of the 'double individuality'. It must be read in the constant modification that this transaction introduced in the lasting relation with the system of reality to which the affectionate, dispassionate, and realistic love relation led us: to the acceptance of the determinations of the system of production.

This is why Freud moves on from pathology to normality. For in the former case identification, through the hiatus between the subjective and the objective, still makes visible for the others the discrepancy that denounces the senselessness of the transaction. The transaction in the case of illness was only subjective, as the body took itself to be both part and whole. Whereas here, in the projection that links me to the real and external objects, this transaction becomes invisible because it coincides with objective reality. The illusion covers the real form of the external love object, and this coincidence is no longer relevant with regard to the individual but presents other demands in order to be perceived as that which it is in reality: a generalised form of social transaction. The hiatus shown in the individual, because it appears subjectively as complacency and satisfaction, can be read only at the level of the global contradiction of the productive system.

The important thing to retain from all these Freudian analyses in our view is the following: how even the most narrow and singularised relation with the other, in its closest carnality, appears determined by the cultural form that split in us the rational signification by separating it from the corporeal power that gives it meaning, and which is its point of affirmation in reality. The human form that thus is organised, even in its closest relation with the heterogeneous other, in its most intimate and most personal desire, is a form of depersonalisation. It is the presence of the system insofar as it covers up and destroys the understanding and intelligibility with regard to its own origin, installed in the very depths of the human subject who emerges into the real.

This determination of the system, as we saw, conforms both the subject and the object. This is why the object – the other – is not for Freud mere sensibility: what prevails in it is a determinate 'form'. And this conjunction of the ego ideal, which forms and confuses itself with the sensible form of the other, thus gradually shows us the congruence of the form of the human being and its content: the extreme case of the object relation, in which the object of the external world is the heterogeneous other – man for woman, woman for man – within the homogeneity of the human being. There where apparently we have maximum proximity to the sensible other, where one body welcomes the other at the level of all the senses, there also appears, as setting the rules for this relation, the ideal determination, the form of the other extended and completing the object so as to turn it into a possible object of our desire. And without which it could not be such.

This dominion of ideality is verified in the case of the adolescent, when being in love, in the state of sexual overestimation, leads to the total repression of directly sexual satisfaction. It is here where 'the object has, so to speak, consumed the ego', because out of love for the object I give up precisely on the satisfaction that led me to it. Here it is no longer 'the shadow of the object' that falls over the ego, as in the case of melancholia, where the object lives the subjective life that we lend to it in our own bodies. No, here it is 'the object' that has consumed the ego, the real and external object, which exists outside of me, in which therefore it would seem to be confirmed, at last, that my ideality meets up again with the objective conditions of material reality.

4   *The Ideality of the Subjected Flesh*

What does Freud wish to show here? That the apparent renouncing of sensuality is in fact the renouncing of ideality. That ideality passes into the sensible and conforms the sensible presence of the other. That it is this ideality, in other words, which gives meaning to the other's corporeality – just as it gave to mine. And I would say that this ideality, which is ignored and which prolongs itself in the ego ideal, is determined by the superego, hence, by the prolongation of the sensible father who is introjected and now converted into the formal model, the regulating and normative conscience that gives expression not to the subject's normativity but to the normativity of the system that produced this subject. But, even more: that this normativity incorporated into the ego *ignores its origin*. Therefore, it is an ideality which, because it is elevated into the absolute and transcendence, continues to rule not only my own flesh but also every relation with the others, as if it were their 'natural' personal form, where the farthest converges with and determines the nearest. This happens to such a point that the form of the system of production already ends up being engraved in the personal form as the only possible form of being.

This is why Freud can say:

> Contemporaneously with this 'devotion' of the ego to the object, which is no longer to be distinguished from a sublimated devotion to an abstract idea, the functions allotted to the ego ideal entirely cease to operate. The criticism exercised by that agency is silent; everything that the object does and asks for is right and blameless. Conscience has no application to anything that is done for the sake of the object; in the blindness of love remorselessness is carried to the pitch of crime. The whole situation can be completely summarised in a formula: *The object has been put in the place of the ego ideal.* (113, emphasis added)

Why is love for the object not differentiated from love for an abstract idea? Because here the flesh, together with the meaning that emerges and prolongs itself from it, disappears as effective index of reality. Here there appears a form without quality, the predominance of the rationality – the ideal of the ego – that covers over the object and inscribes it, whatever its real objective and historical meaning may be – *in the system itself*: in the repressive system. This is then the most important consequence: any relation that implies the affirmation of my body implies essentially and necessarily, at the same time, that its cultural signification be inscribed in a manner that is coherent with the repressive system. What appears as devotion to purely sensual love, the kind of love that rises up from the deepest and darkest viscosities of nature present in me, already carries with it the rationality of the system as the track along which its irresistible impetuousness is nevertheless steered.

This is why 'devotion to an abstract idea' is no different from this kind of love: what is different between them is not the fact that one would involve the flesh and the other a mere idea. No: both in reality involve the ideality without body – already constituted and consolidated forms and orderings. In both what prevails is the rationality of one and the same structure *without verification*. To think or to love, within these cultural determinations, means the same thing: not to be able to broaden the field of rationality that confines us, limits us, besieges us, and installs us in the impossibility of broadening the true meaning of the world, of assuming the contradiction of a reality that remained *halted* within us, no matter how much we love or how much we think.

And so there is no criticism with regard to the other nor any criticism of the truth of the world in which we live as thinking and loving beings. In our submission to the object or to the abstract idea, the only thing that is affirmed is the persistence of the repressive system. To establish any relation to the world, whether felt or thought, means to affirm as its foundation the system on the basis of which we affirm this reality. And it will not do to say that this cannot be known or felt: therein lies precisely its power. Not being able to feel or think except within the limits of this homogeneity, outside of which to love implies precisely that the object of love is inadequate and not lovable, that the abstract idea of thought is incoherent and false. In both areas we are besieged either by the inability to know or by the absence of affectivity, which appear *as if* they came from the object or the idea when in reality we are the ones who are unable to feel or think that which does not agree, not only with what we believe ourselves to be but also with what we were ordered to be. In other words, we are acting out the negation in the domain and element in which the true dialectic is at play, but without being able to see it. We live in relation to the other, but the other in truth is not connected to the system of reality: the first identification, in which we were whole and part at the same time, finds in this totality internalised as model the meaning with which we invest the signification of everything that is real. The totality of the real, which comes to us from the objective organisation of the historical system of production, does not configure the framework to be conquered so as to inscribe in it the meaning of our actions. As adults we continue to be governed by a pseudo-totality, which once it is incorporated continues to segregate and determine the meaning of our loving and our thinking. And, within this opposition, all the openings onto the real appear to have been jealously and terrifyingly guarded: in the kind of love that does not have the form of the other what sticks out is the anxiety of death opened up by the negation of the superego that gives us life, just as in the act in which to think would imply to put ourselves at stake, in our own corporeality, as signifying difference. And, because it has its origin in the negation of what sustains us, the difference is a deadly difference. The anxiety in the face of death makes sure that we do not confront life, and that we cave in to a simulacrum in which narcissism, the curling up into the same, boxes us into the infinite illusion of being outside of time and in the absoluteness of the most profound kind of loving and thinking, which is only the profundity of the abyss and the void that opens up before the lack of reality – other than what is given.

However, what this process shows us, in synthesis, is the moment in which *the ego has made itself into the object*: it alienated itself in the other. It reified itself in the form of the other and now attempts to reach itself in the other, having made itself in the other into that which the ego itself cannot be without negating itself. Thus an impossible comprehension rides on top of the sexual need, an understanding which nevertheless is situated in the time of development of history and turns into its opposite: in the illusion of an instant in which *the coincidence of the ego ideal with the ego* becomes materialised. It is consumed in the time *outside time* and in the materiality *outside matter*. In the time of the sexual relationship, where the flesh of the other animates our impulses with which the atemporal and anonymous id passes over into reality, this impulse in order to erase its own meaning pairs up with the time of the ego ideal, which becomes transmogrified in the 'coincidence' with its object in absolute verification, the infinity of an hallucinated flesh.

Identification, then, does not belong only to the domain of illness, which would cease to be the only one in which the dialectic of whole and parts would appear to be negated. In normality, too, this process of identification has a generalised applicability. Its difference consists only in a nuance, albeit an important one. This is why Freud asks himself: 'Can there be no identification while the object is *retained*?' (114). That is to say, retained as such, objectively, in external reality, which is something that in the case of illness turned out to be suppressed in favour of the introjected object.

All this means that the object, whether it is retained or not, *loses in both cases its reality* so as to become integrated, either outside or within the subject, into the field of fantasy and subjectivity. *The essential point therefore is not that the object subsists or disappears as empirical object. What matters in both cases is the exclusive predominance of its psychic existence and, thus, of its ideality*, which also means of its predominantly subjective existence, *even though the object, as the support of ideality, remains*. Its function is not restricted to its empirical reality, but its reality serves only as the support for the form that we impose on it. And here, in the analysis of the essence of identification, it is a matter of indifference whether this operation becomes realised within, on our own body (illness), or without, on the body of the other (normality): in both cases it lacks the part of verification and the particularity of the individual fails to be developed.

This is why, no matter how paradoxical it may seem, the problem revolves neither around one's own body or the body of the other in the conduct of the subject. The problem is necessarily that of the relation of the human subject *with the cultural system's domain of reality* in which this conduct acquires meaning and determines its true or false signification. Because what normality and sickness shows us as difference is the following:

1. In the case of 'illness', the agreement concerns only the subject with itself: with the world internalised in its subjectivity, itself being part and whole, at the same time.

2. In the case of 'normality', the agreement occurs only with the conventional outside milieu, but it is also a semblance that here appears. The objective domain is nothing but the domain of an agreement that does not effectively broaden the limits of the individual, in spite of giving itself the semblance of 'materially' being inscribed in the world. Its solution continues to be narcissistic, and the repressive immobility of the external world substitutes itself for the immobility of fantasy. But to this end the structure of the cultural system displays a simulated agreement, one that the subject 'rediscovers' as its own, but that only provides the persistence of the system itself. The subject turned itself into a structure that produces the agreement in its own irreducible sameness. The limits of the subject remain immobile as much as the limits of the world.

This is why the difference between one case and the other is clearly expressed in Freud's analysis: it depends on 'whether the object is put in the place of the ego [melancholy] or of the ego ideal [being in love]' (114).

5   *From Individual Dependency to Social Dependency: Hypnosis*

However, it is not only in the condition of being in love that the object is situated in the place of the ego ideal. The same occurs in hypnosis, except that here the difference is a difference between form and content.

In the case of being in love the object remained invested with the maximum of individual libido: the relation was one of body to body, sense to sense, organ to organ, sex to sex. In hypnosis we are going to arrive at a 'purer' form of identification: 'with sexual satisfaction excluded' (115). As we will see later on, here the relation is the least embodied, almost purely 'spiritual', only gaze to gaze. But this is why it shows as a purer form: because *it is a social form of dependency on the other, any other, which exerts this power over us, linking us to him or her.* Almost disembodied, the hypnotic relation actualises the power of the pure form of the other and imposes it on us.

Thus, being in love would only be a particular case of the relation with an object situated in the place of the ego ideal, whose *general* form is the one that appears in hypnosis: 'it would be more to the point to explain being in love by means of hypnosis than the other way round' (114).

Humble subjection, compliance, absence of criticism, sapping of the subject's own initiative: these features are all common to being in love and hypnosis.

> The hypnotist is the sole object, and no attention is paid to any but him. The fact that the ego experiences in a dream-like way whatever he may request or assert reminds us that we omitted to mention among the func-

tions of the ego ideal the business of testing the reality of things. No wonder that the ego takes a perception for real if its reality is vouched for by the mental agency which ordinarily discharges the duty of testing the reality of things. (114)

This is obviously the most important consequence to be stressed: in both cases, being in love and hypnosis, *the testing of reality is suppressed in the ego under the appearance of its exercise*. The real is what coincides with the ego ideal, which is only the ideal of the other. And generally: the ideal of the cultural system that produced us as subjects adequate to it. Except that here, Freud tells us, this form is purer, and we will see that it is precisely in this purity that its eminently social and generalisable character consists. Here the other, the hypnotist, is only the material support in the exercise of a social function, the most primitive function of all, which is renewed in the collective relation: the first relation, in which the other emerged originally for us with his absolute character – the father – to whose fascinating gaze we remained subjected, and it is renewed in the social other – the leader – whom libidinal indifference and the lack of social satisfaction turn into an absolute external object, *but which now is shareable*, in its gaze without flesh.

> But on the other hand we may also say that the hypnotic relation is (if the expression is permissible) a group formation with two members. Hypnosis is not a good object for comparison with a group formation, because it is truer to say that it is identical with it. Out of the complicated fabric of the group it isolates one element for us – the behaviour of the individual to the leader. (115)

It is here where the apparent contradiction, presented both in social psychology and in individual psychology, coincides in one and the same object: the *social* aspect of the system is present in the individual relationship, as dependency and subjection; the most personal *individual* aspect is present as foundation of the social relationship, because its origin lies in the other that determines it. This is why Freud is ably to say that this bi-personal relationship is *identical* to the collective formation: the collective already determines it, and conversely the collectivity becomes actualised in this bi-personal relationship. The 'identity of opposites' here reveals its dialectical character: they are the same and not the same. They are the same: *it is* a collective form; they are not the same: *it is* an individual form.

It is this concealment of the social *in* the individual, and of the individual *in* the social, that leads to the impossibility of reaching the true reality test. The separation between parts and whole sends us back to this embodied logic in which, in being in love as well as in hypnosis, *one becomes the whole* but in a different manner. In *the sensible whole, a body in love*, as the model of all relations to the flesh, in which my sensible extension toward the world is halted; in *the rational whole, a gaze in hypnosis*, in which the other, without flesh as the model of all dependency, halts and configures my extension towards the collective system.

Thus, it is not only in illness that the testing of reality takes the form of an imaginary and merely subjective testing. What interests Freud is to show us how in the normal relations, in which we remain fascinated by a woman or a leader, this reality test is a semblance: it is a fantasy test.

Let us consider this in greater detail: in the 'whole scale of possibilities within the range of the phenomena of love' (111).

Freud found an essential form: hypnosis. This is a double relationship, in which identification revealed the maximal libidinal distance – typical of collective phenomena – in the minimal personal distance – typical of individual relationships, because this is 'the unlimited devotion of someone in love, but with sexual satisfaction excluded' (115).

And *this would then be*, of all the forms of relationships among human beings, *the foundation of the relation of dependency and collective submission*. Because here we are not dealing with the directly sexual impulses, referred to the sexual couple. Here the impulses are inhibited in their aim, therefore *the only ones recognised as social*, those that derive from a repressed libido and corporeality, the ones that can take as object the ego ideal situated in the *external other, but generalisable and shareable*, which thus appears purely as support of the ego ideal, *transition of the individual form to the system of production that through its mediation also includes me*. But it includes me *already* as a subjected human being.

> Hypnosis is distinguished from a group formation by this limitation of number, just as it is distinguished from being in love by the absence of directly sexual trends. In this respect it occupies a middle position between the two. (115)

Here the other is the *individual-social* form in its mere gaze, just as the couple was the apparent *individual-individual* form ('double individuality') in its mere sexuality. In both cases the true extension of my libido and my rationality ends up being closed off; in the couple my libido only takes as object the sensible other without rational signification; in hypnosis, my desexualised body only takes as object the other whose social signification excludes the materiality of the system in which I prolong myself.

6   *From the Instant of the Couple to the Duration of the Institutions*

The hypnotist – the leader – would mark the human place where the ego ideal and the superego prolong themselves and become unified in the contradictory unity of a human subject-support. The latter thereby verifies, in an apparent objective coincidence, the correspondence present in the subjective demand, which remains closed around the first form that by way of identification took shape in the child. In the reality of the adult, in the adhesion to the other brought out by the hypnotist, the circuit becomes closed in which the sensible form that sits at the basis of the organisation of both the superego and the ego ideal rediscovers *one* actual sensible form in which the re-encounter with the infantile fantasy can take place in 'reality'. The superego and the ego ideal do not extend themselves from the infantile normative form so as to rediscover the systematic and true rationality that might enable it to disentangle the first dependency that in this way was prolonged. Returning to the most infantile foundation, to its most regressive sensible content, it once again locks itself up in the sensible form of another actual substitute, and the adult thus finds in the official reality the consistency of his or her flesh with an object in its social function that is adequate for such coherence. It prolongs the infantile sensibility in the adult sensibility, which is the only one, moreover, that its ideal-form contains as capable of being filled with an incomprehensible reality in which all criticism and all difference have been inhibited.

> It is interesting to see that it is precisely those sexual impulsions that are inhibited in their aims which achieve such lasting ties between people. But this can easily be understood from the fact that they are not capable of complete satisfaction, while sexual impulsions which are uninhibited in their aims suffer an extraordinary reduction through the discharge of energy every time the sexual aim is attained. It is the fate of sensual love to become extinguished when it is satisfied; for it to be able to last, it must from the beginning be mixed with purely affectionate components – with such, that is, as are inhibited in their aims – or it must itself undergo a transformation of this kind. (115)

Thus, as we saw in the case of being in love, the satisfaction of the instant was followed by the experience of duration. And we went from the shining infinity of the id to the temporal finitude of the affectionate social sentiments. In this alternation, the satisfaction reached in the discharge was prolonged as a future promise, which made it tolerable to live the everyday in preparation for when weakness once more would become fortified. And the new instant and the newly complete satisfaction once more included us in the time of unsatisfactory reality in which the fantasy of a coincidence, though instantaneous, would really be accomplished. In the sexual realm, satisfaction did not consist in the duration but in that which this duration promised. *By contrast, in the conventional social realm, satisfaction lay in the duration itself*: in the permanence of the absolute other who becomes transparent in the submission to the hypnotist. Thus, at the moment when apparently it rediscovers finitude, the time of history, the latter appears as repetition: as the repetition of its lasting permanence and, thus, *as infinitude*. Satisfaction lies in the fact that the bonds are lasting, in that they last eternally, and in that the promise of its duration is repeated. This presumption of infinitude without a body, which is prolonged in the affectionate instincts of the couple in the bonds that tie me to the leader, and in which the latter, as model, ties me to reality, only expresses the desire that the foundation of my being should remain. I mean that the primordial father should really be validated in the new relation of submission. *This is the social transaction: it is satisfied in the instant with the couple, and in duration with the institutions*. Both are satisfied, in alternation, as if they were not contradictory. But in this way I keep myself from understanding that the foundation of my being is no longer the other who is gone and disappeared forever, but the system of production that produced us all: the father, the mother, the partner, and the leader. The affectionate feelings, even in their vanishing corporeality, continue to tie me to the precise human form of the other that takes the place of the other; and they keep me from gaining access to the structure of the system of which the latter is only one model of control. My wish is for the foundation of my being to remain eternally in place and for it to serve as the subjective support for the invariable permanence of the system's institutions and the negation of historical time. The lasting bonds with the father reaffirm themselves – through the leader – in the duration of the bonds that tie me to the global society.

It is clear, however, that hypnosis is not the relation of the human being in a mass or multitude, nor is the hypnotist truly a leader or caudillo. The relation of dominion is here strictly individual: 'the relation between someone with superior power and someone who is without power and helpless' (115). But the form of resistance is different too: the subject can oppose the hypnotist 'due to the fact that in hypnosis as it is usually practised some knowledge may be retained that what is happening is only a game, *an untrue reproduction* of another situation of far more importance to life' (116, emphasis added).

What comes to the foreground for the first time in this process is the elementary character of 'the complicated fabric of the group', and therefore the *subjective foundation of social dependency* in the conventional individual. The form of dependency, which originated at the heart of the social form that is the family, is prolonged in the social institutions (e.g. the Church or army), preserving the same form of dependency that the self-enclosed adult maintains in the presentation of his or her infantile sensibility. Thus the adult only repeats, in broader social forms, the structure that was determined in the midst of the family, as a model of being that conceals its social determination.

How, then, in the subject of the artificial mass, can we unravel this adhesion to the political and economical system in which this subject finds itself integrated? It is clear that the imbalance of this subject includes all the determinations that affect its relation to reality. Therefore, it is difficult to envision its transformation, its 'cure', as if its illness did not consist precisely *in the corroboration of its infantile structure that occurs in the social system and institutions.* Or even more strongly put: the corroboration of the infantile structure that the system requires, organises, and solicits. Thus the dimension of abnormality acquires its true meaning in the signification of the subject's action when it is read only on the basis of the rationality of the system of production, because from the individual point of view the subject's conduct is considered socially normal. Perhaps for the 'sick' person the individual perspective of the doctor can be considered valid: it so happens that the doctor acts as a model of the system, with regard to which the normality or abnormality of the patient is interpreted. A psychoanalysis that only treats 'sick' people is already showing, in the restriction it applies to the domain of official reality, the acceptance of the only possible field to which the system of production steers it, by signalling as its task the adaptation of the residue that its own social organisation segregates, *but nothing more.* The delimitation of the domain of sickness at once has a restrictive social character and includes a value judgment: to mark as sick only those subjects who reveal, in their conduct, the repressive character of the system. But at the same time to signal to them that this domain for the interpretation of the imbalance is the only one, *and not the whole reality.* Even though this is not the criterion of sickness for Freud. The classical figure of the sick person is only an opportunity to lay bare the sick structure of the presumed 'normal' person in 'normal' society.

What should we then make of the analysis of groups? Let us say that these groups, at the conventional level, constitute the maximum level of society that psychoanalysis, in its bad conscience, takes in. But then, in the extent to which it does not extend itself to the point of showing the integration of the individual into the system, this group analysis is only the repetition of the very structure of the artificial group or mass in the psychoanalytical task. And this is so because it maintains as unmovable precisely the index of objectivity on the basis of which the testing of reality appears for Freud: that of its integration in the institutions of domination. The psychoanalysis of groups, like that of the individual, reaches its moment of verification in the fact that both constitute a 'collective formation', whether formed by two persons or by various. The truth of this bond appears not in their number but as a function of the form of the social system to which both belong. And this is why Freud, as the only proof of reality in the 'normal' case that we just studied, offers the reference that necessarily situates it beyond the individual: in the broader social form of the historical system. He verifies it in the fact of group belonging, that is, in the artificial forms of institutions in which we are all, in one way or another, included.

We thus see why the psychoanalyst could not move beyond the individual model. When he was curing individuals, because his own form of being 'healthy' appeared as a model of integration to those who had not even reached this still conventional level, they could not adapt themselves to the institutions, whether the family, or work, or the Church, or the army. But when he is curing groups, how should we situate this little 'artificial mass' that is the analytical group? If here the psychoanalyst does not disarm the trap of the system, if he does not bring out the group as the 'cellular form' of every repressive social institution, he necessarily occupies the role of the leader, in that he too, by force, solicits the same adhesion that in the broader social field is demanded of every artificial social mass. Because, in order to disarm this trap, the regional scientific knowledge that Freud elaborates in psychology must necessarily give way to the scientific truth of the social system of production that Marx elaborated for the science of history. If the strict rationality of the system of production does not appear included explicitly in the analysis of the group or in the individual analysis, this ignorance of the analyst does not save him: it simply appears as one determination that the system imposes on his 'science' and on his person. If he omits this knowledge and its application, he only shows his adhesion to the system, in which the act of curing is the privilege that he supposedly ascribes to himself while at the same time he ratifies, as an unspoken contract, the scale and hierarchy of people in the contradictory social system. Thus, the case of the psychoanalyst is one of the most sensitive in terms of the evident trap it presents: at the very moment when I believe I am curing the sick person it is I who ratify myself as healthy. Before whom? Before the unreason of the sick person. The more I cure, the more I certify my own health, my presumed truth: the more I save myself. We should recognise that even the poor capitalist runs more risks. At least he will have to confront a rebellion: the strike that the workers may bring against him. But who is going to rebel against the psychoanalyst if he is the one who, by the very definition to which we adhere from the moment we enter submissively into analysis, has reason on his side?

This reduction of social relations to individual relations, from which the determination of the system would be excluded, is a bourgeois category in the very midst of science.

> From the very first individual psychology, in this extended but entirely justifiable sense of the words, is at the same time social psychology as well. (69)

For Freud the individual relation is originary in the child, but not in the adult. Every relationship in the case of the adult is, at once, a social relationship. And it is not even original for the child: it just so happens that the child cannot know this. But in that case what should we make of an analyst who limits himself to understanding the situation as if he were a complacent child in its self-enclosed asocial individuality, finding support for this in the neurosis of the adult he is treating, whereby ideology forms a system with illness?

Let us go back again to Freud's presentation of the problem, and let us try to understand the passage through hypnosis in order to reach an understanding of the spontaneous mass or group.

From the hypnotist to the mass; from the covering up of the social to its uncovering; from the implicit to the explicit: such would be the moment of comprehensive transition that Freud is trying to capture, whereby at last the elementary unity of the collective *appears in its ambiguous and preparatory modality of a possible transition or of its newly submissive permanence.*

> ... after the preceding discussions we are quite in a position to give the formula for the libidinal constitution of groups, or at least of such groups as we have hitherto considered – namely, those that have a leader and have not been able by means of too much 'organisation' to acquire secondarily the characteristics of an individual. A primary group of this kind is a number of individuals who have put one and the same object in the place of their ego ideal and have consequently identified themselves with one another in their ego. This condition admits of graphic representation:

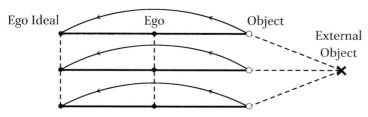

FIGURE 1

Let us analyse this schema from Freud. Between hypnotism and the mass there is a similarity and a difference: 'limitation of number', Freud tells us about the first: relation of *one to one*. This is the visible element. And yet, implicitly, what is invisible as social dependency is the historical determination of the 'one to the many' in this 'one to one'. And it is this invisible aspect of the hypnotic relation that becomes visible when we move on to the group or mass. But when we pass from the one to the many, it is also *the domain of the world* that appears together with the others: *the common situation*. In the 'libidinal formation of the group', the collective becomes objectified: the many that are implied make themselves effectively present. But this does not mean that the implicit becomes explicit: the objective collectivity appears only at the perceptive level as collectivity, but within it the previous mode of linkage, which was individual, still subsists.

The *ambiguous* character of this libidinal formula of the spontaneous mass would be found in the following characteristics:

1. Each individual of the group or mass is determined by his or her own ego ideal, which orients him or her toward a new external *object* (the leader). Each one is thus oriented by an individual superego that *reanimates the first reality test* and converges toward a *new* real individual as its support. Except that *it is the many who are doing this, now simultaneously*, by choice, *from within a new common objective situation*.
2. The individual subjective element that so far was lived as self-enclosed and completed in the artificial mass becomes unified in the affirmation of a *new* common objectified subjectivity: the leader, although this leader here still maintains the individual dependency toward him. The objective power becomes realised in this convergence, in which once again *all depend on one, but in a different manner*.
3. The formula of the spontaneous mass, then, is not a *contradictory formula of transition*, which only acquires meaning if we include it in a real process: *where each mass or group comes from and where it is going*. The formula, as the contradictory moment of a broader development, allows us to grasp this moment of passage and elaboration in which, in the midst of the old, something new announces itself and takes place. Therefore, this static and synchronic cut must include, as part of its signification, the formal diachronic and dynamic determination of its historical process.

7 *Where Does the Spontaneous Mass Come From?*

Let us then complete Freud's static and partial schema by including this implicit dimension without which it would lack historical meaning: where does the spontaneous mass come from? It is evident that it comes from the traditional groups, as the product of the contradiction in which people cannot remain. This question 'where does it come from?' is furthermore endorsed by Freud himself in his previous analyses in the first chapters.

Let us note (Figure 2) that the movement of return of the external object onto the ego ideal is the same as the one effectuated by the external repressive model, Christ or army general, on the historical system of production. Here the ego ideal, which each individual retains as the most subjective element, in reality results from a cultural process, in this case the system of capitalist production. Within this system the isolation of 'free' individualities does not recognise this common origin, which is concealed in the world of official culture or civilisation. But the identification with Christ or with the Commander-in-Chief, as models, already shows their consistency with the system and once more integrates them within the institutions, that is to say, the artificial groups. The social form thus closes in on itself while dragging the apparently free individuals with it.

But at the same time the external model with which the free individuals identify themselves opens out, not onto the true rational signification of the productive system but onto the domain of an abstract totality (ideology): God, Country, and Home. In this way the splitting of the system becomes ratified under the rubric of the subject.

So then: *the spontaneous mass emerges from within this artificial mass. Where does it go?*

Freud himself indicates that the spontaneous mass cannot remain in this pure spontaneity when he says that his 'formula' treats 'at least of such groups as we have hitherto considered – namely, those that have a leader and have not been able by means of too much "organisation" to acquire secondarily the characteristics of an individual' (116). It is, then, a form of transition. As opposed to the artificial masses or groups, in which the contradiction appears consolidated in the stability of their form, here by contrast the alternatives of a passage are present: they come from the destruction or dissolution of the artificial group and they may or may not go towards another stabilised form. But the disjunction is as follows: whether or not this stability towards which the spontaneous mass is tending once more reproduces the contradictory reality from which it derives.

Each spontaneous mass in its rebellious emergence in other words would be a new testing ground for putting into play the instant and the permanent: of how the signification discovered in the spontaneity of rebellion is prolonged or not, developed or inhibited, in the stable permanence of a new social form. Whence the ambiguity of the formula, which in itself presents the possibility of

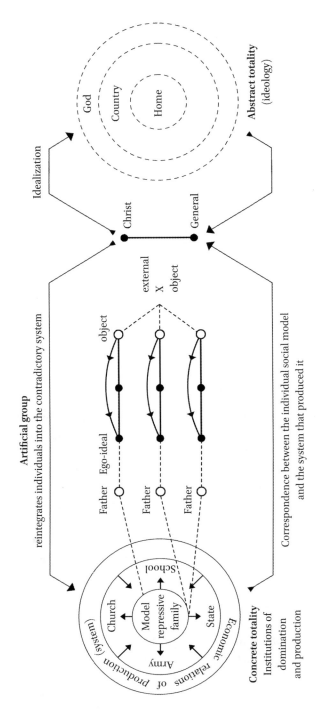

FIGURE 2

an opening as much as of its closure. Grasped as an instant of rebellion *opposed* to the institutionalised permanence, this opposition once more submerges us, as in the cases of identification and being in love previously analysed, in the scission between fantasy and reality, between the real world and the imaginary world: this is the ambiguity of the spontaneous mass.

Let us recall Freud's analyses about the dissolution of the individual form that takes place in the spontaneous mass. There the libidinal expansion augmented the affectivity of its members, while the official rationality of their consciousness appeared to be negated. Here we will once again see the appearance of the human form of the leader with which the group identifies as the one that may either produce a return to the rigidity of the previous form or, on the contrary, create the opening of a new form of sensible relationships as well as the emergence of a new field of rationality.

This is then the problem that Freud is analysing: how the form of the leader may break the previous relation, which still prolongs itself at the affective and libidinal level in the leader's person, and open out onto a form of rationality that would discover the truth of the historical process for the collective process. Freud's analyses inscribe themselves precisely in the scientific contribution that in the historical transformation attempts to foreground the permanence of forms of dependency that are not captured at the political level, together with the depth of the transformation without which there could not be a revolutionary process.

VIII The Return to the Historical Origin

1 *The Mass, Place of Historical Elaboration*

In this chapter, in which Freud analyses the herd instinct, we will verify whether our interpretation of the group or mass is adequate. We had established that the 'formula' of the group formation, when it was considered statically, was an ambiguous formula. One that only when it was integrated into a determinate social structure could acquire its true signification, given that Freud indicated to us the existence of three basic types of group: artificial, spontaneous, and revolutionary. And as a result we established that the signification of the 'formula' of the mass or group could not remain restricted to the mere union of convergent individualities, each one of which took a common object, the leader, as its own. The problem is that of the origin: what led them to seek out this *same* external object? If we remain in the individualistic and merely psychological – and, I would go so far as to say, psychoanalytical – interpretation of the phenomenon, this formula could be interpreted by affirming that there is a subjective determination that naturally, by way of the convergence of individualities driven by a certain herd instinct, leads to unity. But what happens if we integrate the perspective of a historical genesis into the qualitative determination of the mass, and therefore also in its *mode of being* a mass or group?

Freud's 'formula', insofar as it expresses the 'cellular' character of the mass, in other words admits both perspectives:

1. The individualistic and psychologist perspective: it admits the 'miracle' of individualities that converge on one and the same object, the leader, as a determination present in the subject's own ego. There is nothing specifically historical that we should include in the individual element. Each human being tends to seek out the image of his or her father in the leader, and this *is* the collective. Here the formula preserves its character as an abstract formula: it exhausts itself in the synchronic description. But this is the conventional outlook, which starts from the abstract, isolated individual as the basis for constructing the collective. Obviously, what is not included here is the history of the social process that produced this abstract individual.

2. The Freudian and historical perspective: if we include the dialectic of the historical process, and thus the revolutionary transformation as a determining factor of its movement, the formula of the mass changes its meaning insofar as it becomes part of an artificial or a spontaneous group, for example. This explains why the 'formula', in its ambiguity, seems to include this possibility of transformation. Because there is a process in the group itself, *the group or mass can appear in its origin as having one meaning, but it can end up having another*. The artificial group falls apart and, within it, there appears a different form of group, which preserves the previous qualities even while transforming them. Here the perspective does not start out from the individual but from the totality: the individual acquires the meaning of the totality of the system that determines it. *Here the outlook starts from the collective in order to understand how it determines the integration of the individual within the collective, and how, subsequently, this collective expansion from the individual takes places*. And it is in this direction, in the bond that unites them, that Freud's first question finds its destiny: 'there must surely be something to unite them' (73). The common is not always the desired object: the common is also the present situation. This is why:

> We cannot for long enjoy the illusion that we have solved the riddle of the group with this formula. It is impossible to escape the immediate and disturbing recollection that all we have really done has been to

shift the question on to the riddle of hypnosis, about which so many points have yet to be cleared up. And now another objection shows us our further path. (117)

The path will be the following:

a) To differentiate the artificial mass from the spontaneous mass in terms of the signification they acquire in the historical process.

b) To understand that collective action is not the result of a natural instinct: what determines the collective relations are the interests that are at stake in the productive process.

c) To explain that there is a historical development present in the masses: this process is regulated by the incorporation of individuals into a universal field of reciprocal and coherent relations, in which the satisfaction of the shared desire determines the collective bond.

This analysis requires that we previously establish what the masses have in common, in order to see how their difference emerges. The *same*, what they have in common in the abstract 'formula' of the mass or group, thus admits two readings depending on the mass in question. If we read this formula only from the perspective of individualism, we see only Le Bon's devalued mass or group; if we do so from the revolutionary and creative perspective of the mass, we see its historical function appear. Freud chooses this last reading.

The description of the mass or group, seen from the perspective of bourgeois individualism, retains only one common feature and this is why it generalises without seeing the differences:

> It might be said that the intense emotional ties which we observe in groups are quite sufficient to explain one of their characteristics – the lack of independence and initiative in their members, the similarity in the reactions of all of them, their reduction, so to speak, to the level of group individuals. (117)

This is the 'abstract', generalising perspective, which is what individualism retains, from its point of view, in the mass: to be only a unit within the multitude, at 'the level of group individuals'. And, it is true, this is what defines the common for every mass or group, both the artificial and the spontaneous one. But depending on the function it performs, artificial or spontaneous, the signification of this mode of being included in the group also varies.

> But if we look at it *as a whole*, a group shows us more than this. Some of its features – the weakness of intellectual ability, the lack of emo-

> tional restraint, the incapacity for moderation and delay, the inclination to exceed every limit in the expression of emotion and to work it off completely in the form of action. (117, emphasis added)

This difference appears in the masses or groups only when we adopt the point of view of the *whole*, the totality which discovers for us the meaning of each particular group in terms of the function it performs with respect to the whole. Because the features just indicated are certainly not the ones that every group has in common, but they correspond *only to the spontaneous groups or masses*. This difference is what allowed Le Bon – who distinguished as groups only the spontaneous ones – his distinction between good and bad groups: between those regulated by the 'genius of the race' and the revolutionary masses regulated by their 'own interests'.

> ... these and similar features, which we find so impressively described in Le Bon, show an unmistakable picture of a regression of mental activity to an earlier stage such as we are not surprised to find among savages or children. A regression of this sort is in particular an essential characteristic of common groups, while, as we have heard, in organised and artificial groups it can to a large extent be checked. (117)

In the spontaneous groups or masses, there is a regressive emergence of the repressed. In the artificial groups repression was triumphant. It is not that the repressed that appears in regression would not exist in the artificial group: it is hidden, beaten down. This emergence of the repressed in other words is what differentiates the two: actualised in one kind of group or mass, tamed in the other.

Thus, what Freud gives us in the 'formula' of mass or group formation is only what they have in common: the lack of independence and initiative on the part of individual members; the identity in their reaction to all the others; their descent to the level of being a unit in the crowd at the level of group individuals. But Freud, we should remember, adds other characteristics, which *appear only in the spontaneous mass*: the weakening of intellectual ability, the lack of emotional restraint, the incapacity for moderation and delay, the inclination to exceed every limit in the expression of affectivity, and the tendency to work it off completely in the form of action. Therefore, we ask ourselves: *how do the differences emerge that are* signalled *from within the common*? How does the same produce what is different? This is a process that can be understood only from within the historical development. And, if we recall that Freud had signalled the existence of three modalities of the mass or group:

1) the artificial or institutionalised mass (e.g. the Church and army)
2) the spontaneous mass
3) the revolutionary mass (e.g. in the French Revolution),

then, intervening in the understanding of the differences we see that previous questions come back: where does the spontaneous mass come from and where does it go? And we can give an answer: it comes, Freud told us, from the artificial or institutionalised group. Where is it going? It goes towards the revolution.

We thus understand that the features that appear in the individuals of the spontaneous mass express the *negation* of the form of individuality that is retained and confined in the rational and affective dimensions of the artificial groups or masses. In this temporal and historical development, we witness a rupture of the limits of the institutionalised mass. Thus the spontaneous mass is here opposed to another form of mass or group. The same generates difference; the same was not homogeneous: it was a contradictory unity. Dissociating itself from within, one mass or group produces another that is opposed to it. Hence, *the spontaneous mass, Freud would be telling us, produces itself as the rebellion against its previous form as an artificial group or mass.*

But this difference, which Freud extracts from his general 'formula' of the group or mass formation when it becomes historically specified in terms of the function it performs with regard to the totality, is complementary to another specification: that which is different in the artificial mass. Only because Freud did not maintain the artificial and institutionalised group as invariable and understood its meaning, only for this reason was he able to differentiate it from the spontaneous group or mass. And this is what could not be done in the case of someone like Le Bon, who considered the existing institutions as natural and absolute.

The artificial groups presented the following characteristics: heterogeneity, duration, unity due to exterior constraints, high degree of organisation, directors (not leaders). These characteristics in turn signal where the artificial masses come from: they show the subdued, defeated, collective power of a prior revolutionary mass, now obliged to remain in permanence without change. The homogeneous aspect of the common desire, which previously was shared, gave way to the undifferentiated heterogeneity; the creative temporality gave way to the duration that now excludes it; the organisation of the bureaucratic revolution determines it as a mechanism for the repetition of the same; the revolutionary leaders gave way to the bureaucrats: to the directors. The understanding of the historical process, which includes the spontaneous mass in the active project of overcoming the artificial group, indicates its historical genesis looking backwards, revealing its origin in other spontaneous and revolutionary masses. And the 'where is it going?' part of the current spontaneous mass is determined by the 'where does it come from' in a double sense. It comes from the previous form, but it comes from even farther back: it comes from a prior form that must be discovered as having been produced in a historical process that has its point of departure in the origin of the human subject.

What has disappeared from the artificial group when compared to the revolutionary mass? Precisely the originary creative sense, the historical process that led from spontaneity to its permanence, which Freud justly calls 'artificial'. What disappeared is the power that necessarily had to be present in its originary formation, that is to say, its prior revolutionary being, which ended up hidden, expulsed from its own history, in the present system to which it belongs. And this is what reappears, albeit restricted, in the spontaneous mass: the repressed, which is *acted out* now. The product, albeit incipient, of its own production.

The spontaneous mass thus shows us the ambiguity contained in Freud's formula: *the attempt to satisfy the repressed within a regressive social relation*. Indeed, what we must come to know is
– whether or not the leader returns the power that each individual reflects onto him;
– whether the individuals learn to read themselves as produced as a collective and not an alien power.

All this indicates the necessity for a new form of sensibility and thought to emerge from within the spontaneous mass. And one emerges as a function of the other. If the leader shows and gives back the power that has been delegated to him, and does not conflate his being a part as if he were the whole, in this destruction of fetishism there occurs at the same time a return and a recuperation of the material bonds that tie human subjects together. The whole is no longer hypostasised in the leader; it remits us, as its foundation, to the material domain of the process of production and to the rational comprehension of its structure.

The fact that this is the path that Freud pursues becomes clear in the following affirmation, which brings to the fore the need for the spontaneous mass to move on to another form, both individual and collective:

> We thus have an impression of a state in which an individual's private emotional impulses and intellectual acts are too weak to come to anything by themselves and are entirely dependent for this on being reinforced by being repeated in a similar way in the other members of the group. (117)

This is then the origin of the difference between the artificial group and the spontaneous group: the discovery that the individual forms of thinking and feeling must be amplified by recuperating the collective power from which they derive. At stake is not something that, as power, would already be contained as a capacity within each individual. Once again: neither the individual affective element nor the personal intellectual element has the force of energy necessary, Freud says, to affirm themselves socially and confront the state of dissatisfaction. The group or mass, outside the limits that inhibit and rigidify it, is an activity that *generates power*, that creates a capacity that was previously concealed and at the individual level was impossible to discover. Or, which is to say the same thing, the truth of the individual, both affectively and intellectually, lies in this return to a capacity for creation that only the incorporation into the collective process of history gives back to him or her. And something fundamental appears: the fact that the common truth is worked out on the basis of *new* individual bonds among the members and not only based on the unilateral dependency on the leader: 'too weak to come to anything by themselves and ... entirely dependent for this on being reinforced by being repeated in a similar way in the other members of the group' (117). By contrast, the individualism that is compatible with the institutionalised groups means the destruction of this power:

> We are reminded of how many of these phenomena of dependence are part of the normal constitution of human society, of how little originality and personal courage are to be found in it, of how much every individual is ruled by those attitudes of the group mind which exhibit themselves in such forms as racial characteristics, class prejudices, public opinion, etc. (117)

2 *The Mass, Place of Cultural Individuation*

We should understand that when Freud calls human society 'normal', he is speaking of the artificial society congealed into institutions of domination.

What is contained in the historical process in other words is the attempt on the part of people acting collectively to acquire an individual form that would open up the limits both affective and rational that check their relation to the world and condemn them to repression. But what this shows us is at the same time the search for a human form of passage *into the other*. The other is taken as a model, as a form of being distinct from one's own, which at last discovers and places in our reach this limitlessness that apparently is present in the other. This fervent desire projected onto the other as the one who would be capable of amplifying, by way of identification, their own limits is what gives meaning to the formation of spontaneous groups or masses. And this is precisely what the theory of the 'herd instinct' cannot explain.

If the form assumed by the 'leader', as opposed to the 'director' of the artificial groups, were not a determining factor in the process of social transformation, the signification that its human figure acquires would not result from a need common to a group of people who, in their convergence, discover precisely in this figure those qualities they desire to have as their own. But then the collective forms also would not accomplish a historical function: they would be a natural phenomenon, prolonged in human society. Thus only the elites – through God – would be able to provide them with their orientation, the 'spiritual' sense that the true subjects, not massified, would impose on it from the outside. Freud, by contrast, in criticising the notion of the 'herd instinct', returns to the creative specificity of history and gives it its meaning by understanding the mass or group as a collective process that creates new forms of being human. And, therefore, beyond dependency and submissiveness, which the spontaneous mass also generates, he is interested in showing the movement of particularisation in the midst of the universal exchange opened up by the masses, which is the 'element', or the milieu of their development. And how, as a result, people are differentiated and unite themselves in a common signification that brings them together – the leader – who is nothing but a social model in which the contradictory signification of the system of production is incarnated.

Precisely, Wilfred Trotter's affirmations cover up this process with their recourse to the 'herd instinct':

> Trotter derives the mental phenomena that are described as occurring in groups from a herd instinct ('gregariousness'), which is innate in human beings just as in other species of animals. Biologically, he says, this gregariousness is an analogy to multicellularity and as it were a continuation of it. (In terms of the libido theory it is a further manifestation of the tendency which proceeds from the libido and which is felt by all living beings of the same kind, to combine in more and more comprehensive units.) (118)

We see the confusion that results from Trotter's analogy: human individuality here does not carry any meaning distinct from biological individuality, which consists in the mere reproduction and dissemination of *the same*, but not the development of difference in the universal exchange. The homogeneity of the biological form, in this dualism, turns into the homogeneity of the content. But it so happens that it is precisely in human history where this homogeneity does not have a natural sense. This homogeneity is what would be expressed, in the eyes of the privileged, in the artificial group. But Freud, as we have seen, had distinguished in the midst of the spontaneous groups or masses the production of a *new* homogeneity derived from the negation of the heterogeneous artificial groups: it was a homogeneity without meaning. However, Trotter insists on conceiving of the mass or group as a noncontradictory and homogeneous totality, as a mere sum in which the personal particularity once again is dissolved, except for his own:

> But Trotter's exposition is open, with even more justice than the others, to the objection that it takes too little account of the leader's part in a group, while we incline rather to the opposite judgement, that it is impossible to grasp the nature of a group if the leader is disregarded. The herd instinct leaves no room at all for the leader; he is merely thrown in along with the herd, almost by chance; it follows, too, that no path leads from this instinct to the need for a God; the herd is without a herdsman. (119)

Let us note the final irony: why do the dominant classes have recourse to the model of the divinity, to Christ as their 'good herdsman' or 'pastor'? Freud aims to undo this game that only considers those models that are compatible with the dominant system. And it is precisely the necessary introduction of the leader as the new 'model' of the human form that, at the collective level, expresses the development of the form of the human subject in history. History is a process that produces human subjects. The negation of the part of the leader implies the negation of the historical debate that produces new forms of being human that the masses bring forth. Every system of production possesses the truth of the human models that it installs in the same process. This saliency of the mass or group, the leader, only expresses the aspiration to another possible form of being human in which the mass recognises itself and identifies itself: this new form is the current human form of its dilemma and its new aspiration. In this way we see the ideological result to which the theoretical explanation of the herd instinct is tending: to remain in a consolidated cultural form as if it were natural, as if the current directors of the artificial groups were the most elevated forms of human being possible. And it is against this naturalisation of the social that Freud's subsequent analyses are aimed in this chapter: to show the appearance of this process in the child as the access to a growing field of universality.

3 Genesis of the False Collectivity in the Child

Except that in the child this access is accomplished in the midst of a repressive civilisation that makes it conform with the institutions of domination and turns it into the subject of the artificial group or mass. The first form of unsatisfied desire, Freud shows, already has the form of the other from the start: the mother, 'which the child does not yet know how to deal with in any way except by turning it into anxiety' (119). Why anxiety? Because the child does not know how to satisfy its desire fully; it does not know how to make the transition from the unsatisfied desire to reality. This form of the unsatisfied desire, which is hostile in its dissatisfaction, how could it take on the transition toward reality if it were not through the model of this other who traces the outline of the human form of all possible satisfaction? The unsatisfied infantile desire here is the originary one: to have the object, the mother, *all to oneself*. But then it turns out that one's object is the object of another: of the father. Envy draws the scheme of this first relation, against the other because of the other. From the very first the object of desire and of opposition has a precise human form: between the fear of losing its object and the envy of that other who really has it, anxiety is the only answer compatible with the real inefficiency of the child in the adult world: the anxiety of *not being for not having*. In the midst of this first collective cultural form – the family – the child rises up to reality feeling that every other is a stranger and an opponent: an anxiety-inducing obstacle. In the beginning, in other words, the herd instinct does not exist for Freud, but rather its opposite. Freud's description here rediscovers the 'formula' of the artificial group:

> ... for a long time nothing in the nature of herd instinct or group feeling is to be observed in children. Something like it first grows up, in a nursery containing many children, out of the children's relation to their parents, and it does so as a reaction to the initial envy with which the elder child receives the younger one. The elder child would certainly like to put his successor jealously aside, to keep it away from the parents, and to rob it of all its privileges; but in the face of the fact that this younger child (like all that come later) is loved by the parents as much as he himself is, and in consequence of the impossibility of his maintaining his hostile attitude without damaging himself, he is forced into identifying himself with the other children. So there grows up in the troop of children a communal or group feeling, which is then further developed at school. The first demand made by this reaction-formation is for justice, for equal treatment for all. [...] This transformation – the replacing of jealousy by a group feeling in the nursery and classroom – might be considered improbable, if the same process could not later on be observed again in other circumstances. (119)

There exists an analogy between the child's social anxiety and the subjects of the artificial group or mass. The analogy, contrary to what happens in Trotter, does not operate here between nature and culture, but between culture and culture. The form of this first infantile relation remains afterwards as the matrix of every adult relationship. The form of accepting the failure of the unsatisfied infantile desire – nobody among the children, who are all similar, ever satisfies it – configures the acceptance of the failure of desire in the artificial group. In this group nobody reaches satisfaction either, even as adults, and in both cases it is with love that we are rewarded, that love which equates us all in equal dissatisfaction, which offers consolation for the failure and turns it into a success: if we accept it, we will no longer suffer from anxiety. 'Christ or the Commander-in-Chief, Freud said, love us with the same love with which our father loved us'. In this way, at the heart of similitude (the field of human subjectivity) an essential and originary difference finds its origin: between the inferior and the superior. But this difference, someone will say, is only a temporal difference concerning one's insertion into society, which the process of maturation overcomes: one is born a child but every child becomes an adult. Except that this difference relative to time is lived as absolute in the atemporality of childhood. We could say that the first social battlefield is also, in its own way, a class struggle: the class of dependent children, in whom the unsatisfied desire by nature and culture is condemned to remain as such; and the class of dominant adults, where the father is king. In the child this 'class struggle' presents it also as inevitably defeated: as belonging forever to the class robbed of the object of its desire and condemned to dissatisfaction. But this struggle ends with the collective submission of the children, with only one possible consolation: the consolation that all are treated equal. Justice consists in this equality of all those subjected before the law of the father, and this implies as its foundation that they give up on satisfaction – if all accept that nobody will be fully satisfied. And the 'affectionate feelings' are only the index of the child's radical weakness: having renounced the direct satisfaction of the libidinal body.

This form of relation gives shape to and prolongs itself in the 'normal' organisation of the adult. And this is how the adult class struggle requires, at the political and economic level, the intensifying of the infantile solution in the first 'class struggle':

> Originally rivals, they have succeeded in identifying themselves with one another by means of a similar love for the same object. (120)

In this way, there is a double identification at work in the access to reality of our desire. The first, with the father, in which we end up recognising that our initial similitude has a limit: not being able to be like the other on the basis of which my own being conformed itself as similar to him. I am and at the same time I am not like him: I begin to take part in similitude in the extent to which I accept difference. And the difference consists in not having what he has. In this not being fully similar to the one who gave me my being there resides nevertheless my belonging to the domain of the similar. To be and not to be at the same time: this is the point of departure. To be means: to be unsatisfied desire. The second identification, with the other children, is based on the foundation of this first limitation and negation, which is recognised as essential. Here the affirmation of the power that gave me my being is founded on the recognition of its absolute sovereignty. This implies, at the same time, that the radical foundation of my being is the renunciation for the sake of love: to love for the sake of the security that at least I can continue to exist under its shelter. And it is only thus that I identify with the others: on the basis of renunciation. But I identify with similar others of inferior rank: with the ones who, like me, come from the same dilemma and arrive at the same acceptance. We are equal before the law, which means: we are equal before the father but he, as the foundation of the law, is not equal to us. This second identification is already a diminished identification: it internalises the real similarity into a state of dependency and the acceptance, which is objective, external, and visible for all to see, that there is no satisfaction for anyone from the same class: that we are, as the class of children, an unsatisfied collective desire.

Once again the 'formula' of the group is verified, but in its meaning as artificial group: the group of children does not know – but in this infantile case it is necessarily so that it does not know – from where it comes; it also does not know where it is going. Without past and without future, devoid of memory, the class of subjected children depicts the collective form of a synchronic structure of dependency, where dependency is perennially dependency, with neither beginning nor end; where domination is perennially domination, with neither origin nor end point: things are necessarily the way they are, from the very first beginning. It is here that synchrony reveals itself in its psychic reality as eternal repetition of the same, outside time and history.

4 *Social Justice as Having without Being*

This form, we said, is prolonged in the human subject as if, as a form of relationship imprinted on the child's flesh, it continued to confirm its persistence in the traditional groups, now that its content is the adult:

> What appears later on in society in the shape of *Gemeingeist, esprit de corps*, 'group spirit', etc., does not belie its derivation from what was ori-

> ginally envy. No one must want to put himself forward, every one must be the same and have the same. Social justice means that we deny ourselves many things so that others may have to do without them as well, or, what is the same thing, may not be able to ask for them. This demand for equality is the root of social conscience and the sense of duty. (120–21)

If in the child the father is the law, now the law as the regulatory formula of the whole is in the hands of the leader. This is why he can express the whole: because as the incarnated presence of the law, every cultural regulation has its base in this figure, its point of departure and confirmation. In this way social justice, thus understood, implies that we consider the satisfaction of 'needs', but outside the desire's framework of appearance: outside the social origin of the dominant human form. Social justice, as being and having the same, covers up the original foundation of the struggle over the human being, in which being and having implied always the development of a dialectic of which similitude and difference were the two poles. Here, in the conventional social justice of the artificial mass, *the problem of being is omitted, and all that appears is the problem of having*. This reduction of being to having implies the conversion of being into an invariant structure, as something that cannot be put into question. *The being of the human subject is not in play in the conventional type of social justice: once the origin of the difference between masters and slaves has been dislodged, all that remains as domain of development is the field of similitude – in which the differences of the masters are not included.*

Social justice, which situates itself outside the origin of subjection, only prolongs its demand in the wake of the transition from the primitive envy – which is also cultural – towards the world of culture or civilisation. The primitive envy was the envy of the dependent being before the absolute being of the father: the child confused the passing determination of the biological maturation process and inscribed it as psychic determination in the form of being an adult. The initial biological incapacity, turned into an absolute, prolonged itself in the form of a cultural and historical incapacity. This generalisation of dependency, which at the origin corresponds to the specific 'class struggle' between parents and children, thus gives shape in the child to the inscription of a collective and social form. Why? Because in the transition to the world of culture or civilisation this form is not negated but on the contrary confirmed in the social institutions: *it is having, as in the origin, which fully gives being*. The private property of things prolongs itself in the private property of being.

> Thus social *feeling* is based upon the reversal of what was first a hostile feeling into a positively-toned tie in the nature of an identification. (121, emphasis added)

Indeed: the child had no other model that from within the similarity that was its own, the humiliated kind, could offer it a way out. Coming from the children the father has no rival: among the children there could be no hero to redeem them (except in children's tales, in which the infantile desire prolongs itself in the adult-child who writes them). In their looks of sweetness and vanquished love, the children are the eyes of subjection: they are forever beings without a way out – other than in fantasy – to confront the adult world. There are revolts of slaves, savages, women, even animals: outside the stories in which the adults already from the other side avenge themselves, there never has been a children's revolt.

This is the feeling that is preserved, because that is how strong it was, but not the understanding of the rationality for the transition, which did not exist. The *feeling* of dependency prolongs itself, without discontinuity, in the *reason* of the social law, and the affective submission ratifies itself under the rubric of adult legality. And finally the hostility that was necessarily repressed in the child continues to be repressed, for the most part, in the adult as well:

> So far as we have hitherto been able to follow the course of events, this reversal seems to occur under the influence of a common affectionate tie with a person outside the group. (121)

Thus the manliness of the male subject is limited only to the sphere of sexuality in the artificial group. He is a good man: he has everything in order. Where? There where the other signalled the place for it: to place his possession only in the woman, and to manifest himself as a man in the couple. In the sphere of sexuality the totality of masculinity is exhausted in the sexuated body as its centre: in everything else, with the powerful, the adult man is affectionate. When we move from the family to the broader social relationships of the artificial institutions, we are aided only by the infantile corporeality. All we have left is the desexualised affectionate feeling and the repressed flesh, affection almost devoid of the body: the homosexual libido, vanquished before the other who has what is lacking in our being in order to be like him. The duration and objective temporality only reach a body in which the unitary energy of sex prolonged itself as submission and prostration. In this way social justice reaches an abstract universality, without libido. The merely distributive rationality, at the level of things, is not a true vindication if it does not include the drama of the passage of the child into the drama of the adult as a problem of *being* that is fought out at the level of *having*: to be non-contradictory, to be non-dependent, to be non-humiliated. As a form of objectivity without subject, it keeps repressed the meaning of history: the production of human subjects through things. To have without having.

> Do not let us forget, however, that the demand for equality in a group applies only to its members and not to the leader. All the members must be equal to one another, but they all want to be ruled by one person. Many equals, who can identify themselves with one another, and a single person superior to them all – that is the situation that we find realised in groups which are capable of subsisting. (121)

Whence the modification that Freud introduces in the concept, which now turns out to be partial, of man as political animal. Neither political animal nor herd animal. Its 'animal' form of being, that is, its form of 'naturalising' itself as cultural being and of remaining in the incomprehension of its origin, is that of being a 'horde animal' in the artificial group. And from this follows later its political or gregarious being.

> Let us venture, then, to correct Trotter's pronouncement that man is a herd animal and assert that he is rather a horde animal, an individual creature in a horde led by a chief. (121)

Let us understand this well: *in his origin* man is a horde animal, an animal in the 'primal horde' prolonged in the repressive world of culture or civilisation. But not a member of the 'fraternal alliance' that makes its transition to history through the revolution.

IX Dialectic of Collective Forms: From the Primal Horde to the Fraternal Alliance

1 *The Always Present Origin*

Individual psychology opens out – now we understand the complexity of the first presentation of the problem – onto social psychology: the relation between parts and whole. But at the same time it opens out onto the past and the future: onto the meaning of history. And if the first developments led us to show the whole inherent in each individual, now the problem refers to the *potential* existence of the past in the present. That is to say: how the collective history is present in the individual history.

> Just as primitive man survives potentially in every individual, so the primal horde may arise once more out of any random collection .... (123)

Put differently: there is an illusion of being an individual, which hides the collective determination that constituted us, even in the midst of the collective itself. But there is still more: once this determination that ties us to the social is discovered, this does not mean that we have arrived at the foundation and the meaning of our social existence. The point is not that Freud, as a psychologist, does badly what sociology does well. The point is not that he tries to produce an 'applied psychology' and invade, inadequately, the field of sociology by unduly extending its limits. Freud seeks to develop that which sociology is lacking to be a truly human science: the inclusion of the subject in the collective process. Whence the recourse to the past *in the subjective element*.

Something important took place in the beginning of history, Freud would be telling us, and this transition that led from nature to culture even now continues to realise itself, except that it is hidden for the human subjects who accomplish it. We therefore need to go back and awaken this first signification, that of the first social act, so as to include it in the understanding of that other, present-day act which necessarily continues to repeat itself in the renewed access of human beings to the world of culture or civilisation. Freud thus tries to understand the basic presuppositions that lie at the beginning of history. For this he has recourse to an initial hypothesis, which attempts to recreate the conditions without which this transition from nature to culture would not have been able to realise itself. And he does so starting from the current forms. In the same way Marx, in 'Economic Forms that Precede Capitalism', must show on the basis of the 'natural' family the historical process that led to the development of the later forms. In both cases, it is a question of understanding what had to happen so that the *first step*, which opens up history, could be taken. This first step, which can be enunciated in science only as a hypothesis ('scientific myth', Freud says), but deduced from the terminal form of which we are part, is the only one that holds up as being necessarily in the beginning.

What characterises this first step in history? The generation of a collective mode of conduct that entails the formation of a new power: the collective power of producing human beings and transforming nature, both the nature 'proper' to us and nature 'out there'. This is what is common, the most general, in the first form of production as much as in the last. And this is what appears hidden in the individuality of the artificial group, where the seriality of integration does not lead us to perceive as our own the power that human beings generate collectively. In the case of Freud, on the other hand, the point of departure is the affirmation of the constitution of a new human power for cooperation. But this new power that was constituted at the origin presents a fundamental difference with regard to the traditional groups of the present: instead of obeying the director of the crowds, the transition from nature to culture on the contrary takes place because this figure has been suppressed, because he has been put to death.

At the origin the individual who dominates the primal horde *dies*: at the end, the officer or priest of the artificial group *lives*. But both are collective acts: the first is put to death, collectively; the second is given life, collectively. In this distance that opens up between the death of the chief of the primal horde and the life of the chief of the traditional mass or group, what plays itself out is the meaning of the process of history. And the dilemma for the human being from the world of culture or civilisation would be the following: to be born into the collective, as child, from within the individual relationship (the family); but for the real emergence of the historical collective to be a collective deed of the adult (the primal horde). There is a lack of consciousness of the collective on both ends: in one's own personal historical past, where the origin of my collective being is nevertheless individual (mother, father); in the past of the society to which I belong, whose collective origin is lost 'in the night of history' where it is hidden by the already constituted power. Therefore, when seen from the perspective of psychology, human beings are besieged from two extreme points. On the one hand, by the concealment of the historical origin of their being at the beginning of their life, by the specificity of their carnal origin, which conventional psychoanalysis continues to hide at the same time that it provides us with the appearance of restoring it to us, because it refers it solely to individual relations and to a nuclear minimum, the family, but without integrating in it the historical system of production of which the latter is merely a social cell. And, on the other hand, human beings are also besieged at the end point, as adults, by the fact that in the broader forms of society in which they participate this collective origin also disappears: because in the different groups of which they will be part they do not acquire the historical consciousness of the collective power that produced them, and because this real power that subjects them also returns to them, misleadingly, the consciousness of their individual being as if it were prior to and not constituted by the social.

Presented in these terms, the question that Freud would formulate is the following: what was present at the origin, which now remains hidden? What was necessarily part of the first civilised individuals, which now is sidestepped as if it were not part of their subjective and individual determination? What should we postulate, on the other hand, in order to understand that without which human conduct would lack all meaning? On the basis of what minimal reality did this maximum reality open up in which we are participating, as if the meaning of the former had disappeared, having been negated, in the latter? What element of the historical unconscious is repressed in the individual consciousness today, which nevertheless must be present to give meaning to the individual element? It is as though Freud wanted to trace the minimal temporal coordinates of the psychic space in order to locate in them the historical structure of subjectivity, the coordinates without which human beings cannot include themselves in the truth of history nor can psychology include itself as a human science.

Therefore, the inclusion of human beings in the logic of collective forms, while situating them in the element of the social and making them participate in history, does not for this reason fulfil the meaning of the historical, since *it excludes the historicisation of subjectivity*, without which the true signification of this collective participation is lost. The example of this, as we saw, is the artificial group. If there is no personal subjectivisation in the midst of the collective, there is no true collectivity.

And it was in the context of this attempt that Freud had to move on to the analysis of identification and to the prolongation of his path. Because this is where the struggle was fought out over the forms through which individuals assume the relation to others, while hiding the structure that gave them meaning. The forms of identification that were analysed are only those in which the prolongation of the body was halted in its signification. But they were also the matrix from within which the other opened or closed the possibility of serving as the mediator and model of my insertion into the collective reality: the form of the other is always the one that lays out the synthetic character of my social relation. The others opens for me a real totality, allows the libidinal extension of my body, or else closes it off into an abstract, imaginary whole, in which my body restricts itself narcissistically and by way of a transaction inscribes the halted relationships. And every social structure, no matter how rational it may be, no matter how broad its limits may be or how far its objects are from a sensible affirmation, is determined – as the basis that makes it understandable – by the human form from which all meaning is constructed and understood. But this is so not because we would decide, rationally or voluntarily, to place this form at its basis. It is present in its very absence, indicating the void of what remained hidden and repressed.

In other words, the group presents for Freud the following contradictory aspect: that sitting at its origin as the collective foundation of the individual form that it generated, it appears in its endpoint as dissolved into the individual form. This contradiction between the origin and the endpoint is the one that we are going to confront. Why this hiding and this dissolving of the collective power? What irrepressible access, what unstoppable amplification, what essential creation finds in this the only domain for the production of all things cultural? Our interpretive hypothesis is the same as the one Marx proposes for every historical moment: the productive forces, the creators of all wealth, are necessarily the producers of all subjective capacity and force.

> Not only do the objective conditions change in the act of reproduction ... but the producers change, too, in that they bring out new qualities in themselves, develop new powers and ideas, new modes of intercourse, new needs and new language.[6]

2   The Transition from the Natural Collective to the Cultural Collective

Let us go back to the myth of the origin of civilisation, the new 'hypothesis [...] to lighten the darkness of prehistoric times' (122). Freud picks up on his work from 1912, *Totem and Taboo*. There he showed the transformation of the primal (natural) horde, 'ruled over despotically by a powerful male' (122), into a fraternal (cultural) community. This transformation is the result of having confronted a limit situation: the rebellion against this despotism and the violent death of the chief, who at the same time was the father. The killing, in other words, of the most hated and at the same time the most beloved being, the crime against the despotic father, *the violence of all against one*, sits at the beginning of human history. The latter, says Freud, is only a new hypothesis to be added to the many hypotheses produced by the historians of primitive humanity. It is, therefore, a hypothesis that attempts to link the nearest with the farthest, with an origin that has disappeared forever, but which nonetheless must be formulated from within the present, because the present contains it as that from which its actual meaning is derived. And, I would say, because this origin continues to repeat itself, in its generality, in every moment when the human being, qua collective organisation, repeats this transition from a prior situation, lived as 'natural', to the following historical situation, discovered as a true cultural field of development.

But between that origin and this present, something that did not exist in its beginning is present in its endpoint as concealing its origin: there is 'religion, morality, and social organisation' (122). It is this dense historicity that therefore must be reanimated with its original sense.

The argument proceeds from the beginning between the primal horde and the actually existing group:

> Human groups exhibit once again the familiar picture of an individual of superior strength among a troop of equal companions, a picture which

---

6   Marx 1973, p. 494.

> is also contained in our idea of the primal horde. The psychology of such a group, as we know it from the descriptions to which we have so often referred – the dwindling of the conscious individual personality, the focusing of thoughts and feelings into a common direction, the predominance of the affective side of the mind and of unconscious psychical life, the tendency to the immediate carrying out of intentions as they emerge – all this corresponds to a state of regression to a primitive mental activity, of just such a sort as we should be inclined to *ascribe* to the primal horde. (122 emphasis added)

Here, however, we should retain a first difference: the comparison between the primal horde and the current group is established between two collective forms that are situated in different spaces. The primal horde, *before* history, in *pre*history, therefore as a natural collective, before the death of the father-chief and its conversion in fraternal community. And the current group or mass, which for its part is indeed already situated, *afterwards*, in the space of history, in the thick of civilisation, but nevertheless repeating a form that reproduces a relationship among its members that would correspond to the state of nature, now in the condition of culture or civilisation.

Let us try to understand the transition from nature to culture, the emergence of the civilised human form. This 'origin myth' is, as we saw, a hypothesis, and it could not be otherwise. But, we ask ourselves: does this contain, yes or no, the consideration of the origin such as from within our present we must infer it and deduce it to explain to ourselves *the present origin of our present*? This question amounts to having to answer for *the essence of the social in the human subject*.

Let us recall that individual psychology was defined, from the beginning of this book, as being 'from the very first ... at the same time social psychology as well' (69). How should we understand this 'from the very first' and 'at the same time' of the individual and the social? In our present actuality, yes, we see that psychology is as Freud demonstrated already *at the same time* individual and collective. But, we ask ourselves: what does 'from the very first' mean? In other words, what does the origin have to do with the present?

> Thus the group appears to us as a revival of the primal horde. Just as primitive man survives potentially in every individual, so the primal horde may arise once more out of any random collection; in so far as men are habitually under the sway of group formation we recognize in it the survival of the primal horde. We must conclude that *the psychology of groups is the oldest human psychology*; what we have isolated as indi-

vidual psychology, by neglecting all traces of the group, has only since come into prominence out of the old group psychology, by a gradual process which may still, perhaps, be described as incomplete. (123, emphasis added)

How then should we understand the difference between the first affirmation (on page 69) and the last (on page 123)? Here it would appear that collective or group psychology is prior to individual psychology. And that the psychological individual gradually differentiates itself from within the collective. Is the whole then prior to the parts that it determines? How then should we understand the 'formula' of the group formation, in which it was the set of individuals that constituted the collective totality in function of the leader? There is an ambiguity, an oscillation in the concept of the collective and the individual, which leads us to establish the predominance of one aspect, the part or the whole, the individual or the mass, over the other. But the problem is that of regression: if we establish that first there was the group or mass as collective psychology, and individual psychology as a result thereof, the return of the present-day group to its originary foundation would be the return, the regression, to a level where the psychological individual did not exist. With that the present meaning of the group disappears: it is not only a regression within our civilisation with everything constituted as cultural wealth, but also a historical regression towards prehistory and nature: a descent into the animality of the collective without subjectivity. This is why it is not a matter of establishing the origin in a *point* of departure. At the origin there is no point, no instant of thought, but a situation in time and space, the capture of a new structuring, and the appearance of a new form of relationship. Freud must recreate in the past, deducing it from the present, the drama of transition of the origin of our present situation on the basis of the essential form of a past situation that ours prolongs as its meaning.

This is why Freud immediately adds:

> Further reflection will show us in what respect this statement requires correction. *Individual psychology must, on the contrary, be just as old as group psychology,* for from the first there were two kinds of psychologies, that of the individual members of the group and that of the father, chief, or leader. The members of the group were subject to ties just as we see them to-day, but the father of the primal horde was free. His intellectual acts were strong and independent even in isolation, and his will needed no reinforcement from others. (123, emphasis added)

Therefore, a conclusion imposes itself: in a first moment, there was no individual psychology in the horde but there was in the father. This is how it is possible to consider the problem of the emergence of this individual psychology from within the midst of collective psychology. On the one hand, there would be *only* individual psychology, in the father; and, on the other, in the horde, *only* collective psychology. *There would be a contradiction between the individual and the collective.* Because the problem would be the following: could this individual psychology, that of the father, be extended so as to determine each one of the individuals who find themselves determined by collective psychology? Or, put differently: was the father's individual psychology compatible with the individual psychology of the members of the horde? Let us note that Freud in this hypothesis of the origin proposes to consider the congruence between part and whole, between individual and society: between individual psychology and group or mass psychology.

3 *The Last Natural Individual*

Thus, according to Freud, there would be no anteriority of one kind of psychology over the other, but simultaneity: at the same time the one and the other. And yet, both forms of psychology move, separately, still in the domain of nature: that of the father, as *natural individual*; that of the children, as *natural collective*. The individual, the father-chief, who dominates the whole, in this way would appear to have constituted *from the beginning of the whole*, that is to say, *he was not constituted by the development of the collective relations as a function of the cooperation of the members among themselves*. This is why at the origin the primal horde presented the opposition: on one side, the individual; on the other, the collective.

> The members of the group were subject to ties just as we see them today, but the father of the primal horde was free. His intellectual acts were strong and independent even in isolation, and his will needed no reinforcement from others. Consistency leads us to assume that his ego had few libidinal ties; he loved no one but himself, or other people only in so far as they served his needs. To objects his ego gave away no more than was barely necessary. (123)

Here we are in the domain of animal need, not in the shared desire that constitutes the human form of need. This natural exteriority of the individual with regard to the collective appears clearly expressed: his individual freedom was based on the submission of the others, but *as if* he did not depend on them. The intellectual acts were strong and energetic, *as if* his energy and strength were not based on the dominion over the others. His individuality was the result of a natural process. His libido did not extend itself so as permanently to encompass the others, and the other appeared only fleetingly, disappearing as soon as the need disappeared, *as if* need were not determined by the others in his satisfaction without memory. And the barely necessary attention his ego gave to objects was only what was needed to make them exist, for them to remain as objects of domination, *as if* his own existence was not founded upon theirs. And he could not do anything else, because his representations were individualistic: they did not result from the thoughtful exchange among the group's members. The others were nothing and he, as individual, was everything. He was the only individual, and his very privileged existence presupposed the non-existence of the others as individuals.

In this way Freud situates in the beginning what Nietzsche locates at the end of history:

> He, at the very beginning of the history of mankind, was the 'superman' whom Nietzsche only expected from the future. Even today the members of a group stand in need of the illusion that they are equally and justly loved by their leader; but the leader himself need love no one else, he may be of a masterful nature, absolutely narcissistic, self-confident and independent. We know that love puts a check upon narcissism, and it would be possible to show how, by operating in this way, it became a factor of civilisation. (123–24)

The existence of the superman would presuppose only the lack of consciousness of his power and the recognition, by the others, of the power that they nevertheless grant him as if it did not come from them. It would presuppose, in other words, not a process of culture or civilisation but a return to nature within culture. Because the narcissism in the world of culture or civilisation, which Nietzsche would express, is not equal to the natural narcissism of the first man: *he could not know it*. The narcissism of the primal father was anterior to the love that would encompass all; the narcissism of the chief of the current artificial group or mass, by contrast, becomes possible against the backdrop of a civilisation that *extended love and then withdrew it*. This second narcissism appears against the backdrop and from within a totality of cultural or civilised individuals, which is not the case of the first. Only in this way does narcissism become an important factor of civilisation: it imposes abstinence on the others, not on the basis of nature and the lack of individuality but against the backdrop of the production of culture or civilisation – work – and the existence of individuals whose limits are restricted, hiding the community and launching them into the struggle of opposition and pillage.

But this last individual, the natural superman, was not a narcissist by civilisation: he did not have the superego that would allow him to take himself as object. He was the strict complement of his biological ideality, restricted to his body without signification: without ego ideal. In the beginning there thus would be only a natural individual psychology. Or, what is the same, there would be a biological narcissism, anterior to the social, primary kind, without presupposing a totality of individuals but only a indiscriminate whole in which he, and only he in his biological sufficiency is in truth the unique individual, whose existence does not presupposes the recognition of the individuality of the others. The others were fused into the collective. Which also presupposes that the collective is not internalised in him; the whole is not part of the subjectivity of the natural individual, despite the fact that it refers to him. While the horde as a whole bordered on him, he was nevertheless the only one who, as individual, bordered on the whole. Yet not from within the whole, but from the outside and on top of it. The dominant natural individual lived out his life in the totality, as external to it. This situation is therefore necessarily anterior to civilisation, because civilisation implies the existence of an individual psychology that at the same time and from the very first would be group psychology, *within the individual element itself.* Thus, an individual psychology that emerges as a collective product. This is the problem that Freud brings up next. The individual psychology that is the work of civilisation, then, is not the mere prolongation of the natural individual psychology, because in the world of civilisation or culture the whole determines the part, the individual, and enters this social form in order to organise its individual structure.

> The primal father of the horde was not yet immortal, as he later became by deification. If he died, he had to be replaced; his place was probably taken by a youngest son, who had up to then been. There must therefore be a possibility of transforming group psychology into individual psychology; a condition must be discovered under which such a transformation is easily accomplished, just as it is possible for bees in case of necessity to turn a larva into a queen instead of into a worker. One can imagine only one possibility: the primal father had prevented his sons from satisfying their directly sexual impulsions; he forced them into abstinence and consequently into the emotional ties with him and with one another which could arise out of those of their impulsions that were inhibited in their sexual aim. He forced them, so to speak, into group psychology. His sexual jealousy and intolerance became in the last resort the causes of group psychology. (124)

4   *The Inaugural Violence of History*

The problem of the transformation of collective or group psychology into individual psychology comes up *after the assassination and death of the father*. But this death could happen only because there was a passage from natural group psychology to cultural group psychology: from the horde to the alliance. And in this passage resides the secret of civilisation, and of its concealment. Another field thus opens up, which is qualitatively new: the transition from the instant of satisfaction in which the primal father remained caught, sensible without rationality, to the open infinity as a symbolic domain separated from the sensible due to the assassination whose memory was repressed. He was the finite whole for the children, and his death opens up a process of psychic but common internalisation, in each one, of this totality which now is infinite and turns into an abstract subjective totality, from which the carnal and sensible figure of the father disappears as conscious content – in spite of the fact that his sensible form necessarily ended up written in blood on the flesh of each child. Because of his death there is the advent of the first individual of civilisation, because he is the one who now emerges from within the collectivity of culture or civilisation, from within another real totality: the youngest son was only 'a member of the group like any other'. And it is at this point that Freud initiates a movement of return, in which he must cast doubt on his prior affirmation, the *simultaneous* existence of the primal horde and the first civilised individual. This first simultaneity, projected as origin, reveals itself to be a retrospective illusion, the product of our present that represses the origin: it only appears projected onto the past by virtue of the simultaneity in which *we today* live their coexistence in the present world of culture or civilisation. But this is not how it was in the historical origin. Now we remain in the 'idealist', abstract vision of a negated origin: the origin of the assassination and of death. In the present it would be the expression of this concealment that we thus project back onto the origin and, therefore, it would be the projection sent back to the past of a current situation that we do not want to see, or cannot see. 'There must therefore be a possibility of transforming group psychology into individual psychology', Freud tells us (124). But this must occur from within the acceptance of the collective origin, of the violent power exerted and recognised as common; only from there can the individual of civilisation emerge. But to recognise the past origin we must be able to see it, as a similar matrix, showing up in its form, *for us*, from within the present. Not against the backdrop of an imaginary totality, an abstract whole, but starting from a real and present situation that is the historical endpoint of that past which, in retrospect, proves us right. And this is how it is revealed that the first collective or group psychology, the one that we consider to be natural, *in reality was an imposition*: the father imposed the group psychology on them in order to control them, when he imposed abstinence on them. And that this is, in reality, our own point of departure, except that now – and the difference is crucial – it is *cultural*:

> One can imagine only one possibility: the primal father had prevented his sons from satisfying their directly sexual impulses; he forced them into abstinence and consequently into the emotional ties with him and with one another. (124)

At the historical origin, the collective relationship of the union with others is a fact that comes *after* the union with the father. The primal father, prolonging a natural privilege, that of his paternity, separates himself from the totality by emphasising his difference and imposing privation on all the others in order to prolong his own pleasure against them as a function of his force and his anteriority. From this there follows, as a secondary consequence, *first* an affective tie of submissiveness; and, *then*, as a result of this submission, the establishing of bonds of similitude among the brothers, all subjected to the same figure. The horde, as natural collective, thus appears to be determined as a function of privation by a bond in which each member, indistinct in his individuality, reads off his nonbeing in the being of the father. But this nonbeing *is*: qua being, each member has his biological individuality restricted to its animal corporeality; qua non-being, he has his psychic dependency restricted to the being of the other, the father. This then inaugurates a nonbeing that, as lack, comes from the father and is given back to each member as the negative form of an individuality that emerges as the obverse of the father. It is in this natural collective where the negative identification with the father as nonbeing opens up the domain of a collective recognition, in which each individual nonbeing, defined in this nonbeing as lack, recognises himself within a collective being as *collective lack*. The collective being in a first moment consists in the recognition of being through the establishing of individual bonds on the basis of nonbeing: on the basis of a lived negation. Thus at the heart of the biological collective we would have a form of being that, because of the relation with the paternal form, allowed the individualisation of its members in the contradictory form of a nonbeing, and this created the possibility of conceiving its affirmative being as collective from within the negated individuality. From the midst of a natural collective, fragmented in bilateral dependency, imposed by the father figure, there emerges the cultural collective of civilisation, based on the determination of each member as individual negated by the father's individuality. But this individuality, which emerges in the fraternal alliance, is not the same as before, in the primal horde. The individuality of the horde would be biological, and, therefore, an individuality without others, only side by side with others. In the fraternal alliance it would be cultural, an individuality with others, determined in its very form by the others. The second is the collective or group psychology, which is at the same time, and from the very first, individual psychology – the one which Freud asked about from the very beginning (on page 69).

5   *The Concealment of Death in Painless Pleasure*
The later individual psychology, which we found in the domain of culture or civilisation, is the result of the sexual satisfaction that liberates the members from the cultural group psychology (reciprocal identification). But above all it is the result of the concealment of the collective action, the real community, which made the individual psychology possible. This is why Freud insists on bringing this out as an essential discovery: because it is this origin that continues to be concealed in the current form of individuality. Thus what happens is that in the transition from nature to culture the process that made it possible, the first historical act that, according to the first hypothesis, continues to take place in history in each advent of an individual in the individual psychological sense, what makes this possible is precisely what *disappears*.

> Whoever became his successor was also given the possibility of sexual satisfaction, and was by that means offered a way out of the conditions of group psychology. The fixation of the libido to woman and the possibility of satisfaction without any need for delay or accumulation made an end of the importance of those of his sexual impulsions that were inhibited in their aim, and allowed his narcissism always to rise to its full height. (124)

The last natural collective was a whole without any satisfaction: with neither woman nor property. The first cultural collective is a whole in which sexual satisfaction, in the social family, is possible. The liberation of individuality that thus is produced continues to happen, however, as if it happened within the first natural totality. It reproduces the individual psychology of the father, so much so that in its origin the collective force that led to the fraternal alliance, to the exercising of a historical power that led to its satisfied cultural individuality, was able to do so thanks to this plural act of the exercise of a real power, in which the nonbeing of the biological individuals recuperated itself as the being of a cultural individual. It forgets the fact that it did so from within the collective power and in the confrontation of the obstacle: the killing of the individual who imposed privation on them. Thus, the presupposition of their own existence, that which keeps sustaining this existence in its satisfaction, pass from the real into the virtual. And, at another level, the dissolution comes back:

sexuality reappears, satisfied, on the limited model of the ferocious father. The meaning of the social death and of life disappears in the instant of satisfaction as if it were 'natural' to find enjoyment with the female partner. And what disappears in the collective is the meaning of that power which produced it as fraternal alliance, in order to install itself as a form of naturality of the cultural collective. What happened is that the originary transition was negated, the reality of the act was negated, and the source of individual power lost sight of the real origin that gave rise to it: the force of the collective. The subjective domain opened up as an infinite totality by the negation of the death of the father did not allow an opening in the psychic apparatus, in consciousness, for the real and temporal dimension of the passage in question: it could not take responsibility for the violence and necessary pain of having removed the obstacle that was opposed to life – the obstacle that, in spite of being loved as well, was removed for the sake of living. The subjective domain remained in the false infinite whole, without prolonging itself in the internalisation of the real categories that would reflect the truth of what was lived. Here, in fact, the whole was the real and temporal totality of the fraternal alliance: a historical totality from which the possibility of individual satisfaction derived thanks to the exercise of its collective power. The cultural individuality, in its enjoyment, ignores the historical origin that made it possible.

This is why, even though the successor, the youngest son, liberates himself at the origin from the collective or group psychology, in reality he liberates himself from the natural group psychology from within the new cultural group psychology that thus is created. But this transition remains concealed, because the killing of the father, as we saw, is repressed as if it did not sit at the beginning of his individual being. This guilt that is not assumed, by hiding the meaning of the collective past and remaining only at the level of individual enjoyment, conceals the collective and cultural meaning present in the access to individual enjoyment. And it conceals the opposition between the finite and the infinite: the finitude of affectionate ties, which in the social duration acquires the ahistorical infinitude of a collective whose signification ends up being reduced to the form of the dead father, who was the whole, and who continues to persecute the individual consciousness. And the direct satisfaction of the sexual drives appears to convert the instant of yearning, previously sent back to the fantasy of an imaginary satisfaction, into the only individual reality. The libido, which previously encompassed the brothers in the fraternal alliance, becomes dissociated so as to centre all its love on the sexual form of woman, in her empirical form, and limited to the sensible corporeality of the sexual object. In the extent to which the origin of their capacity for love and pleasure disappears, because it conceals the foundation of pain and hatred from which it proceeds, the collective signification of this 'double individuality' also disappears, as well as the social signification of the individuality of the other. The withdrawal of libido produces a withdrawal of our sensible prolongation into reality as well as a retraction of the field of thought. If the lived relation of the body with the others disappears, it is because the consciousness disappeared that inhibits its thinking. But this totality which thus restricts itself for this reason does not stop keeping them alive in the relations of production, in collective property or in private property: they cannot drop out of the material reality in which they continue to subsist. The truth that has been relegated from individual consciousness remains engraved in the inevitable persistence of the relations of production, on which the individualities are based. Thus, the lack of consciousness of the collective, erased from individual and social consciousness, effectively subsists in the collective materiality of the relations of production, which for their part cannot be erased. The aim-inhibited tendencies, which united themselves in the fraternal alliance in search of their object so as not to remained inhibited, by returning from what was inhibited to its foundation in sexual satisfaction become separated: in their place appears narcissism, that is to say, what in history will culminate as the dissociation between the individual and the collective, in bourgeois individualism, precisely there where, as Marx said, the collective relations are the broadest and the most complex. In this way the social collective totality once again comes to exist *side by side* with individuality, and in opposition to it.

6 *The Concealment of the Origin Prolonged in the Negation of the Present*

It is precisely in this social space, which is that of the forgetting of the origin of the collective power that made possible the psychic individuality, where the artificial group or mass appears. And this form, insofar as it is real and is part of the productive system in which, through labour, everybody is newly integrated and subjected, is the result of an 'ideal transformation' for Freud:

> We may further emphasize, as being specially instructive, the relation that holds between the contrivance by means of which an artificial group is held together and the constitution of the primal horde. We have seen that with an army and a Church this contrivance is the illusion that the leader loves all of the individuals equally and justly. But this is simply *an idealistic remodelling of the state of affairs in the primal horde*, where all of the sons knew that they were equally persecuted by the primal father, and feared him equally. This same recasting upon which all social duties are built up is already presupposed by the next form of human society, the

totemic clan. The indestructible strength of the family as a natural group formation rests upon the fact that this necessary presupposition of the father's equal love can have a real application in the family. (124–125)

We saw that the domain of reality produced by the fraternal alliance as the first historical act was internalised, out of guilt, as the ideal form expelled from reality, and the realm of the finite inaugurated in this way was transformed into an abstract infinity: the distance that separates precisely the life preserved from the death that was given to the father, whereby the finitude of one's own is separated from the infinitude of the other, as internalised absolute. Let us note, once again, the similarity that Freud perceives *only* between the primal horde and the artificial group, that is, the collective formations that are those, for example, of the capitalist system. Within a cultural collective domain, the latter reproduce anew the natural group formation of the horde, prior to the recognition of its power and the exercise of violence that led to the removal of the obstacle opposed to satisfaction. But, in the case of the artificial group, we are dealing with a cultural form, one that inhibits that which constitutes the essential aspect of the historical process: *to know themselves to be equally persecuted*. It inhibits therefore the collective power that would be required to exercise violence *one more time* in order to oppose the present obstacle. Therein consists its idealism: in transforming the persecution into the adhesion to the power that persecutes us. The material reality, which expresses itself in the relations of production that ties us to the appropriation of labor without any return, but under the appearance of exchange, is socially instituted in individual consciousness by an abstract totality. There the form of the father, elevated to an infinitude without time or space, continues to regulate our relation to reality. In terms of culture we have the direct sexual satisfaction in the family, but without duration. In terms of nature we have the atomisation of the collective and the submission to power, which robs us now, not of woman, but of the only thing of interest within the domain of culture or civilisation: the collective force of labour and the property of nature. The social duties of labour and productivity are thus imposed as if they were the result of the fraternal alliance, which was a community meant to overthrow power. At the heart of the most intensively collective forms, what is actualised, as if they were cultural, are the forms of biological collectivity, in which the father was the only property-owner: of the earth and of women. Insofar as what dominates us now is no longer an individual form but a collective one – capital – its need no longer requires all women, who are conceded to us, but all of labour, which is extracted from us. From within the subjected individual form that is being fought out in the collective, there is thus no amplification either in feeling or in thinking that would include in the individuals their true collective signification. (And this is what was prolonged in the science that Freud is criticising.) For the only social field in which the individual has the illusion of being loved is in belonging to the social form of the family.

The latter, the family, is the social form that spontaneously is considered as the 'natural' form: it preserves the production of man-woman from the origin until today, without technology having been able to supply this form of production. This is why the artificial group or mass finds in the bourgeois family the form in which the group is already contained as its necessary social extension. Because here the family, which in its very structure that is lived as 'natural' ignores its historical origin, excludes that its members gain consciousness of the social determination that is lost therein. The 'natural' family, in spite of its being a fact of culture or civilisation, would seem to be the same family as that of the primal horde. In it there is no room for the social determination, which also did not exist in the first whose archaic cellular structure is prolonged into the present:

> The indestructible strength of the family as a natural group formation rests upon the fact that this necessary presupposition of the father's equal love can have a real application in the family. (125)

In the family, considered as natural, what disappears is the effective reality of the system of production, given through relations of opposition and class struggle. And what appears in its place? An effective reality, which conceals the other one, which is the global truth of the system: the father's equal love toward all of his children. Thus the love of the bourgeois family, as an island of love, conceals the hatred that from the outside rules over it as well as the struggles and conflicts that its members necessarily encounter, once they cross the threshold of the family. In this way the family gives itself, internally, the archaic and prehistoric presumption that cancels out the current social determination of the system that shapes it. But since it is not really natural, and since the love of the father in the family leaves open the satisfaction of the direct impulsions *outside of it*, the domain of the social appears *later* as conceding that which the father, in his family, did not concede. The problem, the only one, that the members of the bourgeois family would admit outwards, is nevertheless present from within the family as if it were its true origin. It is the only problem that the family admits as the familiar origin of the human subject: as a one-to-one relationship, which later, as collective society, it presupposes as already resolved in our transition towards it. And yet, the father of the family, in which 'the father's equal love can have a real application', is not the archaic *Ur*-father. Ours carries within himself, as the form of being the father, the social form of the superego that rules over him. This is why Freud says that the superego is that of the grandparents and that is why he talks of a collective superego. The cultural father, who necessarily appears as natural to the child, is qualitatively different from the father of the horde. *Our father in the family is the subjected individual in the artificial group*, who repressed the assassination of his own father and who gave himself up to the power that subjects him. And, in so doing, he is the one who in producing us inhibited himself and kept himself from inscribing in his paternity the system of production as the real producer of human subjects. By usurping his production as absolute, before the child, he conceals his own production by the system, as subjected father. The 'real application' of this love he has for us, therefore, is not an appearance: he treats us, the children, as different from him, the father. The class struggle in the social system is reduplicated in this struggle of the children against the truth that the parents conceal in the family system. He loves us in the way he, in his abstract solution, is loved in the system: loved by the dominant love that the reigning models to which he is subjected impose on him, by the collective superego and by the individual superego. His cultural form of love drags along with it the rationality of the whole system and imposes it on us in his love. Because he himself ignores it, the latter is thus *a form of love that covers up what is real*.

Thus, we discover that *our family is produced* not only by society, as people say, but *by a determinate form of society: by the artificial group or mass*. That is to say, by the social forms that impose the form of their own being and the modalities of repression onto the father and mother. All of which is based on being in love, which led to procreation. But our father, who in turn is a member of the artificial group, is lived from within the family, by the children, as if he were the terrorising father of the horde. And this is what the child, because of its infantile insufficiency, cannot see: it is taken advantage of. The arrogant family father is the terrorised member of the subjected group.

Thus, from within the family, the social signification disappears that really constituted it as family. And, as a result, what disappears is the social signification of each of its members in their most profound individuality: in their narcissistic core. This signification is not meant to be seen: it is meant to be known. Only on the basis of knowledge does a new cultural capacity for seeing open up. The question, therefore, comes back to the problem: what keeps us from knowing? What keeps us from reading off the meaning of the social system on the basis of the family? And once again we will see that it is the blinding splendour that the figure of the father projects and expands.

7   *The Gaze without Consciousness*

To explain the appearance in the subject of a seeing without knowing, Freud steps back from the social form and picks up anew the problem of hypnosis and suggestion, now within this wider framework at which he has arrived thanks to the preceding explanation. And we will understand why hypnosis for him was 'a group formation with two members' (115). This was because the foundation of this social relationship of two already included the social frame that had determined both terms: the hypnotist, in his paralyzing power, which is a power that is not individual but social (the place of the father); and the hypnotised, in his submissive dependency, which is a delegation of power that also is not individual but social (the place of the child). The result was the paralysis of one of the extremes: the omnipotent person here confronted an impotent subject. The asymmetry was not biological but cultural: both omnipotence and impotence were a collective result. Now the importance of this analysis becomes evident: it tends to explain the form of individual dependency as a minimal form that is already collective, already social. And we arrive at the following result: the power for which the father shines in his splendour is the outcome of the infantile vision, as the vision of that external being who in his presence expresses the whole reality that through its domination opens up for us. This power, which makes the father be *all* for the child, is what elevates him into transcendence while being only a *part*, which in fact he is. Presence and signification are united here: the child sees him as a whole and, in its presence, it is the whole for him.

Let us have a closer look at this process. Freud says:

> But we expect even more of this derivation of the group from the primal horde. It ought also to help us to understand what is still incomprehensible and mysterious in group formations – all that lies hidden behind the enigmatic words 'hypnosis' and 'suggestion'. And I think it can succeed in this too. Let us recall that hypnosis has something positively uncanny about it; but the characteristic of uncanniness suggests something old and familiar that has undergone repression. Let us consider how hypnosis is induced. The hypnotist asserts that he is in possession of a mysterious power that robs the subject of his own will; or, which is the same thing, the subject believes it of him. This mysterious power (which is even now often described popularly as 'animal magnetism') must be the same power that is looked upon by primitive people as the source of taboo, the same that emanates from kings and chieftains and makes it dangerous to approach them (*mana*). The hypnotist, then, is supposed to be in possession of this power; and how does he manifest it? By telling the subject to look him in the eyes; his most typical method of hypnotising is by his

look. But it is precisely the sight of the chieftain that is dangerous and unbearable for primitive people, just as later that of the Godhead is for mortals. Even Moses had to act as an intermediary between his people and Jehovah, since the people could not support the sight of God; and when he returned from the presence of God his face shone – some of the *mana* had been transferred on to him, just as happens with the intermediary among primitive people. (125)

In a first beginning before entering history, at its starting point, we should recall that the familiar and the collective coincided: the natural collectivity was the family. It was there, moreover, where the power of the father, in the infancy of the human being, naturally imposed itself on the children. He was all, the others nothing. But at the same time he was the one who generated the totality of the family, and each one was a child only with reference to his power of generation. But together with the adult father, the current family lost the privilege of this coincidence. *The current family does not coincide with the collective*: global society contains the family as a partial form that it determines. But for the child born within the family, who passes from the natural to the cultural, this appearance of the origin once again repeats itself: the father is the whole and the family is the domain where this power displays itself. The system of production, which determines the family, does not appear directly in its interior. Everything that is real reaches us and actualises its power only through the father. The power of the father is the prolongation of the social power, but we live this in inverted form: we do not know it. We know what we see, and we see him, but the vision of him is a shining splendour. It shines with his power. Thus, what in hypnosis once again is reawakened is 'something old and familiar': the unbearable presence of the look of the father, and the renewed subjection to his power. The father was like God: we could not bear his sight. And his command was like God's: it imposed its fulfilment. Freud here reaches the moment in which the other is and reappears as absolutely other for oneself. And he shows us one more time the real origin of an actual illusion. In the beginning, he tells us, we were all slaves of the father's power. In the end, we all have to confront the risk and free ourselves from him. What the fraternal alliance did, which was to assassinate the father, each human being must necessarily do in order to gain access to existence. Nobody made us, in fact, free once and for all. Each human subject must face up, from his new emergence, and newly enter the battle of his or her own liberation. But a basic and essential difference subsists between the child and the primitive: the fact that the child lives an experience as real, whereas reality and appearance coincide for the primitive. This is why the child, from his infantile incapacity, remains restricted to an unavoidable dependency – until it reaches adulthood. But being an adult implies transforming the paternal dependency and including in it the broadening that opens the family to the social form that determines it, just as the power of the father prolongs itself until it finds its foundation in the power of the system. This is precisely what the members of the horde did in order to reach their cultural individuality: to inscribe their power in that of the fraternal alliance and confront the father's power with a new power, the collective power, which was the common discovery.

Primitive man, the man of the horde, as an adult confronted an adult submission that was based on a real domination. But the child emerges from the infantile submission in which the father's domination, as real, is only figurative: his power is the result of the fact that he is already an adult, whereas the child is only a child; and his law is the result of the power that the system exercises over him. In this way the child does not know that the father, whom he experiences as master, is also a slave. Between the child's sight of the father as master and the knowledge of him as slave, the system of production introduces itself, the recognition of the social source of the true power. The recognition that discovers that we, the father as well as the child, are *both slaves of a power to which we are both subjected*. But to reach this it is necessary for the child to have made the transition from the infantile appearance to the adult truth, and for the former to extend itself, by including itself, into the latter. One must not subsist side by side with the other. The adult flesh must not become the seat for the felt infantile dependency. It must reawaken the same terror and the same stunned reaction before the gaze of the other. It must reveal within itself, at last, the source of all power: *expel from its flesh the seat of transcendence*. To liberate oneself here does not mean to liberate oneself *from* the father but to liberate oneself *with* the father: to understand him too as the slave of power. As Hegel said about the power of the master: to see behind him the true power, the 'absolute master', to whom both the slave and the master are subjected: death. But here what is at stake is not death, which in itself is invincible as endpoint, but to vanquish those who use death in order for them to remain alive. As long as the distance between father and son remains as an atemporal distance, without the introduction of the time of history that links one's own origin to the common origin, the distance also will not open up for the social field in which to recognize the true enemy.

This transformation, as shown in the analysis of hypnotism, repeats the relationship in which, once more, a man returns as if he were all and the other, who sees him thus, is reduced to nothing, to an infamous part at best in total dependency to the other. This is an extreme case, in other words, in order to underscore the process of identification. But no longer in sickness, but playing it safe in health: looking for salvation in the other. We already saw the distortions that occurred in the dialectic of whole and parts when we took the human form as the point of departure of logic. But here we have the basic form in which the libidinal relation appears reduced to its minimum and the dependency, by contrast, reaches its maximum. Though based at the origin on a very precise other, the father, this form of identification is the one that was decanted in ourselves as *general disposition for dependency and submissiveness*, as exaltation surrendered to the gleaming splendour of power. Every relation with the other invested with power repeats the relation of dependency: 'some of the *mana* has been transferred on to him' (125). What is of interest in hypnotism is this submission and surrender to the other that causes the disappearance of the adult intelligibility of reality, of the effective connections and relationships that structure it, and from the very depths of the presumed affirmation of individuality cause the uncontainable appearance of a blinding and yearned-for dependency. What is Freud showing here? That together with and next to the normal understanding of reality, and from within an intellectual grasp that corresponds to the rational comprehension of the world – and, I would say more: even in those in whom a dialectical form of thinking predominates – there is something uncontainable that emerges from the flesh that the other all of a sudden reanimates with his look: a complete destruction of this rational connection with reality. And thus we once again immerse ourselves in the elementary forms of relationships, in which the dialectic of whole and parts appears once more subverted, reduced to the mere primordial sensibility without reason:

> The situation is the same as if the hypnotist had said to the subject: 'Now concern yourself exclusively with my person; the rest of the world is quite uninteresting'. [...] The hypnotist avoids directing the subject's conscious thoughts towards his own intentions, and makes the person upon whom he is experimenting sink into an activity in which the world is bound to seem uninteresting to him; but at the same time the subject is in reality unconsciously concentrating his whole attention upon the hypnotist, and is getting into an attitude of rapport, of transference on to him. (126)

The mechanism is clear. The hypnotist asks his subject to concentrate *not on his whole self* but on a *privileged part* of his body: on his eyes. Apparently, this is the habitual form of all perception. Indeed, all perception focuses on a part of the world, and the whole tied to this salient part then appears as the *backdrop* of the perception in question. But in the part of the eyes, we see with our own eyes the eyes of the other looking at us: we look at the other at the very centre through which his being makes itself seen. And from seeing we go on to be seen. This is the crucial moment of every perception of the other: to see that with which the other sees us. We accept to see the other in a part of him, but it is that part from where his whole being radiates out. It is no longer 'something' we see: we see the other in his *power* of seeing us. Here the gaze oscillates in its most profound ambiguity, where what is at play is my being in the face of the being or nonbeing of the other: do we see or, in reality, in a process where our intention falls in the trap of the other's gaze, are we seen by him? All looking the other into the eyes presents a challenge: to be able to continue looking there where the other sees us from. This means the self-assertion of our own power to see the other, without being negated by him in our autonomous capacity for seeing. But the hypnotist already starts from a minimal relationship of dependence: he *obliges* the other to look him in the eye, he *subjects* him by means of his gaze by *imposing* on him the condition of being looked at by him. But he imposes on him the condition of being seen in the very centre of his being: he forces him to let himself be seen there where he does not see himself. Therefore, the hypnotist gives up his sight for the sake of the other's seeing: he makes him 'sink into an activity in which the world is bound to seem uninteresting to him' (126). It is no longer he who is looking: he only sees with the eyes of the other. He disappears in his being in order to be the other: 'the subject is in reality unconsciously concentrating his whole attention upon the hypnotist, and is getting into an attitude of rapport, of transference on to him' (126). What did the hypnotist demand from the hypnotised subject when he asked him to look him in the eye? *Without saying it* (and this is why Freud, saying that which the hypnotist does not say, reveals his 'unavowed intention'), he conceals what he is pursuing: 'The situation is the same as if the hypnotist had said to the subject: 'Now concern yourself exclusively with my person; the rest of the world is quite uninteresting'' (126). He does not say so, he does not confess his project of control, because in the concealment of his conscious intention *he solicits from the other a gaze without consciousness*. This is why, from the start, the apparent symmetry of the reciprocal gaze, the equality of the situation, has been falsified; the conscious intention of domination in one is opposed in the other by the credulous incomprehension of the conscious but unavowed intention with which this gaze is solicited: 'The hypnotist avoids directing the subject's conscious thoughts towards his own intentions' (126). There is one who remains conscious; and there is another in whom consciousness surrenders itself and disappears. One is the dominator; the other turns out dominated. To surrender consciousness in relation to the other means to surrender the whole field of signification where the gaze of the other acquires meaning, so as to return exclusively to a *corporal seeing without consciousness*, which reanimates, by means of repression, the first terror of being seen by the other: when 'the people could not support the sight of God' (125).

8   *Fathers or Brothers?*
In a footnote Freud highlights this subtraction of the signification of reality in the very moment when we most surrender ourselves to the presence of the other. Our interest splits into two: the real ceases to attract us, while our conscious attention focuses only on the hypnotist. The other monopolises our conscious interest, as if it were everything. It is not the *form* of gaining consciousness that here gives itself up, which would leave consciousness free as a capacity to integrate the perceived into knowledge. It is the subject's conscious capacity that delegates itself in this aspect in which the object erases the world or makes it insignificant.

> This situation, in which the subject's attitude is unconsciously directed towards the hypnotist, while he is consciously occupied with monotonous and uninteresting perceptions, finds a parallel among the events of psycho-analytic treatment (126 n. 2)

To the dependency with respect to the hypnotizer there corresponds an immobility in reality; the external world loses its temporal and cultural signification, which is parallel to the subject's own development, even as the latter depends on the former. This case would be diametrically opposed to the one at work in the scientific decentring. Whereas the individual, in order to reach the truth of the system that determines him, must decentre the reality away from himself so as to centre it in function of the structure of the totality, here the decentring is displaced in order to centre itself anew, but this time on the other as if here where all. The other assumes, in his corporeality, the structural *function*: he is the one who gives meaning to the world, which radiates out from him.

We are clearly seeing in what sense Freud's analyses inscribe themselves: in the attempt to understand the mechanisms of displacement of the totalising function of thought in the subject. Its application to the analysis of the group is only one of its aspects, perhaps the most important one. But we must also indicate that this problem arises precisely at a determinate moment in history: when the rational capacity of human beings has reached the scientific knowledge of the structure that determines them so as to be able at last to organize their action in function of a rational truth prolonged from within the flesh. The aim is to analyse these obstacles.

By the measures that he takes, then, the hypnotist awakens in the subject a portion of his archaic heritage which had also made him compliant towards his parents and which had experienced an individual re-animation in his relation to his father; what is thus awakened is the idea of a paramount and dangerous personality, towards whom only a passive-masochistic attitude is possible, to whom one's will has to be surrendered, – while to be alone with him, 'to look him in the face', appears a hazardous enterprise. (127)

It would remain to be shown that this Freudian analysis, the need to have recourse to the archaic heritage in order to explain these phenomena, is an unnecessary hypothesis, or at least one that is not the most economical. The mass or group would actualize the archaic situation in one of three possibilities: submission to the father in the artificial group; rebellion in the spontaneous mass; effective revolutionary organisation in the fraternal community. And our question would be: from where does the artificial group receive the meaning of its organisation, which is precisely the one in which the archaic heritage appears most strongly to be the determining factor? At issue is not only that the individuals would actualize in their own individuality only *one* archaic content, and for this to constitute in and of itself the phenomenon of the artificial group. We have seen that this emergence of the archaic opens up several possible forms of being a group or mass: the three forms that Freud presents. There thus must exist *from the outside, now*, a power external to the individuals that obliges them to enter into a relationship, to come together in a bond, to fuse *in some way*. To internalize *one* element of the heritage. This external power does not appear clearly in Freud's text, unless we take the work relationship, on which he insists so much, as a determining factor of this pressure in the direction of fusion. We will say then that the broader system that unites them into a totality, or in various totalities, is the social relationship of work or labour, which organises them in function of production.

What Freud wishes to show in other words would be the following: within a collective organisation whose meaning stems from an actually existing relation to the totality of the system of production, the individual in function of having been a child without undoing the trap of the primary process goes back to participate in this organisation *as if* the real content of its social and historical determination did not appear to give meaning to it. It is here that the personal determinations of the subject's own formation re-encounter the social determinations of its historical formation, and coincide with them.

This would be why for Freud, coming solely from within the current social condition, the subjective features that appear so uniformly to determine the individual of the artificial group: passivity, masochism, renunciation of the will. It is as if he had said that now there are groups *because* in the human subject there persists the archaic, proto-historic heritage, an individual thread that ties each individual, already separately, to an origin that for its part was collective and which the current collectivity retrieves when it is already determined. But these reactions, which would have to be, Freud says, those 'of the individual member of the horde' (127), as we have seen, are not the same *now*. The determination of dependency on the father would govern his individual being in the family in the stage close to the child's birth and, therefore, only in an individual who neither knows nor has a relation with the others, who is still in a relation of parental dependency. By contrast, for the determination in the individual who would correspond to the situation of the fraternal alliance, there is no moment in the child that would be homogeneous to it: the analogy comes into play only in the individual's relation to the others, from within the specific situation that occurs in an adult social formation. Once more, then: the archaic heritage is inadequate for explaining the current situation in the child, and the analogy would be explicable not as coming from the past towards the present, from the archaic towards the contemporary, that is to say, from the origin of history up and until today's child, but on the contrary *from the present towards the past. We infer and we deduce*, based on the dependent character of the child today – and this in turn from within an explanation that discerns its current motivation from its own birth – the origin of this dependency, and we create the scientific myth of the origin. And in so doing we translate it by conceiving of the origin of history on its basis. The current organisation of the mass or group explains and gives meaning to the prehistoric masses or groups, and not the other way around. It is because human beings *today* must confront the meaning of their dependence that the understanding of their belonging to the group is produced. It is because human beings *today* subject themselves that we study how this dependency originates in the child. And it is *from here* that we conceive of an origin that led human beings to pass necessarily from natural dependency to the community: because both are present in our time. Marx shows how, whatever the human being may be capable of, it is impossible to think of the past without previously determining the categories of the present that make it thinkable and allow it to be reconstructed by following those categories. This is not a hypothesis: it is the result of a methodological analysis that disentangled at last the historical method for science. But the problem in Freud would seem to reside in the fact that, in spite of everything, he endows the human being with a power that acts beyond this limit: each one would have the capacity to actualize the prehistoric form of the initial drama which in the individual outlives itself and continues. Would the reconstruction of the past from the present then have no meaning, given that it is present, albeit without history, in the present? We think not, because, as we saw, Freud himself in spite of his hypothesis has to reconstruct the truth of this original situation from within the present: whence the scientific 'myth'. But not only that: he has to give it its new meaning from within the present, supplementing it with that which, because of the determinations of *our* current system of production, specifies it in its true meaning.

What we are interested in retaining is furthermore the notion that the character of 'individual psychology' is the product of a historical process; that the return to the first form for dissolving oneself in the archaic mass is impossible, since we *already* are, through and through, cultural individuals. The return to the form of the 'primal horde', then, is historically nonsensical when looked at from the vantage point of the necessary transition that each one has already effectuated. If in the archaic origin there was first the fraternal alliance and *then* the first individual, this real generation, which leads from the collective to the individual element, is inverted in the child: first, there is the individual, by itself; then, little by little, the social totality appears. First there is the power of the father; then, the power of the system. Everything then is turned upside down: coming from the family, the necessary decentring, which the structure demands for inserting oneself into the family as true individual, must be conquered against the illusion centred on one's own being, on oneself. The child is born as if it lived in the primal horde, but it develops itself – if it really does so at all – as if it made its transition to the fraternal alliance.

In this way what is actually primary in the child's origin coincides only with one aspect of the initial drama of the prehistoric origin of the human being: with the primal horde. For all these reasons, Freud completes his analysis by establishing once more the character of the current group formation by referring it to its origin in the primal horde, to which it may be 'traced back' (127). This is why he rephrases the problem: if it descends from the primal horde, its current meaning can only be understood by confronting once more today the same problem of the horde, which marked the beginning of history: by confronting the power that, among us, oppresses us. Whence the fact that this historical origin becomes readable only in the present, because it is always repeating itself. We never have won it over definitively: it must be put back into play, time after time, in a new way. This is true not only in the case of the group but also in the case of the individual. The historical process demands, therefore, both conquests, both forms of independence, and one cannot exist without the other. The conquest of personal independence, in the extent to which we live in the artificial group – institutions of domination – necessarily passes through the independence of the whole, *without which there can be no individual solution.*

This is why Freud makes the artificial group accountable for the resurgence within it of phenomena referring to suggestion and hypnotism. Only in this way can he affirm:

> The primal father is the group ideal, which governs the ego in the place of the ego ideal. ((127)

If we have understood that the artificial group is the only one in which the drama of transition to history proper is held back, in the individual as much as in the institutions to which he or she belongs, it is clear that only to such a group can we assign the social persistence of the domination of the primal father and, thus, the predominant form of the horde. Those masses that rebel against domination and objectify the actuality of its archaic prolongation, then, separate themselves from the artificial group. The rebelling masses interrupt the sense of history and promote its dialectic, by assuming their historic function, the one that reveals to them the key to the collective power that at last has been recuperated. Thus appears with great clarity the historical rationality of the masses: to incorporate themselves into history by destroying the model of social organisation that keeps them in the condition of culture or civilisation as if it were a natural state, as if there were no meaning for human beings except to submit to the same, the constant repetition of the forms of imbalance and dependency that currently rule.

Can we consider this consequence, which implicitly is contained in the prolongation of Freud's thinking, as something optional, to be accepted or rejected? Can psychoanalysis, as the discovery in the subject of the historical determination that gave rise to it as human subject, elude the moment of its collective determination? And can it elude the confrontation and the rebellion before the repressive power that includes it, in history, in a form that is prior to history? Can human beings reach their historical and therefore most personal meaning, without accomplishing this act of assuming the social determination of their subjectivity? Does the sick character of a civilisation not reside in this impossibility? The conventional psychoanalyst, restricted only to the forms that this same civilisation defines as normal, stops seeing his own abnormality, his own participation in the artificial group, his insertion into the horde: *individuality without brothers*, without fraternity, reduplicating in concealment the presence not only of the repressive father but also, qua model, the activity of the repressive power that is prolonged in the father.

X The Mass, Stage or Battlefield

Implicit in the 'amplified' notion of love was the amplification of the ego, the broadening of the field of subjectivity of each human being: the transition from the I to the we. The 'amplifying of love' is only the synthetic expression of the amplifying of the I who passes from the ego ideal to the group ideal: from the ideal of the one to the ideal of all. And the 'ideal' here expresses the distance between what is actual and what is only possible. In other words, it appears to present the demand of a transformation: to convert a merely subjective, internal distance into an external, objectified distance – one that is both historical and collective. But we also already saw how there is a trap in the realm of the social for thwarting this process, by converting the matter of this ideal – the group or mass that in its collective expansion includes the material field of domination and transformation in which it lives and produces – into a merely symbolic incarnation. It 'incarnates' the group ideal in the leader: it confers on the group ideal only the miserable materiality of an individual body.

In this chapter Freud is going to analyse the vicissitudes that affect this passage *from the ego ideal to the group ideal*, which is nothing but the *passage from the I to the we*, from individual psychology to its true extension in collective or group psychology.

The repressive system, as we saw, presented as the ego ideal what was only the ideal of the other and, thus, the ideal of the system, which nonetheless govern us from without our own being as if it were desirable for the ego. But I am a narcissistic ego, who remains within the realm of similitude and the limits of my own restricted body. And in this scarce and isolated materiality that I live as my own, in which the limits of my skin are the limits that separate me sharply from the alien corporeality of the other as well as from nature, which also is alien as private property, in this bit of flesh that is all I have – and there is nothing that will remedy this – I symbolically inscribe the material transformations that I dared confront in the field of the others. To transform my ego ideal, substituting its miserable geography with the group ideal, would imply to open my subjectivity and verify it in the collective domain whose meaning must be inscribed in the material objectivity of the historical process. But, and this is Freud's implicit question: is every traditional, spontaneous group, every new group or mass, by the same token a revolutionary mass?

The problem, as we observed already, resides in the necessary transformation of the subject without which there can be no collective transformation. If psychology is at the same time individual and social, the transformation of the totality implies necessarily the transformation of the parts – the individuals – that compose the whole. This is why Freud, in his search for a true way out, begins by underscoring a problem he had already laid out: what happens in the ephemeral groups, in which the individual personality disappears, even if this separation as he indicates may be *only fleeting*. This 'prodigy' of the complete, if also fleeting disappearance of the individual's particularity does not occur in the artificial or institutionalised groups:

> Each individual is a component part of numerous groups, he is bound by ties of identification in many directions, and he has built up his ego ideal upon the most various models. Each individual therefore has a share in numerous group minds – those of his race, of his class, of his creed, of his nationality, etc. – and he can also raise himself above them to the extent of having a scrap of independence and originality. Such stable and lasting group formations, with their uniform and constant effects, are less striking to an observer than the rapidly formed and transient groups from which Le Bon has made his brilliant psychological character sketch of the group mind. And it is just in these noisy ephemeral groups, which are as it were *superimposed* upon the others, that we are met by the prodigy of *the complete, even though only temporary, disappearance* of exactly what we have recognised as individual acquirements. (129, emphasis added)

Let us recall that, contrary to Le Bon, Freud considers as a group *any* collective formation, including those institutions that the bourgeoisie does not consider to be groups, because they constitute the collective formations most proper to it. As a point of departure we all belong necessarily to numerous groups. Each one of us, as a person, is the result of the crisscrossing of various spheres of belonging that determine the constitution of the ego ideal: race, social class, Church, State. Freud therefore starts out from the determinations that are biological (race) as much as economic (social class), political (State) and religious (Church). This rigidly defines the sphere of the ego ideal, the field of its possible unfolding in all these dimensions of reality just indicated: what it is customary to call the 'realisation of one's personality', or 'the most intimate vocation'. But Freud reminds us, further down, of the meaning of this notion of the ego that thus constitutes itself as what is most proper to oneself:

> ... the ego ideal comprises the sum of all the limitations in which the ego has to acquiesce (131)

This is why the ego ideal is mediated, in the world of culture or civilisation, by models of the human that were elevated to the category of forms-of-being-human, models of being authorised into existence, which converge on the ego and offer themselves as the unreachable ideal: that to which human beings must aspire in vain. All of them constitute the 'collective superego'. But as such, we will see, *the collective superego is not the ideal of the revolutionary mass: the collective superego is only the ideal of the artificial mass or group*. For the revolutionary group or mass the model to which it aspires as its ideal must, on the contrary, be created. It is not realised in the past: it is present in the group itself as collective future, irreducible to the sole form of *one* individual. But in the self-concealment of the system the ego ideal reproduces subjectively the forms of being that are compatible with their system of production. And this is why each system, each 'civilisation', both for Marx and for Freud, can be defined as a system for the production of human subjects. If the system verifies itself in the contradictory subjects it produces, the transformation of the social structure must also rediscover, as a necessary moment, the transformation of the human subjects. Not, however, as some kind of luxury or excess relegated to the future but not yet meant for now that we find ourselves in the urgency of 'reality'. If we do not assume this contradiction, necessarily contained in both extremes, the human being and the social structure, any revolutionary process turns out inexplicable and impossible. And Freud gives us the theoretical proof of this impossibility.

The social formations that Freud adopts as his point of departure to explain on their basis the new emergence of ephemeral groups in which we see the complete, even though only temporary, disappearance of exactly what we have recognised as individual acquirements are the artificial or institutionalised groups: stable and lasting group formations, established in the consolidated framework of the system of production. The effects produced in the human subjects by these lasting group formations to which the spontaneous masses will try to oppose themselves, are 'uniform'. They similarly repeat forms of being a congruent human subject and, Freud tells us, raise themselves above this uniformity only 'to the extent of having a scrap of independence and originality' (129). To what extent? Precisely in the extent to which they do not contradict the maintenance of the repressive structure. Therefore, there truly exists no way of being a different human subject, without breaking through the limits rigidly defined by the artificial groups, even in the appearance of originality, as a form compatible with this structure. There is no possibility for individual 'originality' by maintaining the repressive social scheme.

It is interesting to note in Freud's analysis of the artificial structure that this effect of massification or group formation implicit in the system itself, the fact that institutions too are 'masses' or 'groups', is not visible to the subject who is congruent with them. They are 'less striking to an observer' (129). This is why this fact does not become visible as a 'scientific' object for the observer who is part of them – obviously in this case that would be Le Bon. The scientific observer, apparently impartial and objective, in reality is nothing of the kind: he too finds himself determined by this artificial group or mass that gave rise to his individuality as separate and conceals, in the presumed originality of his thinking, the rationality of the social system that produced him. What is it that becomes visible and striking only from within the blindness to what is proper to oneself? Not the totality of the system but that part of it that would contradict it: the revolutionary mass that is opposed to it and breaks the peaceful monotony of the social organisation that wanted to think of itself as lasting by dissolving the correspondence – the adequacy that pretended to be without residue – between individual and institution.

Thus, from within the artificial, stable, and lasting groups or masses, we see the irruption of the 'noisy ephemeral groups' or multitudes. We might say that they are the symptoms of the dissolution rather than the dissolution itself. Because these 'spontaneous' multitudes do not contradict the basic structure or existence of other artificial groups: they are only 'superimposed', Freud says, upon the others. And it is in the context of this setting that we see the complete, if also temporary disappearance of all individual particularity. And Freud is right to call this a 'prodigy': only in this way could all particularisation disappear and everything return to the same, as if nothing at all had happened.

1   *The Vicissitudes of the Embodied Ideal*
What happens in the complete, even though only temporary disappearance of individuality in accordance with the traditional institutions? Something that from the descriptive point of view could appear to be a transition from the subjective element to the social objectivity:

> We have interpreted this prodigy as meaning that the individual gives up his ego ideal and substitutes for it the group ideal as embodied in the leader. And we must add by way of correction that the prodigy is not equally great in every case. In many individuals the separation between the ego and the ego ideal is not very far advanced; the two still coincide readily; the ego has often preserved its earlier narcissistic self-complacency. (129)

The 'prodigy' therefore must find its explanation in the way in which the individuals who compose the spontaneous mass have succeeded in separating their own ego from their ego ideal: this is the measure of their transformation. This means: how they managed to become independent, in themselves, from the cultural regulation that organises them as subjects congruent with the repressive system. Here the individuals who make up the new 'spontaneous' mass did not complete, merely by coming together, a transition toward the revolutionary mass. Because the ego, returning to its ideal, may either open itself onto the effective domain of collective power and give itself the ideal of the revolutionary mass, or remain in the ideal of the spontaneous mass, but *incarnated in the leader*. In the first case, the individual body opens out onto the common collective body; in the second the body persist in the individual relation despite being part of the group, and the power of the group is once again usurped by the form of another human being who appears as if he were the whole: the leader. In this way Freud sketches out a line of amplification of the field of social transformation, not limited to the base of economic or political claims in the restricted sense. The index of social transformation, of its revolutionary depth, lies above all in the capacity of the masses to recuperate their own collective power with such profundity that the result from the individual point of view is also radical: to the point where the independence from the repressive power dissolves, within the revolutionary subjects themselves, the forms of the previous system – the models – that remained in place as shaping their individual connection to the system. But no prodigy can make this happen: this requires a slow and arduous transformation.

Whence the persistence in 'narcissistic complacency' (129). If the form of the father was determining for the relation of dependency, this was so above all because the flesh of the subject, its entire psychic structure, was invaded by the alien form of the other. Therefore, it is not only the collective form – the artificial or spontaneous group formation – that must undergo a mutation in its merely external organisation. For there to be an effective transformation Freud is showing that the mutation must necessarily include the reciprocal transformation of each of the human subjects who compose the group with respect to the others. Their power alone will be able to recuperate one's own creativity, not delegated, which exists in us as collective power. By contrast, in the spontaneous mass it is the system that usurps this collective power. This externalisation of the ideal, *embodied in the leader*, in other words would be the social equivalent of the neurotic way out. And yet, we cannot fail to understand that these are attempts to give oneself an external object in which the ideal is not the individual ego ideal but the group ideal. But is it not the case that this group ideal embodied in the leader continues to be the ideal that the social form of the repressive system continues to offer as collective form? Is the group ideal perhaps not the objectification of the desire that is unsatisfied but still governed by the human form of the repressive system? And is it not the case that the repressed contents of this desire continue to take the form, burned into the flesh, in which the other as a privileged being reached its satisfaction? And because of its origin in the exclusion of the others, does this form not drag with it the impossibility of integrating them into the universal field of shared desire?

Let us analyse this possibility in Freud's interpretation.

Spontaneous Masses in Which the Personality Is Not Dissolved: The Bourgeois Leader

Freud writes:

> ... we must add by way of correction that the prodigy is not equally great in every case. In many individuals the separation between the ego and the ego ideal is not very far advanced; the two still coincide readily; the ego has often preserved its earlier narcissistic self-complacency. (129)

And he adds:

> The selection of the leader is very much facilitated by this circumstance. He need often only possess the typical qualities of the individuals concerned in a particularly clearly marked and pure form, and need only give an impression of greater force and of more freedom of libido; and in that case the need for a strong chief will often meet him half-way and invest him with a predominance to which he would otherwise perhaps have had no claim. (129)

In the spontaneous group Freud thus analyses a moment of the dialectic of historical development, the one in which the group or mass, stirred up by the repressive system itself, concludes by including rebellion within its own system. To reach this point it relies on a *symbolic substitution*, in which once again the logic of whole and parts appears to negate its foundation in the materiality of the system of production, which remains unchangeable. When there is no real transformation and the selection of the subject in the group or mass continues to be narcissistic, meaning that it invests its ideal with heavy doses of libidinal energy, what predominates in this case is the election by substitution: I 'substitute' the ego ideal with the group ideal, but *incarnated* in the leader or chief. What is the group ideal? The satisfaction of the unsatisfied desire, from which the group as dominated group has seen itself excluded. It is the same ideal that corresponds to the subjective moment of the individuals in the horde, now in the world of culture or civilisation: to be *as if* I were the father, to substitute myself for him. But we saw that in the transition from prehistory to history this individual desire, by recognising itself as collective, gave way to the fraternal alliance and to a new form of individuality, which for its part was determined by the collective – albeit still without any consciousness of this determination. Let us recall: to gain consciousness implied, at the origin, consciousness of the assassination, the violence, and the guilt for having put the primal father to death. Here we have the case where, within the spontaneous group or mas, there is *not* a complete, though only temporary disappearance of personality: there is only the permanence in narcissistic complacency and identification by substitution. Therefore, there is also necessarily no violent transformation of the repressive system, even though – as we will see – this last solution, which for its part is really only temporary – may be continuously effective. This means that not every horde all of a sudden leads to the fraternal alliance.

From this we can infer what for Freud are the features that make possible the emergence of a revolutionary mass, just as in the case of individual sickness we must always deduce what are the characteristics that enable to passage to health. Freud clearly lays out the model of the revolutionary mass in the historical transition from the primal horde to the fraternal alliance, *as an incomplete process*, in which what subsists as not integrated into each individual is the collective domain from within which, through the alliance, they effectively came into being. What is never fully integrated is the violence exerted in the transition and, therefore, the exclusion from oneself of the collective force which is the basis for the privilege of one's own individual force, of its prerogatives and its pleasures. And this collective process will only reach the truth of history, and human beings will become conscious of this collective element including in their own individual genesis, when they become independent from the form of the other that guiltily continues to govern over them on the inside *for not being able to confront it on the outside*. The crucial step for the spontaneous mass, its transition to the revolution, thus appears as a possibility only through this process *where the father objectified in the system*, prolonged in the structure, as an impossible model, *must be put to death, destroyed, once again, but now on the outside*. Now as the embodied social model of an impossible satisfaction, which also entails as part thereof the sustained impossibility of all collective satisfaction. And this is why, in these frustrated forms of rebellion, Freud is going to show us which conditions are sketched out, as perhaps necessary stages presented negatively, in these false ways out of the collective sickness.

In the case of the substitution of the ego by the group ideal incarnated in the leader or chief we see another example of the conversion of the internal into the external, within the regressive scheme of narcissism. But here its inscription as a real collective process introduces a fundamental difference with regard to the individual regression. This one is a *collective regression* and, therefore, with regard to the previous situation, it is also a *collective progression* from the subjective to the objective: to the field of history. Here the categories of individual analysis, in the extent to which they are maintained, completely conceal the sense of the process in question.

Let us first analyze its *regressive character*. Instead of encountering in the prolongation of the ego ideal into the group ideal the objective historical field that produced this ideal in one's own individuality, we go back to substituting the infantile father with an adult supplement: the leader or chief. Apparently the group ideal, which here replaces the ego ideal, would express a process of objectification of a subjective agency, now verifying itself in the collective convergence. But this objectification, which apparently tends toward another form of being, remains within the similitude of the narcissistic choice. Here there is no desire shared with the others at the level of reality. The only thing shared is once again the desire to be loved by the leader: they share, by way of identification, the real satisfaction of the other.

> He need often only possess the typical qualities of the individuals concerned in a particularly clearly marked and pure form, and need only give an impression of greater force and of more freedom of libido; and in that case the need for a strong chief will often meet him half-way and invest him with a predominance to which he would otherwise perhaps have had no claim. (129)

Even though the individuals transform their individual ego ideal into the group ideal, the collective nature here is secondary, while still being a component part: *the collective ideal is an individual ideal*. Once again it is embodied in a form of human being in which the contradiction persists, though faded away. This is why the leader is selected: as a substitute-transaction within the repressive system. The model of the leader who embodies the group ideal only expresses the desire felt by a group of individuals to obtain the same thing that he reached as a privileged being. The leader here expresses the ideal that has been repressed in each one: it is the impossibility of being that each one carries within as what is most desirable but at the same time unreachable.

But the *progressive character*, which is *what is lacking in the individual regression*, consists in the fact that the meaning of the group or mass, if there is history, will always be to struggle against the oppression that closes off the path toward satisfaction. In the domain of history the personal incarnation of the group ideal in the leader is only a moment of transition – even though, in certain periods, it may end up being halted. The leader of the revolutionary mass destroys this incarnation and, as we will see, opens up the rational signification of its personal form. The one, therefore, in whom this possible universal form of being human is embodied, but not as already constituted, not as an already accomplished model of satisfaction. Because actual satisfaction is only the privilege of those propped up by the necessary dissatisfaction of the masses. The revolutionary leader will only be the model of the necessity of a collective transition: the one who with his actions and his project expresses the embodied form of the necessary transformation, and of the assumed decision to make this real, up to its extreme limit.

And what does Freud show us? That precisely in those spontaneous masses that rise up in rebellion, in which the traditional personality of the individuals who are its component parts does not disappear, the latter at the most aspire only to an impossible ideal: to become equal to those who already conquered or obtained their privilege. This is why they incarnate their ideal in the chief: in that man who already, in actual fact, from within the same system enjoys the privileges of power and command that they would like to obtain by way of substitution. The chief is he who 'need only give an impression of greater force', which therefore would not derive from the collective power but would emerge only from his individual body that, against the backdrop of those who have been subjected, would dominate the power of the others with an independent force of his own. As a result they see in this model the illusory possibility of its magical universalisation. Without understanding that this model of being is possible only thanks to the necessary dependency in which they live and to which they once again, through the mediation of his person, submit themselves. Once again they gather in the submissiveness and admiration of that unique being who in his enviable particularity owes to nobody, except to himself, the absolute power with which he is invested. The ego ideal, which is the ideal that is common to the group, now becomes materialised in the person of the other in which *the ideal became real*. It is clear therefore that here we are dealing with a bourgeois leader. The – typical – qualities are no different but the same ones that the individuals in the group desire or already possess. They are, in other words, qualities produced as normal by the system. The leader must give 'the impression' of a considerable force, but this is no more than an 'impression': it had to appear as a force exerted from within the domain that the same bourgeoisie provided for him, all the while concealing its origin. If he impresses them as being strong it is because he continues in a superlative manner the same form of indifferent freedom that the primal father assumed before the son. And the power he discovers for us is not ours: on the contrary, we the people of the mass are the ones who count on *his* omnipotent power – which on the other hand we assign to him and to which, without this assignment, 'he would otherwise perhaps have had no claim' (129). Where else could this power come from if it is not from the extension of the power that the system itself grants him but that we continue to assign to him as his own, until the moment when now we invest him with our power? All we will have done, Freud would tell us, is elect – within the context of models of the system that oppresses us – someone who gives us the impression of not being determined by this same system, of having liberated himself – while preserving his enjoyment – from that to which we continue to be subjected. But under this model the same power of the system will continue to prolong itself, only adding the force that we ourselves keep lending to it, thus renewing the pact of love with the new father, within the historical scheme of the horde.

Thus we see what is the ideality that became real in the leader. It is a reality that does not prolong the ego ideal in the direction of the social *system* wherein resides the rational key of the desire that is dissatisfied in the masses, namely: their collective domination. Rather, by substituting it with the leader, it returns in the present, through an inverted, regressive process, to the material form of the model – the father – on the basis of which the form of all satisfaction took shape. We do not prolong the sensible form of the other, this other who necessarily is present in each one as the foundation of the ego ideal, to the point of reaching the rational form of the productive process that produced this ideal as cultural model in our individual history. Rather, what we do at present, under the presumption of moving on to the objective moment, is going back to the point where the other was configured, in our primary sensibility without intellect, as absolute other. We substitute once more the first object with a second object, an infantile object with an adult object that takes its place. But this substitution maintains the absolute character of this new other, who is the leader: we renew the pact of submission in which once again the relation of master and slave of the primal horde is reproduced. What do we encounter here once again? A substitute-father, who prolongs the same form of being subjected, for now in a bond that adapts us, through its mediation, to the same social structure. What the embodiment of the leader conceals in its sensible presence, without conscious intellect, is the rational signification of the real.

2   *The Human Form as Mediator of the Collective Process*

However, just as in science there is no sudden discovery of the rationality of the real, there also is no such thing in history. To be creative in history presupposes an arduous process of discovery insofar as *the collective process creates history while making history at the same time*. In this sense, *the process of historical creation implies the equivocal moment of transitioning through the form of human subjectivity*, which as in the case of the leader announces itself by signifying another human form of possible transition. As a signifier, the leader effectively expresses the totality of power that converges on and is announced in his figure. But as a human being, this power once again has a tendency to appear at the same time as being merely one's own. This ambiguity, as a moment in the dialectic transmitted to the human subject as an index of the sense of the whole process, cannot always be avoided. There is no leap from the sensible to the rational. Therefore, the contradictory form that appears in the spontaneous mass or group, which attempts to move from subjective dispersion to the domain of objectivity by means of a new collective unity, nevertheless also has a positive side, even as it once again turns out to be concealed or covered up. This is why bourgeois group psychology detects in it a danger that throws it into doubt once more, like the eruption of some seismic movement throws into doubt the apparent stability on which the city rests, having forgotten the earth underneath. And this is why it tries to reorder itself through a leader or chief from within its own ranks, who fulfils an unexpected function. Just as Claude Lévi-Strauss used to say about every new marriage that it actualised all the others and brushed up against incest by actualising the repressive pact, the same could be said about every group or mass in which the contradictions once again become condensed around a repressive scheme: they brush up against the previous revolution from which they necessarily derive, and actualize as an ambiguous moment the transition from nature to culture, from the primal horde to the fraternal alliance.

As Freud indicates, this is an ambiguous moment, which once again lapses into a form of dependency for lack of a rational understanding. Let us analyse this process. The ego ideal corresponds to an individual human form that by prolonging the first identification became amplified to the point of determining my inclusion in various artificial groups, which are the institutions. In other words, it is the transition effectuated by an individual human form, unknown to itself in its origin, invading a reality that revealed to it the social forms that were compatible with it and without which it would not reach its adult reality. This regulatory individual form, which is the ego-ideal, did not discover the origin of its power in me: it was experienced as transcendent, if I dared think of it, and as absolute, insofar as I felt it. But at the same time my inclusion in the artificial groups – social class, religion, State, etc. – was not the integration into a totality that might open a new dimension of power for me, in function of the collective domain of which I became part. Even within the collective social form, the relation with the general, with the priest, with the political organisations of the State, etc., was a relation of one-to-one, of dominant to dominated, of omnipotent to impotent, master to slave. In the shock that gives rise to a spontaneous group or mass when the latter superimposes itself upon the artificial groups, the place of the ego-ideal is taken over by the group-ideal: it is discovered in a new collective form. Therefore, it is the moment when the individual discovers *at present*, like the first human beings at the origin, the possibility of a fraternal alliance as opposed to the relations of submission to the repressive power, which is the current prolongation of the primal father. But this situation in order to be effective would necessarily imply a break with the form of one's own individuality, because this is where the traditional repressive power is founded. And that means to internalize a new objective order into the subjective element. The conservative success of the artificial groups, which are already constituted in stable social institutions, consists in avoiding this rupture by sealing off the permanence of the current repressive power and validating the contradictory system of production as if this were a necessity for one's own individuality. And what should be the goal of the substitution of the ego-ideal by the group-ideal is the destruction of this submission in which we are all caught by virtue of our necessary belonging to the artificial groups. Such would be the discovery: the ego-ideal conceals the fact that, at its historical origin, it was necessarily the ideal of the fraternal alliance, even though now in its current individual origin in the child, this origin may be ignored and only one's own family history occupies its site. This is what we brush up against in every spontaneous mass, even if it goes no further than to include itself in the same system. That is why from the side of the existing repressive power, with Le Bon as its mouthpiece, we can hear screams in a last-ditch effort to stop us: your personality is being dissolved! Then follows the moment of verification, in which the omnipotent father, internalised in each one of us so as to open the complementary domain of fantasy and infinitude, now opens out onto an embodied form – the leader – who would verify the limits of the human extension of my libidinal body: the leader for Freud *embodies* the group-ideal. But if the group-ideal means *to be like the father in a group*, the ego-ideal by contrast, when it *embodies itself* in the leader, 'objectively' verifies the limits of this subjective ideality: the field of its effectiveness is the field of the external world's reality. And this transformation, which reached the objective domain of the system of production, already has its own dialectic, which escapes the realm of subjectivity and in its vicissitudes reaches the definitive domain of history. The leader must give proof of his omnipotence in reality. And here the laws that govern the rationality of the real, in the long or in the short run, cannot totally be broken. This passage from the ideality of the superego to the rational idea, but from within the embodied form of the other, constitutes a key moment in the access to the history of history. The leader incarnates the ideal: he gives body to an idea, anticipating the ideal in combination with a similar flesh, in which we are now shown the father's real counter-figure from where we may confront his imaginary form. But for this to happen the leader who embodies the group-ideal would have to express with his presence both *the flesh* of the human subject and *the idea* that gives it meaning, both the sensible presence and the rational signification of the new structure in which his presence is inscribed as a possible form of being human. Only thus would his flesh cease being abstract in order to become concrete, the index of a new social form of which he presence would be the anticipatory model. But in that case the signification of his presence as model would have to allow for those human beings who converge towards him to *verify* the ego-ideal in this counter-figure and, by way of a new identification, to replace the ego-ideal with the revolutionary ideal of the fraternal alliance.

But, in the individuals that Freud describes, 'the separation between the ego and the ego ideal is not very far advanced; the two still coincide readily' (129).

This is why, if there is no transformation and verification of the ego-ideal in the system of production, what is preserved is 'its earlier narcissistic self-complacency' (129). Or, put differently: what is preserved in me, ruling over me, is the other. And thus the bourgeois leader simply comes to extend, while also ratifying, the form of the system of production that I cannot leave behind. But in that case what is the function of the leader in the spontaneous group or mass? Perhaps he could modify reality with the help of the group. Except that the modification necessarily has to be superficial, without tackling the repressive power in its true foundation: neither in the social system that produced us nor in our own subjectivity. Since at present, as adults, the form of being an individual and the ego ideal rest only on their lived ratification in the system of production, the permanence and contentment in what we already are necessarily implies that we remain in the same repressive system of production and are not even capable of seeing why this is necessarily the case. This is why the models of leaders offered by the bourgeoisie, in their solicitation to keep to what we already are, the narcissistic complacency of the masses that take the leader as the ideal object of their own group ideal, always imply the maintaining of the same system, in spite of the real or apparent variations introduced on the surface. The human subject is not invited to make a radical change; and this is why the system also does not change radically.

Thus the leader is selected in this case for what he has in common with the form of individuality of the subject who make up the group, and not for the rational signification that the situation assumed by the group finds with regard to the social contradiction. *And in the beginning it could not be otherwise*, if we take seriously what Freud says: that, as individuals produced by the repressive system, we necessarily start out from the form of the ego-ideal and make the transition to the group ideal *incarnated in the leader. In this way it is impossible not to pass through the contradictory moment of incarnation: this is its real historical path.*

3 *From the Subjective Infinitude to the Historical Time and Space*

So as not to leave any doubt as to the direction in which his investigation inscribes itself, Freud pinpoints the specificity of his contribution to the problem of the groups or masses:

> We are aware that what we have been able to contribute towards the explanation of the libidinal structure of groups leads back to the distinction between the ego and the ego ideal and to the double kind of tie which this makes possible – identification, and putting the object in the place of the ego ideal. (130)

Let us recall what we took to be the meaning of the fact that Freud in the social process put forth the problem of the libidinal relation in the group. This implied that we recognize to what degree the social integration broadened or restricted, in one's own corporeality, the field of the subjective relationship and converted the body into a cultural body. This meant integrating into the body a power that extended itself in the discovery of a body shared in common with the others from within the same subjectivity: in the material domain of production, the common exterior nature, in which subjectivity objectified itself. The domain of our material development was already inscribed in our own individual body. This objective body of subjectivity – nature – that is strictly determined by the system of production, is what appears disguised in the spiritualism of bourgeois subjectivity and 'depth' psychology: it is lost in the infinity of pure interiority. But it is this objective body of subjectivity that the masses obscurely tend to recuperate in the collective spontaneity by integrating one's own subjectivity in that of others. For we were subjected to a process of historical dispossession, which is not immediately readable in the empirical present, nor in the individual past, and which only opens itself up in the historical comprehension of the process that led to it – the dissolution of the relation of possession of the human being to the common land, to the tools, to the raw materials, and to the means of subsistence that in ancient times belonged to us and today, in the capitalist system, no longer do. This process of dispossession is what led to the narcissistic social form in which the wage labourer currently inscribed. But this was a truly subjective narcissism, without object: in the worker, narcissism has not other material base except that of his father prolonged within the limits of his own body – but no further. The worker who is truly dispossessed is the only one in whom narcissism knows no objective ratification in the process of production, as does occur by contrast with the bourgeois owner, who seals his subjective narcissism with the real and exclusive property in which this narcissism is ratified and on which it is based: the objects of his property. If the workers continue to prolong their narcissism into the form of the leader taken as group-ideal – the bourgeois leader – without claiming the material base that is the foundation of collective power, they continue to lend their power to the very same power they are fighting against, now in the human form that the system itself hands out to them as one more pleasure and another, still subjective form of satisfaction. In this way the analysis of the group's libidinal organisation proves to be consistent or inconsistent in the very materiality of the body that verifies its extension in the materiality of the world.

Let us consider wherein resides the distinction that Freud claims as his contribution to this problem: the distinction between ego-identification and substitution of the ego ideal with an external object.

Identification, which in the beginning forms the basis for the constitution of the ego, was analysed by Freud in his 'On Narcissism: An Introduction' and *The Ego and the Id*. This first identification could lead to two forms for determining any object choice: in conformity with the narcissistic type or the anaclitic type. In the narcissistic type, one continues to be part and whole: this type loves 'what he himself is (i.e. himself); what he himself was; what he himself would like to be; someone who was once part of himself' (see 'On Narcissism: An Introduction', SE 14: 90). It is here that 'the immortality of the ego, which is so hard pressed by reality, security is achieved by taking refuge in the child' (SE 14: 91). The anaclitic type of attachment, by contrast, implies a transition to the reality that finds support in the sensible and welcoming form of the real and external other from within which it prolongs itself: 'the woman who feeds him, the man who protects him' (SE 14: 90). About the long series that follows starting out from these two forms, we could say that the narcissistic type leads to an imaginary dialectic, whereas the form of anaclitic attachment is inscribed in the possible transition to a real dialectic. In the first my own body is the material domain in which is inscribed every relation with regard to the real; in the second, by contrast, my own body can amplify itself to the point of really extending itself in the others and including itself in the material reality of the world as a part thereof.

In the analysis of identification in cases of illness and in the state of being in love Freud found that:

– *In sickness*: the ego identifies itself with an object internalised into itself. 'The shadow of the object fell upon the ego', for example. The subject itself is part and whole at the same time.

– *In being in love*: the ego searches for an object, whose form was already blurred in the ego itself. 'The object has consumed the ego'; 'the object has taken the place of the ego-ideal'.
– *In the spontaneous mass*: the individual 'substitutes for the ego ideal the group-ideal, incarnated in the leader'. The collective social whole is confused with the part: the leader.

And the conclusion that imposed itself was the following: *in all three cases the truth of the relationship did not reside in the object of the outside but in the object of the inside. It resides in the true connection with the world in which this relationship is inscribed*. For, even while finding an *outside* object, narcissism persists. And in the collective domain what does Freud discovers for us? That here again the relation to the social world is what likewise determines the possibility or impossibility of any experience of true affirmation with reality. Because even in the search for solutions that would transform the repressive reality, this historical and collective framework, too, can constitute a false way out.

This is why in the individual case (in sickness) the ego identified with the other or with a part of the other. The ego made itself into the other: in order to be or to have the other. There is no distance from the other in this relationship: it is a prolongation of the primary identification. But in the (normal) case of being in love as well, what appeared was the identification of the ego-ideal with an external object. Apparently, I did not make myself into the other, who was indeed external to me, but I loved him out of love for the other. In neither of these two cases could I develop difference on the basis of primary similitude. And when, at last, beyond any individual possibility, I tried to rise up in rebellion, this time collectively, against the social determination that was opposed to the satisfaction of my desire, I once again relapsed into the same subjective mechanism in which the new social subject, the spontaneous mass, once again was substituted qua totality by a part – the leader – taken as if it were the whole. *As if*, in one case, I were or had my mother or my father; *as if*, in the other, I had the woman of my desire; *as if*, in the mass, I transformed my subjective ideal into a collective one by substituting for my ego-ideal the embodiment of the leader. All these *as ifs* indicate the substitution, in the real dialectic, of the part for the whole.

Let us try to shed more light on this problem of the substitution of the group ideal, incarnated in the leader, for the ego-ideal. For this we must start from the relation between the ego and the ego-ideal. In this subjective relation there is only an internal distance for the subject who lives it: the ego-ideal rules over the ego from within, as its own moral conscience. But when, in the passage from the individual to the field of the collective I substitute for the ego-ideal an external object, the leader, in reality I am replacing an internal distance with an external distance: the internal becomes external. But with this I do not reach the truth of the objective sphere, since I only accomplish an externality in which the genesis of this distance is not imbricated with my subjective determination: this does not mean that I *know* and *understand* the historical process that determined me as its individual. The external realm that I thus reach covers up its historical signification and, therefore, my own access to the world of culture or civilisation: the formation within me of my ego-ideal. It is true that now, objectively, a distance opens up that previously was internal, welded into the subject. But this objectivisation in which the leader replaces the ego-ideal as if in his own exemplary individuality he himself were the ideal of the group itself, at the same time closes us off in an apparent verification in which all the other human subjects included in the group, my fellow subjects, accept the rule and preeminent existence of the same subject. Here, in the model of the leader of a spontaneous group or mass, we see the consolidation of that which previously, as individual ego-ideal, kept me in place in the paternal duty a *must-be*, in order to integrate me, in the group-ideal, as the *social must-be*. I close in the subjective lack onto an objective model, which will continue to govern me within the same repressive scheme.

We thus come to the point where we are able to establish a point of departure to understand the inefficiency in which the spontaneous mass is inscribed *in its first moment*. What was repressed and yearned for satisfaction therein, what unconsciously tries to accomplish itself in reality – to satisfy not only the *need*, as read in the economy, but the unsatisfied *desire* – *cannot be realised by preserving the same framework in which the other artificial and lasting groups are installed*. This superimposition of the spontaneous mass on top of and next to the artificial groups – next to the Church and even the very same army – indicates with great clarity that the form of the system is maintained without any variation: such groups or masses appear *suddenly*, Freud says, next to the other artificial groups. They appear like a form of delirium in the case of a sick person: bringing with them a forgotten content of historical truth, but emerging within the domain defined by the logic of the official system as something illogical, irrational, incomprehensible. It coexists side by side with the normal logic but without radically throwing it into doubt, without considering in this sickness the existence of a broader system in which the emergence of what thus was repressed becomes validated in its truth-content. As long as the spontaneous mass 'incarnates' its ideal in a human being whose presence is closed in on his empirical individuality without prolonging itself in a new rationality that he would contribute to forming and making manifest, there will be no transition to another social form. In other words, the transition from the artificial group (the primal horde whose form now repeats itself in the world of culture or civilisation) to the revolutionary mass (the fraternal alliance which rediscovers that this origin must be continuously actualised) implies the passage from the individual affective element to the rational collective element. The logic of narcissistic individuality corresponds to the simple materiality of the separated body; the logic of the revolutionary mass discovers its reason in the rationality of the collective domain, which finds nature transformed by human labour and the other human subjects as that totality from which all individual power derives. There is then no mere substitution of an internal object (ego-ideal) by an external object (leader). What must occur fundamentally is a substitution in the framework of fantasy. It is not, then, 'another scene' or 'another stage': it is a new domain of materiality and signification.

The substitution of an internal object, blurred in the normative and rational guise of the ego-ideal, replaced by an external object, is a poor solution to the problem: *the rationality behind the norms does not reside in an individual but in the system of production*. If I replace what constitutes a rational form, qua ideal, with an individual content that would realize this ideal, *what disappears is the rationality absorbed by the object*. The illusion of a primordial agreement continues to subsist in the adult: it is stamped with a hot iron as origin and as destiny. This is why the object that replaces the ego-ideal with the group-ideal cannot be an individual whose presence is exhausted in the merely sensible, like the bourgeois leader, in which this ideal is incarnated. It must preserve the sensible and the rational elements that were present in the constitution of the ego-ideal, but in order to reframe it within a new rationality and a new sensibility.

4 *Carnival or Revolution*

Freud's analysis, in what we have seen so far, was referring to the 'spontaneous' masses, that is to say, masses or groups that were not institutionalised and constituted themselves in reaction to the limitations of the existing social system. But, he indicated, in these groups the personality of the individuals that comprise them is not dissolved: the bourgeois leader who guided the spontaneous masses preserved and imposed a human form that was consistent with the system, against the backdrop of his privilege and his exceptional being. Now, by contrast, we are analysing a second form, complementary to the first, and also delimited in its apparent dissatisfaction by the repressive structure. But here, as opposed to the masses led by a bourgeois leader, there is a total, even though temporary, loss of personality.

The transition from the individual to the collective, such as Freud shows it to us, appeared as 'a differentiating grade in the ego' (129): the passage from *identification* – which constitutes the basis of individuation – to *substitution*. In this process, of which the ego is the stage, we substitute the form of the other, given in identification, with an external 'object', that is to say, with another human being – in this case the leader – who prolongs the first and objectivises its function. From the point of view of psychology, therefore, his transition is part of the process through which the ego would amplify its relations with the external world. But this was only an appearance. As we saw, this substitution does not necessarily imply a firmer grasp and confrontation with reality. The substitution of the primary other – turned into the superego – that continues to rule over me from within the subjective sphere, no matter how much it ends up being displaced by the objective and external presence of a man who serves as leader, continues this amplification – when it follows the bourgeois model – within the scheme of the primary process and the repressive Oedipal system.

But now Freud will try to show us this new activity of substitution that starts out from the individual solutions by prolonging itself, qua structure, in the collective solutions. In the individual ego, as we saw, this process of apparent amplification presented two extremes. One in which the ego took an 'object' from the external world (being in love); and the other, in which the ego offered itself as 'object' (psychosis). But only psychosis is what most clearly shows us the vicissitudes of the apparent object relation – in which its existence is fully subjective. About this extreme case of subjectivism Freud says:

> ... the ego now enters into the relation of an object to the ego ideal which has been developed out of it, and that all the interplay between an external object and the ego as a whole, with which our study of the neuroses has made us acquainted, may possibly be *repeated upon this new scene of action* within the ego. (130, emphasis added)

Here, in psychosis, 'the ego enters into the relation of an object to the ego ideal'. As a result, the relation to the external world is replaced by a subjective simulacrum: the individual subjectivity acts as a 'new scene of action' where what is played out is the drama of an existence that is eluded and not lived in its external prolongation. But, Freud will show us, also the 'normal' human beings who amplify their relation to the world and give themselves, as opposed to the sick persons, *effectively* a real external object may nonetheless convert this external reality itself into a 'new scene'. Except that, in order to accomplish this and give themselves the complete illusion that the sick individual obtains in the form of hallucination, here what is required is a collective framework that would suggest the reality that is missing in it. Between this extreme limit of individual psychosis (individual 'new scene') and the relation of the ego to a collective external object (collective 'new scene'), there would thus be a whole gradation whose different pathological forms can be ordered in function of the modalities of failure experienced by the ego in its pretence to extend its relations with reality. These failures are the results of the difficulties that each new access to the reality of the external world – of the system of production – presents:

> Each of the mental differentiations that we have become acquainted with represents a fresh aggravation of the difficulties of mental functioning, increases its instability, and may become the starting-point for its breakdown, that is, for the onset of a disease. (130)

Seen from this angle, then, the criteria for speaking of disease become amplified: the mental or psychic differentiation, which comes into view when we discover the magnitude of the obstacle that impedes the amplification of the ego's relations with reality, also increases its instability, and this is due to the risk of death that it implies. But *it is precisely this failure, this retraction and, thus, this disease that the repressive system rewards if we manage to include ourselves within the limitations marked off by its institutions*. This is what happens when the failed individual remains within the 'artificial' institutionalised masses or groups (Church and army), where the 'unstable' person is remitted to the appearance of an agreement, which is the seal of normality.

This is the crucial point: the contradictory society also creates a 'new scene' so that the merely symbolic realisation of unsatisfied desire in the domain of its institutions may find a collective substitute in which, just as in individual psychosis, satisfaction may be fantasied. Except that now the 'new scene' opens up in the external world, in the objective reality, and exists in the margin allowed by the institutions. How does this pseudo-objectivisation occur in the collective field, where the imbalance therefore is not detected as such but may exist *together with* and *next to* the normal condition? Freud goes on to explain this mechanism of pseudo-objectivisation as being an integral part of the same system, inseparable from the series that starts out from the individual sickness all the way to its collective solution because both, the former no less than the latter, are *at the same time* individual and social.

In this chapter, in other words, Freud extends the reach of psychopathology from the individual to the collective, which thus appears inseparable from the first. Because, as we have been seeing, it is only from this last form, from the collective and directly social sickness, that the individual sickness becomes meaningful. Thus, the different modalities of subjective rebellion (individual sickness) and objective rebellion (cultural and collective) are nothing if not modulations of one and the same failed relationship, different scenarios that play out the drama of an existence that is avoided and not assumed in its true prolongation with regard to the structure of the world that produced them.

Both forms, in spite of their differences, have recourse to regression and to the satisfaction of its contradictory demands, whether in alternation or successively. In both cases, the individual and the collective, the 'solutions' preserve within the ego the form of dependency that the ego-ideal imposed on them. In one case, in individual sickness, the material field of transformation is one's own individual body; in the other, in the collective social solution, the individual body is included without extending itself within the collective body that the 'artificial', institutionalised group frames and limits. But both are determined by the ego-ideal, which is nothing but the ideal of the other and, as a result, the ideal of the repressive culture. From the individual superego to the collective superego, it is the same determining structure of the system that organises both the head and the subjugated body.

Let us see how Freud describes this process and the mechanisms he invokes to explain it. He begins, once again, with the child:

> Thus, by being born we have made the step from an absolutely self-sufficient narcissism to the perception of a changing external world and the beginnings of the discovery of objects. And with this is associated the fact that we cannot endure the new state of things for long, that we periodically revert from it, in our sleep, to our former condition of absence of stimulation and avoidance of objects. It is true, however, that in this we are following a hint from the external world, which, by means of the periodical change of day and night, temporarily withdraws the greater part of the stimuli that affect us. (130)

With the child's entrance into the world there necessarily occurs a first amplification of the social field: the opening onto reality from within the primary narcissism. But periodically there is a return to the previous situation, due to the fact that 'we cannot endure the new state of things for long'. What makes this new state so difficult to endure? Not only the biological birth but the transition from a natural form to the cultural dimension, which here occurs *abruptly*. The cultural dimension appears as a leap: the temporality of the world of culture or civilisation in the instant of the passage becomes welded into the biological temporality and does not show us – nor could it – the historical dimension that produced the transition.

The child in the world of culture or civilisation in other words uses the fact of biological alternation, of sleeping and waking, which as a subjective mechanism coincides with the objective alternation of night and day. There is a subjective-objective coincidence: the subjective pair 'sleep-wakefulness' corresponds to the objective pair 'night-day'. The pair 'sleep-wakefulness' serves as a pivot in the transition from nature to culture or civilisation. When the child was not yet born, it slept in the maternal womb: it had no external reality but was sufficient onto itself. Birth, as radical change, inaugurated the day of wakefulness coming out of the night of self-sufficient narcissism. And in going to sleep the child has recourse to a biological mechanism that prolongs the narcissism from before birth in the reality of its cultural existence.

But in the biological realm, the alternation of sleep and wakefulness that regulates the bodily ego, which knows only the natural rhythm, does not have the same meaning that appears in the cultural alternation of the psychological ego.

What happens when this natural body finds itself already inscribed, as adult, in the world of culture? What happens is that the limits met by the child do not present the radical incompatibility that they had in the first moment:

> The second example of such a step, pathologically more important, is subject to no such qualification. In the course of our development we have effected a separation of our mental existence into a coherent ego and into an unconscious and repressed portion which is left outside it; and we know that the stability of this new acquisition is exposed to constant shocks. In dreams and in neuroses what is thus excluded knocks for admission at the gates, guarded though they are by resistances; and in our waking health we make use of special artifices for allowing what is repressed to circumvent the resistances and for receiving it temporarily into our ego to the increase of our pleasure. Jokes and humour, and to some extent the comic in general, may be regarded in this light. (130–131)

The child went back to sleep so as to find rest in the midst of its access to reality: it took respite so as to become free and take a new step forward. But, Freud tells us, now, in the adult, the biological alternation remained as a model to confront a mental or psychic differentiation that is cultural: the opposition between the consistent ego and the unconscious ego. And in this alternation the adult finds the scheme for a solution, which is no longer one of respite but of flight: a flight away from reality *within reality* itself. The neurotic is an individual who dreams while being awake, we said, and it is here that fantasy alternates, as a refuge, with the repressive reality in which it lives. The alternation here is not between sleep and wakefulness but between the official ego and the repressed ego: two aspects of a cultural and historically constituted division. Between the light of day of legal coherence and the clandestine nocturnal existence of the outlaw.

Thus, analogically, the unconscious ego is the sleepless night of the conscious and wakeful ego. But since, contrary to what happens in sleep, it is always present, alive next to and together with the conscious ego, the unconscious ego knows no respite. The coherent ego is the official ego that offers itself as an object to the ego-ideal: it is consistent, but with itself, not with the flesh of the subject. And, therefore, it expresses the coherence with the repressive system. By contrast, the unconscious ego is the incoherent ego, seen from the point of view of the subjugated ego: it is the leftover of the being that remains alive in the sleepless flesh and against which it is necessary continuously to exercise violence. It is the 'exiled' aspect of the subject, landless and without a home to welcome it: lacking the right of property in itself. It has been expropriated from within the bosom of its own repressed corporeality; and yet we continue to be this expropriated part because it lives on obscurely – like the night – within our own flesh. How does this solution take place that does not want to confront 'any limitation' in reality and, nevertheless, find satisfaction? By simulating, in the alternation, its access to satisfaction. I wake up the incoherent ego and put to sleep the conscious ego, so that it may not see this. But, as we now see, this means that we avoid the confrontation with the repressive reality. If the conflict is presented as taking place within the ego between coherence and incoherence, the solution necessarily must refer to the domain in which this coherence, assumed as such by our official ego, came to us from within the world of culture or civilisation. *But if we prolong the opposition sleep-wakefulness, it is because we gave the opposition coherence-incoherence, which is cultural, a natural status.* We would have had to formulate our problem from within the coherence of the social system in order to verify ours as an agreement between the subjective element and the historical and material objectivity. We already saw the sequence: primary narcissism, coherent ego, superego, ego-ideal, collective superego, system of production. In Freud this also finds expression as development of libido in self-love; the love of one's parents, siblings, and friends; the love of objects; and the love of humanity and of abstract ideas. And at the level of collective participation the development went from the family to the school to the artificial group to the spontaneous group or mass to the revolutionary mass. The struggle between the coherent ego and the repressed ego in the organisation of the individual is thus a debate that refers us back to an homologous opposition in the organisation of society: the one that in society opposes the conscious and coherent official rationality (ideology), with which the systems conceives of itself, and the real and contradictory organisation of the productive forces, which remain subjected to an energetic compulsion, unable to gain access to the consciousness of the system. Freud has shown that this subjective opposition at best opens up a 'new scene', but not a new reality. It is the refuge of the night when we cannot take it anymore: when we fall back on the alternation of the neurotic transaction, in which both systems are affirmed alternatively – even though they are contradictory with one another. But these contradictions, which play out between the individual and the system, are dealt with symbolically as attempts at a solution within the individual material form: *the contradiction*, which cannot be resolved within these limits, even though we are dealing with an alternation, *is treated as if it were a succession*, based on the logic of biological alternation that is appropriate for its level. It is solved from within the narcissistic scheme that from the child was prolonged in the adult.

This subjective logic is also what appears to regulate the collective phenomena as if they were natural: as if they had the stability and permanence of nature. Do we want more proof of the clarity with which Freud thinks of this sustained failure in the repressive culture, which immobilises the development of the contradiction? We can find it when, prolonging that individual alternation which eludes the time and space of history, he moves on to an example taken from the historical processes themselves:

> It is quite conceivable that the separation of the ego ideal from the ego cannot be borne for long either, and has to be temporarily undone. In all renunciations and limitations imposed upon the ego a periodical infringement of the prohibition is the rule; this indeed is shown by the institution of festivals, which in origin are nothing less nor more than excesses provided by law and which owe their cheerful character to the release which they bring. The Saturnalia of the Romans and our modern carnival agree in this essential feature with the festivals of primitive people, which usually end in debaucheries of every kind and the transgression of what are at other times the most sacred commandments. But the ego ideal comprises the sum of all the limitations in which the ego has to acquiesce, and for that reason the abrogation of the ideal would necessarily be a magnificent festival for the ego, which might then once again feel satisfied with itself. (131)

What the system can provide as a way out for the intolerable, which on the other hand it creates itself through repression, is only a regression within the unmodified permanence of the system. The periodic violence is a social transaction. The emergence of the repressed does not cast doubt on the repressive system with its infraction: rather, it confirms this system. This happens within the same system, without supposing its negation. The ego-ideal, which 'comprises the sum of all the limitations in which the ego has to acquiesce', frees an ego that still, in its collective violation, even as it may ignore this and only feels it, continues to be determined in its rupture by the ego-ideal. Because the violation happens within the law: the law allows, for a brief period of time, its own infringement. It is therefore an appearance it concedes to us: the infraction is part of the very power exercised by the law. Or, put differently, the law, in the very act of the infraction that it imposes, situates itself beyond itself. Where? In its unconscious foundation, where the apparent negation of the law coincides with the apparent liberty of the subject who is authorised to break it. What happens is that the restrictions imposed by the law organize the conscious side of the subject as well as its unconscious reverse side. The law affirms itself in its maximal omnipotence at the very same moment when it orders its own violation. The subject's pleasure does not derive only from the repressed contents that emerge but also from the pleasure produced in the violation of the prohibition itself. This is a new kind of pleasure that only the law in its permanence makes possible.

What is interesting to note here is that within the framework of the repressive system there is no solution possible for the objective distance opened up between the ego and the ego-ideal. This distance always implies the transformation of both terms. And this is what is impossible to achieve *as long as I do not know that this distance experienced as internal is a distance between the subject and the system of production.* As long as I think, with the coherence that is mine – which means that it leaves outside of me the unconscious spontaneity as incoherence – my relation with reality whose structure and law is coherent with my thinking and acting, how could I catch a glimpse of the contradiction in the system? In the periodic violation of the law the system allows me to *act out* the repressed, but *not to think it through*. It opens up a domain where the unconscious may talk, it allows it to unfold, and this is the aspect in which my irrationality coincides with the field of irrationality present at the heart of the law's own rationality. My field of incoherence displays itself in the field of incoherence opened up within the coherence of the law. But it will always continue to be incoherent: I will never have reason on my side, except the kind that the law's reason lends to me. This irreducible margin of irrationality is what the system cannot integrate in its own rationality as reason: that would imply that it transform its own coherence, blow up the foundation of its own power. Thus, this regulated oscillation, which leads from obligation to infraction but then once again from infraction to obligation, is a general form that corresponds not only to the system's imbalance but also to the subject's individual sickness. What the spontaneous group or mass attempts would be to turn this alternation in its favour: to turn the infraction into a continuous infraction. But with this it only confirms its continuous dependence on the law.

5   The Leader and the Revolutionary Mass

And yet, there must be a way out. *Individual power is important to reach the solution*: this is Freud's lesson. To confront the repression we must previously recuperate the power that, though ignored, lies at the foundation of subjectivity. To say 'individual psychology is at the same time and from the very first collective or group psychology', then, is not so innocent. It implies that the categories of the system of production from top to bottom organise the flesh of my individuality. But as long as it remains within the limited space of my own body, its signification will not be able to amplify itself to the point of destroying the narcissistic limitation that the bourgeoisie signed off on in ourselves. This explains why Freud, as we saw, analysed the 'objectivist' tricks by means of which narcissisms pretends to reach the collective externality of the internal: when it makes the collective experience only into a 'new scene' in which to prolong, undisturbed, the distance between the ego and the ego-ideal.

Whence the importance Freud gives to the leader to explain both the relation of subjection and the potential for revolution. For every collective form conveys the form of the human as model of the organisation of the system of production. How could the signification of a new historical situation emerge if not through the human form of the other, who embodies it as the moment of a possible synthesis? If not, how would it be possible for human subjects to condense the rational signification with the event from where someone makes this signification appear, visible to all, in a mode of conduct that assumes it and objectivises it? How would it be possible to open up in the flesh of each subject at the same time the connection between consciousness and body, separated by repression? In the revolutionary leader the human form of the conflict finds the place of a transition where the subjective converges with the objective, the affective with the rational, the individual with the collective, the structure with the event. But here the leader serves as model: he becomes a signifier and irradiates in all spheres of reality showing with his action and his thought the true relation between part and whole, between individual and system. In this sense, the leader is a new model, in opposition to the unliveable models of the artificial groups, which undoes the trap formed in us by way of identification since we were children. In the leader the drama of historical transition becomes the model of confrontation in a body that, through its transformation, also invites our own transformation. The signification incarnated in the leader thus appears to open up a new possible sense within the repressive system and in his action aimed at transforming this structure shows us the path to recuperate the power of the fraternal alliance, renewed once more.

It is through the leader's mediation that the unconscious at last acquires an incarnated form and an actual power: in his figure the irrational element erupts that the system kept alive, in its marginal form, side by side with its own order. But from within its form of being human, it erupts as the unequivocal signal of the domain on which the repressive rationality is founded: in its system of production. It is no longer the unconscious that erupts as a tolerated infraction. It is the unconscious that discovers the historical truth of the repressed and emerges from within a new situated rationality. The transformation of our contradictory individuality thus inscribes itself in the movement for the transformation of the repressive system. There are two levels of verification reached in a single act, which includes them both inseparably: the moment of the subjective transformation and the objective transformation experimented in common, in the material and historical field. These are the two extremes to which the revolutionary leader gives rise synthetically in his proposal: by showing *within himself*, in his own person, the possibility of this transition *for all*. Thus we see that the truth that Freud pronounces in psychoanalysis is assumed by the revolutionary leader as total conduct, as an effective discovery. The scientist says: individual psychology is collective psychology. The revolutionary leader recreates in reality, starting out from this discovery in his own person, the collective bonds enunciated in science.

Thus, in the midst of the spontaneous group's rebellion, we see the preparation and discovery, in a second moment, of *the rationality of spontaneity*, without which the leader who embodies it may appear to be complicitous with power, as a form of flesh without reason. It is this spontaneity that must be organised in order to pull it out of the repressive framework and the repetition of alternation. To do so it is necessary to include within the spontaneous element the theory of the real, just as the psychoanalyst, in the individual cure, finds support in the theory of subjective organisation that allows him to interpret the contradictory behavior. This theory to be included is the rationality that is hidden away by the system in the individual psychic structure, and without which there could be no true psychology.

The rationality lived as subjective and unconscious incoherence now encounters its true domain of verification. This contradiction solidified in the subject, itself divided between the coherent ego and the unconscious ego, has revealed to us the limits of its attempts to find a way out both in the case of the individual and in the spontaneous mass or group. In 'normal' sleep, it was reduced to an alternating satisfaction in which night and day, sleep and wakefulness, rhythmically defined the successive predominance of the conscious and the repressed, each of them in a separate domain of their own, without ever re-encountering the unity and meaning of the opposition: the biological rhythm served as its guarantee. Until someone lost their sleep. Then, in the neurotic, the unconscious would come into the light of day: dreaming while being awake. But, in order to achieve this, the repressed unconscious kept to the irrational domain of a regressive signification, in the imaginary elaboration of childhood fantasies that gave themselves the field of timelessness and the instant as realisation of a desire outside of the historical time and space. Here one's own body actualised within itself this first timeless space of its primal organisation. A meagre materiality, it is true, but lived as though it were all. In the spontaneous mass comprised of 'normal' residual individuals, by contrast, the unsatisfied desire at last emerged in its collective expression. But here the ego-ideal, transformed into the group-ideal, found its real external object in the narcissistic satisfaction of the bourgeois leader who incarnated it. He would thus cover up his ideality without matter with the empirical materiality of the triumphant bourgeois model, transgressor and satisfied, as if we verified in him that alien idealism that the form of the father, prolonged in the direction of reality, discovered for us. And we thereby gave our stamp of approval to the illusion of an insatiable nostalgia, coinciding in the present with a common object that at last covered it.

However, in all these attempts to find a way out the spontaneous group has one privilege, even in its failure. Because this group that objectively lacks satisfaction, determined as it is by the system for dissatisfaction and death, is *the only historical domain where the dialectic of the objective truth can develop*. And this is what the revolutionary leader discovers in his action, just as the revolutionary scientist discovers it in his thinking. This set of subjugated human beings, which in the individualist atomisation of the artificial group appears only as intimate and subjective, now opens itself up for the first time to a possible field of coherence and real objectivity. The subjective distance becomes not only objective but also historical. This unconscious repressed aspect discovers not only its cultural origin, it learns that *today* what produces it are the social relations of production. It is what remains unsatisfied, postponed, left over from the multiple contradictory references to the stable groups or masses, which now converges in 'this commonality that ties them together': the mass that includes us in the organisation of labour. The revolutionary mass is that new collective organisation formed by those who, for the first time, objectivize in a model of being human the synthesis of the coherent subjective order and the unconscious into a new form. The subjective categories of a purely internal opposition thus discover at last the origin of their organisation in an external contradiction from which they derive: the contradiction that exists between the official coherence (institutions and ideology) as opposed to the real foundation of the productive process whose effective rationality and material connections remained unconscious. The opposition between the ego and the ego-ideal now appears between a class of human beings and the system of production.

And if we recall what Freud said about individual creations, when he asked himself if these were really more than perfections of 'a mental work in which the others have had a simultaneous share' (83), then this time we can say that *the leader of a revolutionary mass emerges within it as the figure who was created by the collective situation.*

The revolutionary leader, understood in this sense, expresses and restores to the mass or group the signification of the collective power that allowed him to rise up within it with a prior power that the group communicates to him and in him finds its prolongation. The revolutionary leader mirrors this power, embodying it but by giving it signification, and it is this extended force, incorporated into his individuality, which he returns to the collective with his acts inscribed as proof of a necessary and possible transition. But necessary also for the leader: he discovered that there is no satisfaction of one's own desire if it is not in the desire that is shared. It is his collective being that reveals itself in his individuality. This is why he seeks out the mass of subjected human beings as he seeks the force and orientation towards change that he tries to interpret in order to discover the efficacy of this unconscious power. The revolutionary leader is the one who opens the unsatisfied desire in order to fill it with all the common reality that is possible, and who confers on this very yearning the maximal actuality that it is possible to reach: so that the mass or group may recognise itself in this collective dissatisfaction, which is its force, as the first condition of all desire. It is the first fraternal bond that he returns to them in the risk of his life oriented toward the only possible satisfaction: to include them all in the form of the unsatisfied desire that outlines its content in the very negation of the historical present that denies it. Thus, the desire of the revolutionary leader, insofar as his function is that of creating an opening, traces the limits of the possible and confronts them. But not only as a sacrifice, but as the opening of a real possible that appears when the narcissistic limitations, overcoming the fear of death, opens up the temporality of one's own halted body, but now within the common body. The individual libido, restricted to the limits of my own skin and to the models of the system, becomes what the leader is by way of a liberating identification, because through the mediation of the other it opens itself up by incorporating the common force into one's own. And together with the body that unfolds reason too unfolds itself. It is the function of the 'psychic apparatus' that thus discovers its historical determination in the consciousness that inscribes the body in the mobility of political action. The mass or group thus encounters its transition to reality within the framework of a transformation of reality headed and oriented by the revolutionary leader. It is the passage from the primitive horde to the fraternal alliance, but now already within the context of the knowledge of history and without the guilt of violence.

6   *The Collective Experience Cannot Be a Predicate*

The revolutionary mass, and even the spontaneous mass in its 'noisy and ephemeral' function, would be the ones that lay bare the repressed as historical and social: as the only domain where the difficulties of psychic formation announce the reorganising power oriented towards the whole system, recuperating the true forces that move it along. Only in the mass does the individual repressed surge forth and discover itself in its collective being, in the very domain in which the individual and collective psychology took shape. Its action, as yet unthought, directly inscribes itself in the foundation of the rationality that structures all subjectivities. These acts once again encounter the historical bedrock from which the narcissistic and separated individuality had distanced itself. At last the individual unconscious here encounters the unconscious of the system of production, that wider field which produces them without knowing it. The unsatisfied imaginary desire discovers the only domain of all possible satisfaction, because the material signification of the individual act inscribes itself, in its search for satisfaction, in the materiality of the system. And the result reached is the following: in the system of production that produced them, *there is, in principle, no satisfaction for all*. Its form, therefore, is not a universal one. This limit is also not the obstacle that 'life' encounters in its development as an impossibility in which we would have to acquiesce. It is death and failure that the privileged of the system bring down on the others: it is, in other words, the cultural death for which the human being is responsible.

It is here that the rationality of the new model unites in a new form of life two series that previously were separated: the flesh and the world of cultural significations. Previously that coherence of the ego made it impossible to think the unconscious; the latter appeared only as an individual unconscious. The ego had neither the words nor the social categories to understand it. And yet this unconscious was already, in fact, materialised in the lived connections that in the relations of dependency and labour tied human beings to one another. This is why they could go so far as the spontaneous formation of the group. This 'something common that ties them together', which Freud asked about, lies in that negated bond where what circulates is the unconscious that the cultural system itself produces. It is the unconscious that searches for its satisfaction, but already blurred in its modality by the world of culture or civilisation that simultaneously provokes it and represses it. This synthesis of the group is the first syntheses in which the unconscious rise up anew. It is the spontaneity of the horde, but which here, because we are not dealing with the first historical deed, already produced its first brother. In this way, the spontaneity in which the repressed unconscious surges forth is a spontaneity endowed with meaning: with historical meaning, situated and determined in its form by the system of production as the first synthesis in opposition to the system itself.

Thus, the first content that brought together the prehistoric brothers in the horde no longer corresponds to the possession of the women in the current group or mass that recreates the transition. In order to discover the rationality of the unconscious we have to follow the thread of history from the first need to the current system. We have to trace the historical amplification of the framework in which the content of the unsatisfied desire is inscribed. Freud *does not tell us* that in the beginning the primal father was the owner both of the women *and of the material goods*. This is why psychoanalysis, situated in the prehistory that is alive in the present, may swipe away the material determination of which the father had the enjoyment in dominating the sons. This effect of concealment in remitting to prehistory reproduces and dramatises its complicity with the concealment and disguising currently at work: history is read, as Freud also taught us, *from within the present*. But if we prolong this first dominion, then together with the recuperation of the women the brothers of the fraternal alliance also recuperated the dominion of the land and the work in common. Does this not also form the objective field of the access of desire to the 'reality principle', the cure that leads from dissatisfaction to satisfaction? Is this not perhaps the meaning of the first historical act that continues in our culture, its always present genesis?

This is why the function of the present revolutionary leader is the historicisation of desire, so as to situate it in the true context of historical satisfaction, removing it from the illusory complacencies of the subjective sphere. In the figure of the revolutionary leader we introduce ourselves in the very source of repression, and the sensible similitude with the father opens itself up as difference with the brother. It actualises the repressed and situates it in the time of historical reality, removing it from the periodic and symbolic alternation to which the repressive satisfaction restricted it. It takes us out of anxiety before the nothing, which is anxiety before death, and places us in front of the obstacle. This is why the revolutionary leader takes out the metaphysical death and turns it into a historical death: in the determinate death that the system gives us to live. But it is then no longer the abstract anxiety before death, of the ego before the superego within one's own individuality: it is the risk of the obstacle that is opposed to life, now understood from within the discovery of the common force. It is no longer the subjective id that ends in the limits of my own skin, that private portion of nature delimited by my body. It is the id which, as subjectivised nature, discovers anew the collective anonymity of the common body of nature of which each individual body is part, from which we come and in the direction of which we prolong ourselves. The body of the revolutionary leader makes visible that it is based on our own force and is strong only as long as it invites and depends on this force. And as long as it makes this be known by us and felt by us. Yet its discovery is not the anonymity of nature, to which the repressive system wants to remits it: it is the precise and determinate description of a social system of production that reveals itself as a collective field.

The revolutionary leader is the one who temporalises the ego-ideal and turns it into a group-ideal, which is nothing but the social ideal covered up in the ego-ideal. In the form of the revolutionary leader the archaic father gives way to the new brotherhood: the source of mythic power, which previously was transcendent, ends up finding its true source in the common power. It opens up the force and violence of the unconscious, situating it in front of the obstacle that inhibited it. Its figure integrates and welds together the scission between the conscious and the unconscious, and a discovery is made of the personal movement that integrates them in the creation of a new transition. By unravelling the merely subjective relation, without object, between the ego and the ego-ideal, it shows its origin and makes appear on the outside, as real, what previously dominated ideally, from the inside, as mythical. It puts the right side up of a process inverted by the ratification of an infantile illusion in the official culture: it transforms the mythical inside into historical outside and shows, without substitution, the historical source of its subjectivity. The conscious rationality thus once again encounters the point of its insertion in the prolongation of libido. This convergence of subjectivities, which discover the reason of their similitude and spontaneity, must meet up in its unconscious and postponed subjectivity, in its humiliated content, something more than the yearned-for and dominating father: this content must converge and meet up with the meaning of the world, the imbalance of the system that the revolutionary leader assumed, first in himself, in order afterwards to reveal it as being present in all.

To know that individual psychology is at the same time collective or group psychology means to discover outwards a powerful human universality in the midst of a defenceless and subjugated individuality. Because we ask ourselves: where could the *isolated, lonely* individual, restricted to the limits of bourgeois individualism in which the psychoanalyst himself is situated, find the real force to dominate this power, which furthermore is confirmed by the child's affective development that conceals the historical genesis in the individual genesis? Where could he, if he furthermore realises that this power is ratified by the social formations in which he is strictly included? There is only one answer: *only by returning to a situation of effective domination, in the gathering of forces that converge in the formation of a powerful collective totality, can this abstract ego-ideal once again encounter the foundation and the historical power that is concealed in the individual genesis*. It is not a matter of recuperating only an individual form of *knowledge*: the point is to recuperate a *common power*. This experience of the *recuperated common power* cannot be proportionate, in psychoanalysis, to the power of the individual analyst. We are dealing with an experience that is *radically* different from the one that the analyst may perhaps, if at all, help bring about as the corollary of a beginning, but not terminal analysis. *The experience of collective power is not an experience that the imagination can supply*, because the imaginary contents, even the most exalted ones, continue to be based on one's own individual body, and on the force of the other. The experience of collective power can only be the experience of a hitherto *unprecedented power*, which is necessarily actual because it is the actual presence of the unconscious social power that the individual form in the bourgeois framework could never have lived. Only the narcissism of bourgeois individuality, even when it pretends to be revolutionary, is capable of conceiving of this experience as well as a subject-matter for consciousness that renders the transition to reality unnecessary. It continues to base itself on mere rationality without body, and the extension of libido does not even enter its way of thinking. But if individual psychology is, at the same time, a collective psychology, and historical creativity is not the story of some text written about it but the creativity that rises up within the oppressed mass that liberates itself, then its prolongation in oneself as affective extension of our libido cannot limit its contents to ideas of 'love of humanity': *it must give itself the real object in its actual and effective presence*. It is the flesh itself that once again must rearticulate its relation to this power from which historically it had been disconnected in the successive historical dissolutions that culminate in the capitalist process as collective narcissism. It must understand the path of its subjectivity as that of a historical subject that also prolongs itself in its own subjectivity, historicised at last. This is a subject that, as Marx describes it for us, was first separated from the common land, then separated from the tools of labour, later from the means of subsistence, and now, as *pure subjectivity without object*, finds in individual psychoanalysis the illusion that corresponds to a depth subjectivity *without others*, an abyssal subjectivity that, without re-encountering the cultural nature in which we are all situated, borders only on the infinity of abstract death, without content

But this is not Freud, but only a bourgeois and limited interpretation of a revolutionary Freud, who cannot be heard in the narcissistic reading to which the system condemns us. As Kant used to say about existence, when he refuted the argument for the existence of God, that it is not a predicate, because its being does not reside in the verbal or theoretical affirmation, here too we can say the same about collective power: its existence, for each individual, cannot be a predicate. Freud makes it into a predicate and says: the being of the individual is collective. But he only signals an existence, a real experience: in order for it to exist as the subject's truth, the latter must realise the experience of prolonging its force and its reason into the force and the reason of the others. If my thinking opens itself toward the thinking of the others when the other's idea is appropriated and assimilated – and therein resides the extension of my thinking – how might it open the extension of my libidinal body, as a social subject, if I do not effectively open my body to the common experience of the others? And therein consists the extension of my being. If not, I also would not be able to reactivate the other's ideas: I would not have the body necessary to give them life as true ideas that the body is able to think because it is situated in the materiality of historical life.

Bibliography

Althusser, Louis 1974, 'Théorie, pratique théorique et formation théorique. Idéologie et lutte idéologique' [1965], unpublished manuscript, translated and published in Spanish as part of the booklet *La filosofía como arma de la revolución*, Mexico: Siglo XXI.

Freud, Sigmund 1921, *Group Psychology and the Analysis of the Ego*, in *The Standard Edition of the Complete Psychological Works of Sigmund Freud*, Volume XVIII (1920–22): *Beyond the Pleasure Principle, Group Psychology, and Other Works*, London: Hogarth Press, 65–133.

Sigmund Freud 1932–36, *Civilisation and its Discontents* [1930], in *The Standard Edition of the Complete Psychological Works of Sigmund Freud*, Volume XXI (1927–31): *The Future of an Illusion, Civilisation and its Discontents, and Other Works*, pp. 57–146.

Freud, Sigmund 1932–6, *New Introductory Lectures on Psycho-Analysis*, in *The Standard Edition of the Complete Psychological Works of Sigmund Freud*, vol. XXII.

Freud, Sigmund 1986, *The Complete Letters of Sigmund Freud to Wilhelm Fliess, 1887–1904*, Cambridge, MA: Harvard.

Le Bon, Gustav 1914, *The Crowd: A Study of the Popular Mind*, London: Unwin.

Lukács, Georg 1981, *The Destruction of Reason*, translated by Peter Palmer, Atlantic Highlands, NJ: Humanities Press.

Marx, Karl 1959, *A Contribution to the Critique of Political Economy*, in *Collected Works*, vol. 29, New York: International Publishers.

Marx, Karl 1973, *Grundrisse: Foundations of the Critique of Political Economy*, translated by Martin Nicolaus, London: Penguin.

Index

About the Defeat and the Vanquished (Rozitchner)   7
Althusser, Louis   8, 13–14, 22
America   189
Anti-Oedipus (Deleuze and Guattari)   4, 13
Augustine   2–5, 7

Badiou, Alain   5, 8, 13–14
Balibar, Étienne   14
Bauer, Bruno   11
Being Jewish (Rozitchner)   7
Benezra, Karen   2
Bernheim, Hyppolite   339–340, 342
Beyond the Pleasure Principle (Freud)   95
Bosteels, Bruno   2
Bourgeois Morality and Revolution (Rozitchner)   7
Butler, Judith   8, 13–14

Capital (Marx)   11
Christ   262–263, 281–282, 312, 316, 346–347, 355–358, 360–361, 367–368, 371, 374, 385, 433, 443, 445
Christian Questions (Rozitchner)   7
Christianity   2–3, 5, 7, 9–14, 16, 122, 138, 146–147, 152–153, 162, 164, 167–168, 176, 183, 190, 230–232, 262, 264, 314, 316, 346, 383–384
Civilisation and Its Discontents (Freud)   3, 15, 107–288, 330, 354, 417
'"Civilised" Sexual Morality and Modern Nervous Illness' (Freud)   150
Clotaire   296
Communism   185, 190
Confessions (Augustine)   2–5
Crusoe, Robinson   298
Czechoslovakia   189

Del Barco, Óscar   7
Deleuze, Gilles   4, 13

'Economic Forms that Precede Capitalism' (Marx)   450

Feuerbach, Ludwig   9
'Findings, Ideas, Problems' (Freud)   90, 390

'Formulations on the Two Principles of Mental Functioning' (Freud)   47
Foucault, Michel   5, 14
Francis of Assisi   162, 166
French Revolution   292, 297, 331, 439
Freud, Sigmund
   Beyond the Pleasure Principle   95
   Civilisation and Its Discontents   3, 15, 107–288, 330, 354, 417
   '"Civilised" Sexual Morality and Modern Nervous Illness'   150
   'Findings, Ideas, Problems'   90, 390
   'Formulations on the Two Principles of Mental Functioning'   47
   Group Psychology and the Analysis of the Ego   2, 8, 15, 24, 68, 135, 154, 158, 161, 208, 251, 280, 288–289, 290–510
   'Inhibitions, Symptoms, and Anxiety'   45
   'Instincts and Their Vicissitudes'   43, 210
   Introductory Lectures on Psycho-Analysis   323, 342–344
   Moses and Monotheism   3
   'Mourning and Melancholia'   404–407
   'Negation'   49, 112, 349
   New Introductory Lectures on Psycho-analysis   27–104, 203
   'On Narcissism: An Introduction'   491
   Outline of Psycho-Analysis   85
   Project for a Scientific Psychology   388
   The Ego and the Id   151, 198, 491
   Totem and Taboo   453
Freud and the Limits of Bourgeois Individualism (Rozitchner)   7, 10, 12, 15
Freud and the Problem of Power (Rozitchner)   7
Freudo-Marxism   8, 10, 12–13, 14

Gobineau, Joseph-Arthur (Count of)   292
González, Horacio   1
Groddeck, Georg   83
Group Psychology and the Analysis of the Ego (Freud)   2, 8, 15, 24, 68, 135, 154, 158, 161, 208, 251, 280, 288–289, 290–510
Grundrisse (Marx)   8, 290, 452–453
Guattari, Félix   4, 13
Guevara, Ernesto   189, 281–282

INDEX 513

Hegel, G.W.F.   7, 14, 130, 232, 469
Heidegger, Martin   292
Hermeneutics of the Subject (Foucault)   5
History of Sexuality (Foucault)   5, 14
Holloway, John   11

'Inhibitions, Symptoms, and Anxiety' (Freud)   45
'Instincts and Their Vicissitudes' (Freud)   43, 210
Introductory Lectures on Psycho-Analysis (Freud)   323, 342–344

Jung, Carl Gustav   194

Lacan, Jacques   8, 12
Laplanche, Jean   151
Le Bon, Gustav   290–298, 305–315, 317–322, 324, 326–329, 338, 340, 478, 480, 488
Lévi-Strauss, Claude   487
Levinas or the Philosophy of Consolation (Rozitchner)   7
Levinas, Emmanuel   7
Lévy-Bruhl, Lucien   87
Lukács, Georg   292

Manuscripts of 1844 (Marx)   185
Marx and Infancy (Rozitchner)   7, 9
Marx, Karl   7, 10–13, 14, 20–21, 23–24, 42, 49, 51, 64–65, 94, 110, 116, 127, 165, 185, 209, 243, 254, 259, 275, 290, 298, 329, 348–349, 351, 371, 387, 407, 430, 450, 463, 474, 479, 509
  Capital   11
  'Economic Forms that Precede Capitalism'   450
  Grundrisse   8, 290, 452–453
  Manuscripts of 1844   185
  'On the Jewish Question'   9
Marxism   23–24, 127, 185
McDougall, William   327, 332–335, 338, 340
Merleau-Ponty, Maurice   1
Moses and Monotheism (Freud)   3
'Mourning and Melancholia' (Freud)   404–407
Moses   36, 468

'Negation' (Freud)   49, 112, 349
New Introductory Lectures on Psycho-analysis (Freud)   27–104, 203
Nietzsche, Friedrich   14, 83, 180, 457

Oedipus   14, 36, 63, 67, 228, 231–234, 237, 239–240, 248–249, 251–256, 259, 261, 370, 387, 390–391, 394, 412–413
'On Narcissism: An Introduction' (Freud)   491
'On the Jewish Question' (Marx)   9
Oneiric Materialism (Rozitchner)   7
Ortega y Gasset, José   292
Outline of Psycho-Analysis (Freud)   85

Perón, Juan Domingo   7
Perón: Between Blood and Time (Rozitchner)   7, 10
Person and Community (Rozitchner)   7, 10
Philosophy and Emancipation (Rozitchner)   7
Plotkin, Mariano Ben   2
Political Writings (Rozitchner)   7
Pontalis, Jean-Bertrand   151
Project for a Scientific Psychology (Freud)   388
Psychic Hegel (Rozitchner)   7

Ramos Mejía, José María   292
Rancière, Jacques   14
Ricœur, Paul   252
Rimbaud, Arthur   50
Rodríguez, Simón   7
Rolland, Romain   107–109, 111, 116, 123
Rozitchner, León
  About the Defeat and the Vanquished   7
  Being Jewish   7
  Bourgeois Morality and Revolution   7
  Christian Questions   7
  Freud and the Limits of Bourgeois Individualism   7, 10, 12, 15
  Freud and the Problem of Power   7
  Levinas or the Philosophy of Consolation   7
  Marx and Infancy   7, 9
  Oneiric Materialism   7
  Perón: Between Blood and Time   7, 10
  Person and Community   7, 10
  Philosophy and Emancipation   7

Political Writings 7
Psychic Hegel 7
Terror and Grace 10
'The Left Without Subject' 8
The Thing and the Cross: Christianity and Capitalism 3, 7, 10

Scheler, Max 1, 7, 292
Schiller, Friedrich 190
Sighele, Scipio 331
Simmel, Georg 292
Soviet Union 189
Stalinism 22, 186
Sucksdorf, Cristián 7
Sztulwark, Diego 7

Tarde, Gabriel 338
Terror and Grace (Rozitchner) 10
The Crowd (Le Bon) 290–298, 316, 326, 329
The Ego and the Id (Freud) 151, 198, 491
'The Left Without Subject' (Rozitchner) 8
The Psychic Life of Power: Theories in Subjection (Butler) 8
The Thing and the Cross: Christianity and Capitalism (Rozitchner) 3, 7, 10
Theory of the Subject (Badiou) 5
Totem and Taboo (Freud) 453
Trotter, Wilfred 442–443, 445, 449

Vico, Giambattista 17

Žižek, Slavoj 8

Printed in the United States
by Baker & Taylor Publisher Services